Graphis Inc. is committed to celebrating exceptional work in Design, Advertising, Photography, & Art/Illustration internationally.

Published by **Graphis** | Publisher & Creative Director: **B. Martin Pedersen**
Chief Visionary Officer: **Patti Judd** | Design Director: **Hee Ra Kim** | Senior Designer: **Hie Won Sohn**
Associate Editor: **Colleen Boyd** | Publisher's Assistant/Designer: **Yuan Zhuang** | Account/Production: **Bianca Barnes**
Interns: **Yihan Hua, Diamante Maldonado, Jacqueline Salazar Romo**

Graphis New Talent Annual 2024

Published by:
Graphis Inc.
389 5th Ave.
Suite #1105
New York, NY 10016
Phone: 212-532-9387
www.graphis.com
help@graphis.com

ISBN 13: 978-1-954632-29-5

This book contains some logos that were designed by students for mock clients for the purpose of completing classroom assignments. All trademarks and logos depicted in this book belong solely to the owners of the trademarks and logos. By using the trademarks and logos in these student projects, neither the schools nor the faculty and students intend to imply any sponsorship, affiliation, endorsement, or other association with the trademark and logo owners. The student projects were executed strictly for noncommercial, educational purposes.

Any photography, advertising, design, and art/illustration work must be completely original. No content owned by another copyright holder can be used or submitted unless the entrant has been granted specific usage rights. Graphis is not liable or responsible for any copyright infringement on the part of an entrant, and will not become involved in copyright disputes or legal actions.

We extend our heartfelt thanks to the international contributors who have made it possible to publish a wide spectrum of the best work in Design, Advertising, Photography, and Art/Illustration.
Anyone is welcome to submit work at www.graphis.com.

Copyright © 2024 Graphis, Inc.
All rights reserved.
Jacket and book design copyright
© 2024 by Graphis, Inc.
No part of this book may be reproduced, utilized, or transmitted in any form without written permission of the publisher.

Printed in China.

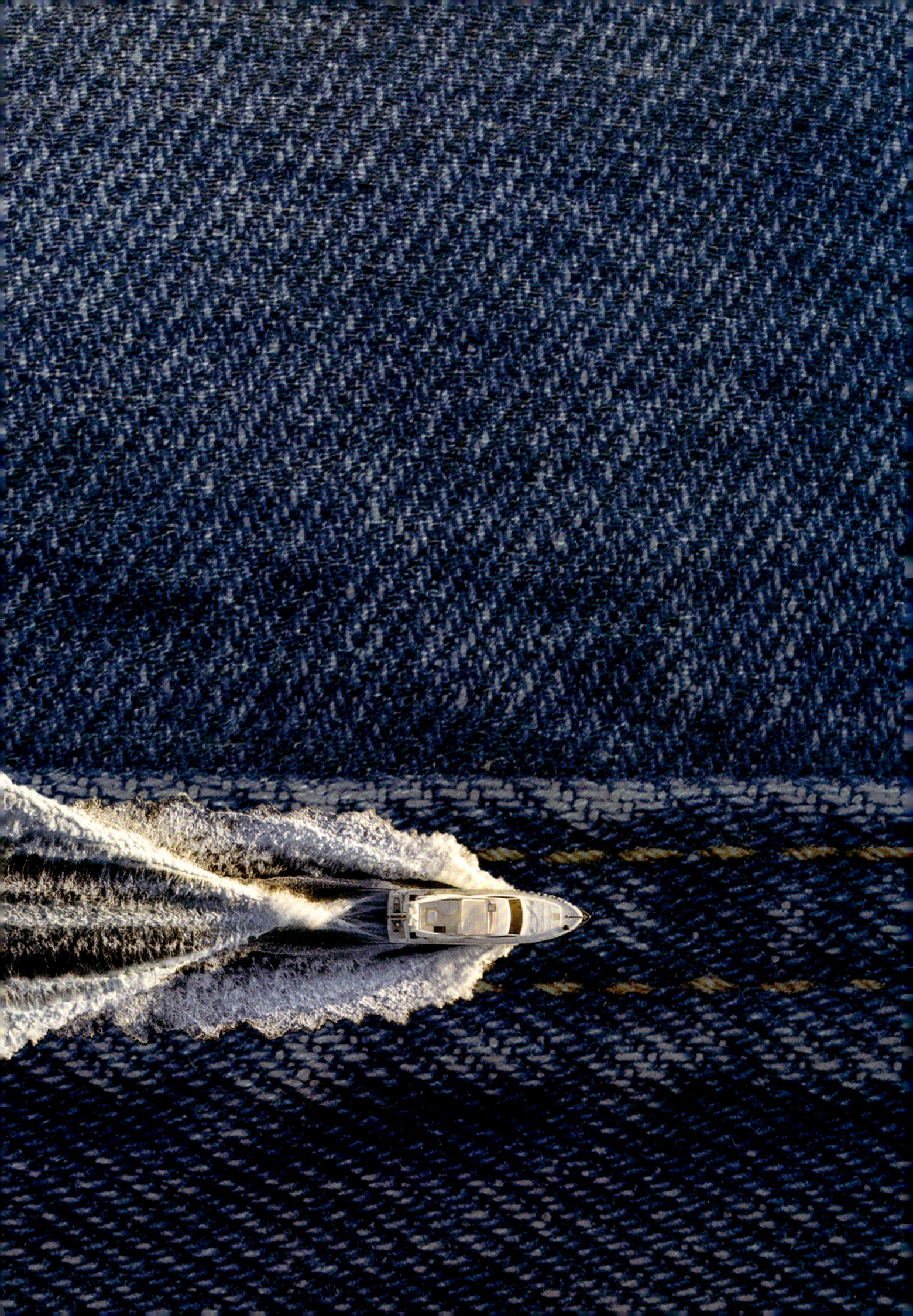

Contents

A Decade in New Talent 6	**DESIGN** **47**	Logo 98	**PHOTOGRAPHY** **227**
Competition Judges 15	Platinum Awards 47	Packaging 104	Gold Awards 227
ADVERTISING **18**	Bios & Headshots 48	Poster 120	Still Life 228
Gold Awards 18	Award-winning Work 50	Product Design 134	Silver Awards 229
Electronics 19	Gold Awards 68	Promotion 136	Credits & Commentary ... 233
Fashion 20	Books 69	Restaurant 138	Index 249
Food 22	Branding 74	Type Fonts A-Z 143	School Directory 252
Product 23	Calendars 90	Website Design 145	List of Honorable Mentions ... 253
Silver Awards 25	Catalogs 91	Silver Awards 146	Graphis Titles 255
Advertising Film/Video 40	Illustration 92	Design Film/Video 216	

Graphis awards have a truly global draw, and if you're lucky enough to win, you get to see your work reproduced in a beautiful book.
David Bernstein, *Chief Creative Officer, The Gate*

The level of work was incredible, and more importantly, the keen conceptual thinking was impressive. It was truly invigorating and inspiring to see the beginning of so many bright futures in the industry.
David Schuemann, *Founder, CF Napa Brand Design*

Page 3: *"Wear the Change,"* Syracuse University, The Newhouse School, Instructor/Professor: Kevin O'Neill, Student: Gabriella Enriquez
Page 5: *"The Crack On Earth,"* ArtCenter College of Design, Instructor/Professor: Dillon Carson, Student: Alicia Cheng

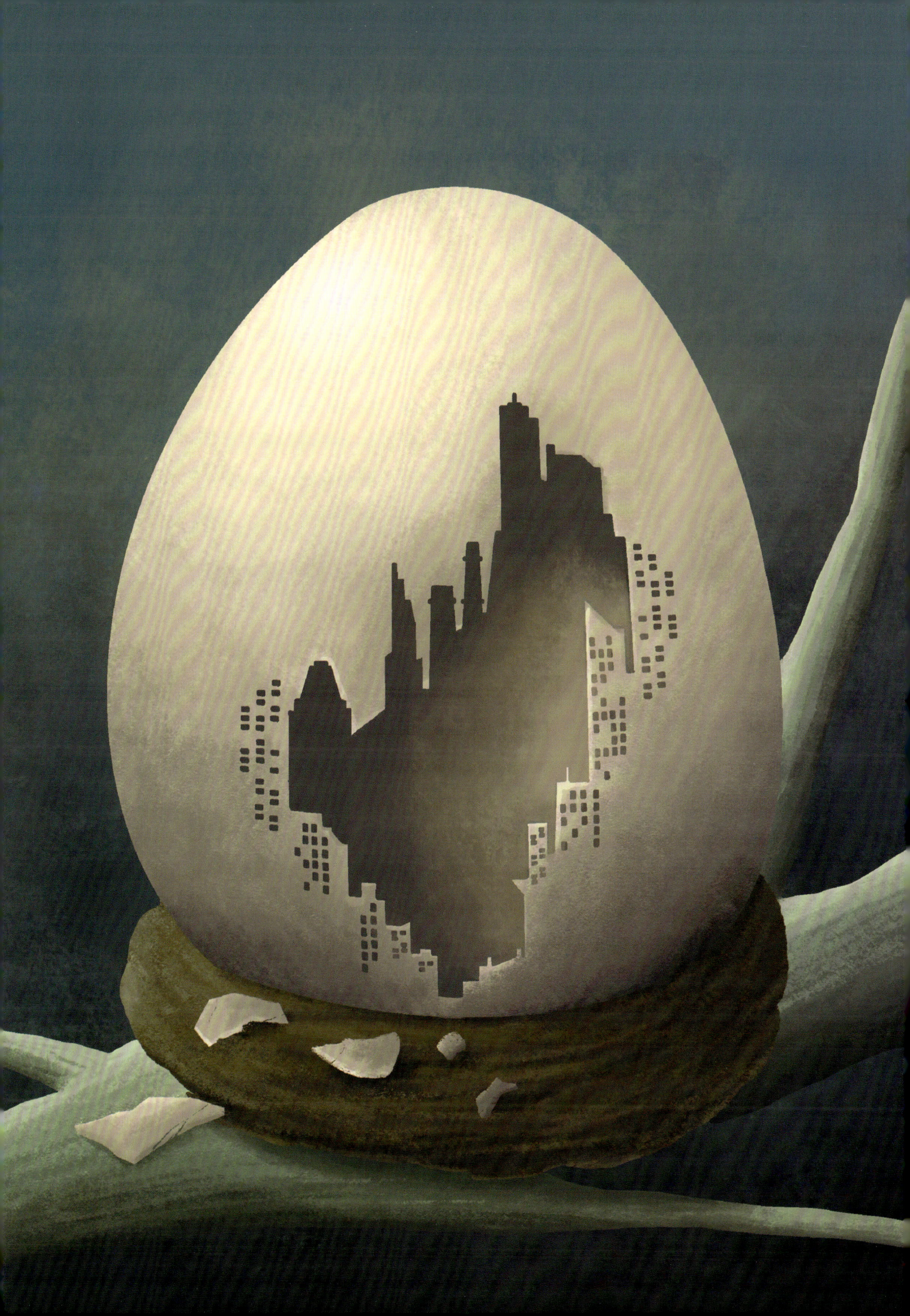

A Decade in New Talent: Winners from 2014

Academy of Fine Arts in Krakow 🇵🇱 Pg. 7
Professor: Piotr Kunce
Student: Katarzyna Zapart

School of Visual Arts 🇺🇸 Pg. 8
Professor: Louise Fili
Student: Ella Laytham

Art Institute of Atlanta 🇺🇸 Pg. 9
Professor: Phil Bekker
Student: Kevon Richardson

School of Visual Arts 🇺🇸 Pg. 10
Professors: Shawn Hasto, Paul Sahre
Student: Sherry Hsin-Ting Kuo

School of Visual Arts 🇺🇸 Pg. 11
Professor: Carin Goldberg
Student: Ben Grandgenett

School of Visual Arts 🇺🇸 Pg. 12
Professor: Bill Oberlander
Students: Sooyoung Jeon, Rina Joonwon Lee

School of Visual Arts 🇺🇸 Pg. 13
Professor: Nic Taylor
Student: Dominika Kramerova

Woodbury University 🇺🇸 Pg. 14
Professor: Behnoush McKay
Student: Logan Miller

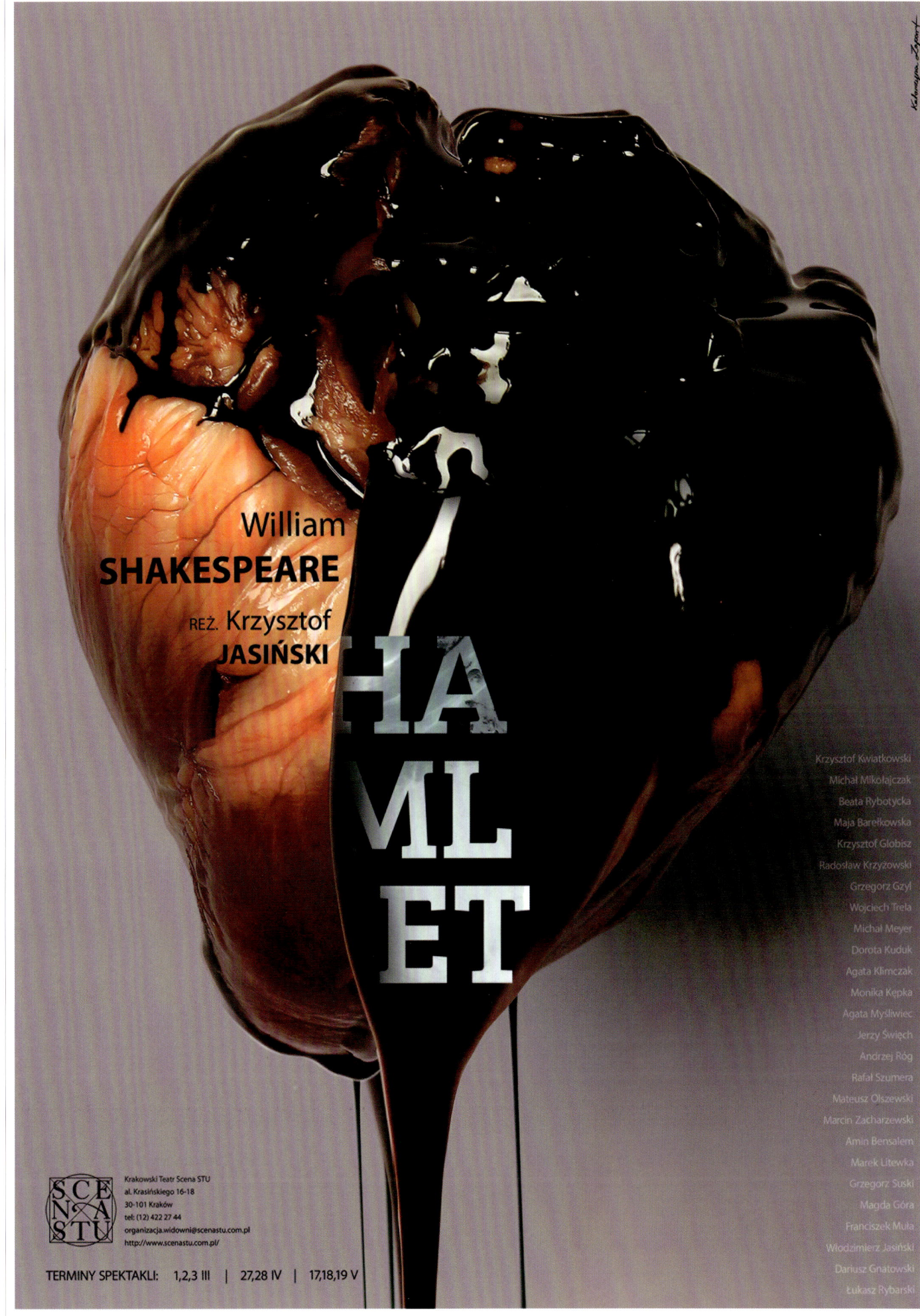

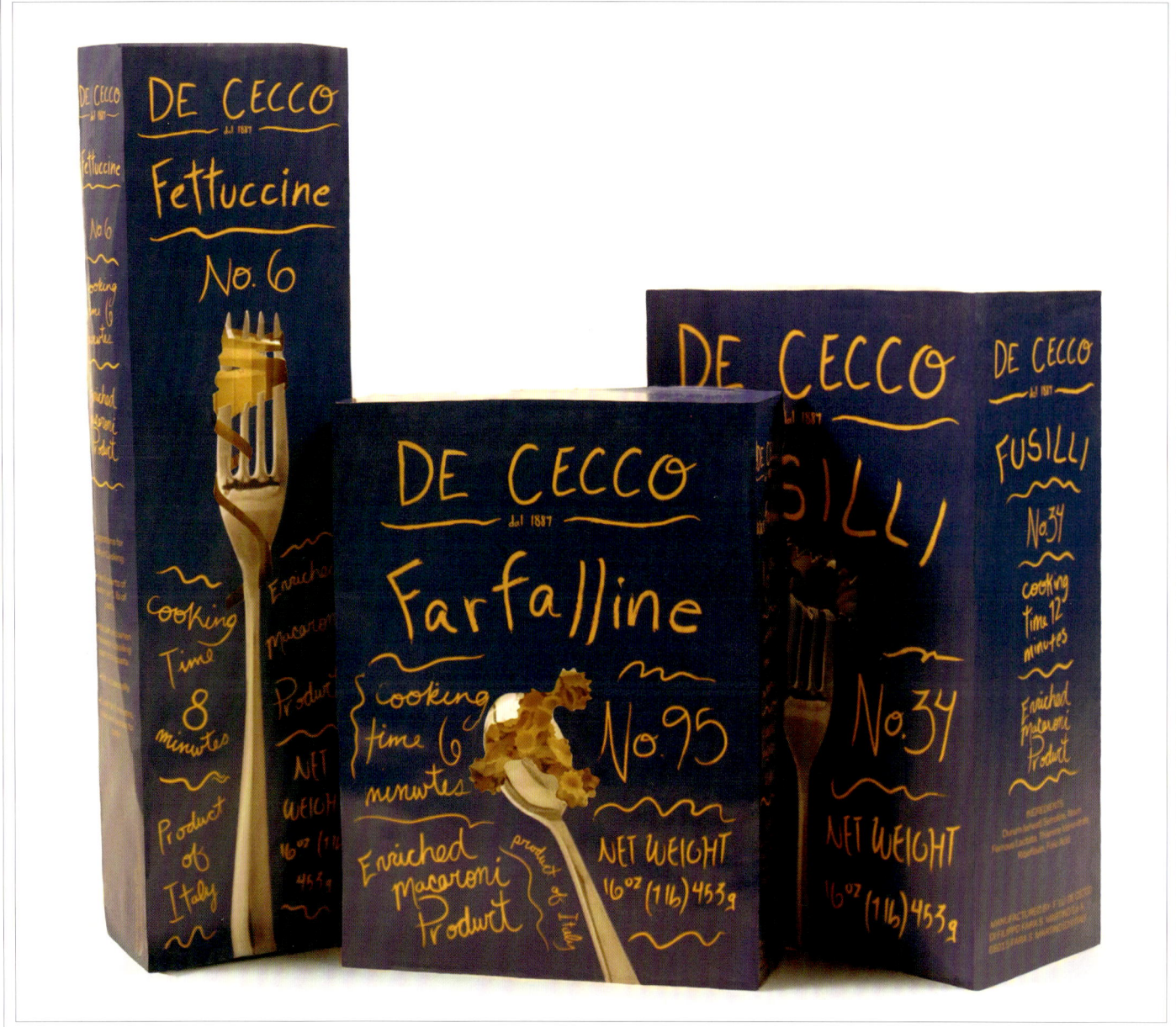

Student: Ella Laytham | **School:** School of Visual Arts

9 INSTRUCTOR **PHIL BEKKER** PLATINUM

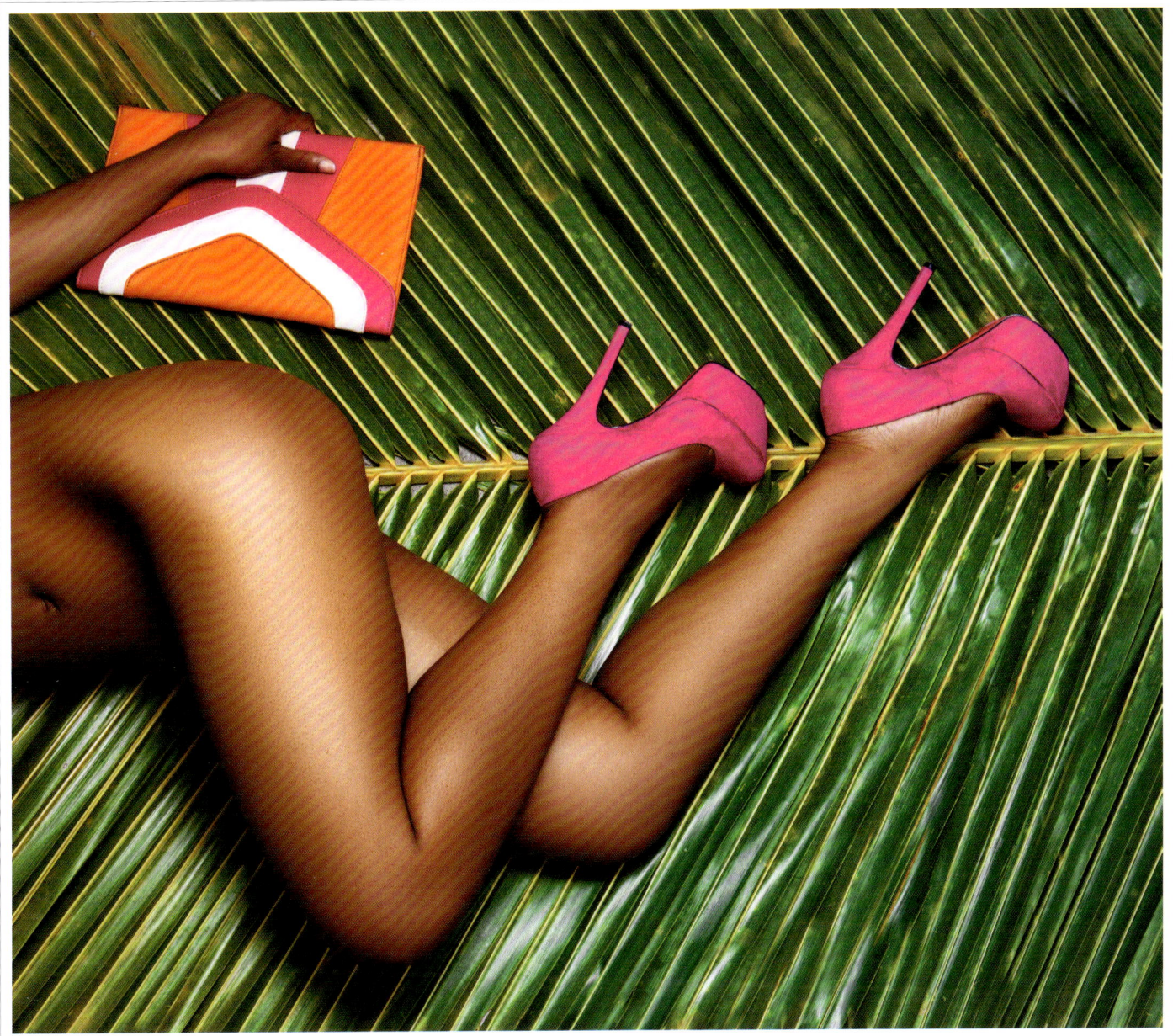

Student: Kevon Richardson | **School:** Art Institute of Atlanta

10 INSTRUCTORS PAUL SAHRE, SHAWN HASTO PLATINUM

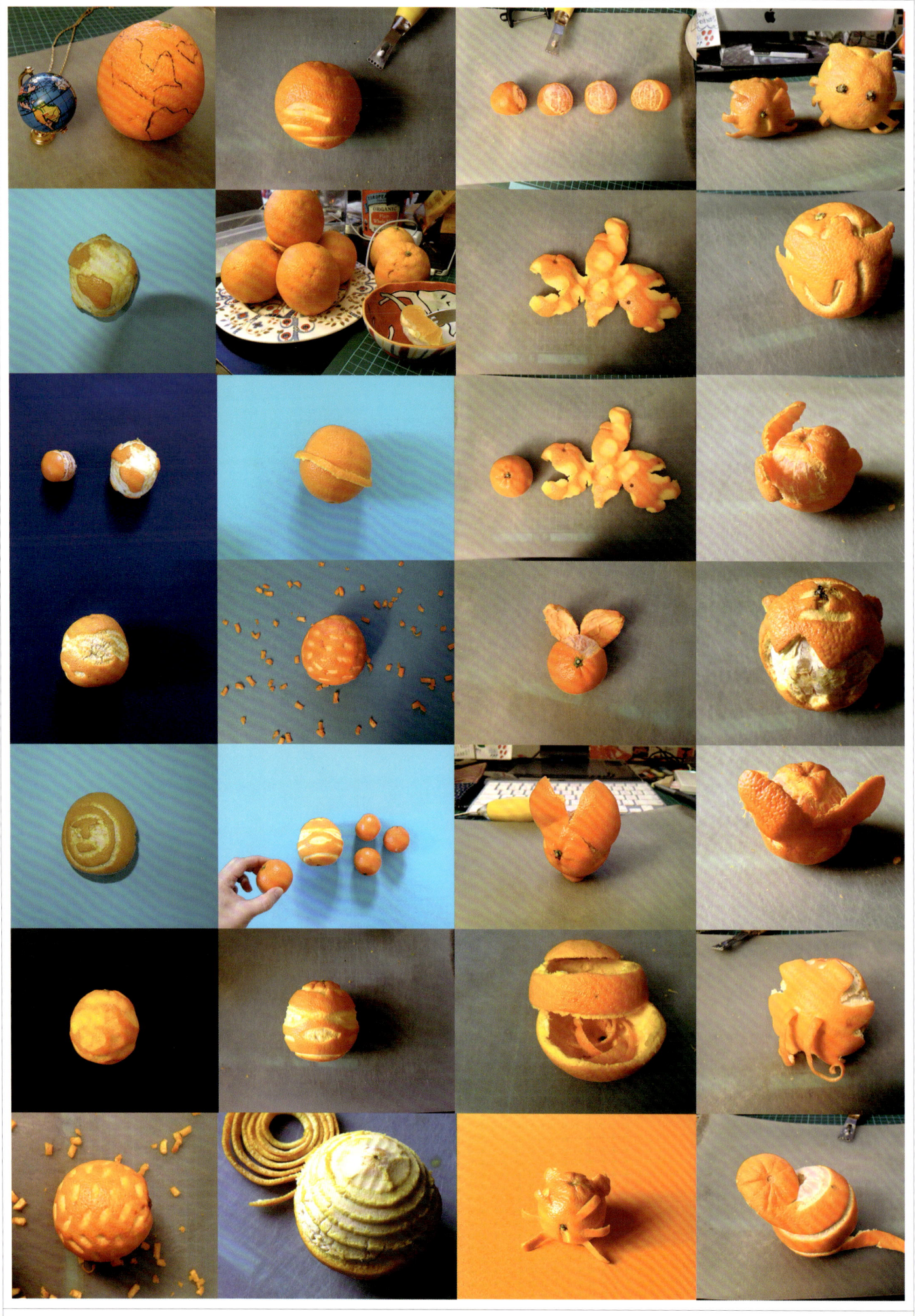

Student: Sherry Hsin-Ting Kuo | **School:** School of Visual Arts

Design | Branding

11 INSTRUCTOR **CARIN GOLDBERG** PLATINUM

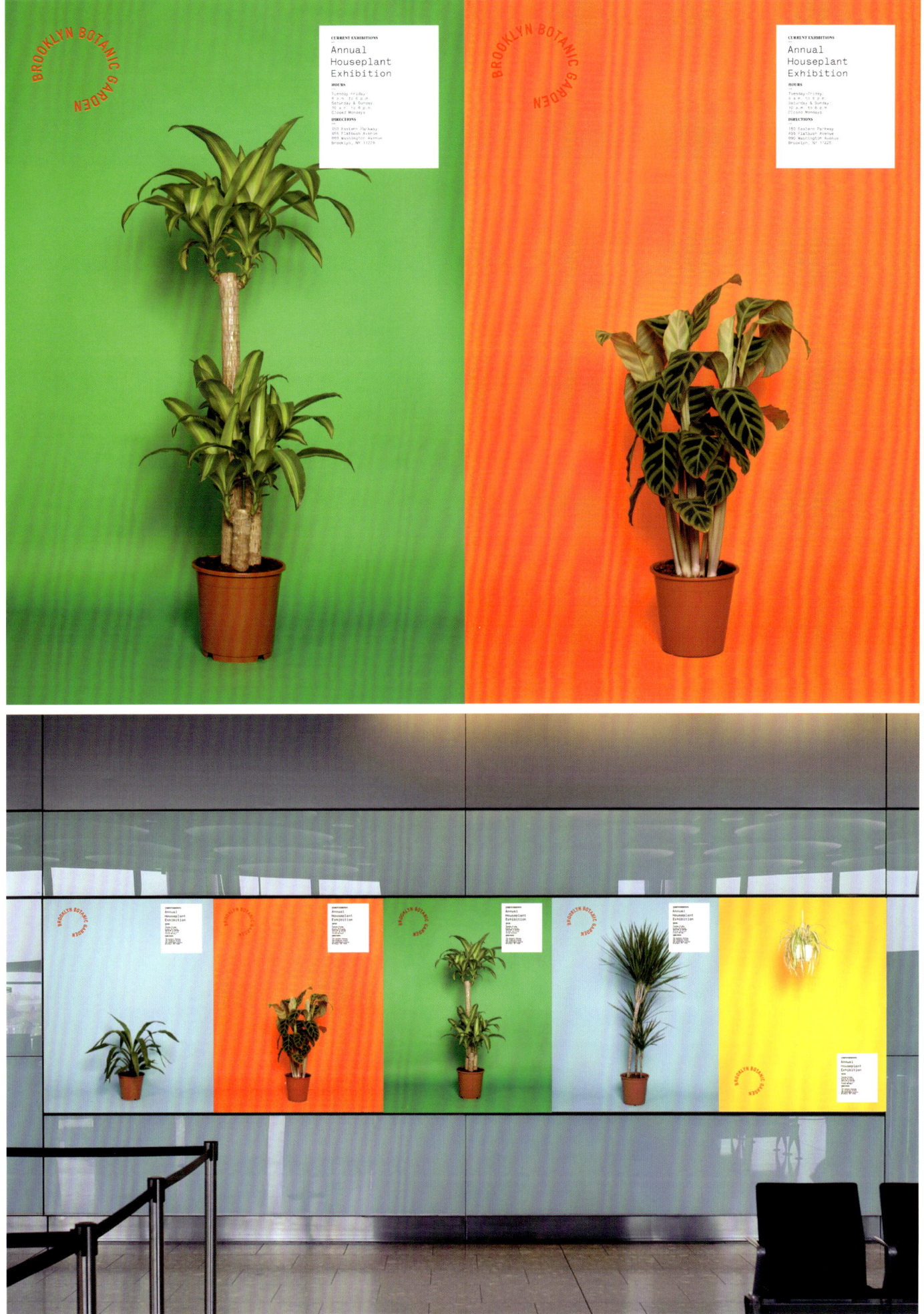

Student: Ben Grandgenett | **School:** School of Visual Arts

Branding | Design

12 INSTRUCTOR BILL OBERLANDER PLATINUM

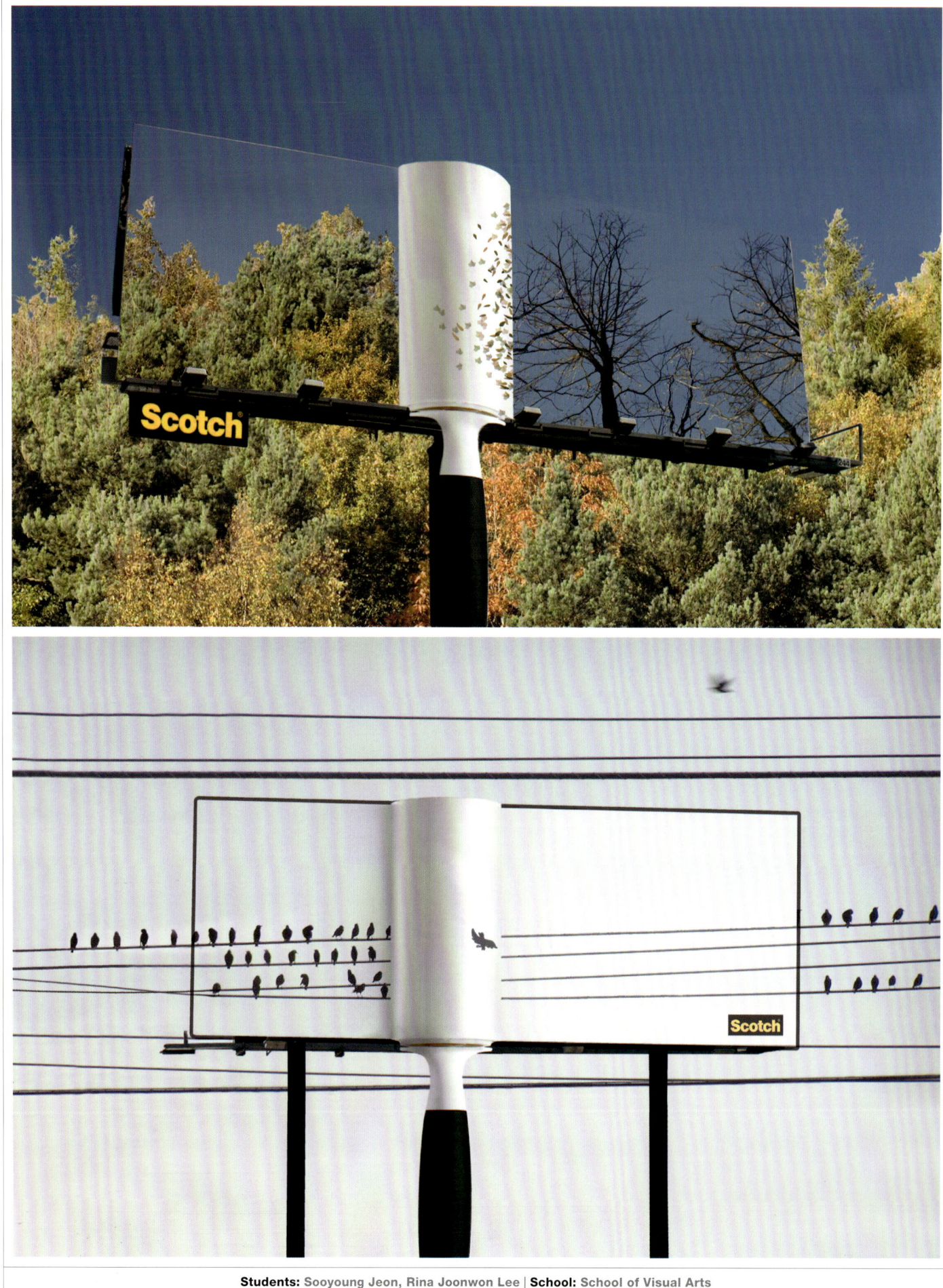

Students: Sooyoung Jeon, Rina Joonwon Lee | **School:** School of Visual Arts

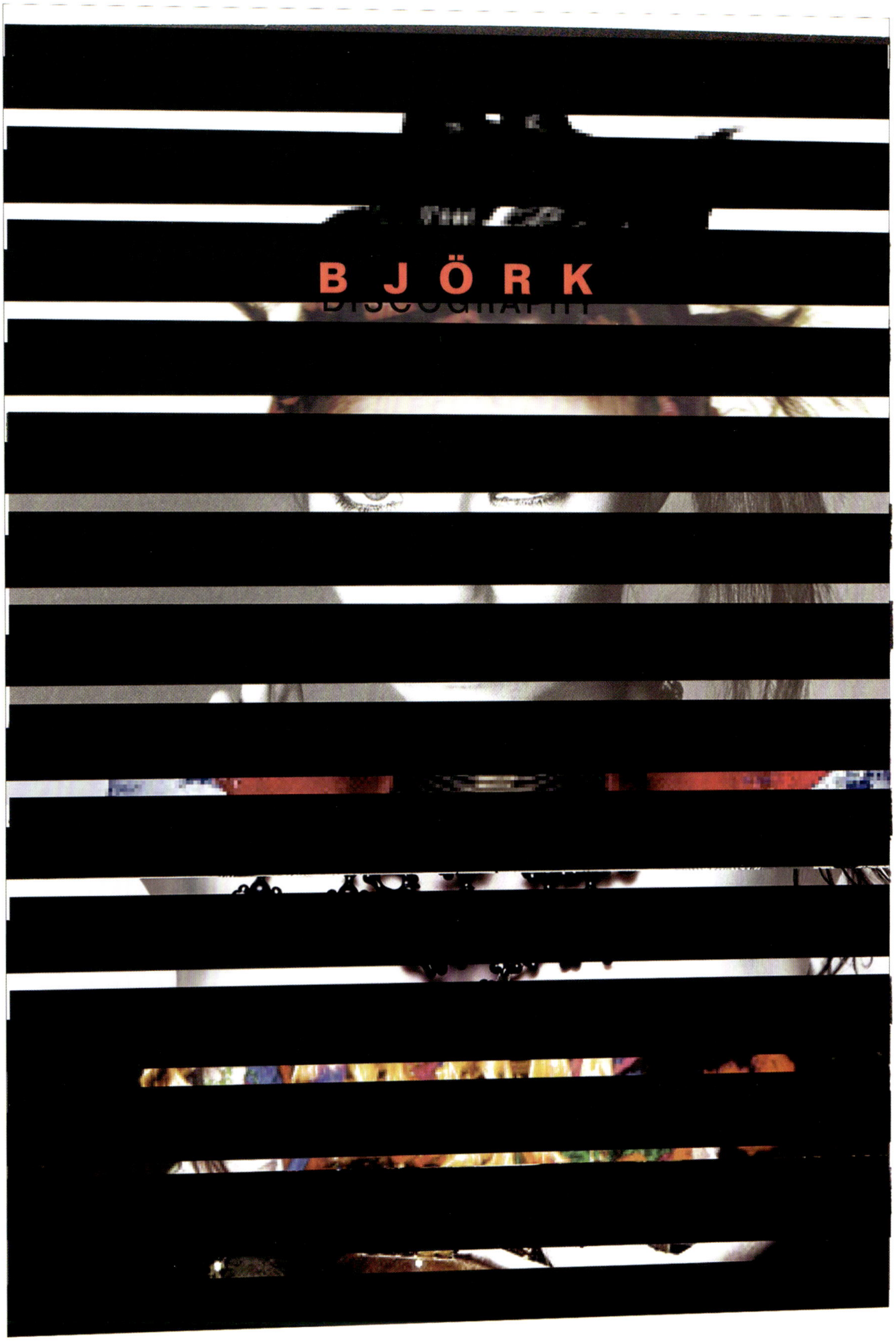

13 INSTRUCTOR NIC TAYLOR PLATINUM

Student: Dominika Kramerova | **School:** School of Visual Arts

Poster | Design

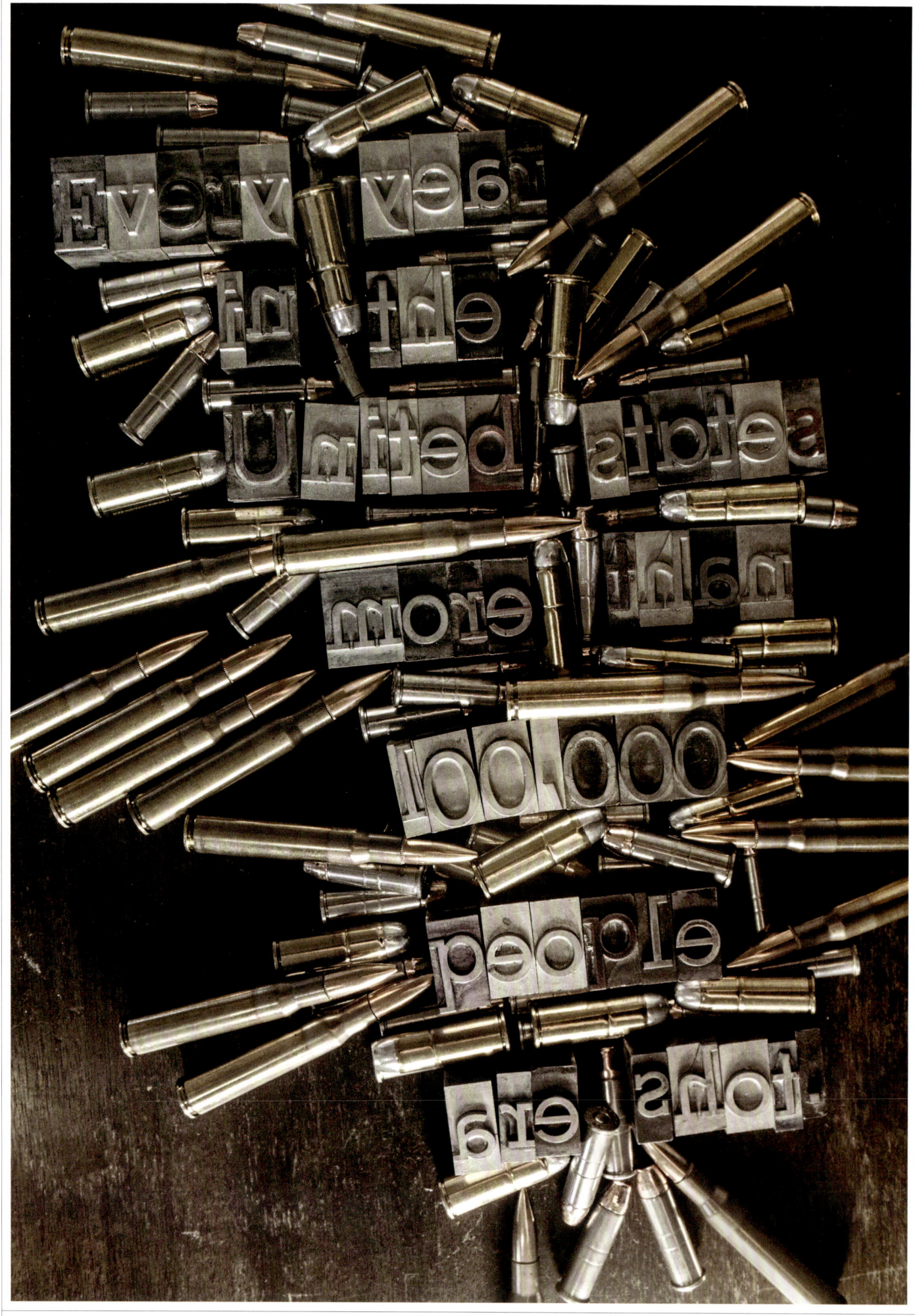

Graphis Judges

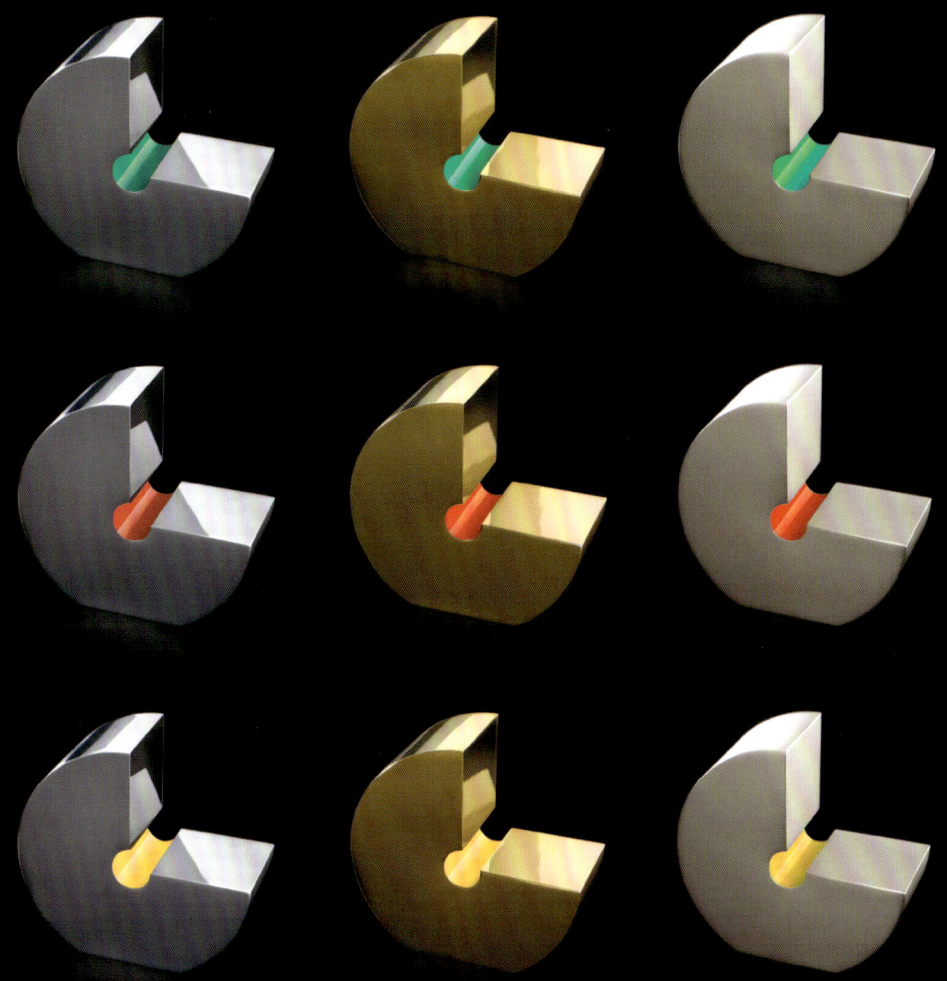

16 NEW TALENT AWARDS 2024 COMPETITION JUDGES

ADVERTISING:

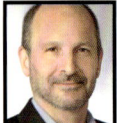

David Bernstein | The Gate | Chief Creative Officer
Biography: David is the chief creative officer of The Gate/New York. During his tenure at the agency, David has won over 100 industry awards and, through an odd twist of fate, co-wrote a best-selling business book, *Death to All Sacred Cows*, after an ad he, Beau Fraser, and Bill Schwab created caught the eye of the editor-in-chief at Disney's Hyperion Books. Before joining The Gate, David worked at creatively driven shops such as Ammirati & Puris, Angotti Thomas Hedge, Merkley Newman Harty, and BBDO.
Commentary: Graphis has always been one of my favorite award shows. It has a truly global draw, and if you're lucky enough to win, you get to see your work reproduced in a beautiful book. I'm not the only one who feels that way. I think I saw about 800 entries in the student competition, and the great majority of them were smart and well-crafted. Congratulations to the students whose work floated to the top. You have a lot to be proud of.

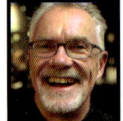

Scott Bucher | Traction Factory | President
Biography: Scott Bucher is the president of Traction Factory, an award-winning advertising and marketing communications firm based in Milwaukee, Wisconsin. "We create strategic, emotive work that lives at the intersection of art and commerce. In the next decade, we will continue to build an irresistible team of strategic thinkers and super-talented creatives and, as a result, reach an even greater level of success by fearlessly elevating the work we do with and for our clients. And we'll do that while adding to the more than one hundred Platinum, Gold, and Silver Graphis Awards Traction Factory teams have been presented."
Commentary: Having the opportunity to evaluate aspiring creative talent in the New Talent Annual was a joy. At Traction Factory, we value the insights gained from the accomplished creative professionals who have served as judges in the evaluation process at Graphis. I am certain that the learning we have accumulated in this venue makes our work better every day. Ultimately, our team and the clients they serve benefit. I applaud the students responsible for the work I saw this year. New creative talent is the lifeblood of our industry, and I am encouraged and excited by the many good ideas the entrants shared.

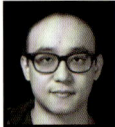

Jim Ma | Bailey Lauerman | Senior Designer
Biography: Jim Ma's world-class design work is anchored in structure and meaning. As a senior designer for Bailey Lauerman's Bosch and Phillips 66 clients, he's crafted nationally-recognized work and won numerous accolades for design on Phillips 66 Aviation, Guardol engine fluid, Kendall lubricants, and Bosch tools, as well as the Lincoln Marathon, Cargill, and Disney, to name only a handful of clients in his ten year career. Jim specializes in thoughtful custom typography, branding, packaging, and conceptual design.
Commentary: Within the realm of visual storytelling, the 2024 New Talent Awards stands as a testament to creativity's boundless potential. Each submission encapsulates a narrative, a message, or an emotion, meticulously crafted into pixels and vectors. From minimalist elegance to vibrant chaos, the spectrum of styles reflects the diverse voices of modern design. As the judging unfolds, may the chosen designs not only inspire admiration but also ignite a deeper appreciation for the power of visual communication.

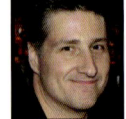

Vinny Tulley | DeVito/Verdi | Creative Director, Art Director, & Copywriter
Biography: Vinny Tulley is a creative director, copywriter, and art director whose work has been recognized in every major advertising award show, including Graphis, The One Show, Art Directors Club, Cannes Lions, CLIO, Communication Arts, OBIE, ADDY's and the Radio Mercury Awards and has been featured in Ad Age, *Creativity Magazine*, *Adweek*, and *The New York Times*. Since graduating with honors from the School of Visual Arts, he has been teaching there, helping hundreds of students break into advertising.
Commentary: After years of helping students win Graphis awards, it was a pleasure to judge this show. Some of the work did the impossible; it surprised me, which, after working in this business for a while, as well as teaching for many years, is a very hard thing to do. Graphis continues to be the quintessential showcase for the talent of the future.

DESIGN:

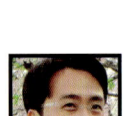

Hoon-Dong Chung | Dankook University | Professor & Designer
Biography: Hoon-Dong Chung is a professor with a Ph.D. in design at Dankook University in South Korea. His works have been shown in international exhibitions and have received more than 200 awards, including the Graphis Platinum Award, the German Design Award, the Red Dot Design Award, the iF Design Award, the Good Design Award, the Creativity Design Award, the HOW Design Award, and others. He also received a commendation from the president of South Korea at the Korea Design Awards. Furthermore, his works are in the collections of the Design Museum Munich, Musée de la Publicité, Dansk Plakat Museum, Ogaki Poster Museum, and more.
Commentary: During the judging period, I felt like I was back in school. It felt like "time travel" for a while. Many high-quality works that professional designers have created were already there. Visually "impressed," I was tremendously delighted. Looking back on that time, it was a pleasant journey. Now, please feel free to enjoy your "journey" in the upcoming future.

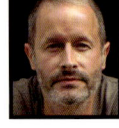

Simon Elliott | Rose | Co-founder & Designer
Biography: Simon (alongside his business partner Garry Blackburn) is a founding partner and co-owner of London-based branding specialists Rose. Simon has partnered and collaborated with hundreds of organizations in that time, from small, owner-managed businesses to global corporations with offices in more than 100 countries around the world. Their work is globally recognized, with over 200 awards, such as Design Agency of the Year from D&AD and International Design Agency of the Year from the Kinsale Shark Awards. Rose is also one of the UK government's Top 100 Creative Agencies for exporting the best of British design around the world.
Commentary: I was delighted to judge the Graphis New Talent Awards and intrigued to see how the next generation of designers view and communicate with the world. The branding category was very well populated, with some exciting and surprisingly mature entries rising to the surface. For me, the best entries were the result of the designer standing in the shoes of the intended audience, understanding what makes them tick, and then finding a relevant and distinctive visual and verbal language to connect with them.

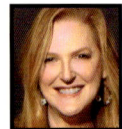

Patti Judd | Judd Brand Media | Founder & Creative Director
Biography: Patti Judd is an award-winning creative director, accomplished marketing and film executive, co-founder of the San Diego International Film Festival, and chief visionary officer at Graphis. Her studio, Judd Brand Media, champions her passion for creating innovative work, receiving over 100 awards in design, advertising, and marketing. Her work includes notable global brands such as WME, Disney, Mattel, Montreux Jazz Festival, Century 21, Aramark, Service America, Hilton, and many others. She holds two executive producer credits for a children's TV series on Nickelodeon and a feature film in association with the BBC. Currently, she is in development as executive producer on an exciting new animated children's series. Patti's nonprofit work includes being a foster youth board member and a past president of an arts and culture board benefiting Balboa Park, the largest urban cultural park in the US. Recently, she was awarded as an Altruist Honoree by *Modern Luxury* magazine.
Commentary: As a judge, I am genuinely impressed by this year's participants' exceptional creativity and innovation. Each project showcases their talent, offering fresh perspectives and solutions. These students are more than simply talented individuals; they are showing their commitment as creative visionaries who will shape the future of their respective fields.

17 NEW TALENT AWARDS 2024 COMPETITION JUDGES

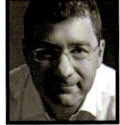

Michael Pantuso | Michael Pantuso Design | Principal Creative
Biography: Michael Pantuso is a graphic designer, illustrator, and fine artist known for bringing a genuine depth of experience and authenticity to his work. As the principal creative at Michael Pantuso Design, he applies a straightforward and innovative approach that is distinctive and immediately recognizable. Born and raised on the south side of Orlando, Florida, Michael now lives in a commuter suburb west of Chicago. This transition from the sunny landscapes of Florida to the bustling creative scene near Chicago has broadened his artistic perspective, enriching both his personal and professional life.
Commentary: The commitment Graphis shows in highlighting the next wave of design talent is profoundly inspiring, and their dedication to discovering, supporting, and celebrating emerging designers and students is pivotal for our industry. Reviewing the submissions, I was captivated by the dynamic energy of these promising students. Their work was a vibrant display of the limitless possibilities in design, marked by creativity, innovation, and passion. Notably, many students spoke fondly of their professors while discussing their projects, highlighting the significant impact these educators have on their growth and development.

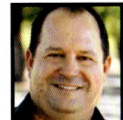

David Schuemann | CF Napa Brand Design | Founder & Designer
Biography: Over the past 21 years, David Schuemann has led CF Napa Brand Design to become one of the world's preeminent brand agencies specializing in the alcohol beverage industry. CF Napa's work has earned recognition from nearly every major design competition, has been showcased in the Museum of Modern Art, and is part of the permanent collection at the Cooper Hewitt Design Museum, the Smithsonian, and the American Design Archives at the Denver Art Museum. David authored *99 Bottles of Wine: The Making of the Contemporary Wine Label*, writes regularly for numerous periodicals, and is a regular industry speaker.
Commentary: Throughout my career, I have viewed Graphis and its competitions as one of the standouts for highlighting the best of the best in design thinking and execution. CF Napa has been humbled through the years by the many Graphis awards we have received, so it was a special honor to judge one of the very competitions I have long been impressed by. I found it inspiring to see so much incredible talent and work on display. The level of work was incredible, and more importantly, the keen conceptual thinking was impressive. It was truly invigorating and inspiring to see the beginning of so many bright futures in the industry.

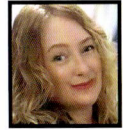

Lisa Winstanley | Lisa Winstanley Design | Designer & Professor
Biography: Lisa Winstanley is an assistant professor of visual communication at Nanyang Technological University in Singapore. With over 20 years of commercial experience and a decade of international research and teaching, Lisa explores ethical and collaborative design practices and pedagogies. Her creative work has received over 80 international awards and has been exhibited across 28 countries. Lisa advocates for creative integrity in the production and consumption of design to support creative communities and foster positive change.
Commentary: It's been a genuine honor to judge the 2024 New Talent Awards. The level of talent and skill showcased by these emerging designers is simply exceptional; I've seen creativity on par with seasoned professionals! Supporting and nurturing our young talent is essential to advance our creative industries, and based on this experience, I can see that we have some rising stars. Congratulations to all participants, instructors, and schools involved.

PHOTOGRAPHY:

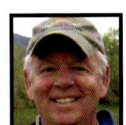

Terry Heffernan | Photographer
Biography: Terry's post photo directorial 40 year career in San Francisco predicated a move to Montana. There, he continues to shoot photos, no longer with his 8x10 camera but with his iPhone. Terry is also involved with a stream restoration project and is always in the company of his beloved bulldogs. When asked his reasons for his move, he is quick to quote John Steinbeck from *Travels with Charley*: "I suppose our capacity for self-delusion is boundless. I'm in love with Montana. For other states, I have admiration, respect, recognition, and even some affection. But with Montana, it is love, and when one is in love, it is difficult to explain."
Commentary: It was very interesting to see the variety of imagery in the photography category. I hope that students will continue to look into the history of photography to find and emulate their heroes. Once heroes are discovered, your fingerprint will evolve around what you know is great work.

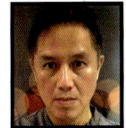

Kah Poon | Photographer
Biography: Kah Poon is a New York City-based fashion, portrait, and dance photographer. A native of Singapore, Kah first came to the US when he was recruited by Brigham Young University's swim team. Kah has also performed and competed internationally with the acclaimed BYU Ballroom Dance Company. In 2021, Graphis honored Kah by naming him a Graphis Master. Kah has also received awards from Polaroid, Communication Arts, FujiFilm, Adobe, Hasselblad, Graphis, Rangefinder, the Tokyo International Foto Awards, the International Photography Awards (IPA), the International Color Awards, and the London International Creative Competition.
Commentary: The range was diverse, and the students showed a willingness to innovate and experiment, each trying to articulate their story and voice. I would recommend these students continue stretching their imaginations and honing their skills. I look forward to seeing their progress. It was fun to judge these students' work.

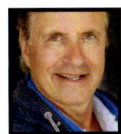

Frank P. Wartenberg | Photographer
Biography: As a kid, Frank Wartenberg got his first camera from his father when he was six years old. When he was a student, he worked as a press photographer at concerts for The Rolling Stones, Pink Floyd, Eartha Kitt, Madness, Astrud Gilberto, and many more. After school, he studied law at university, but never gave up his passion for photography and eventually opened up his own studio in Hamburg, Germany. He worked for magazines like *Brigitte*, *Elle*, *Stern*, *Max*, and more, as well as for fashion and beauty brands like Brax, Goldwell, Wella, and Nivea. In the US, Frank worked in NYC for Coty, ESPN, and more. Today, Frank lives with his family in his hometown, Hamburg.
Commentary: The selection was very varied, and the students illuminated their images well. I enjoyed evaluating the students' work and looking at their talent and their path into photography. I liked the symbolism in some of the pictures. Portraits made up a large part of the photography category, which pleased me. I hope the students improve their skills and see that their imagination and fantasy are limitless.

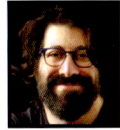

Michael Winokur | Photographer
Biography: Michael Winokur is a film director and still photographer with roots in journalism. Whether it's a three-act story or a single sublime image, Michael looks to express individual identity as well as capture our common humanity. While still in high school, he worked as a photojournalist for city newspapers in Philadelphia, developing an interest in portraiture and a narrative style focused on capturing the essential elements of character. Through overlapping careers as an award-winning documentary photographer, journalist, commercial photographer, and film director, visual storytelling has remained a common thread and driving purpose.
Commentary: To all the courageous young creatives, you're entering a swiftly changing industry where there is at once excitement and risk. Bravo. As you face career highs and lows, you'll need to find a way to keep a score that is as unique as your own goals. I urge you to ignore likes and followers. They will lead you in circles. Clients, awards, and paydays can keep you moving, but you must navigate your own course and seek a way to be honest in your self-assessment. Find your own personal North Star. Now, get back to executing your best ideas.

Advertising Gold Awards

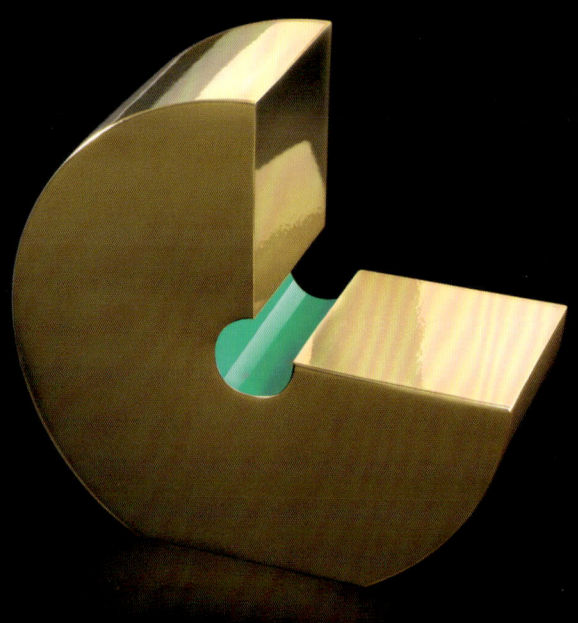

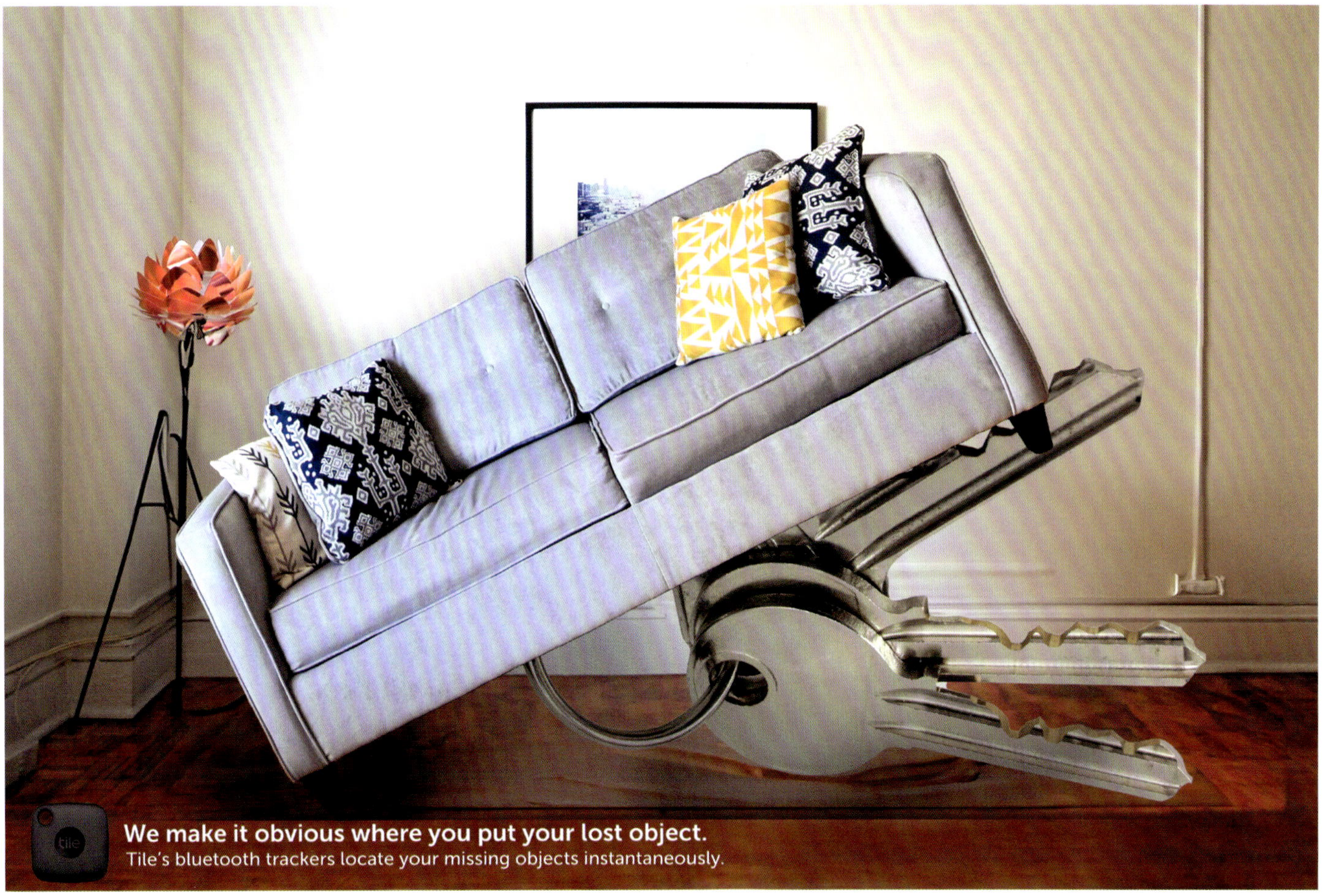

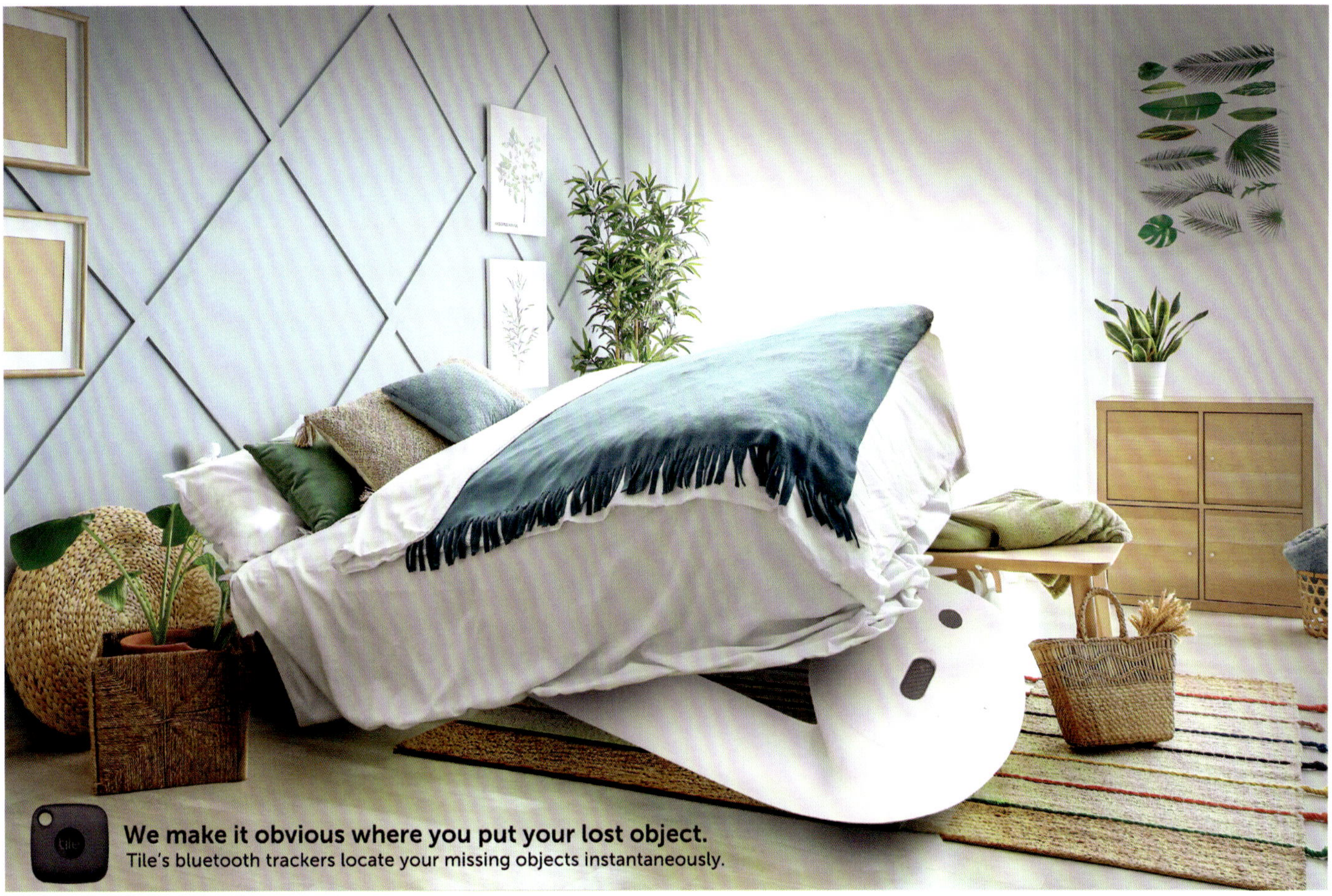

19 INSTRUCTOR **MEL WHITE** GOLD

We make it obvious where you put your lost object.
Tile's bluetooth trackers locate your missing objects instantaneously.

We make it obvious where you put your lost object.
Tile's bluetooth trackers locate your missing objects instantaneously.

| P234: Credit & Commentary | **Students:** Jenna Byers, Sophia Donio | **School:** Syracuse University, The Newhouse School | Images 1, 2 of 3 |

Electronics | Advertising

20 INSTRUCTOR **KEVIN O'NEILL** GOLD

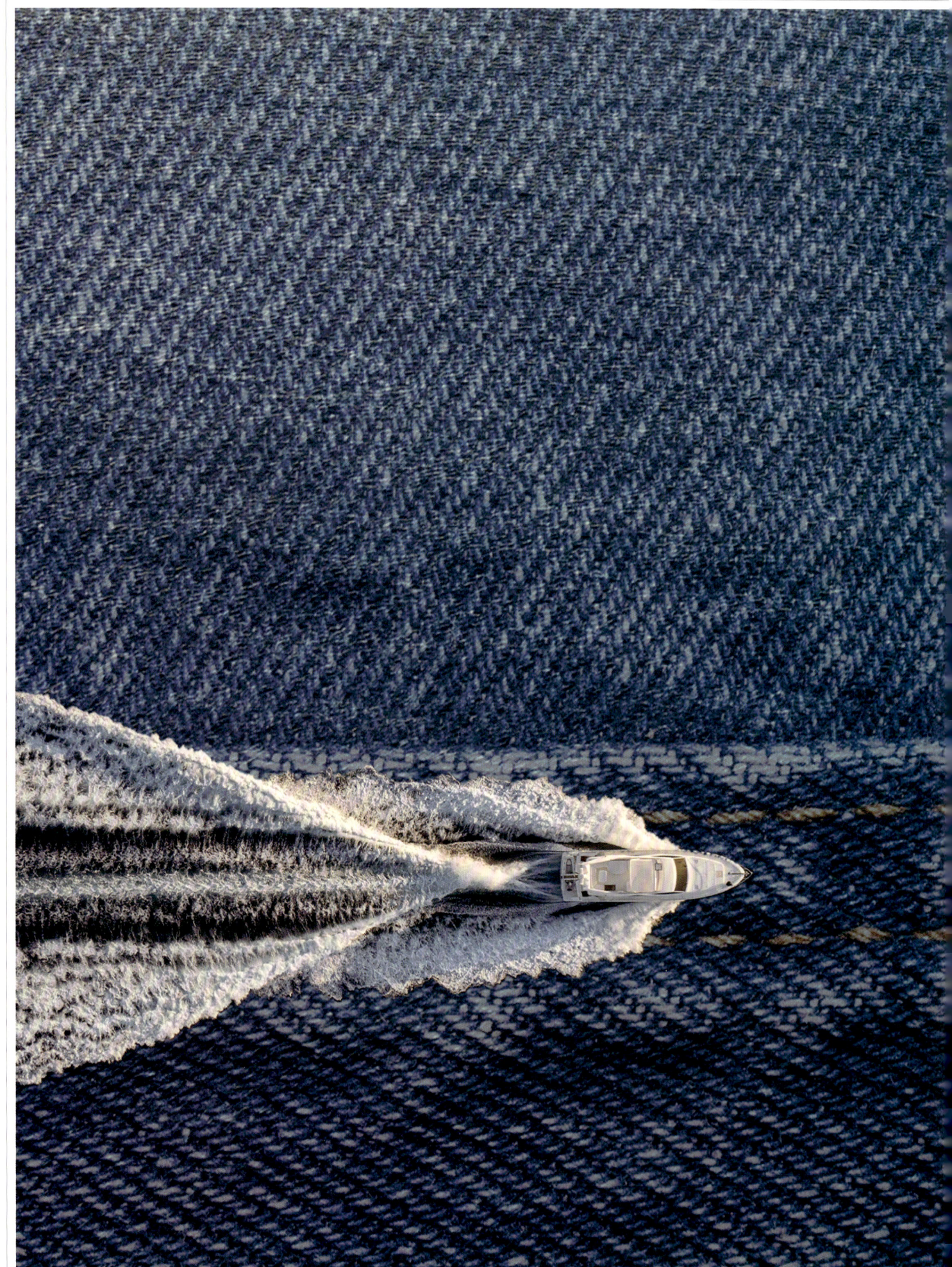

P234: Credit & Commentary

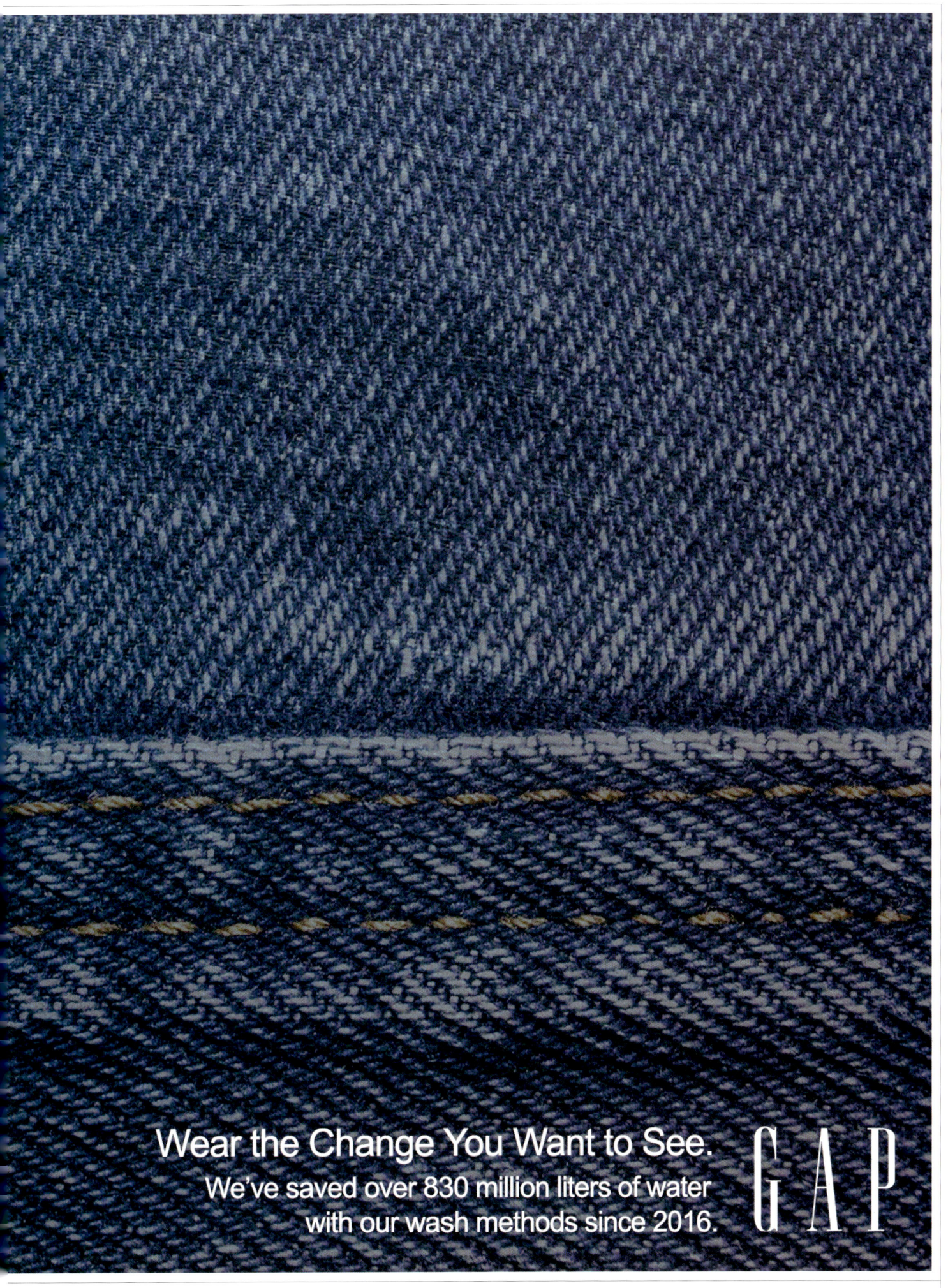

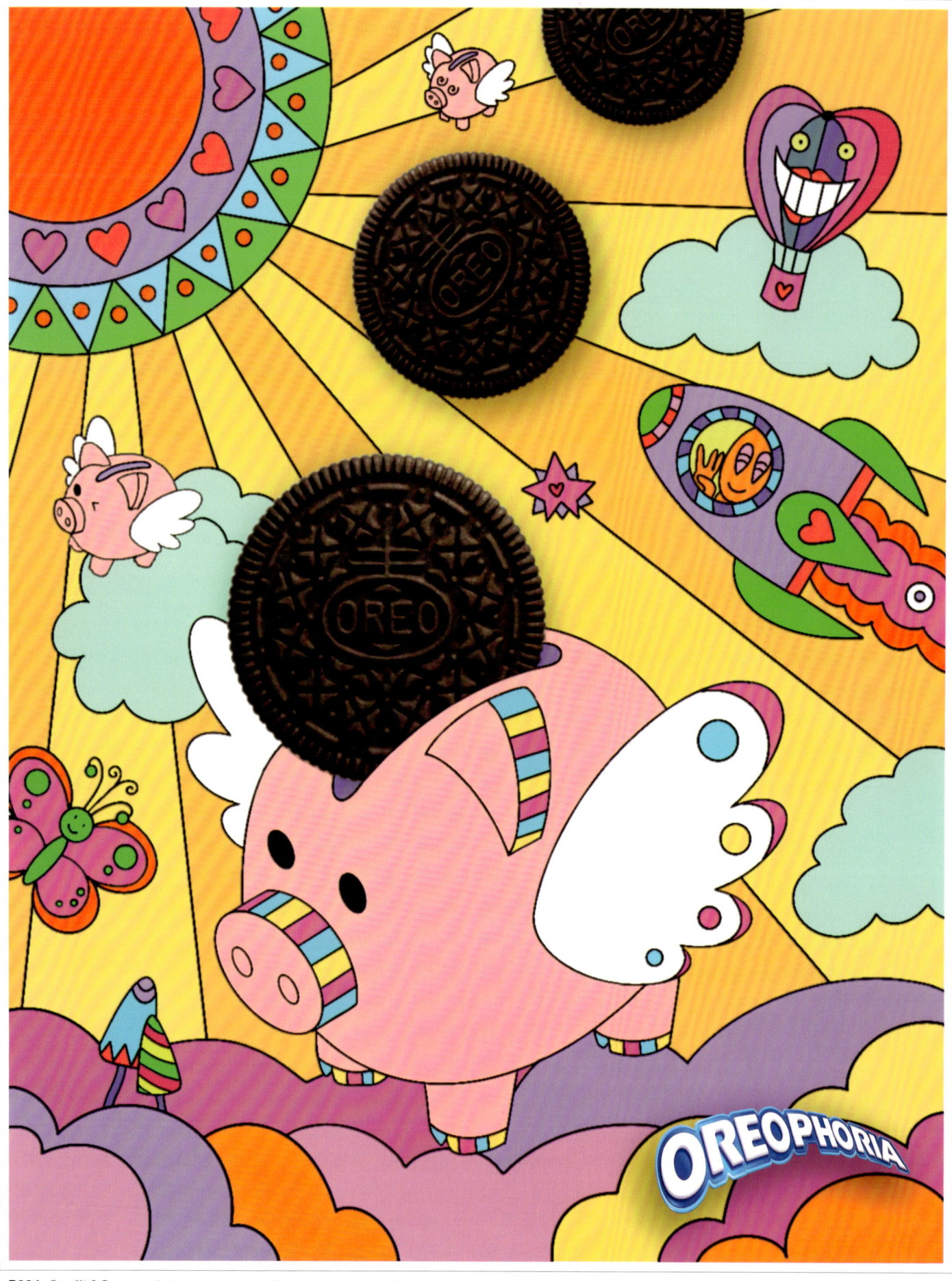

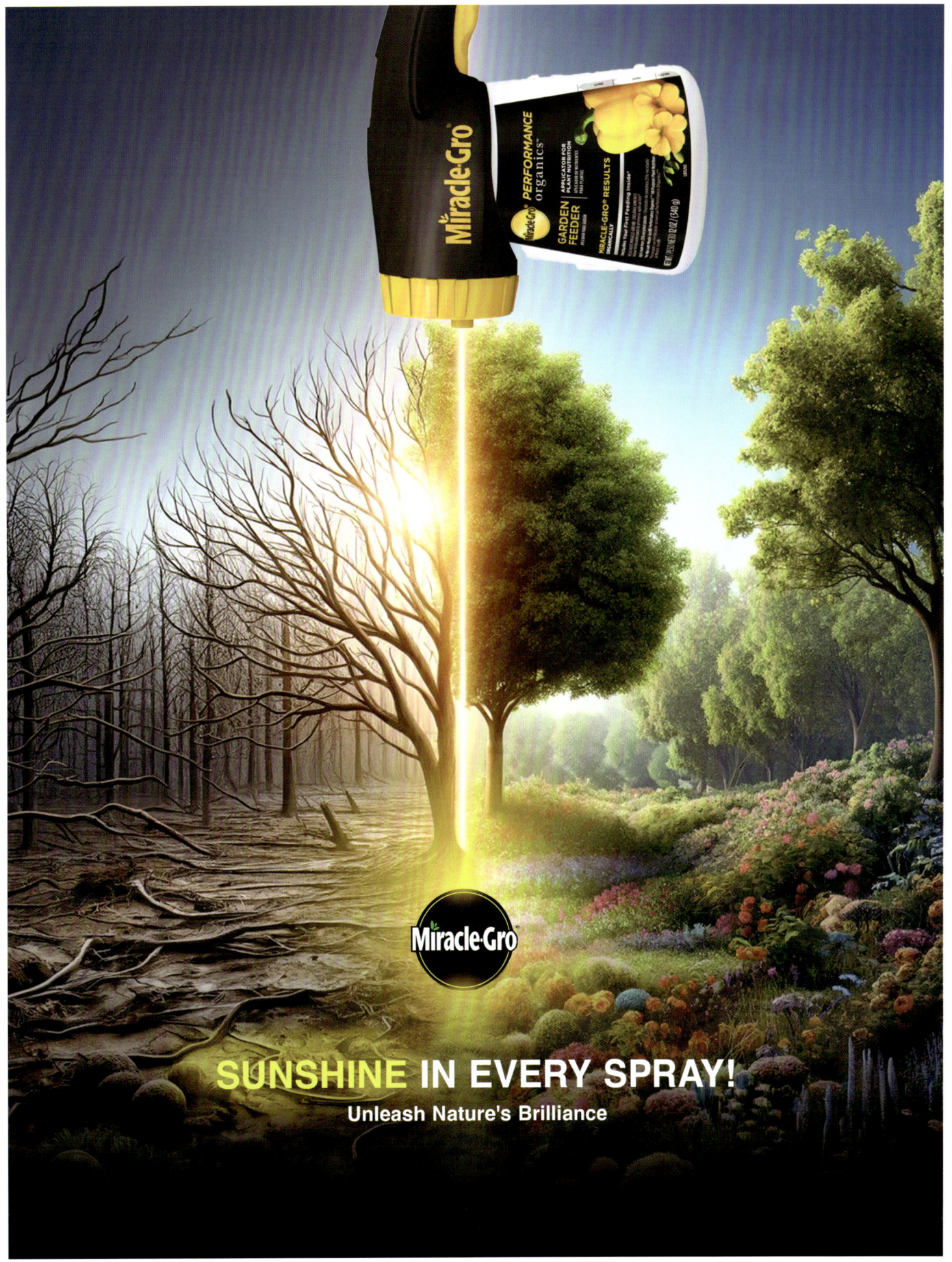

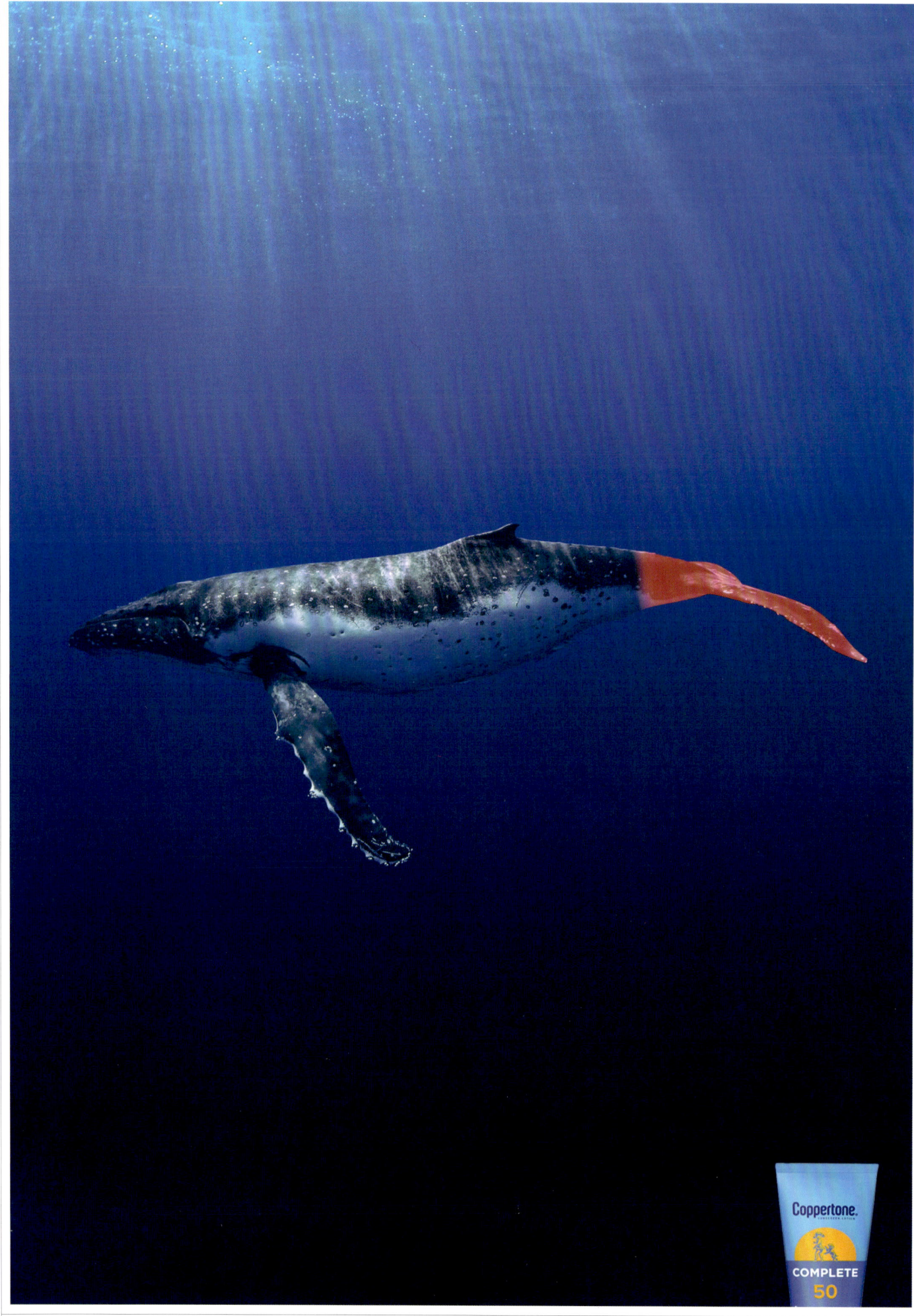

Advertising Silver Awards

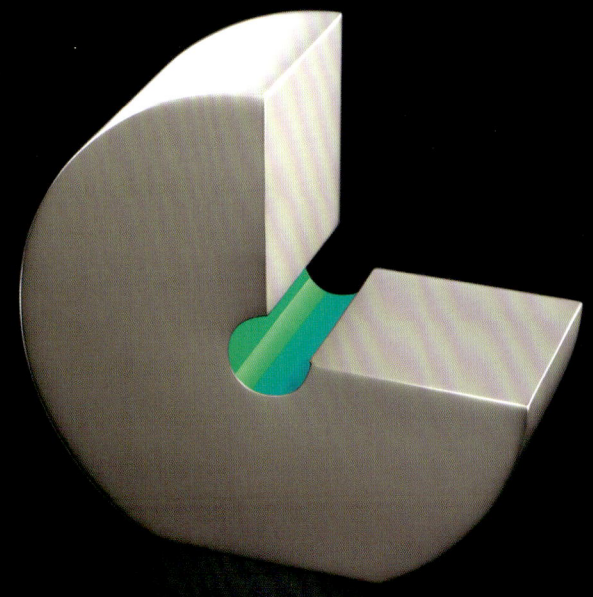

26 ADVERTISING SILVER

INSTRUCTOR DOUGLAS MAY 🇺🇸

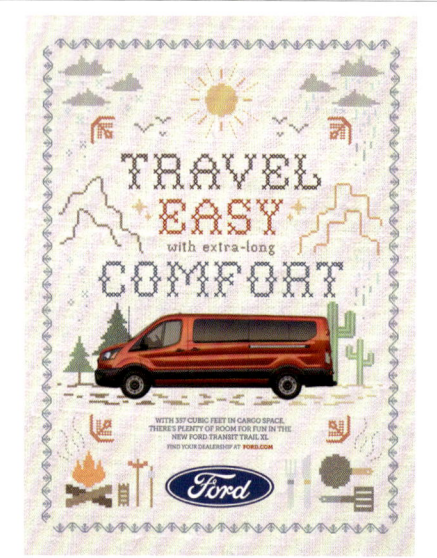

Student: Macy Belton
School: University of North Texas

INSTRUCTOR MARK ALLEN 🇺🇸

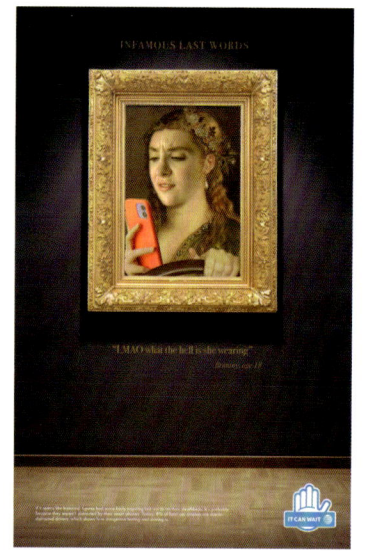

Student: Roshan Gupta
School: Southern Methodist University

INSTRUCTOR WILLIE BARONET 🇺🇸

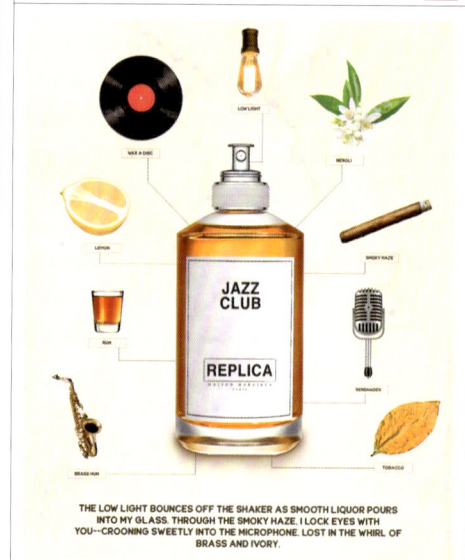

Students: Morgan Martinez, Delaney Gendron
School: Southern Methodist University

INSTRUCTOR DUSTY CROCKER 🇺🇸

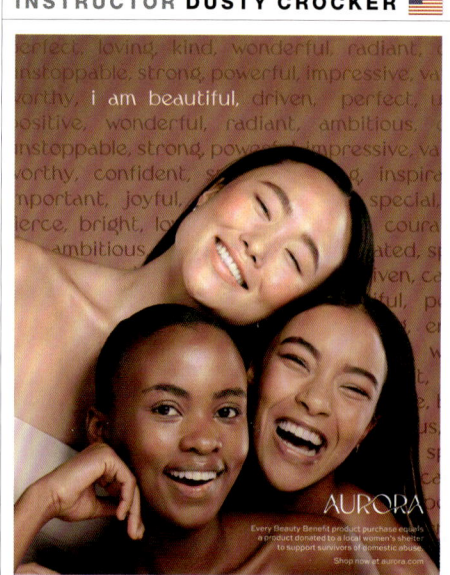

Student: Abigail Lund
School: Texas Christian University

INSTRUCTOR WILLIE BARONET 🇺🇸

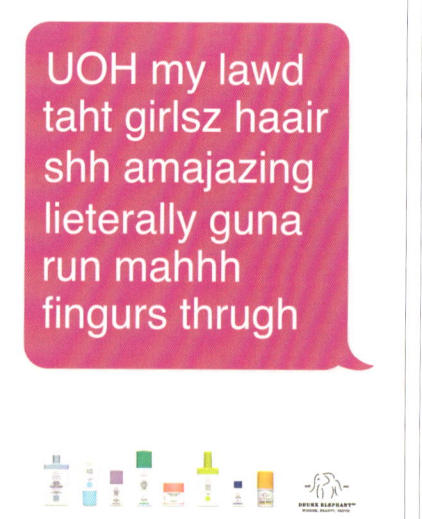

Students: Kaitlyn Blan, Caroline Davis
School: Southern Methodist University

INSTRUCTOR WILLIE BARONET 🇺🇸

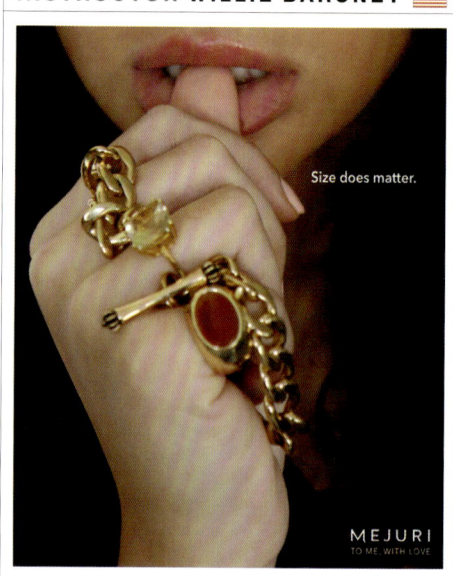

Students: Roshan Gupta, Morgan Martinez
School: Southern Methodist University

INSTRUCTOR BILL GALYEAN 🇺🇸

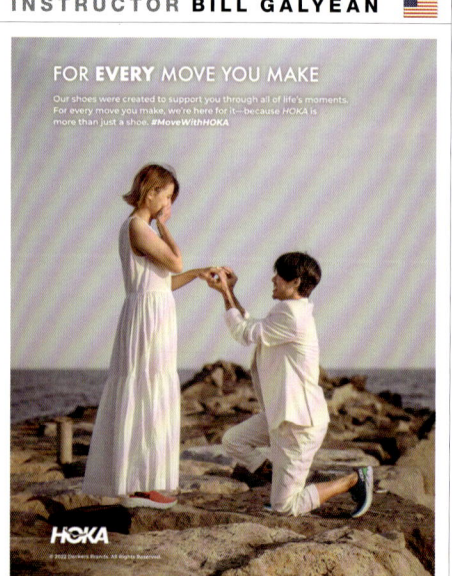

Students: I. Pasino, R. Richard, R. Stegall, E. Wilkie | **School:** Texas Christian University

INSTRUCTOR MARK ALLEN 🇺🇸

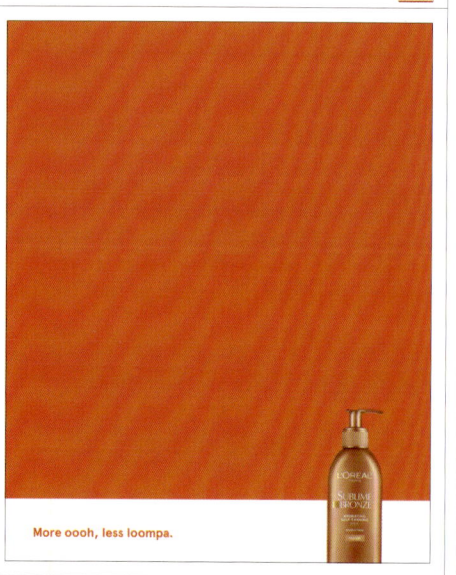

Students: Blake Lyster, Morgan Martinez
School: Southern Methodist University

INST. GENARO SOLIS RIVERO 🇺🇸

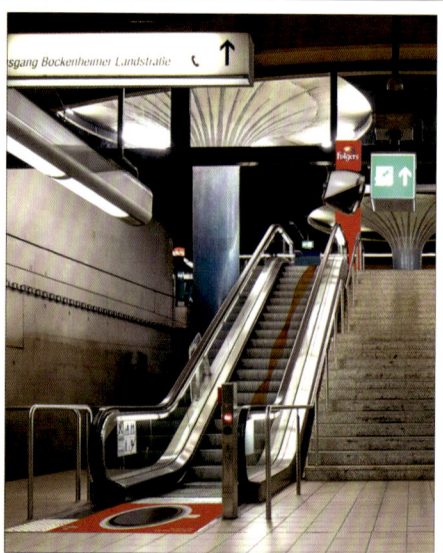

Student: Abigail Sanders
School: Baylor University

Advertising | Automotive, Beauty & Fashion, Beverage

27 ADVERTISING SILVER

INSTRUCTOR MARK ALLEN

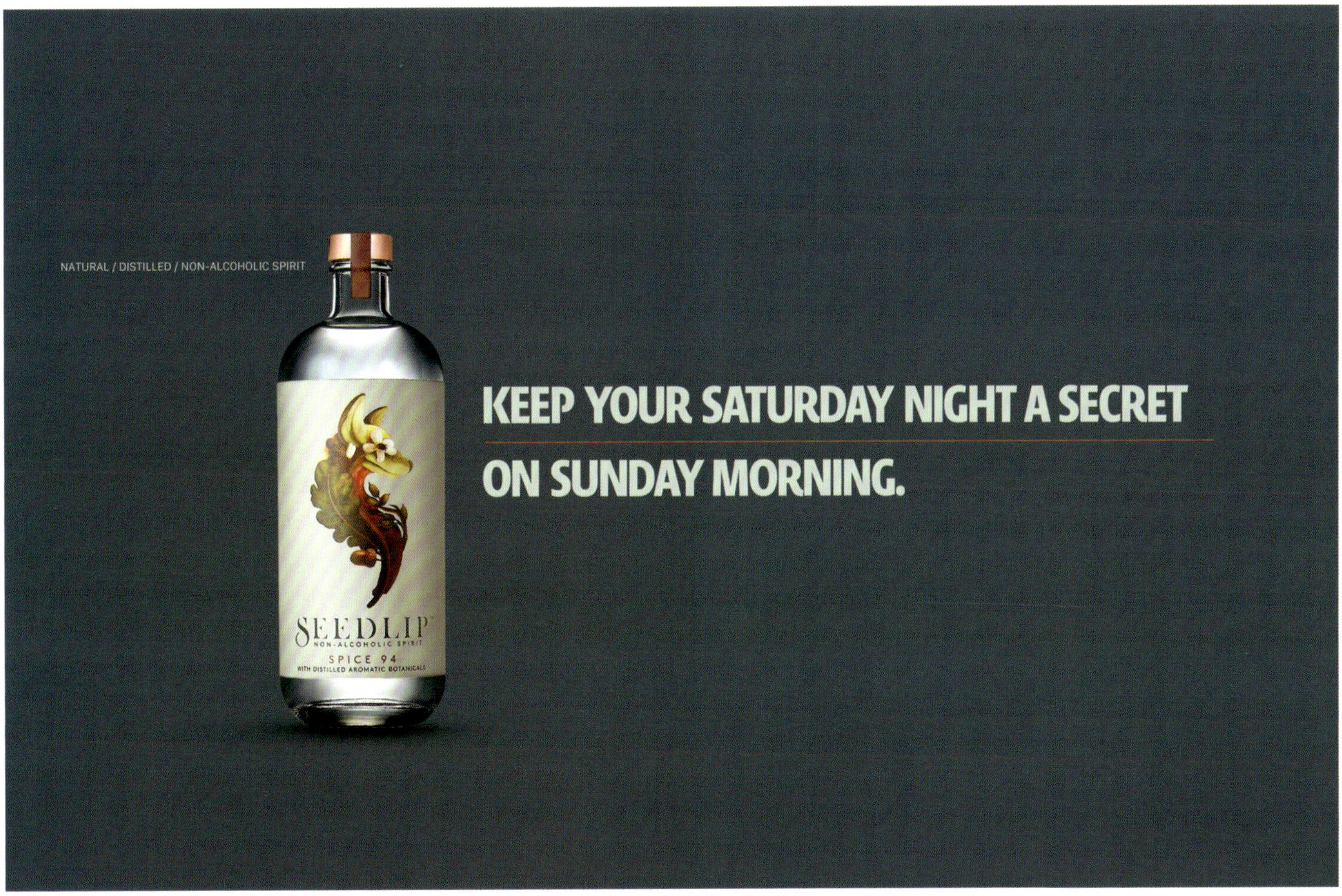

KEEP YOUR SATURDAY NIGHT A SECRET ON SUNDAY MORNING.

Students: Emma Clarke, Callie Oden | **School:** Southern Methodist University

INSTRUCTOR MARK ALLEN

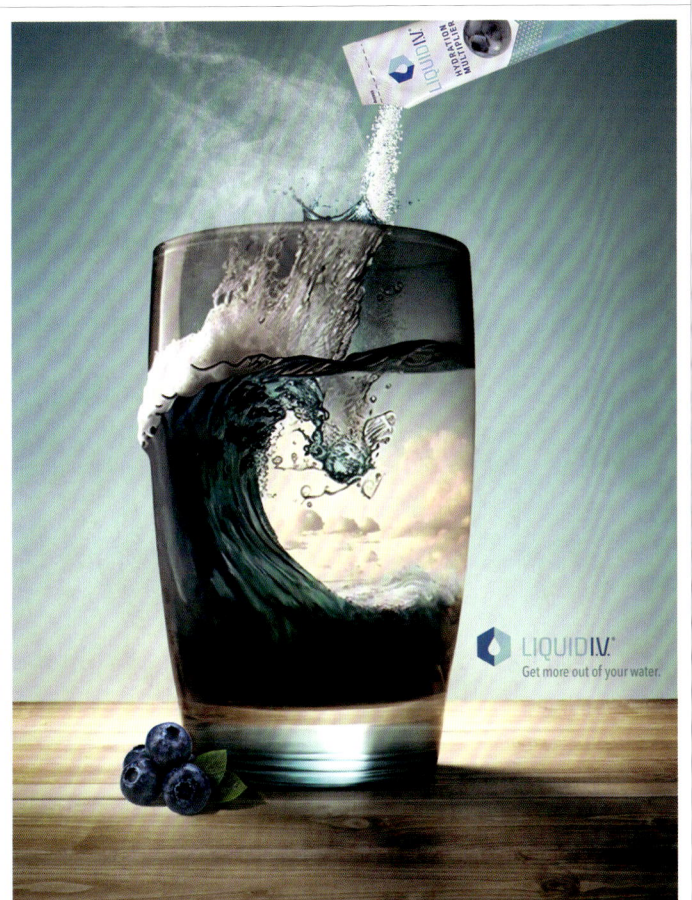

Students: Andrea Torroni, Nicole Zimmer
School: Southern Methodist University

INSTRUCTOR DOUGLAS MAY

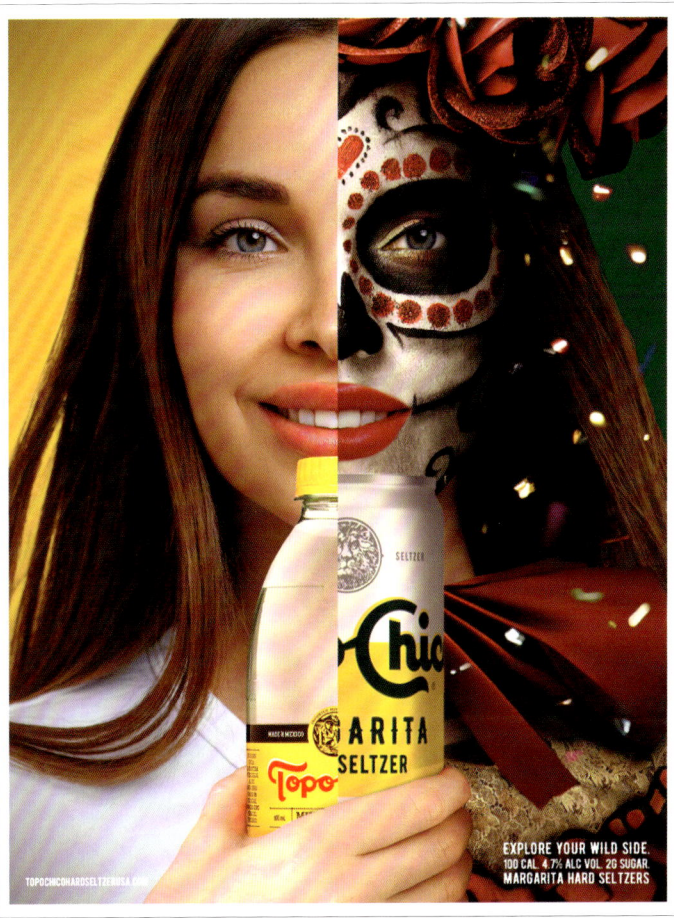

Student: John Paul Nguyen
School: University of North Texas

Beverage | Advertising

28 ADVERTISING SILVER

INSTRUCTOR GENARO SOLIS RIVERO

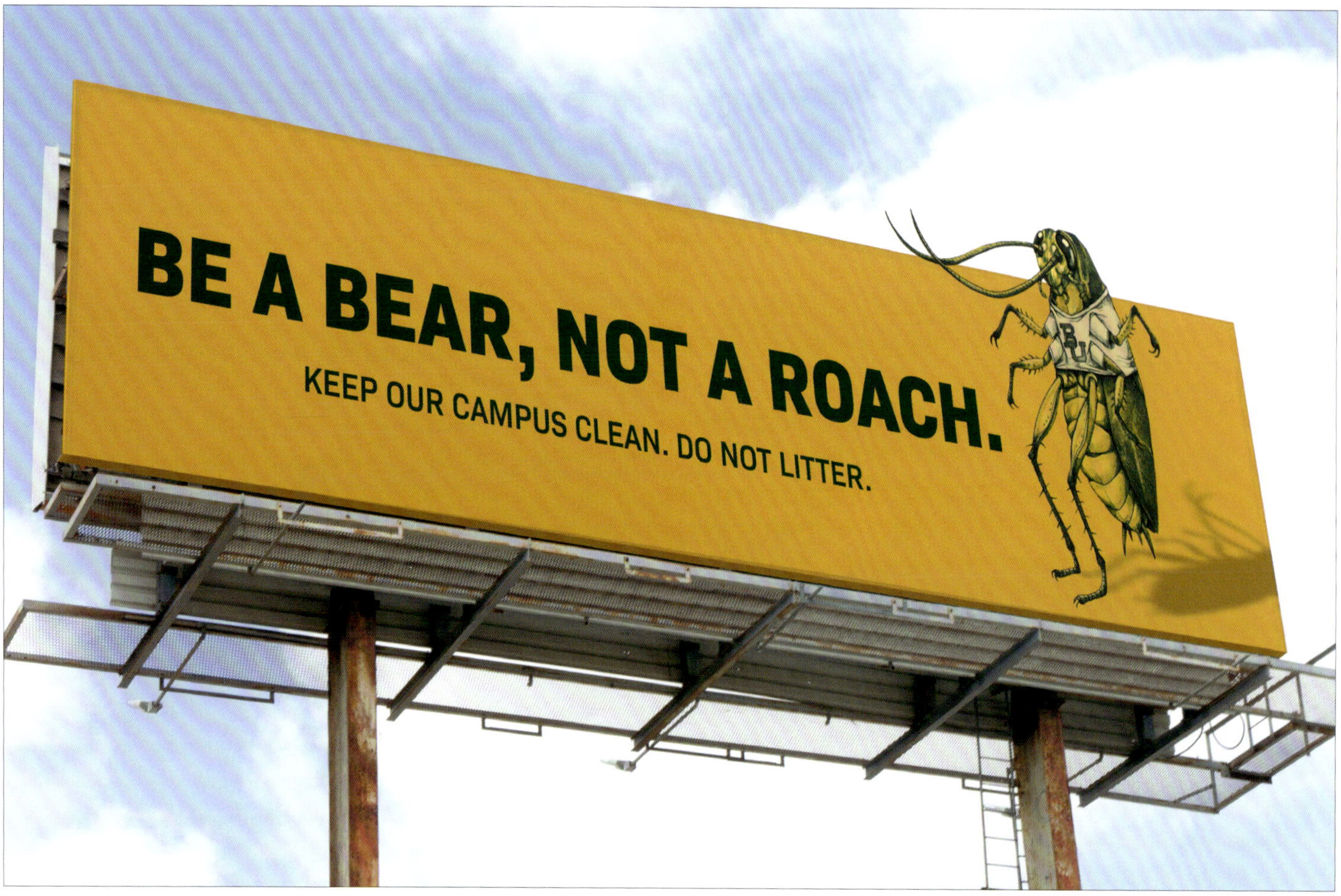

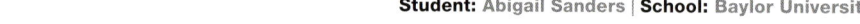

Student: Abigail Sanders | School: Baylor University

INSTRUCTOR BRACKEN HANUSE CORLETT

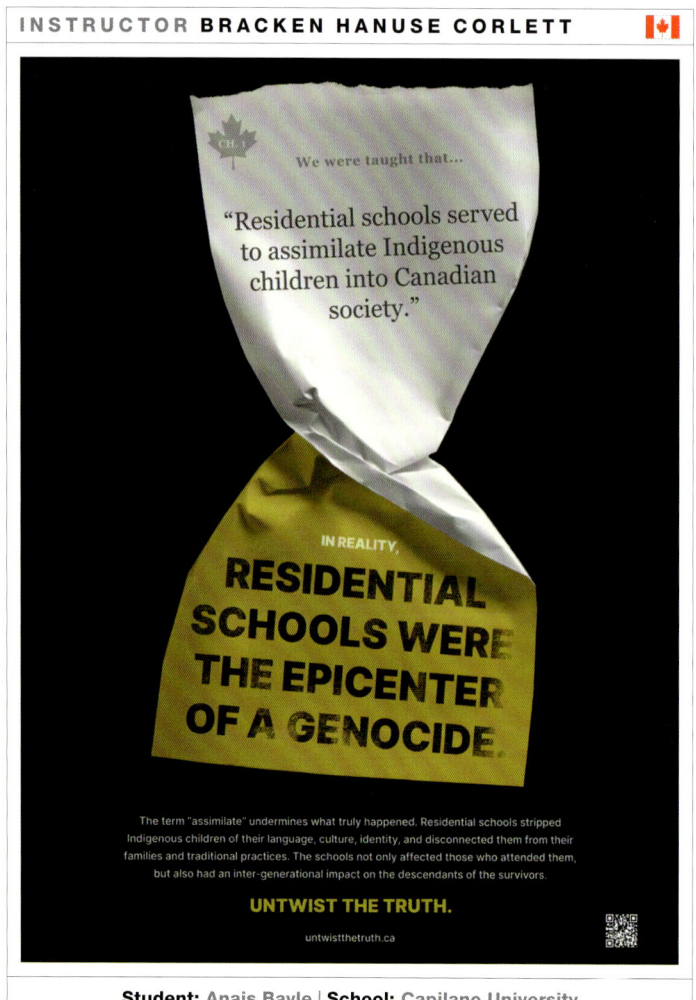

Student: Anais Bayle | School: Capilano University

INSTRUCTOR JOSHUA EGE

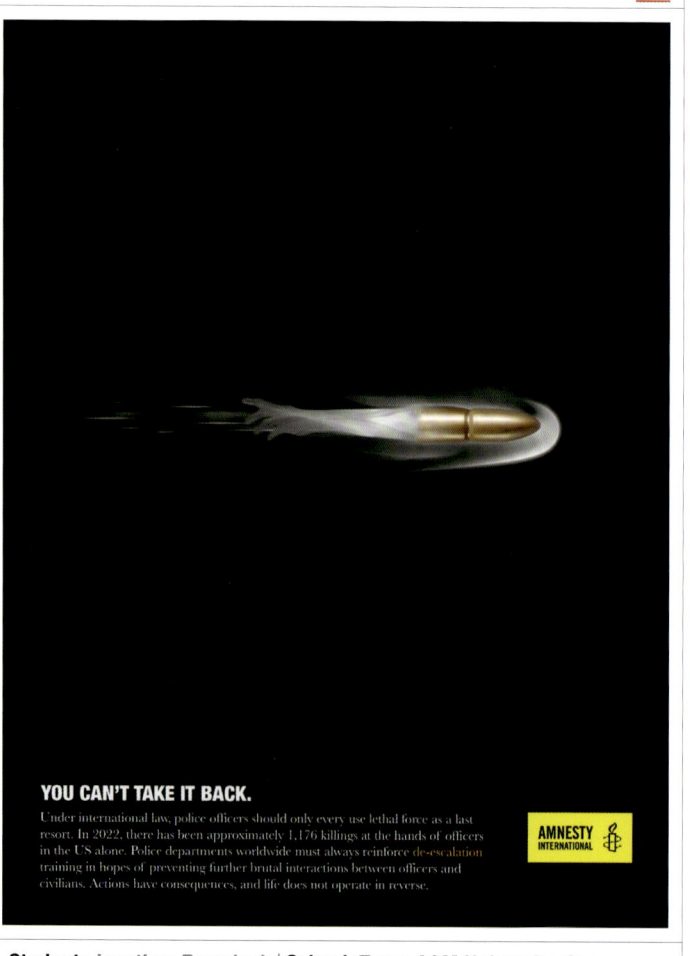

Student: Jonathan Ramsingh | School: Texas A&M University-Commerce

Advertising | Billboard, Education

29 ADVERTISING SILVER

INSTRUCTOR MEL WHITE

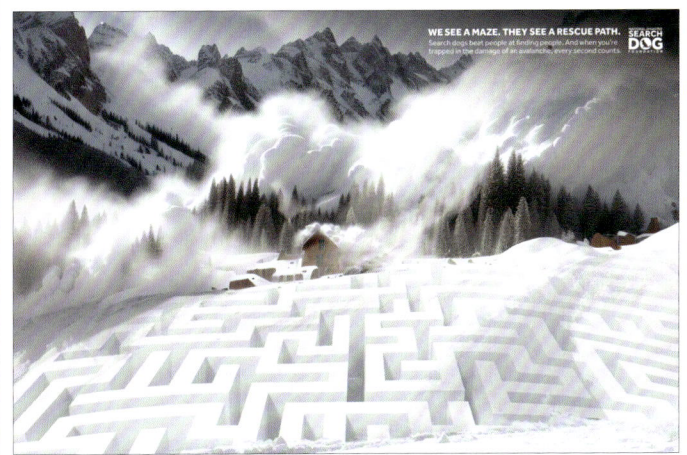

Students: Lang Delapa, Katelyn Hughes
School: Syracuse University, The Newhouse School

INSTRUCTOR MEL WHITE

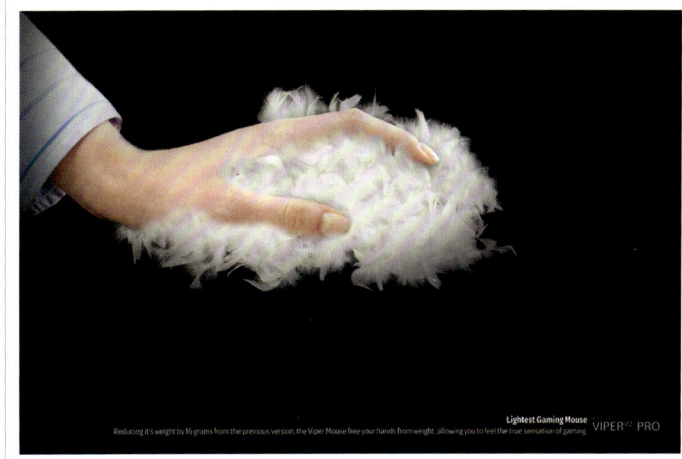

Student: Meiling Xiong
School: Syracuse University, The Newhouse School

INSTRUCTOR MEL WHITE

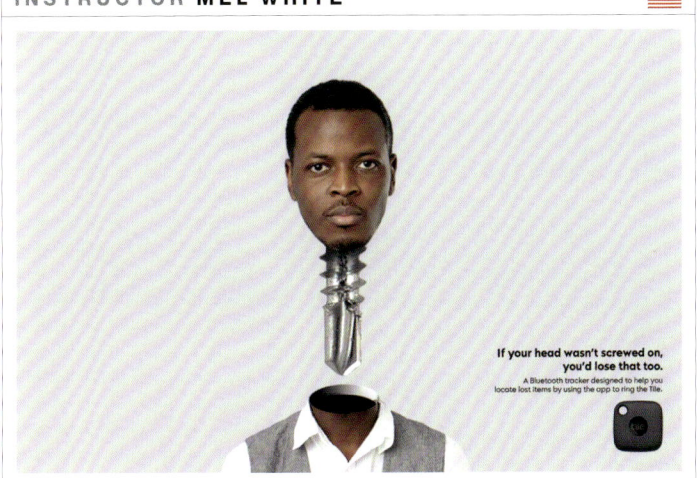

Students: Destiny Erazo, Anastasia Svetlova
School: Syracuse University, The Newhouse School

INSTRUCTOR WILLIAM MEEK

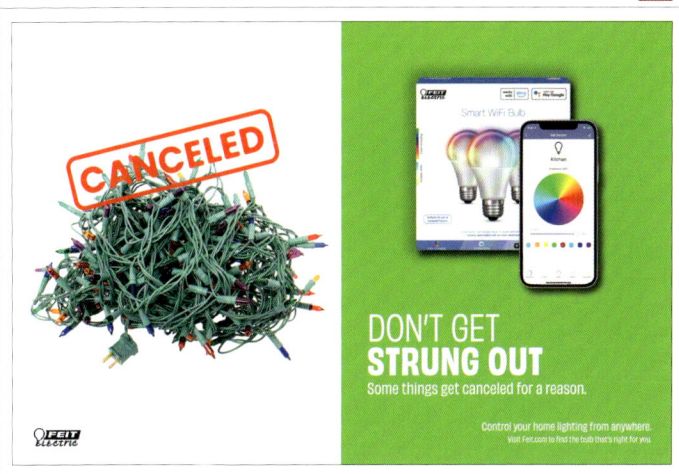

Students: Logan Dorsey, Hannah Kim, Kaliah Orum-Harris
School: Texas State University

INSTRUCTOR MEL WHITE

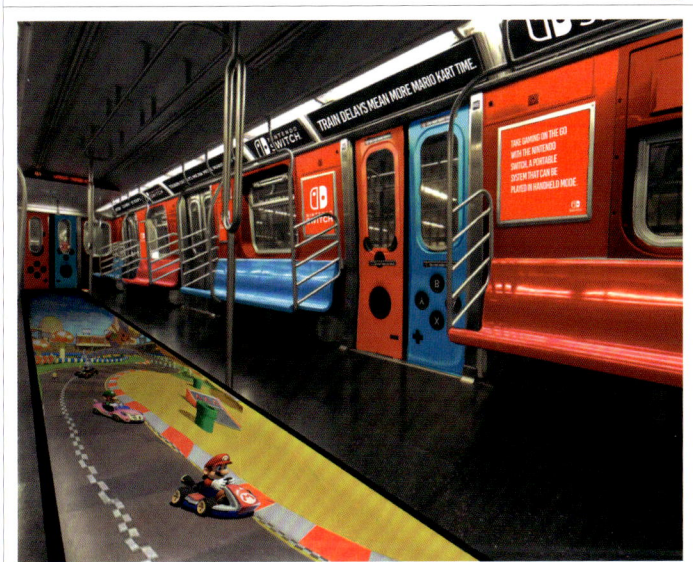

Student: Anastasia Svetlova
School: Syracuse University, The Newhouse School

INSTRUCTOR ABLE PARRIS

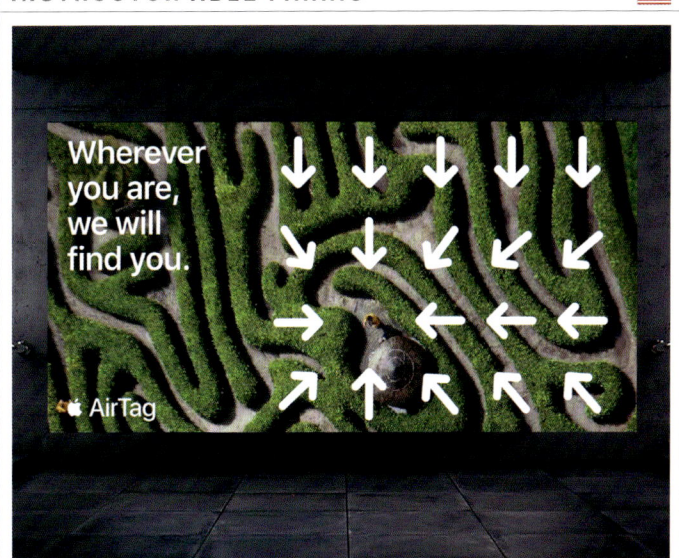

Student: Seongyun Park
School: School of Visual Arts

Education, Electronics | Advertising

30 ADVERTISING SILVER

INSTRUCTOR WILLIAM MEEK

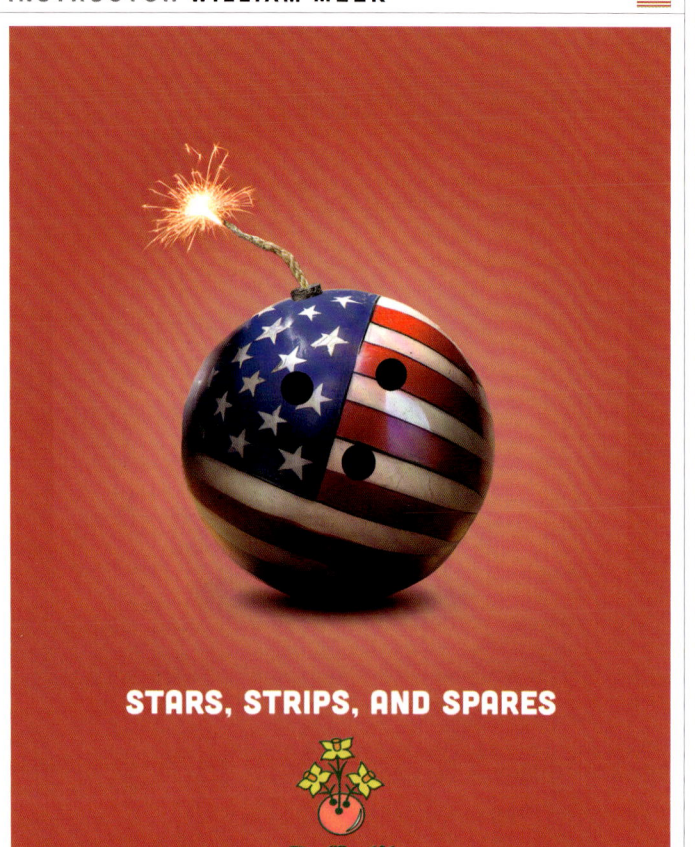

Student: Briana Harris | **School:** Texas State University

INSTRUCTOR EINAT LAHAT-BLUM

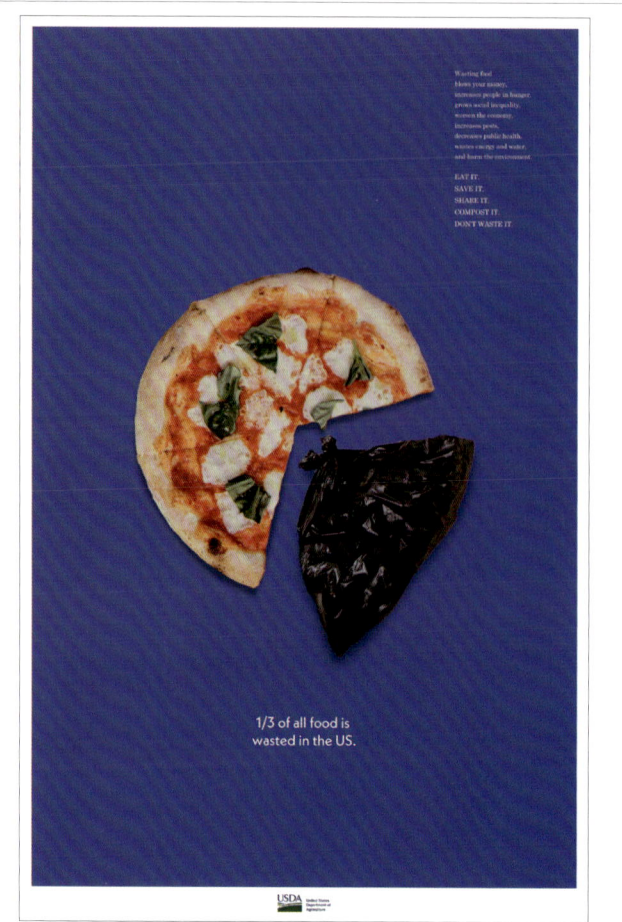

Student: Saki Hinaga | **School:** Pratt Institute

INSTRUCTOR MEL WHITE

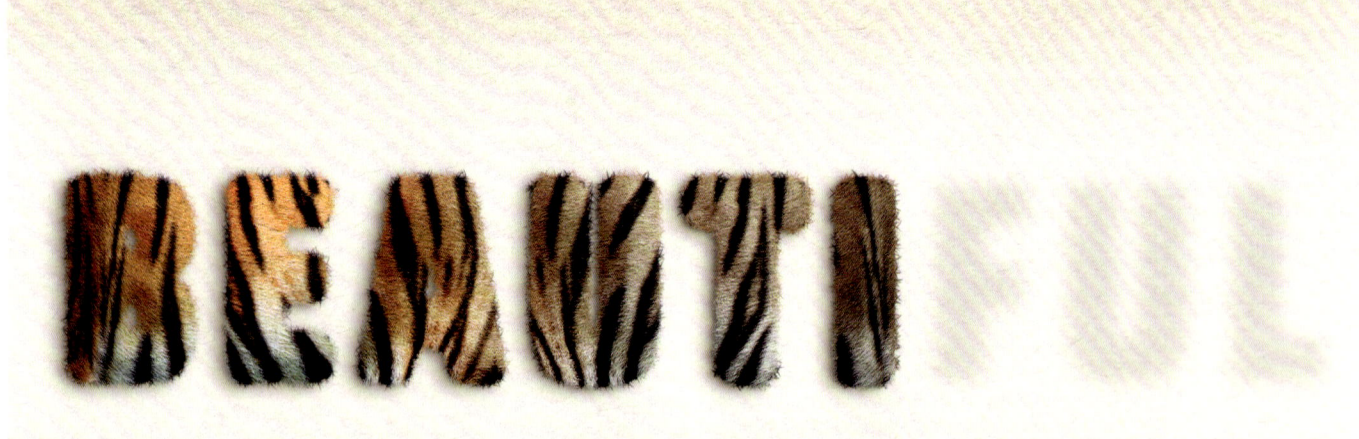

Students: Ryan Garret Conner, Mackenzie Murphy | **School:** Syracuse University, The Newhouse School

Advertising | Entertainment, Environmental

31 ADVERTISING SILVER

INSTRUCTOR MEL WHITE

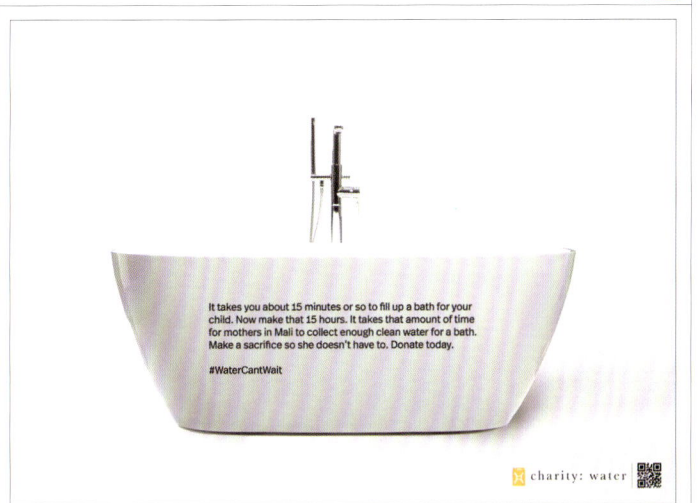

Students: Alex Lund, Ava Schefren
School: Syracuse University, The Newhouse School

INST. DONG-JOO PARK, SEUNG-MIN HAN, NA-MIN KIM

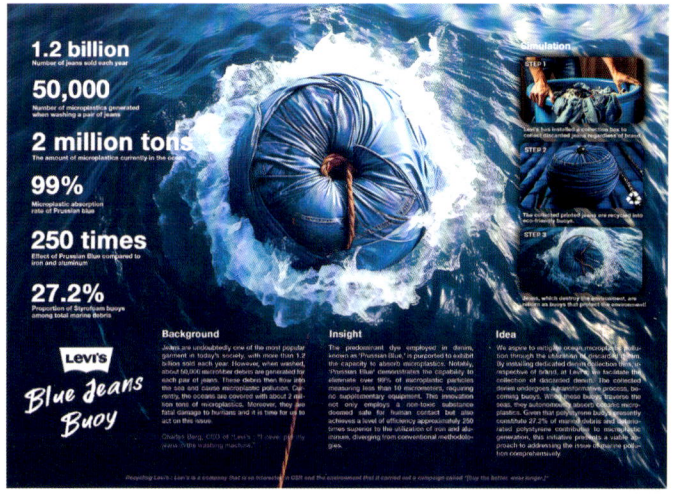

Students: H. Park, S. Jeong, S. Lee, E. Lee, M. Jung
Schools: Hansung Uni., Design & Arts Institute, Kyung Hee Uni., Ewha Womans Uni., Methodist Theological Uni., Kyonggi Uni.

INSTRUCTOR WILLIAM MEEK

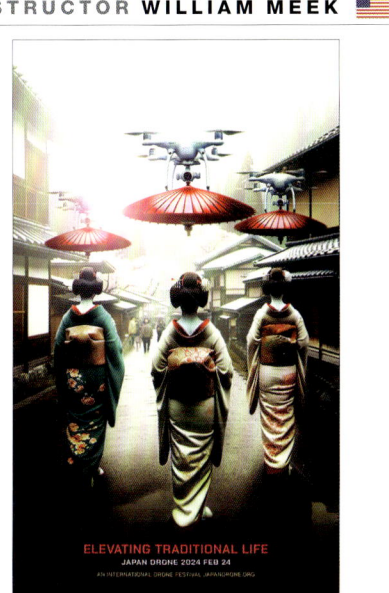

Student: Travis Crawford
School: Texas State University

INSTRUCTOR WILLIAM MEEK

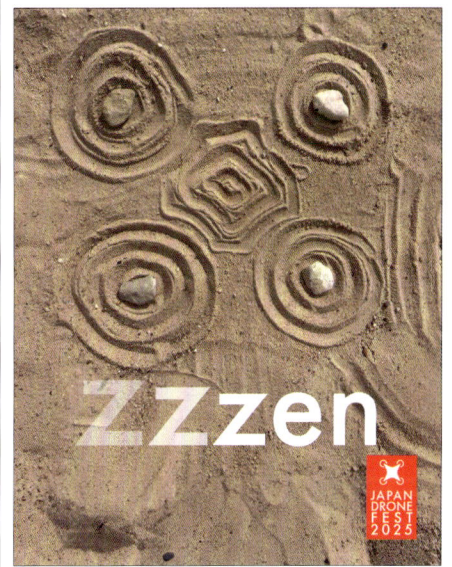

Student: Tina Zurga
School: Texas State University

INSTRUCTOR JAMIE RUNNELLS

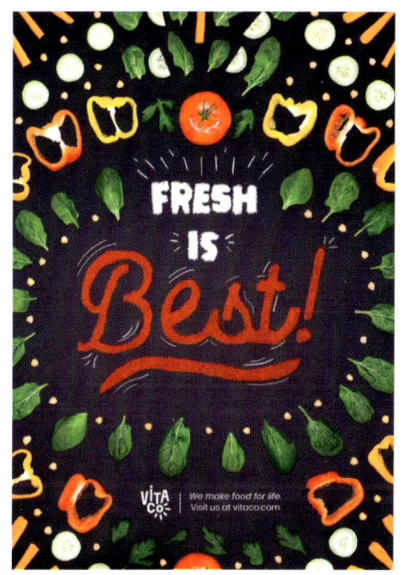

Student: Conner Gayda
School: Jacksonville State University

INSTRUCTOR MARK ALLEN

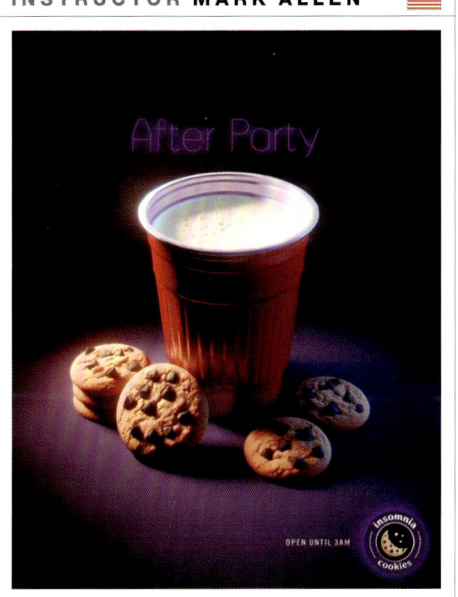

Student: Ross Yenerich
School: Southern Methodist University

INST. KEVIN O'NEILL, MEL WHITE

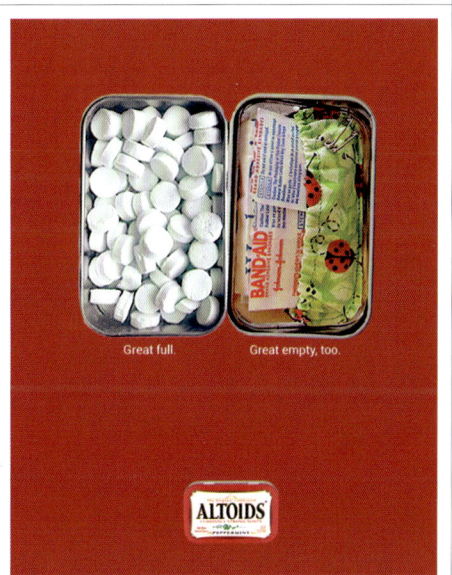

Student: Olivia Doe | **School:** Syracuse University, The Newhouse School

INSTRUCTOR MARK ALLEN

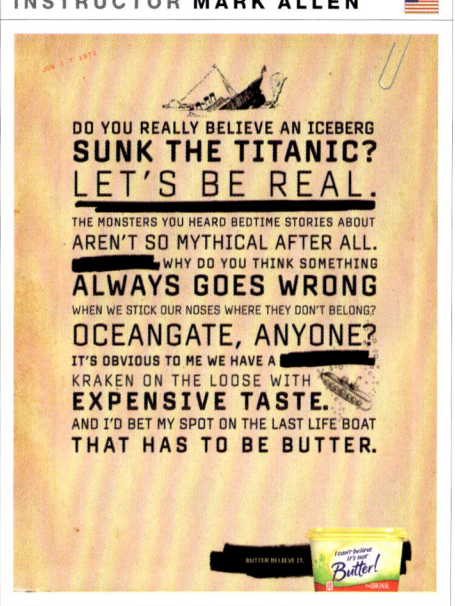

Students: Roshan Gupta, Maddie Otero
School: Southern Methodist University

Environmental, Events, Food | Advertising

32 ADVERTISING SILVER

INSTRUCTOR DOUG REGEN

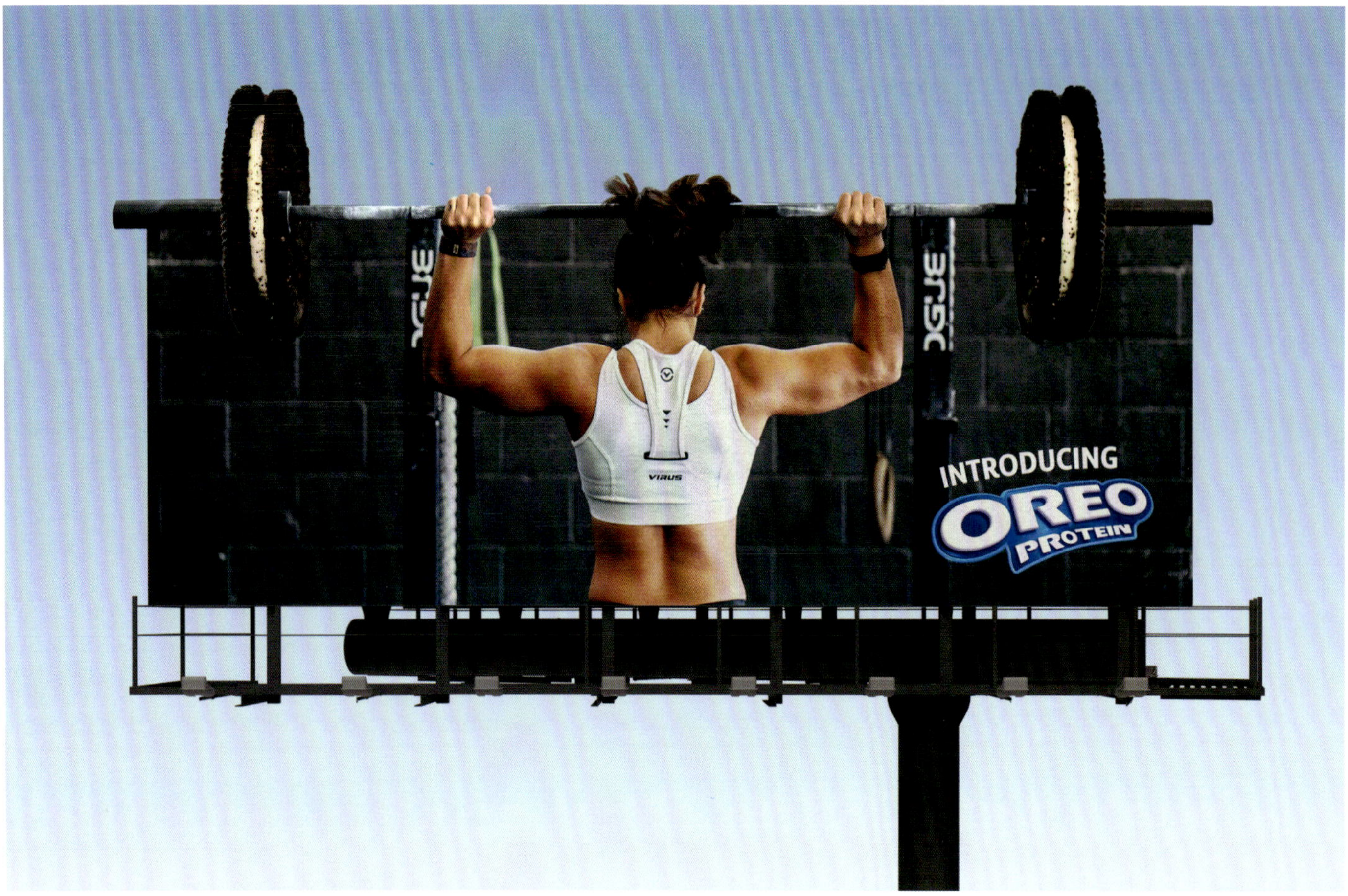

Student: Caleigh Furyk | **School:** Belmont University, Watkins College of Art

INSTRUCTOR GENARO SOLIS RIVERO

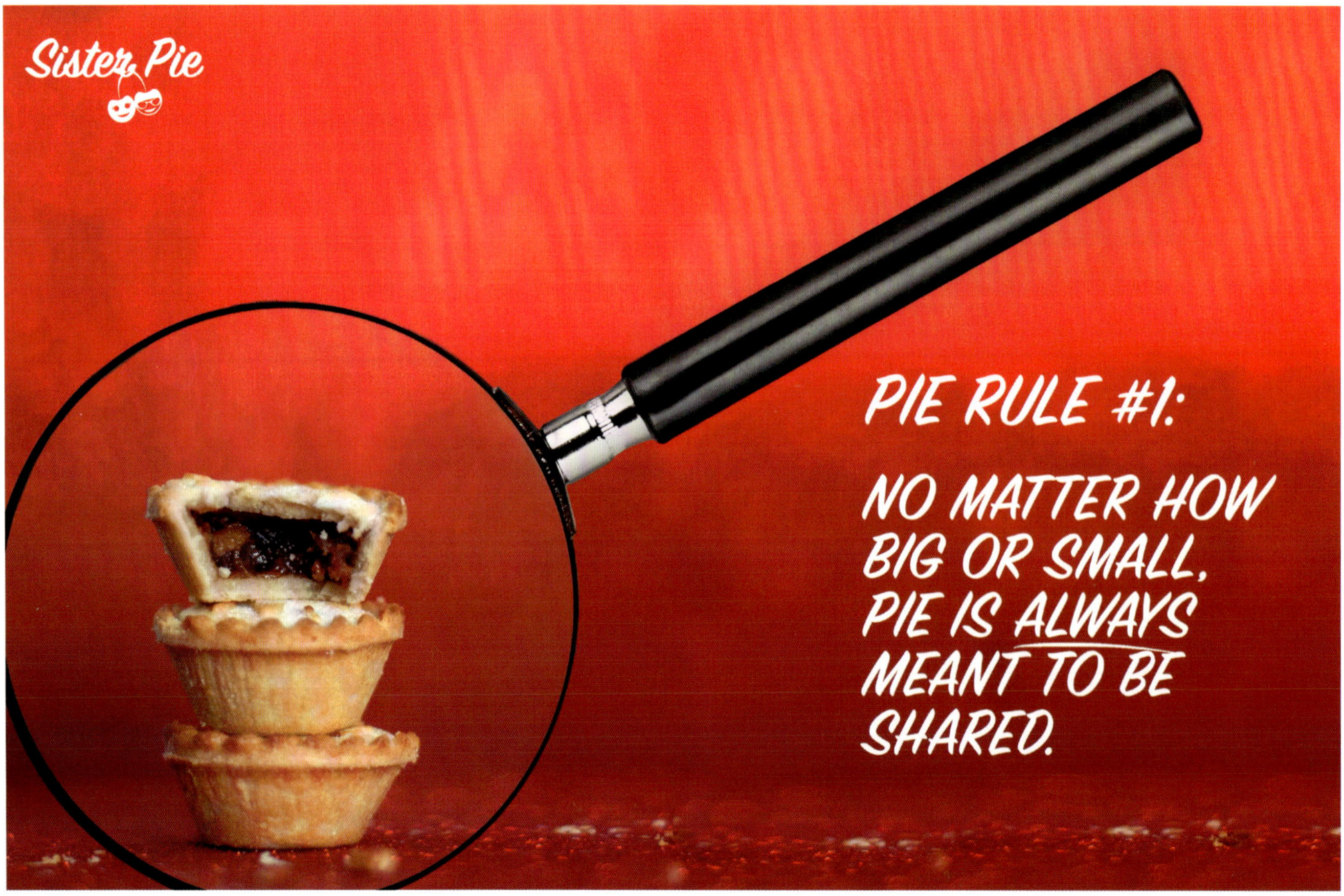

Student: Veronica Jones | **School:** Texas State University

Advertising | Food

33 ADVERTISING SILVER

INSTRUCTOR **DOUGLAS MAY**

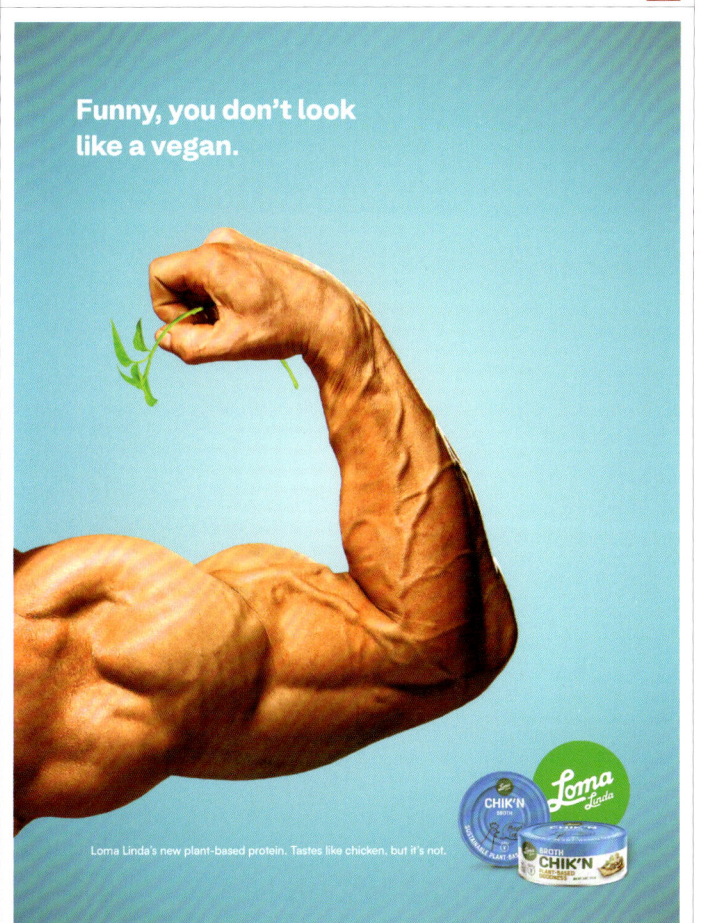

Student: Craig Smith | School: University of North Texas

INSTRUCTOR **DUSTY CROCKER**

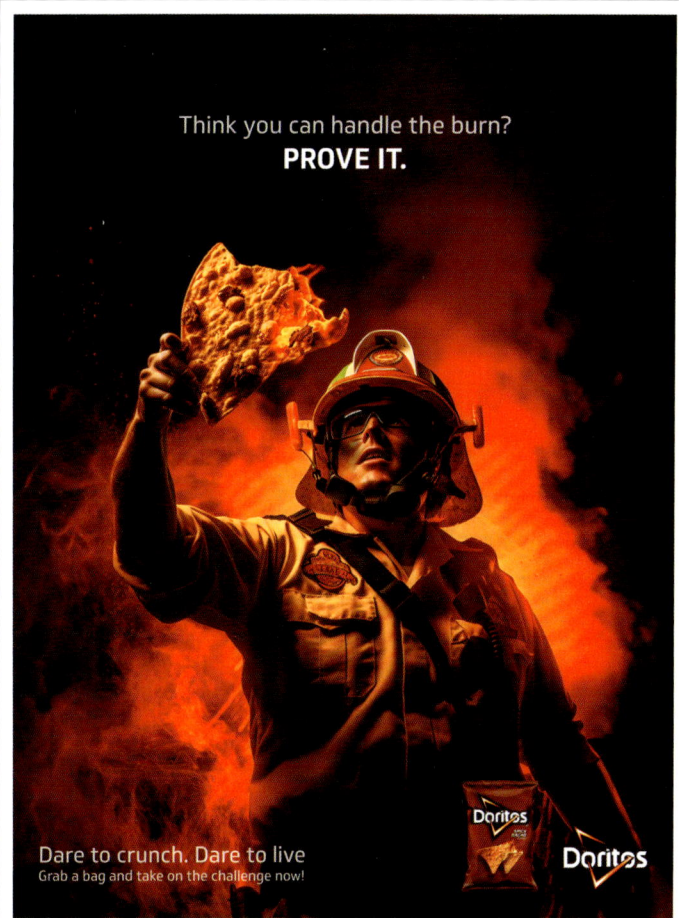

Student: Nhi Vo | School: Texas Christian University

INSTRUCTOR **MEL WHITE**

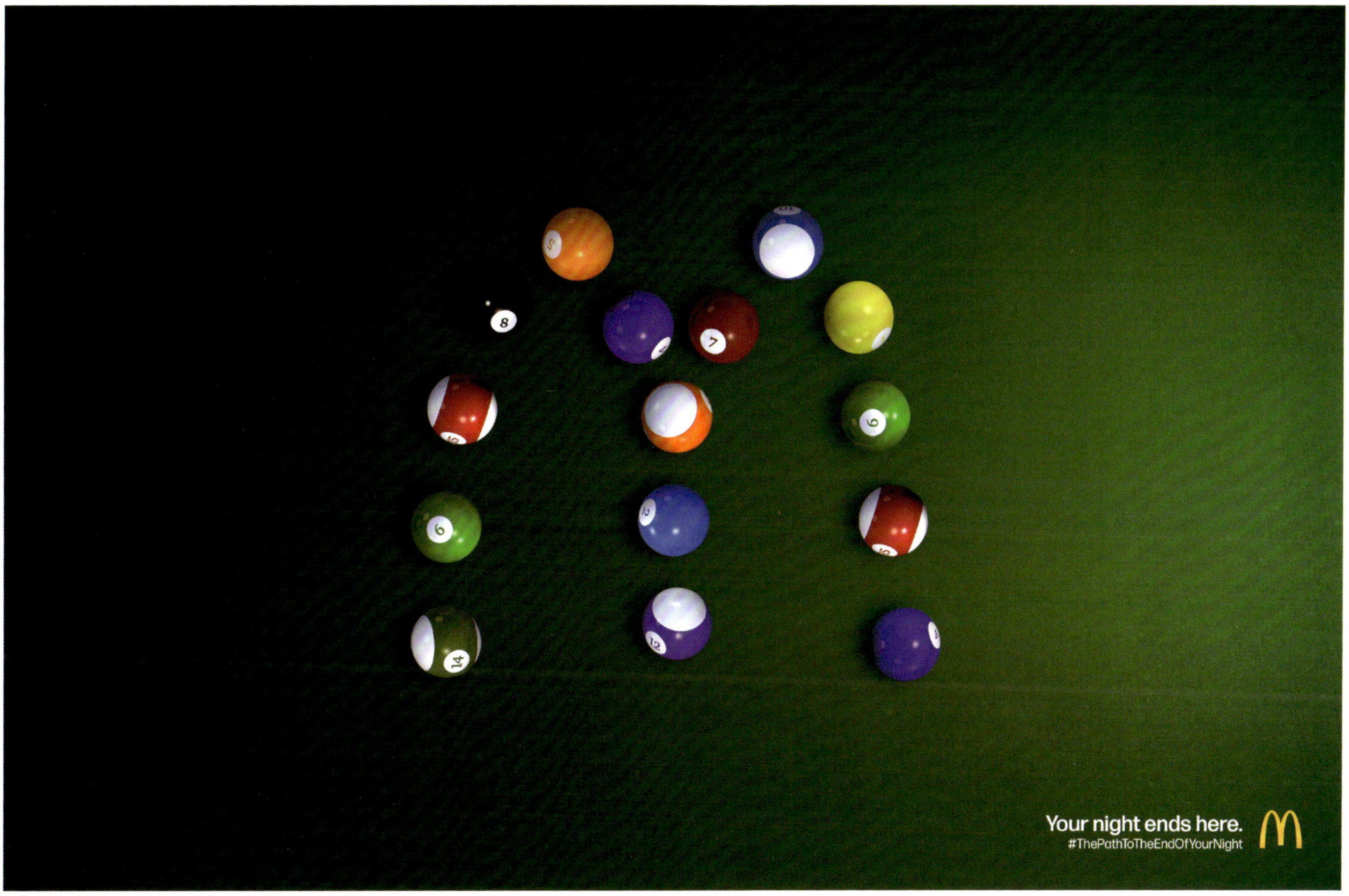

Students: Marlana Bianchi, Lara Molinari | School: Syracuse University, The Newhouse School

Food | Advertising

34 ADVERTISING SILVER

INSTRUCTOR MARK ALLEN

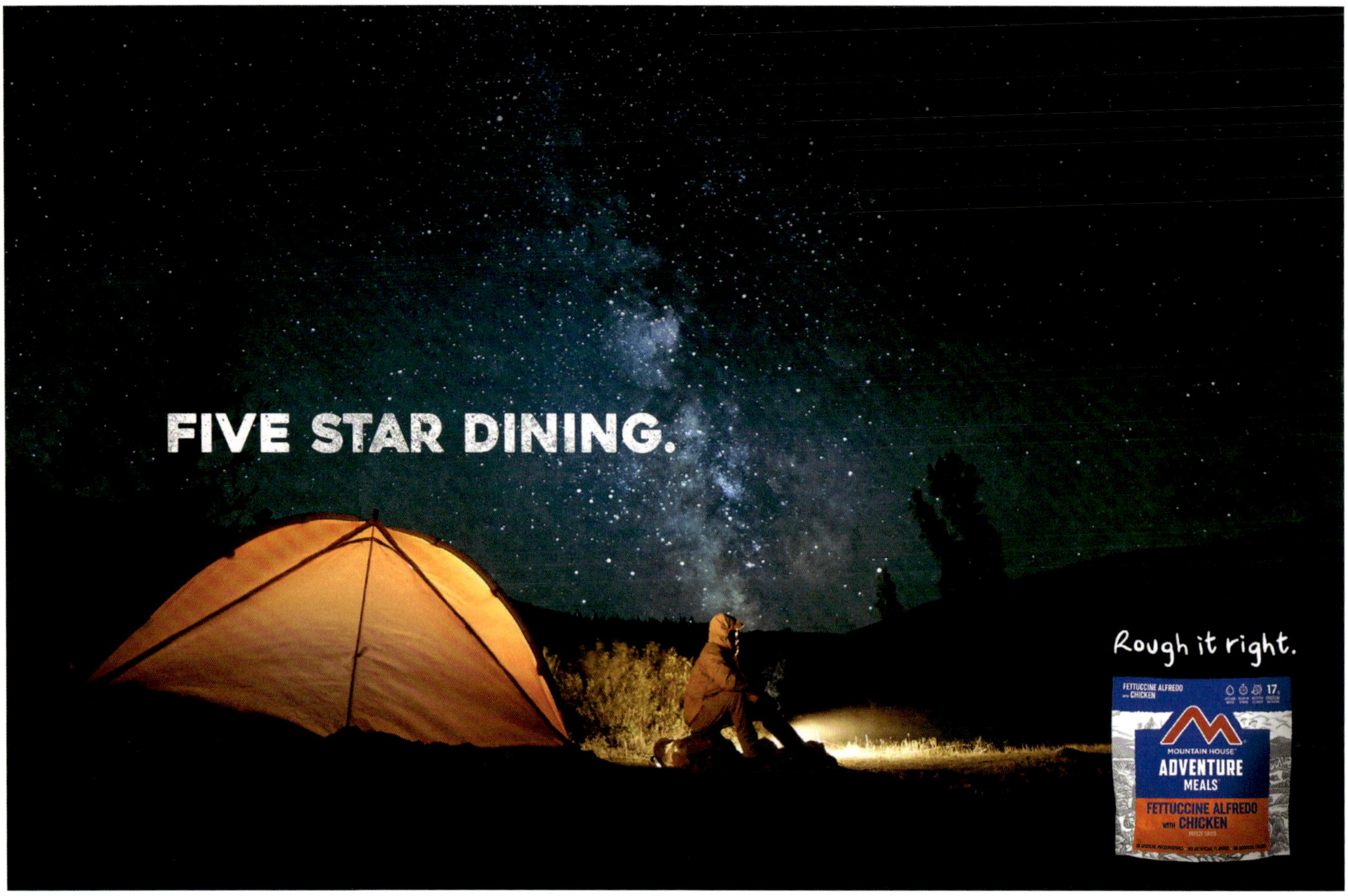

Student: Emma Clarke | School: Southern Methodist University

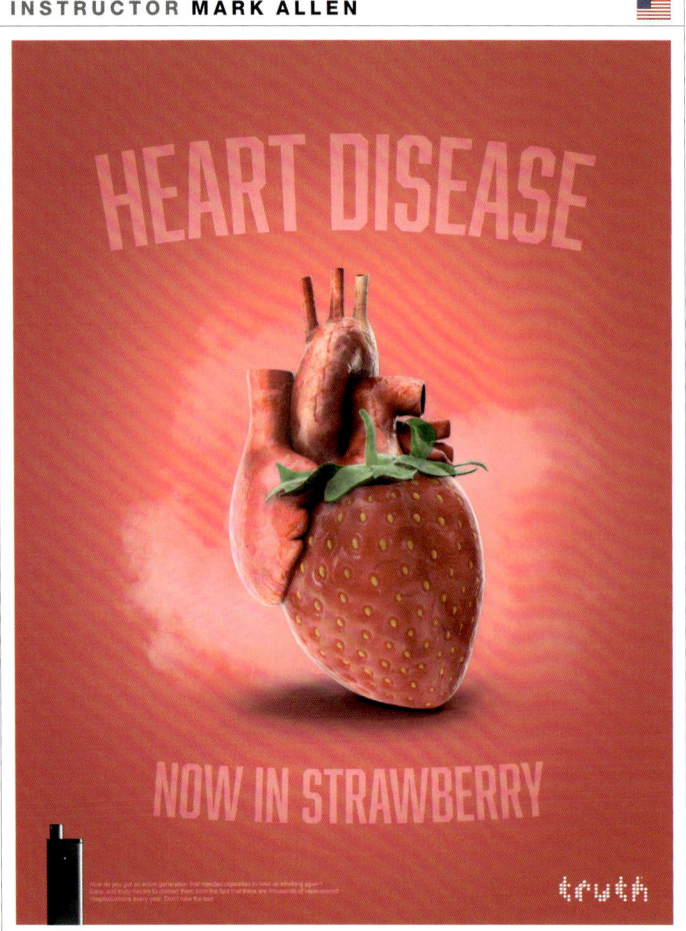

INSTRUCTOR MARK ALLEN

Students: Spencer Hogan, Bella Mac, Allie Weinstein
School: Southern Methodist University

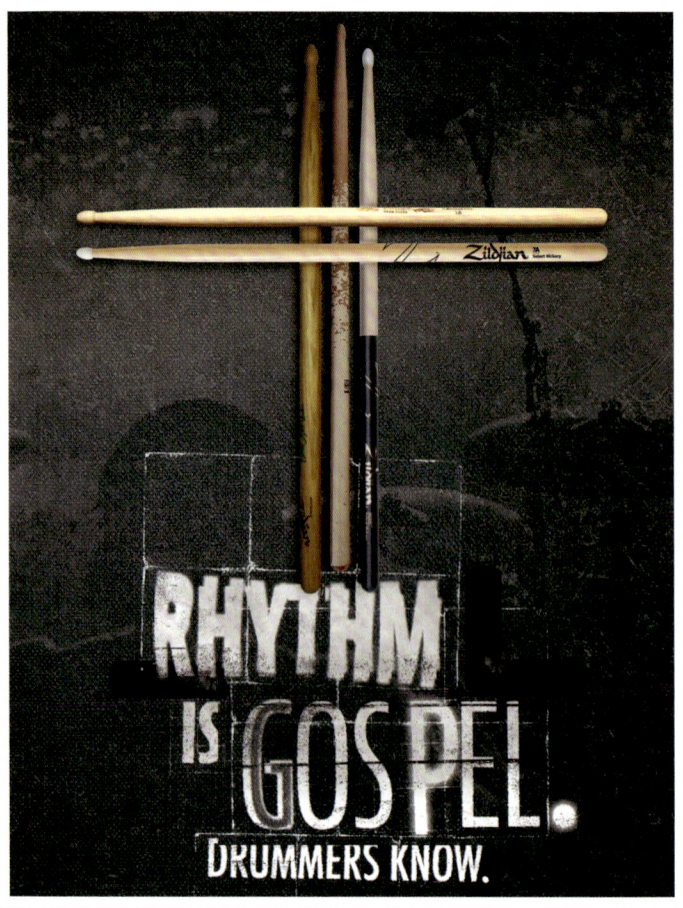

INSTRUCTOR WILLIE BARONET

Students: Timmy Chae, Ethan Jones
School: Southern Methodist University

Advertising | Food, Healthcare, Music

35 ADVERTISING SILVER

INSTRUCTOR MARK ALLEN 🇺🇸

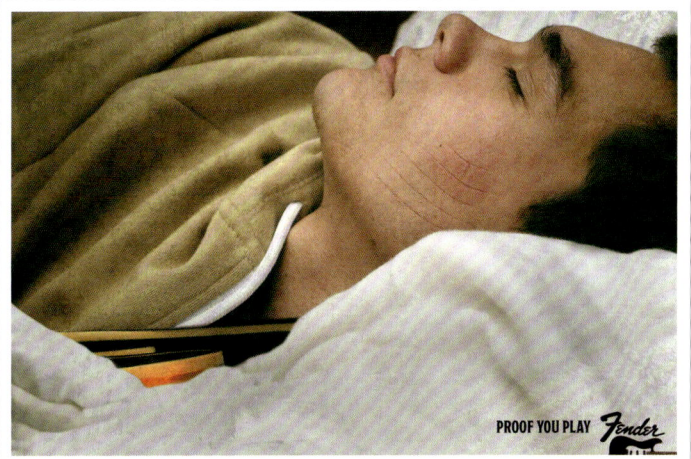

Students: Helena Hargraves, Kailyn Sawhny
School: Southern Methodist University

INSTRUCTOR MARK ALLEN 🇺🇸

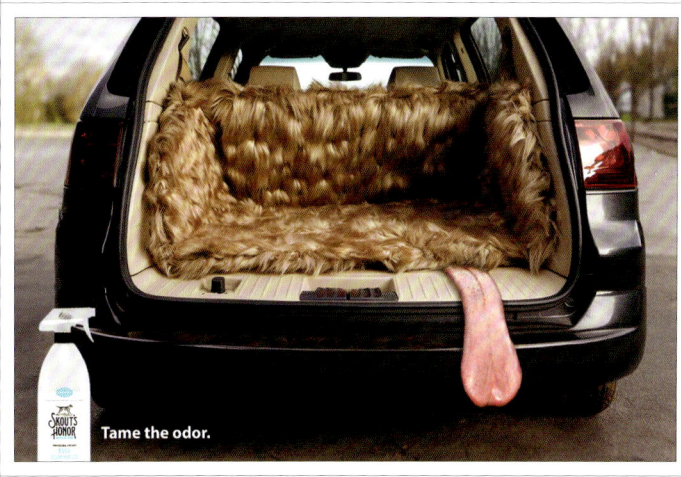

Student: Helena Hargraves
School: Southern Methodist University

INSTRUCTOR MEL WHITE 🇺🇸

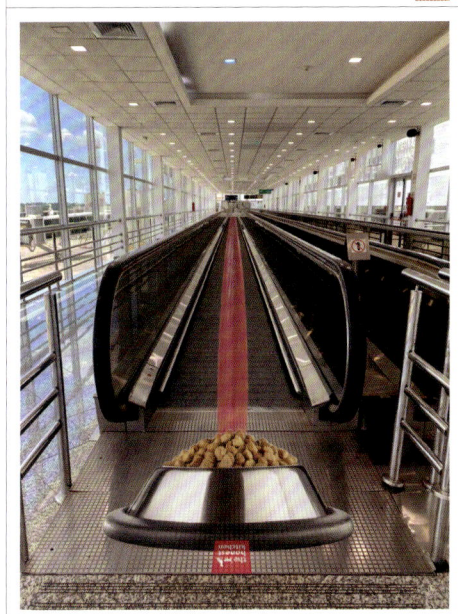

Students: Yaoxinyu Guo, Noah Lourie
School: Syracuse Uni., The Newhouse School

INSTRUCTOR WILLIAM MEEK 🇺🇸

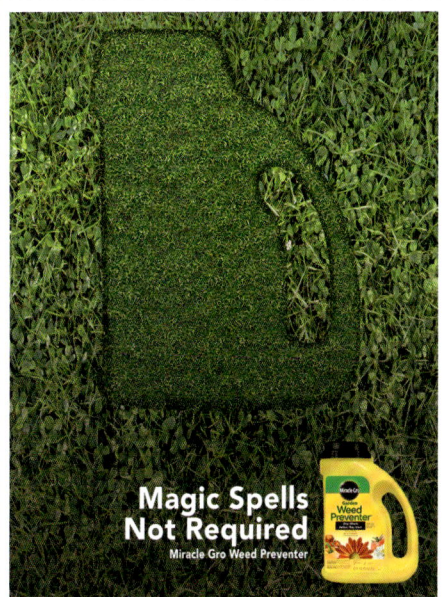

Student: Jayden Wilson
School: Texas State University

INST. GENARO SOLIS RIVERO 🇺🇸

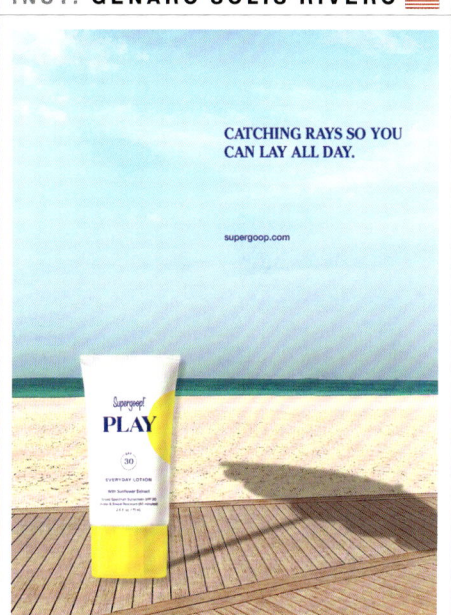

Student: Kennedy Walton
School: Baylor University

INSTRUCTOR WILLIAM MEEK 🇺🇸

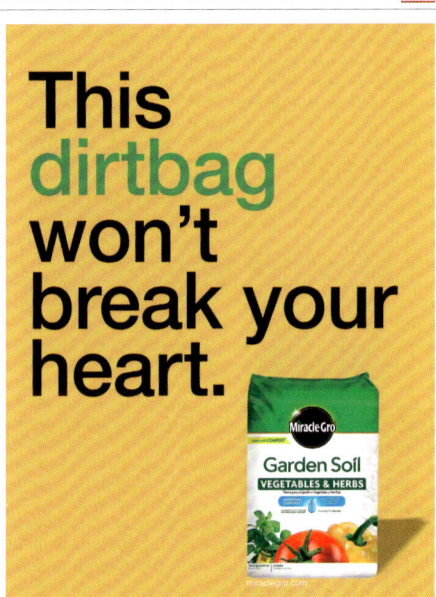

Student: Tina Zurga
School: Texas State University

INSTRUCTOR DOUGLAS MAY 🇺🇸

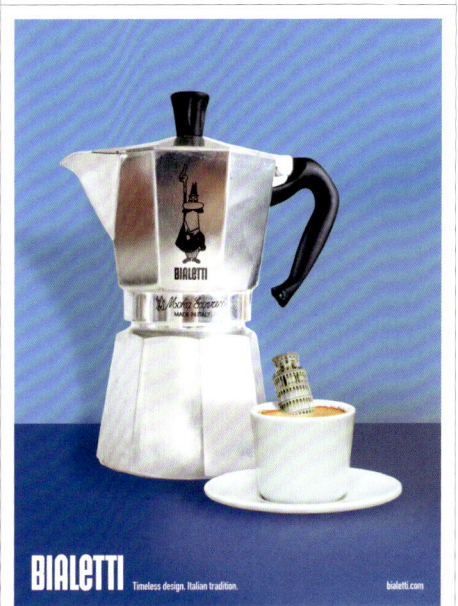

Student: Macy McClish
School: University of North Texas

INSTRUCTOR WILLIAM MEEK 🇺🇸

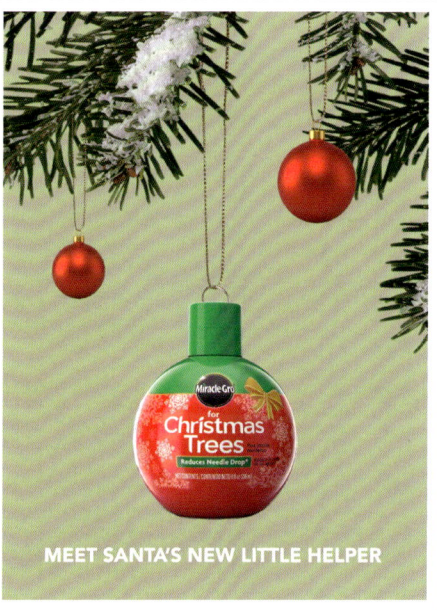

Student: Caroline Koi
School: Texas State University

Music, Pets, Product | Advertising

36 ADVERTISING SILVER

INSTRUCTOR DOUGLAS MAY 🇺🇸
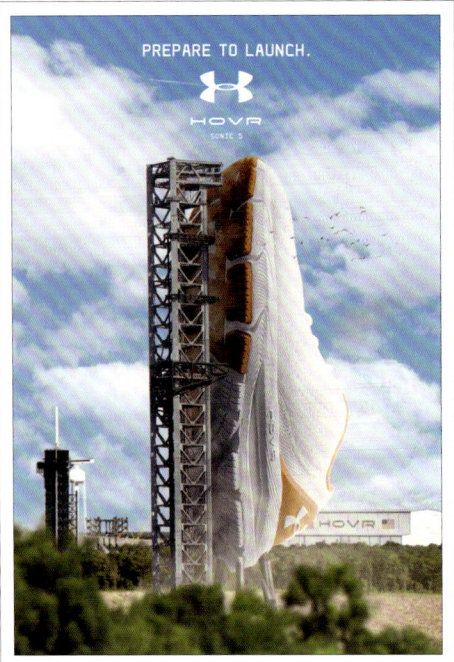
Student: Jordan Heath
School: University of North Texas

INSTRUCTOR DOUGLAS MAY 🇺🇸
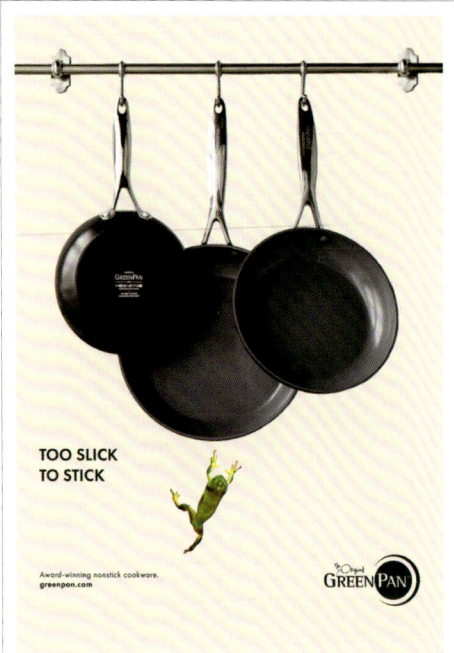
Student: Cuinn Cornwell
School: University of North Texas

INSTRUCTOR DOUGLAS MAY 🇺🇸
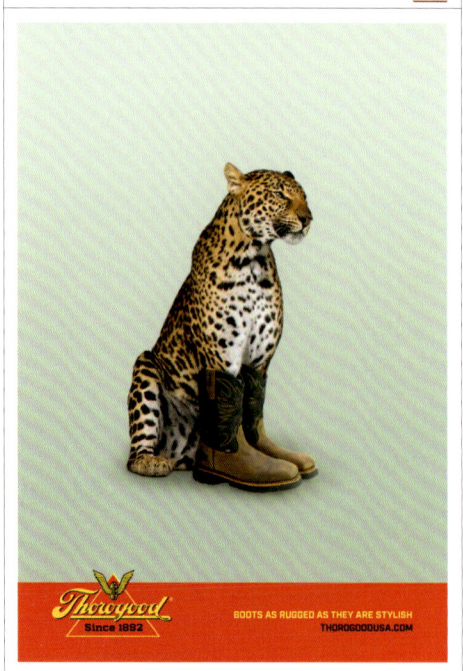
Student: Emily Tran
School: University of North Texas

INSTRUCTOR RYAN PAULSON 🇺🇸
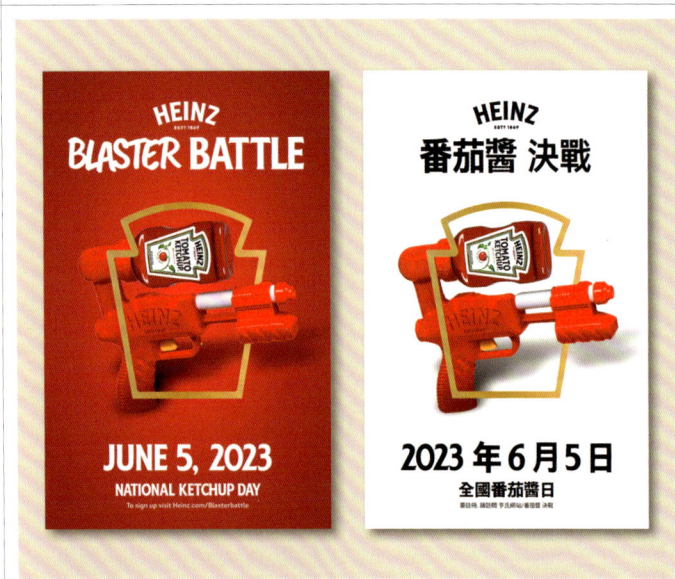
Student: Elyza Nachimson | **School:** School of Visual Arts

INSTRUCTOR DIRK KAMMERZELL 🇺🇸
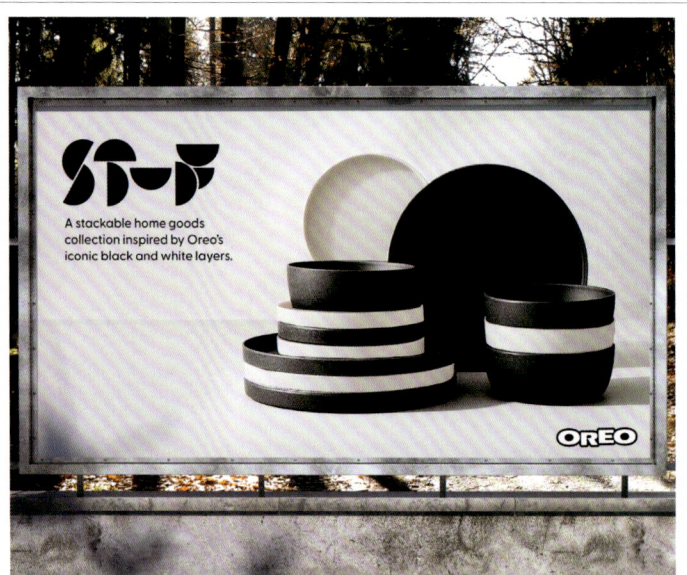
Student: Elyza Nachimson | **School:** School of Visual Arts

INSTRUCTOR VILLY DEVLIOTI 🇺🇸
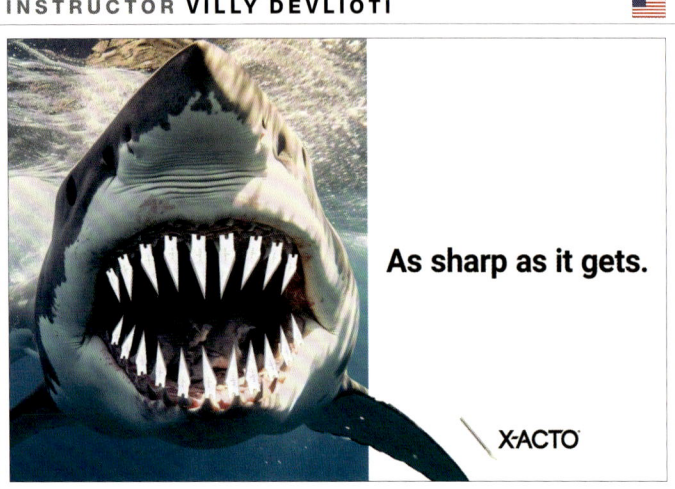
Student: Yuchien Wang
School: M.AD School of Ideas New York

INSTRUCTOR MEL WHITE 🇺🇸
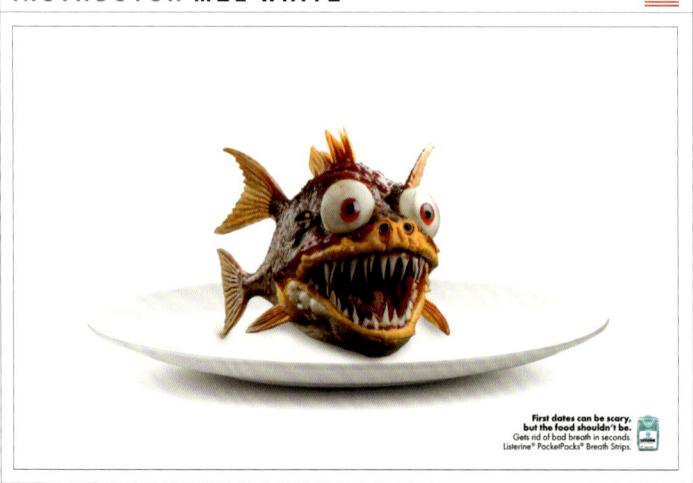
Students: Marlana Bianchi, Lara Molinari
School: Syracuse University, The Newhouse School

Advertising | Product

37 ADVERTISING SILVER

INSTRUCTOR MEL WHITE 🇺🇸

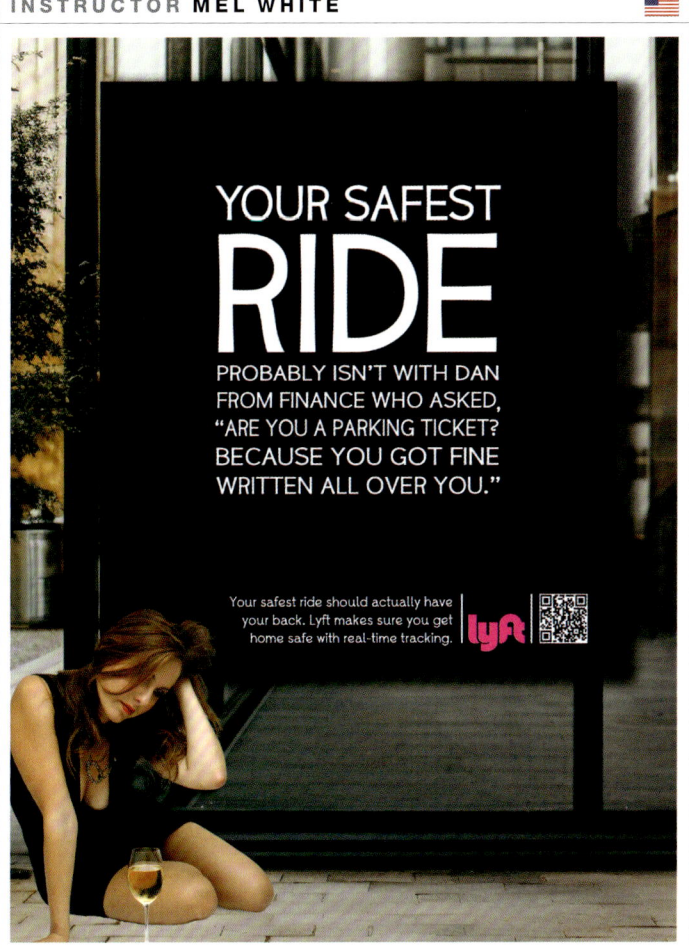

Student: Juliette Keller | **School:** Syracuse University, The Newhouse School

INSTRUCTOR DOUGLAS MAY 🇺🇸

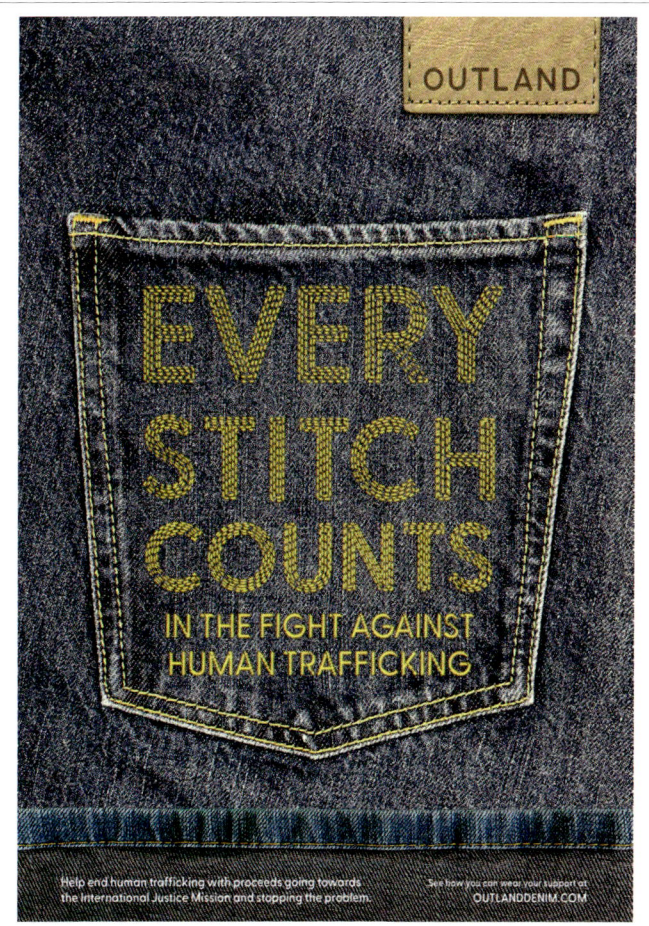

Student: Maxwell Pius | **School:** University of North Texas

INSTRUCTOR GENARO SOLIS RIVERO 🇺🇸

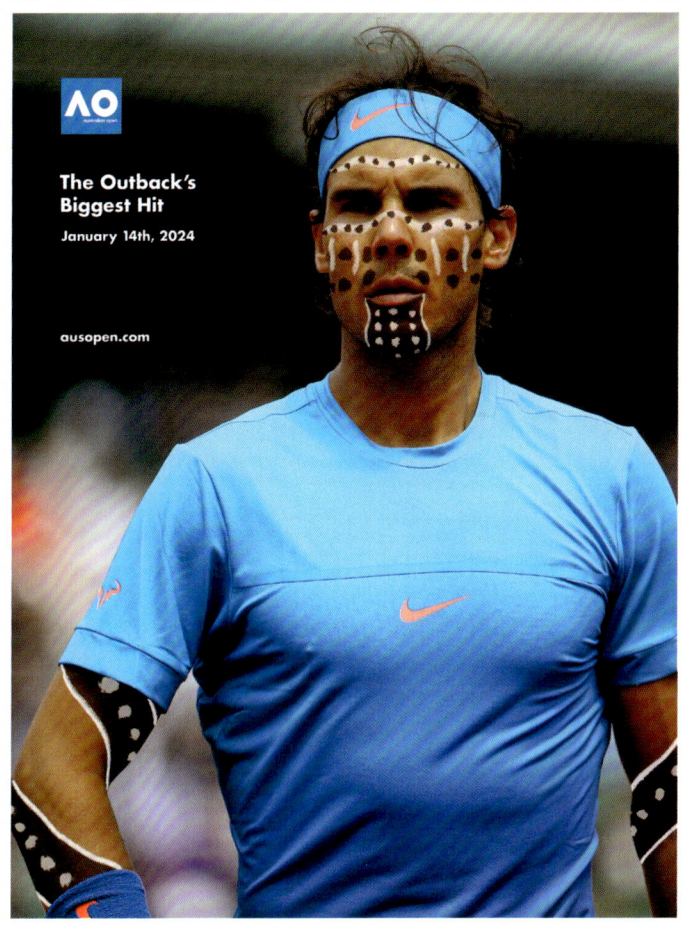

Student: Gabriel Powers | **School:** Baylor University

INSTRUCTORS KEVIN O'NEILL, MEL WHITE 🇺🇸

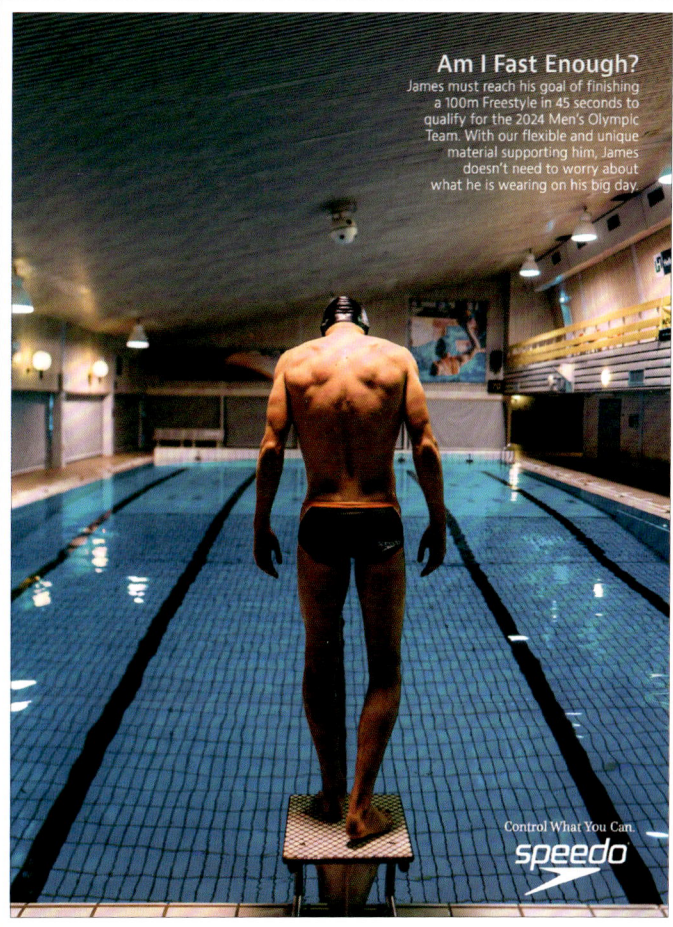

Student: Emily Saad | **School:** Syracuse University, The Newhouse School

Social Services, Sports | Advertising

38 ADVERTISING SILVER

INSTRUCTOR **MARK ALLEN**

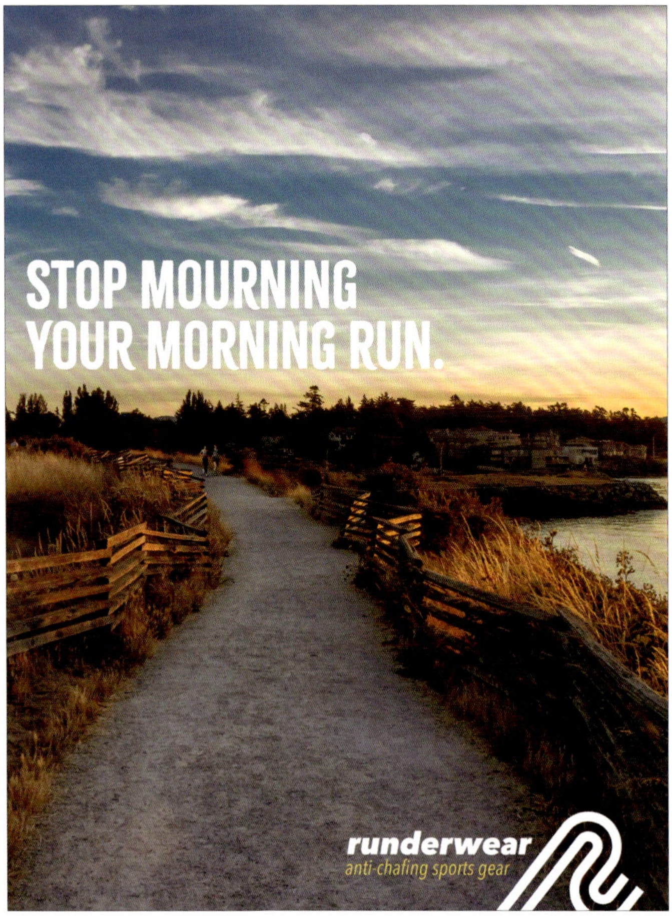

STOP MOURNING YOUR MORNING RUN.

runderwear
anti-chafing sports gear

Student: Callie Oden | **School:** Southern Methodist University

INSTRUCTOR **MARK ALLEN**

IT'S WHAT'S ON THE OUTSIDE THAT COUNTS.

HIPCAMP

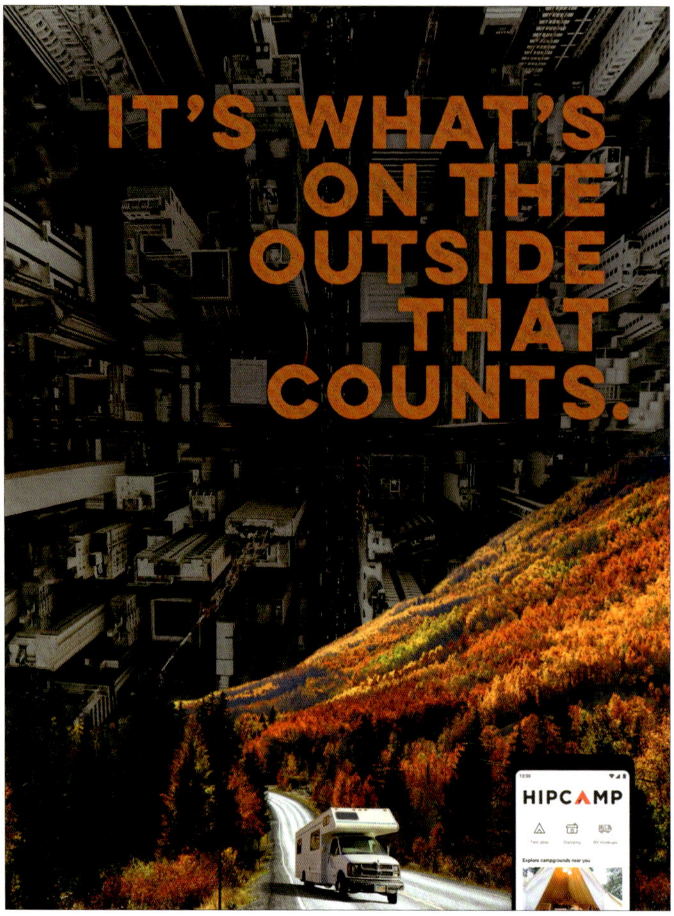

Students: Tyler Chapman, Linh Vu | **School:** Southern Methodist University

INSTRUCTOR **MARK ALLEN**

Unexpected NIAGARA FALL

Allianz (ii) Travel Insurance
Medical and injury coverage.

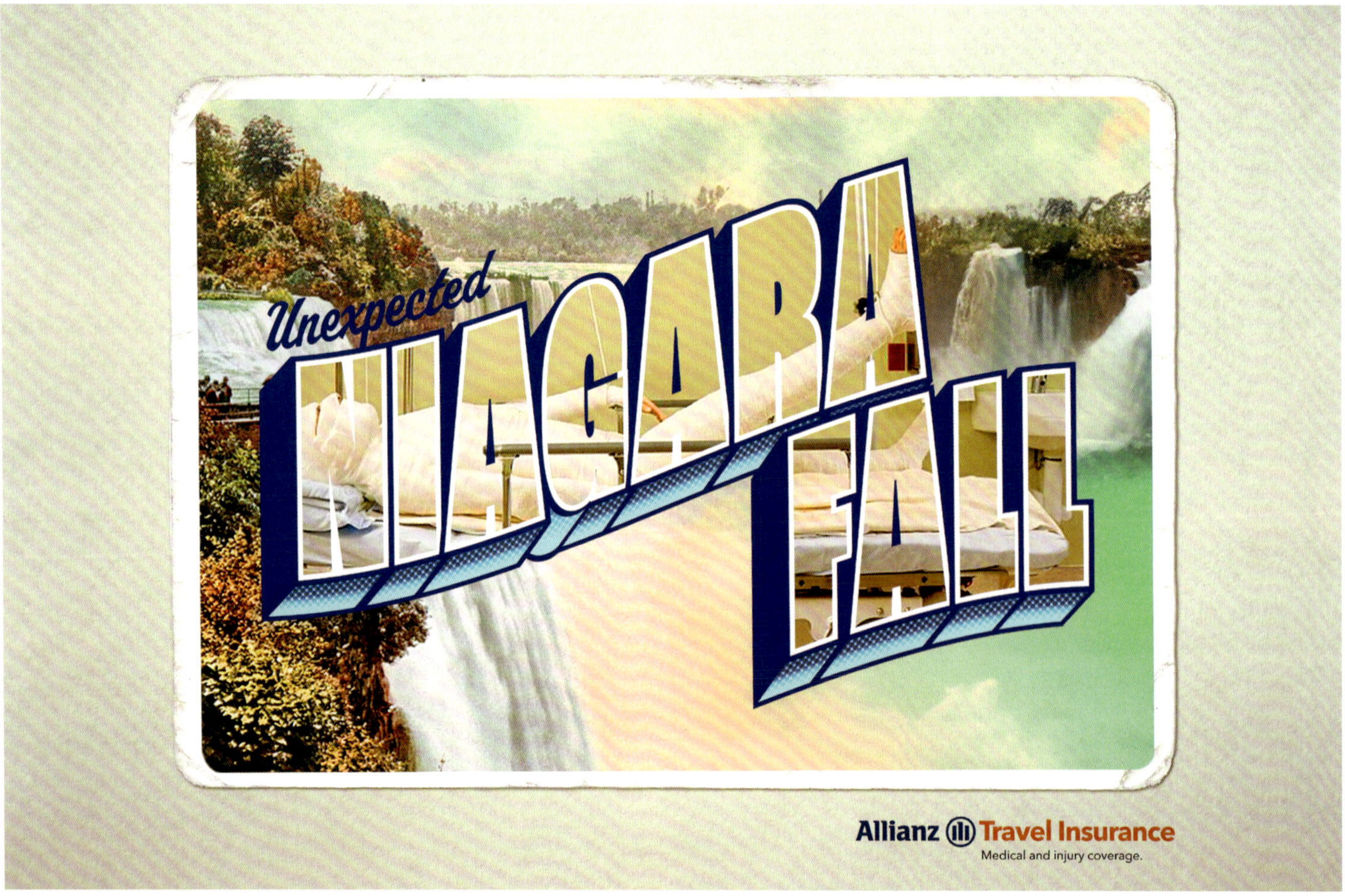

Students: Hannah Jacobbe, Sydney Sam | **School:** Southern Methodist University

Advertising | Sports, Travel

39 ADVERTISING SILVER

INSTRUCTOR WILLIE BARONET

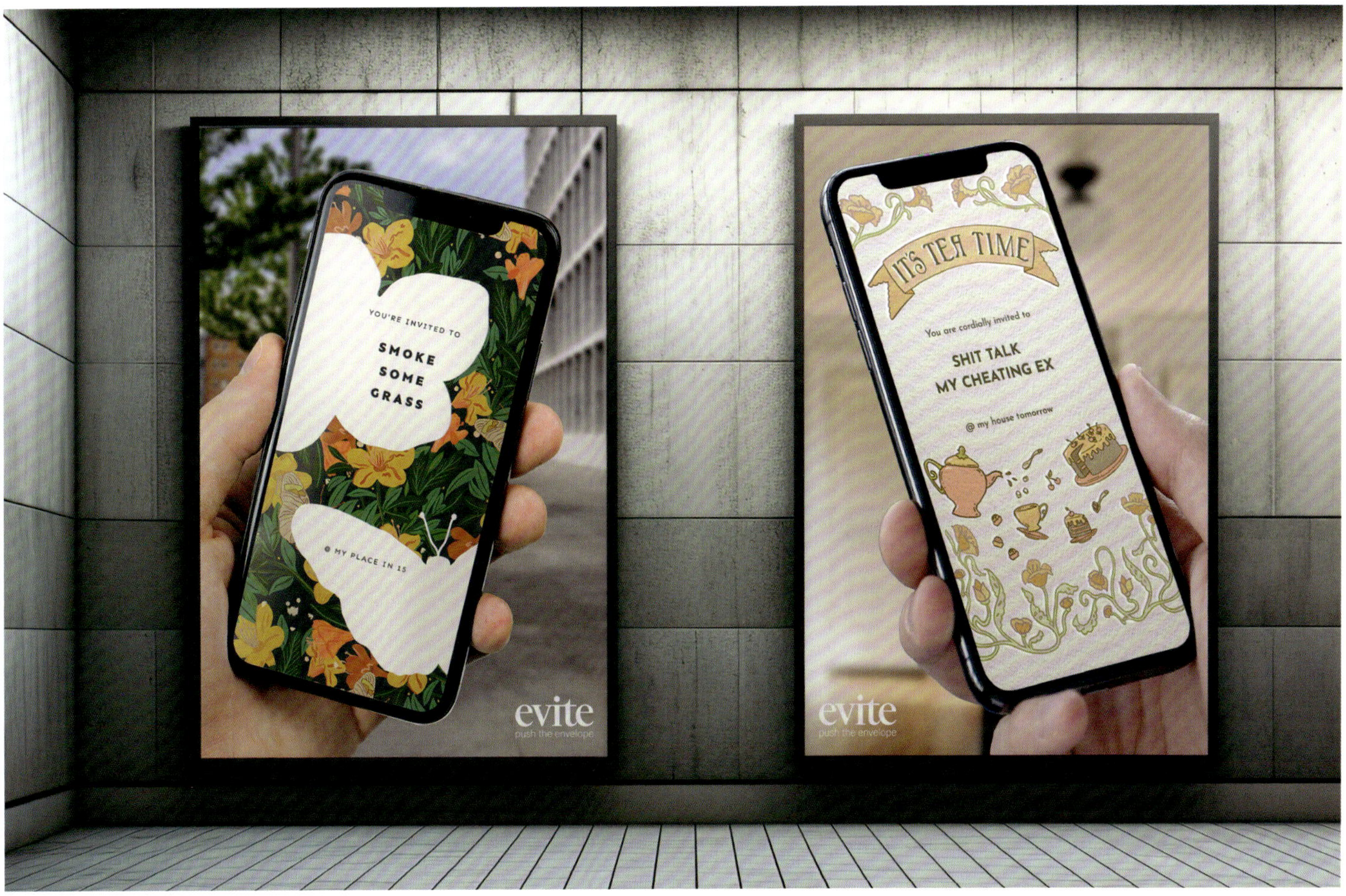

Students: Caroline Davis, Blake Lyster | **School:** Southern Methodist University

INSTRUCTOR KEVIN O'NEILL

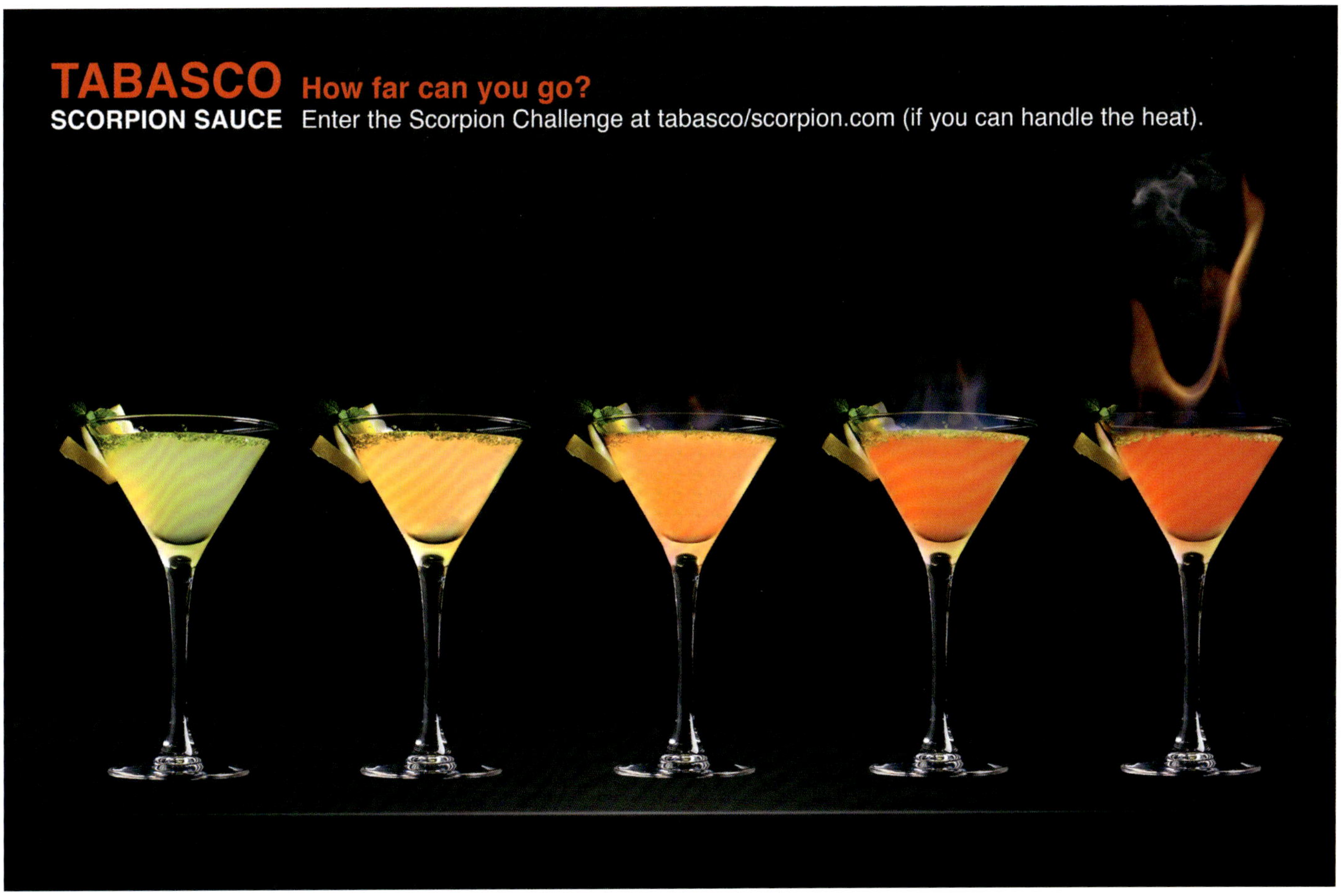

TABASCO SCORPION SAUCE How far can you go? Enter the Scorpion Challenge at tabasco/scorpion.com (if you can handle the heat).

Students: Maggie Mallon, Meiling Xiong | **School:** Syracuse University, The Newhouse School

Websites | Advertising

Advertising Film/Video

41 ADVERTISING FILM/VIDEO GOLD

INSTRUCTOR YVONNE CAO

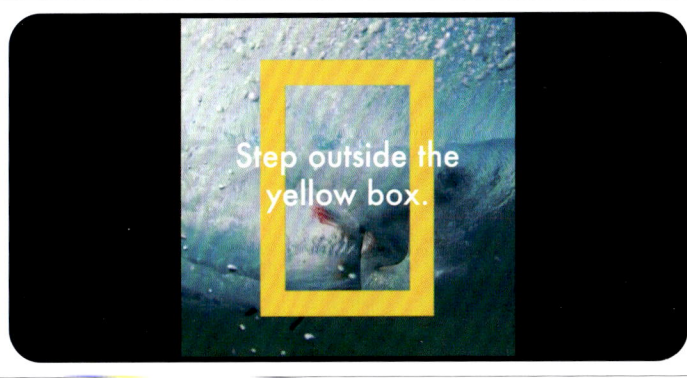
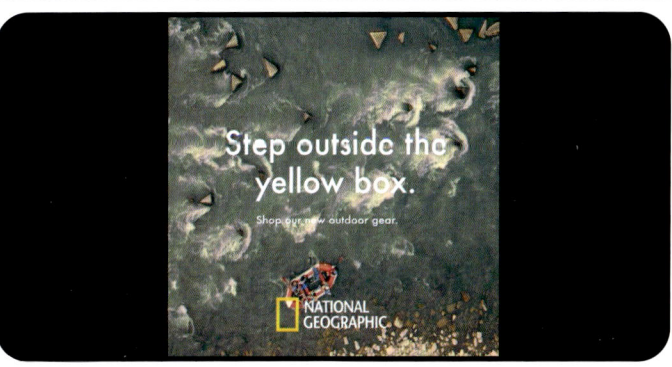

Student: Morgan Goerke
School: Texas Christian University
P235: Credit & Commentary

INSTRUCTOR MARK ALLEN

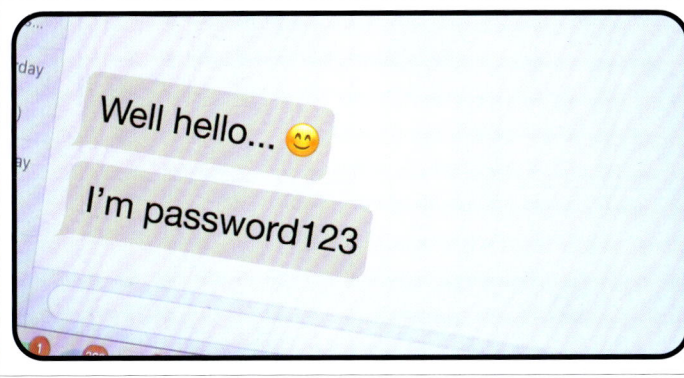
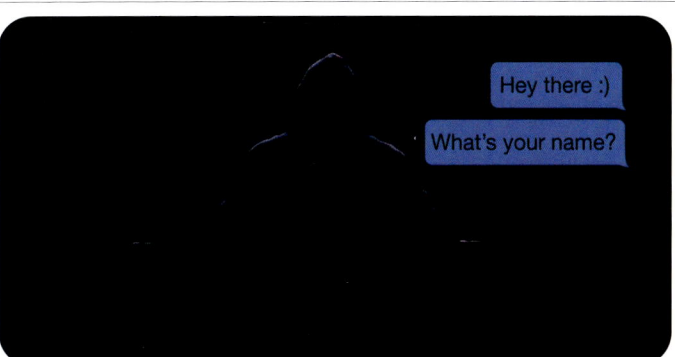

Students: Roshan Gupta, Kayla Hanrahan
School: Southern Methodist University
P235: Credit & Commentary

INSTRUCTOR MEL WHITE

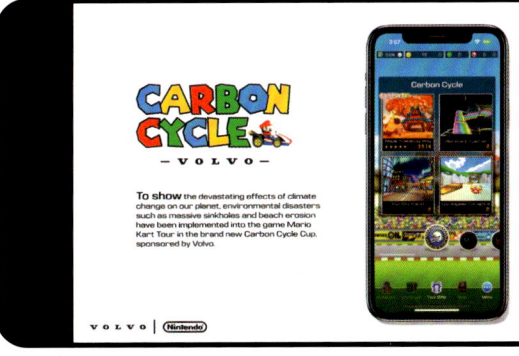
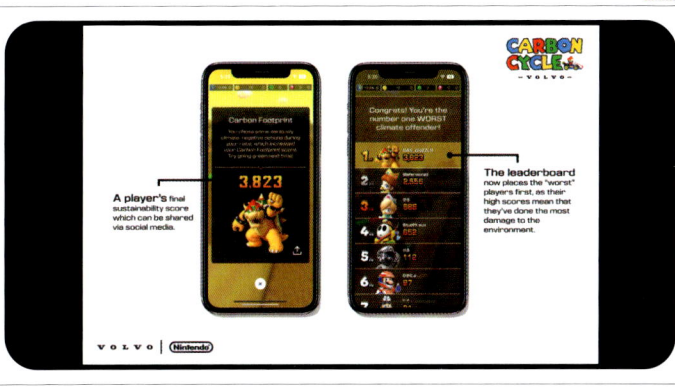

Students: Dianna Higaki, Avery Schildhaus
School: Syracuse University, The Newhouse School
P235: Credit & Commentary

INSTRUCTOR MEL WHITE

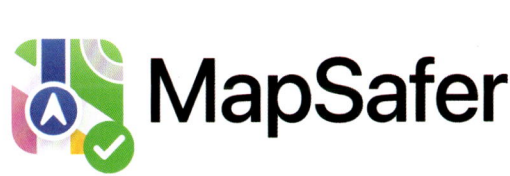
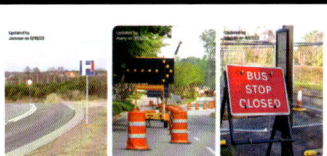

Students: Ava Schefren, Alex Lund
School: Syracuse University, The Newhouse School
P235: Credit & Commentary

Commercial | Advertising Film/Video

42 ADVERTISING FILM/VIDEO GOLD

INSTRUCTOR **MARK ALLEN**

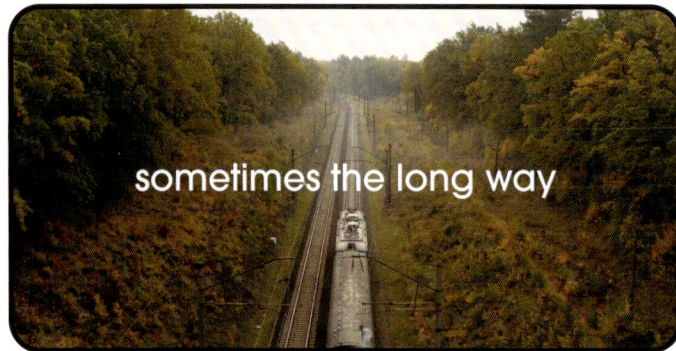
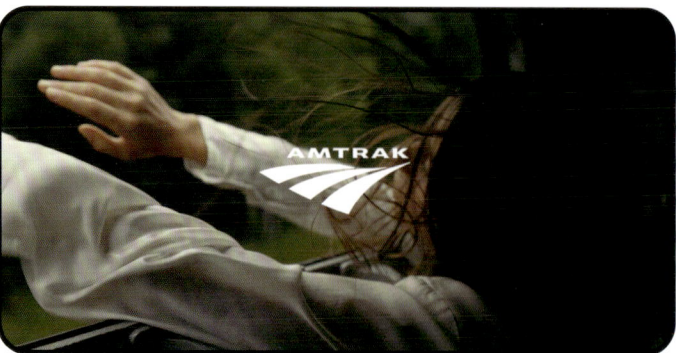

Students: Timmy Chae, Blake Lyster
School: Southern Methodist University
P235: Credit & Commentary

INSTRUCTOR **MEL WHITE**

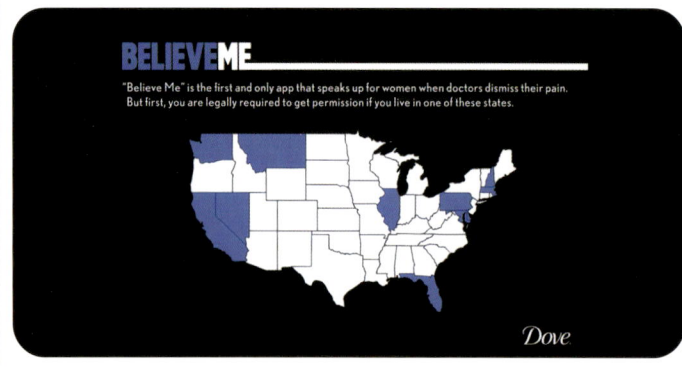
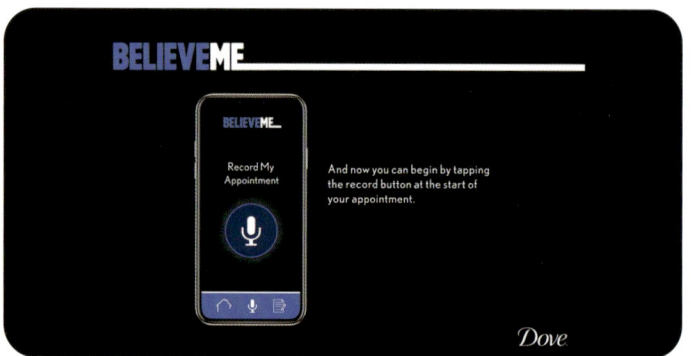

Students: Alyssa Thompson, Juliette Keller, Maggie Mallon
School: Syracuse University, The Newhouse School
P235: Credit & Commentary

INSTRUCTOR **MEL WHITE**

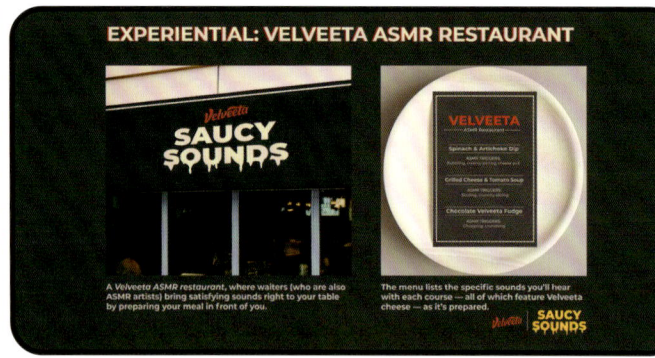
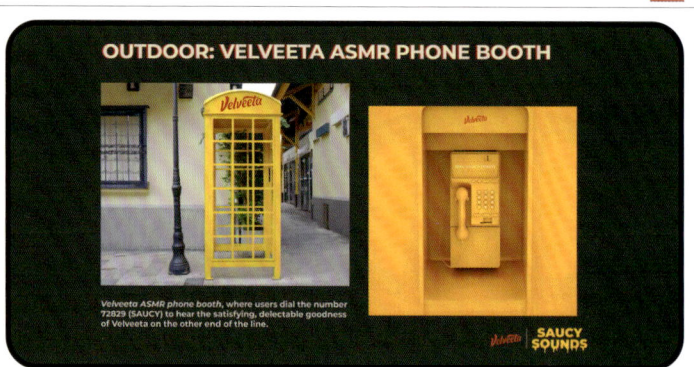

Students: Remi Tsunoda, Avery Schildhaus
School: Syracuse University, The Newhouse School
P235: Credit & Commentary

INSTRUCTOR **WILLIE BARONET**

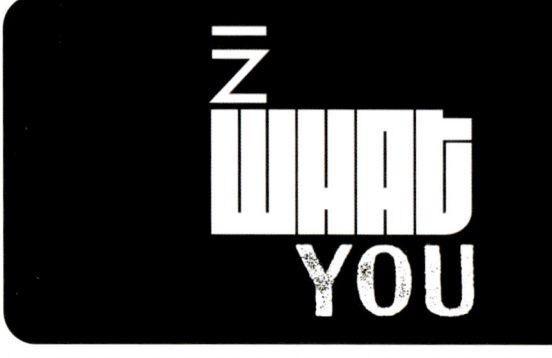
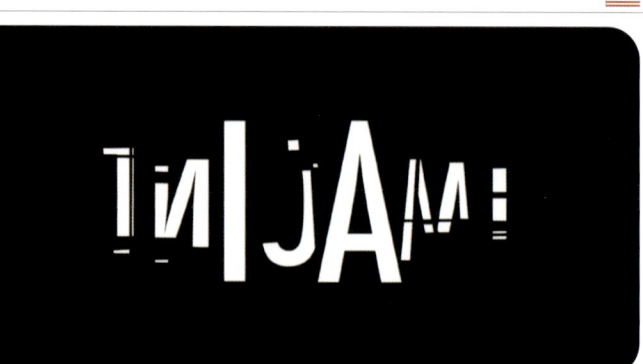

Students: Timmy Chae, Savanna Hodes
School: Southern Methodist University
P235: Credit & Commentary

Advertising Film/Video | Commercial

43 ADVERTISING FILM/VIDEO GOLD

INSTRUCTOR MEL WHITE

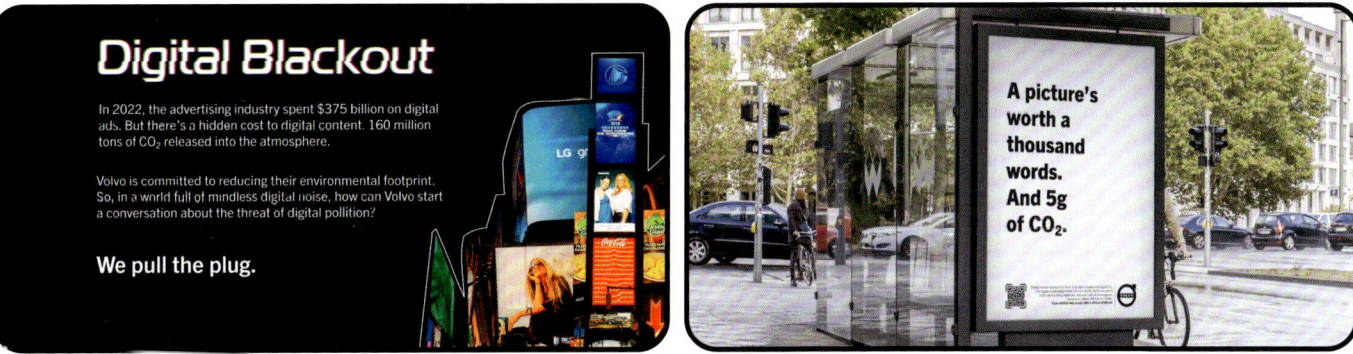

Students: Brooke Hirsch, Charlotte Shea
School: Syracuse University, The Newhouse School
P235: Credit & Commentary

INSTRUCTOR WILLIE BARONET

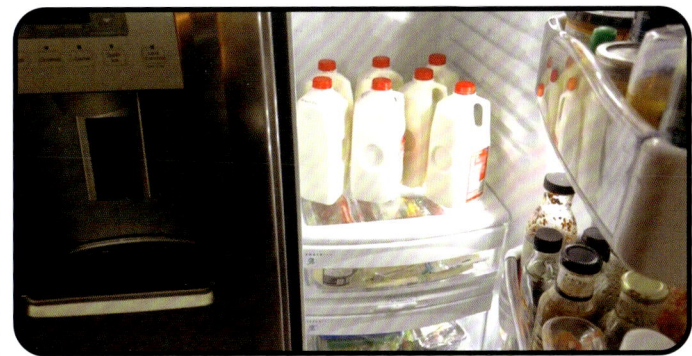 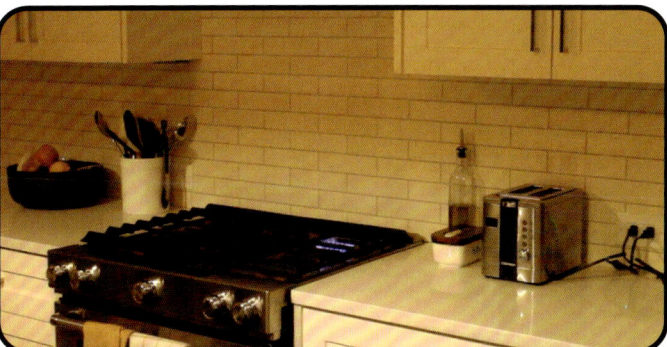

Student: Maddie Otero
School: Southern Methodist University
P235: Credit & Commentary

INSTRUCTOR HANK RICHARDSON

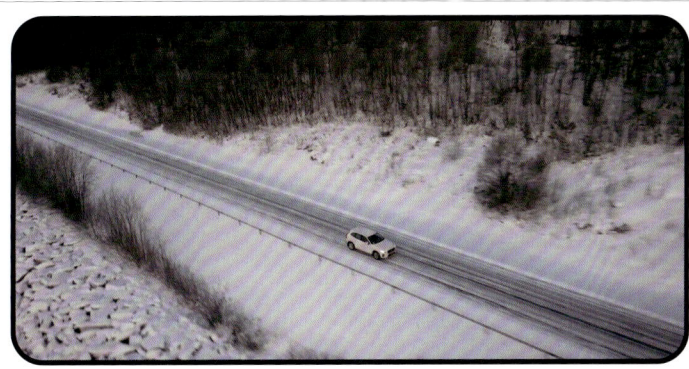 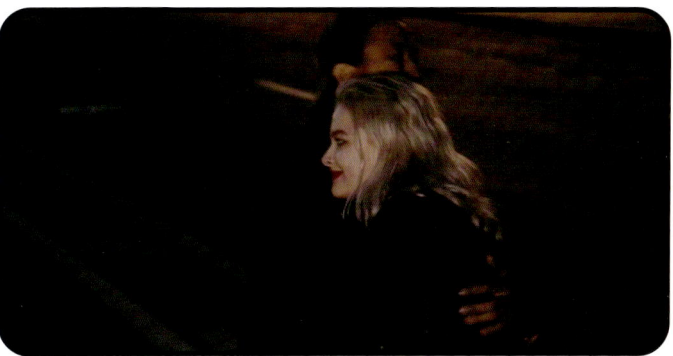

Student: Nikolas Sandevski
School: M.AD School of Ideas
P235: Credit & Commentary

INSTRUCTOR VINAY PARMAR

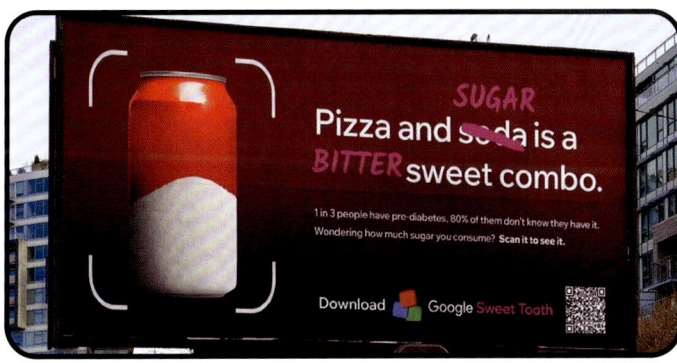 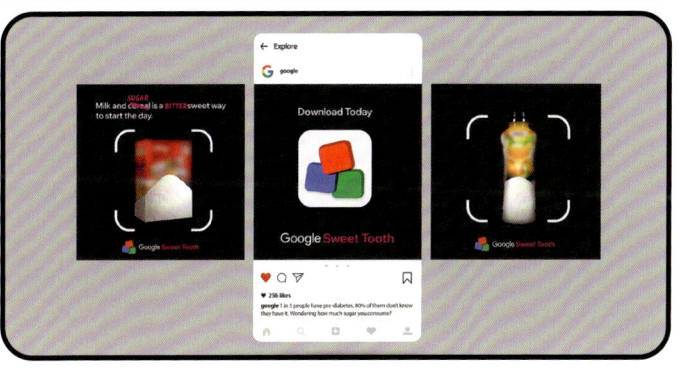

Students: Kailin Zhang, Krishna Betai
School: M.AD School of Ideas Toronto
P235: Credit & Commentary

Commercial, Interactive | Advertising Film/Video

44 ADVERTISING FILM/VIDEO SILVER

INSTRUCTOR PRIYOSHI KAPUR
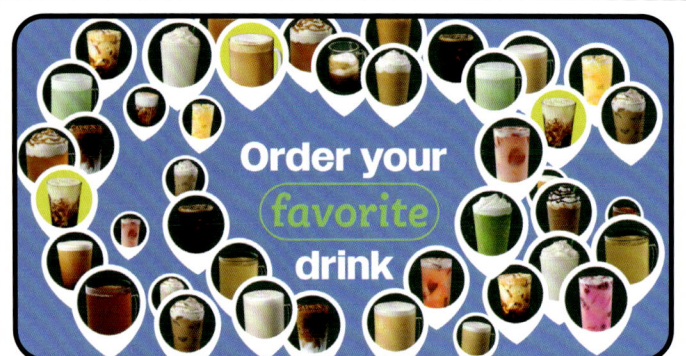
Student: Liz Mathews
School: School of the Art Institute of Chicago

INSTRUCTOR HANK RICHARDSON

Student: Andrea Avila
School: M.AD School of Ideas

INSTRUCTOR MEL WHITE
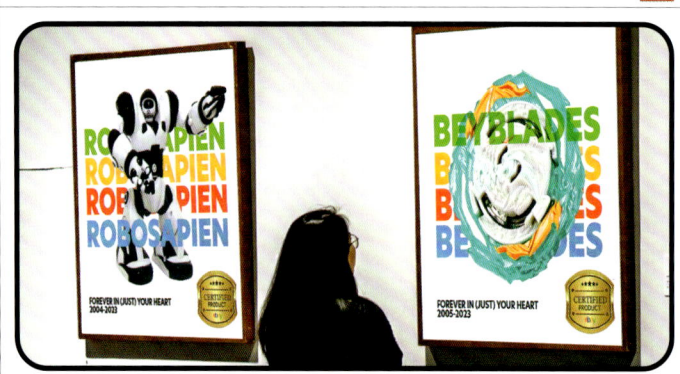
Students: Tori Aragi, Kayla Beck
School: Syracuse University, The Newhouse School

INSTRUCTOR MARK ALLEN
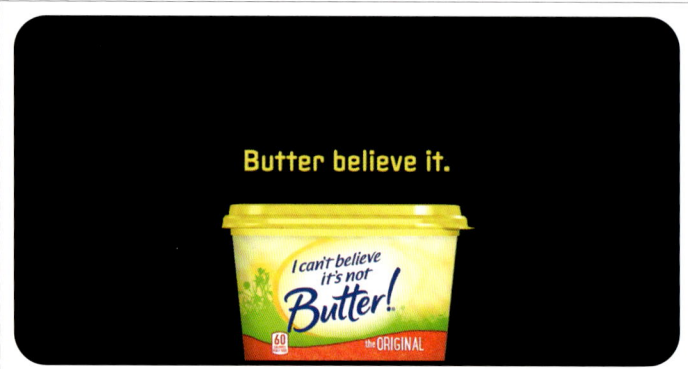
Students: Roshan Gupta, Maddie Otero
School: Southern Methodist University

INSTRUCTOR HANK RICHARDSON
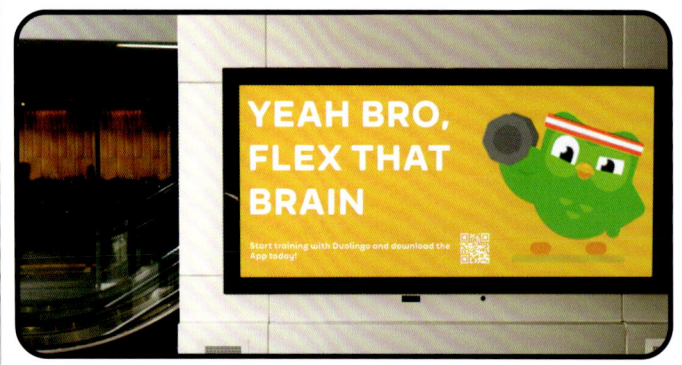
Students: Marie Sophie Baier, Aïna Zaragoza Sostre
School: M.AD School of Ideas

INSTRUCTOR MARK ALLEN
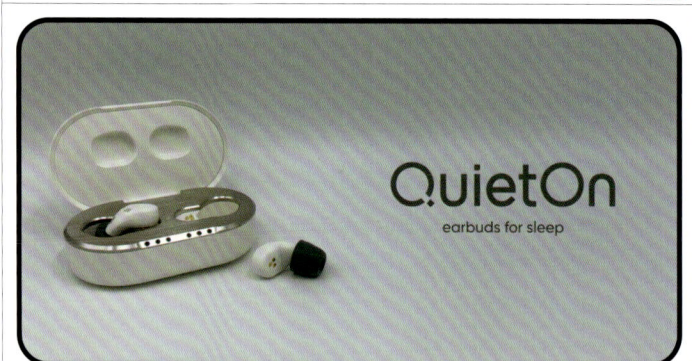
Students: Ethan Jones, Atenas Vijil
School: Southern Methodist University

INSTRUCTOR MEL WHITE
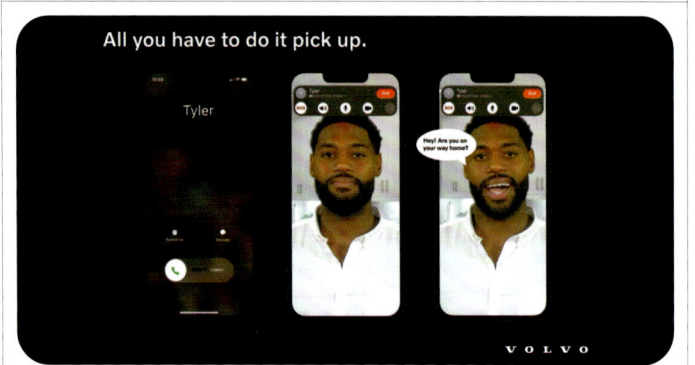
Students: Meghan Gulley, Greta Hartwyk
School: Syracuse University, The Newhouse School

INSTRUCTOR HANK RICHARDSON
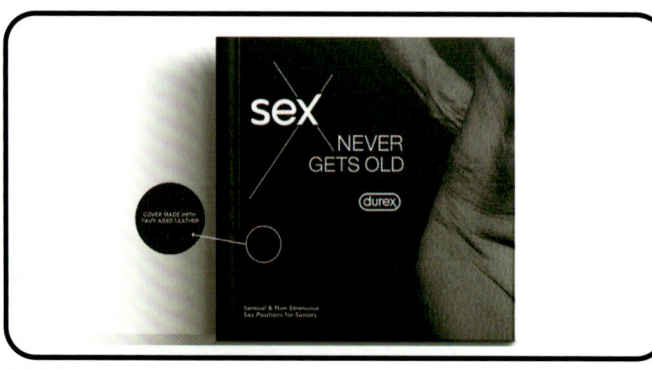
Student: Marie Sophie Baier
School: M.AD School of Ideas

Advertising Film/Video | Commercial

45 ADVERTISING FILM/VIDEO SILVER

INSTRUCTOR MEL WHITE

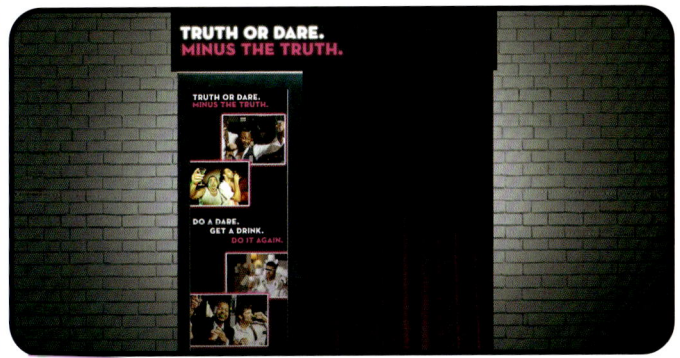

Students: Jenna Byers, Sophia Donio
School: Syracuse University, The Newhouse School

INSTRUCTOR MEL WHITE

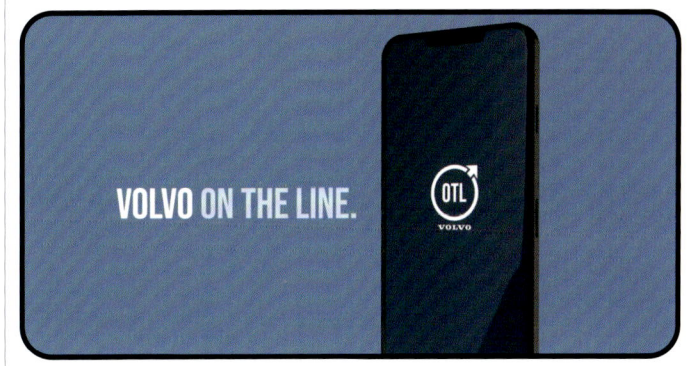

Students: Ryan Garret Conner, Mackenzie Murphy
School: Syracuse University, The Newhouse School

INSTRUCTOR MARK ALLEN

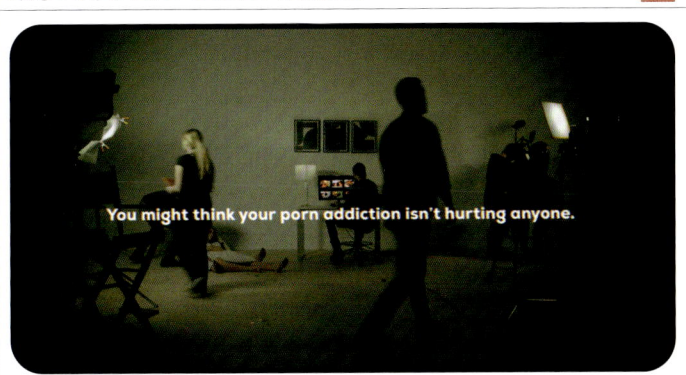

Student: Tyler Chapman
School: Southern Methodist University

INSTRUCTOR HANK RICHARDSON

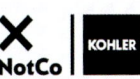

Students: Philip Acierno, Harper Herman, Aleah Jones, Paige Shin
School: M.AD School of Ideas New York

INSTRUCTOR MEL WHITE

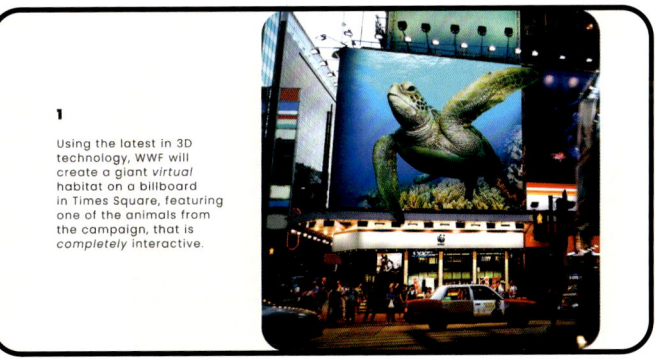

Students: Ryan Garret Conner, Mackenzie Murphy
School: Syracuse University, The Newhouse School

INSTRUCTOR MARK ALLEN

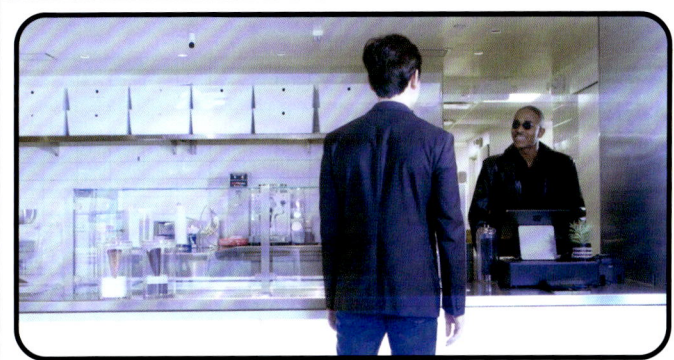

Student: Morgan Martinez
School: Southern Methodist University

INSTRUCTOR HANK RICHARDSON

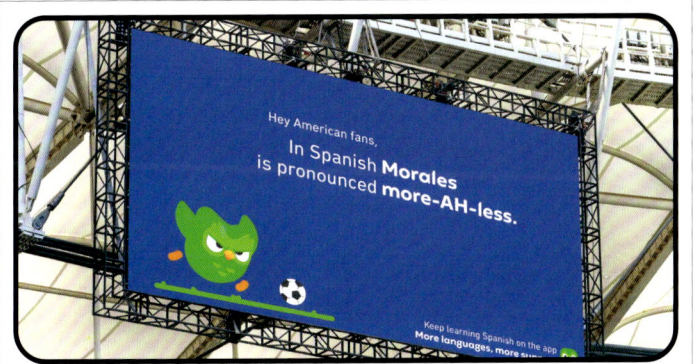

Students: Iuliana Vilcan, Javier Forero
School: M.AD School of Ideas

INSTRUCTOR MEL WHITE

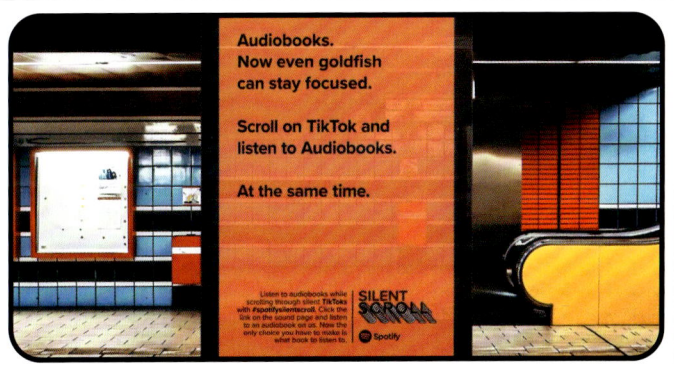

Students: Will Thorpe, Isabella Uribe
School: Syracuse University, The Newhouse School

Commercial | Advertising Film/Video

46 ADVERTISING FILM/VIDEO SILVER

INSTRUCTOR MEL WHITE

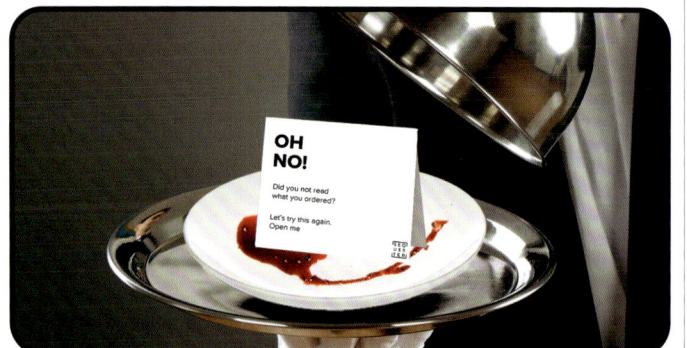

Students: Julia Gershowitz, Amina Shreve
School: Syracuse University, The Newhouse School

INSTRUCTOR MEL WHITE

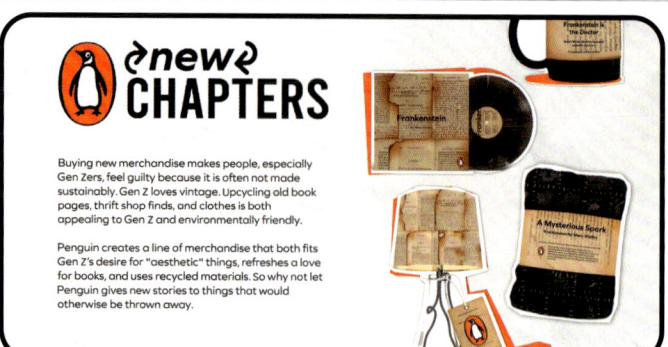

Students: Megan Adams, Dianna Higaki
School: Syracuse University, The Newhouse School

INSTRUCTOR HANK RICHARDSON

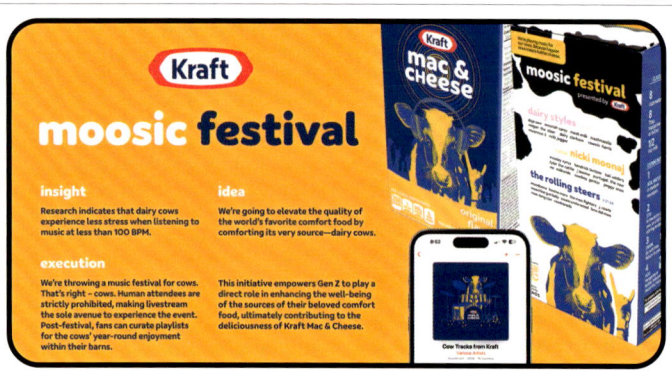

Students: Philip Acierno, Harper Herman, Aleah Jones, Paige Shin
School: M.AD School of Ideas New York

INSTRUCTOR MEL WHITE

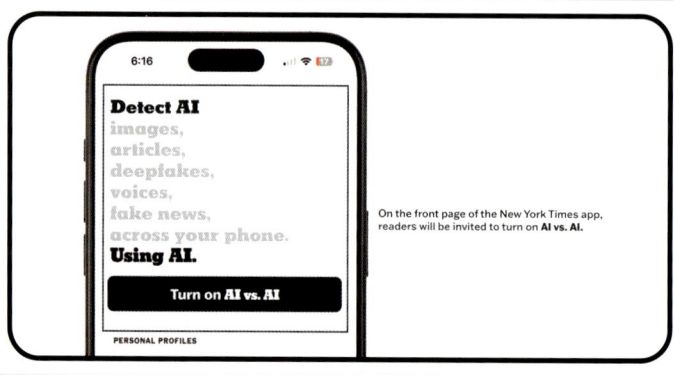

Student: Brooke Hirsch
School: Syracuse University, The Newhouse School

INSTRUCTOR MEL WHITE

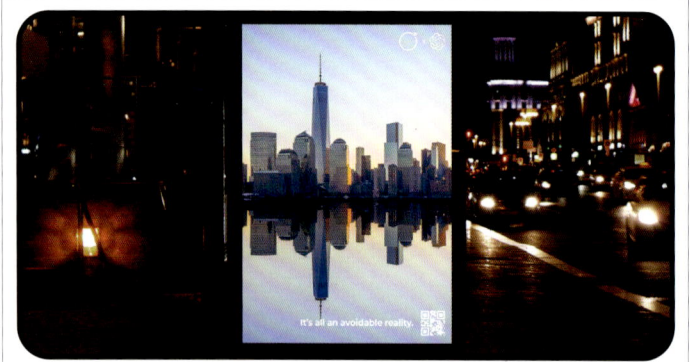

Students: Tori Aragi, Kayla Beck
School: Syracuse University, The Newhouse School

INSTRUCTOR MEL WHITE

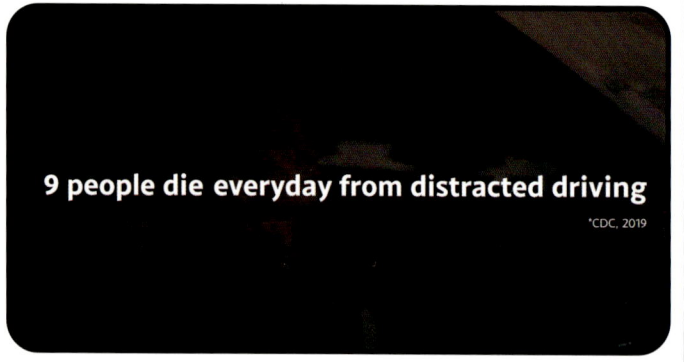

Students: Julia Gershowitz, Amina Shreve
School: Syracuse University, The Newhouse School

INST. T. DUNN, S. BOBACK, M. FARGO, H. EL AKAD

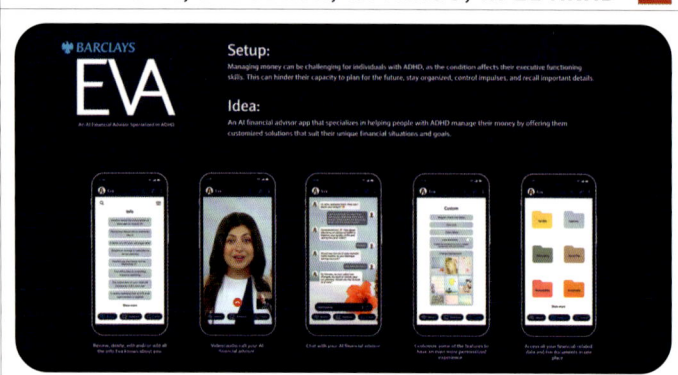

Students: Elena Fernández de Torres, Laila al-Kowatli, Ilu Shilpakar
School: M.AD School of Ideas Madrid

INSTRUCTOR JAMES DAHER

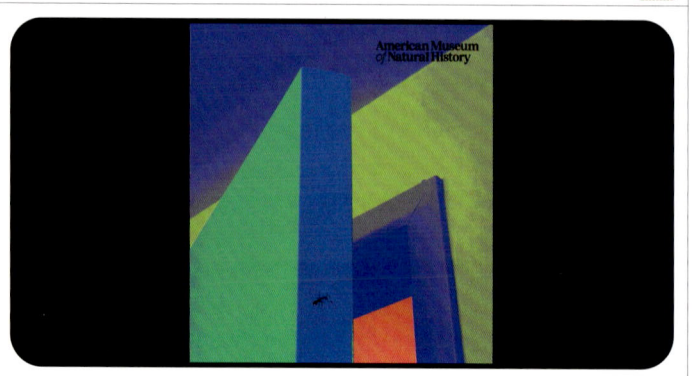

Student: Dong Hyun Kim
School: School of Visual Arts

Advertising Film/Video | Commercial, Interactive

Design Platinum Awards

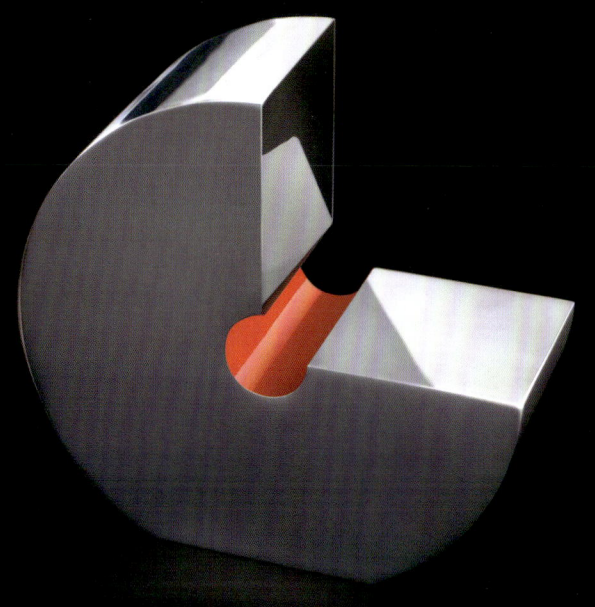

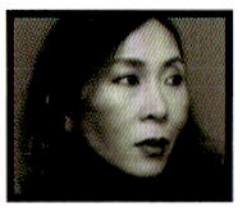

Natasha Jen | **School of Visual Arts** | **Dean: Gail Anderson** | **Pages: 50, 51, 60**
Biography: A designer with a distinctive voice, Natasha's portfolio spans brand identities, exhibitions, and digital systems. Since joining Pentagram in 2012, she's collaborated with global leaders like Google, Pfizer, and Reddit. Her work garners recognition in significant design awards, with an honorary fellowship from the Royal College of Arts and election to Alliance Graphique Internationale. Beyond design, Natasha contributes as a board member and educates future designers at the School of Visual Arts, sharing her expertise globally.
Advice: Surround yourself with excellence and seek mentorship from designers you admire through study, collaboration, or apprenticeships. Deepen your understanding of design and art history to enrich your work. Cultivate critical thinking, and always practice kindness towards your peers.

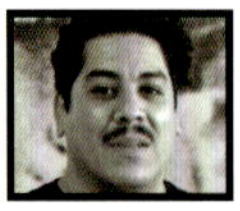

Stephen Serrato | **ArtCenter College of Design** | **Dean: Ann Field** | **Pages: 52, 53**
Biography: Stephen Serrato is an assistant professor for the undergraduate and graduate graphic design programs at the ArtCenter College of Design. In 2015, along with River Jukes Hudson and Dante Carlos Jr., he founded the graphic design studio ELLA. His work has been exhibited internationally and was included in the "Work from California" exhibition at the 25th International Biennial of Graphic Design in Brno, Czech Republic. Most recently, his work was featured in Ellen Lupton's *Thinking with Type*.
Advice: Teachers often use their own process to model for the students. We have years of experience and, over time, have proven that our methods work in and out of the classroom. But ultimately, students glean what they can and develop their own methods. That's the beauty of learning and making your own way. Trust yourself and learn all the rules so you can break them—over and over again.

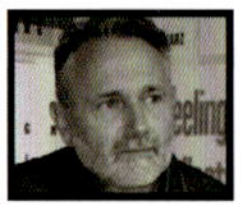

Simon Johnston | **ArtCenter College of Design** | **Dean: Ming Tai** | **Pages: 54, 55**
Biography: Born in England, Simon Johnston was educated at the Bath Academy of Art and the Kunstgewerbeschule in Switzerland. In 1984, he co-founded the London design studio 8vo and was instigator and co-editor of the typography journal *Octavo*. His current design practice, Simon Johnston Design, focuses on publications for artists, art galleries, and museums. He is a professor at the ArtCenter College of Design and creative director of the Hoffmitz Milken Center for Typography. He divides his time between book design, education, and his own art and photography practice.
Advice: With logos and identities, imagine that the best version of your design concept already exists, and it is your job to find it. This means analyzing all of the variables of form and meaning and making sure you systematically try them all out and compare them. The best version will reveal itself to you.

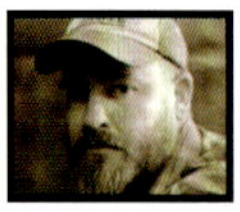

Nathan Savage | **Portland Community College** | **Dean: Gene Flores** | **Pages: 56, 57**
Biography: Nathan Savage leads the Graphic Design Program's faculty and staff at Portland Community College. Before moving to Oregon, Nathan developed Platinum-selling and Grammy-nominated packages for Sony, 15 History Channel program title treatments, footwear branding acquired by Target, and publications galore for Red Herring Design. Nathan's BFA in communication design from Texas State led to interning for the creative teams of Paula Scher and Woody Pirtle at Pentagram. His typography professor, David Shields, officiated his wedding.
Advice: The sooner you embrace typography as your ally, the more creative professionals will respect your work.

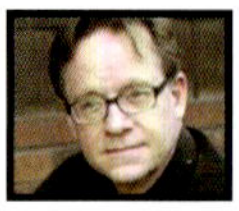

David Tillinghast | **ArtCenter College of Design** | **Dean: Ann Field** | **Page: 58**
Biography: David is the assistant chair of the Illustration Design Program at the ArtCenter College of Design. He has worked in most markets in the illustration industry and has received numerous awards. He has been a lead delegate to the United Nations supporting the Millennium Development Goals and lead faculty on the Anti-Gun Violence Project, a series of award-winning children's books adopted into local public libraries. He has completed training with Al Gore to join climate reality leaders dedicated to community education about the global climate crisis and its solutions.
Advice: Congratulations to all the incredibly talented winners in this prestigious global competition. Remember that talent is the price of entry into the field of art and design, but it is your passion and tenacity that will see you through a lifelong career and gratitude and humility that will allow you to create a life that you can look back on with pride. Good luck to all the talented winners!

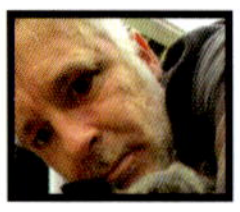

Robert Clayton | **ArtCenter College of Design** | **Dean: Ann Field** | **Page: 58**
Biography: Robert Clayton graduated with honors from the ArtCenter College of Design in Pasadena in 1988. Utilizing skills learned over the past 30 years of art practice and 27 years of teaching, Robert has recently started to explore unconventional means of fabrication generated by a curiosity about self-taught art forms. The focus of his new body of work is pushing the ideas and concepts of narrative and/or illustrative content. Robert currently serves as a full-time faculty member at the ArtCenter College of Design.
Advice: Draw what you want, be who you are, and look under the rocks. There is always something to make.

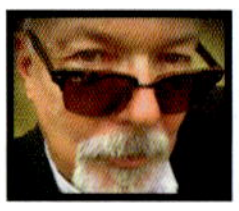

William Meek | **Texas State University** | **Dean: John Fleming** | **Page: 59**
Biography: William Meek earned his MFA from Kent State University and his BFA from the University of North Texas. His professional work and research interests include advertising art direction, trademarks, branding systems, digital technologies like AI, and design instruction. He has been recognized in national competitions and publications such as Communication Arts and *Print* magazine. With 34 years of teaching experience, William emphasizes the importance of strong messaging, thorough audience research, conceptual strategy, design mechanics, and craftsmanship.
Advice: As a communication designer, embrace the dynamic world of AI in problem-solving. From understanding audiences to final production, AI is your trusted ally. Stay open-minded and adaptable as you craft innovative ideas that deeply resonate. Aim for a lasting impact, whether it's making them laugh, cry, or ponder. Maintain a positive outlook and wear your smile proudly—it's your best accessory! With AI by your side, the possibilities are endless, so let your creativity soar!

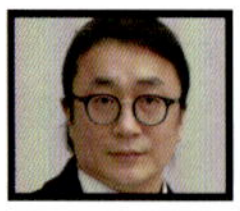

Hyojun Shim | **Dongduk Women's University** | **Dean: Dongbin Kim** | **Page: 61**
Biography: Hyojun Shim currently teaches students as a lecturer for the Department of Visual & Interior Design at Dongduk Women's University in South Korea. He is also a designer and art director at DAEKI and JUN, a multidisciplinary design studio focusing on corporate identities, brand identities, exhibition identities, brand strategy, art direction, moving images, exhibition consultation, and design consultation.
Advice: The important thing is that all of our students are doing well with a solid foundation of fundamentals. If we can free them up a bit more, they'll be even better. Find your own freedom with the basics in place.

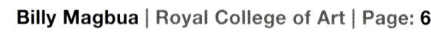

Billy Magbua | **Royal College of Art** | **Page: 62**

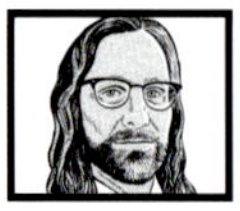

Peter Bergman | **Metropolitan State University of Denver** | **Dean: Shawn Meek** | **Page: 63**
Biography: Peter Bergman combines an academic interest in design, professional experience in printing and print publishing, and an active exhibition and small press publishing practice in which limited edition books and magazines are his work product and art. Areas of research that primarily interest Peter are traditional letterpress printing and its history, typography, self-publishing, artists' books, 'zines (self-published magazines), DIY small press printing and its surrounding ethos, and communication design in the context of web-based social media.
Advice: Some advice I give students, which I gave Courtney for this project, is to art direct your own imagery. Get off the internet and AI, check out a camera, find a friend to model, and plan and execute your own photo shoot. You'll be prouder of the result, and you'll own it 100% legally and creatively.

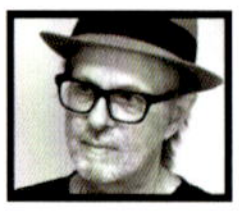

Richard Mehl | **School of Visual Arts** | **Dean: Gail Anderson** | **Pages: 64, 65**
Biography: Richard Mehl is a designer, photographer, writer, and dog lover living in New York City. He is an adjunct professor in the Design Department at SVA, where he has taught since 2002. In his professional practice, Richard has created major visual communication products for J.P. Morgan Chase, Accenture, the Stavros Niarchos Foundation, the Milken Institute, and Morgan Stanley. Richard is the author of Playing with *Color: 50 Graphic Experiments for Exploring Color Design Principles* and the creator/instructor of best-selling online color theory courses for Domestika and CreativeLive.
Advice: Make good rags. Turn off hyphenation. Hang the quotes. Fix the widows. Design the negative space. Create a visual hierarchy. Use color theory. Check the spelling. Simplify. Experiment.

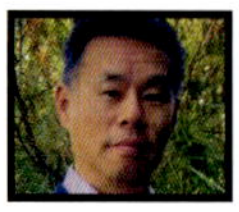

Ming Tai | **ArtCenter College of Design** | **Dean: Ming Tai** | **Page: 217**
Biography: Ming Tai is a veteran art creator and designer with over 25 years of experience in the motion design industry. He co-founded the award-winning motion design company MFactor Inc. in 2002. As a creative director, he has collaborated with such brands as FOX, FX, NFL, and more. Prior to MFactor, Ming was a senior designer at Fox Sports' in-house agency. Since 2002, Ming has been a faculty member at ArtCenter while serving as the faculty director of motion design for the Graphic Design and Illustration Departments. He is also currently the chair of the Graphic Design Deparment.
Advice: Congratulations to all students recognized by Graphis this year. I'm so happy that everyone will see and appreciate your hard work. Your dedication and professionalism inspire all of us to perform to the utmost ability. On behalf of your faculty, we are proud of your accomplishments!

49 DESIGN PLATINUM AWARD-WINNING INSTRUCTORS & STUDENTS

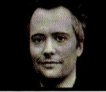
Justin Colt | School of Visual Arts | Dean: Gail Anderson | Pages: **66, 67**
Biography: Justin Colt, a graphic designer and co-founder of The Collected Works in New York City, holds an MFA from the School of Visual Arts, where he also teaches in the Design Program. He has collaborated with notable clients such as Meta, Nike, NBC News, and The New York Times alongside musicians and festivals nationwide. His work has earned recognition from the Type Directors Club, It's Nice That, *Print* magazine, and The Brand Identity, underscoring his contributions to the graphic design industry.
Advice: Pursuing a career in design is among the most fulfilling paths one can choose. It enables you to shape dialogue and influence culture. You have the power to solve problems and define the world as you see it. This career offers the opportunity to collaborate with people and organizations you admire, driving meaningful change. Through the lens of a designer, the world becomes more expansive, exhilarating, and susceptible to your influence. How rad is that?

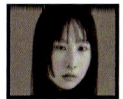
Hyowon Kwon | School of Visual Arts | Dean: Gail Anderson | Pages: **50, 51**
Biography: Hyowon Kwon is a graphic designer based in New York City. With an academic background from the School of Visual Arts, she specializes in strong visual storytelling and image creation rooted in research. She employs a robust visual system to evoke a visceral response to her designs and directly engage with the audience. Her diverse interests in science, photography, history, and fine art, combined with her early experiences in Seoul, South Korea, enable her to draw inspiration from various sources and approach her work creatively.

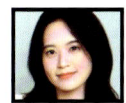
Heejai Park | ArtCenter College of Design | Dean: Ann Field | Pages: **52, 53**
Biography: As a graphic design student at the ArtCenter College of Design, Heejai focuses on brand identity, editorial design, and illustration. She aims to create designs that speak to people, touch their emotions, and form deep connections. Through simple yet powerful elements like typography, images, and colors, Heejai wants her work to show understanding and care for others' feelings. Her goal is to positively influence lives by making meaningful designs that are easy to relate to, aiming for a real impact in making life better.

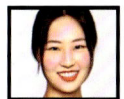
Esther Yeseul Lee | ArtCenter College of Design | Dean: Ming Tai | Pages: **54, 55**
Biography: Esther Yeseul Lee is a designer who balances simplicity and complexity in her design concepts, adding elegance to every detail. She has a passion for discovering innovative approaches to visual communication, particularly in brand identity and motion illustration, exploring ways to better connect with and understand people. After graduating from the ArtCenter College of Design in Los Angeles, Esther is starting her career as a graphic and motion design intern at Hornet Studio in New York.

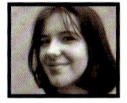
Grace Howard | Portland Community College | Dean: Gene Flores | Pages: **56, 57**
Biography: An upcoming graphic design student, Grace Howard is a passionate and creative designer who loves typography and illustration. She believes that when designing, the research, process, and evolution of an idea is one of the most influential parts of a design. It is only through trial, exploration, and collaboration that she believes designs can reach their full potential. When she's not working on an art or design project, she enjoys cooking, spending time with her cats, and long walks through old Portland neighborhoods.

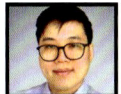
David J. Lee | ArtCenter College of Design | Dean: Ann Field | Page: **58**
Biography: David Lee draws inspiration from personal narratives and nature, crafting emotive illustrations through graphic shapes and vibrant colors. David aims to forge deep connections and evoke powerful emotions through his work. Recently graduating from the ArtCenter College of Design with a BFA in illustration design, he aspires to see his art featured in editorial spreads, entertainment projects, and entrepreneurial ventures, seeking diverse avenues for creative expression and opportunities to infuse projects with fresh, innovative perspectives.

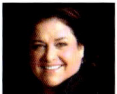
Brandy Compton | Texas State University | Dean: John Fleming | Page: **59**
Biography: Brandy Compton is a non-traditional student at Texas State University, set to graduate in Fall 2024 with a BFA in communication design. She is deeply passionate about creating impact within the communication design community. With years of experience in the hospitality industry and a diverse range of creative outlets, including acting, singing, dancing, printmaking, painting, sculpting, photography, and writing, Brandy brings a unique perspective and skill set to the field. Motivated by a desire to effect meaningful change, she aims to leverage her artistic talents, industry expertise, and academic excellence to drive innovation and inspire others in their creative endeavors.

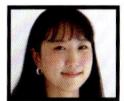
Rachel Pan | School of Visual Arts | Dean: Gail Anderson | Page: **60**
Biography: Rachel is a New York-based designer who creates designs and experiences that evoke curiosity through visual evidence. She is currently a student at the School of Visual Arts studying design with a concentration in UX/UI. Her nomadic upbringing has allowed her to develop a unique perspective on design and aesthetics, and these influences impact her design practices to this day. She constantly strives to create spirited designs, encouraging viewers and users to foster meaningful connections between people and design.

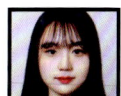
Sojung Won | Dongduk Women's University | Dean: Dongbin Kim | Page: **61**
Biography: Sojung Won is a student majoring in visual design at Dongduk Women's University, a private university established in Seoul, South Korea, in 1950. She is specifically studying packaging design and publication design and is also interested in studying moving images and photography. She recently learned about brand identity in class. When Sojung is not studying, she also has her own YouTube channel and has done comic strips on social media. She used to work for a visual advertising company.

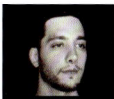
Shahen Markarian | Royal College of Art | Page: **62**
Biography: Shahen Markarian is a seasoned product designer with over six years of experience in the digital product design industry. Throughout his career, he has worked with various clients worldwide, including companies such as Prepply and MantraDao. Currently serving as a team lead within the design department of a Florida-based company, Shahen has consistently demonstrated his expertise in leading teams to create highly innovative and usable digital products. He also contributes greatly as a judge at the Academy of Interactive and Visual Arts. Shahen thrives on the challenge of crafting designs that strike a balance between aesthetics and functionality, resulting in highly usable and impactful digital products.

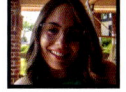
Courtney Meyer | Metropolitan State University of Denver | Dean: Shawn Meek | Page: **63**
Biography: Courtney Meyer is a passionate graphic designer studying at the Metropolitan State University of Denver and is positioned to graduate in the fall of 2024. She has a diverse skill set spanning branding, production, packaging, UI/UX, and beyond. With a keen eye for detail and a commitment to excellence, Courtney strives to craft compelling visuals that resonate with audiences. Her journey through design has been both inspiring and rewarding, and she eagerly anticipates the opportunity to continue making meaningful contributions to the design world.

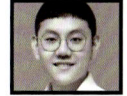
Dong Hyun Kim | School of Visual Arts | Dean: Gail Anderson | Pages: **64, 65**
Biography: Dong Hyun Kim, currently studying graphic design at the School of Visual Arts in New York, stands out as a merit scholar and honors student, having earned recognition in international design competitions. Named a National Merit Scholar for Arts and Sports Vision by the South Korean government, Dong Hyun has showcased his work in esteemed galleries and museums. His proficiency in branding, motion graphics, and interaction design has positioned him as an emerging talent in the international design community.

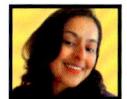
Rabiya Gupta | School of Visual Arts | Dean: Gail Anderson | Pages: **66, 67**
Biography: Rabiya Gupta is a New York-based graphic designer from India and a recent graduate of the School of Visual Arts. She is passionate about creating expressive visual content that transcends convention. Utilizing diverse techniques and perspectives, a handful of which are rooted in her Indian culture, Rabiya's work has a unique voice and can communicate at multiple levels. Her design portfolio includes a variety of projects, such as book covers, album covers, exhibition design, and visual identities. Beyond her interest in design, Rabiya also loves traveling, reading books, and playing the piano.

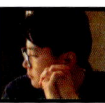
Alan Xu | ArtCenter College of Design | Dean: Ming Tai | Page: **217**
Biography: Alan is a designer who creates elegance and distinction through simplicity, reducing color and form to the bare bones, and then uses that medium in the best way possible to create fascinating results. He is also the designer, organizer, and host for the ArtCenter's Design Speaker Series, where he invited and hosted over 20 renowned designers from around the world and designed over five extensive campaigns for the series. Alan is currently studying at the ArtCenter College of Design in LA.

Visit our Credits & Commentary section in the back of the book to read about the full assignments, approaches, and results from this year's Platinum Winners.

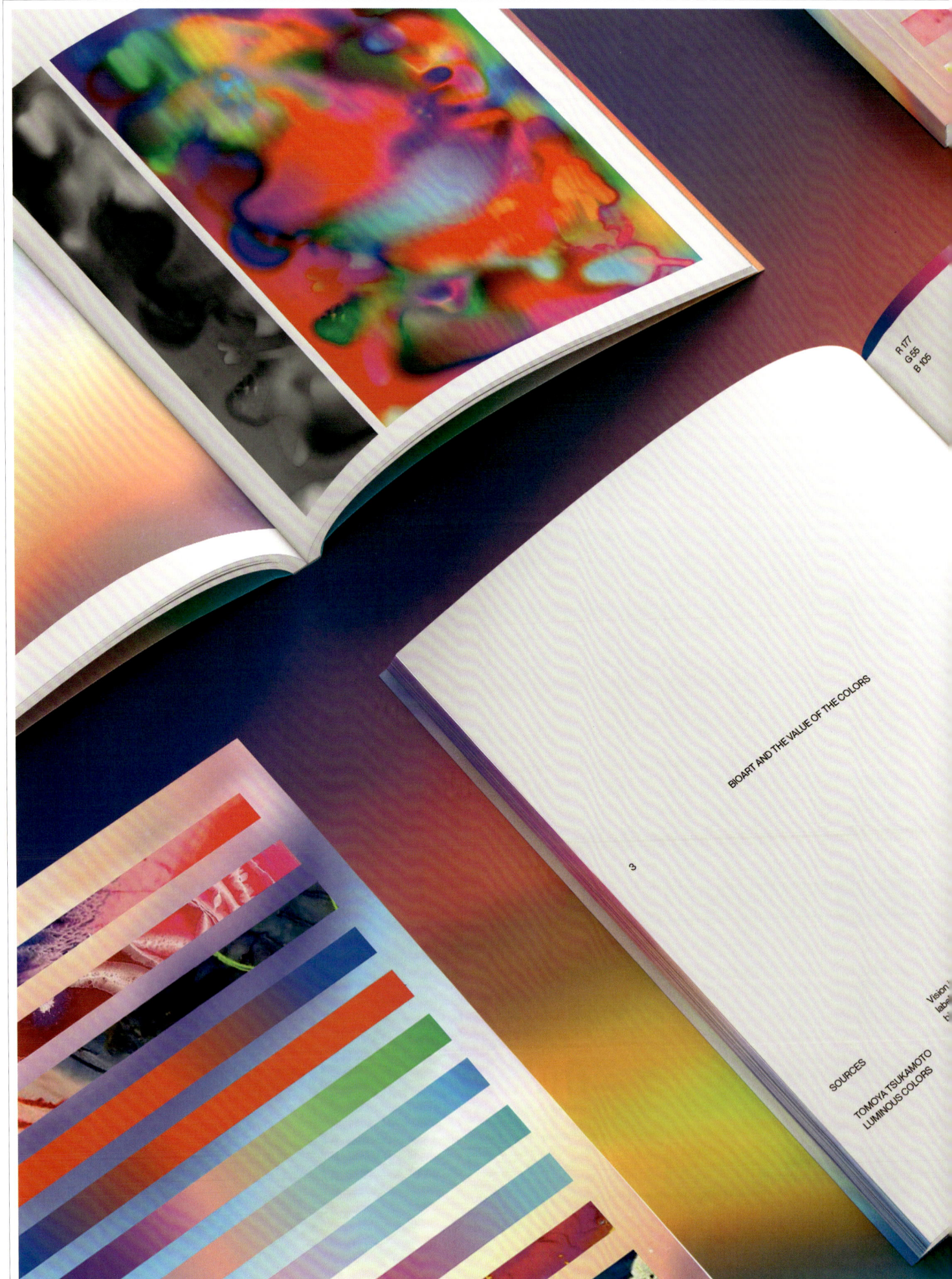

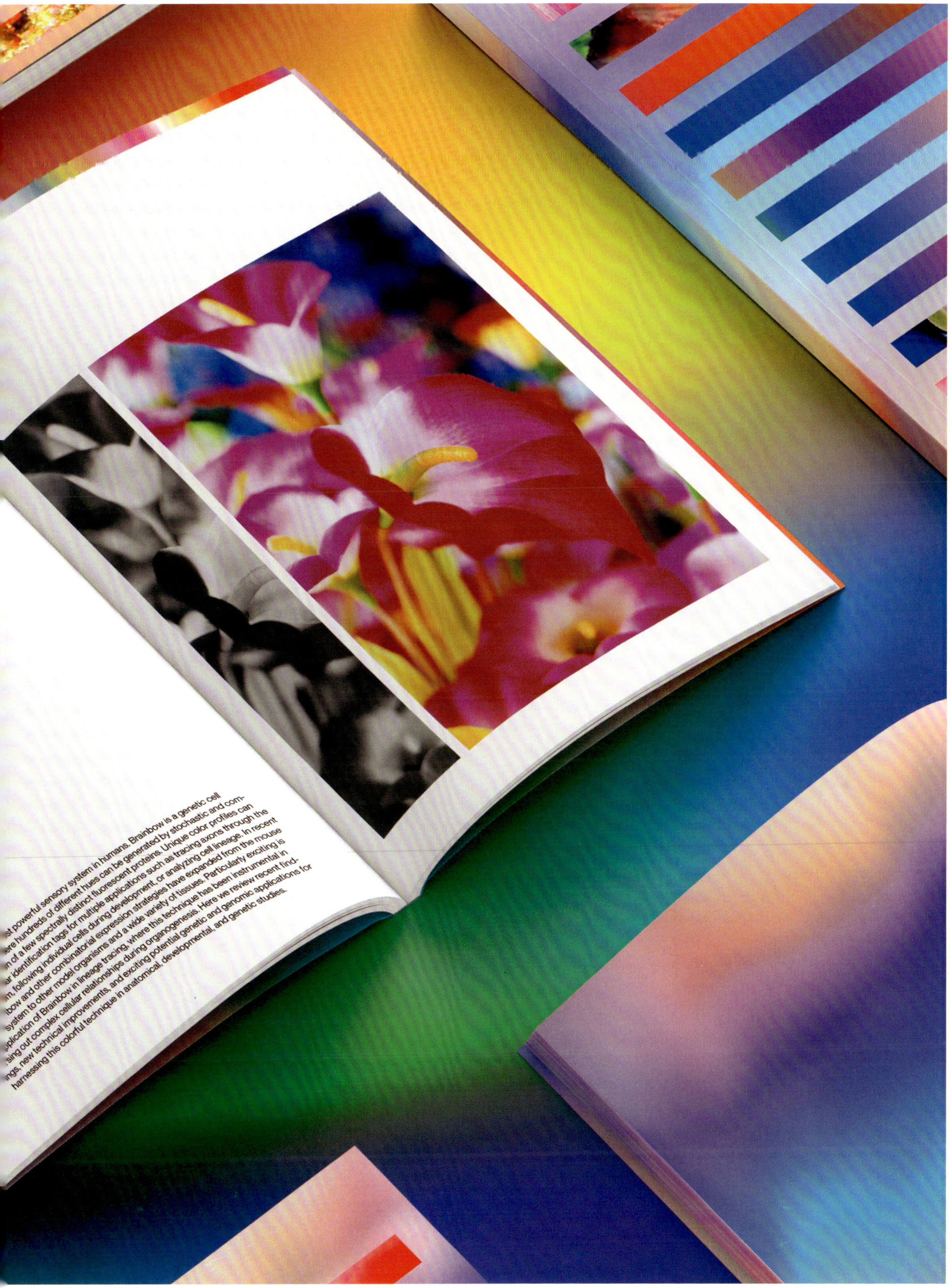

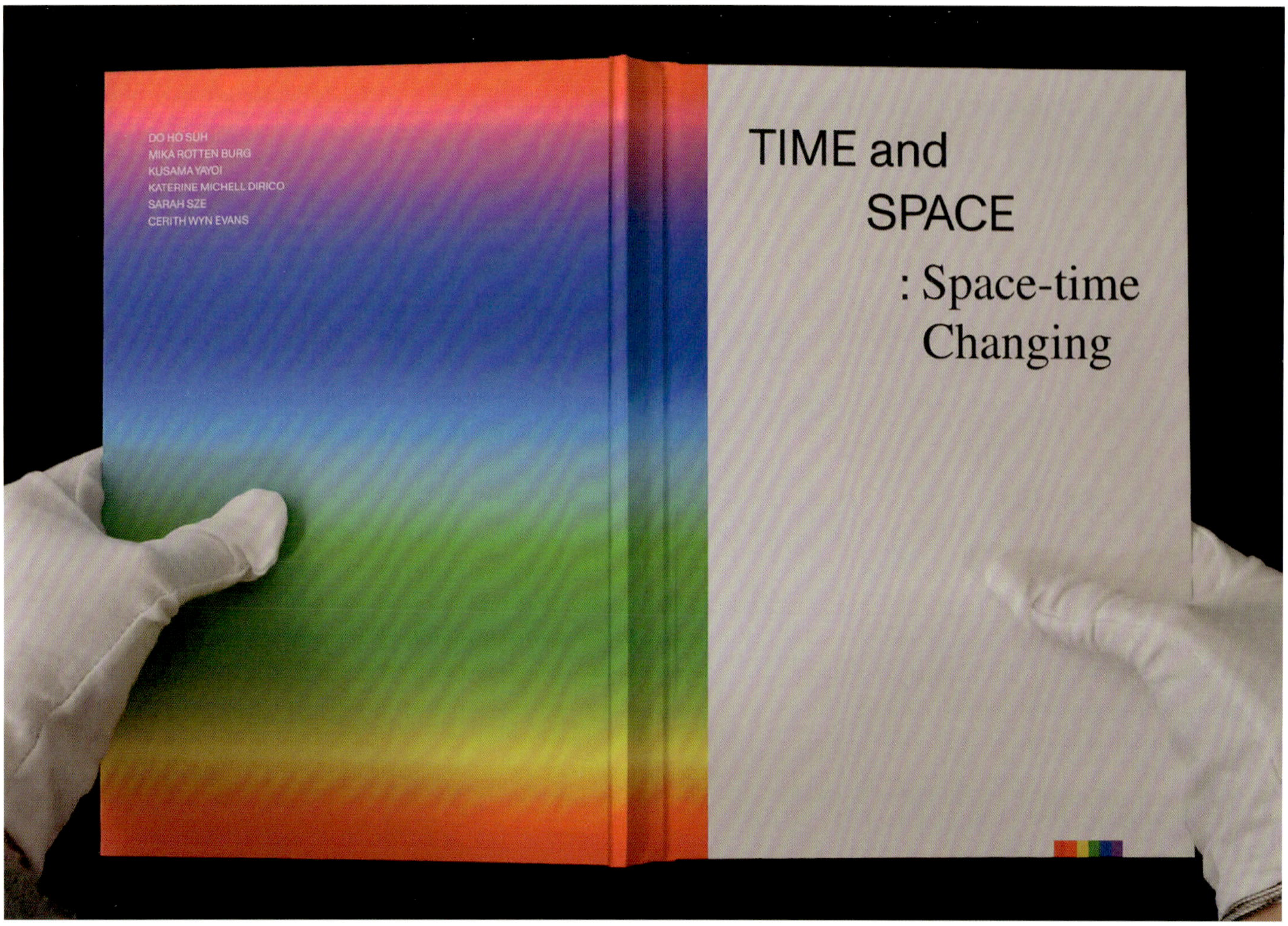

52 INSTRUCTOR **STEPHEN SERRATO** PLATINUM

TIME and SPACE
: Space-time Changing

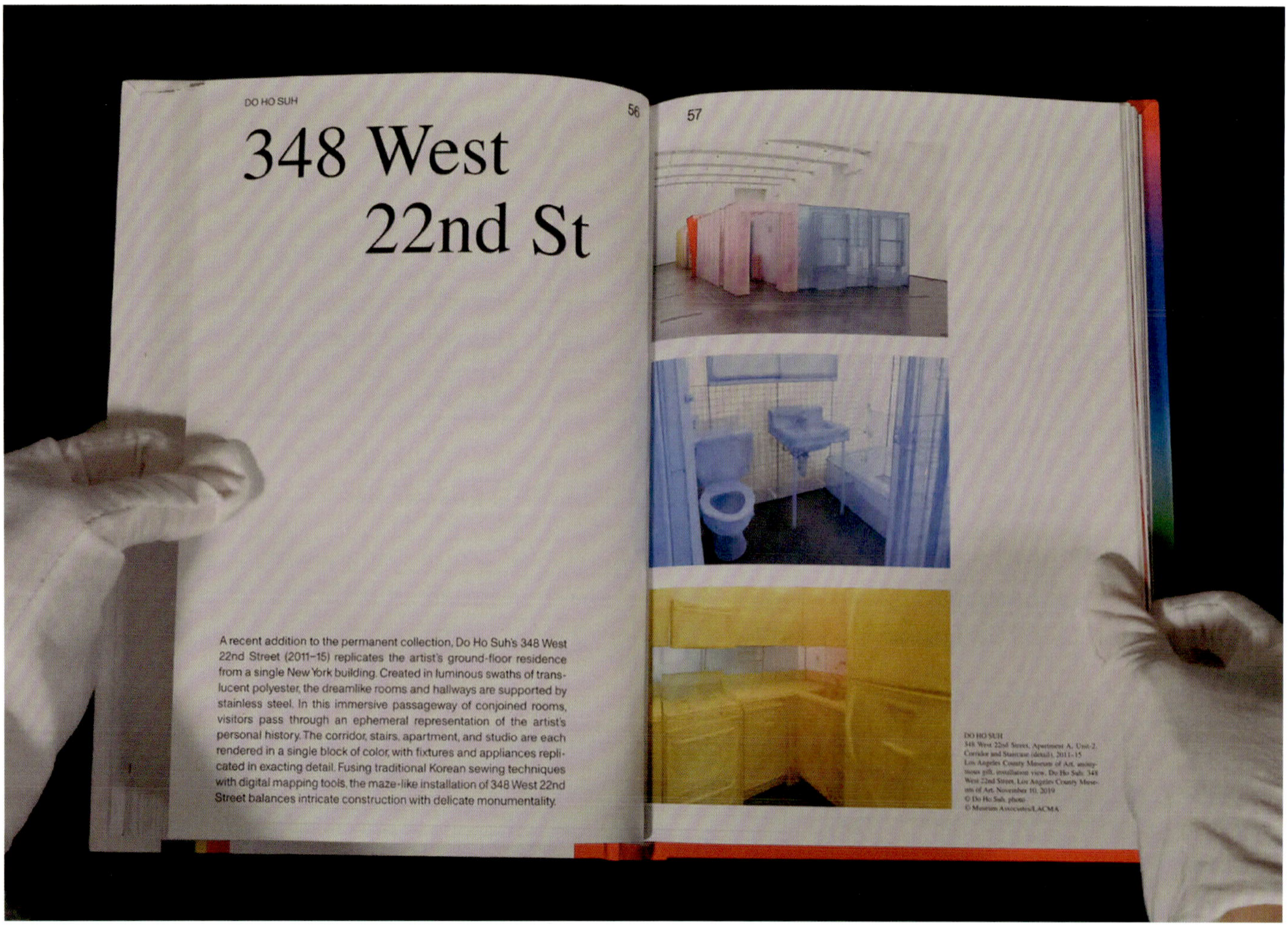

DO HO SUH
MIKA ROTTEN BURG
KUSAMA YAYOI
KATERINE MICHELL DIRICO
SARAH SZE
CERITH WYN EVANS

DO HO SUH

348 West 22nd St

A recent addition to the permanent collection, Do Ho Suh's 348 West 22nd Street (2011–15) replicates the artist's ground-floor residence from a single New York building. Created in luminous swaths of translucent polyester, the dreamlike rooms and hallways are supported by stainless steel. In this immersive passageway of conjoined rooms, visitors pass through an ephemeral representation of the artist's personal history. The corridor, stairs, apartment, and studio are each rendered in a single block of color, with fixtures and appliances replicated in exacting detail. Fusing traditional Korean sewing techniques with digital mapping tools, the maze-like installation of 348 West 22nd Street balances intricate construction with delicate monumentality.

DO HO SUH
348 West 22nd Street, Apartment A, Unit 2, Corridor and Staircase (detail), 2011–15
Los Angeles County Museum of Art, anonymous gift, installation view, Do Ho Suh: 348 West 22nd Street, Los Angeles County Museum of Art, November 10, 2019
© Do Ho Suh, photo
© Museum Associates/LACMA

P236: Credit & Commentary — Images 1, 2 of 7

Design | Books

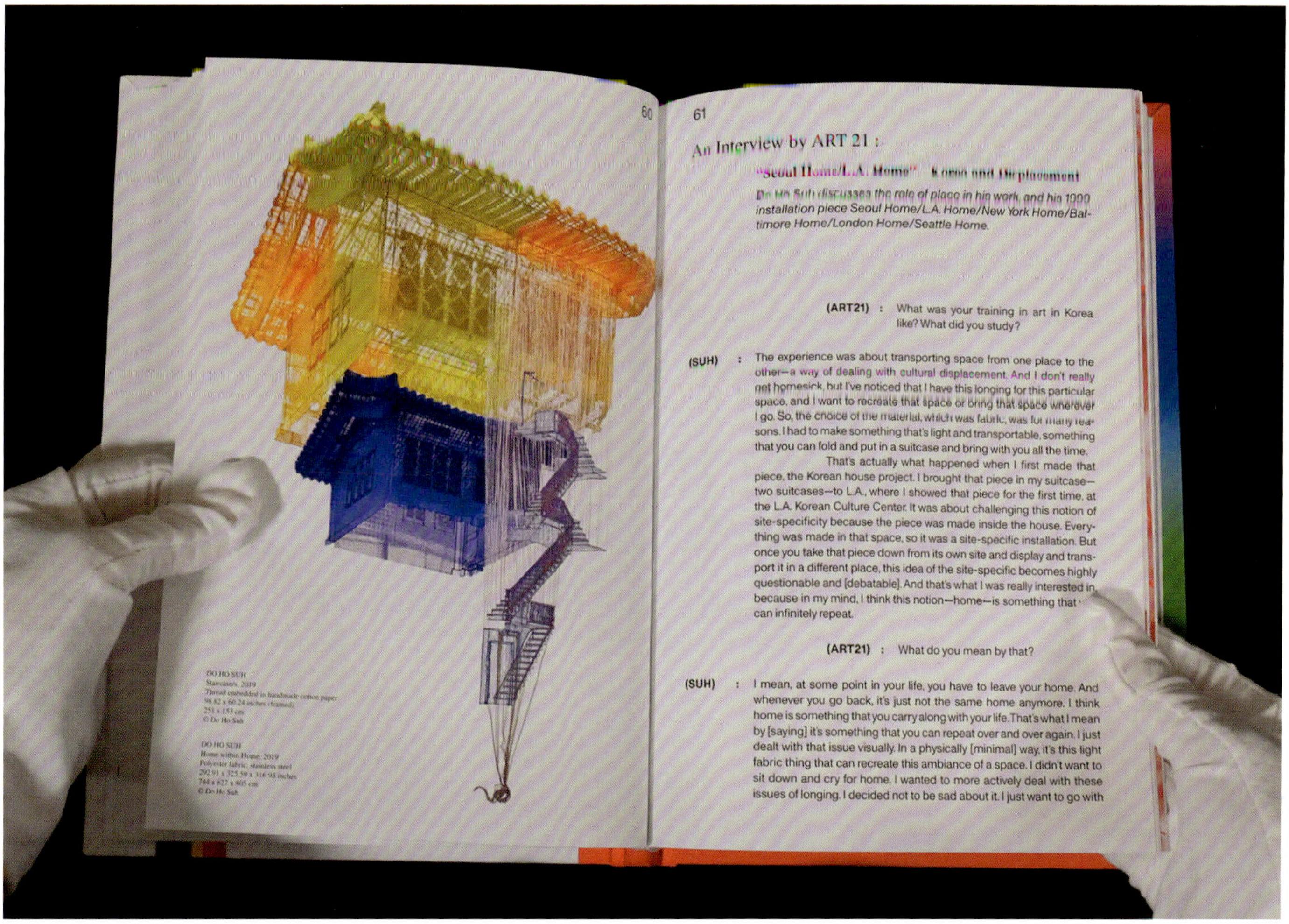

53 INSTRUCTOR **STEPHEN SERRATO** PLATINUM

P236: Credit & Commentary **Student:** Heejai Park | **School:** ArtCenter College of Design Images 3, 4 of 7

Books | Design

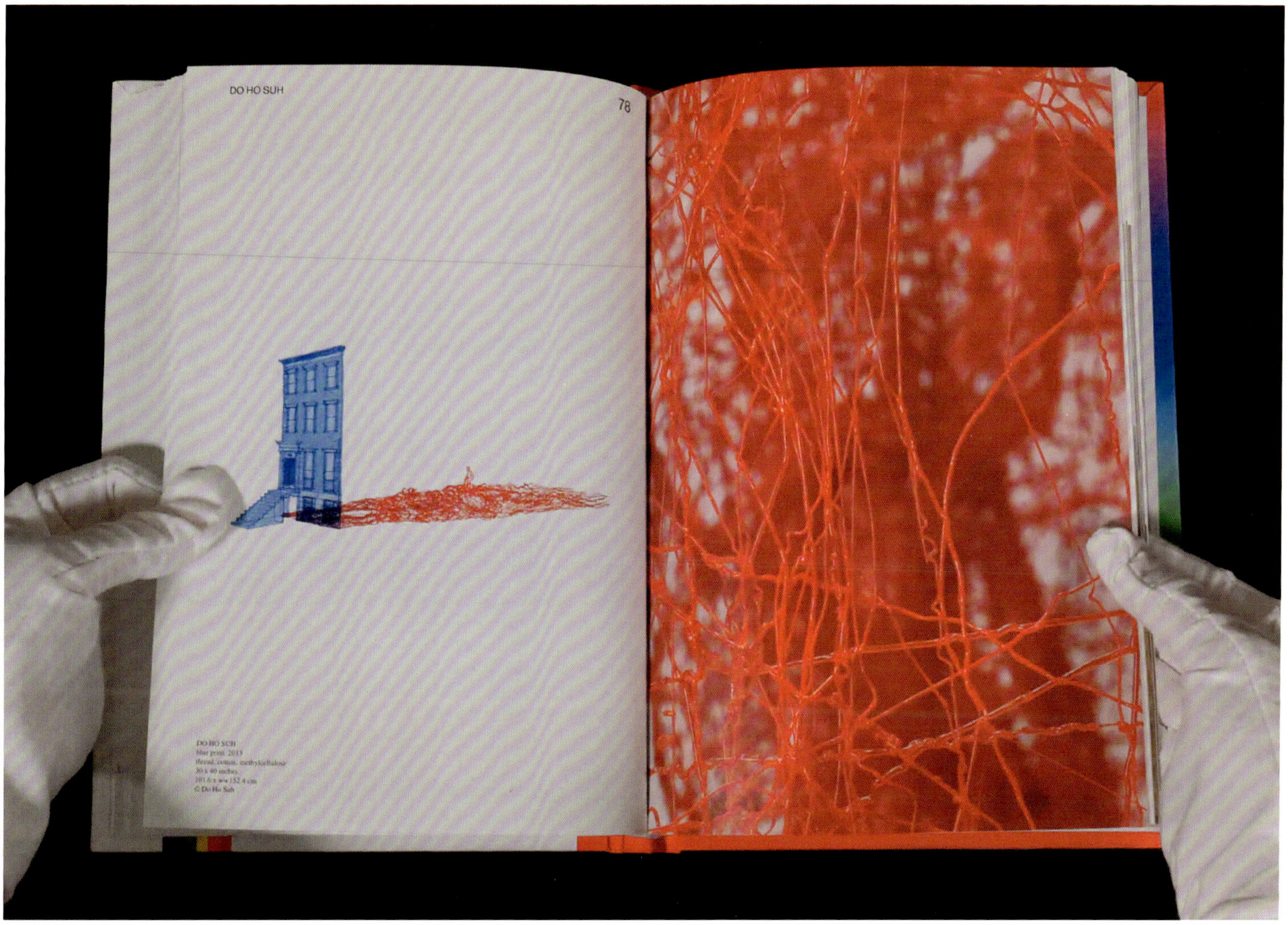

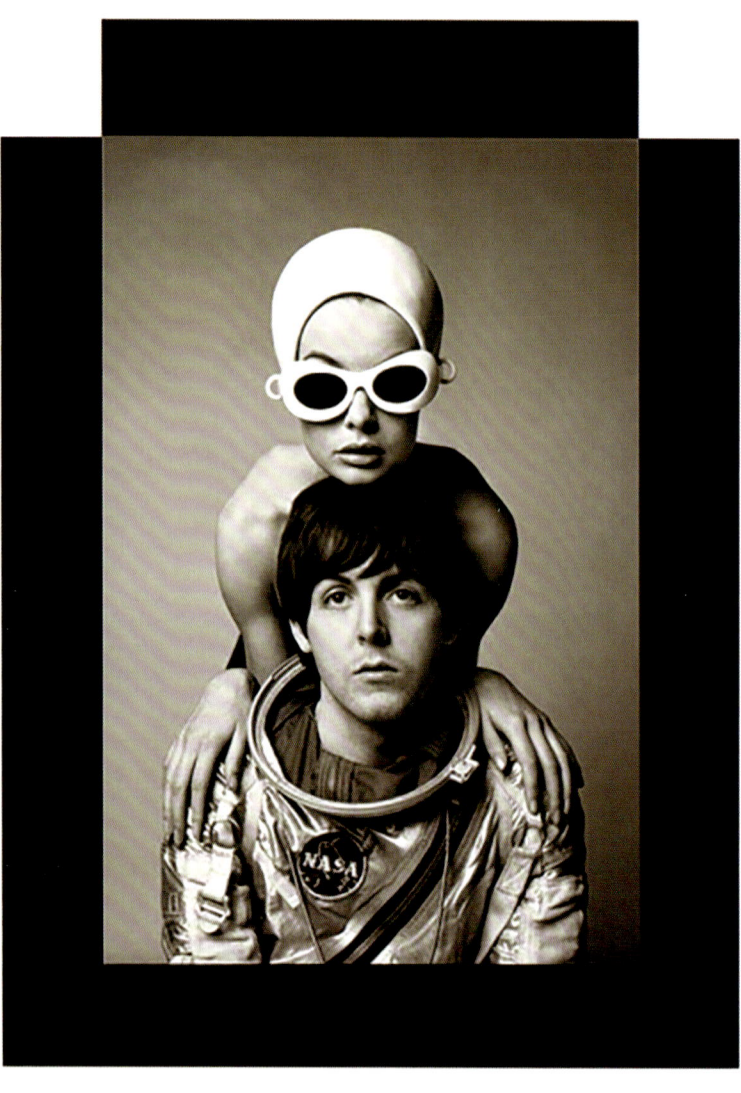

KODAK

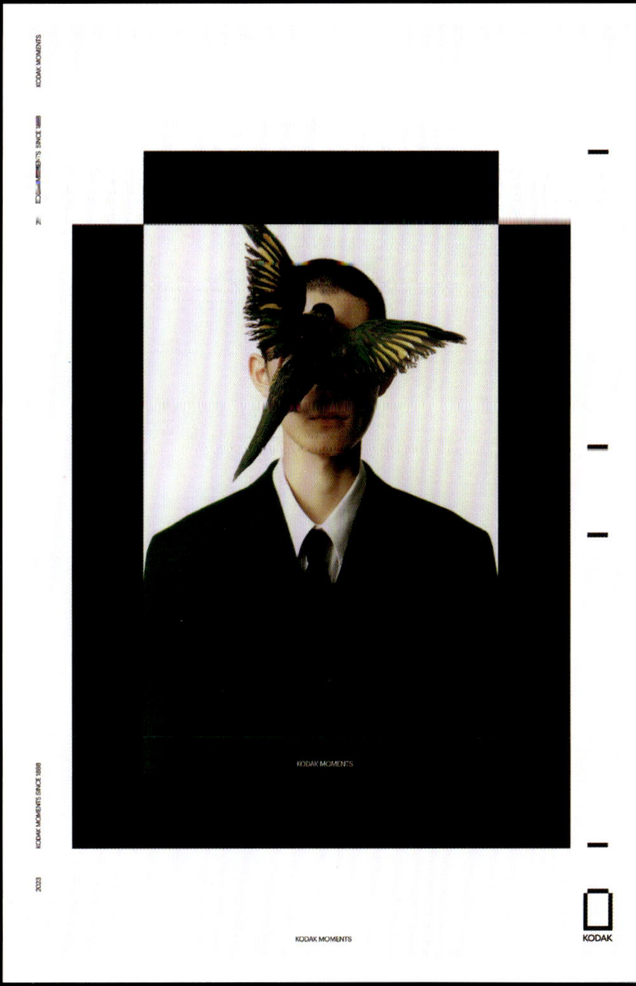

55 INSTRUCTOR SIMON JOHNSTON PLATINUM

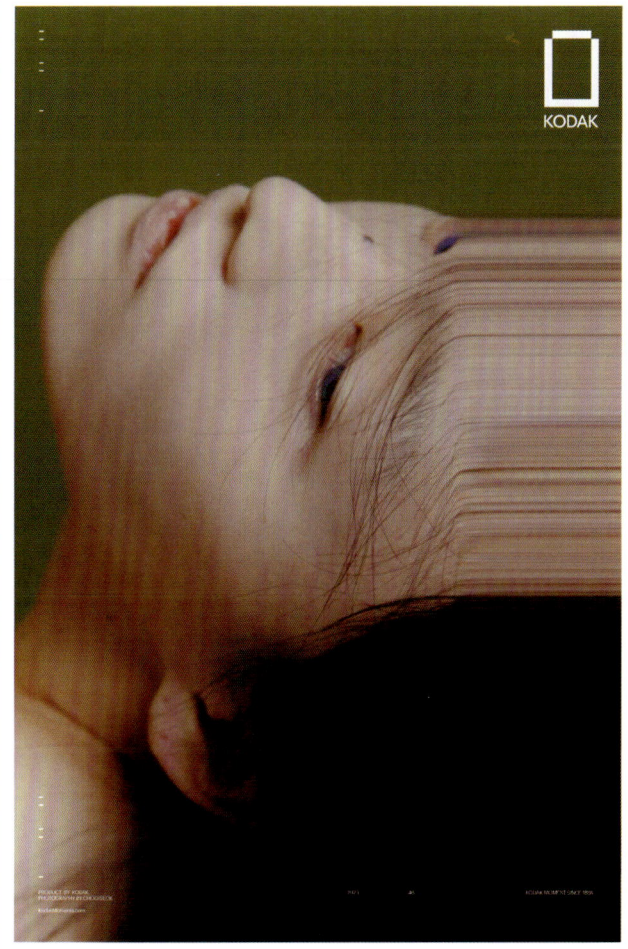
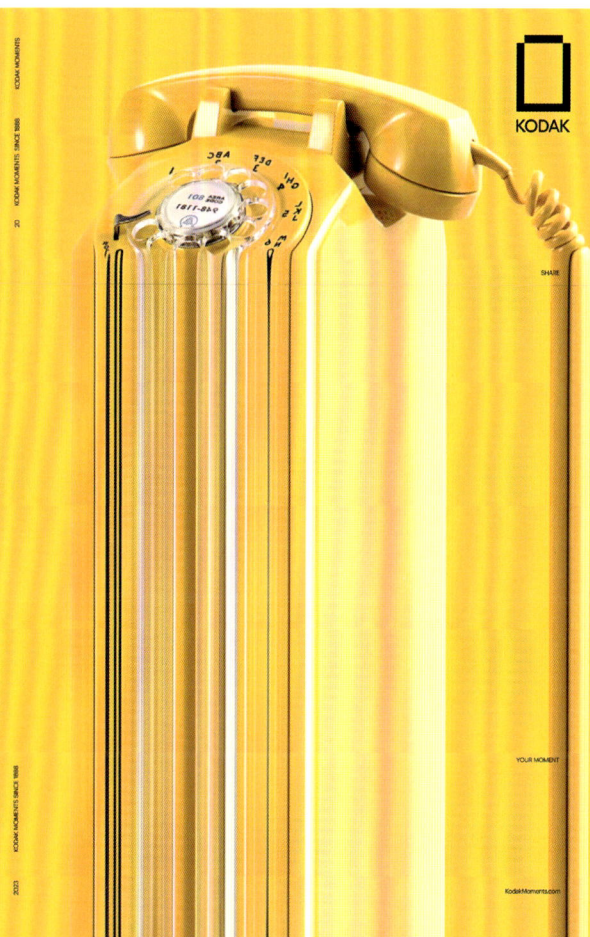

P236: Credit & Commentary   **Student:** Esther Yeseul Lee   **School:** ArtCenter College of Design   Images 2, 3 of 7

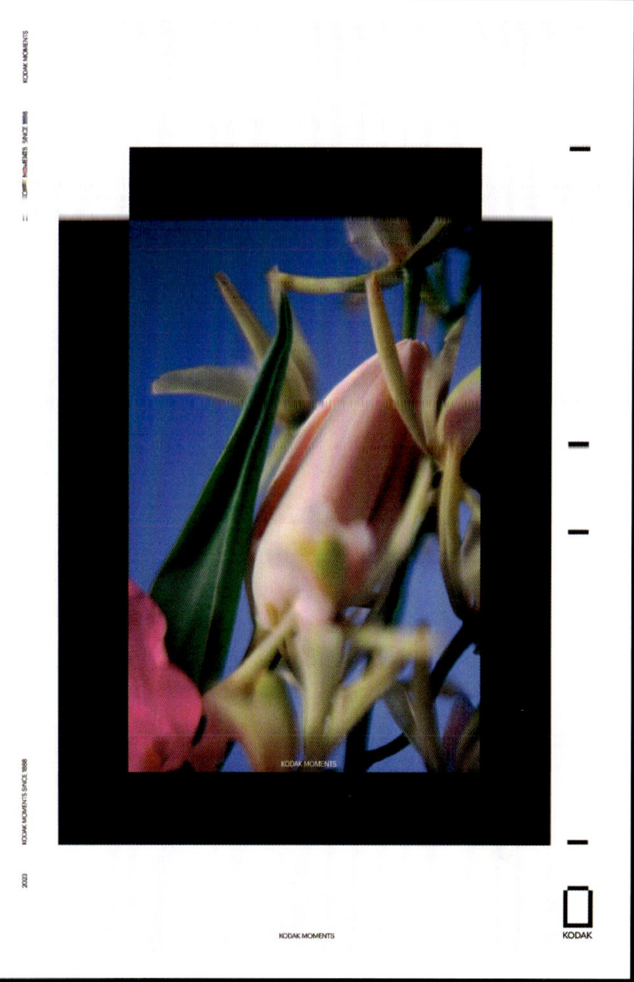

Branding | Design

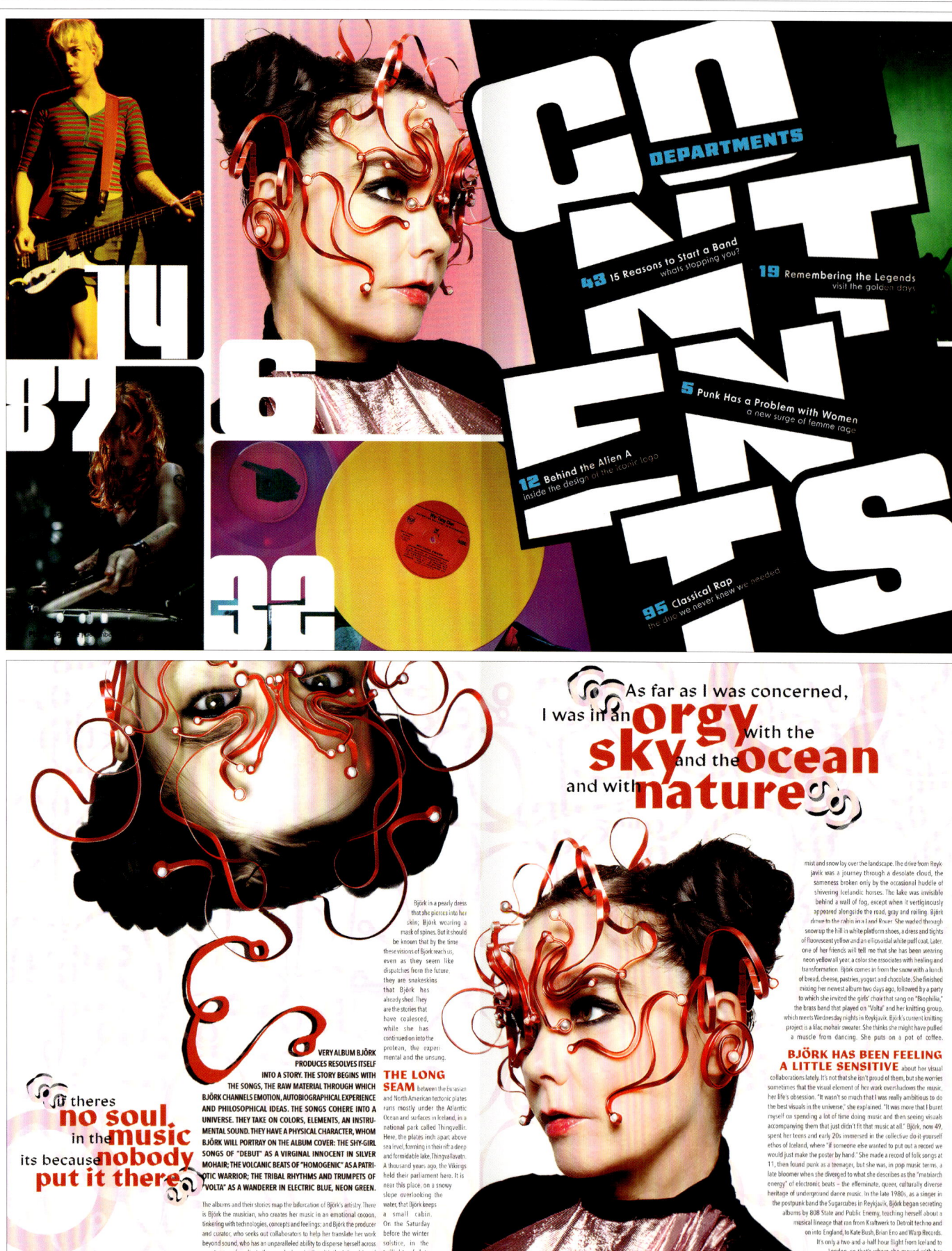

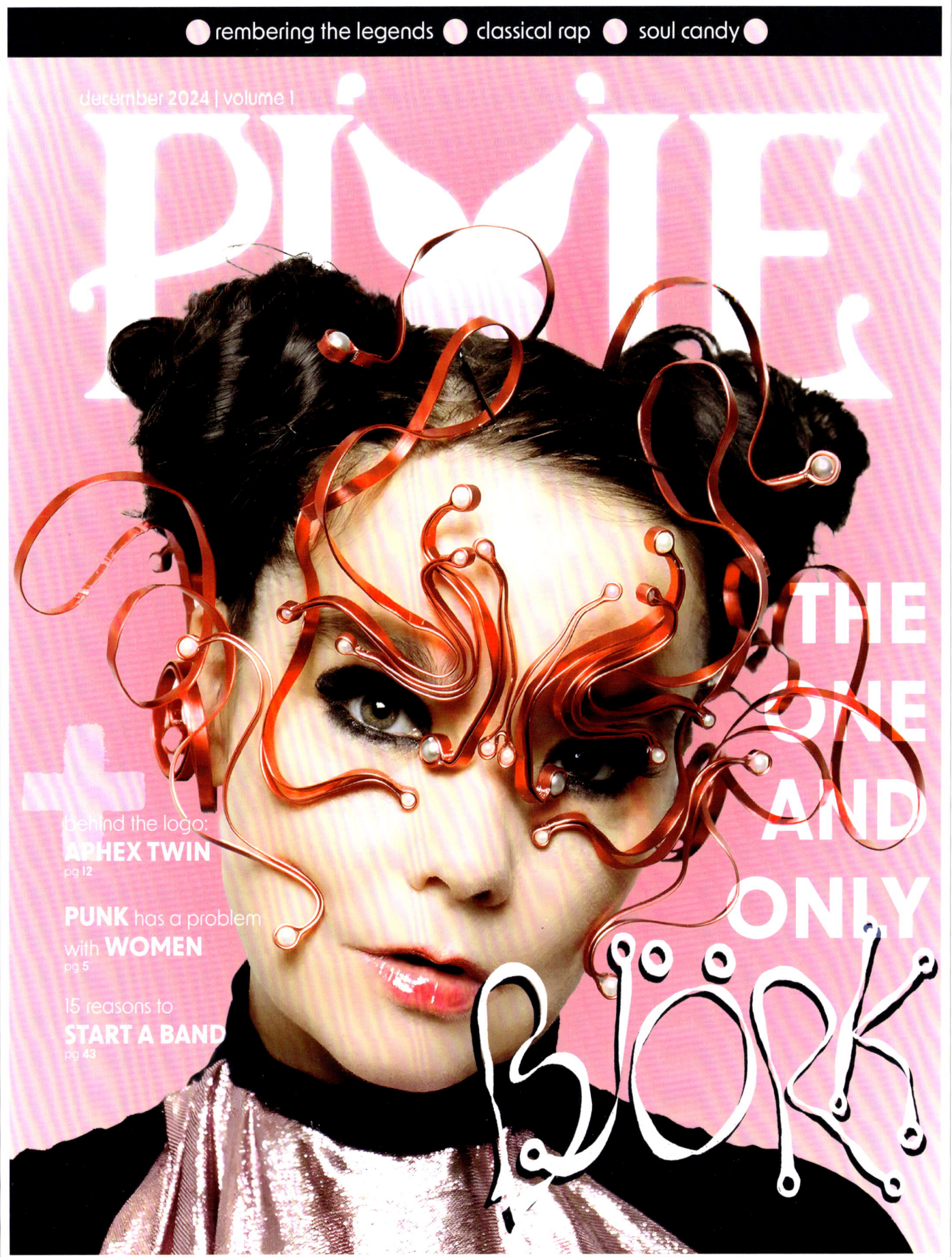

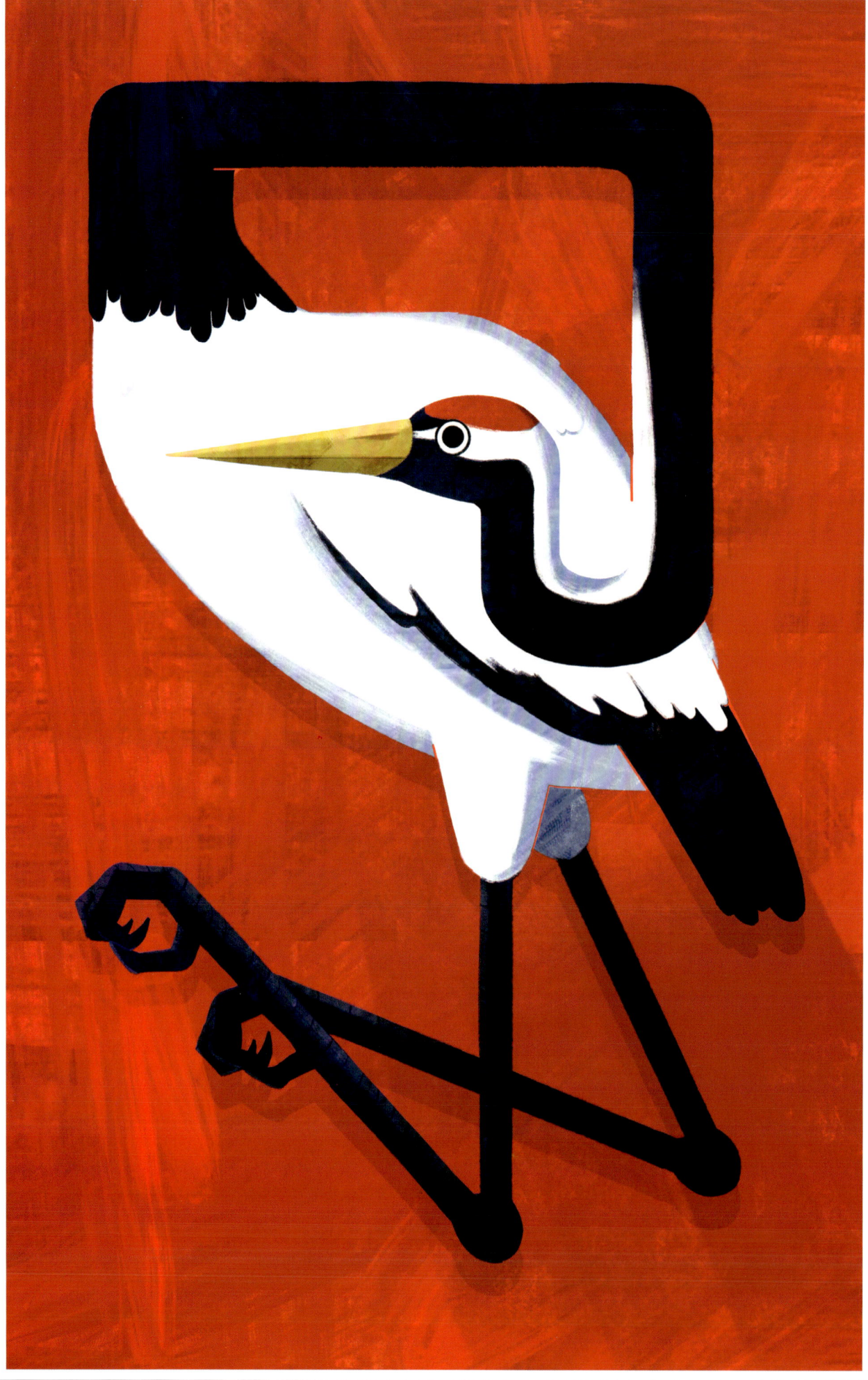

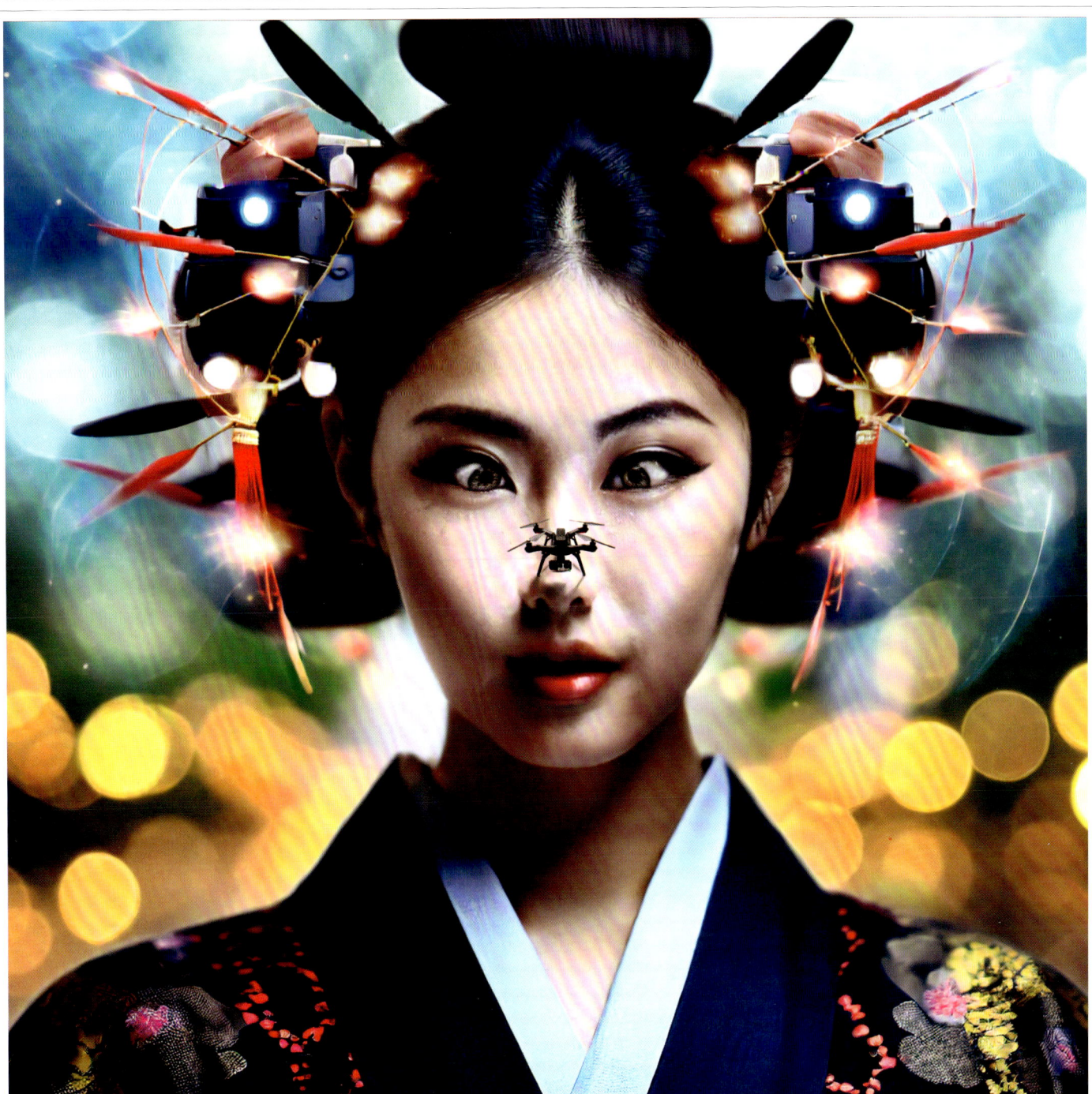

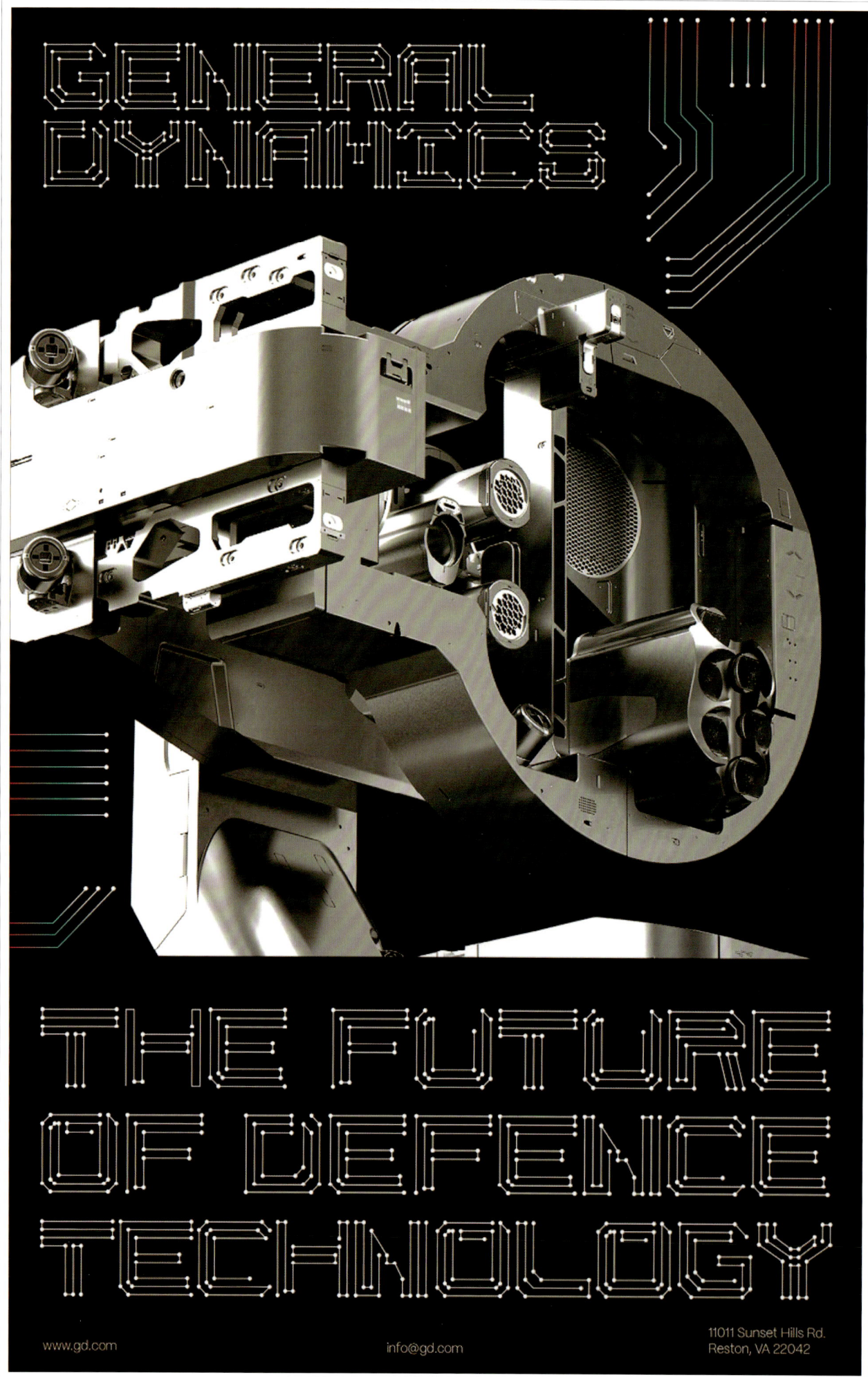

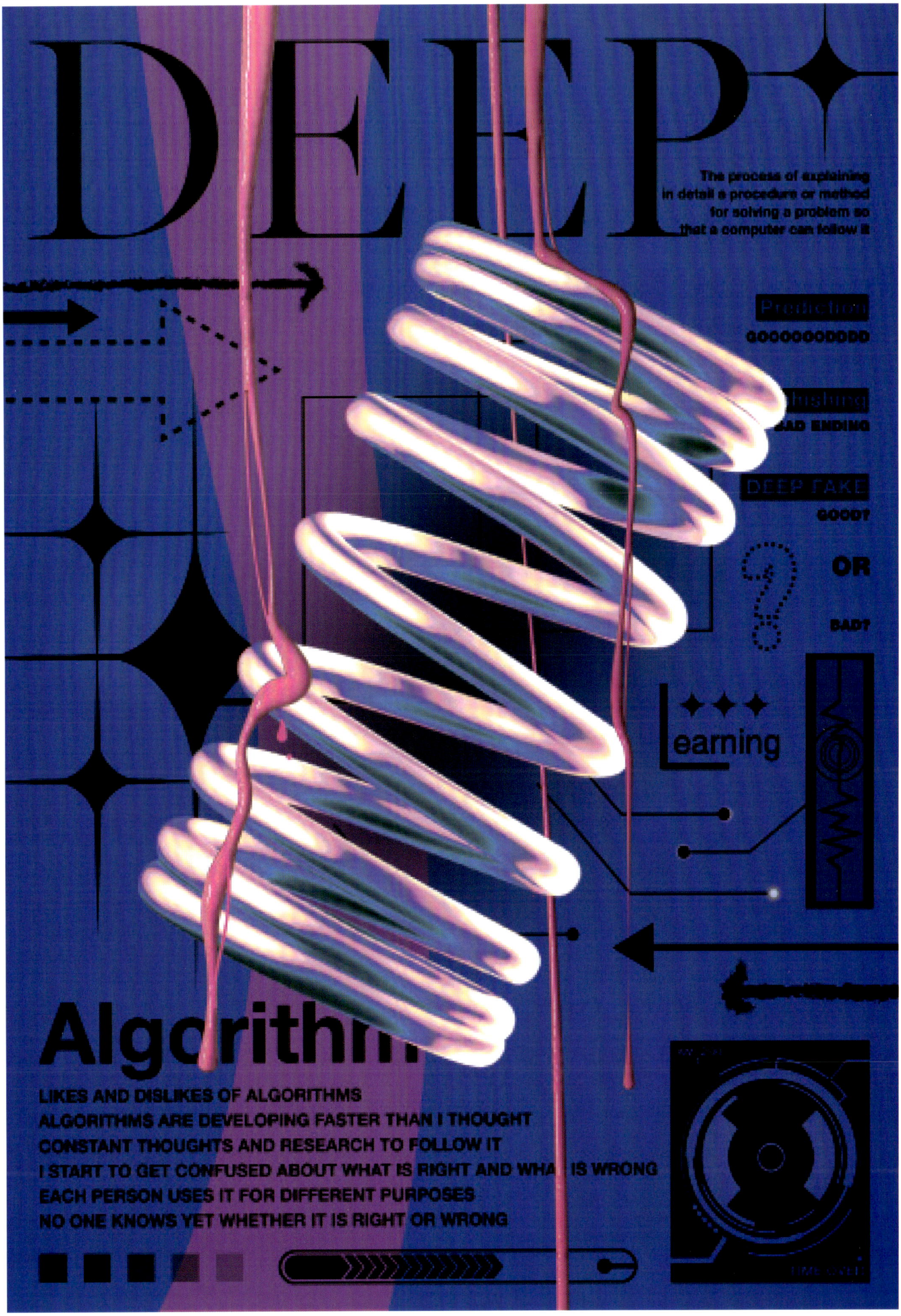

Poster | Design

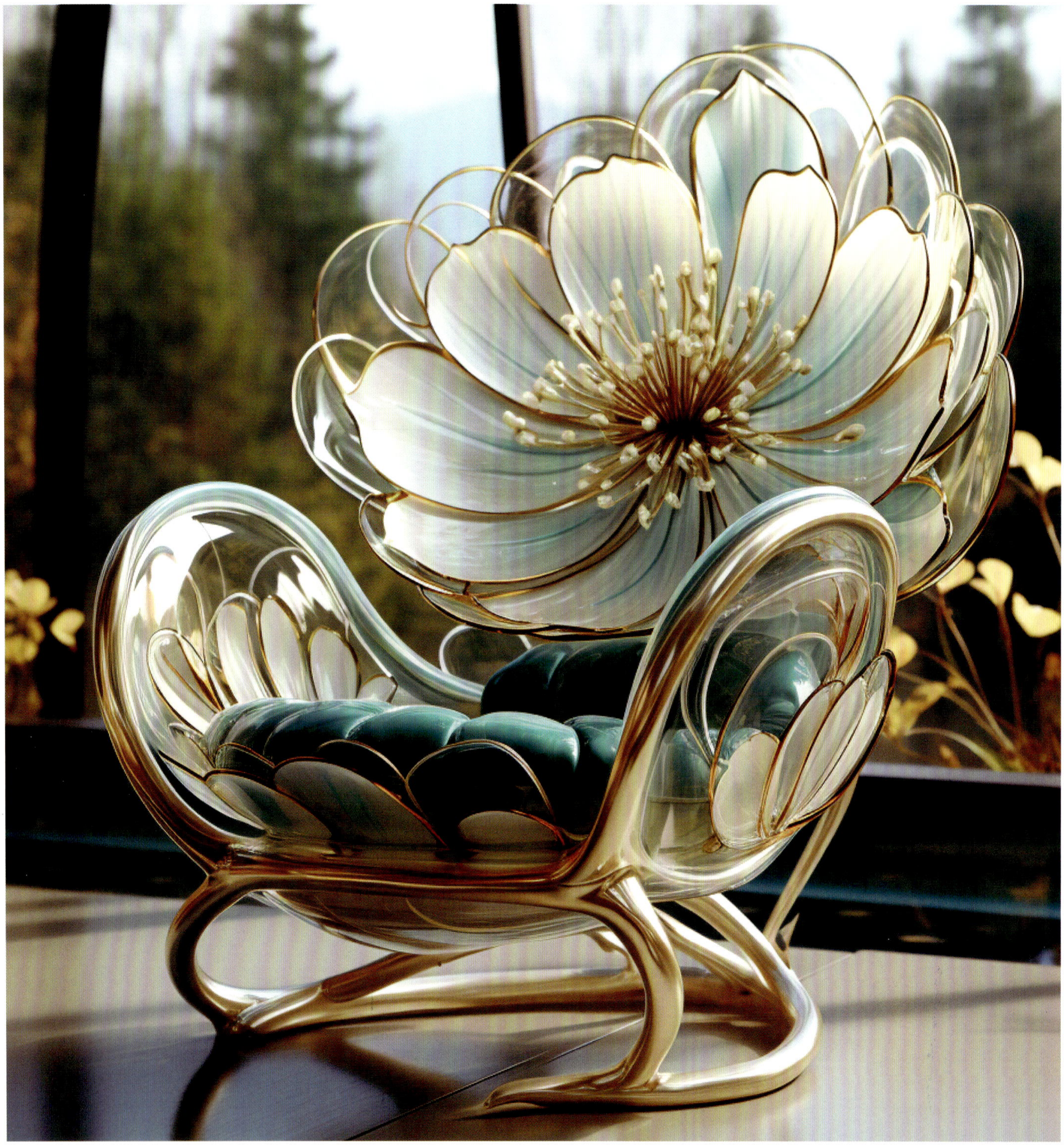

62 INSTRUCTOR **BILLY MAGBUA** PLATINUM

P236: Credit & Commentary   **Student:** Shahen Markarian | **School:** Royal College of Art   Image 1 of 4

Design | Product Design

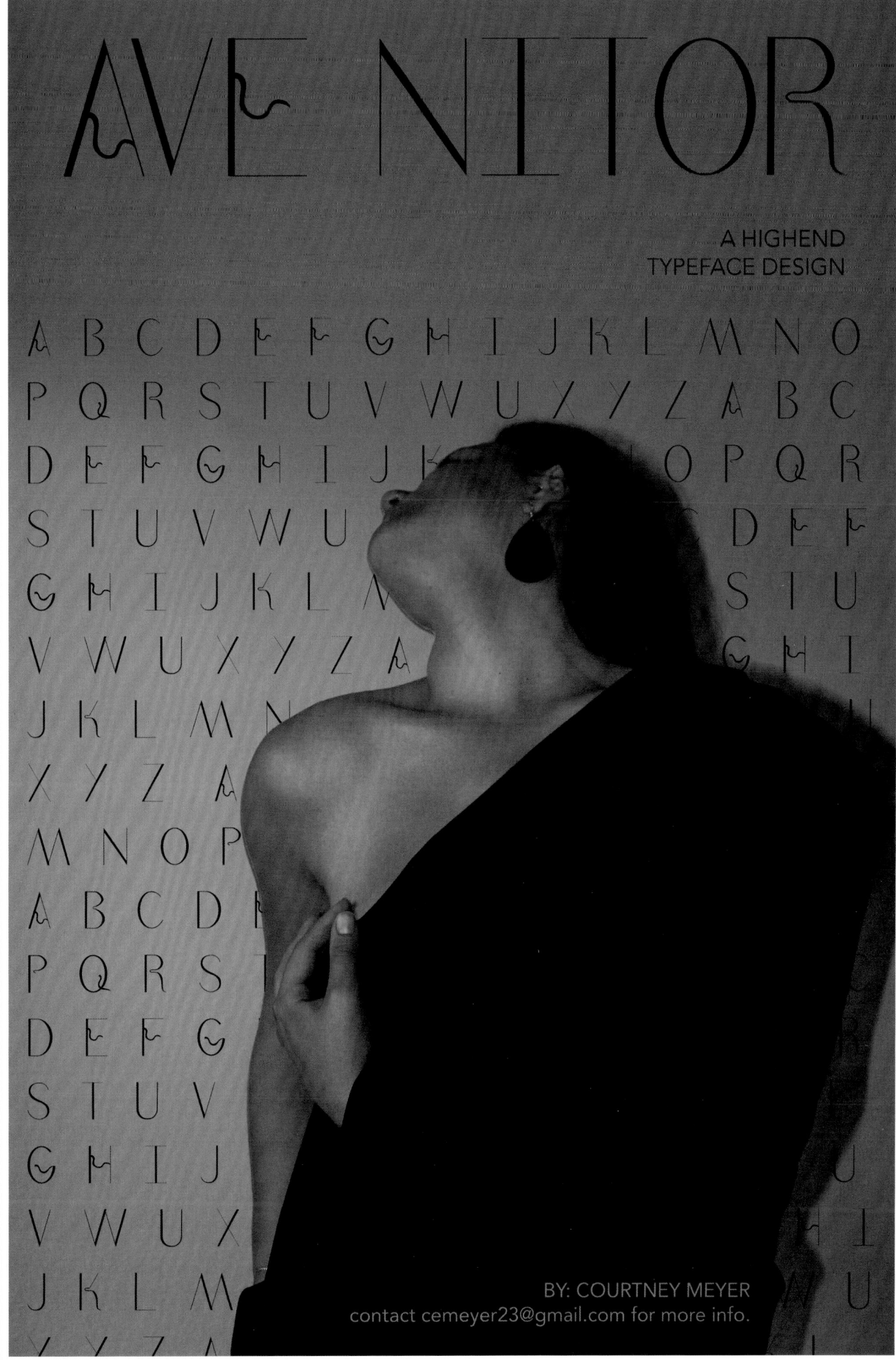

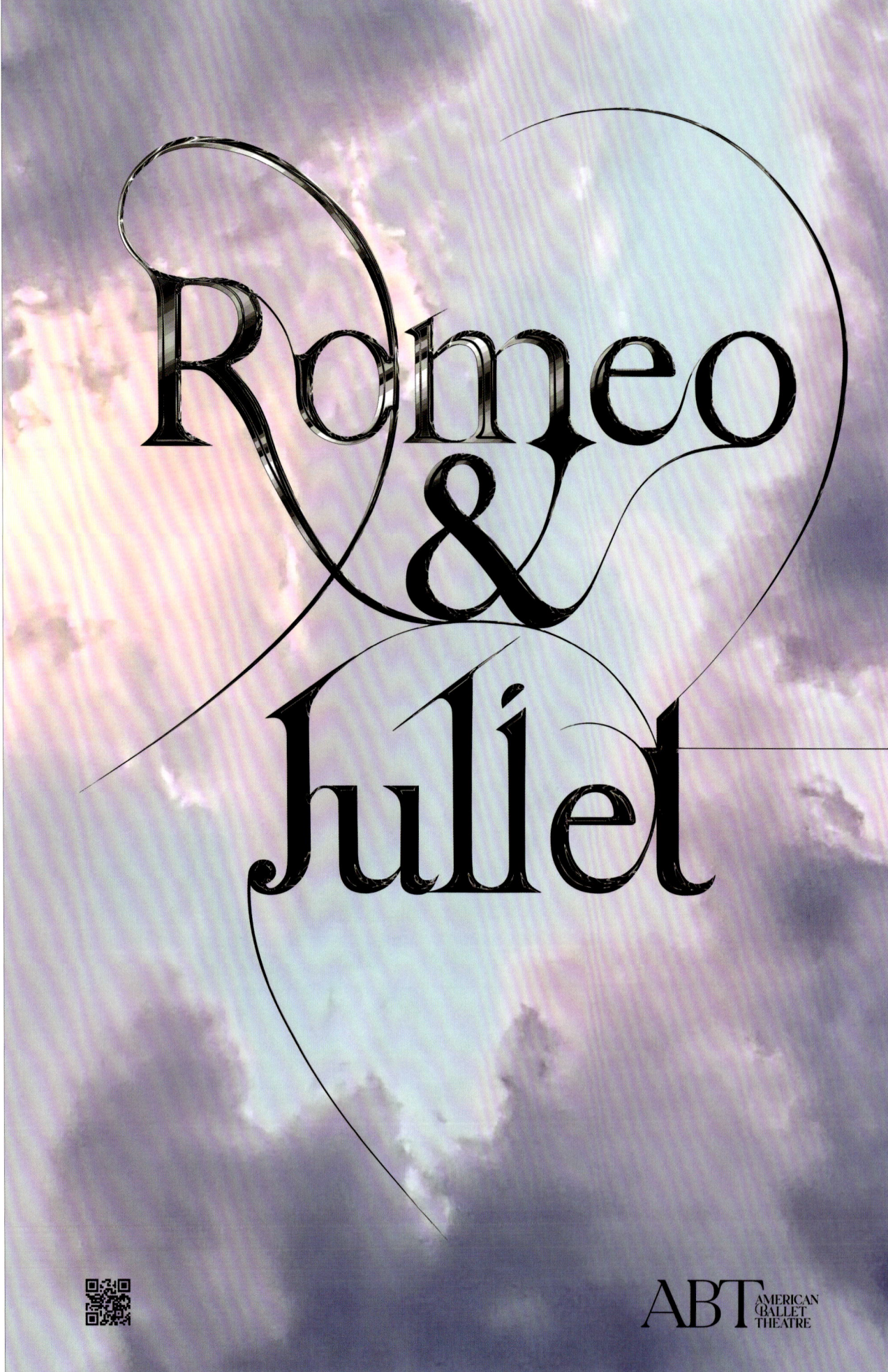

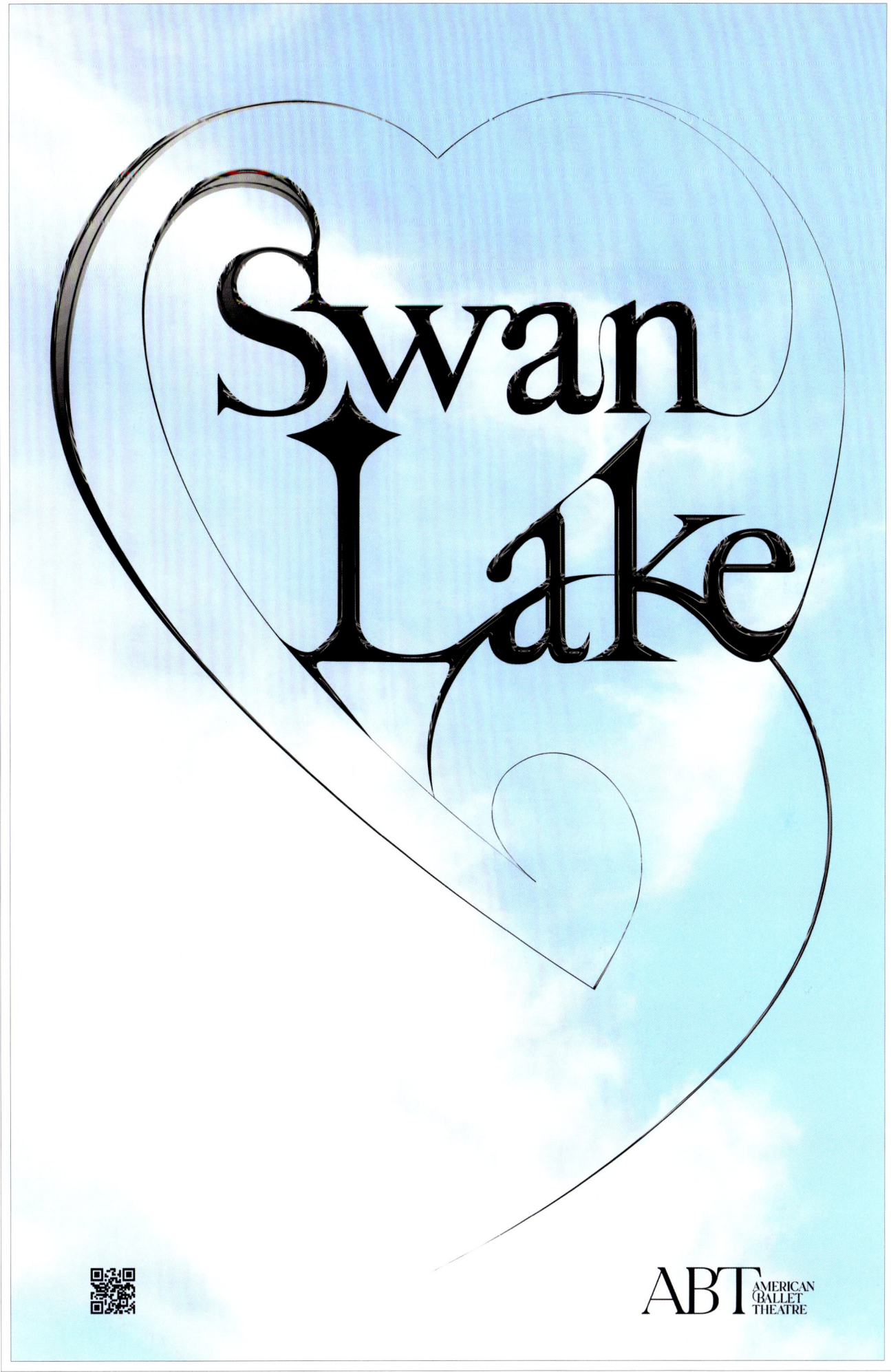

66 INSTRUCTOR **JUSTIN COLT** PLATINUM

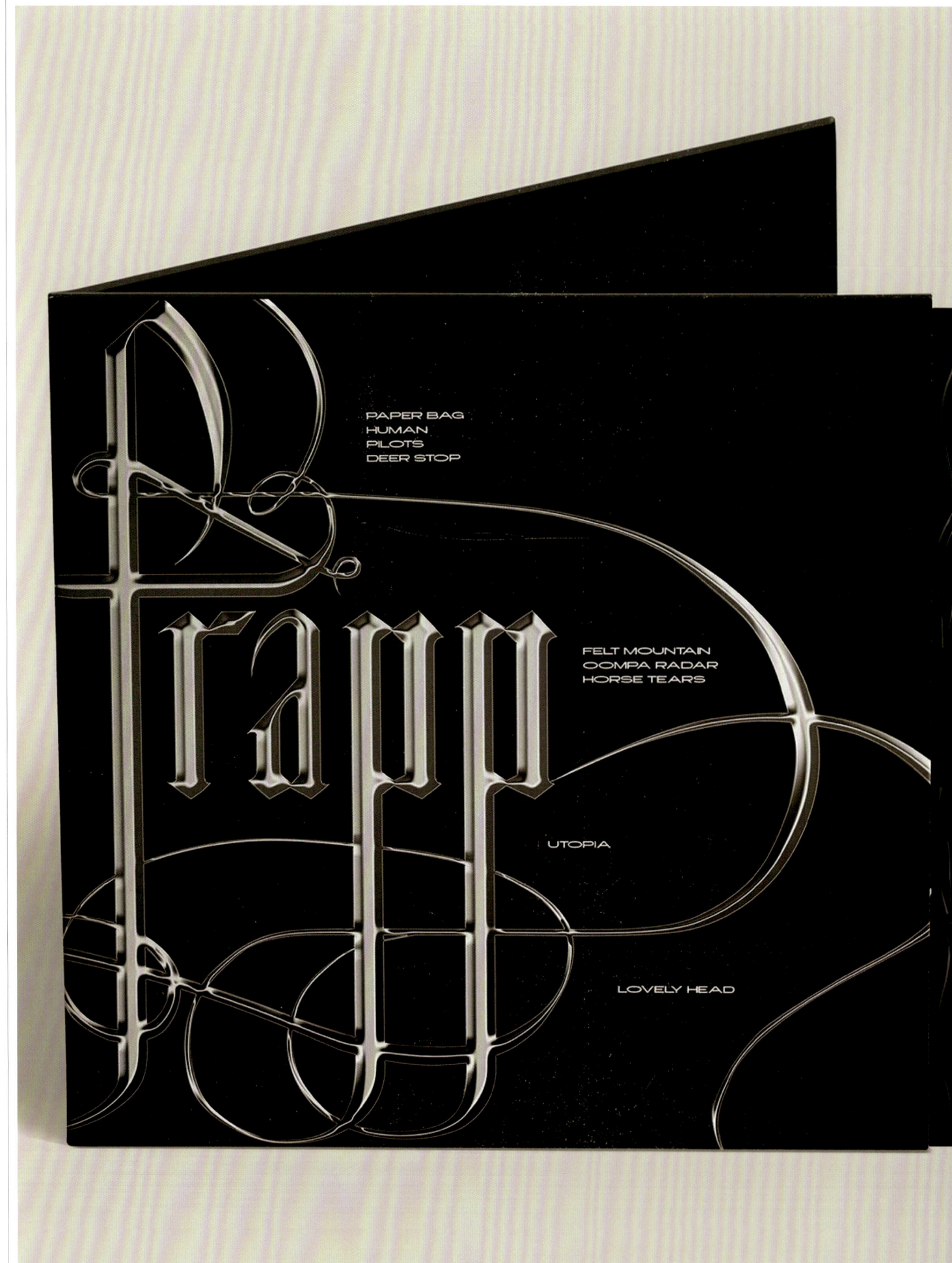

P236: Credit & Commentary

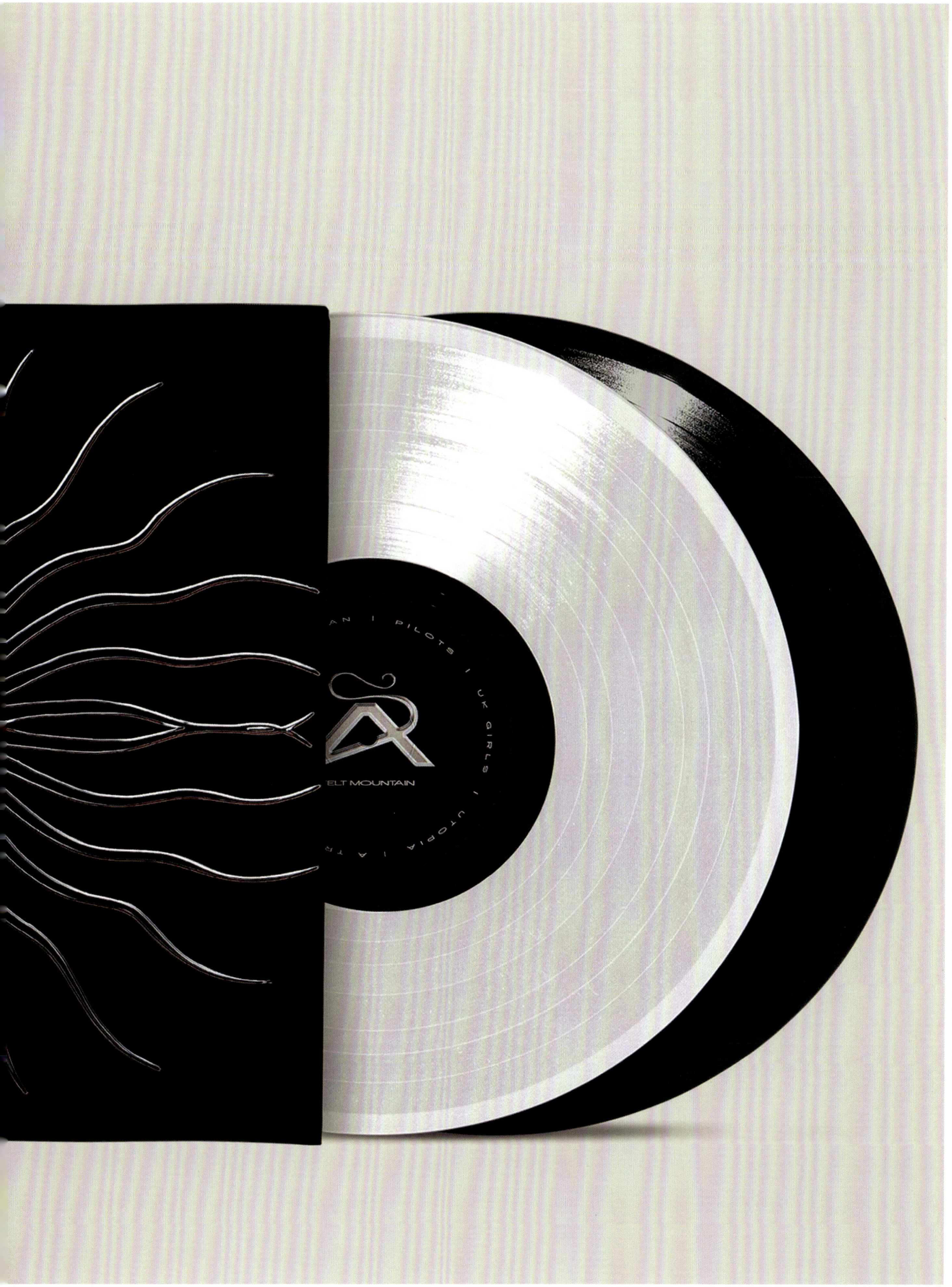

Design Gold Awards

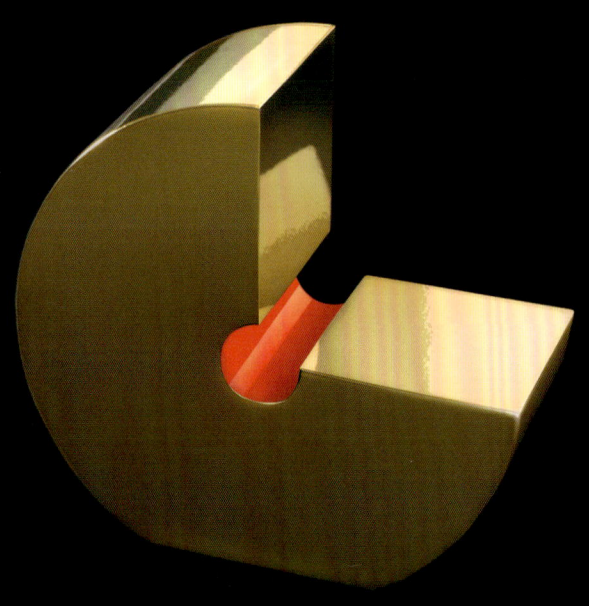

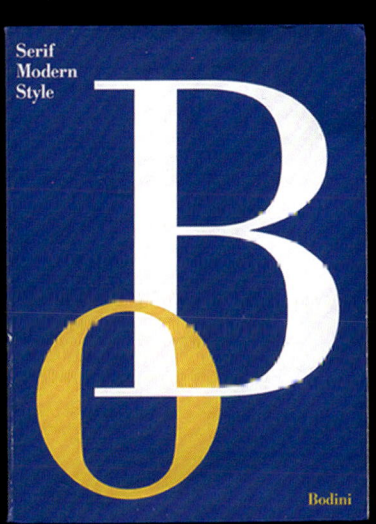
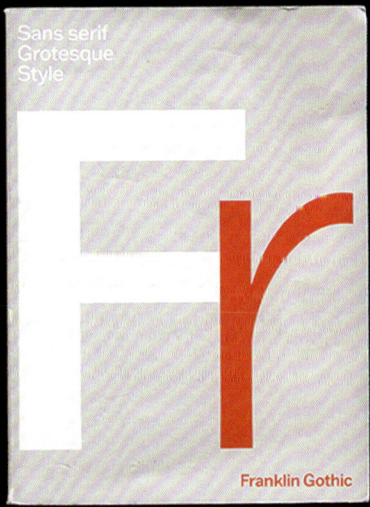
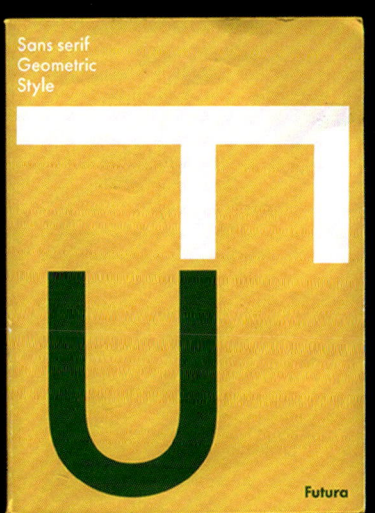
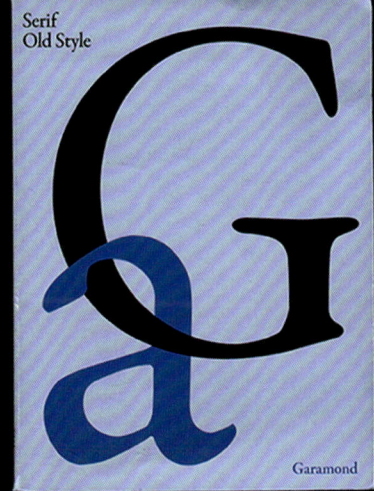
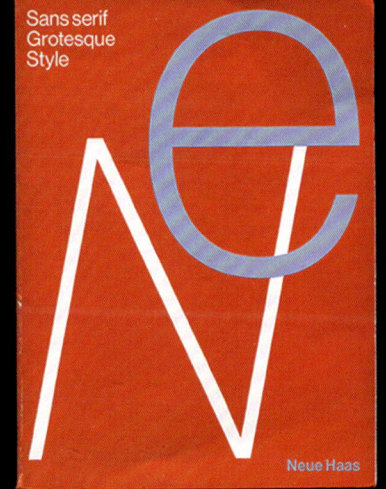
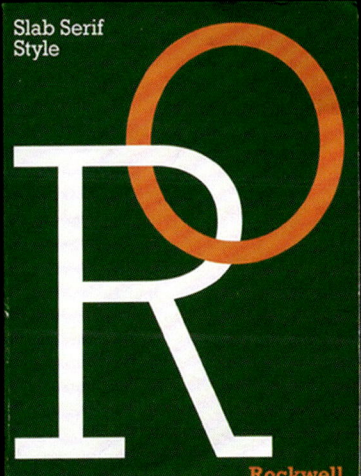

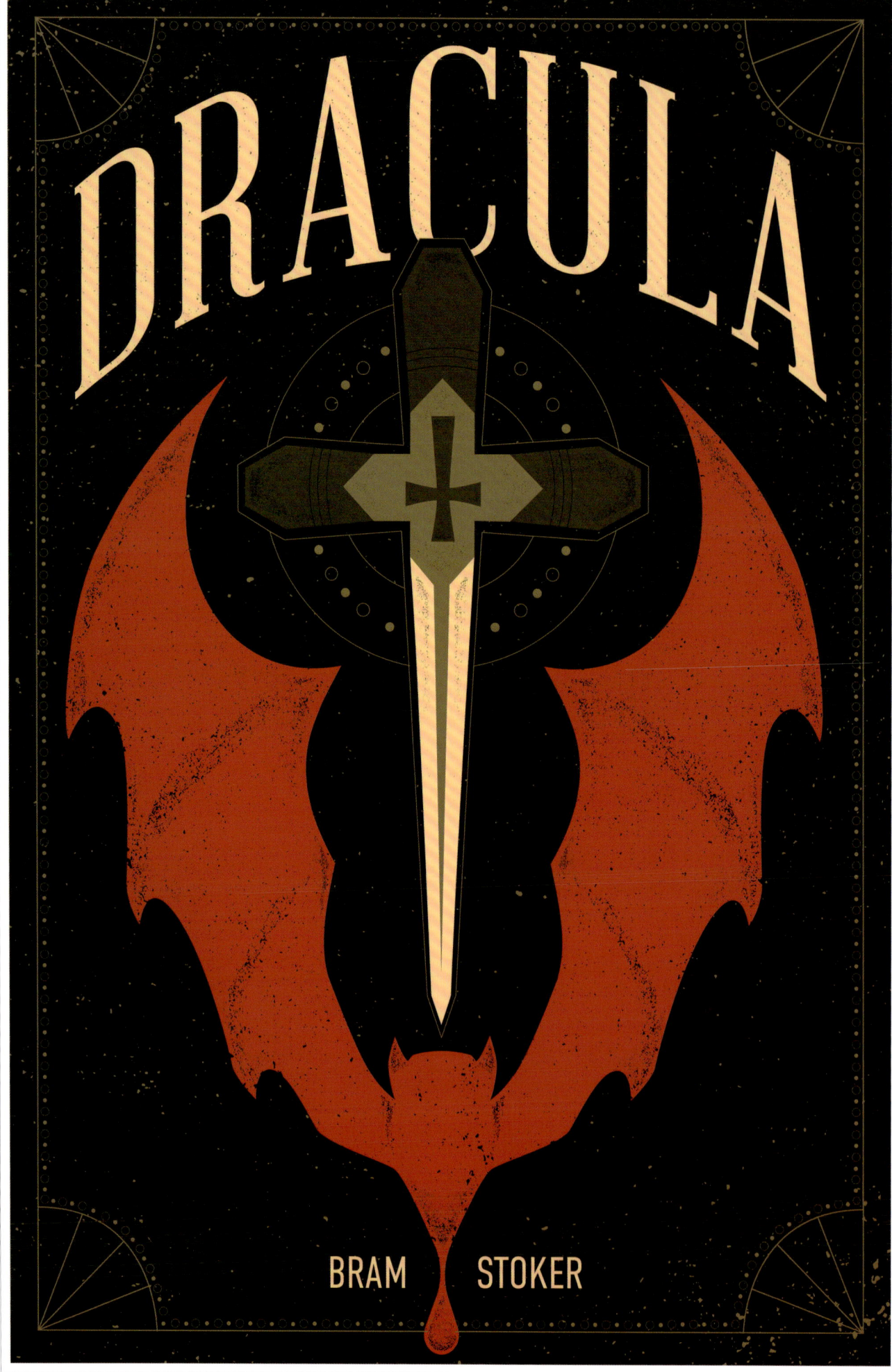

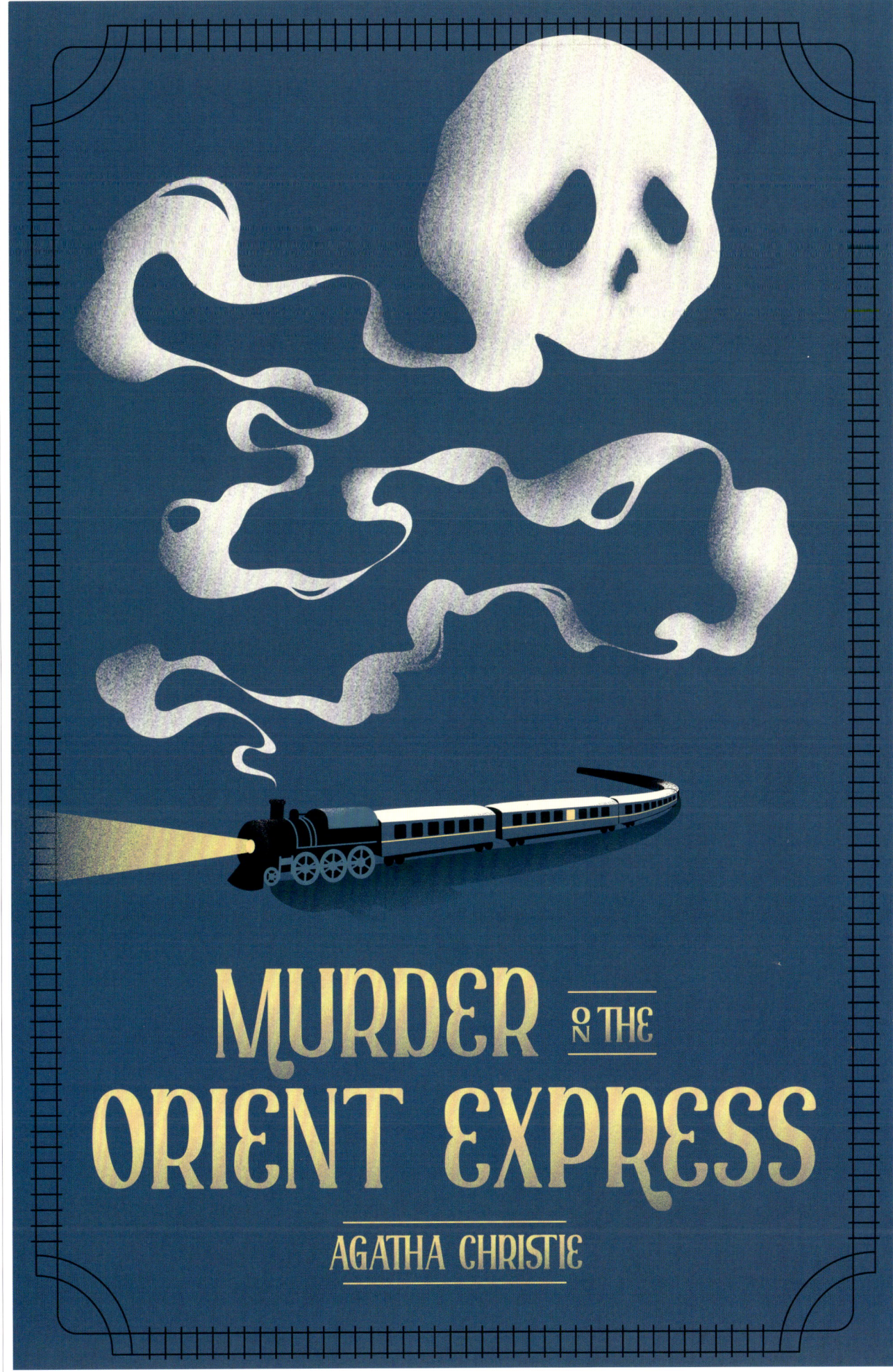

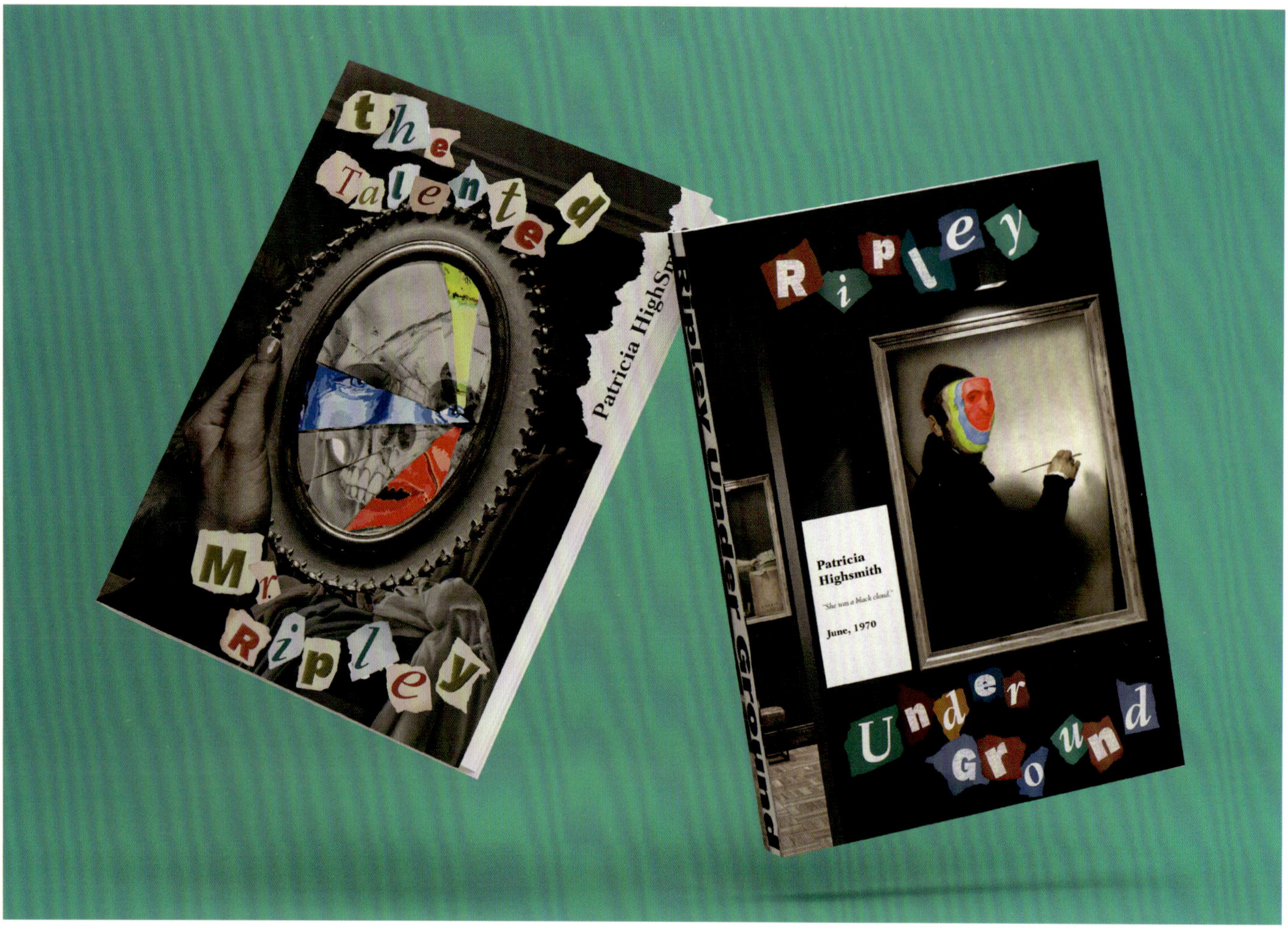

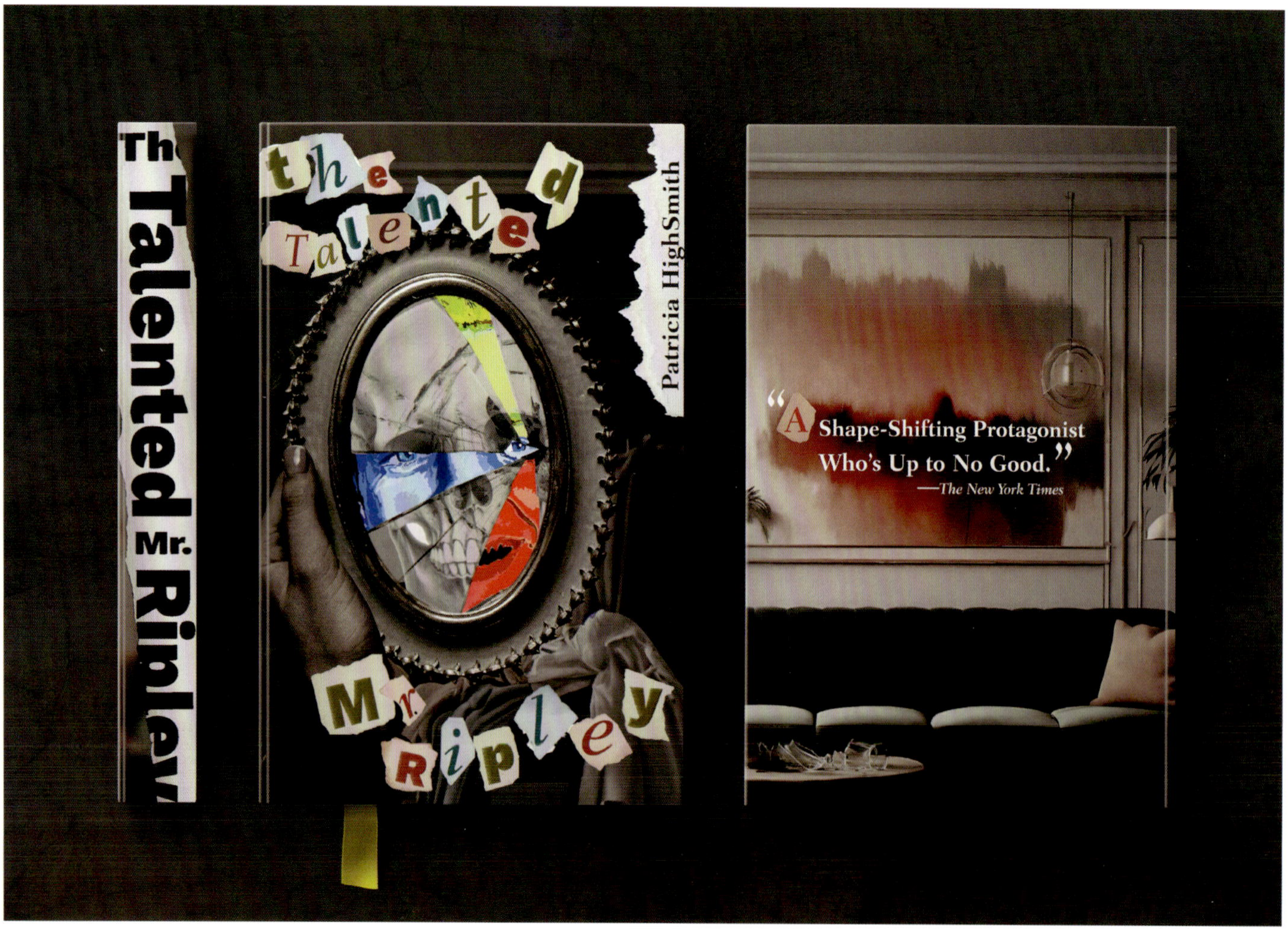

72 INSTRUCTOR **MAURIZIO MASI** GOLD

P236: Credit & Commentary   Student: Zoe LeiLi | School: Lehigh University   Images 1, 2 of 3

Design | Books

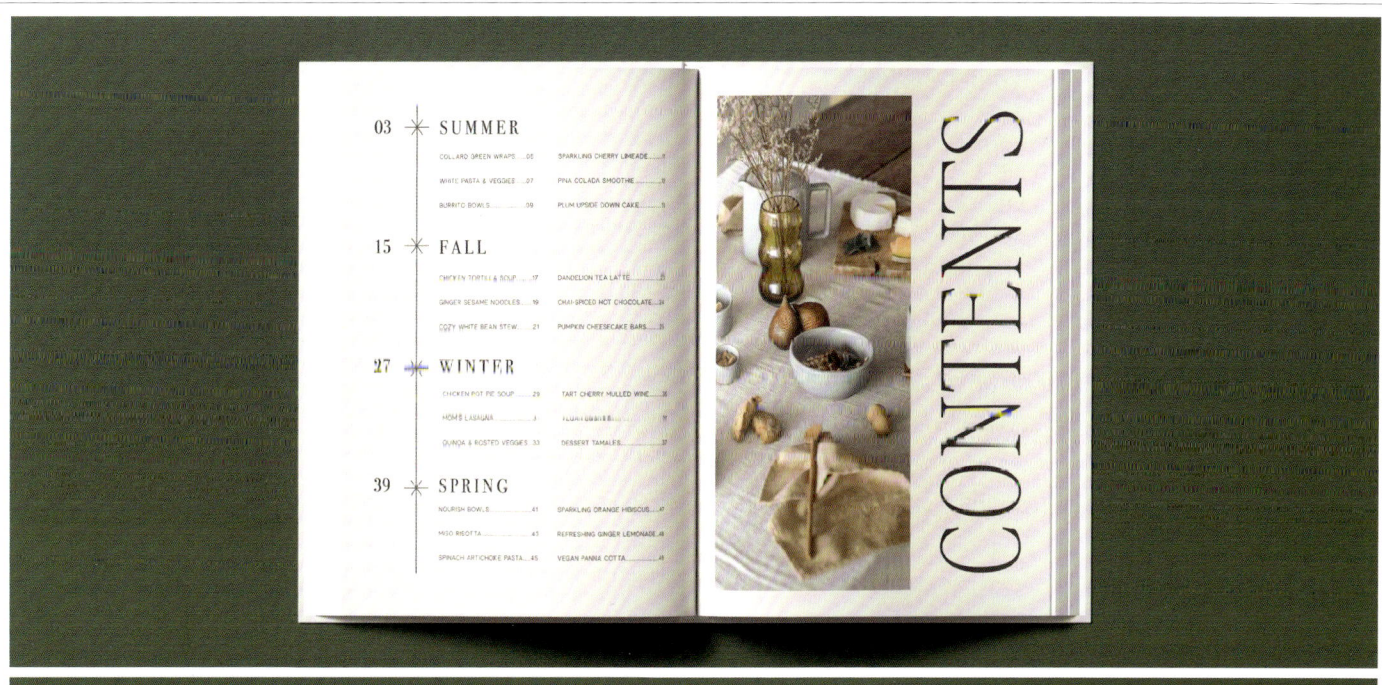
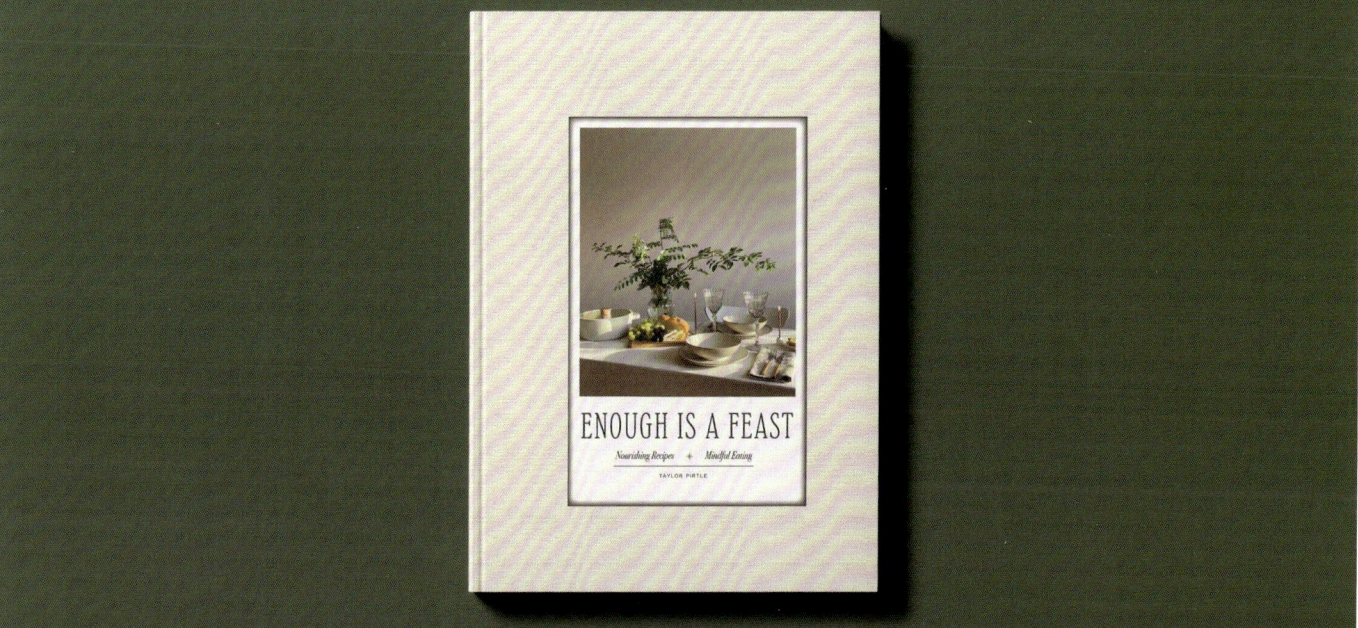
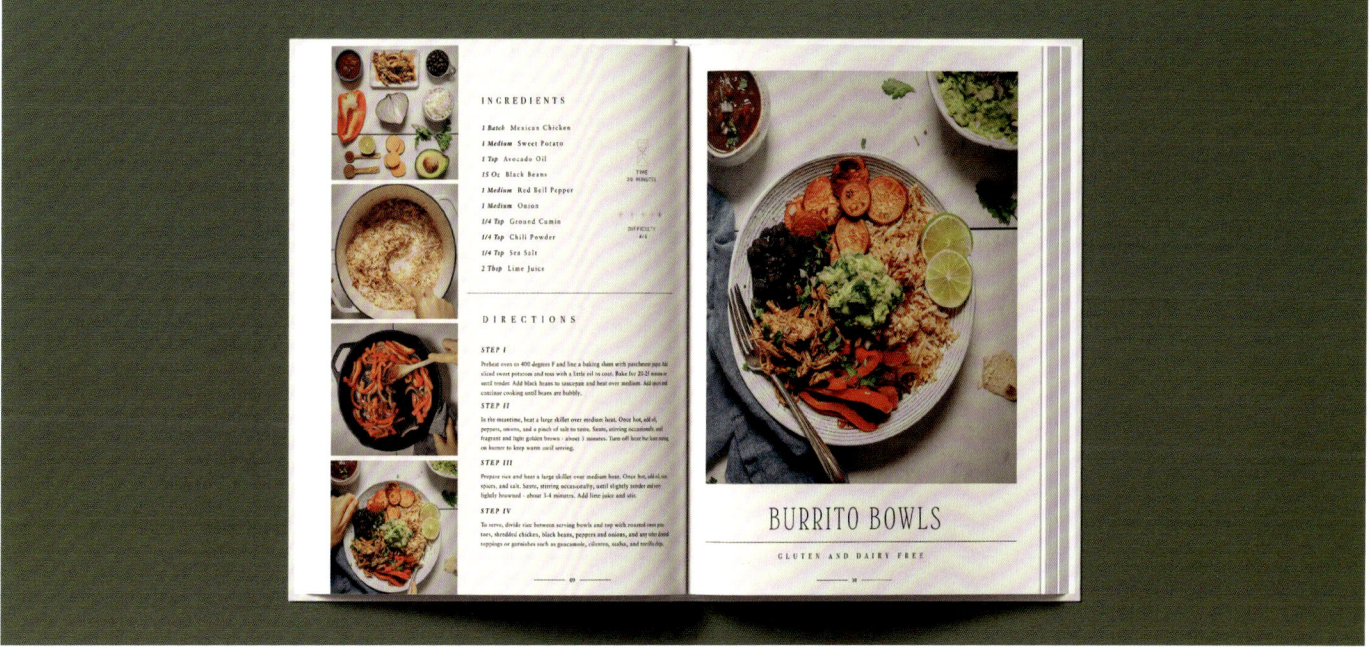

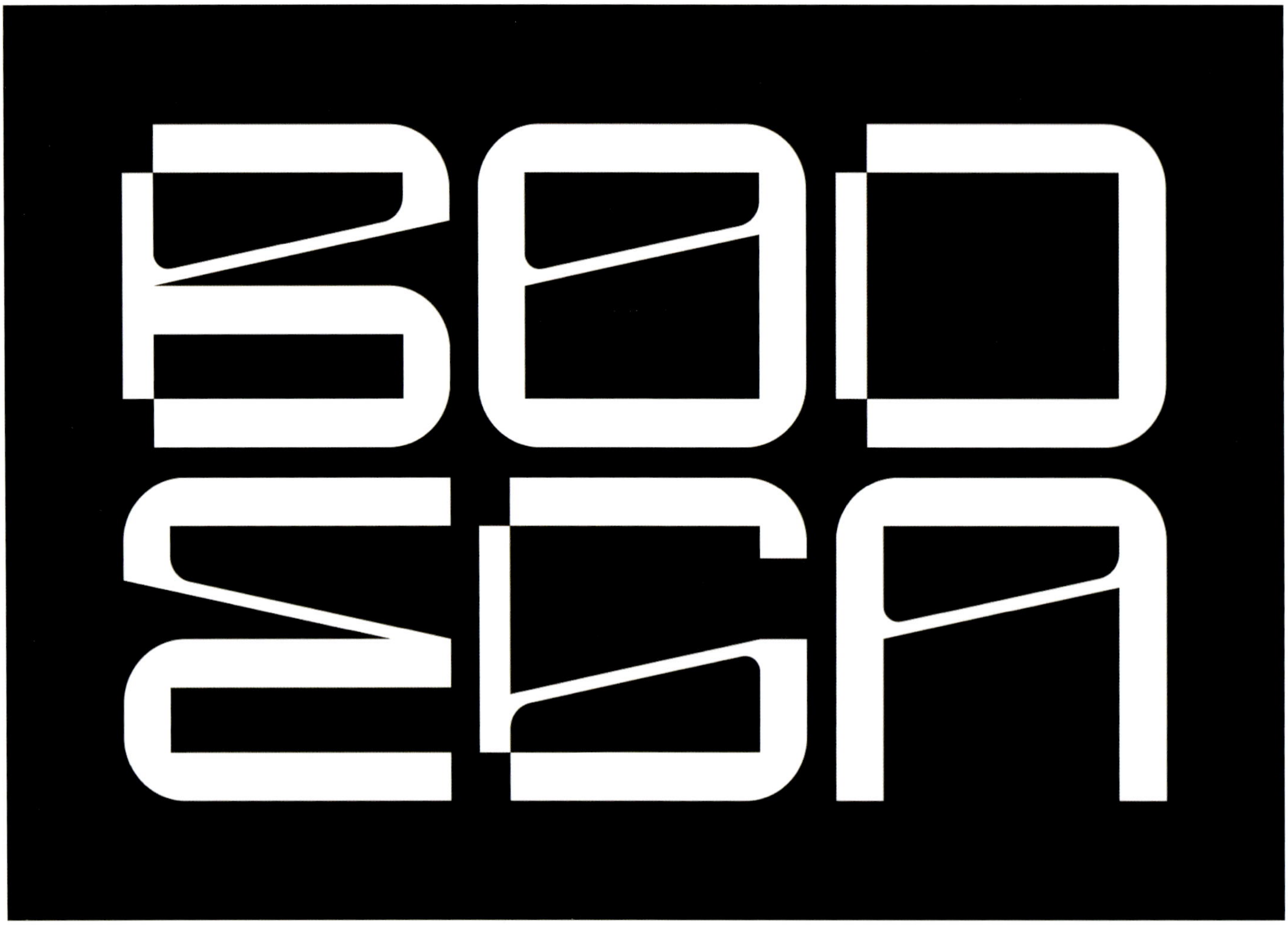

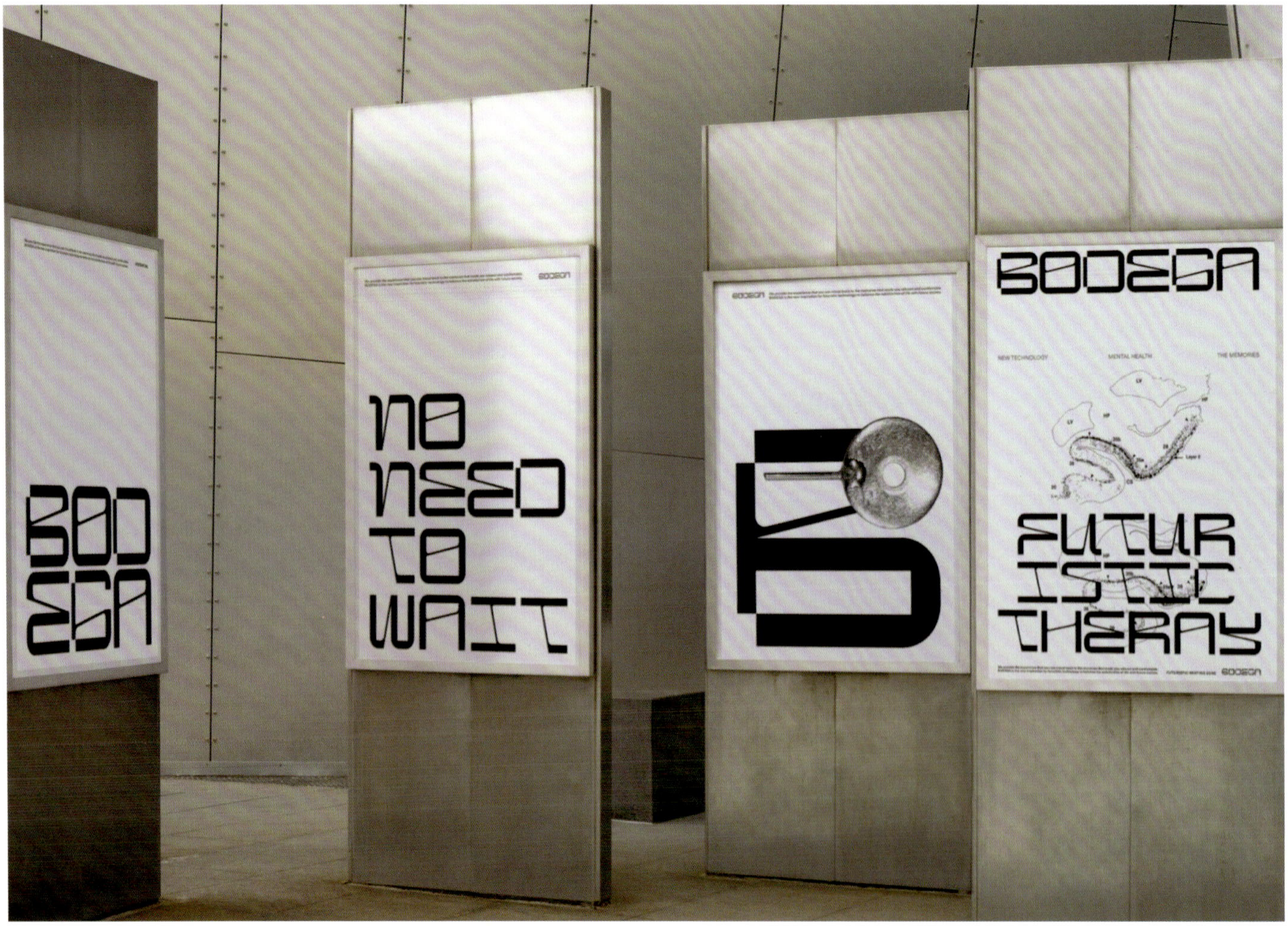

74 INSTRUCTOR **NATASHA JEN** GOLD

P237: Credit & Commentary | **Student:** Hyowon Kwon | **School:** School of Visual Arts | Images 1, 2 of 7

Design | Branding

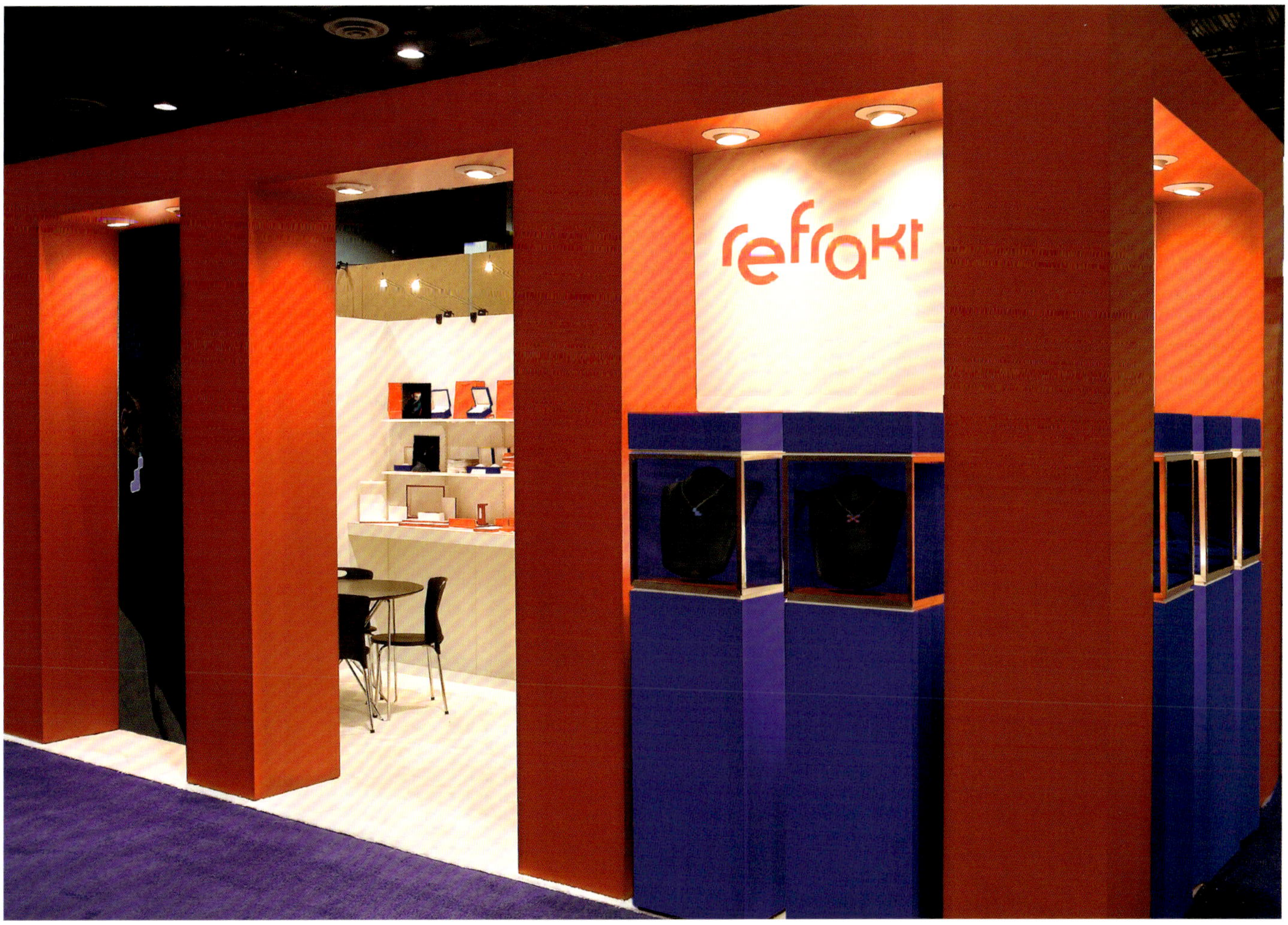

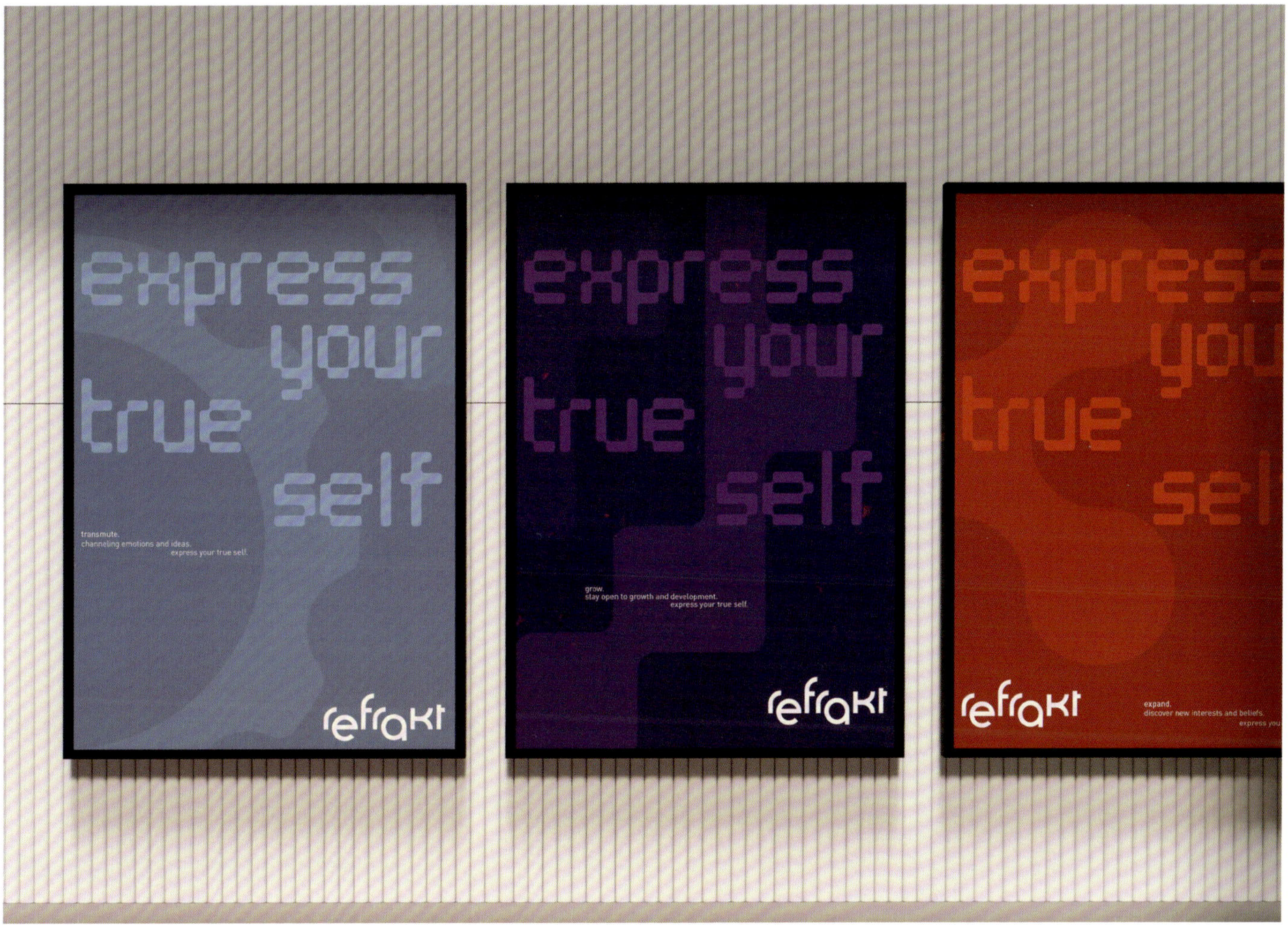

75 INSTRUCTOR **GERARDO HERRERA** GOLD

P237: Credit & Commentary | **Student:** Jamal Abdullahi | **School:** ArtCenter College of Design | Images 1, 2 of 7

Branding | Design

76 INSTRUCTOR **NATASHA JEN** GOLD

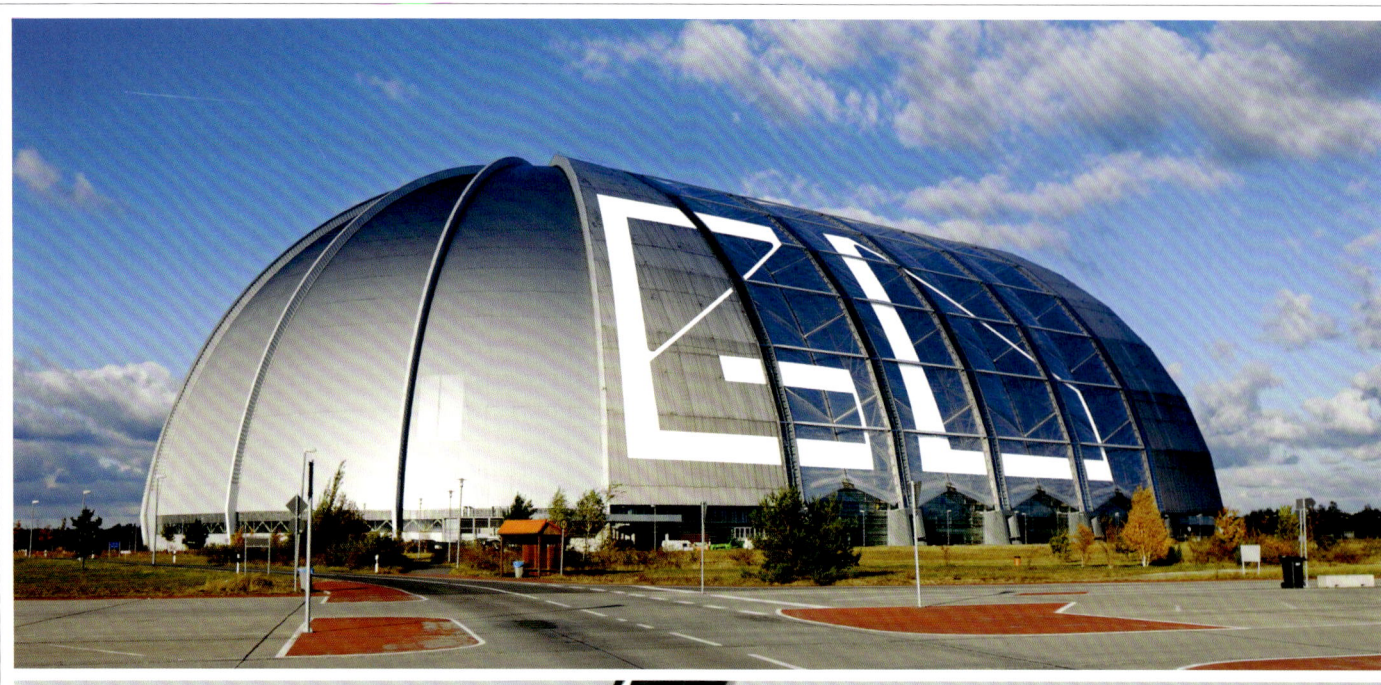
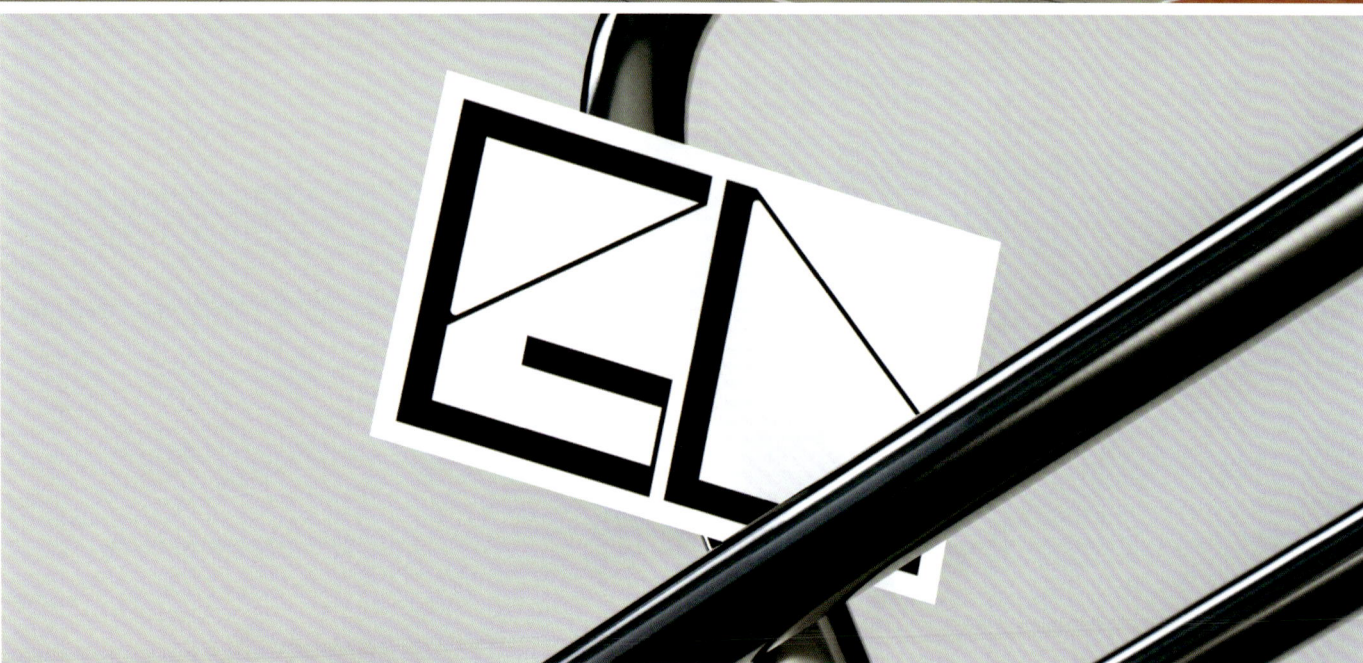
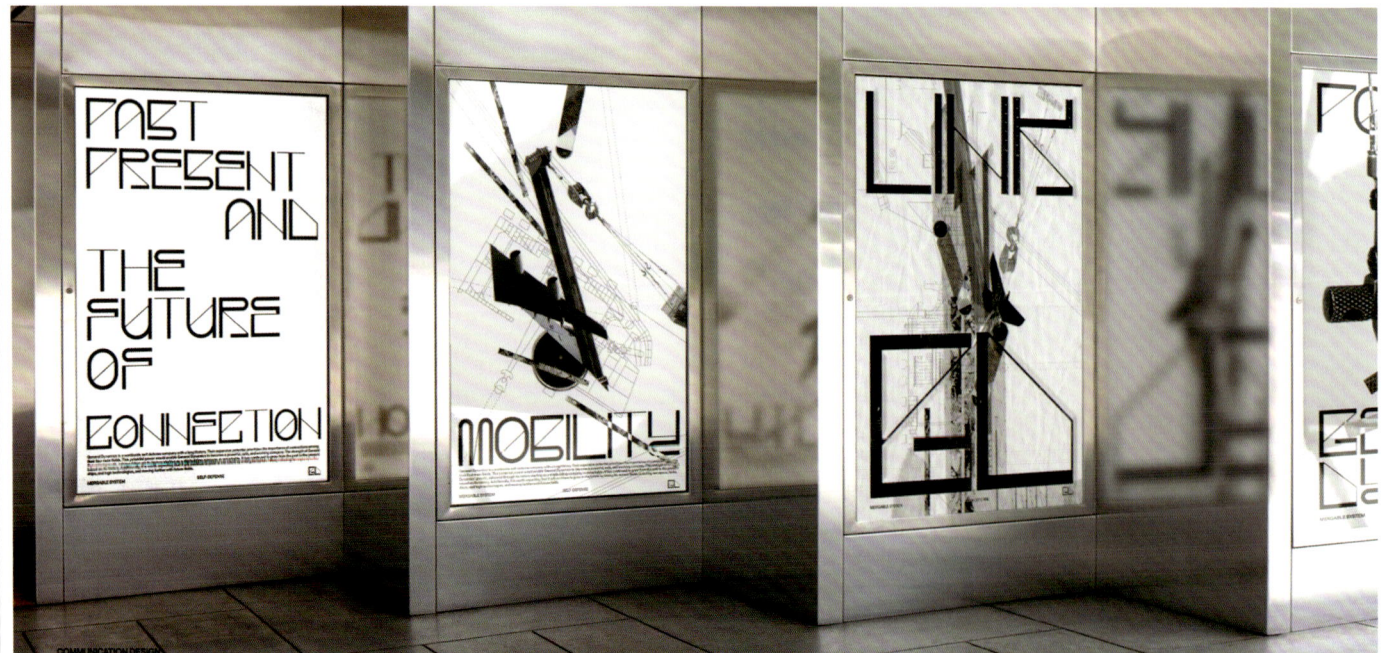

P237: Credit & Commentary **Student:** Hyowon Kwon | **School:** School of Visual Arts Images 1-3 of 7

Design | Branding

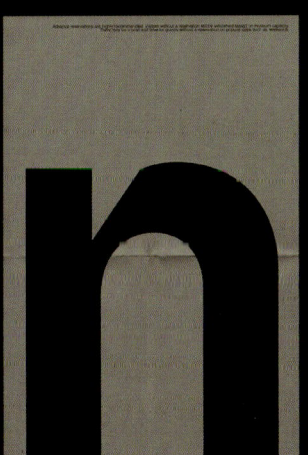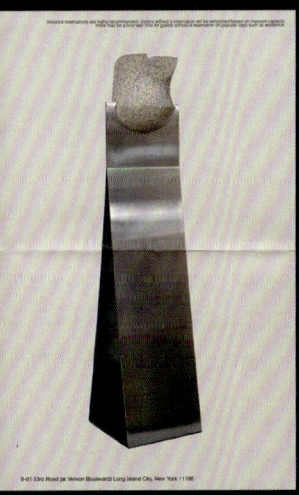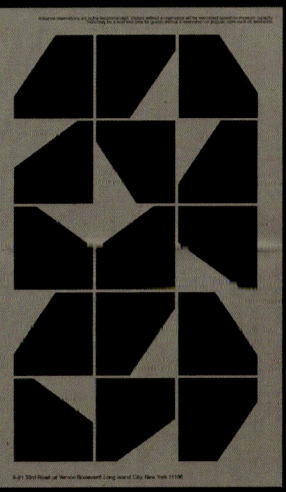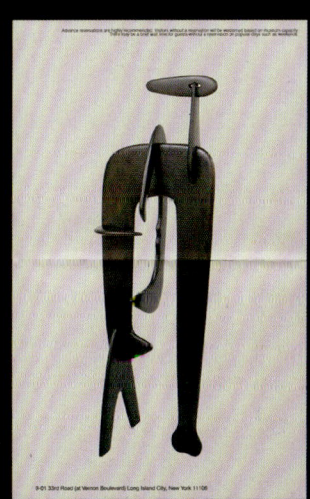
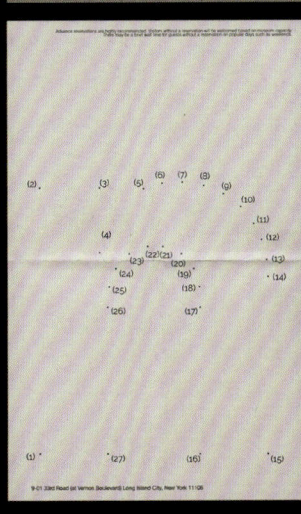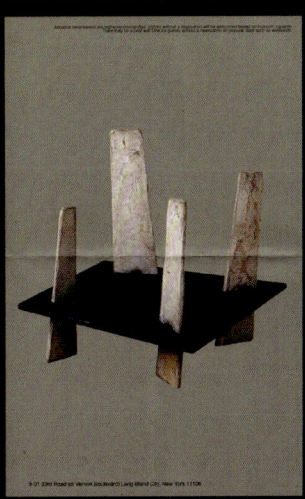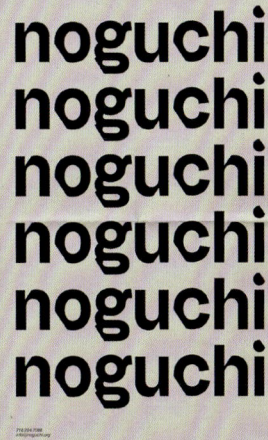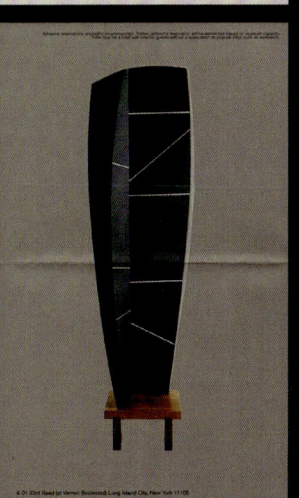
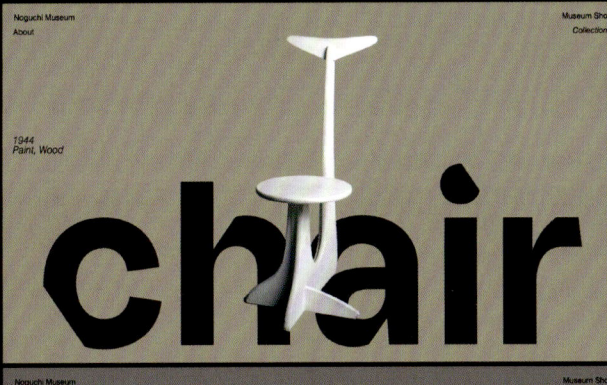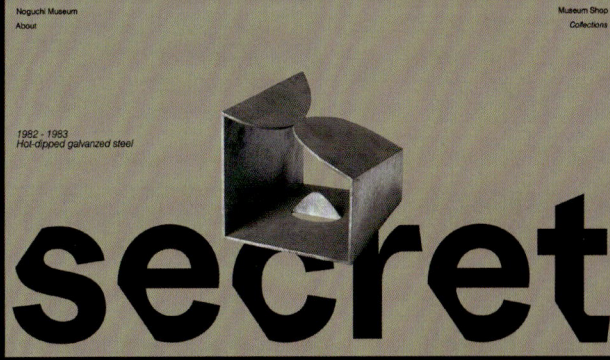
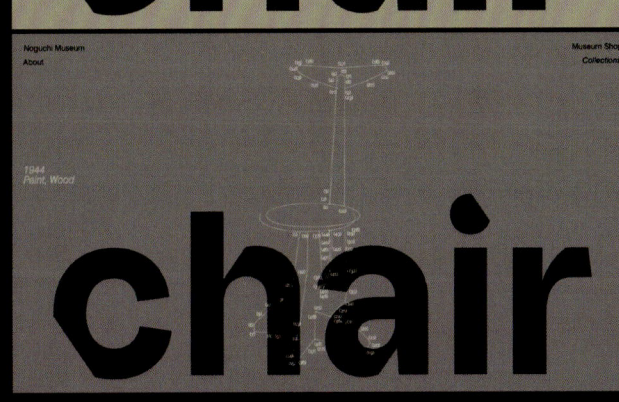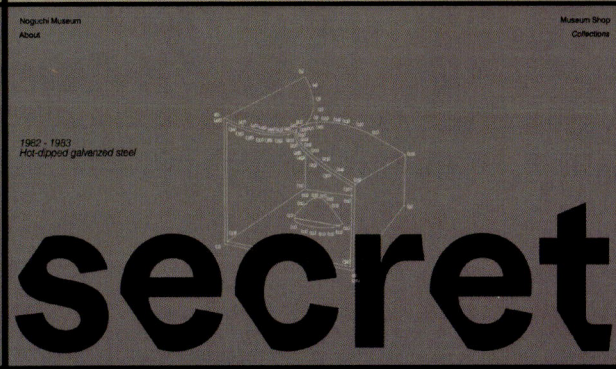

78 INSTRUCTOR **STEPHEN SERRATO** GOLD

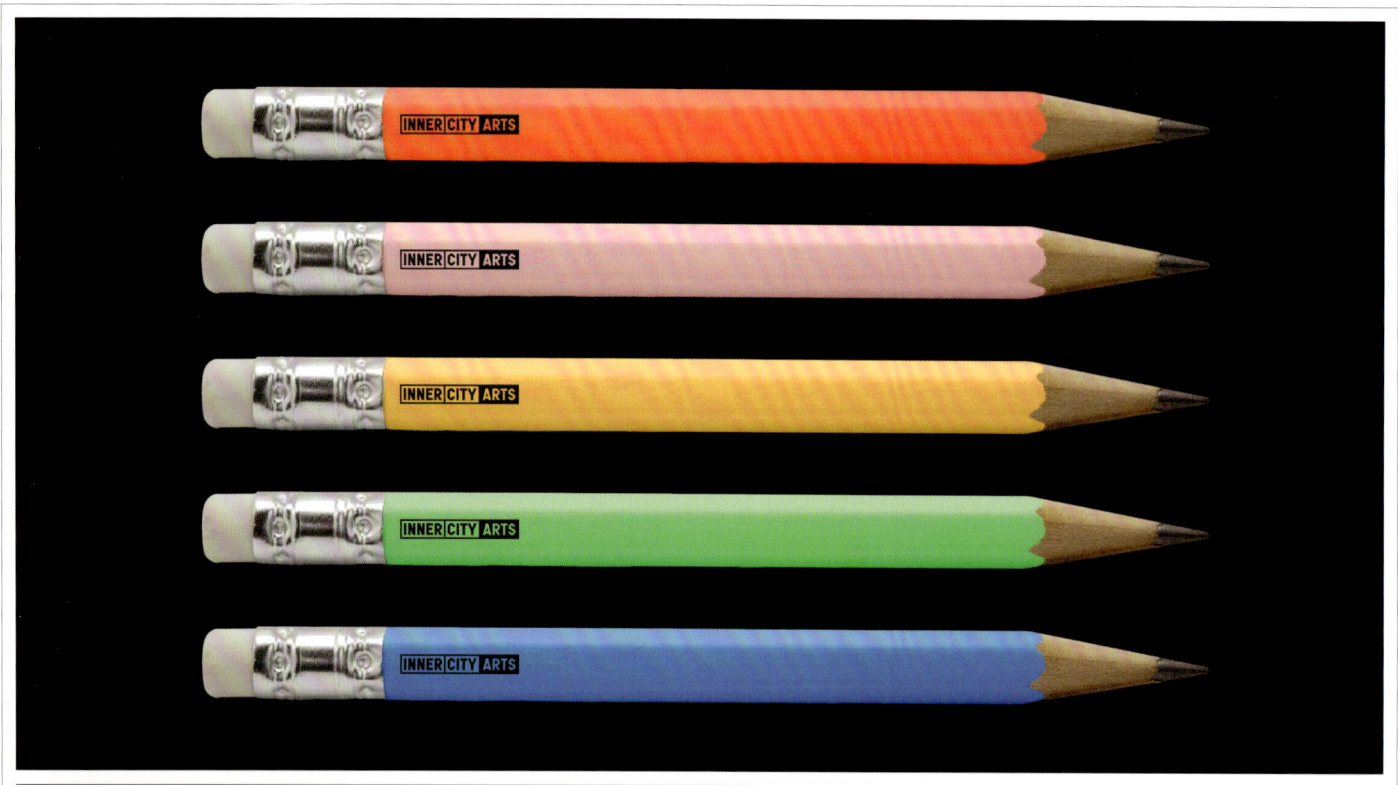

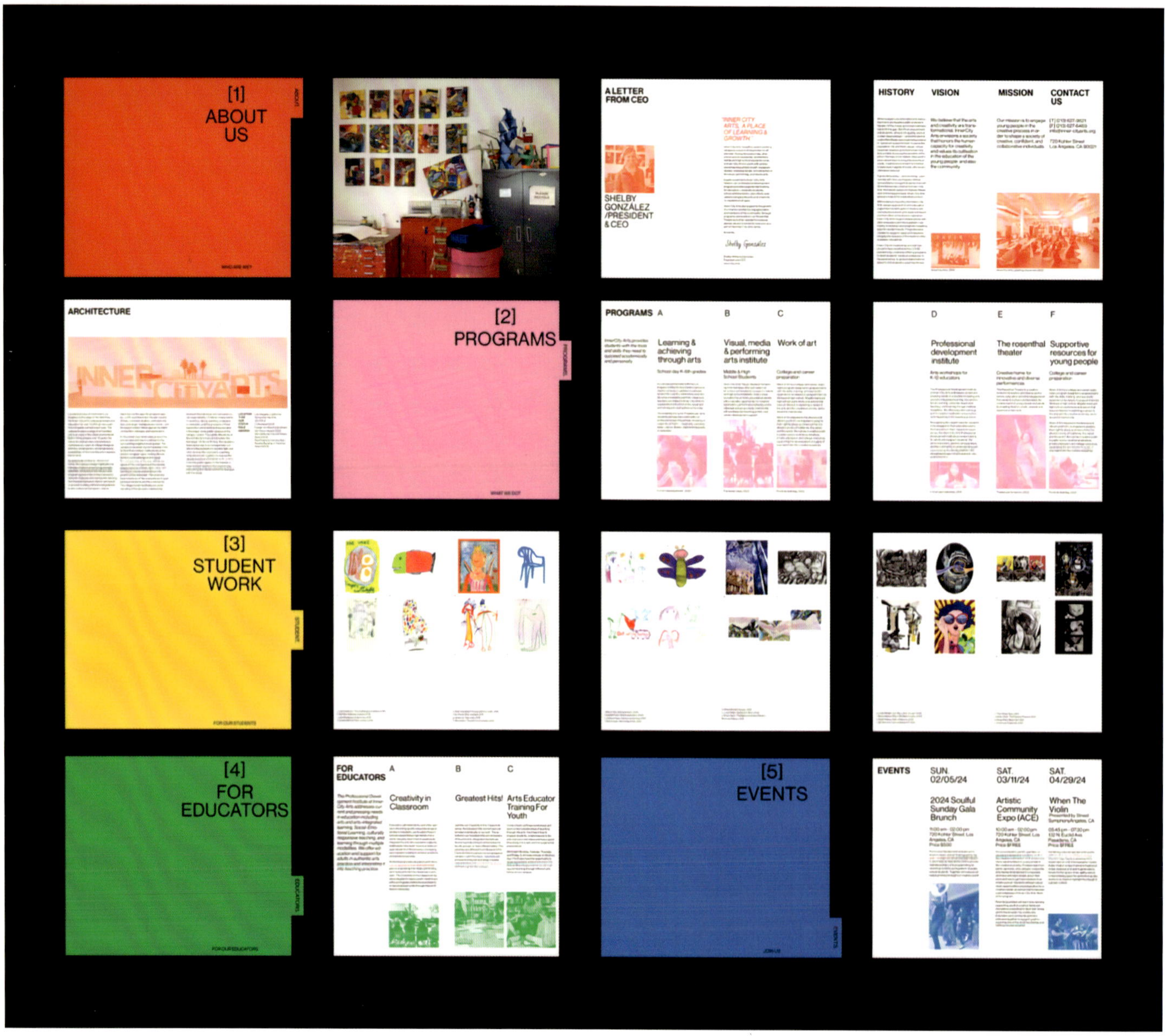

P237: Credit & Commentary — **Student:** Genie Wu | **School:** ArtCenter College of Design — Images 1, 2 of 7

Design | Branding

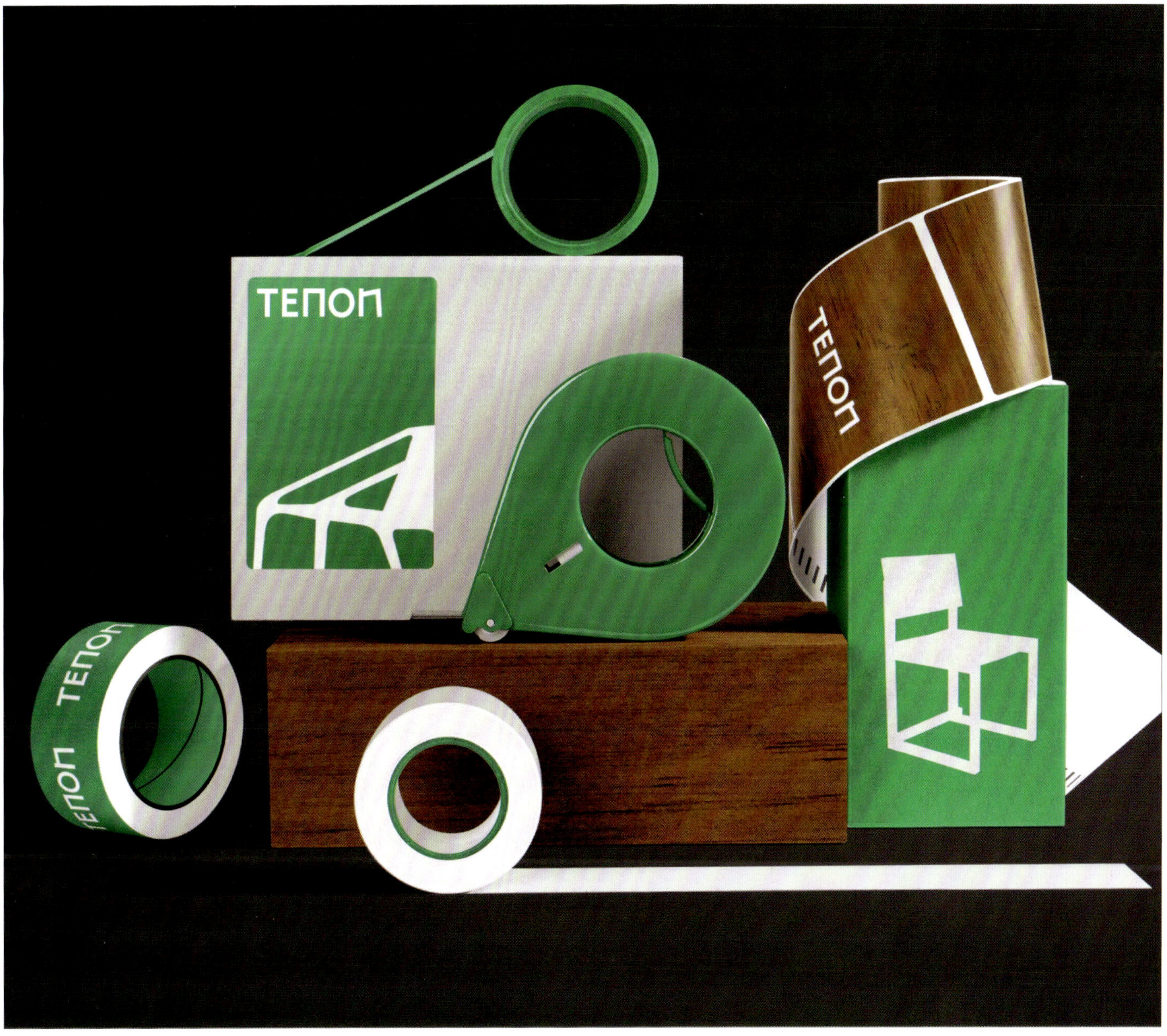

79 INSTRUCTOR **ERIC BAKER** GOLD

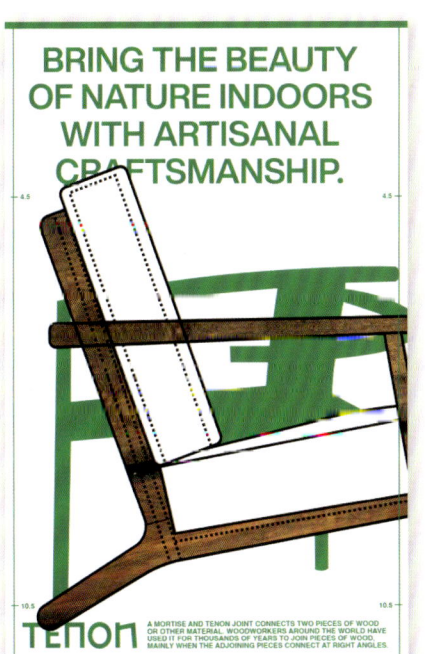
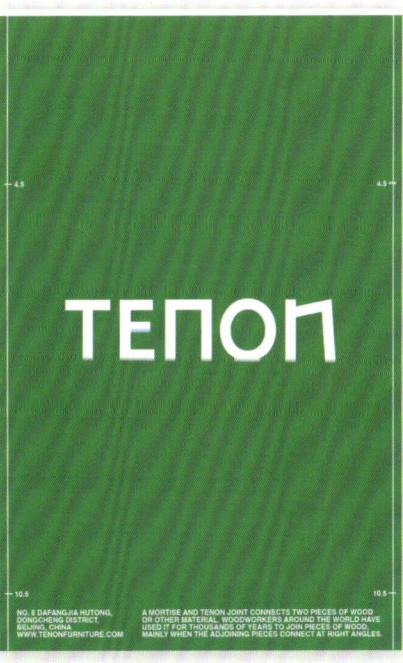
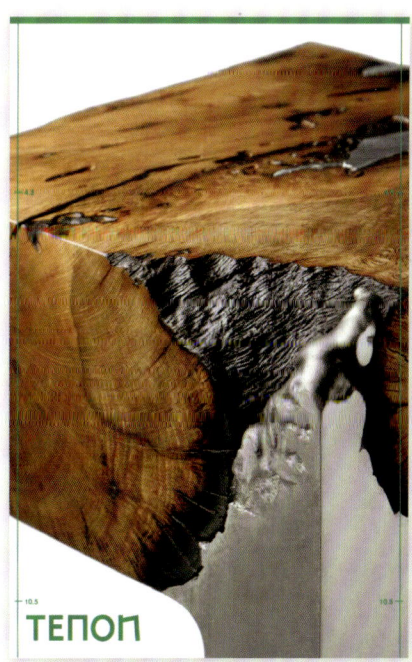

P237: Credit & Commentary **Student:** Jialu Xu | **School:** School of Visual Arts

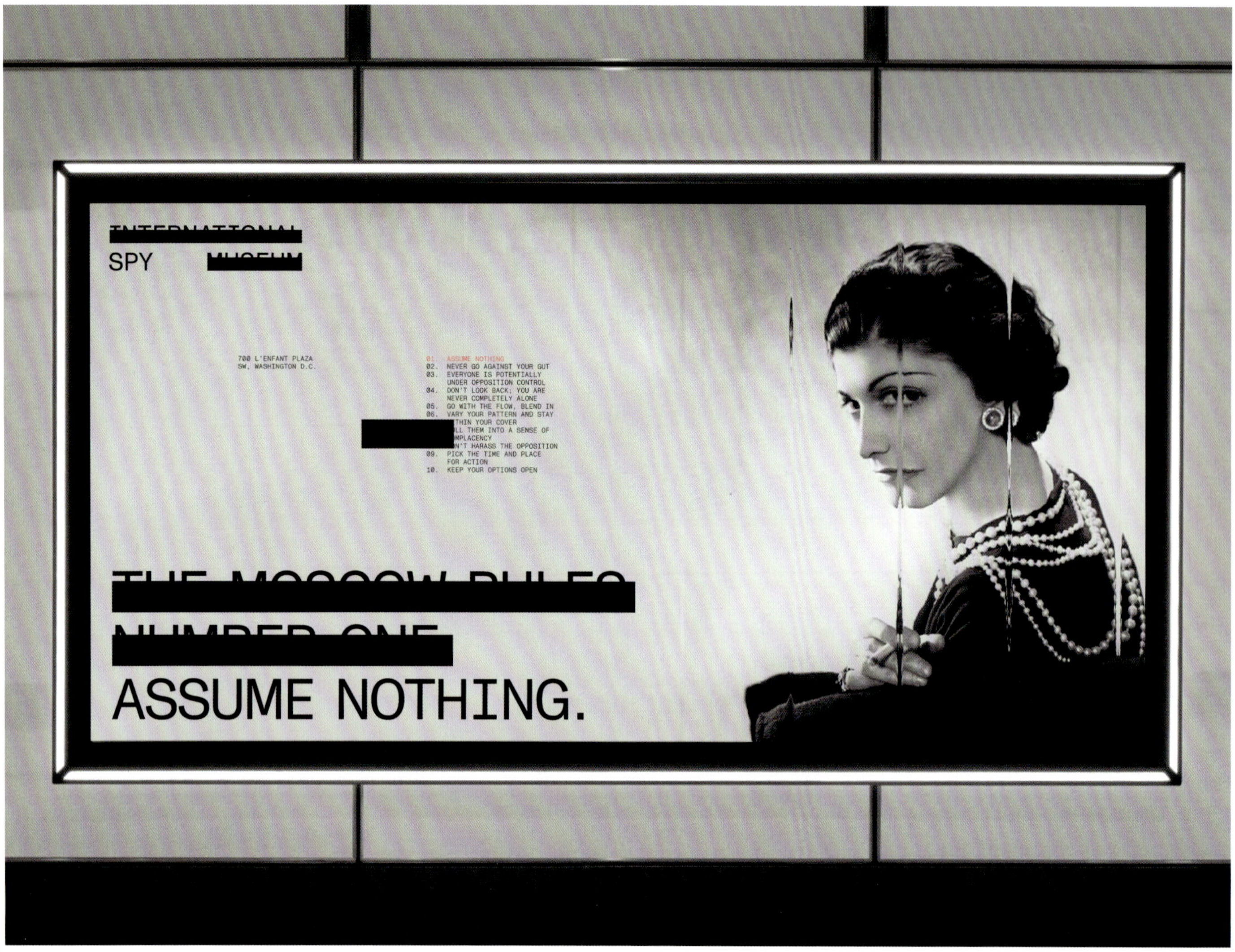

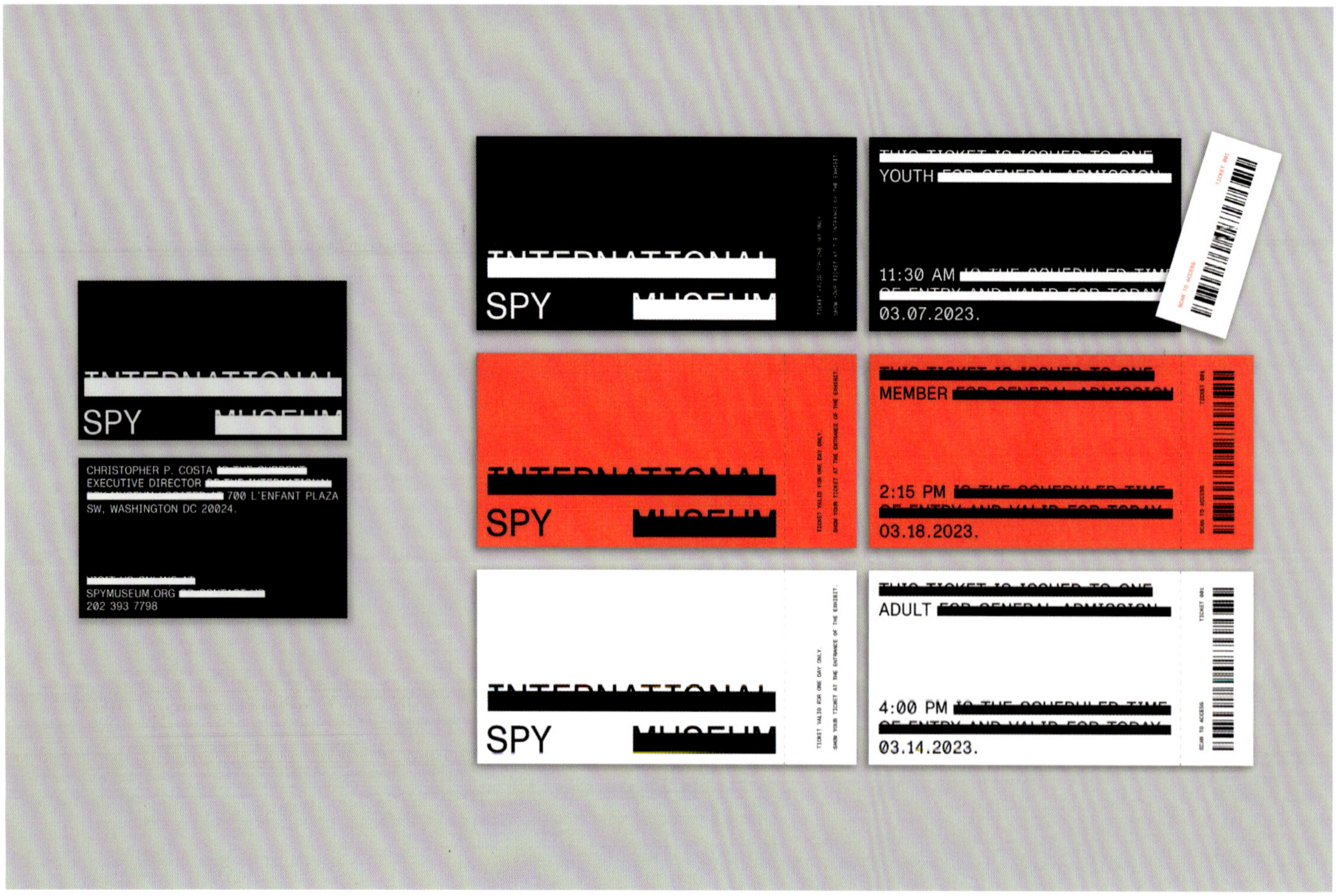

80 INSTRUCTORS COURTNEY GOOCH, RORY SIMMS GOLD

P237: Credit & Commentary **Student:** Ray Chang | **School:** School of Visual Arts

Design | Branding

81 INSTRUCTORS **BRAD BARTLETT, MING TAI** GOLD

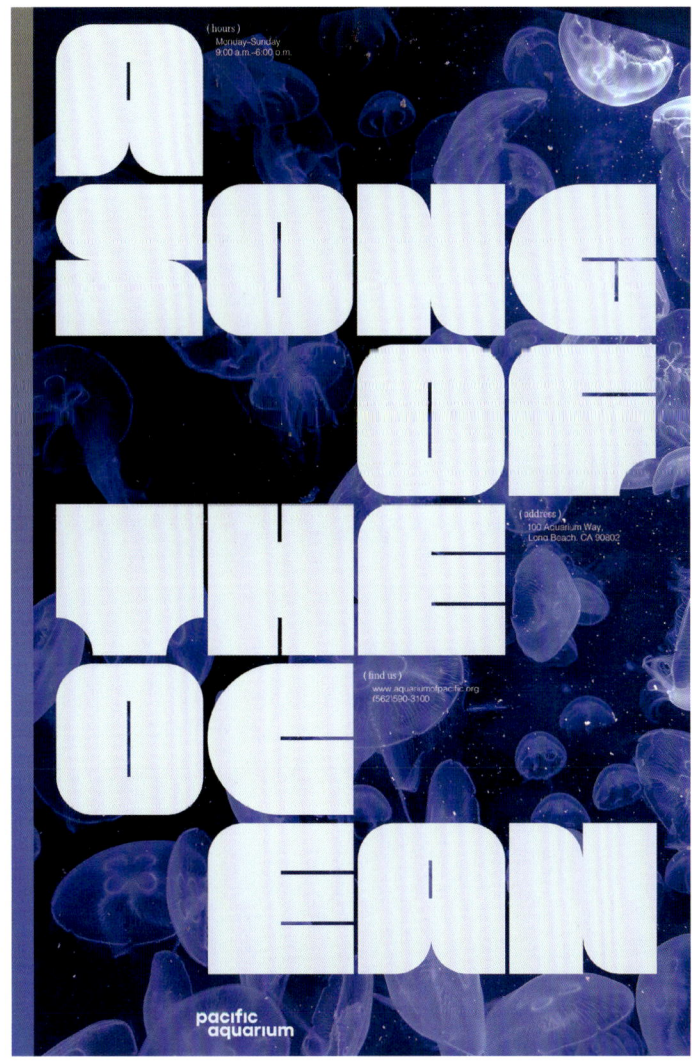
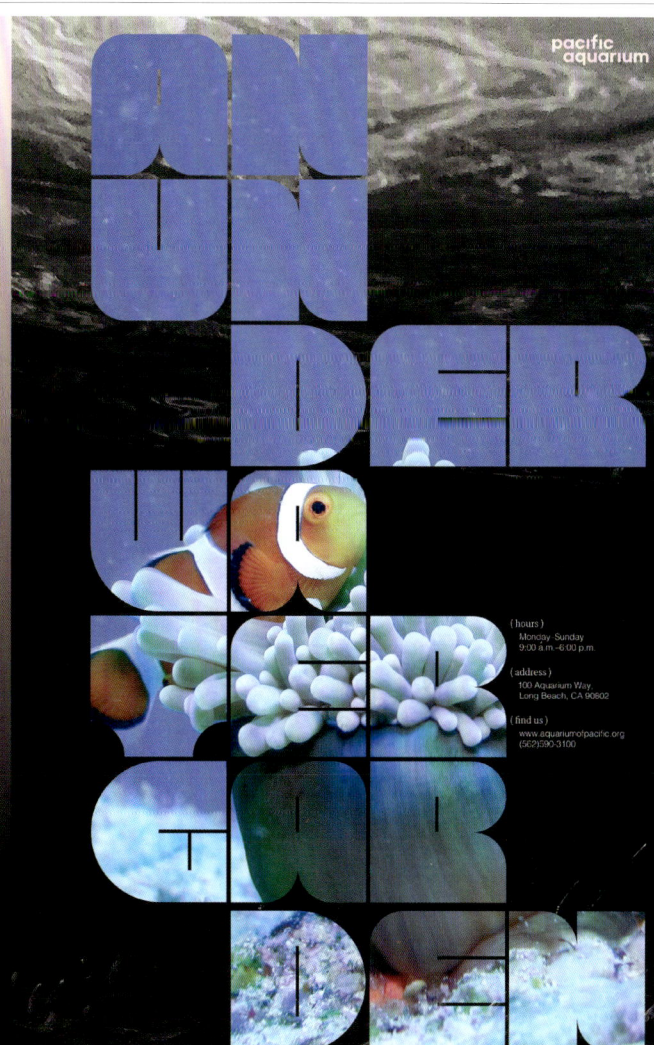
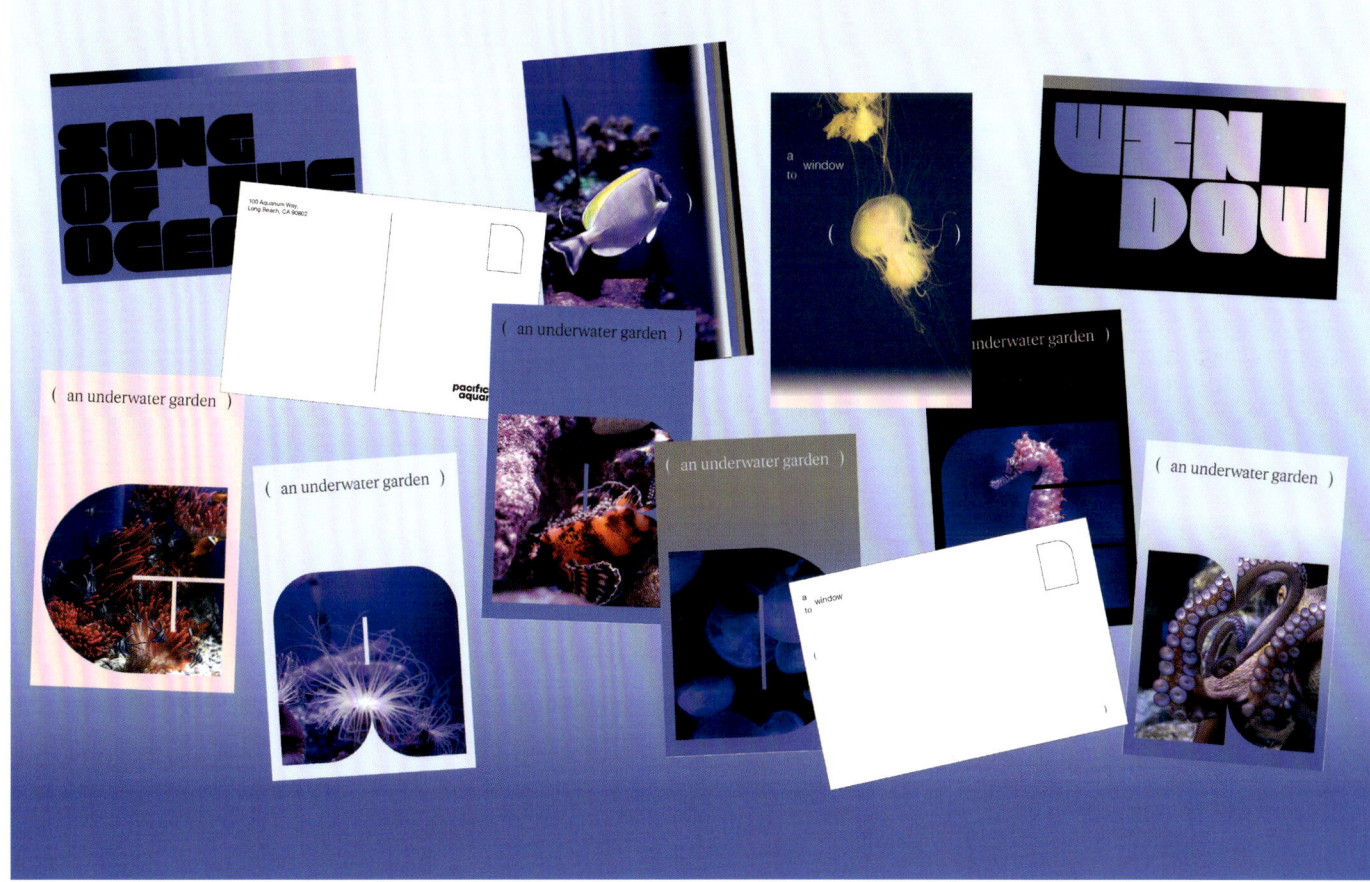

P237: Credit & Commentary   Student: Yuqin Ni | School: ArtCenter College of Design   Images 1–3 of 7

Branding | Design

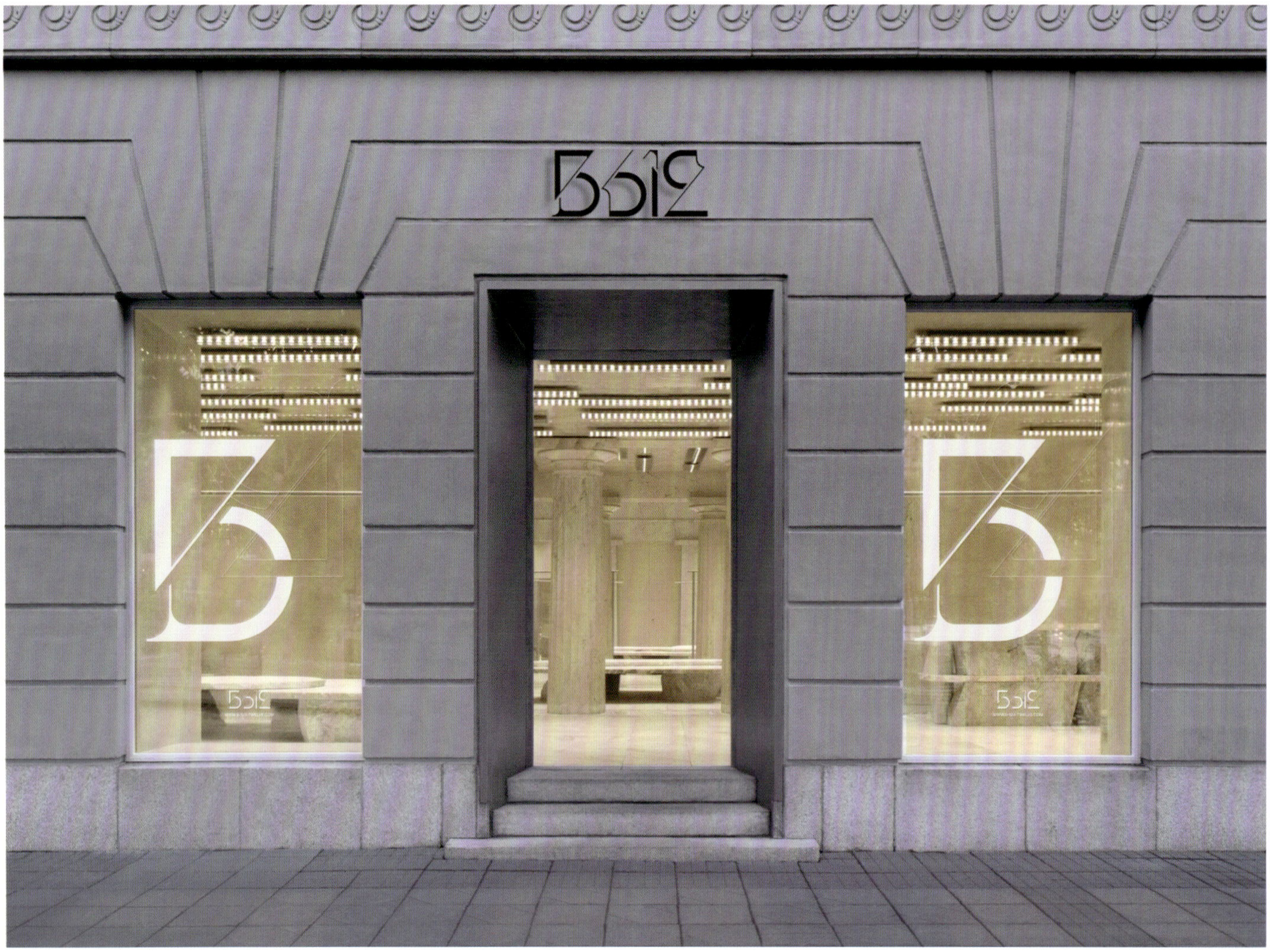

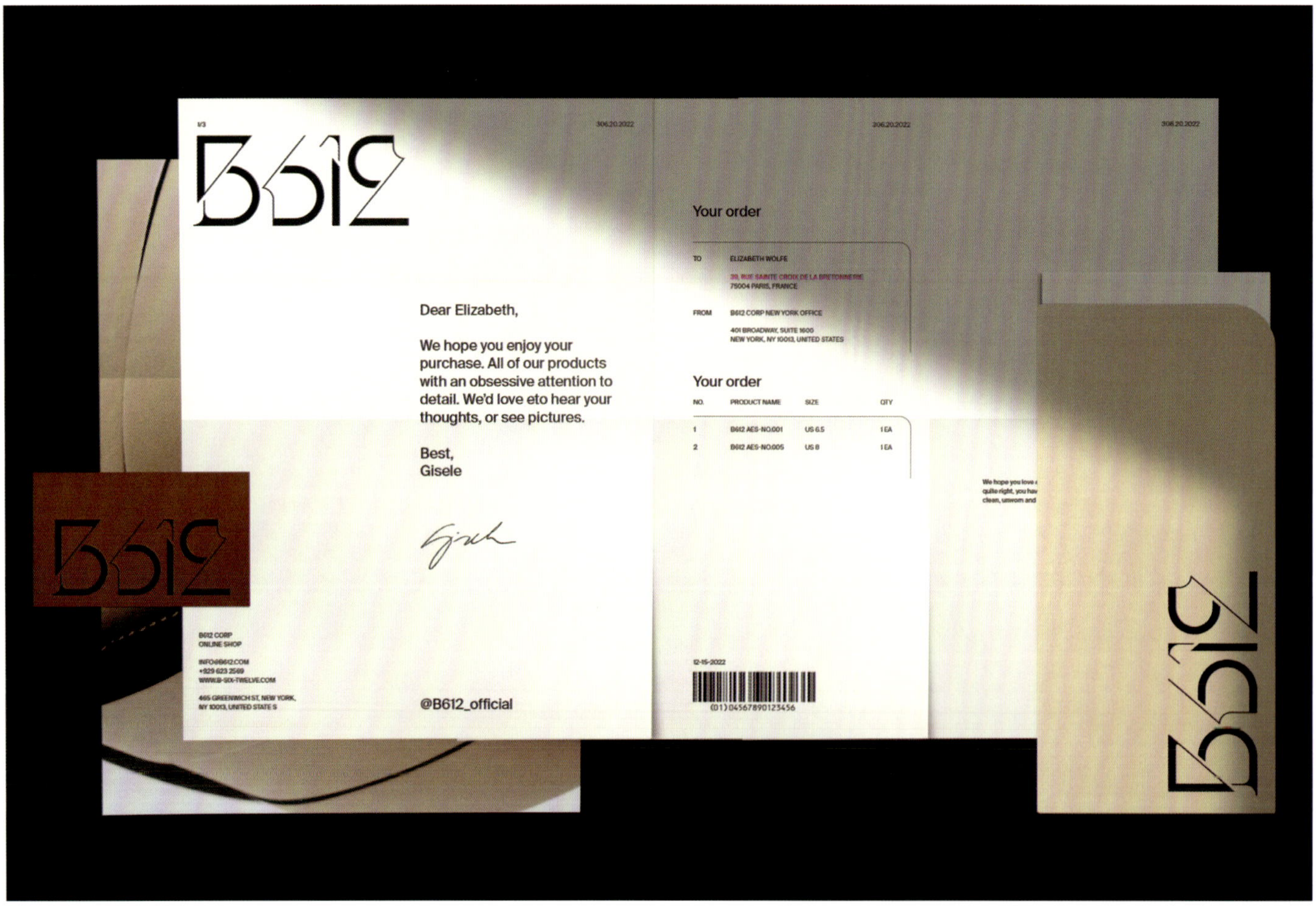

82 INSTRUCTOR NATASHA JEN GOLD

Student: Mina Son | **School:** School of Visual Arts

Design | Branding

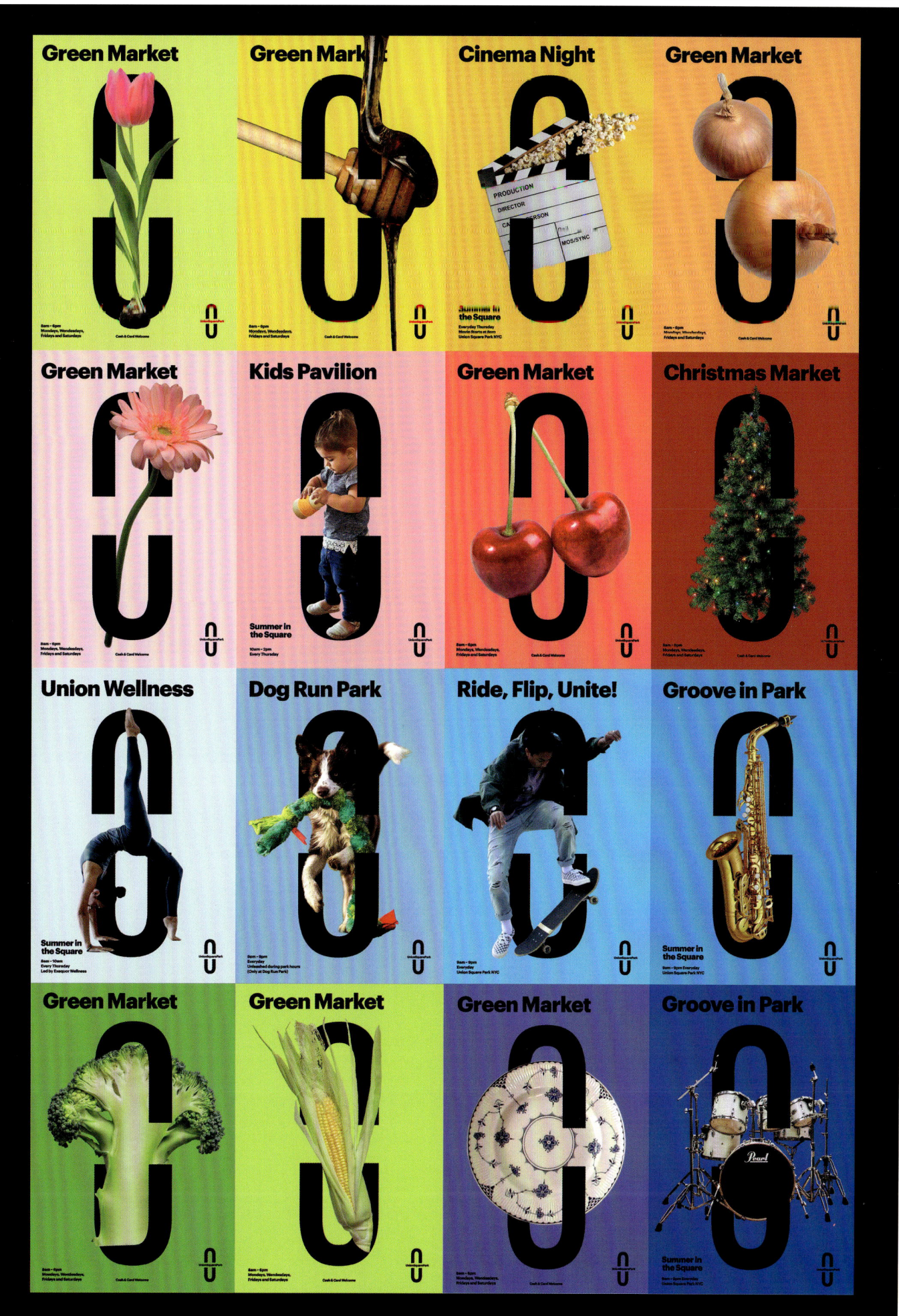

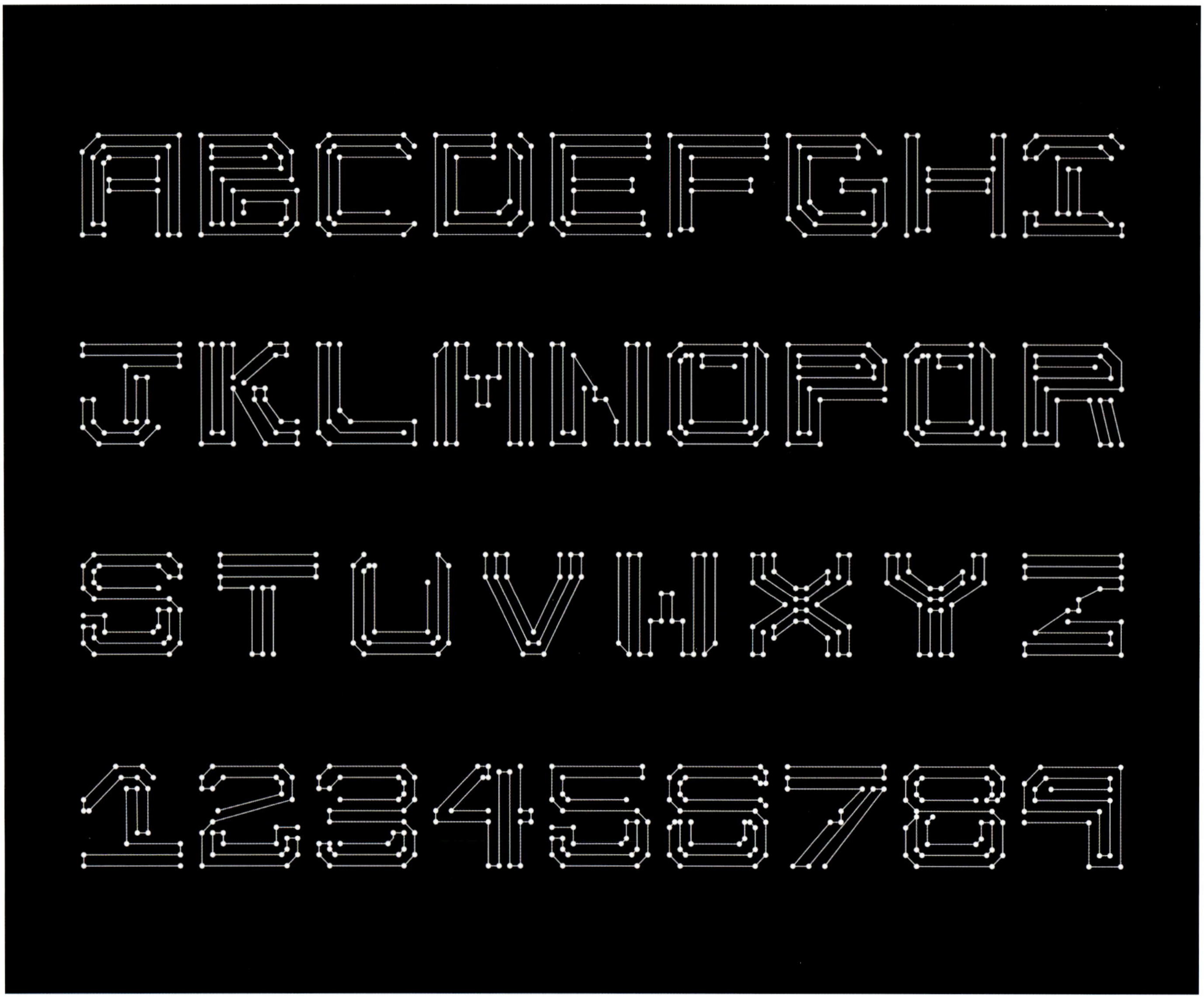

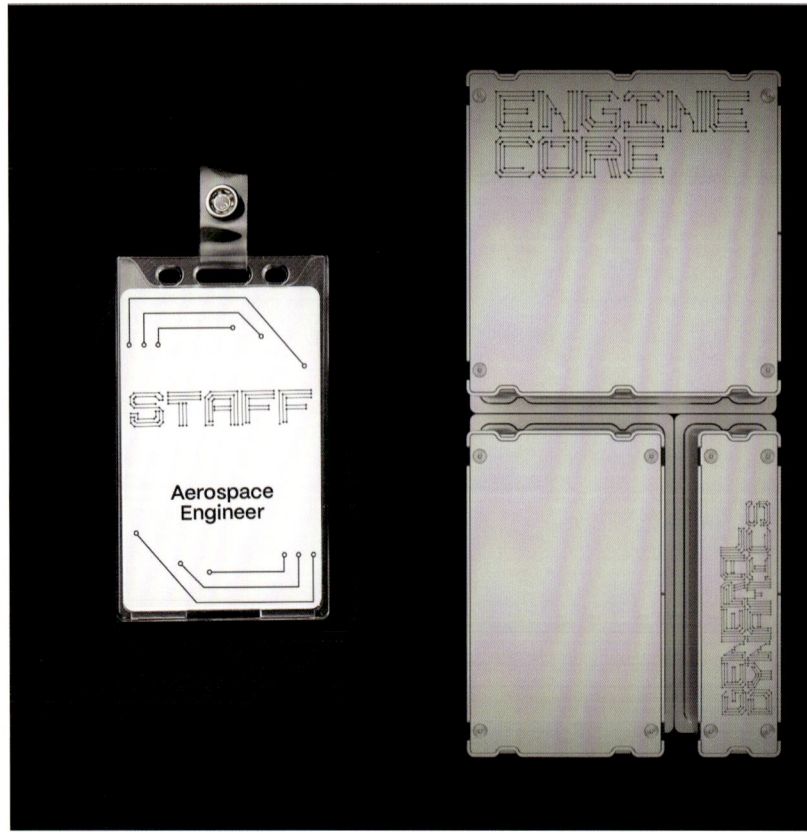
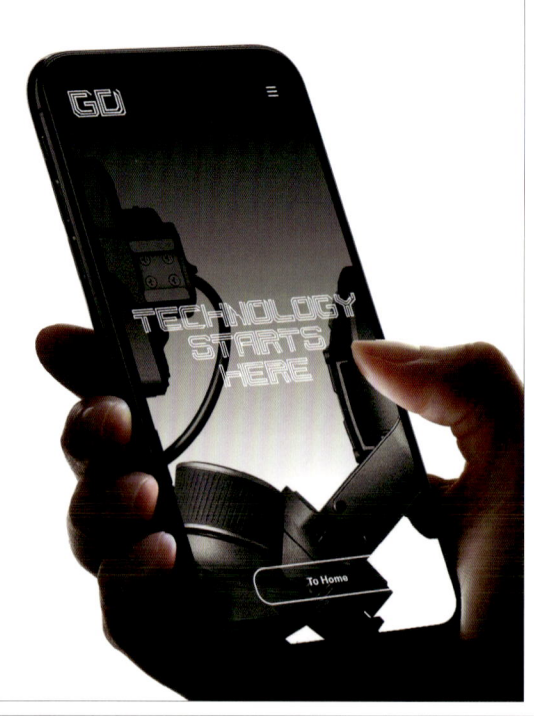

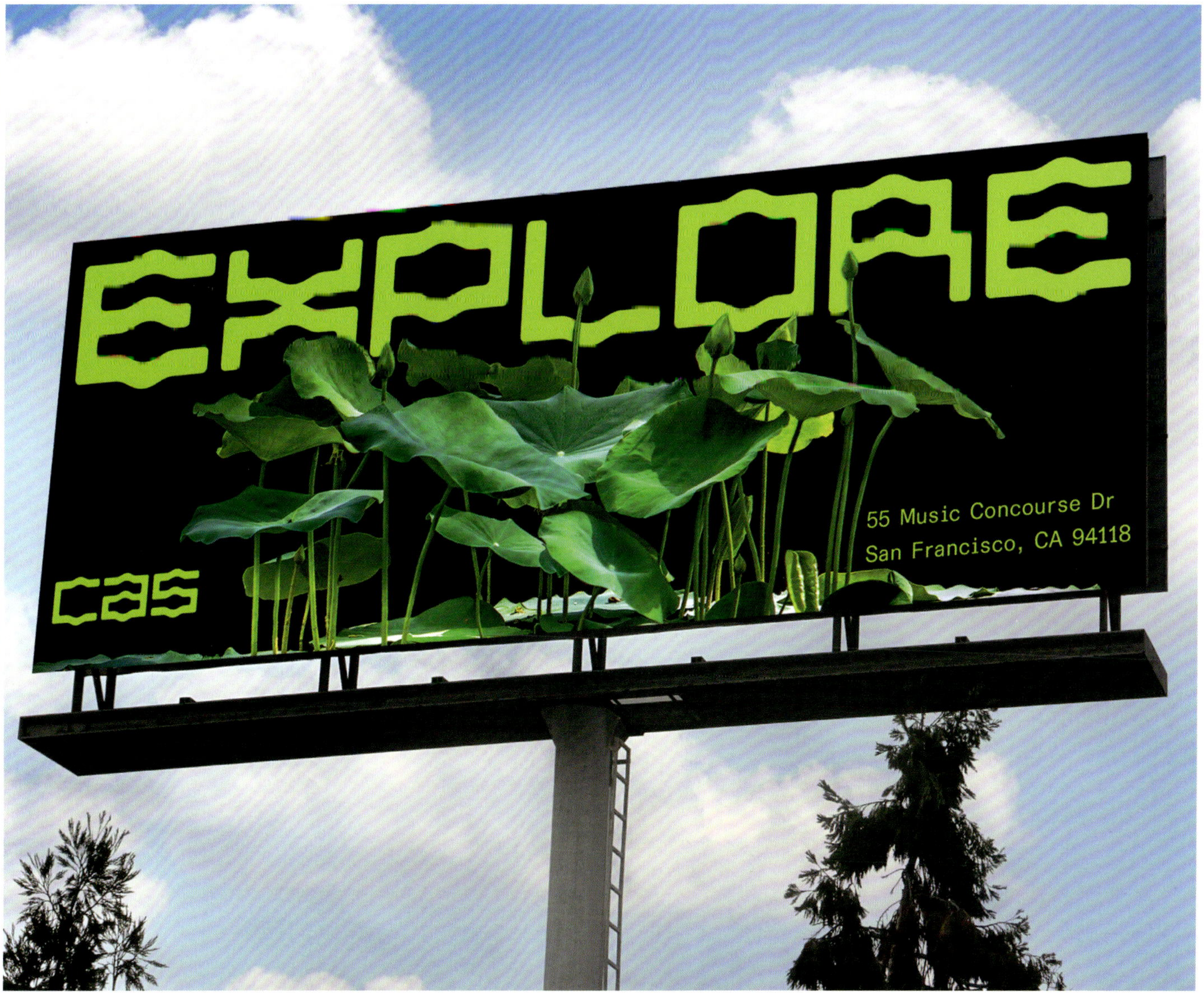

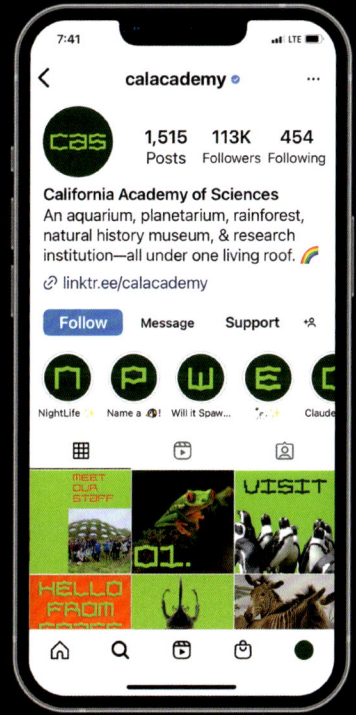
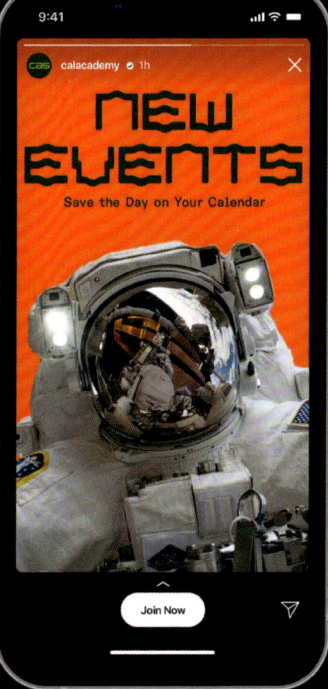
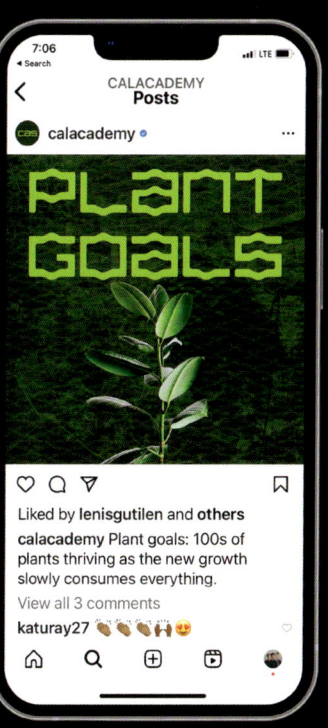

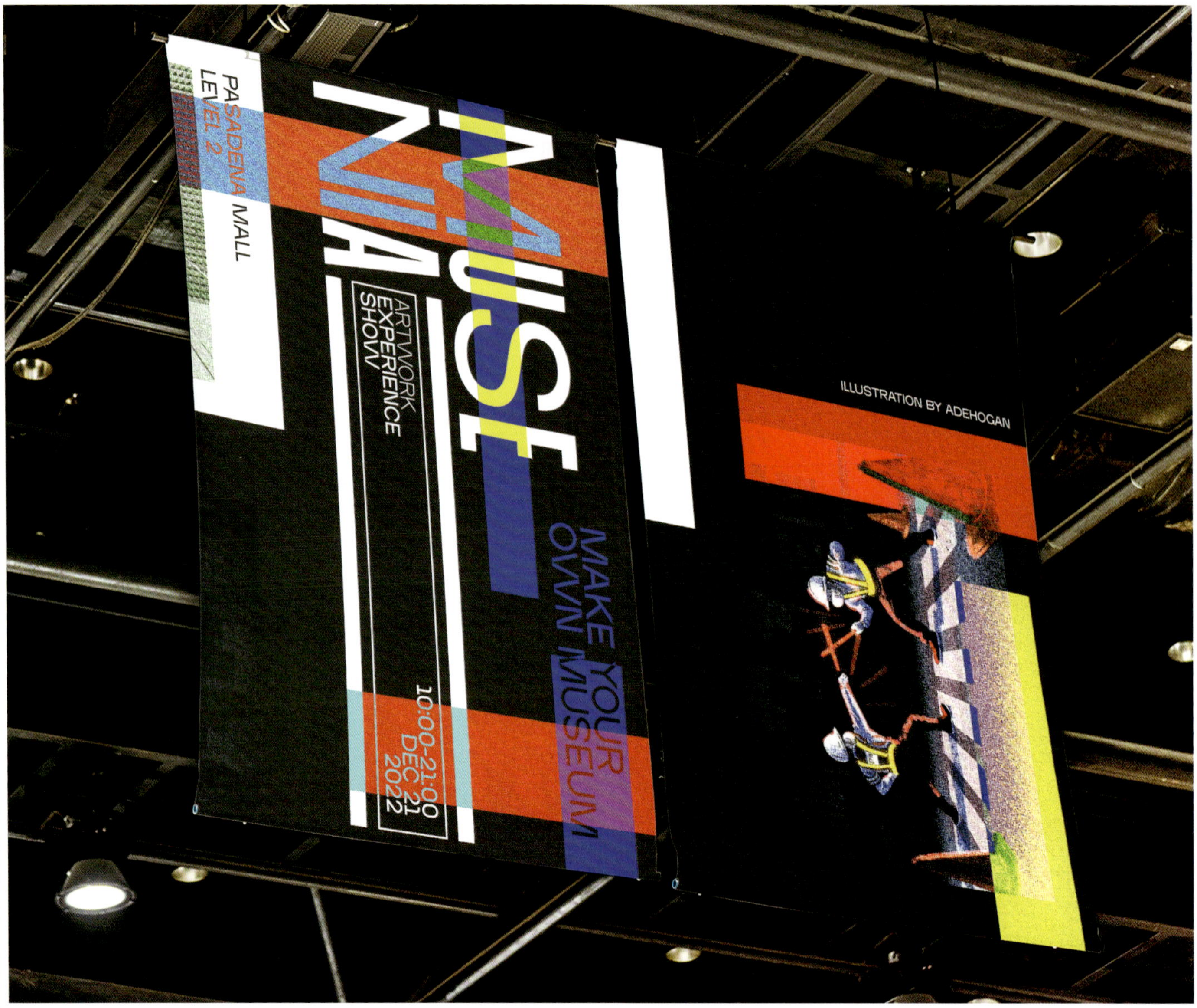

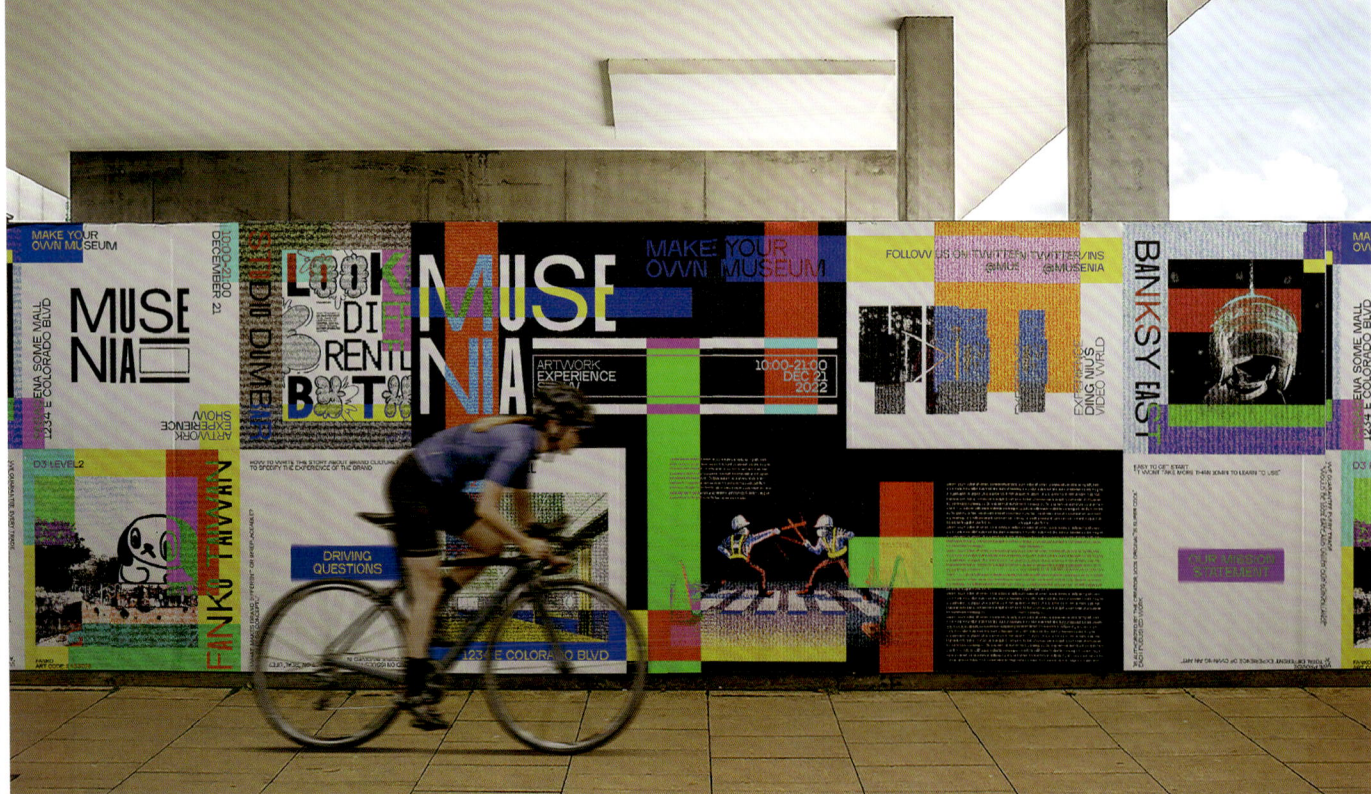

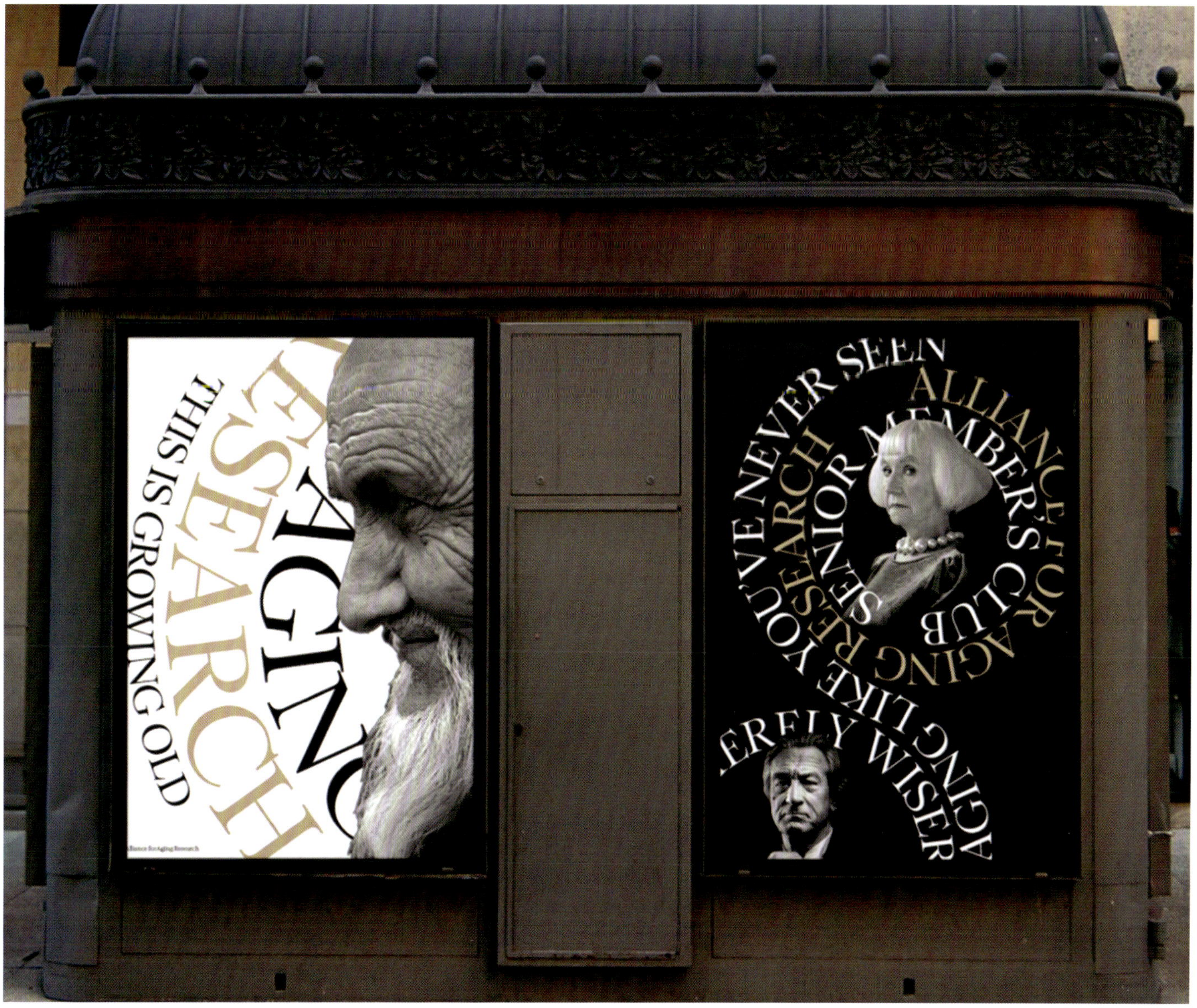

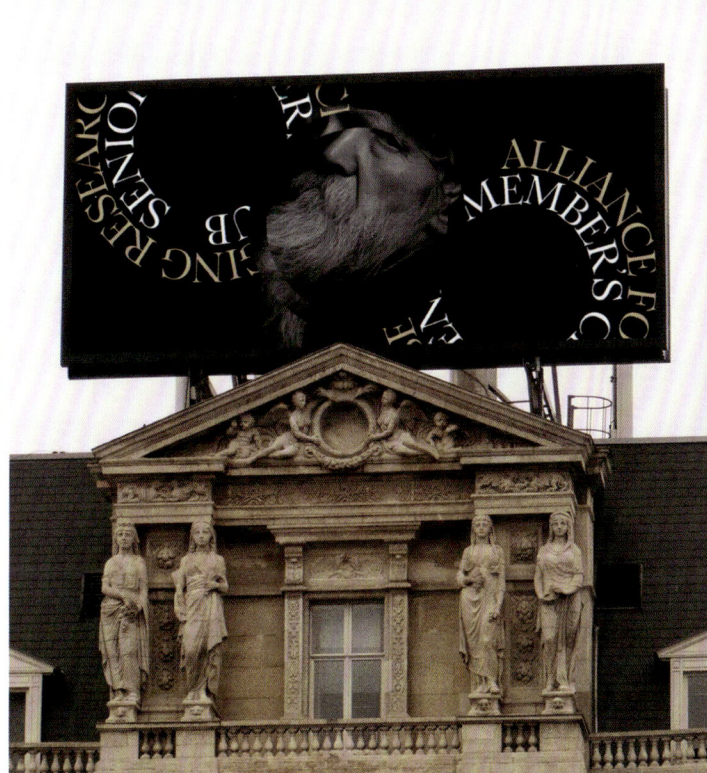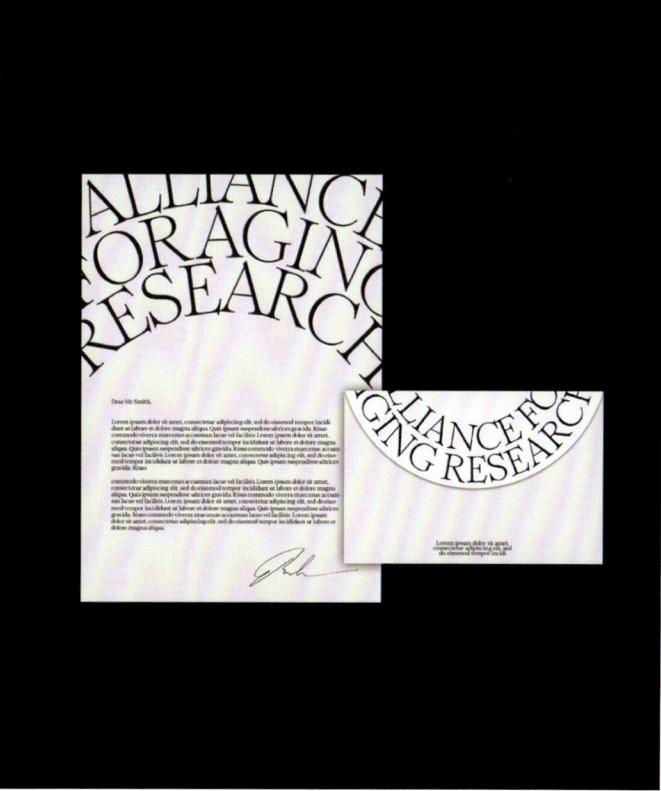

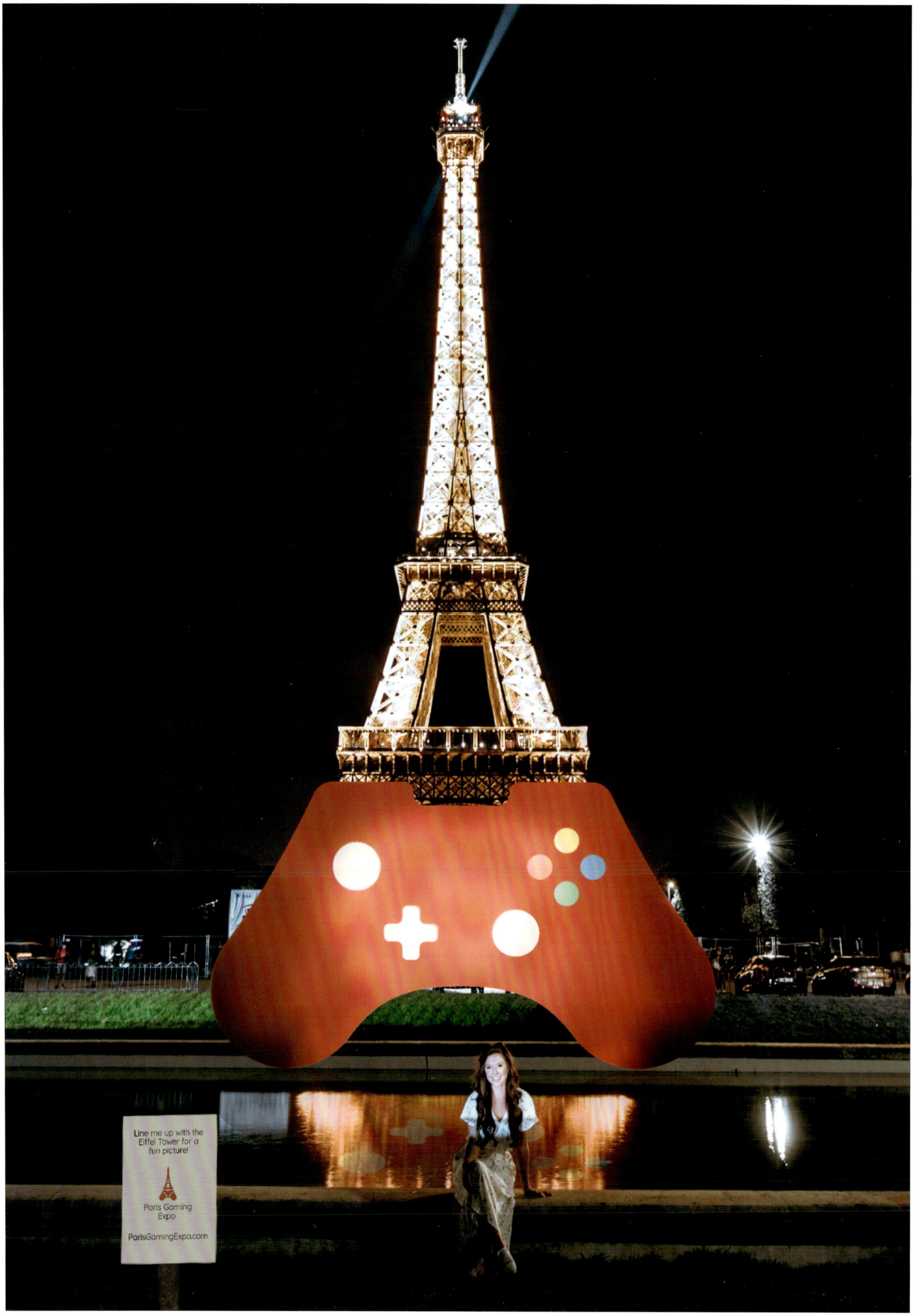

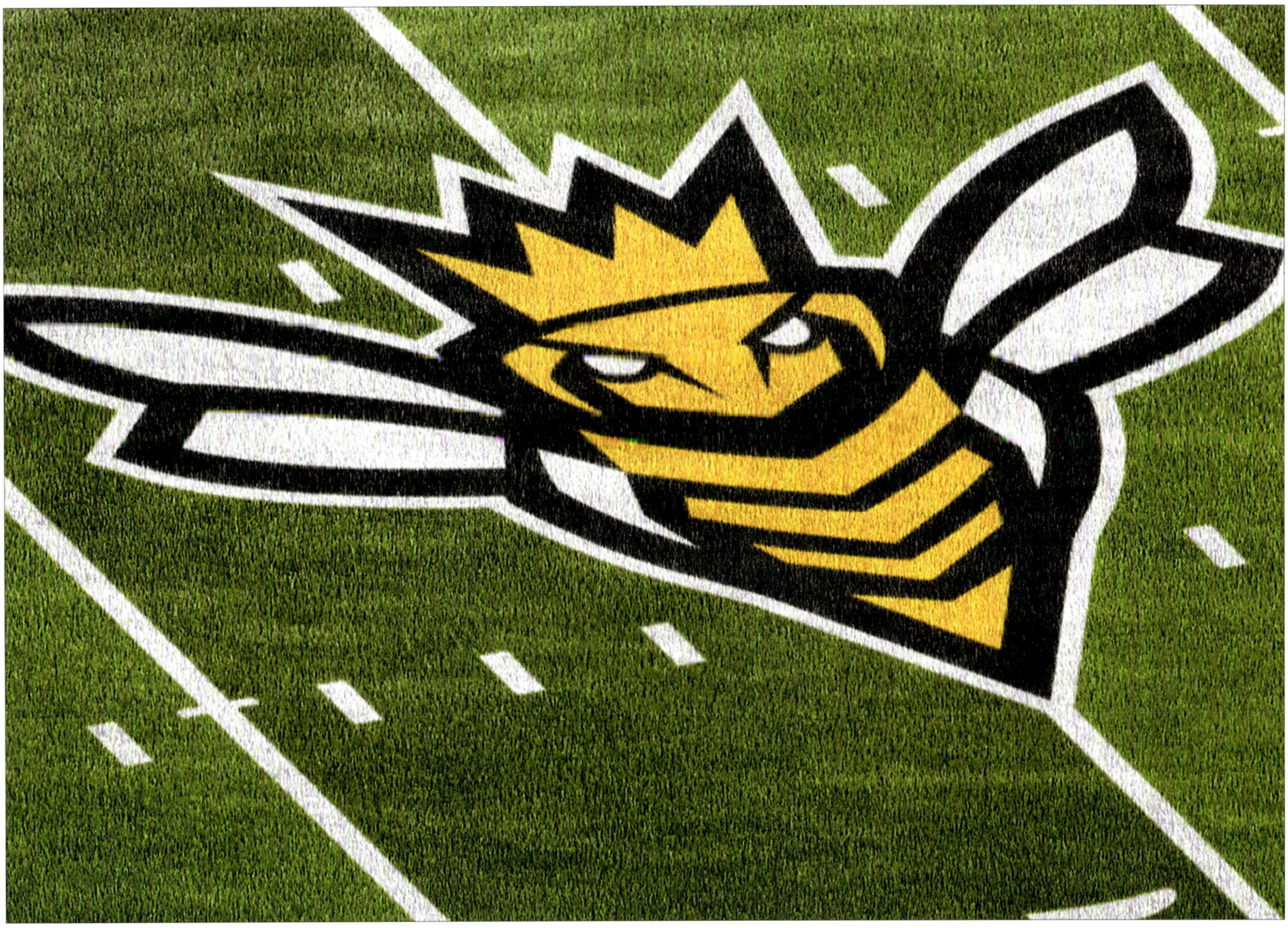

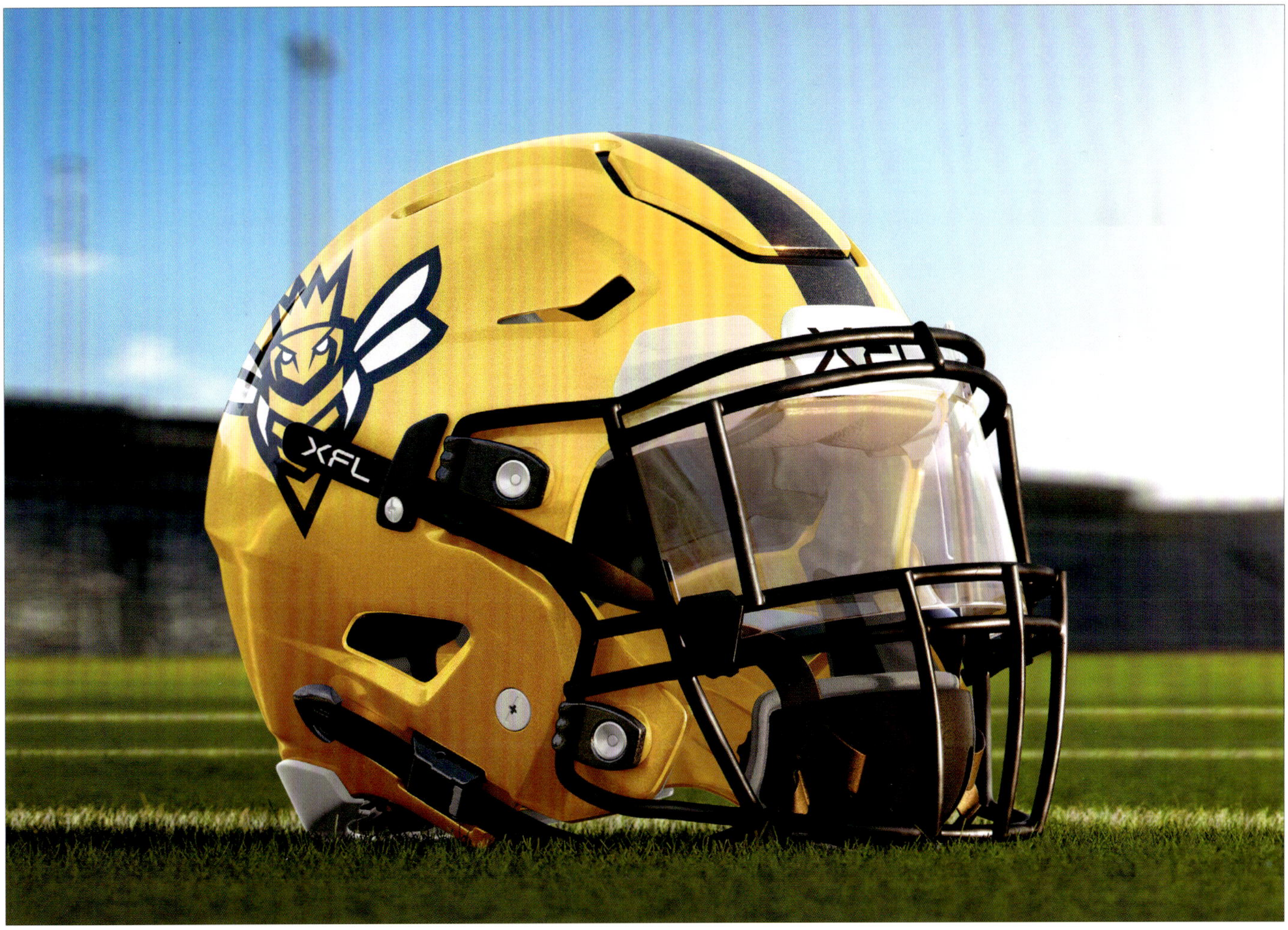

89 INSTRUCTOR **GUS GRANGER** GOLD

P237: Credit & Commentary | **Student:** John Paul Nguyen | **School:** University of North Texas | Images 1, 2 of 7

Branding | Design

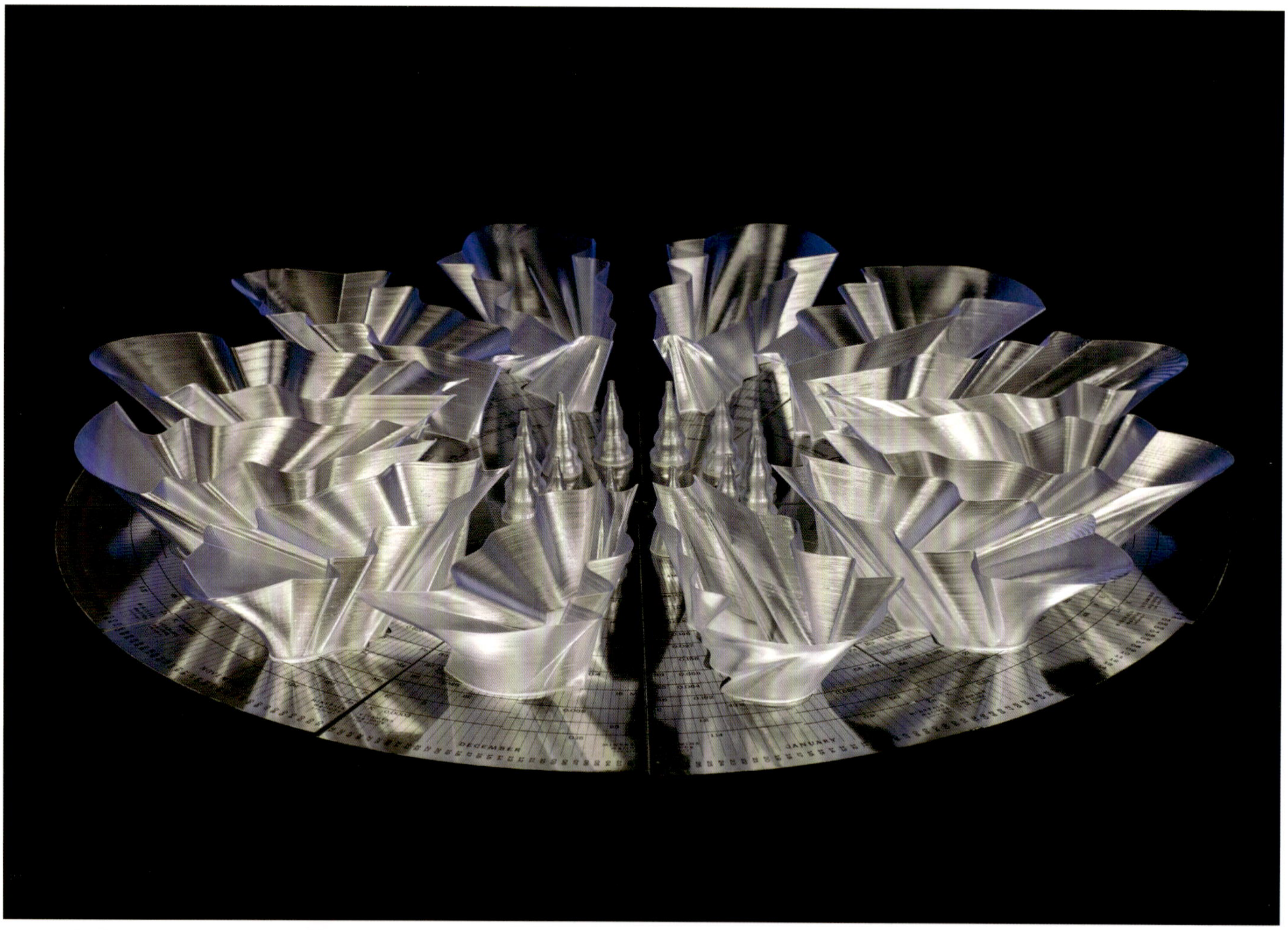

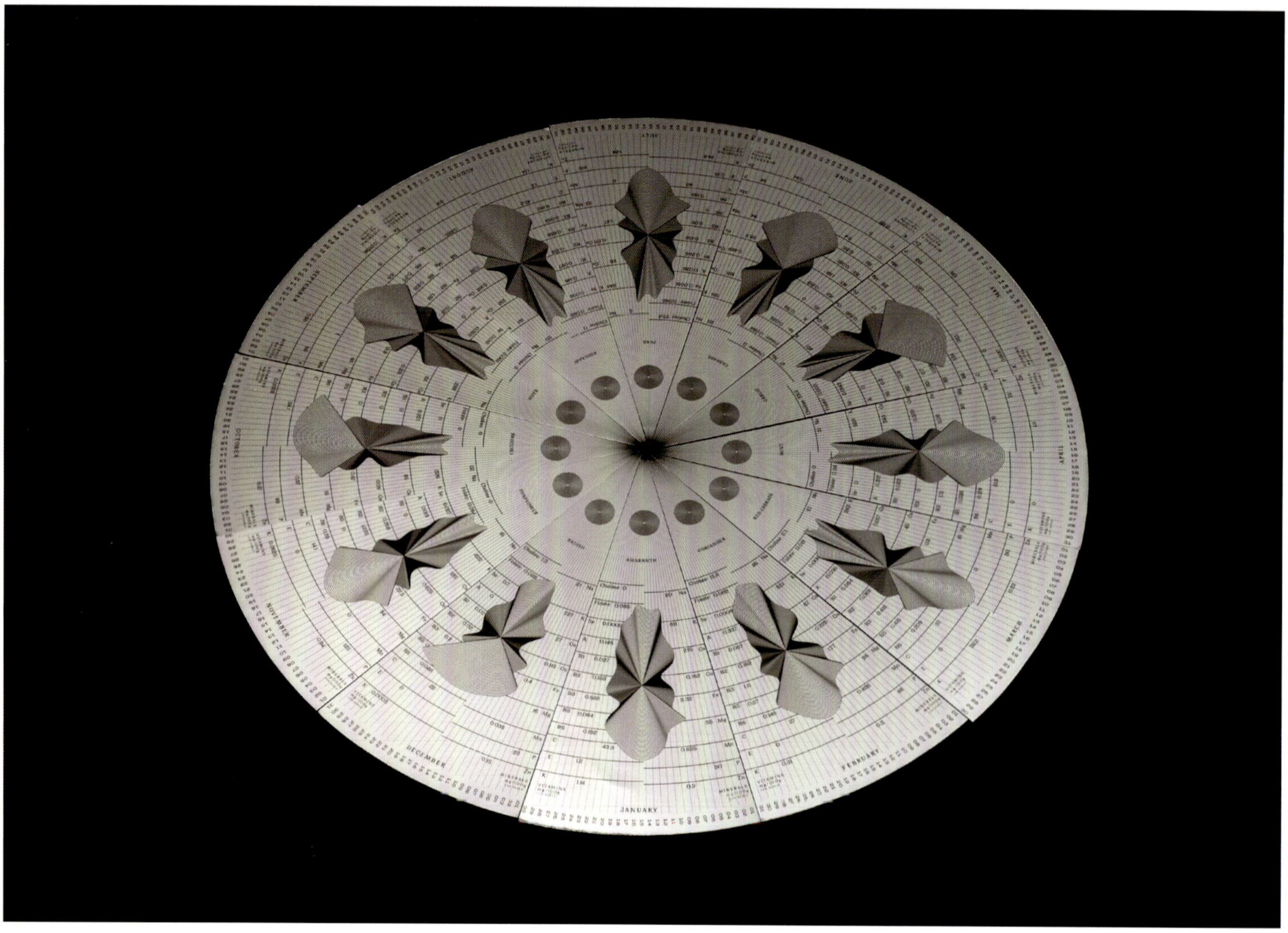

90 INSTRUCTORS **EDUARD ČEHOVIN, RADOVAN JENKO** GOLD

P237: Credit & Commentary **Student:** Strahinja Jovanović | **School:** University of Ljubljana, Academy of Fine Arts & Design Images 1, 2 of 7

Design | Calendars

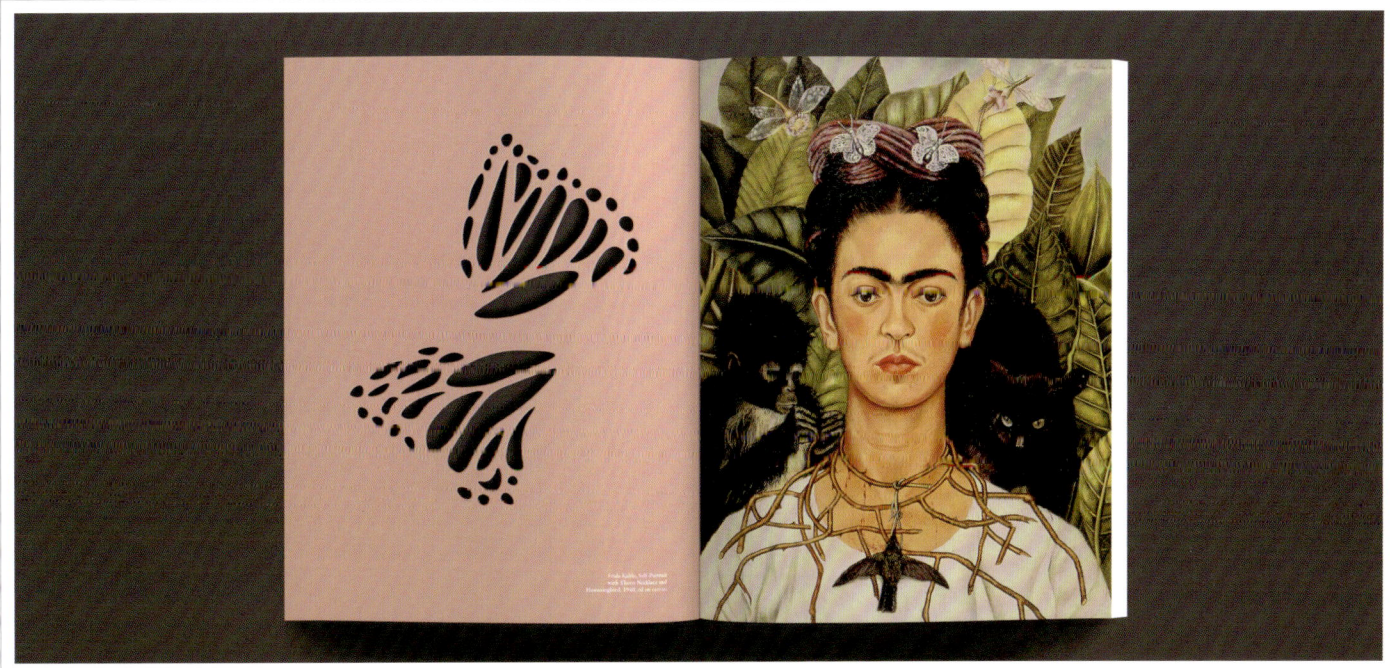
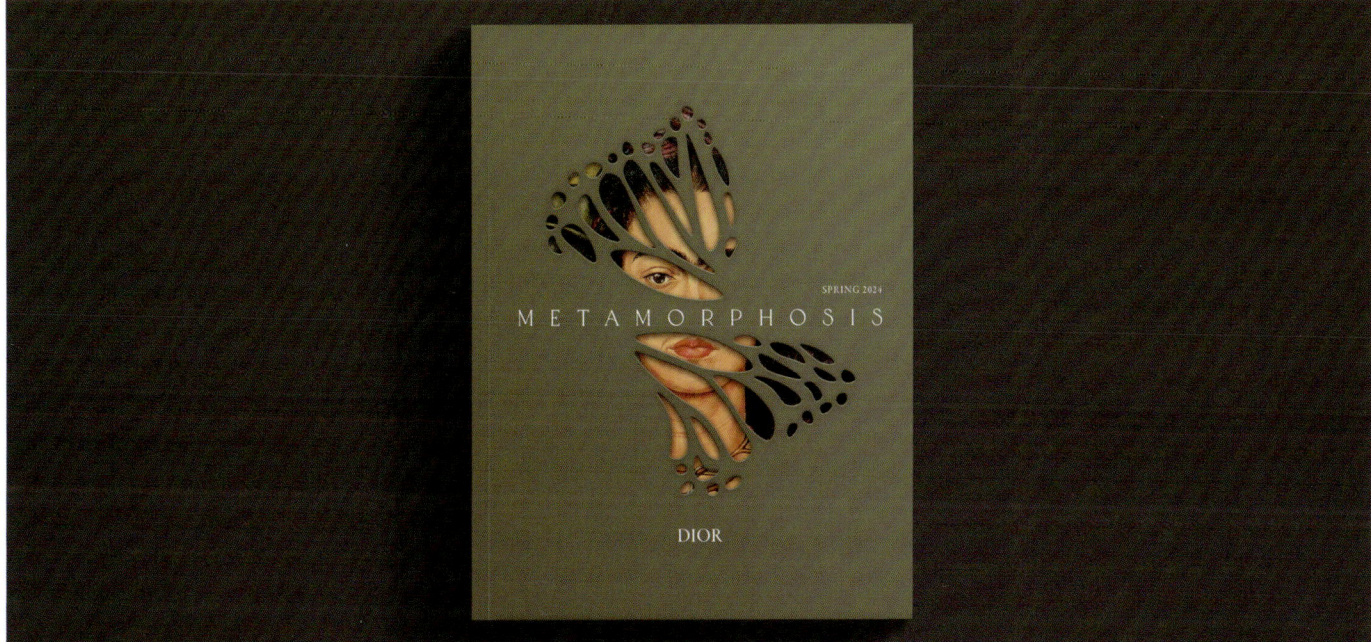
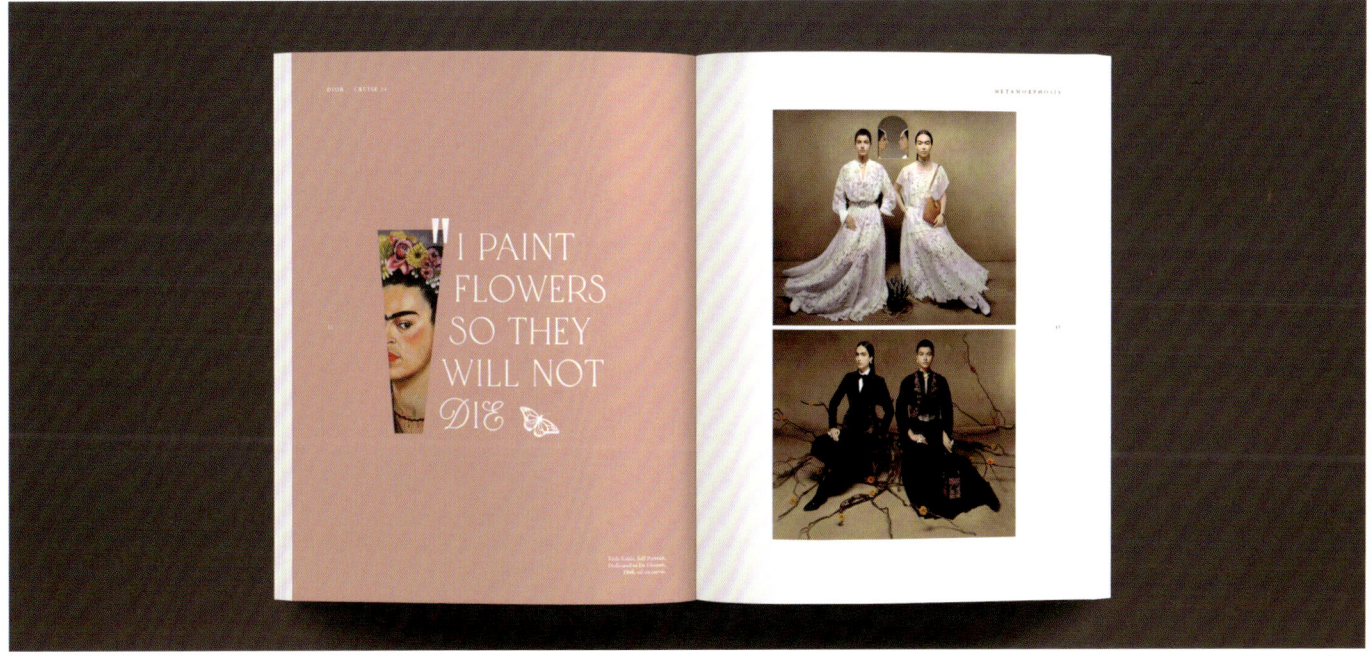

92 INSTRUCTOR **JIM SALVATI GOLD**

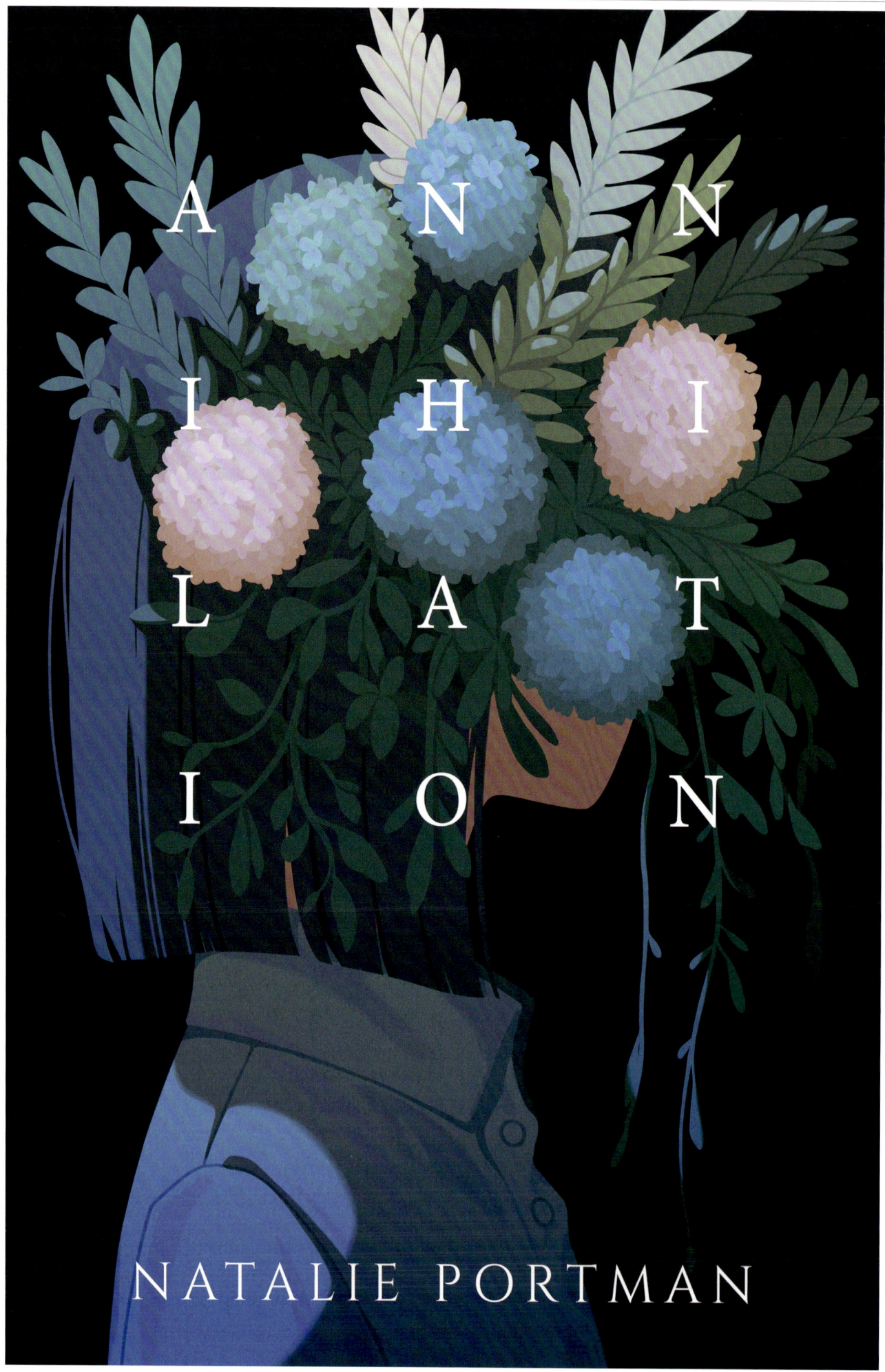

P237: Credit & Commentary **Student:** Rain Gao | **School:** ArtCenter College of Design

Design | Illustration

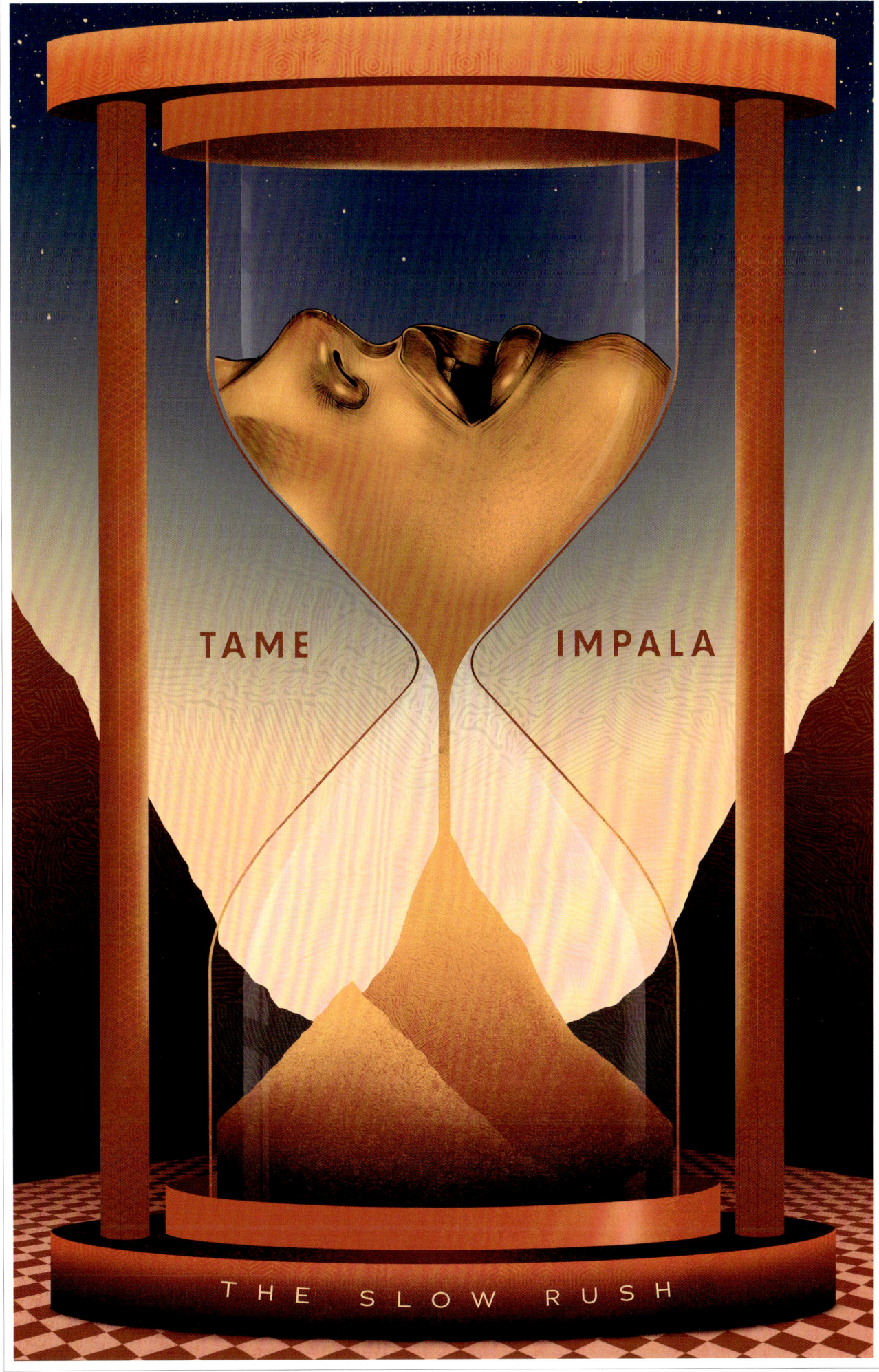

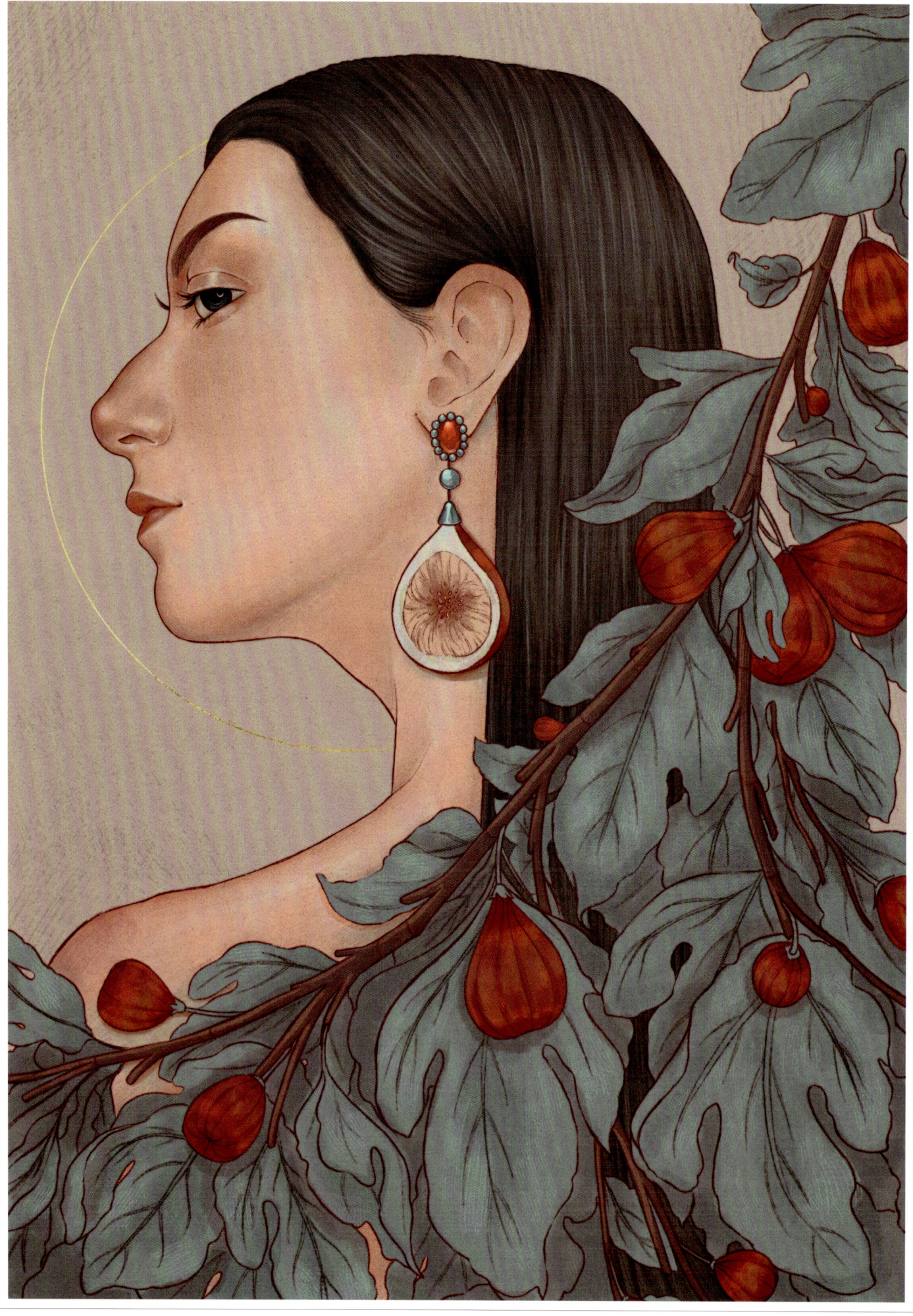

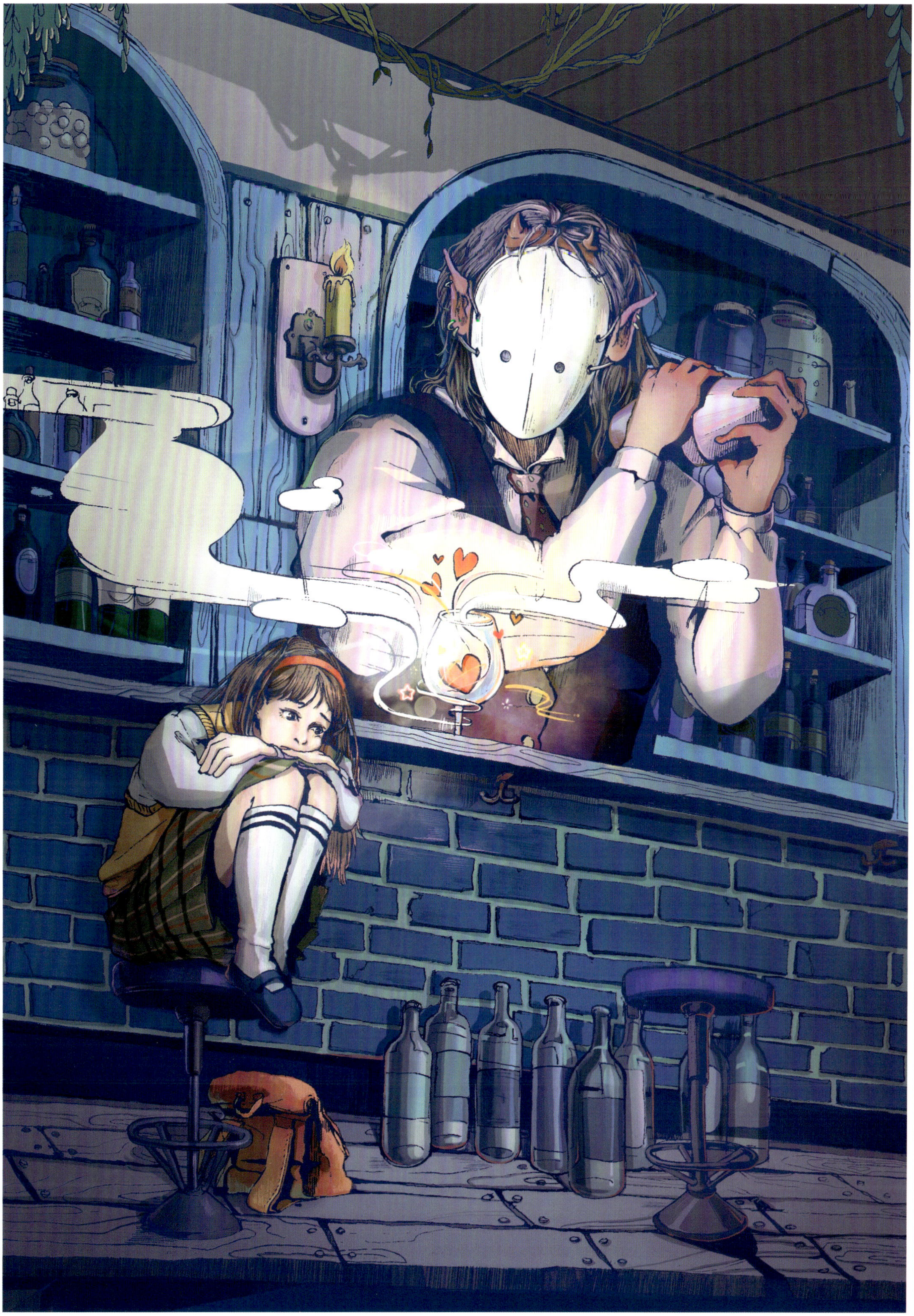

95 INSTRUCTOR **JOSH COCHRAN** GOLD

P238: Credit & Commentary   Student: Jenna Park | School: School of Visual Arts

Illustration | Design

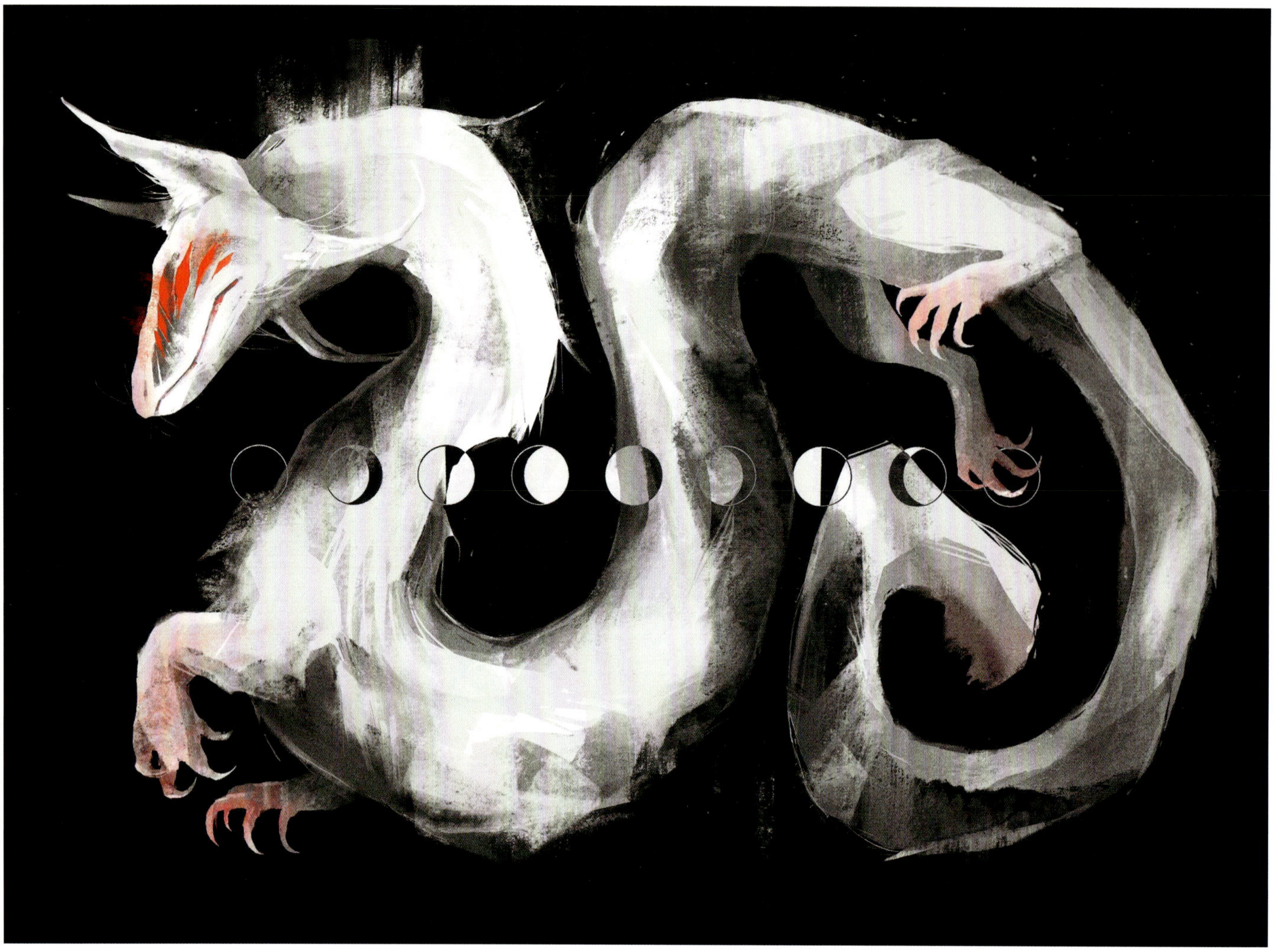

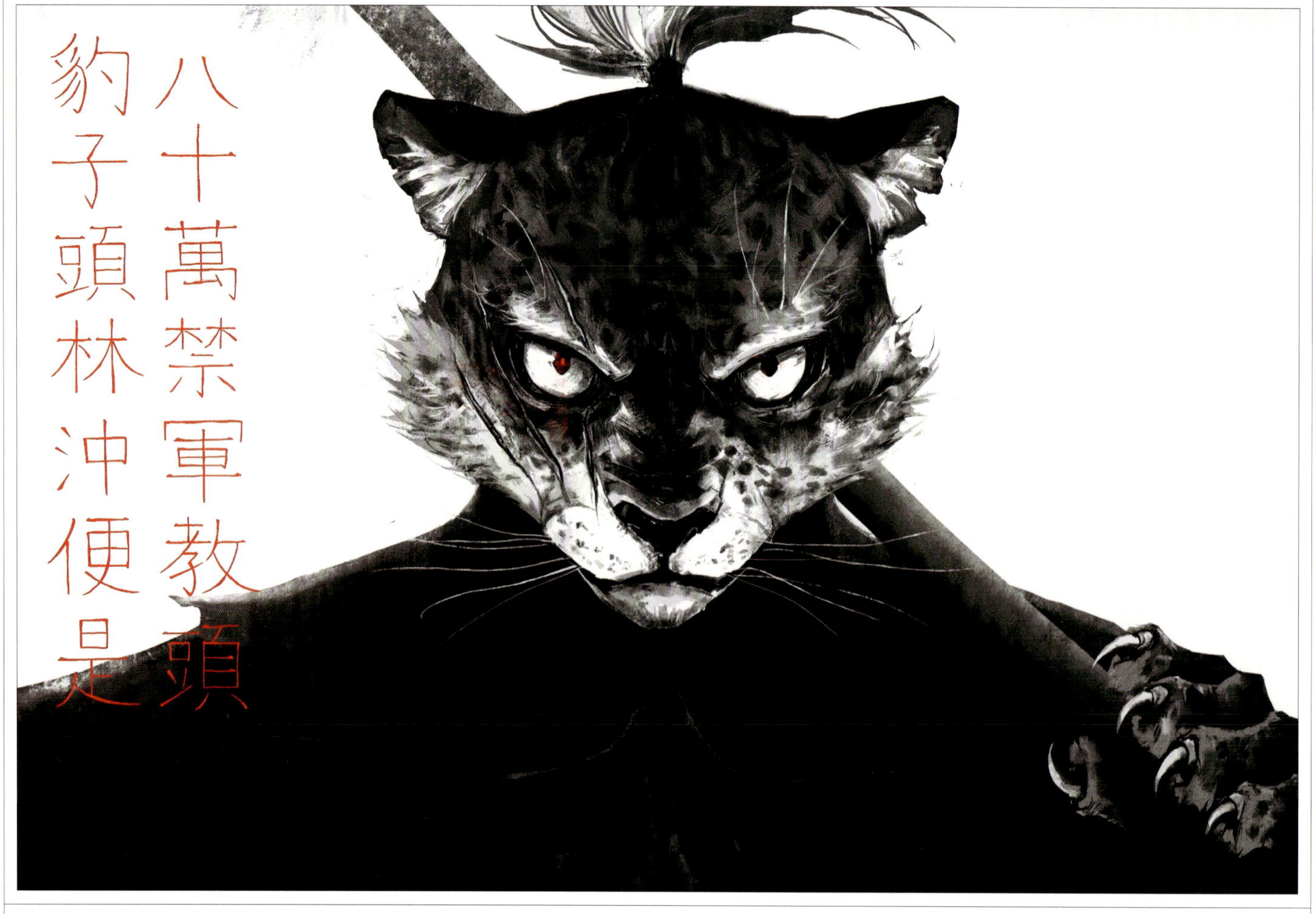

96 INSTRUCTOR **ANTHONY MACBAIN** GOLD

豹子頭林沖便是
八十萬禁軍教頭

P238: Credit & Commentary Student: Yiwen You | School: School of Visual Arts Images 1, 2 of 7

Design | Illustration

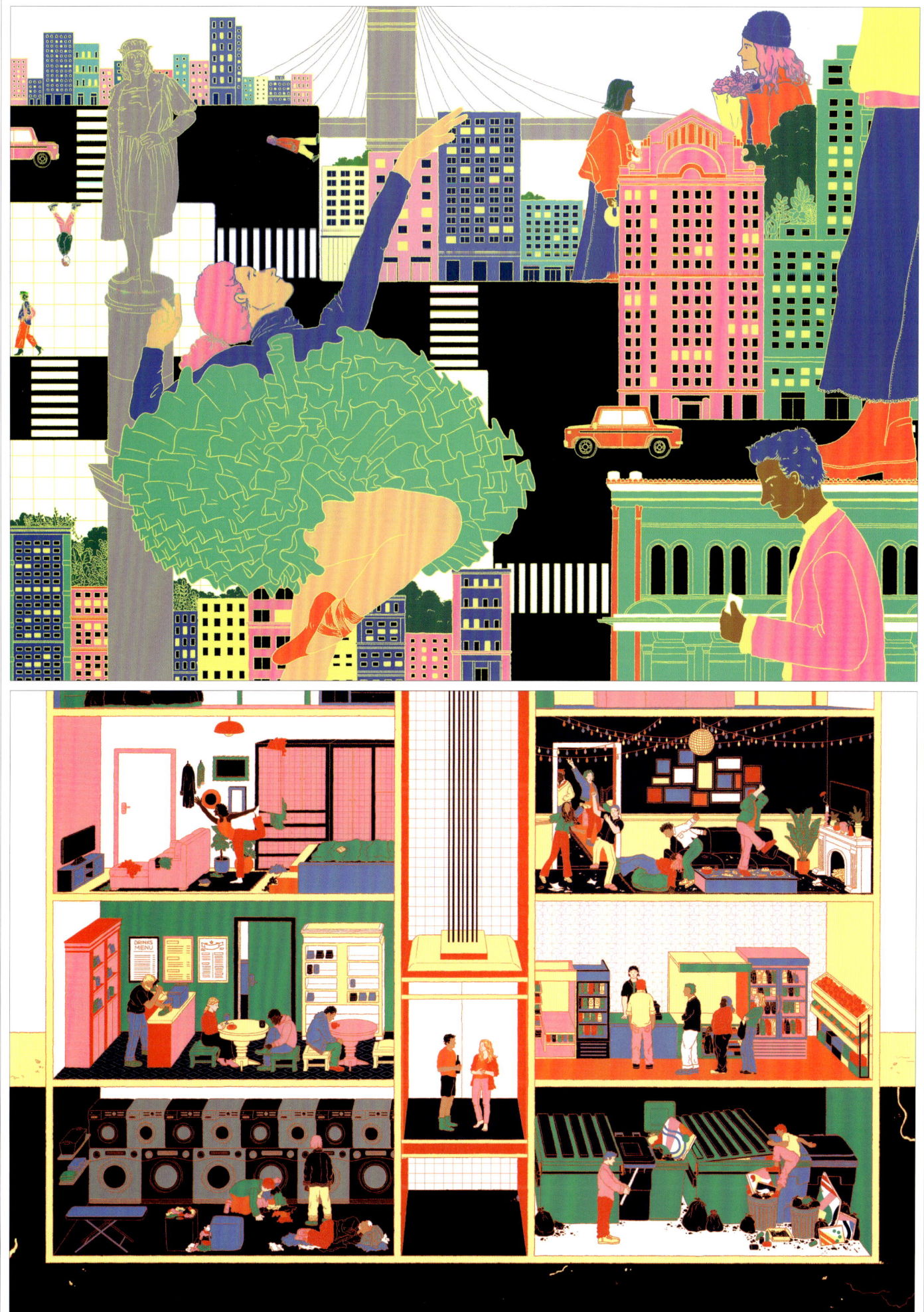

98 GOLD

INSTRUCTORS JEFF BLEITZ, LISA WILLARD

P238: Credit & Commentary — **Student:** Bella Race | **School:** Ringling College of Art & Design

INSTRUCTOR MARK BRINKMAN

P238: Credit & Commentary — **Student:** Danielle Stowe | **School:** Texas State University

INSTRUCTOR CHAD ANDERSON

P238: Credit & Commentary — **Student:** Conner Gayda | **School:** Jacksonville State University

INSTRUCTOR MARK BRINKMAN

P238: Credit & Commentary — **Student:** Courtney Acevedo | **School:** Texas State University

INSTRUCTOR MARK BRINKMAN

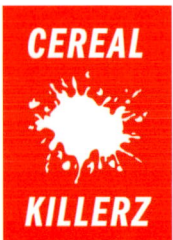

P238: Credit & Commentary — **Student:** Aliya Ibarra | **School:** Texas State University

Design | Logo

99 GOLD

INSTRUCTOR JOSHUA EGE

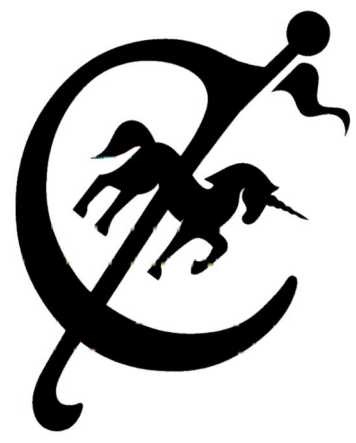

P238: Credit & Commentary   **Student:** Michael Tucker | **School:** Texas A&M University-Commerce

INSTRUCTOR GUS GRANGER

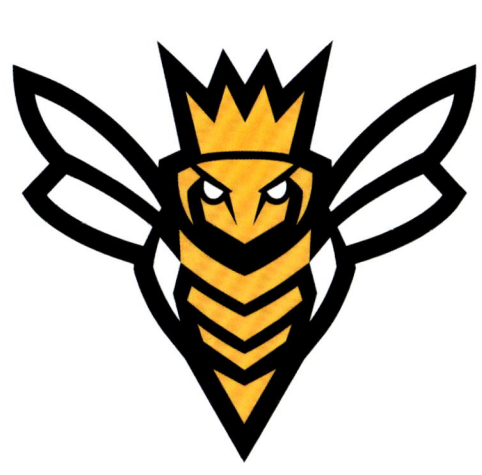

P238: Credit & Commentary   **Student:** John Paul Nguyen | **School:** University of North Texas

INSTRUCTOR DEJAN MRAOVIĆ

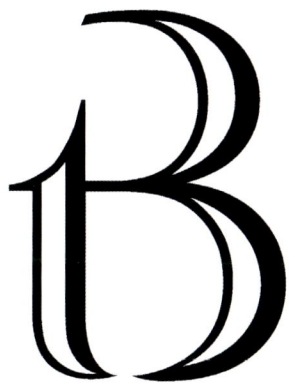

P238: Credit & Commentary   **Student:** Breonna Tolson-Tucker | **School:** Campbell University

Logo | Design

100 GOLD

INSTRUCTOR JOSEPH NEWTON

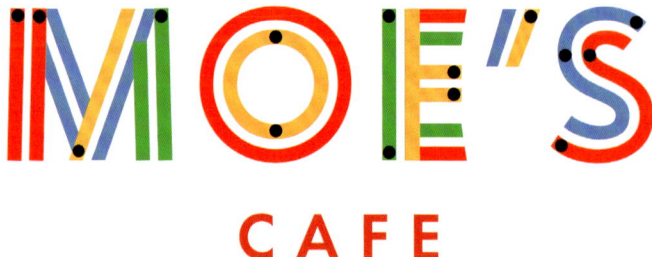

P238: Credit & Commentary **Student:** Yubin Won | **School:** School of Visual Arts

INSTRUCTOR WILLIE BARONET

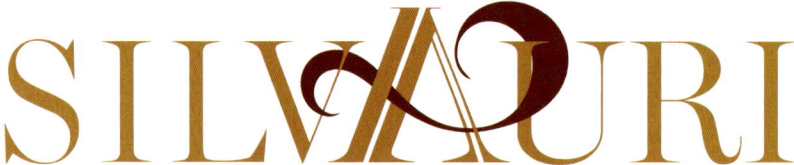

P238: Credit & Commentary **Student:** Juan Silva | **School:** Southern Methodist University

INSTRUCTOR LEILA SINGLETON

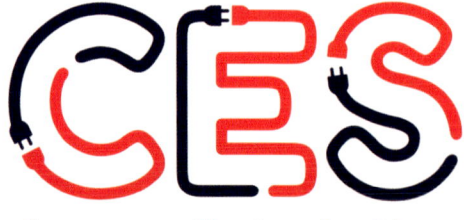

P238: Credit & Commentary **Student:** Darlington Ilukhor | **School:** InFocus Film School

Design | Logo

101 GOLD

INSTRUCTOR DOUGLAS MAY

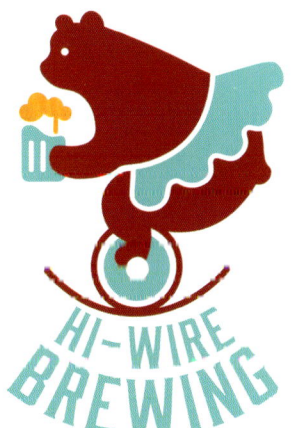

P238: Credit & Commentary   **Student:** Felicia Tshimanga | **School:** University of North Texas

INSTRUCTOR DOUGLAS MAY

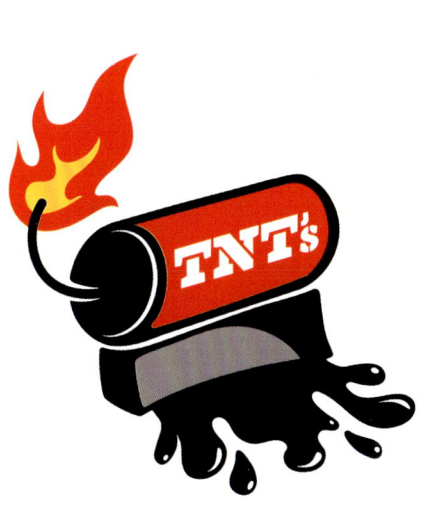

P238: Credit & Commentary   **Student:** Macy Belton | **School:** University of North Texas

INSTRUCTOR WILLIAM MEEK

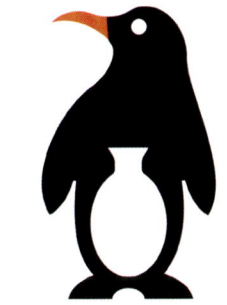

P238: Credit & Commentary   **Student:** Emily Anne Chu | **School:** Texas State University

Logo | Design

102 GOLD

INSTRUCTOR MARK BRINKMAN

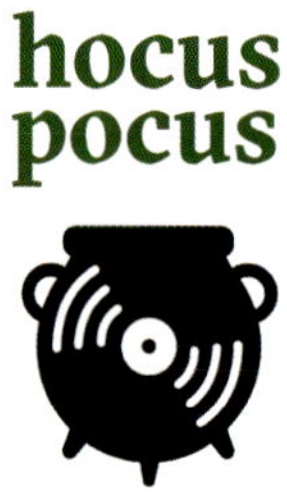

P238: Credit & Commentary **Student:** Hannah Twining | **School:** Texas State University

INSTRUCTOR WILLIAM MEEK

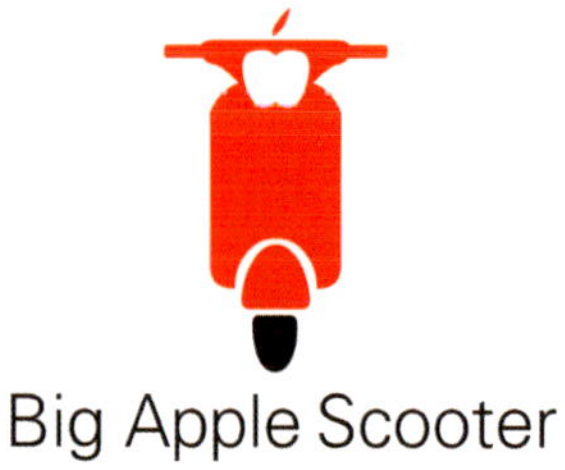

P238: Credit & Commentary **Student:** Emily Anne Chu | **School:** Texas State University

INSTRUCTOR MARK BRINKMAN

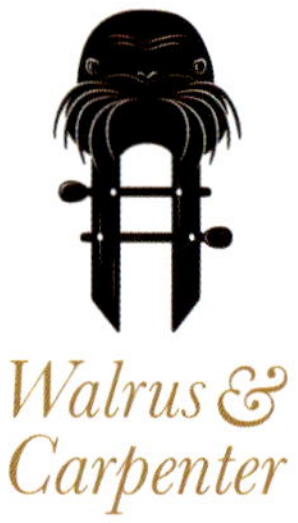

P238: Credit & Commentary **Student:** Brandy Compton | **School:** Texas State University

INSTRUCTOR DOUGLAS MAY

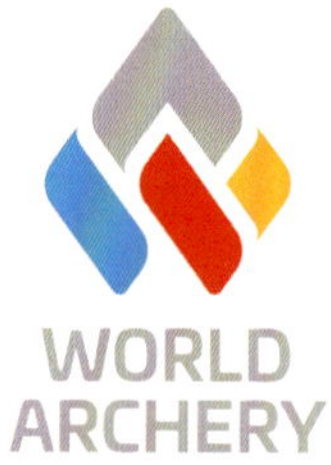

P238: Credit & Commentary **Student:** Jalon Isabell | **School:** University of North Texas

INSTRUCTOR MARK BRINKMAN

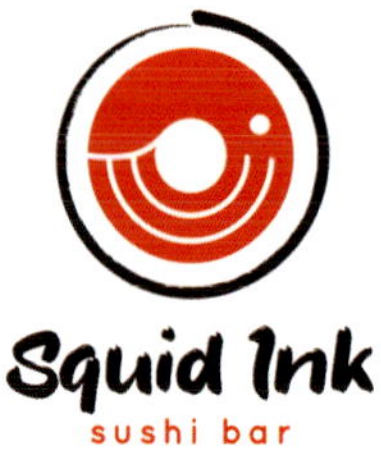

P238: Credit & Commentary **Student:** Sam Roberts | **School:** Texas State University

Design | Logo

103 GOLD

INSTRUCTOR DOUGLAS MAY

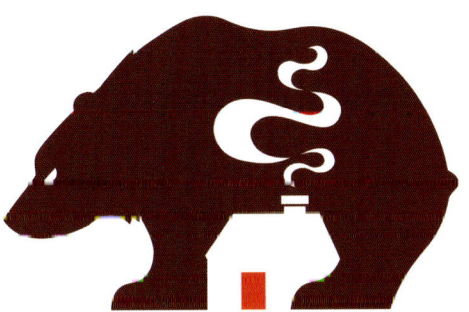

P238: Credit & Commentary   **Student:** Rachel Blow | **School:** University of North Texas

INSTRUCTOR NGUYEN TRI PHUONG DONG

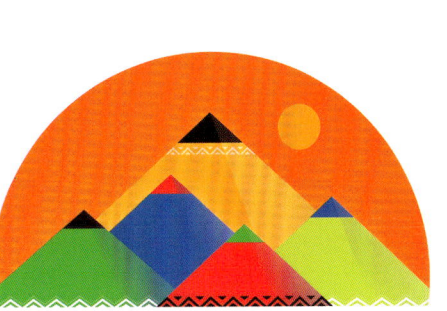

P238: Credit & Commentary   **Student:** Doan Van Huan | **School:** Duy Tan University

INSTRUCTOR DOUGLAS MAY

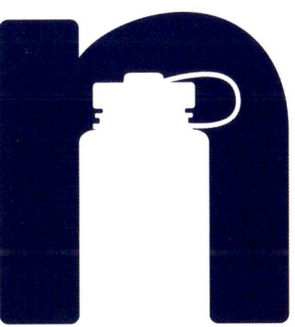

P238: Credit & Commentary   **Student:** Macy McClish | **School:** University of North Texas

Logo | Design

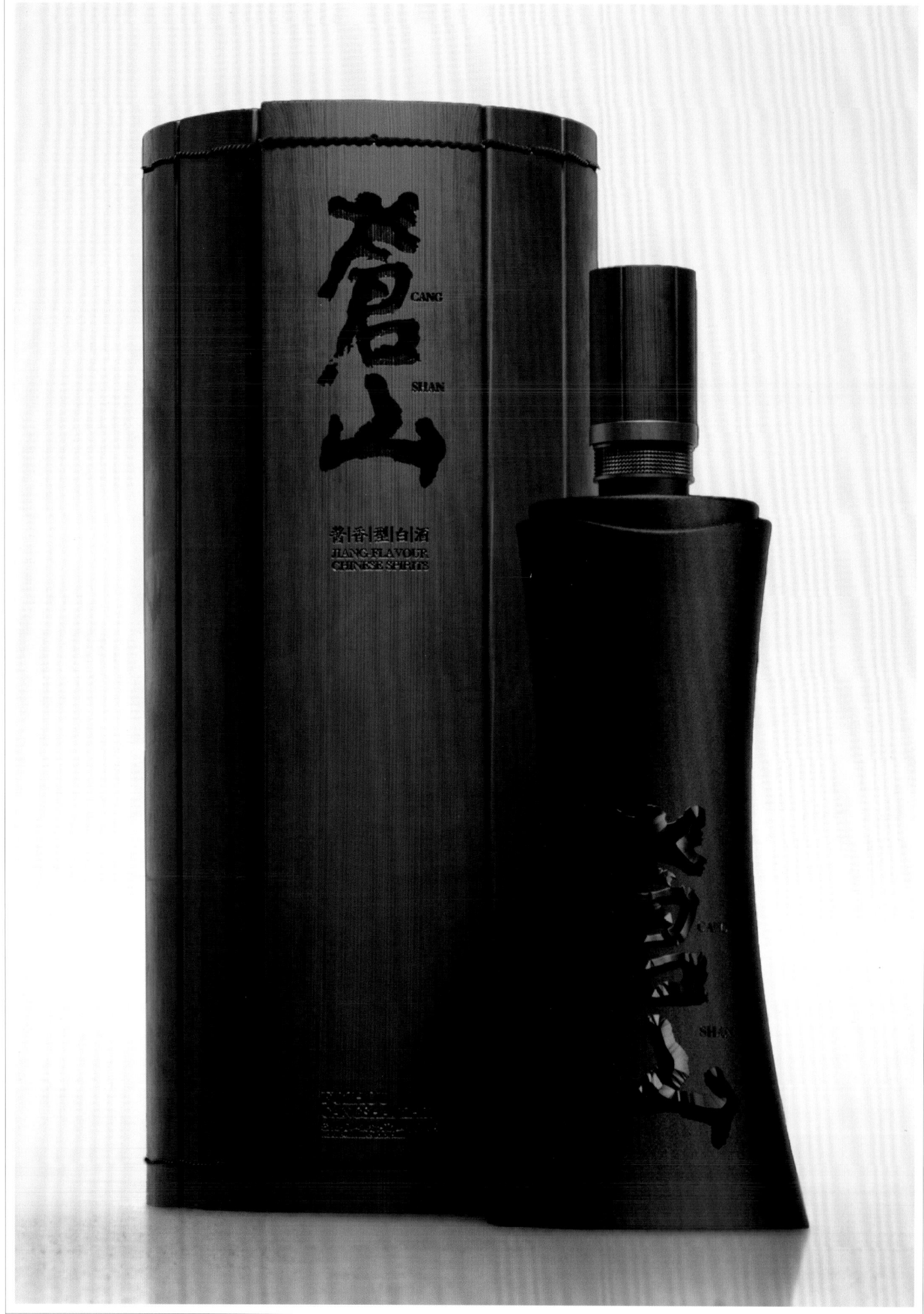

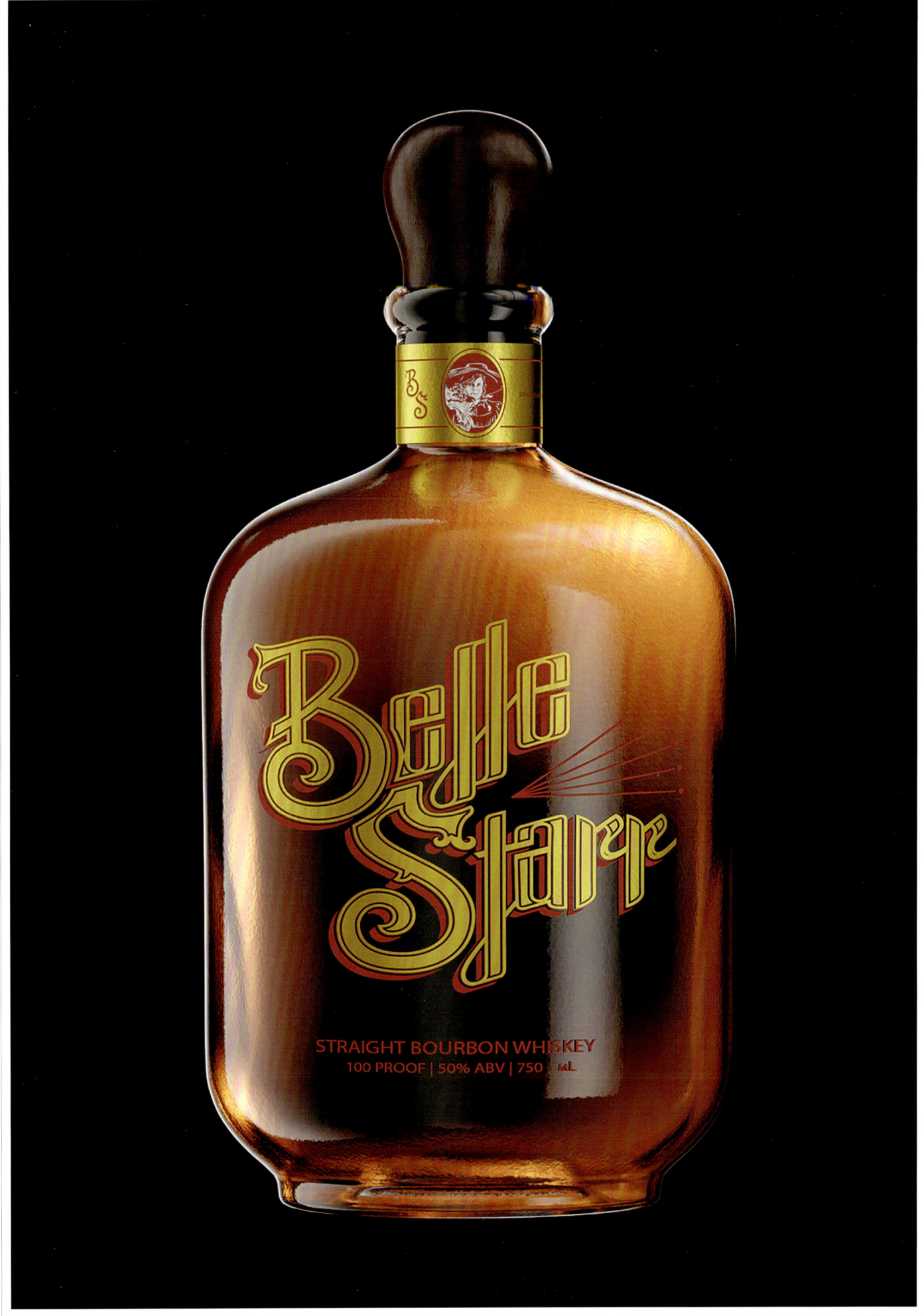

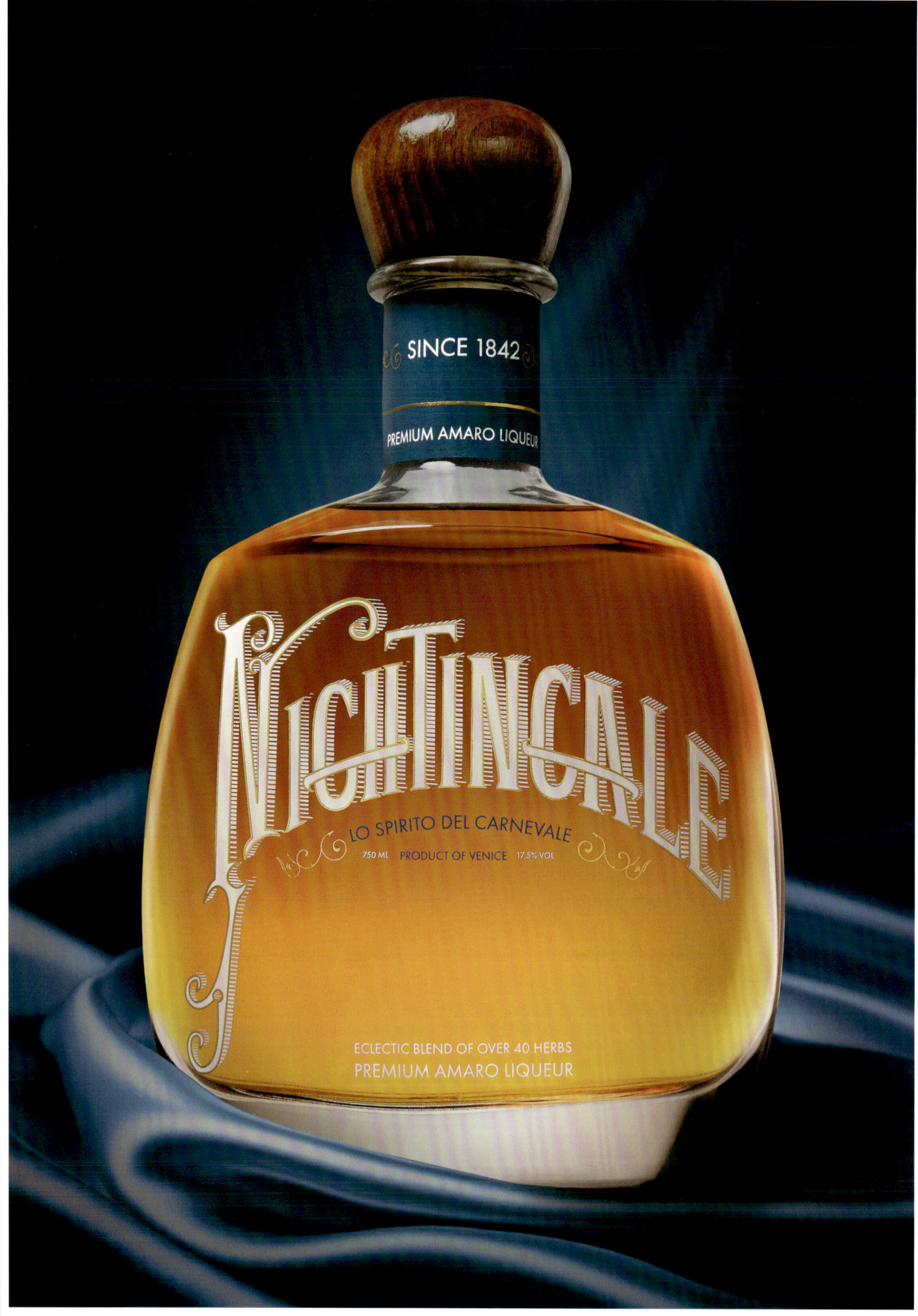

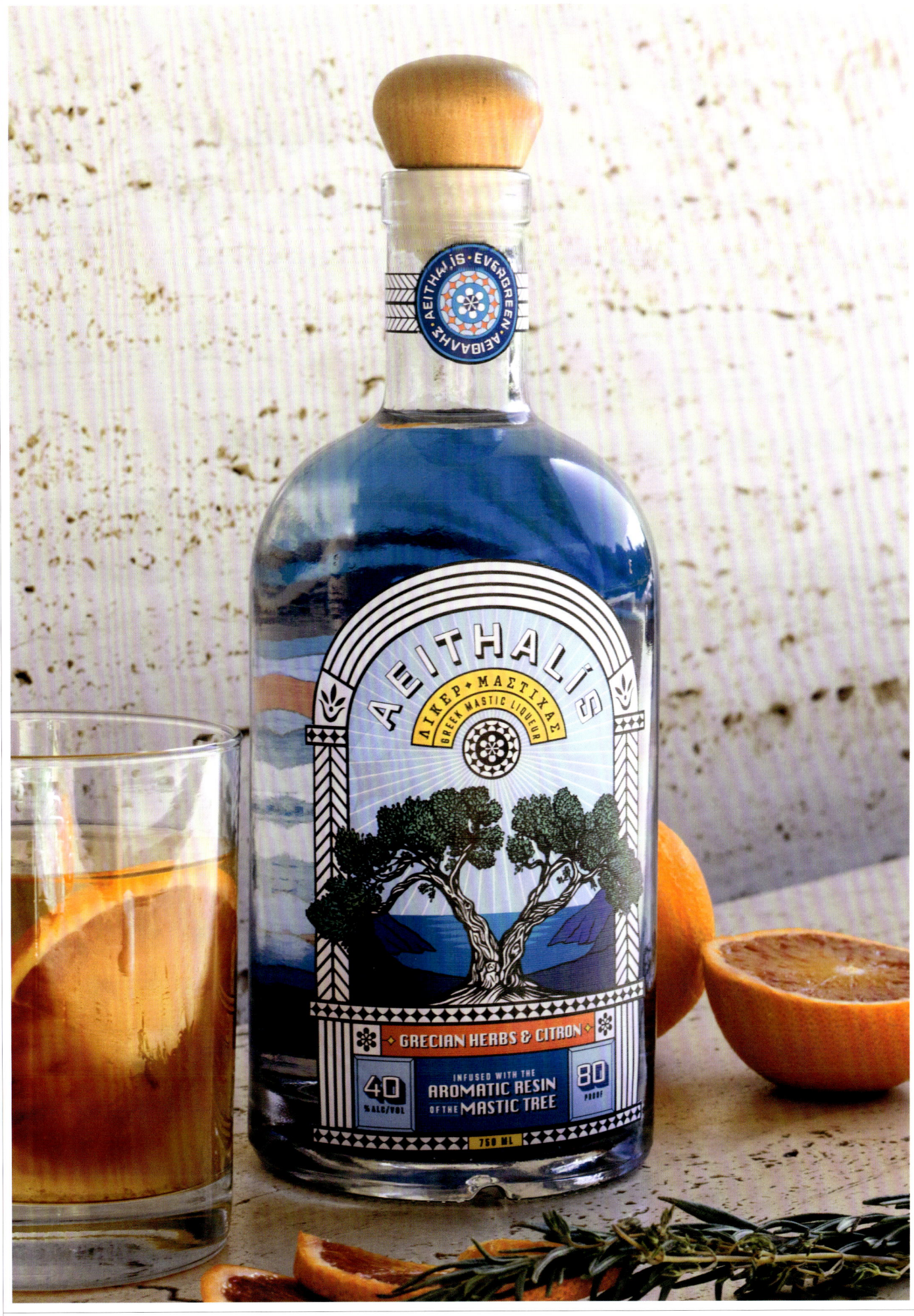

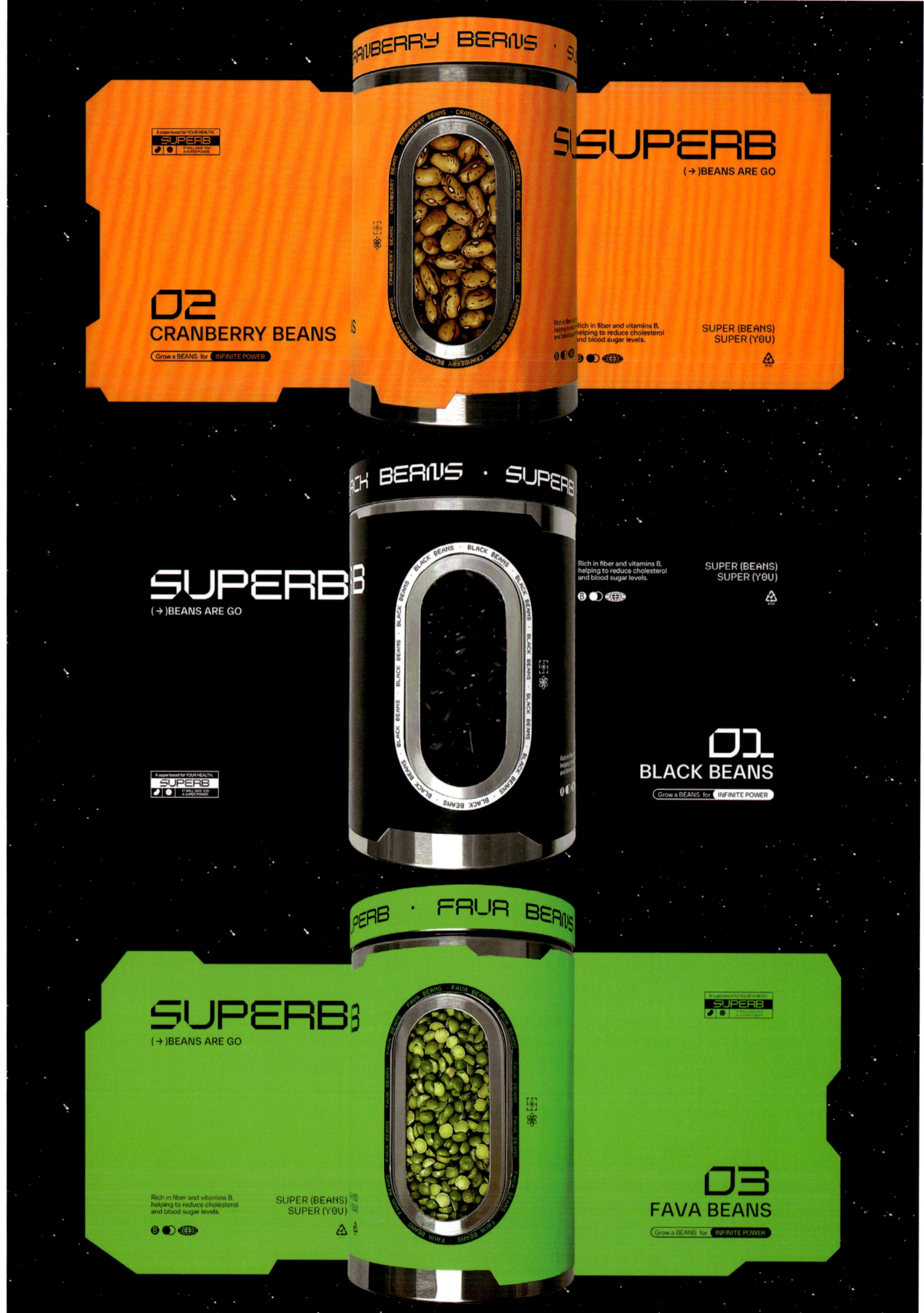

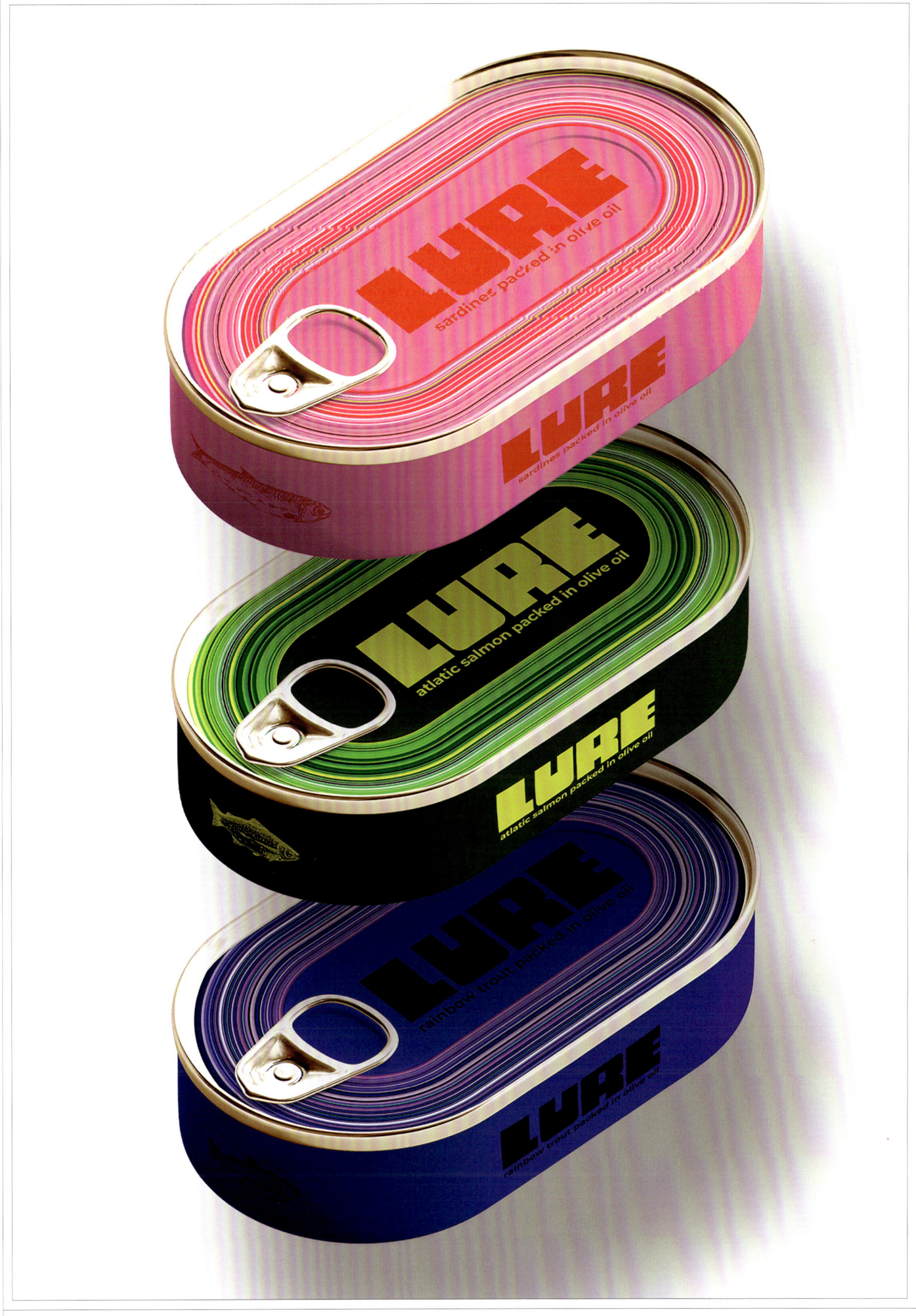

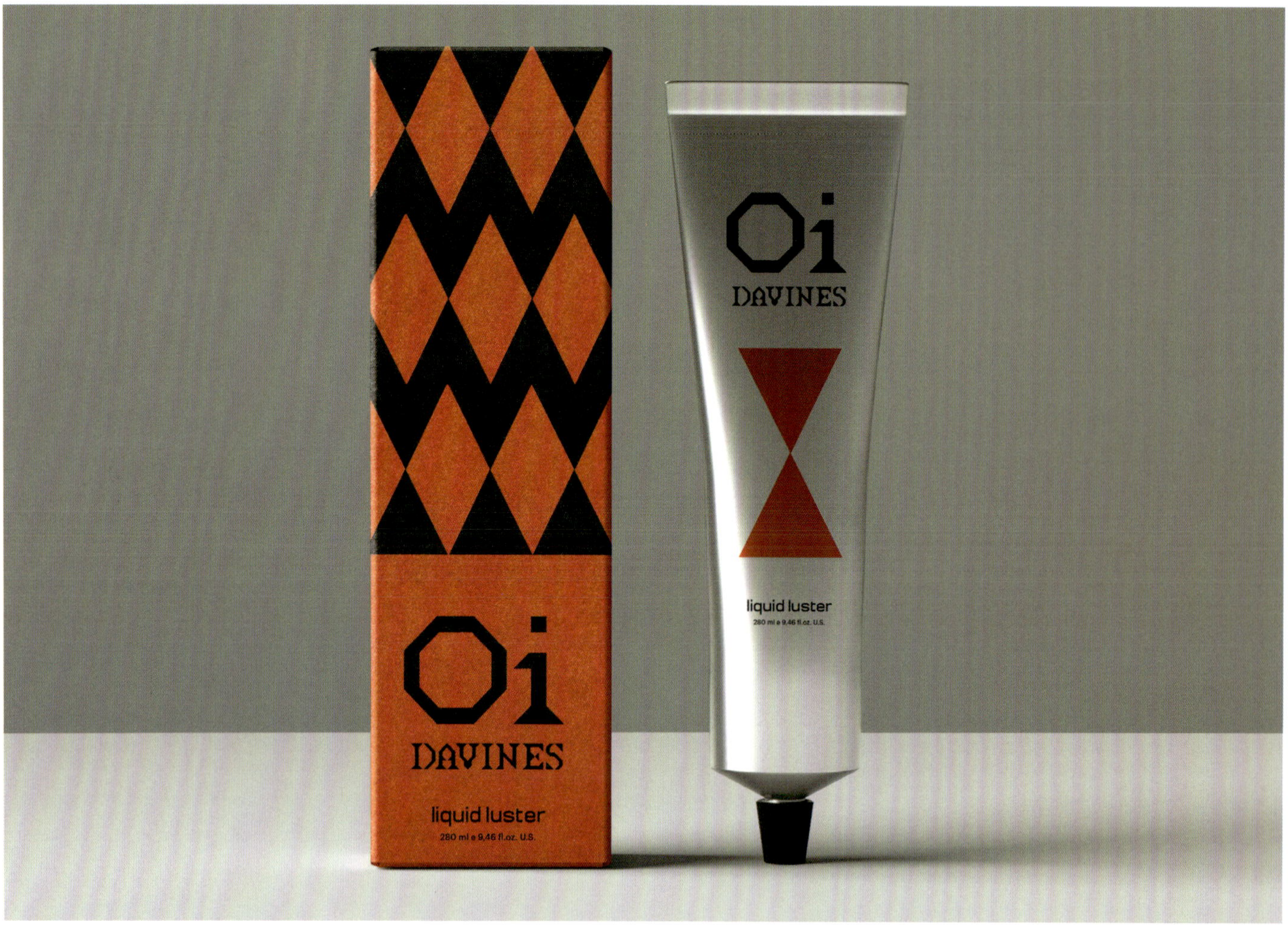

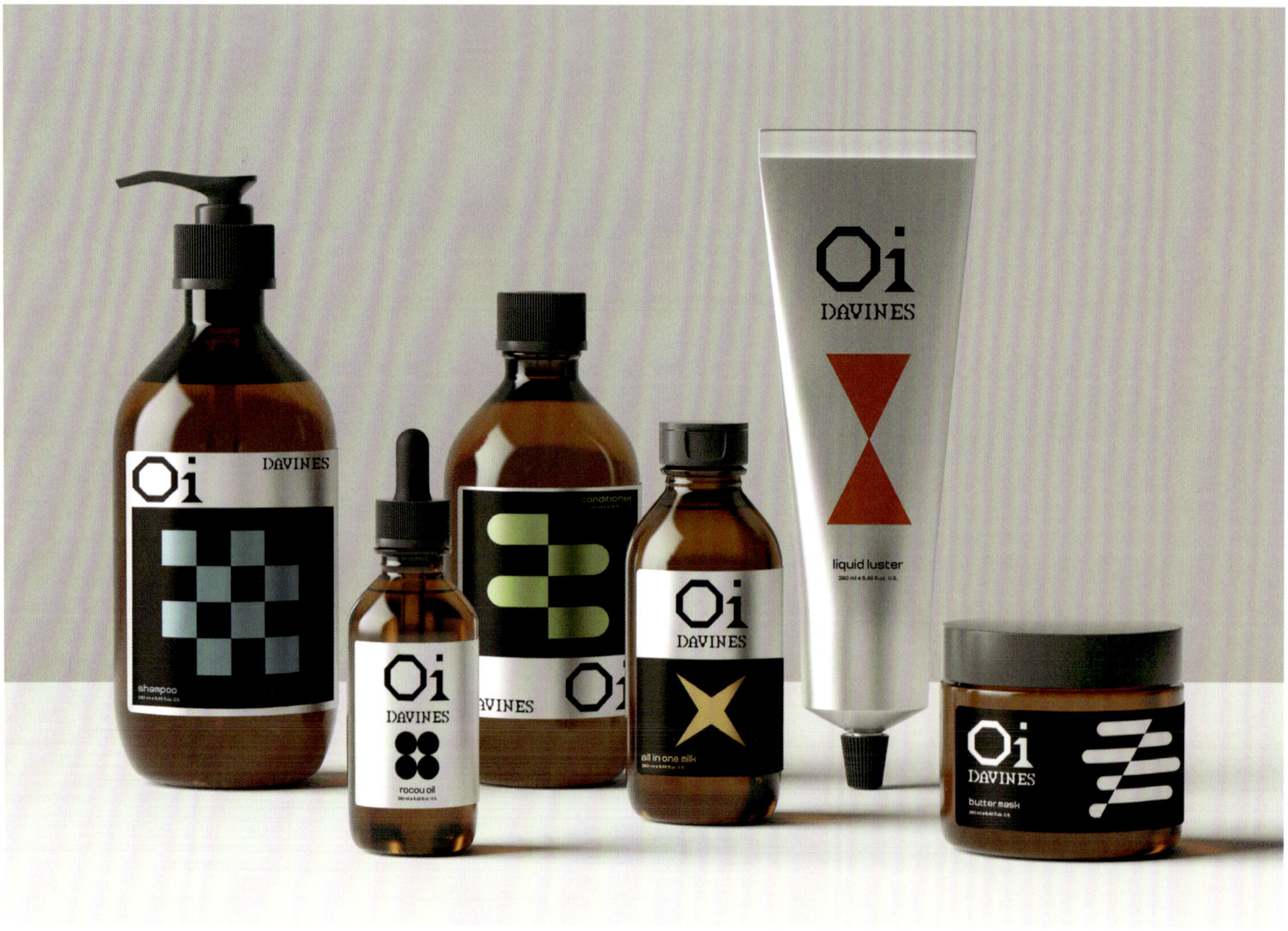

110 INSTRUCTOR **LINDA REYNOLDS** GOLD

P239: Credit & Commentary **Student:** Kate Holmes | **School:** Brigham Young University Images 1, 2 of 3

Design | Packaging

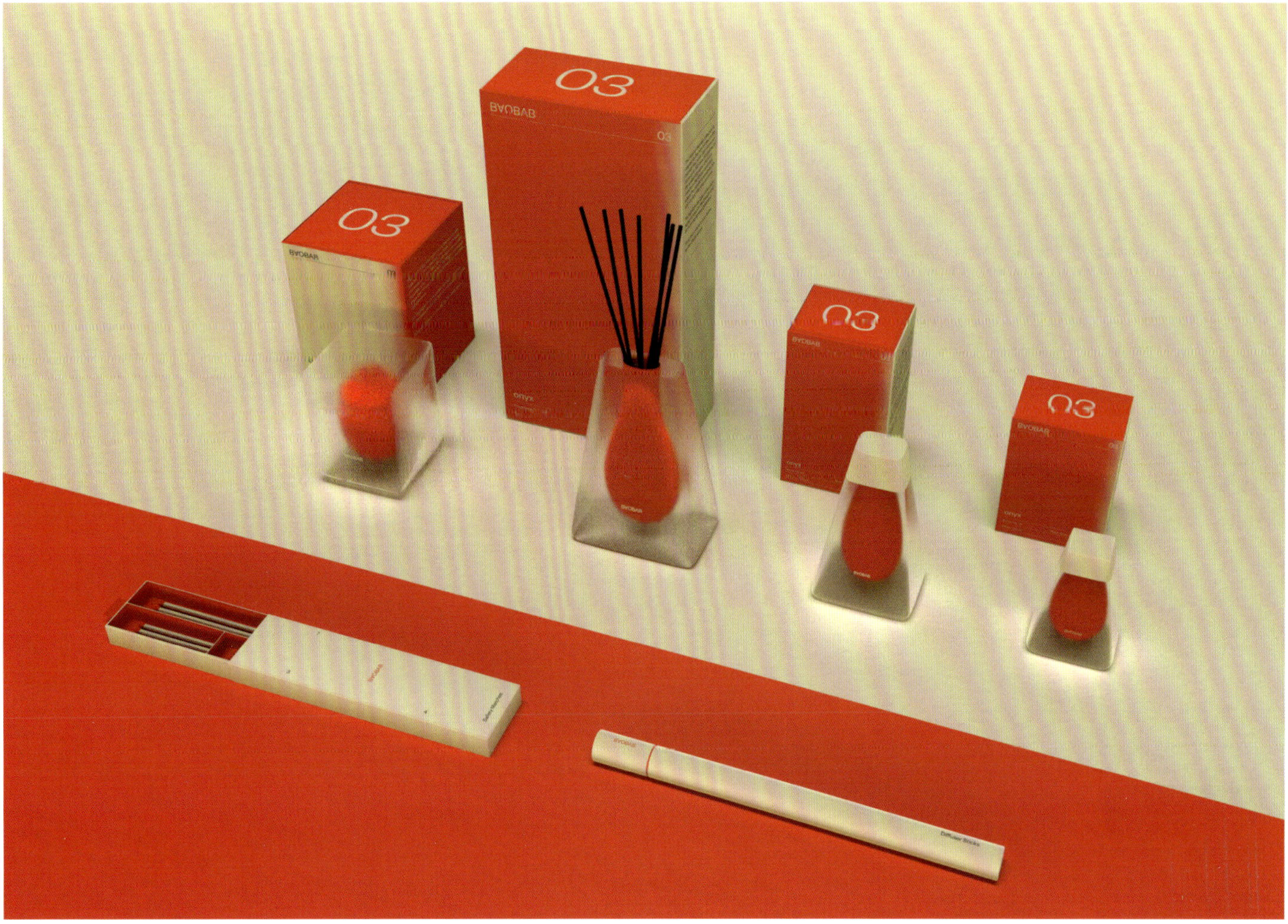

111 INSTRUCTOR **GERARDO HERRERA** GOLD

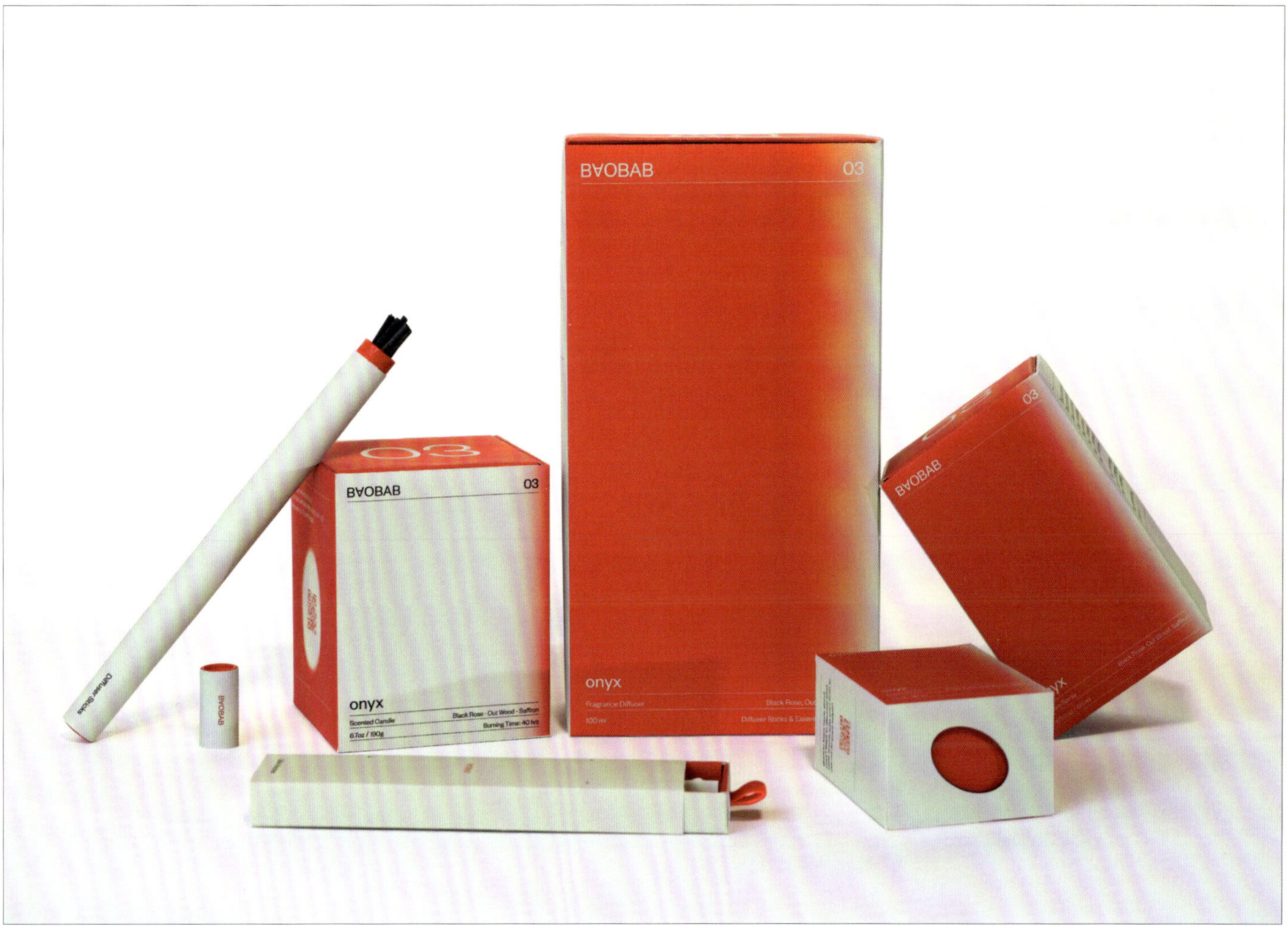

P239: Credit & Commentary | **Student:** Jocelyn Ziying Zhao | **School:** ArtCenter College of Design | Images 1, 2 of 7

Packaging | Design

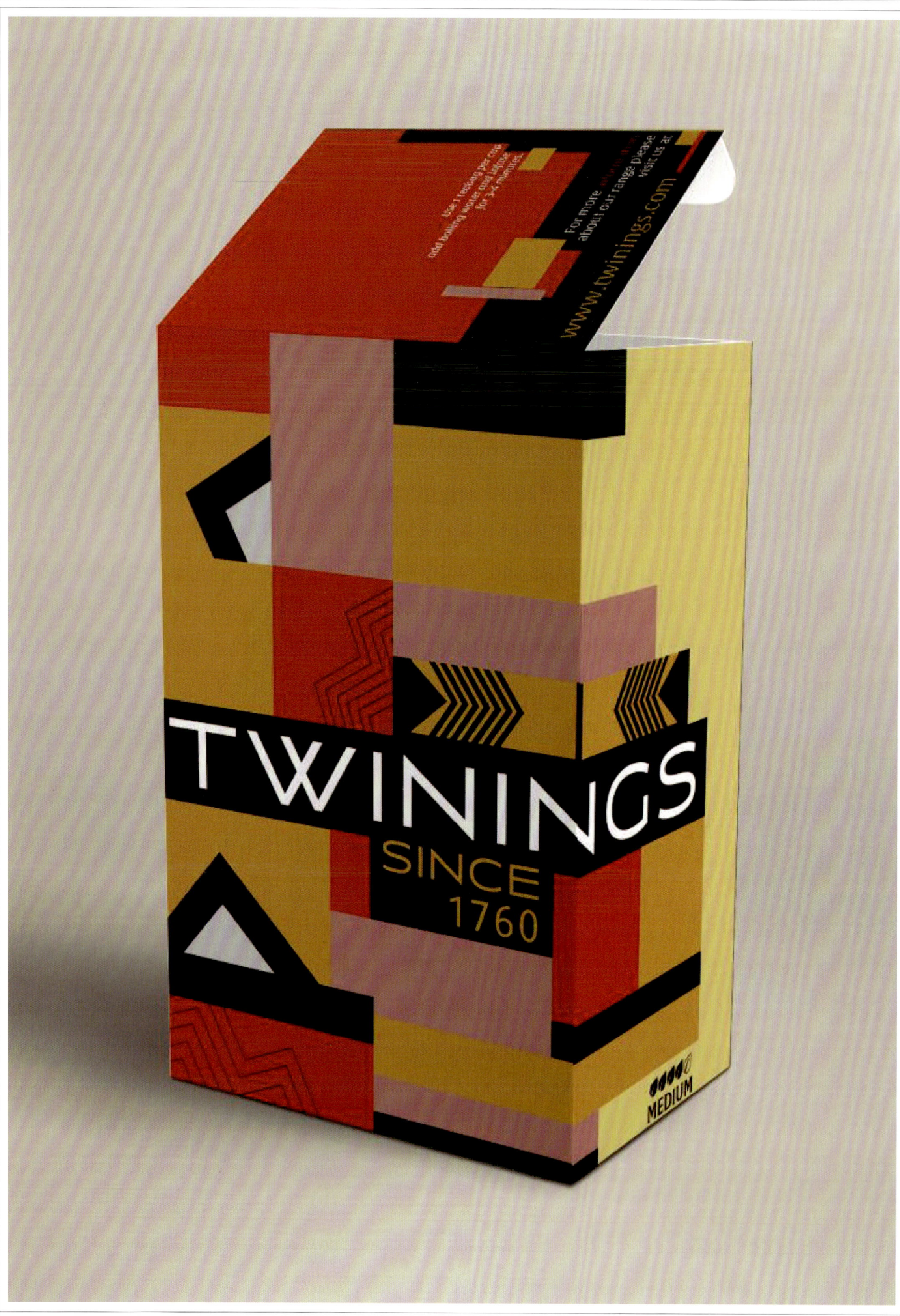

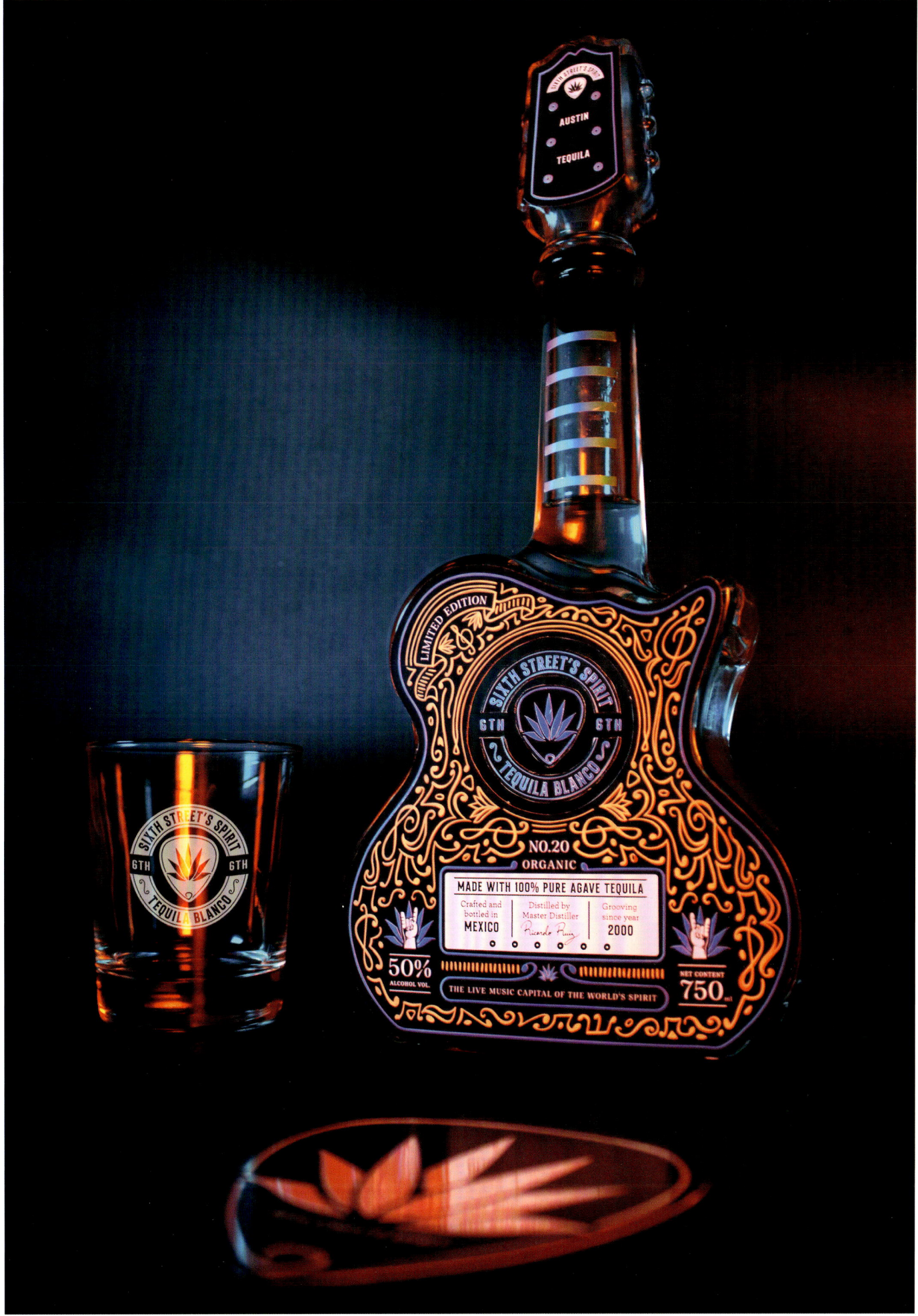

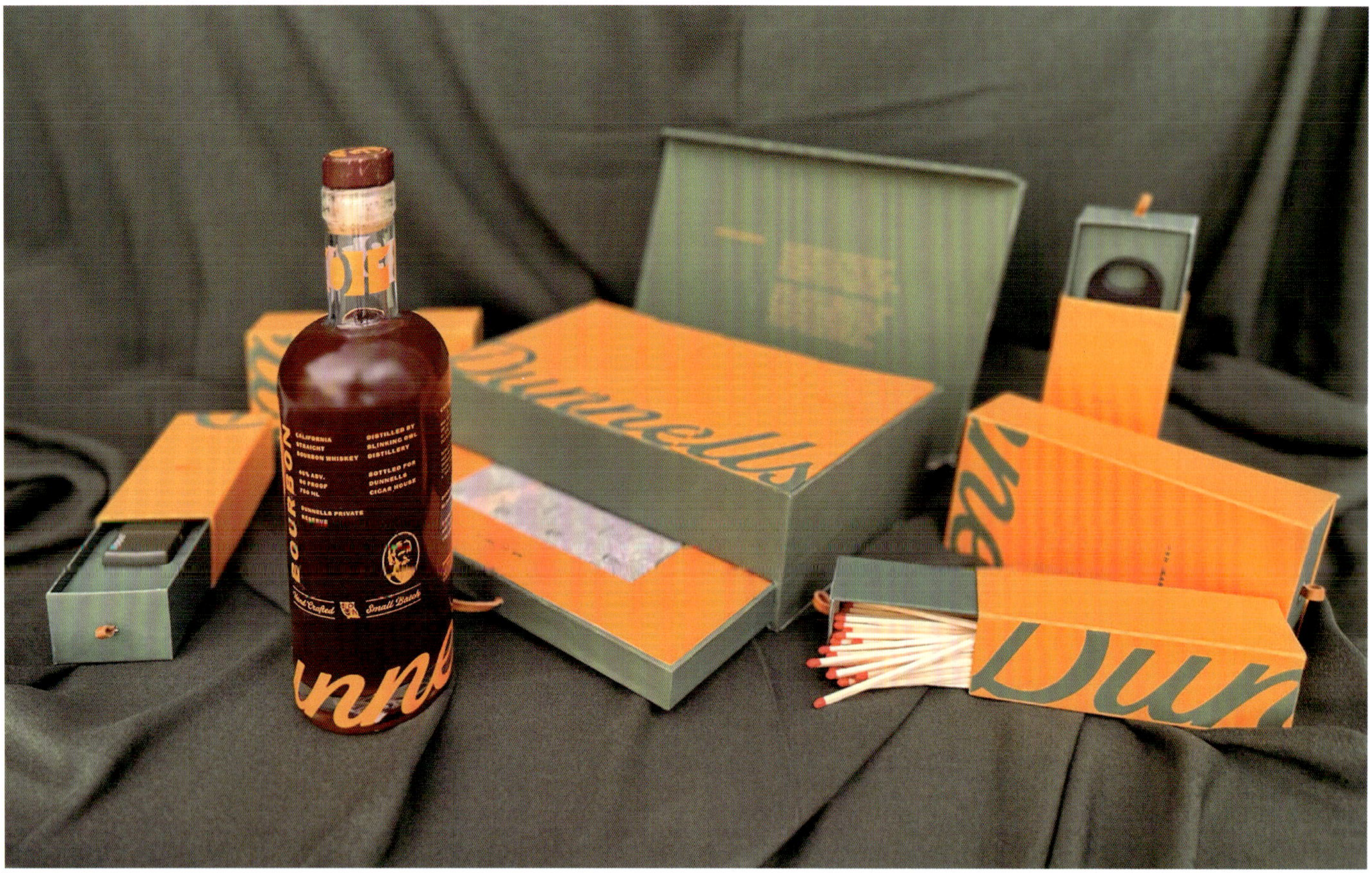

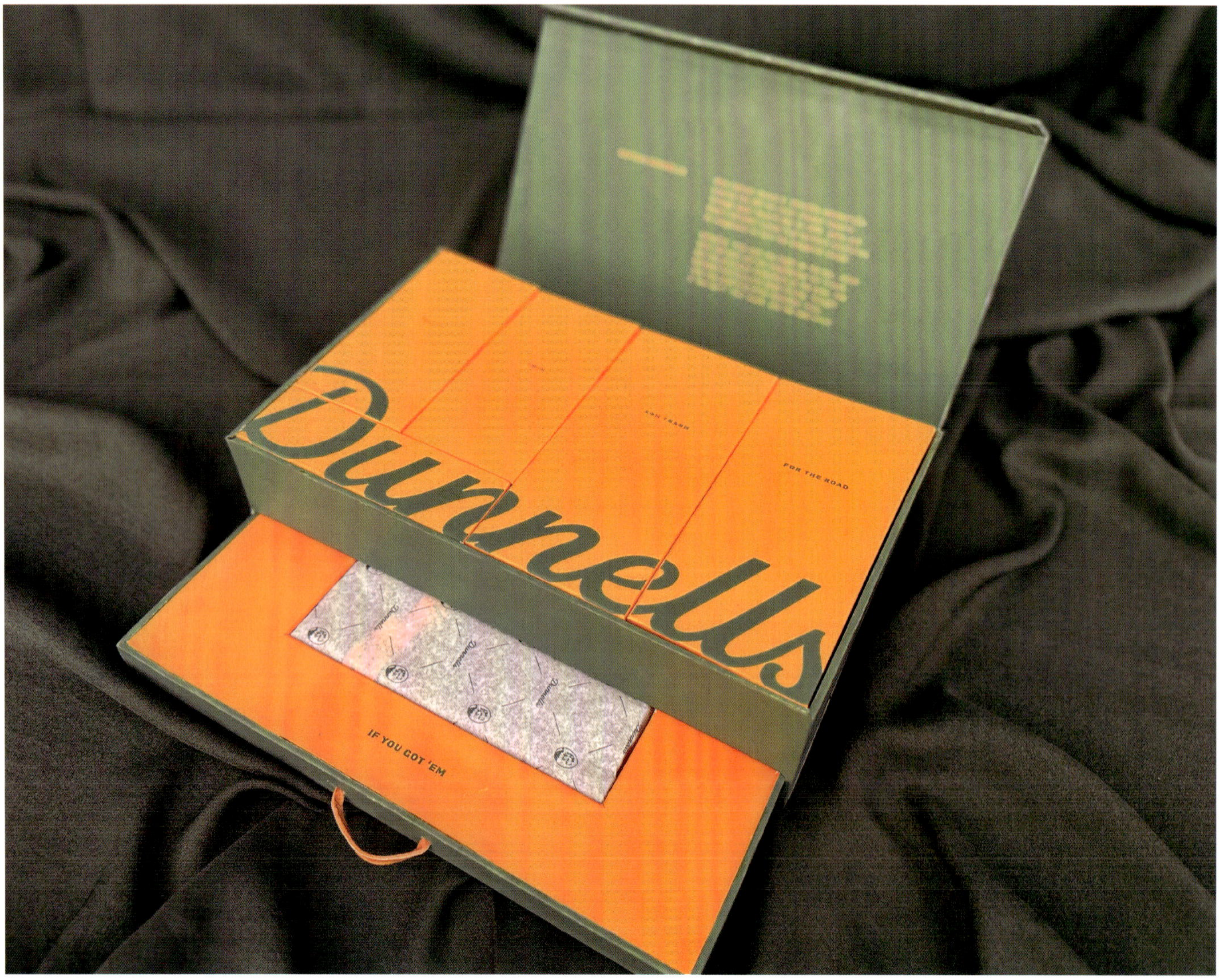

114 INSTRUCTOR **DAN HOY** GOLD

P239: Credit & Commentary **Student:** Brian White | **School:** ArtCenter College of Design Images 1, 2 of 7

Design | Packaging

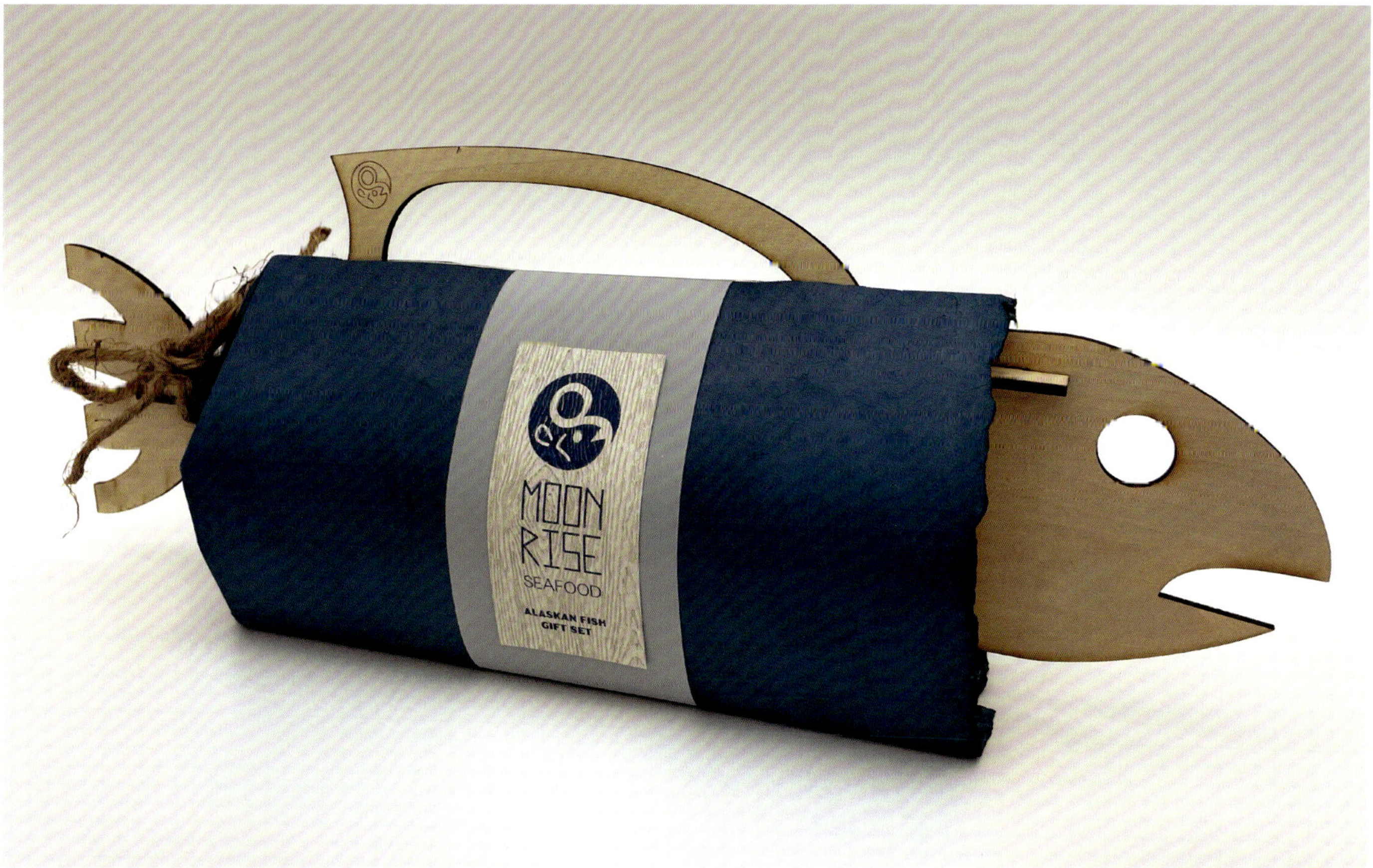

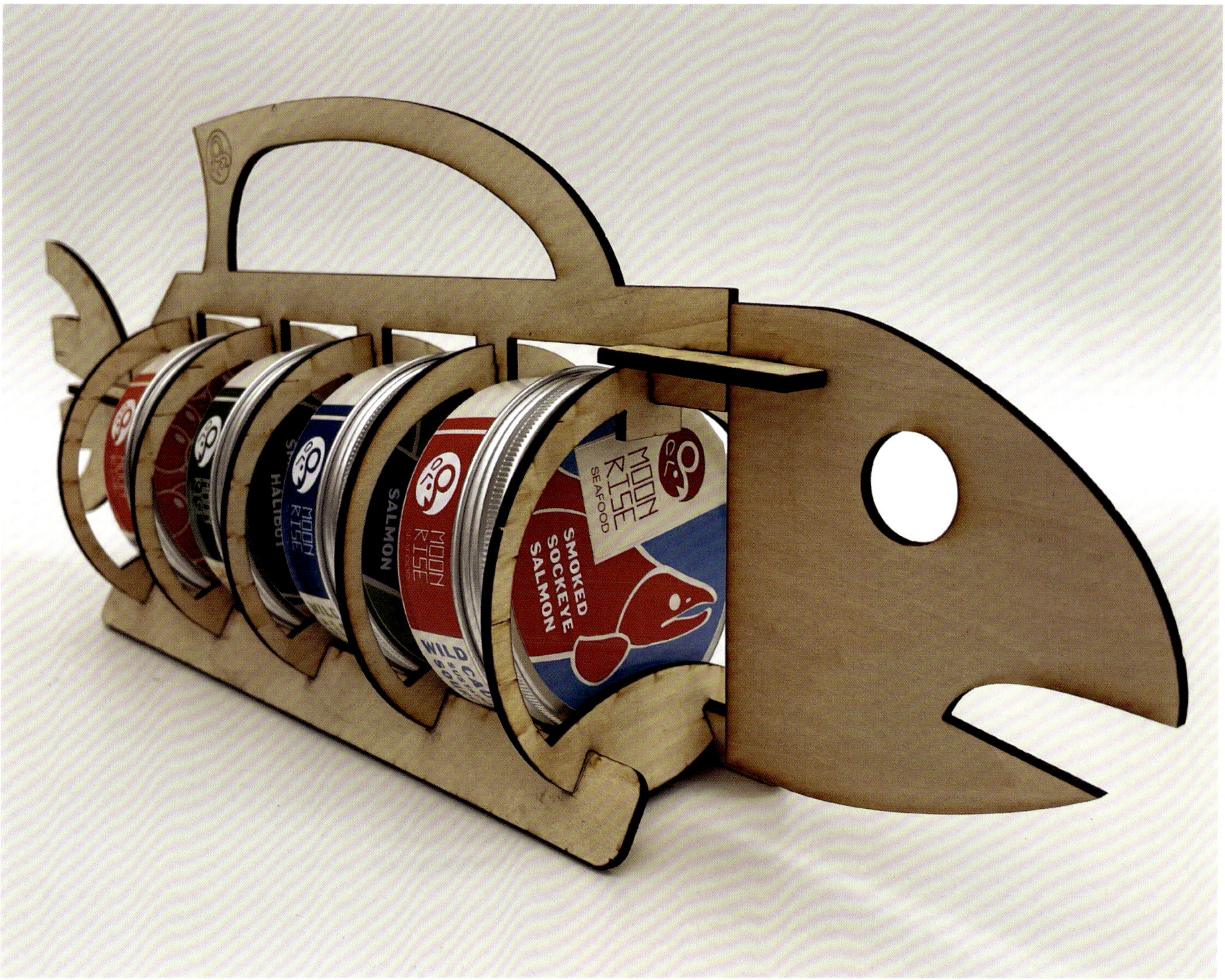

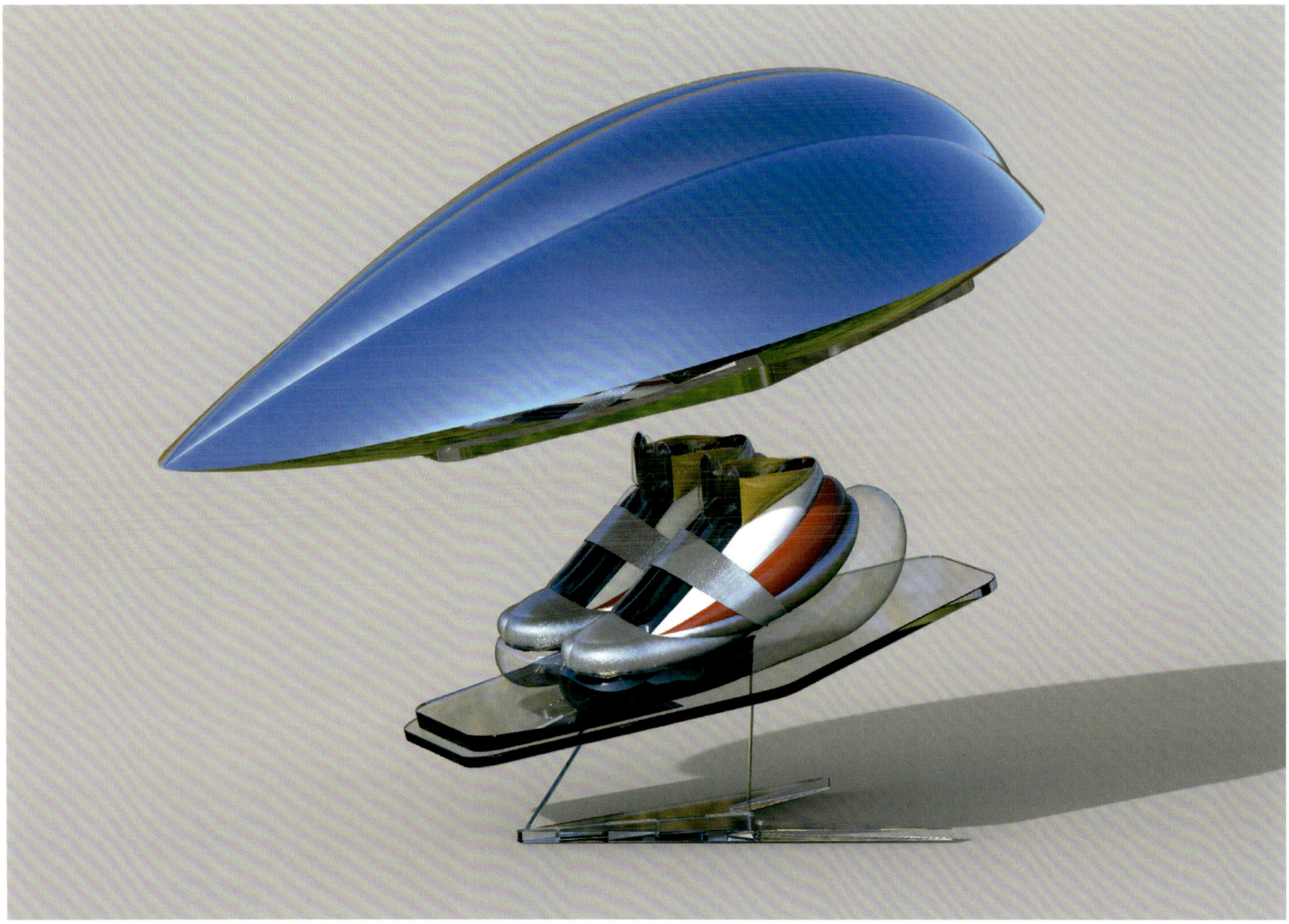

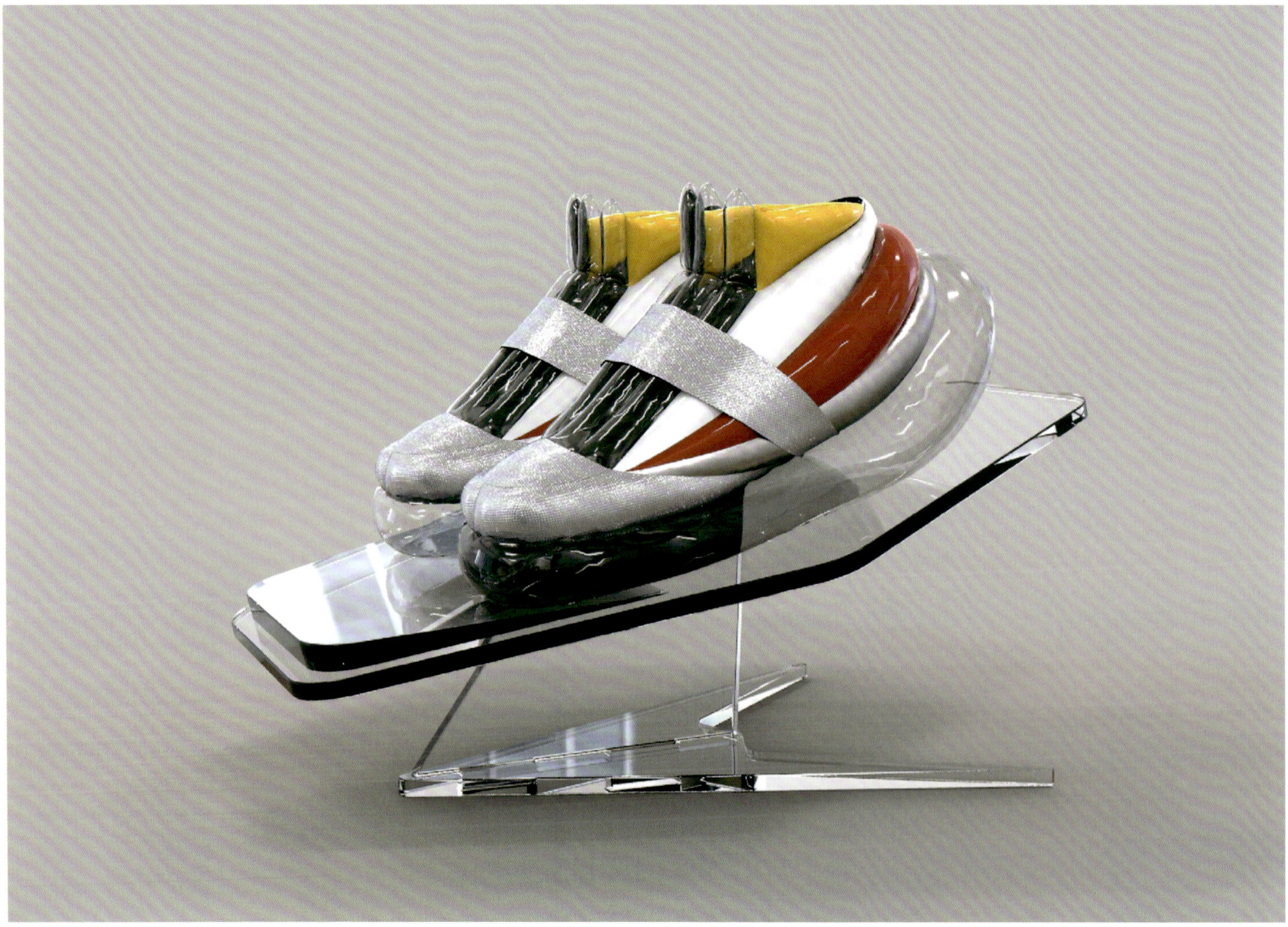

116 INSTRUCTOR **HADAR KFIR** GOLD

P239: Credit & Commentary   **Student:** Wen-Chi Hsueh | **School:** Pratt Institute   Images 1, 2 of 7

Design | Packaging

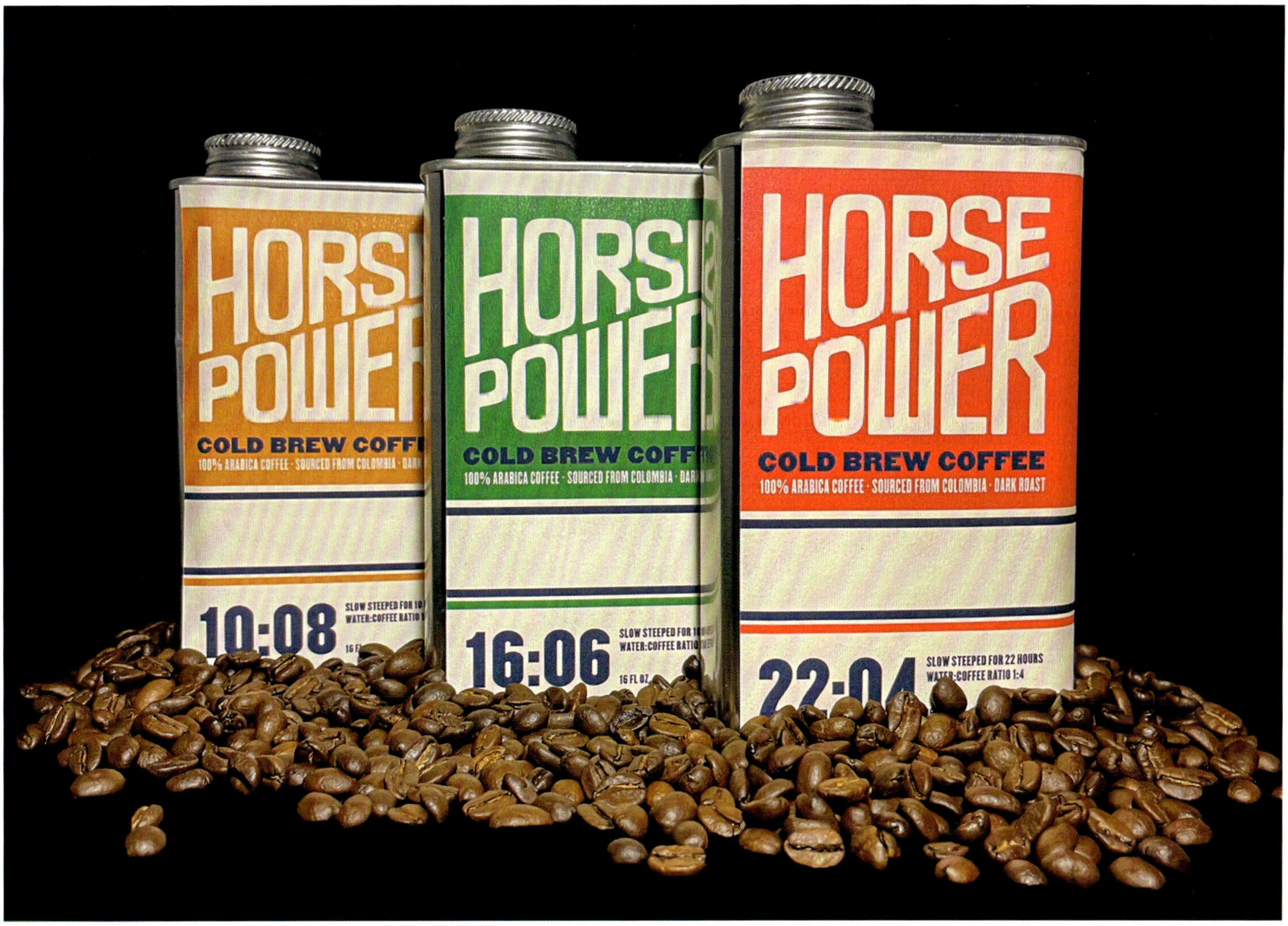

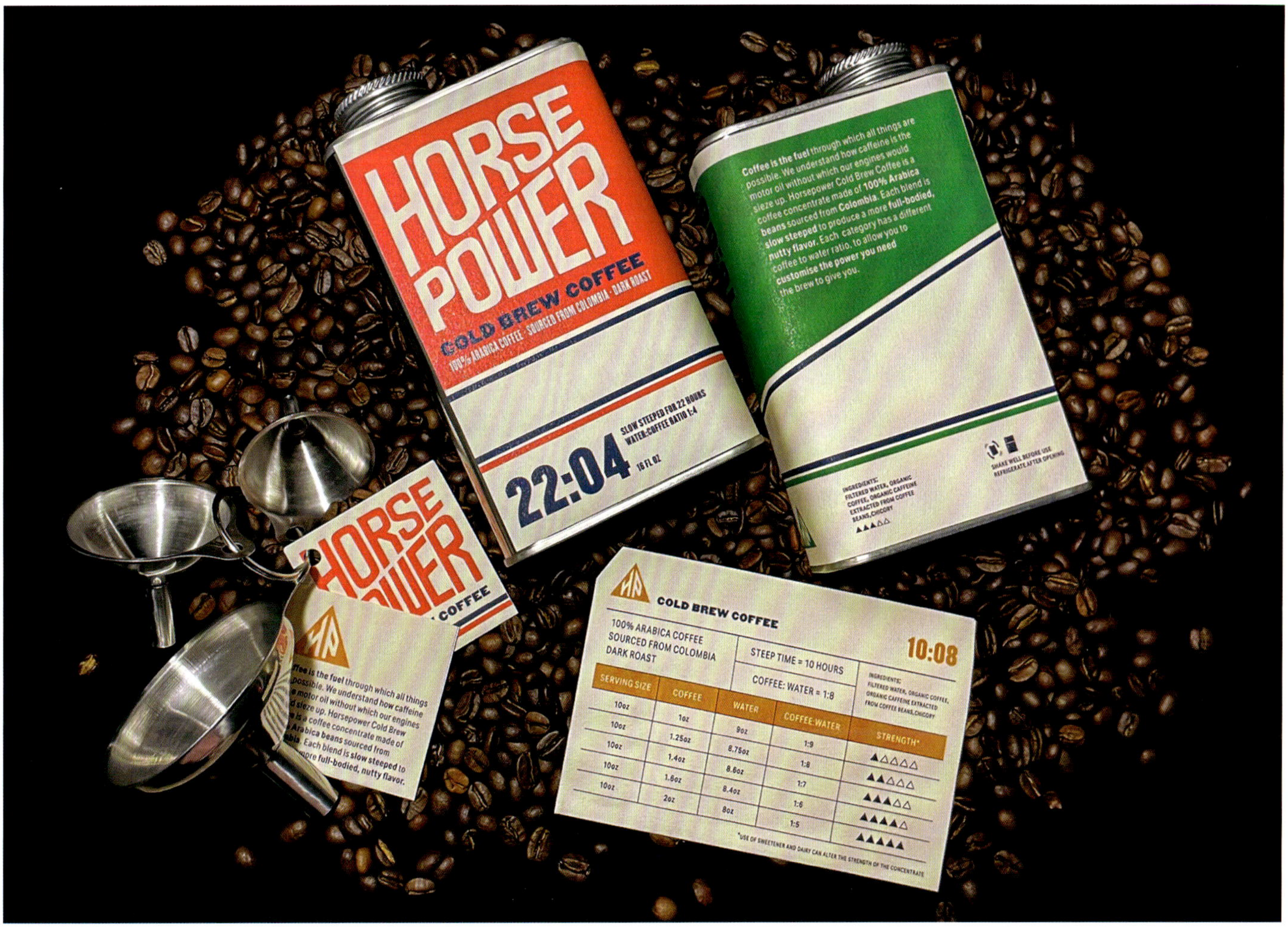

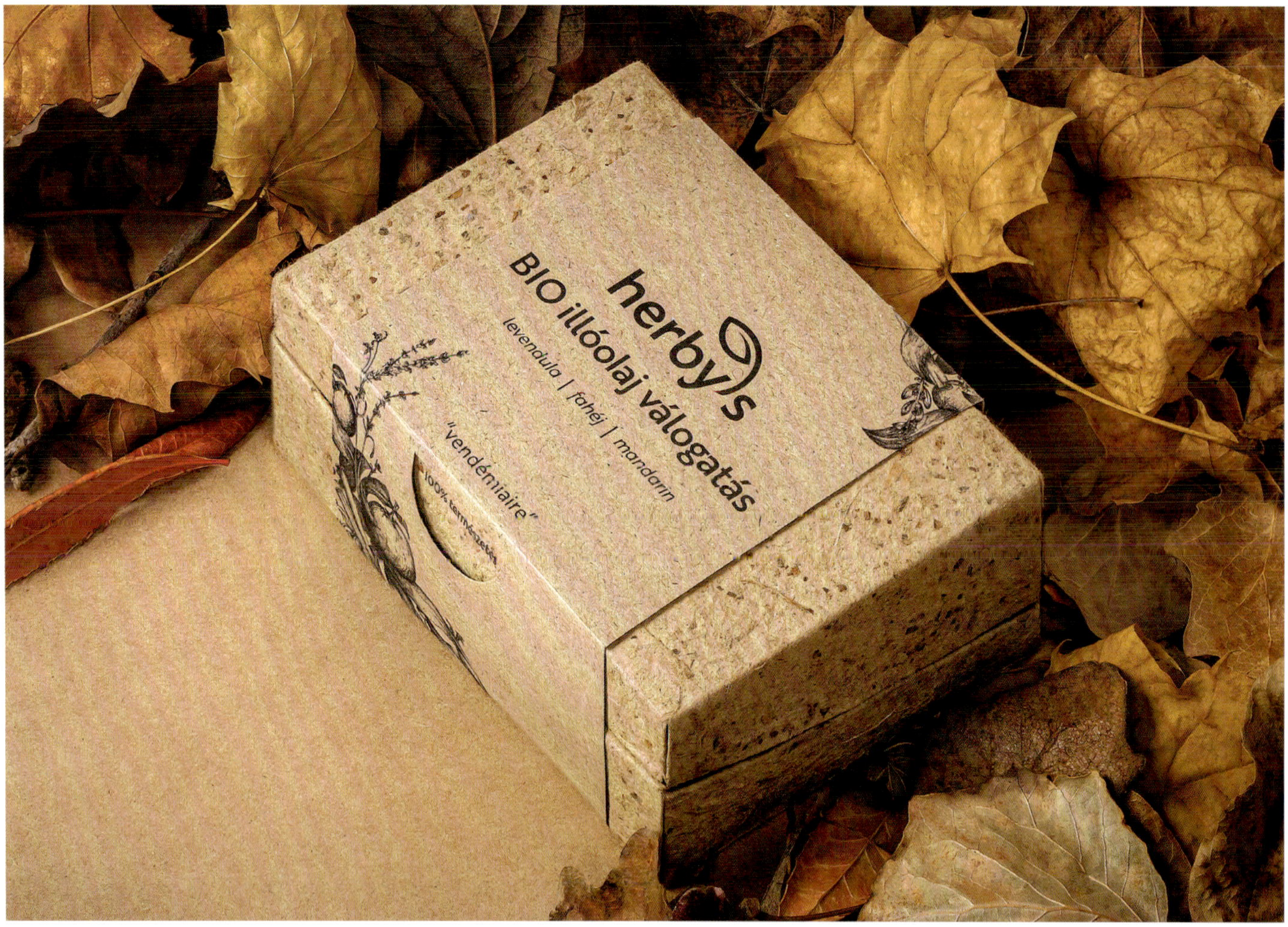

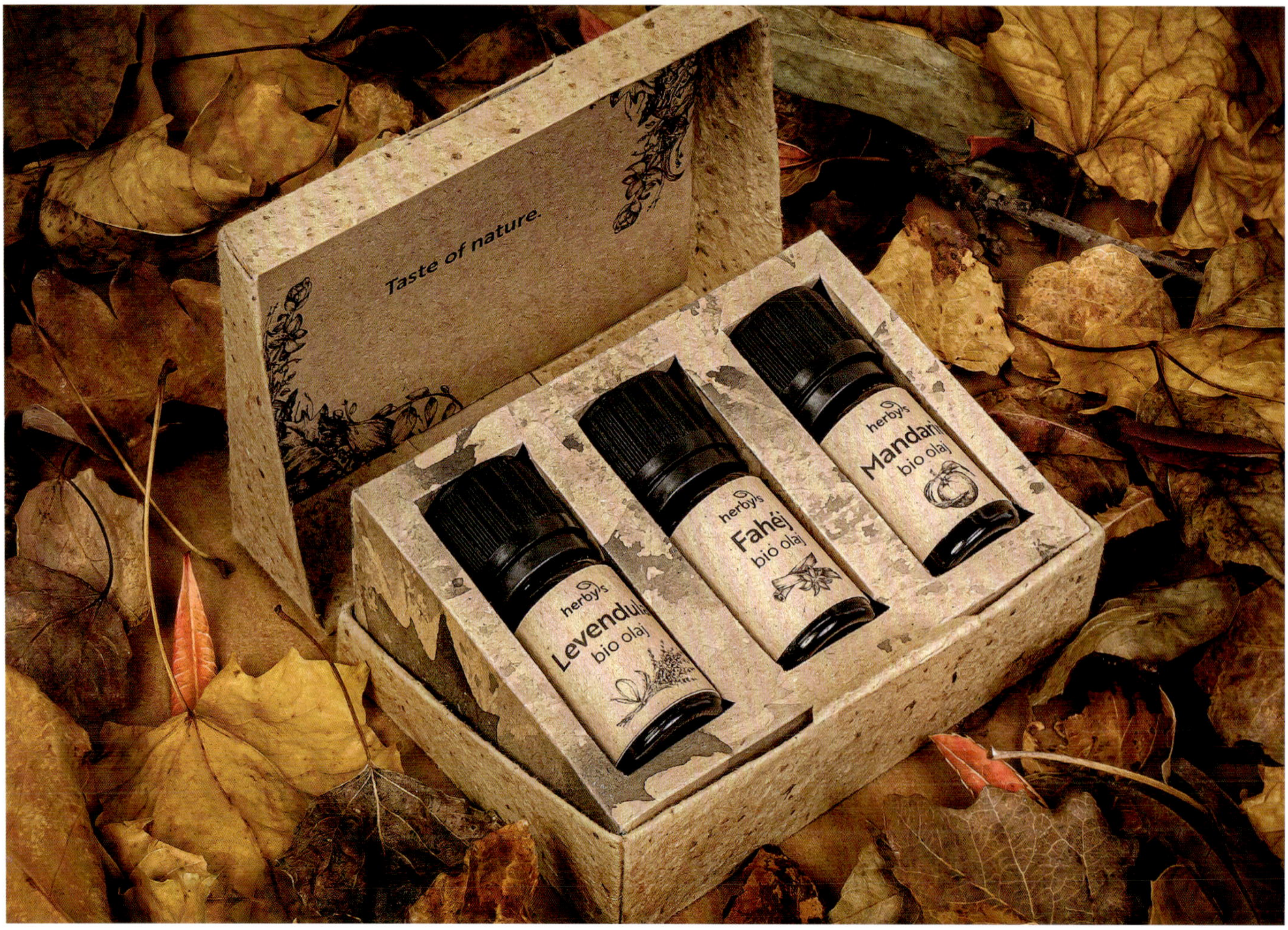

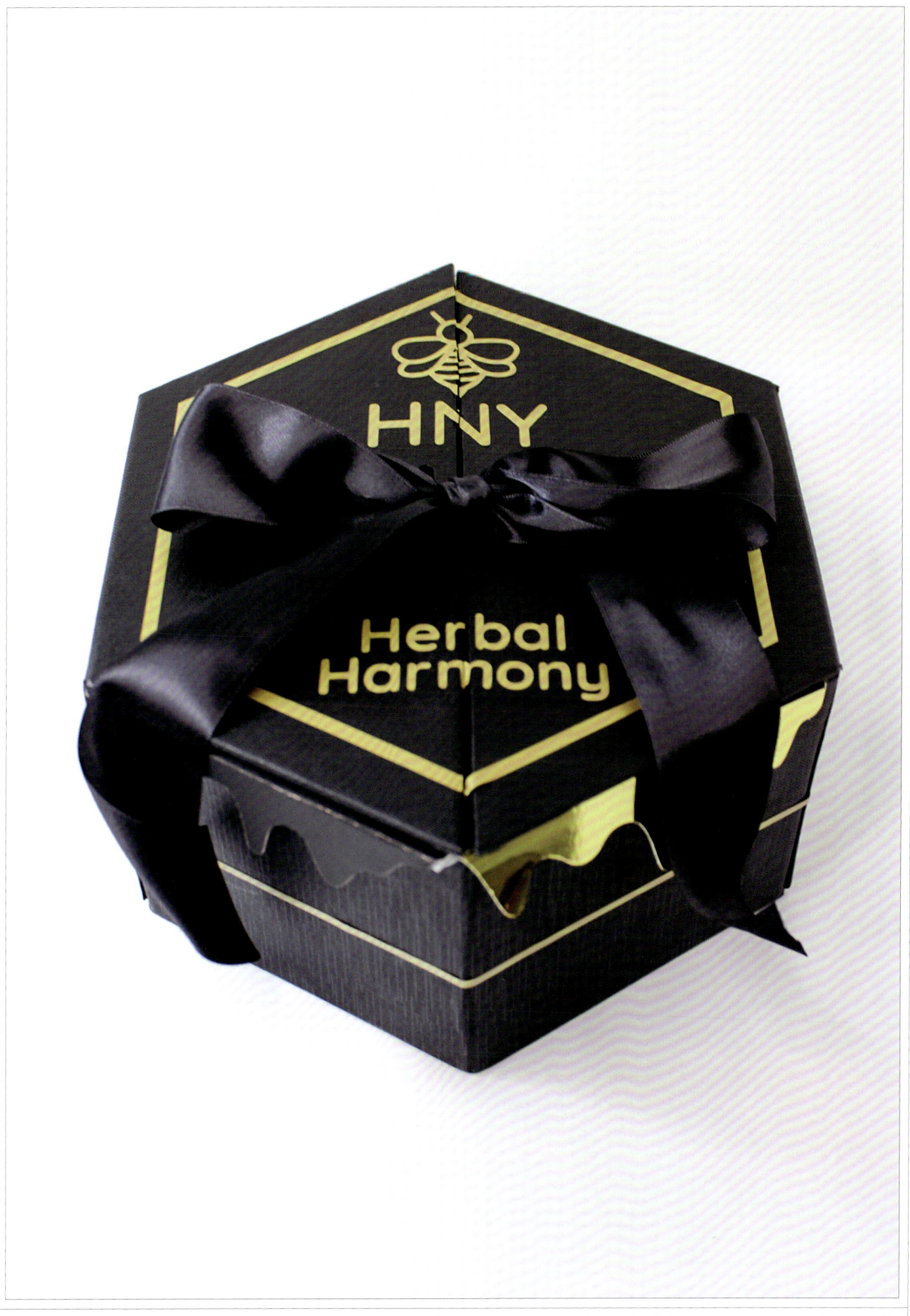

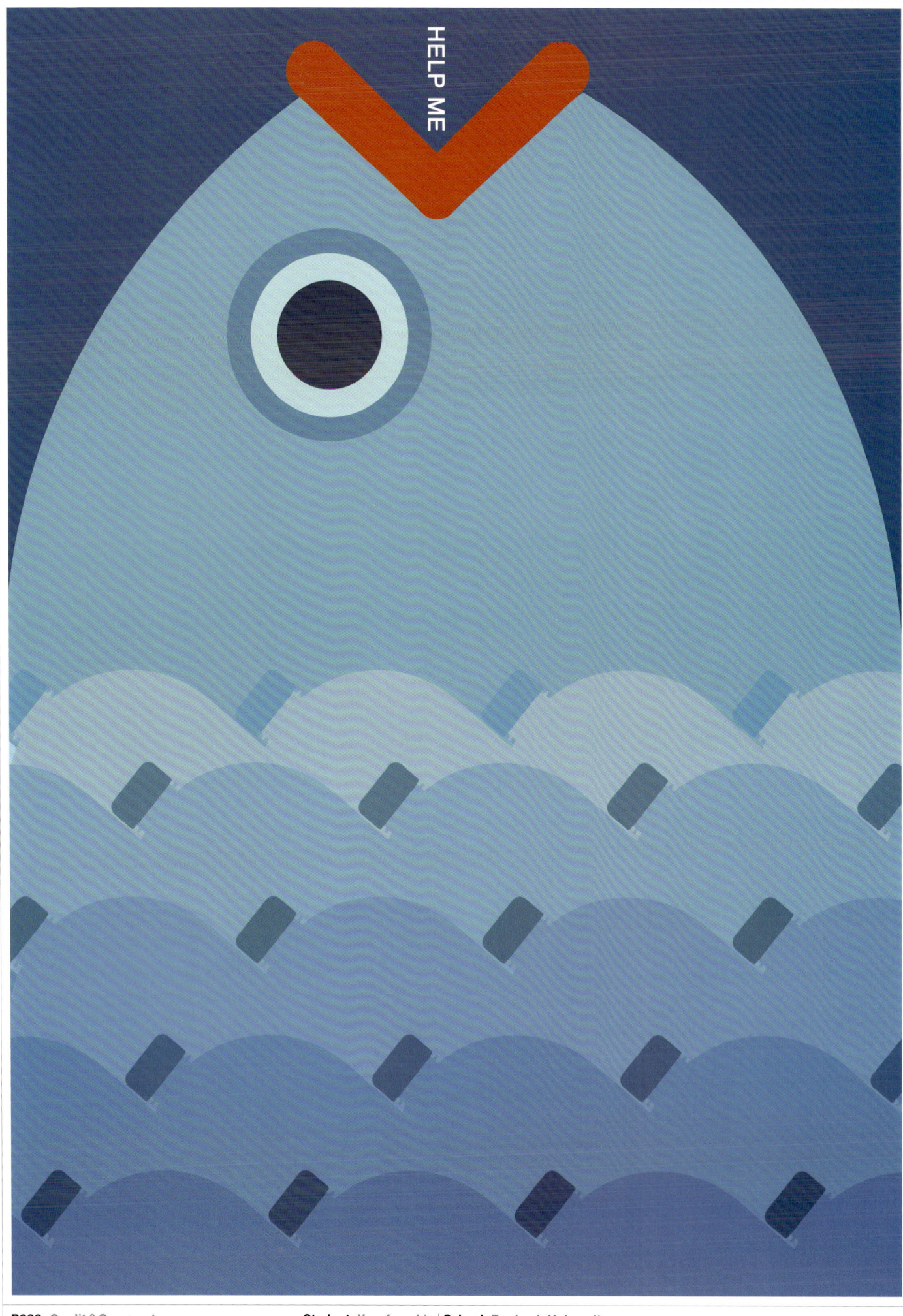

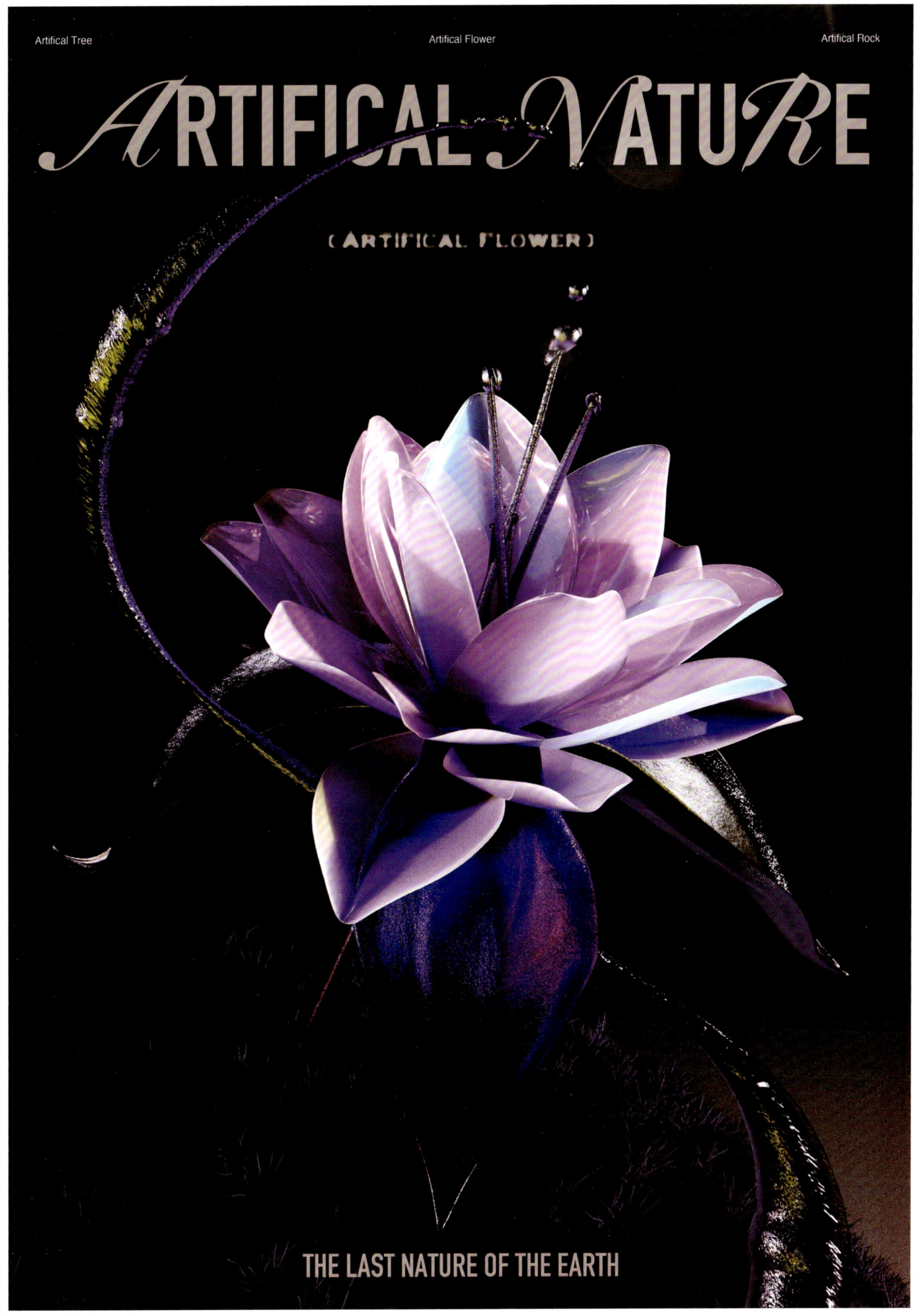

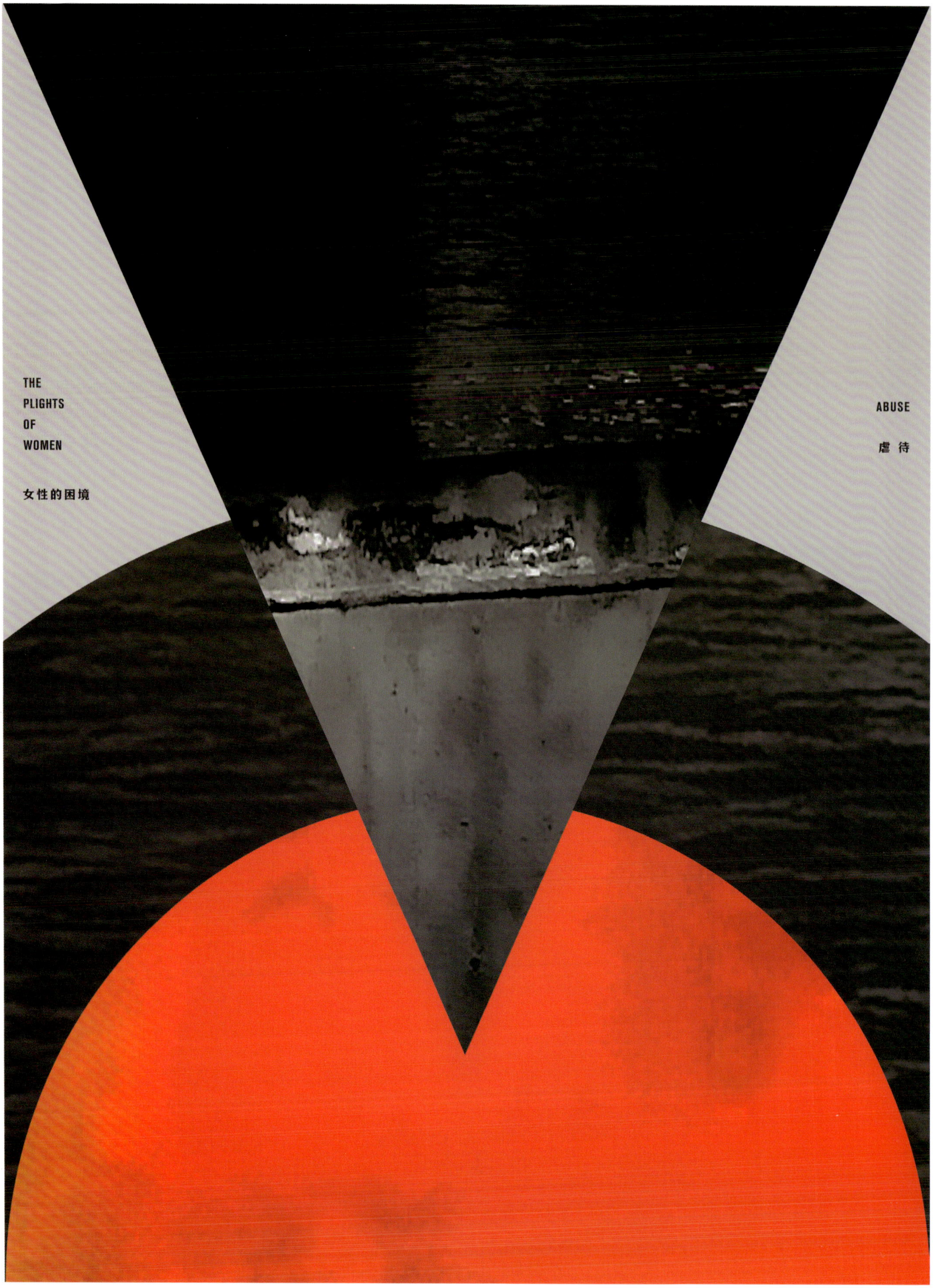

122 INSTRUCTOR **NANCY SKOLOS** GOLD

THE
PLIGHTS
OF
WOMEN

女性的困境

ABUSE

虐 待

P239: Credit & Commentary   **Student:** Shuixin Wang | **School:** Rhode Island School of Design   Image 1 of 7

Design | Poster

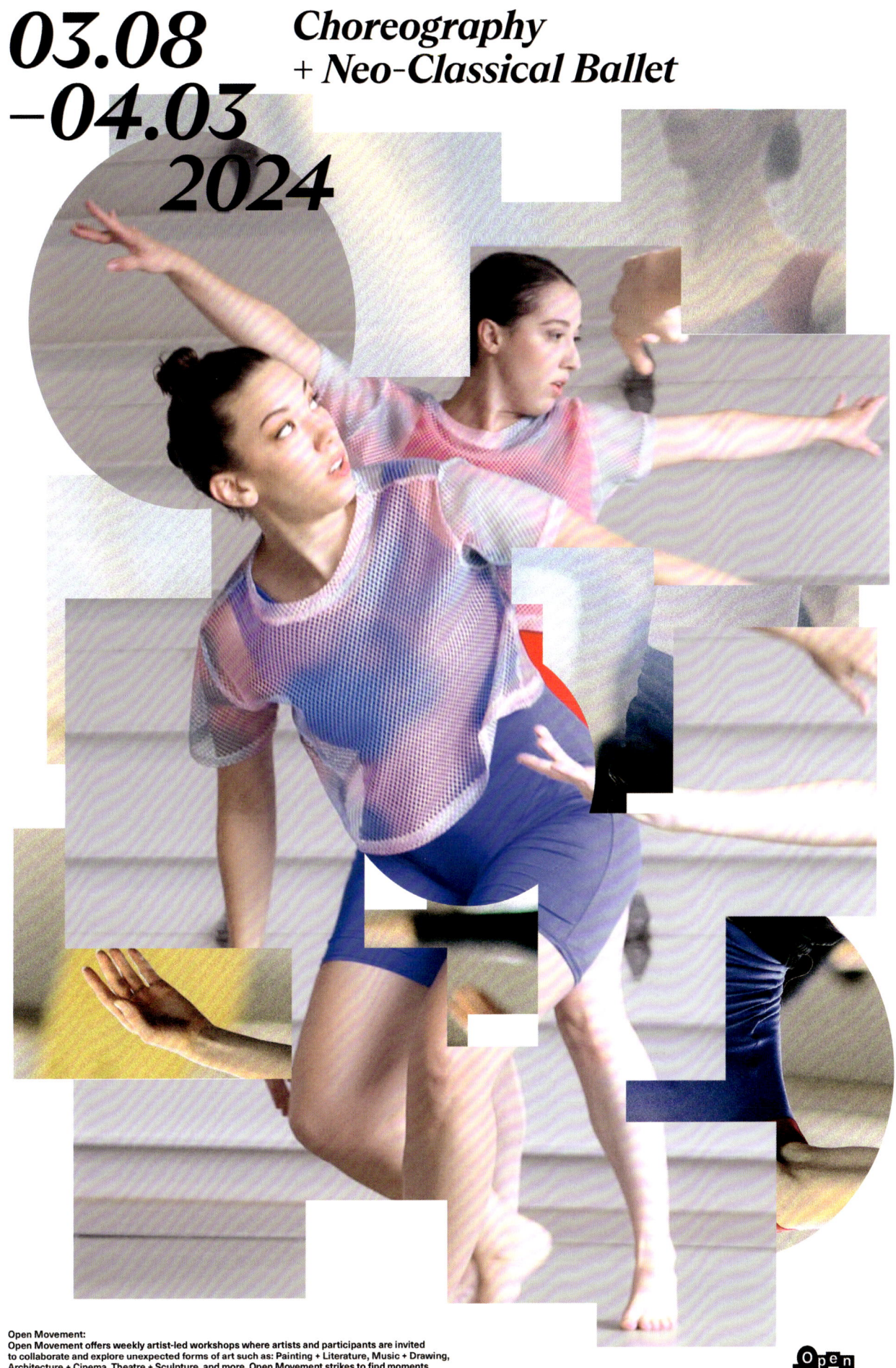

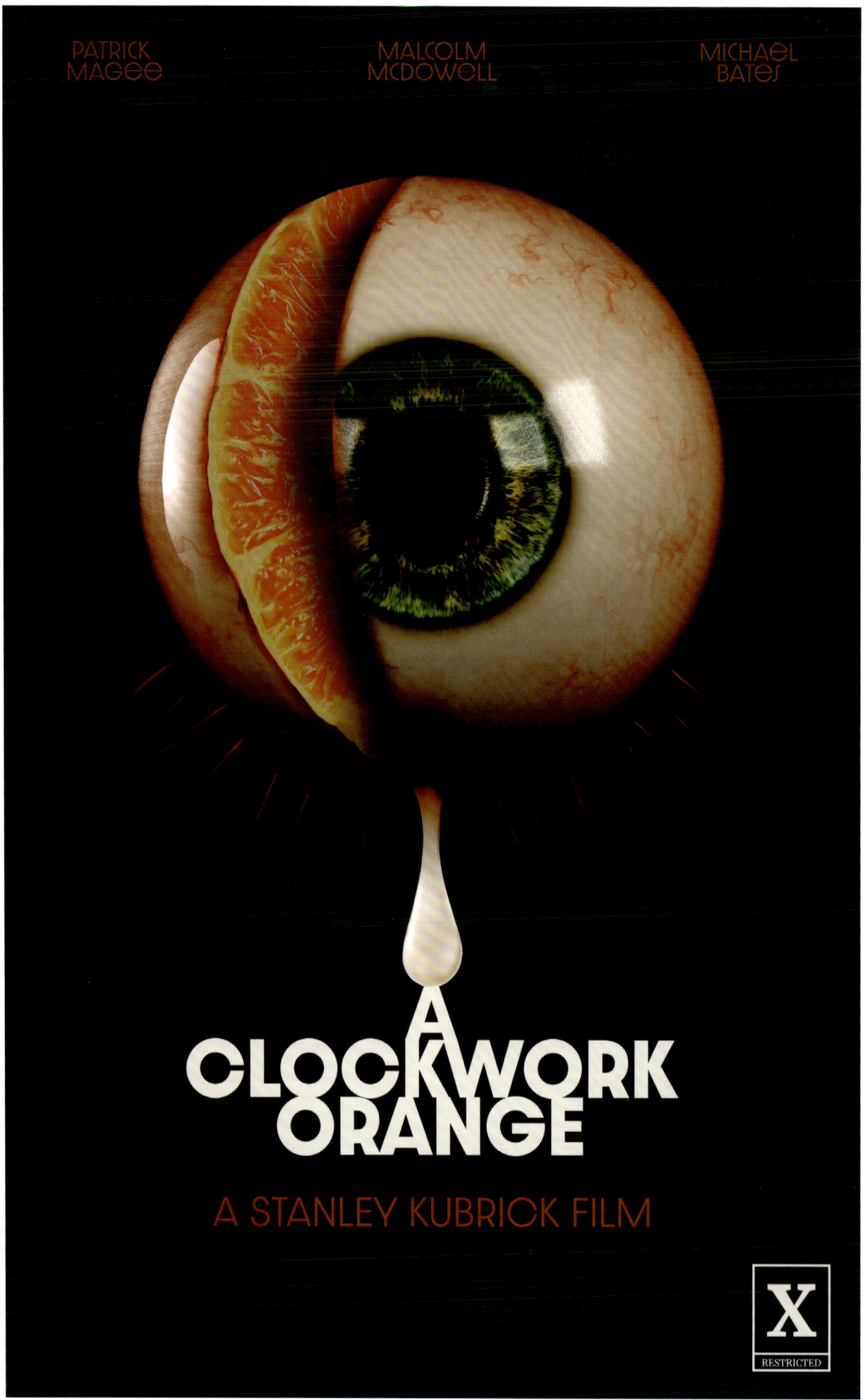

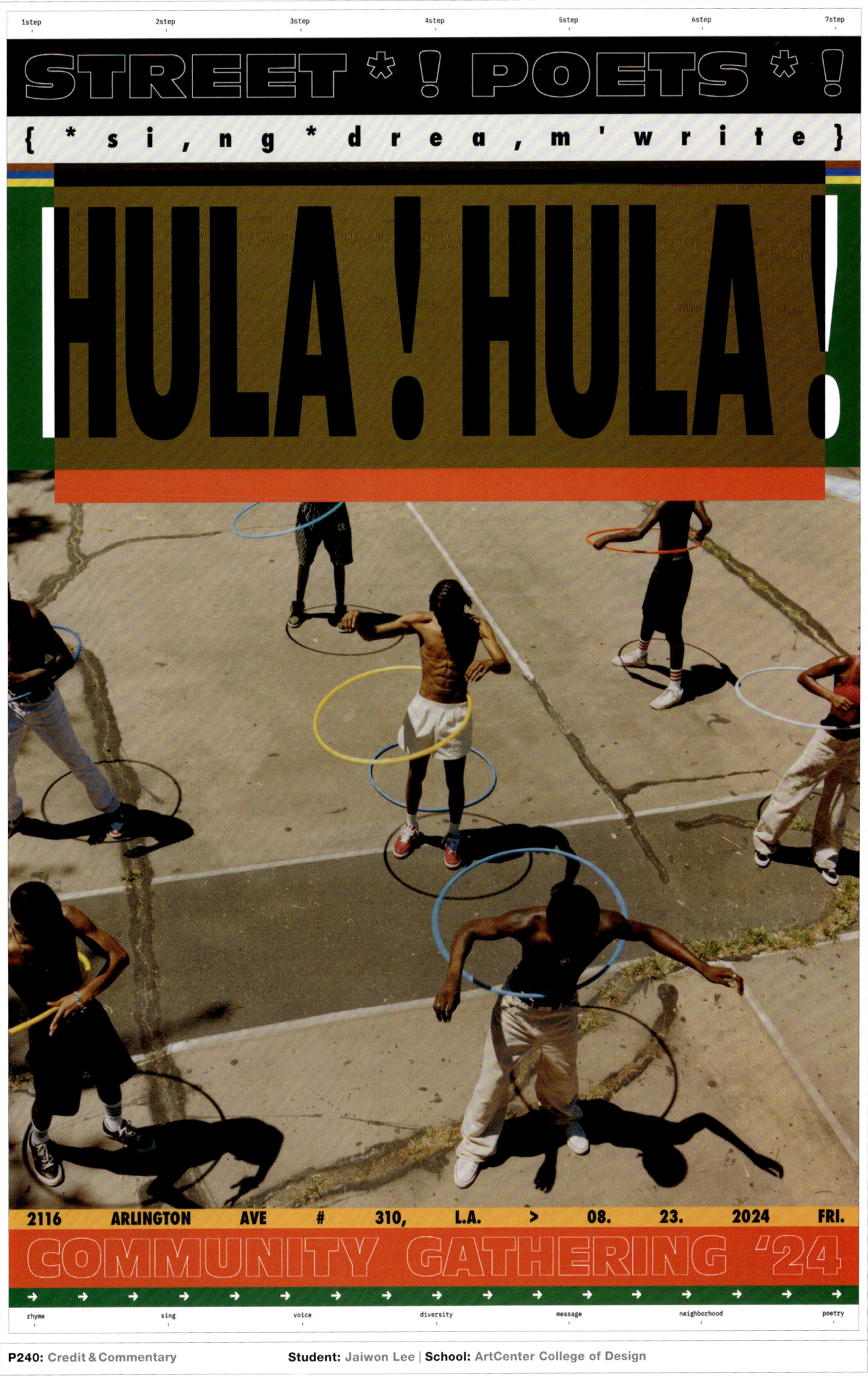

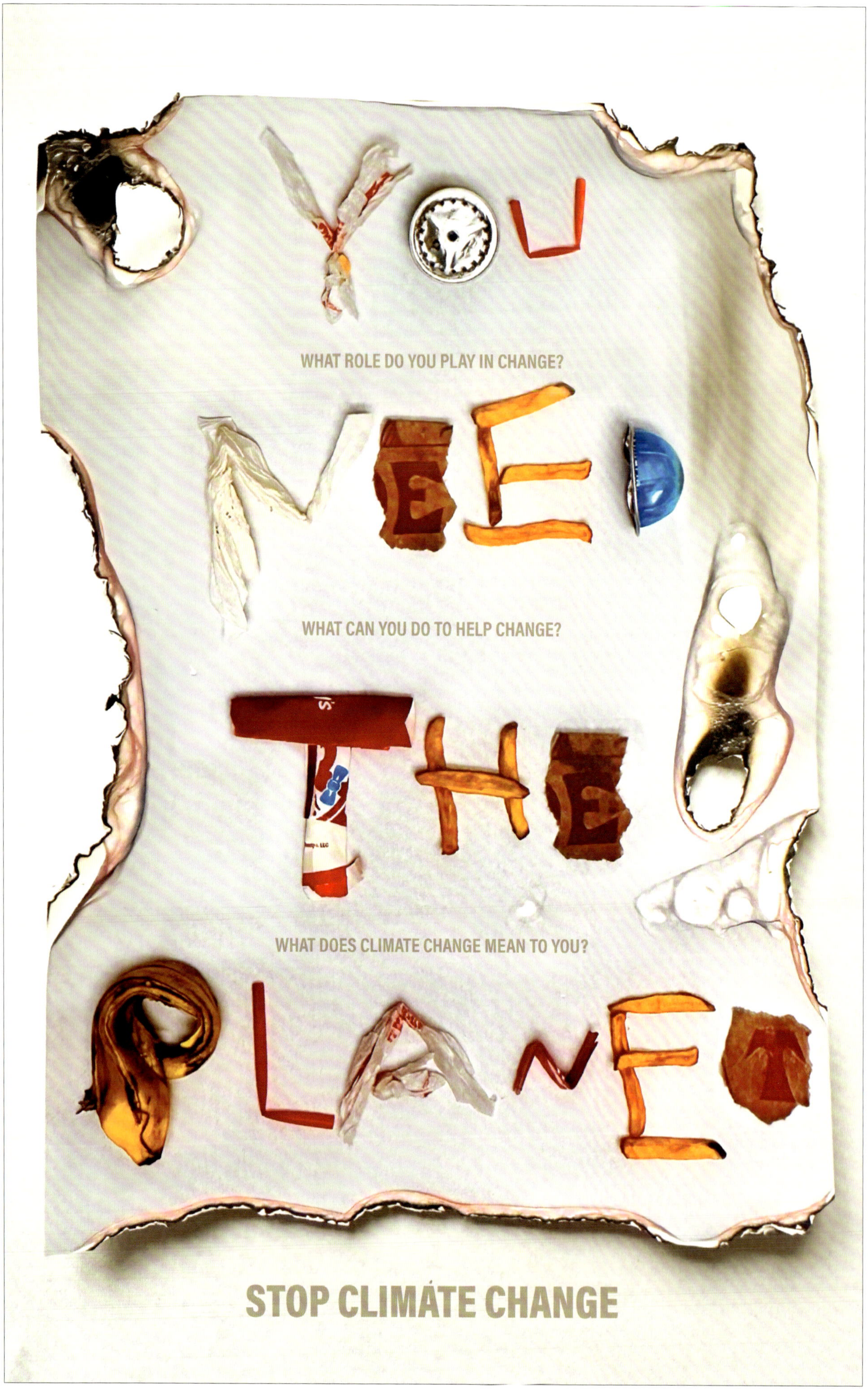

126 INSTRUCTOR **THERON MOORE** GOLD

YOU NEED THE PLANET

WHAT ROLE DO YOU PLAY IN CHANGE?

WHAT CAN YOU DO TO HELP CHANGE?

WHAT DOES CLIMATE CHANGE MEAN TO YOU?

STOP CLIMATE CHANGE

P240: Credit & Commentary   **Student:** Matthew Tweedie | **School:** California State University, Fullerton

Design | Poster

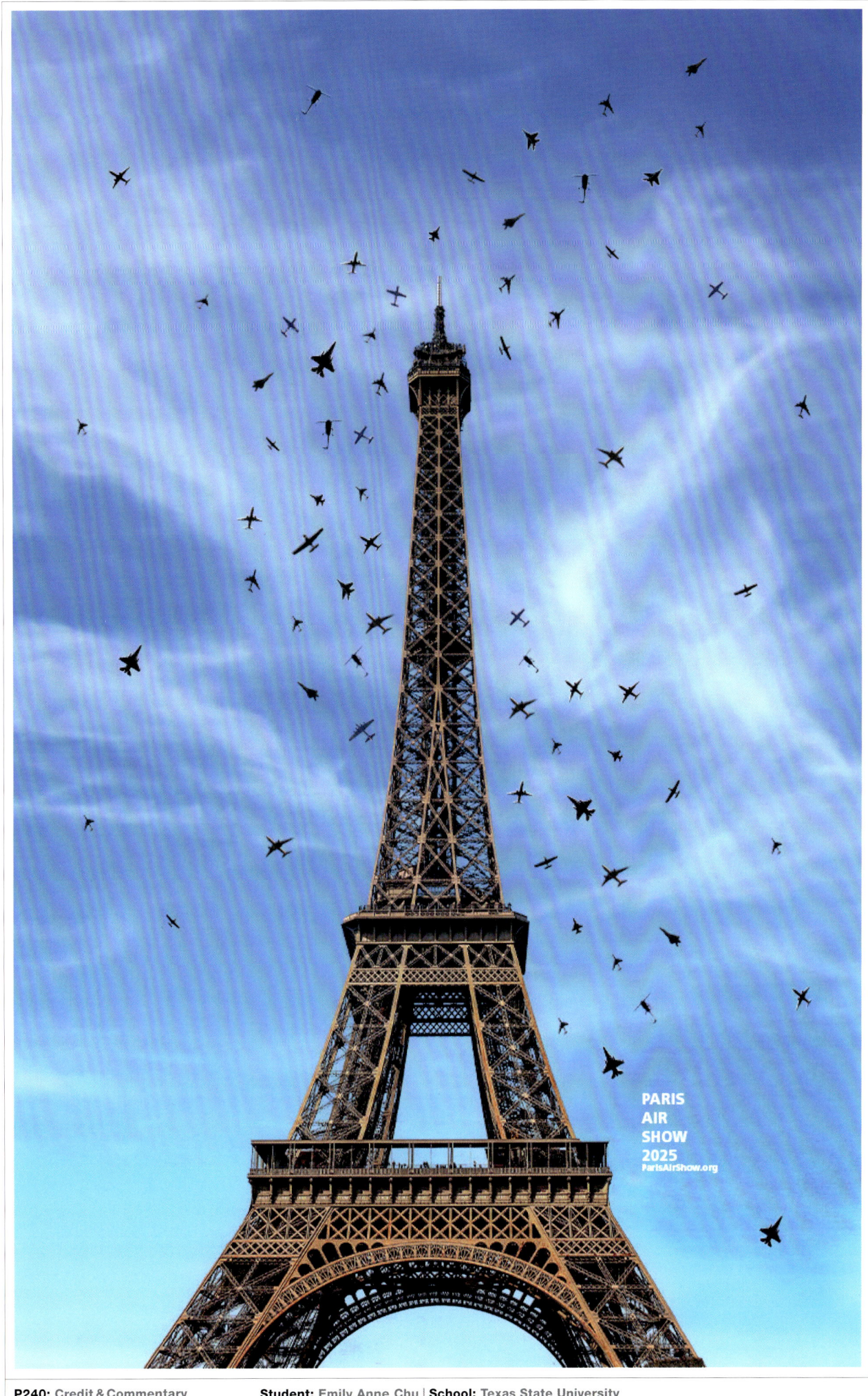

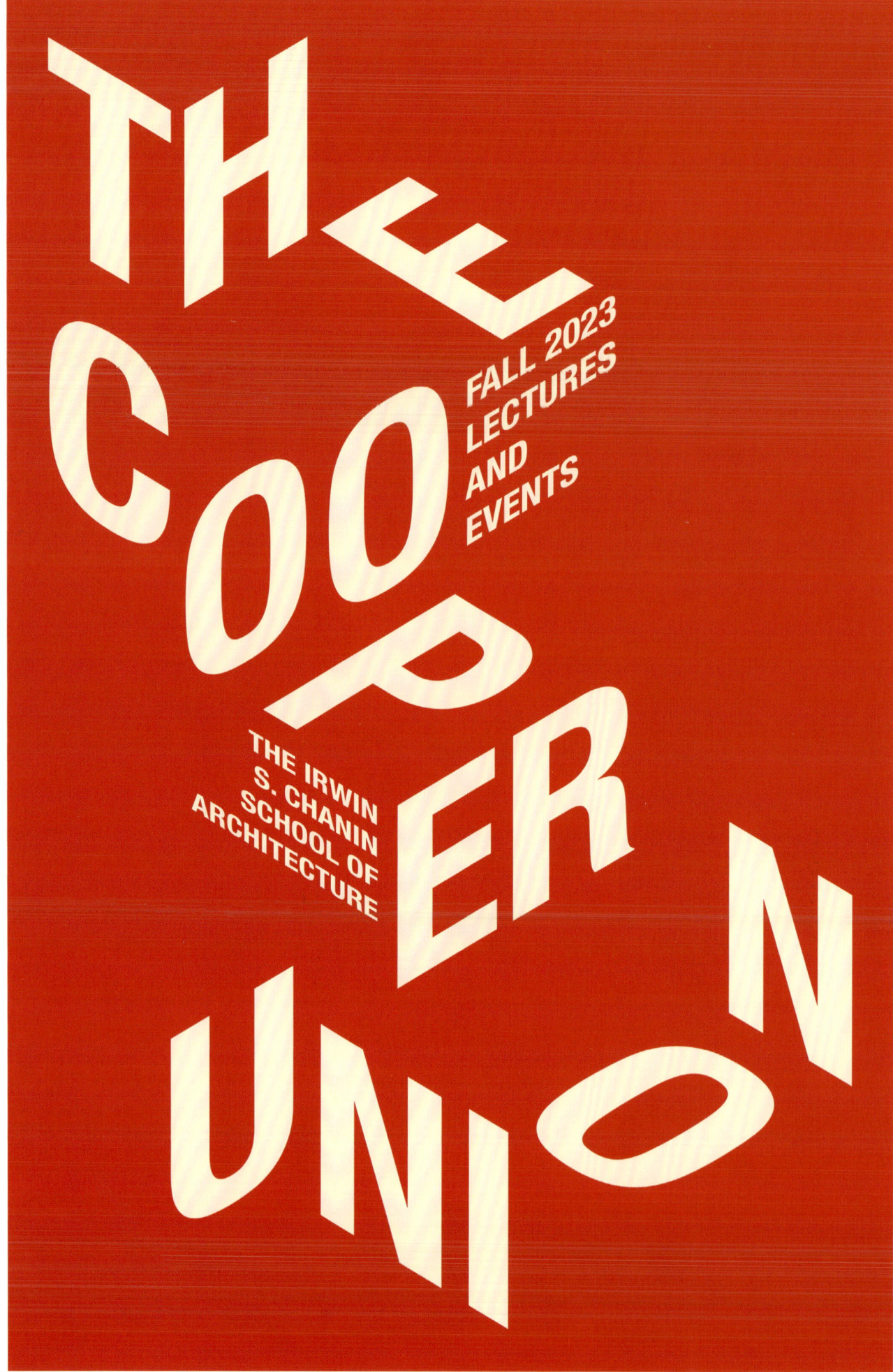

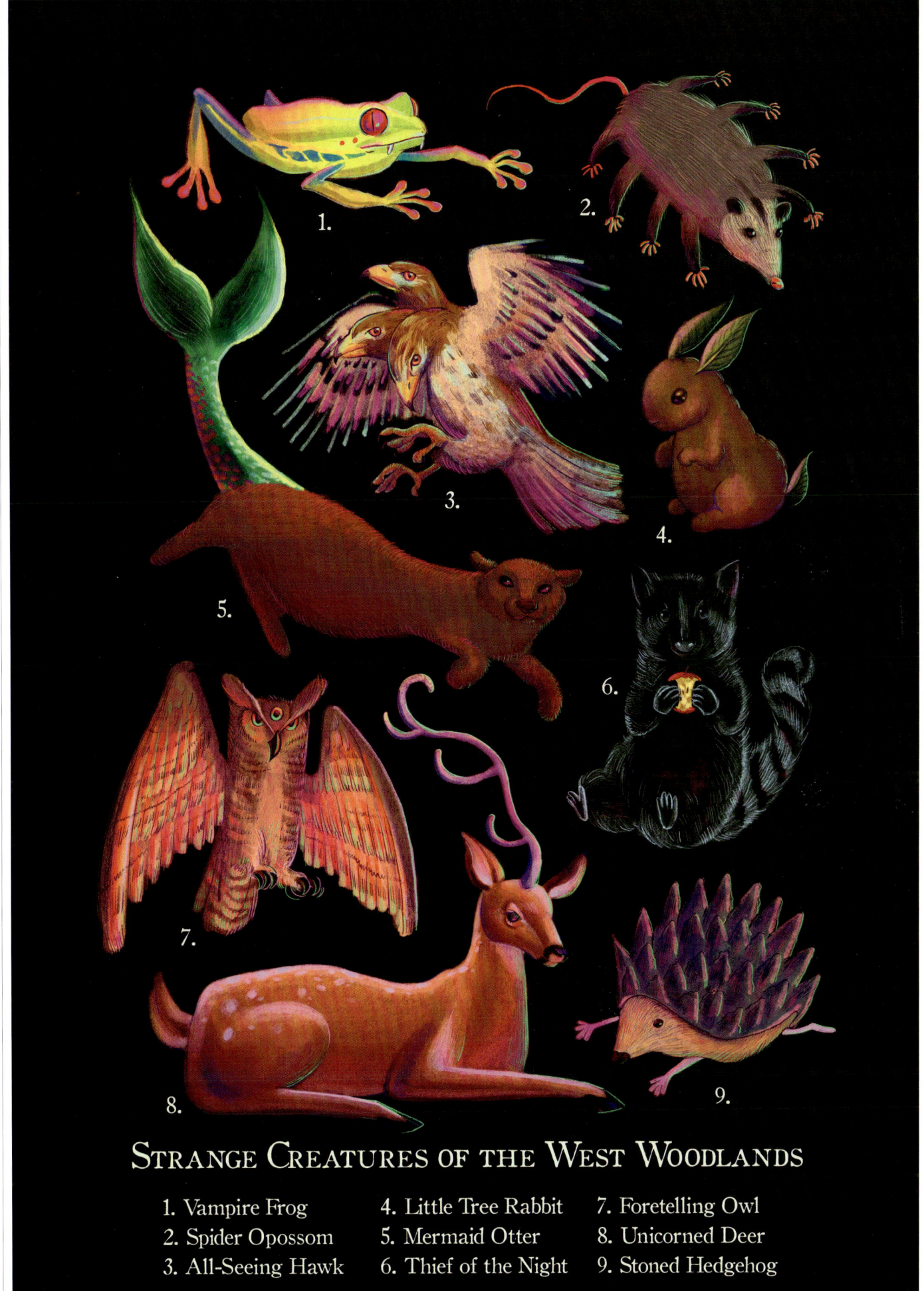

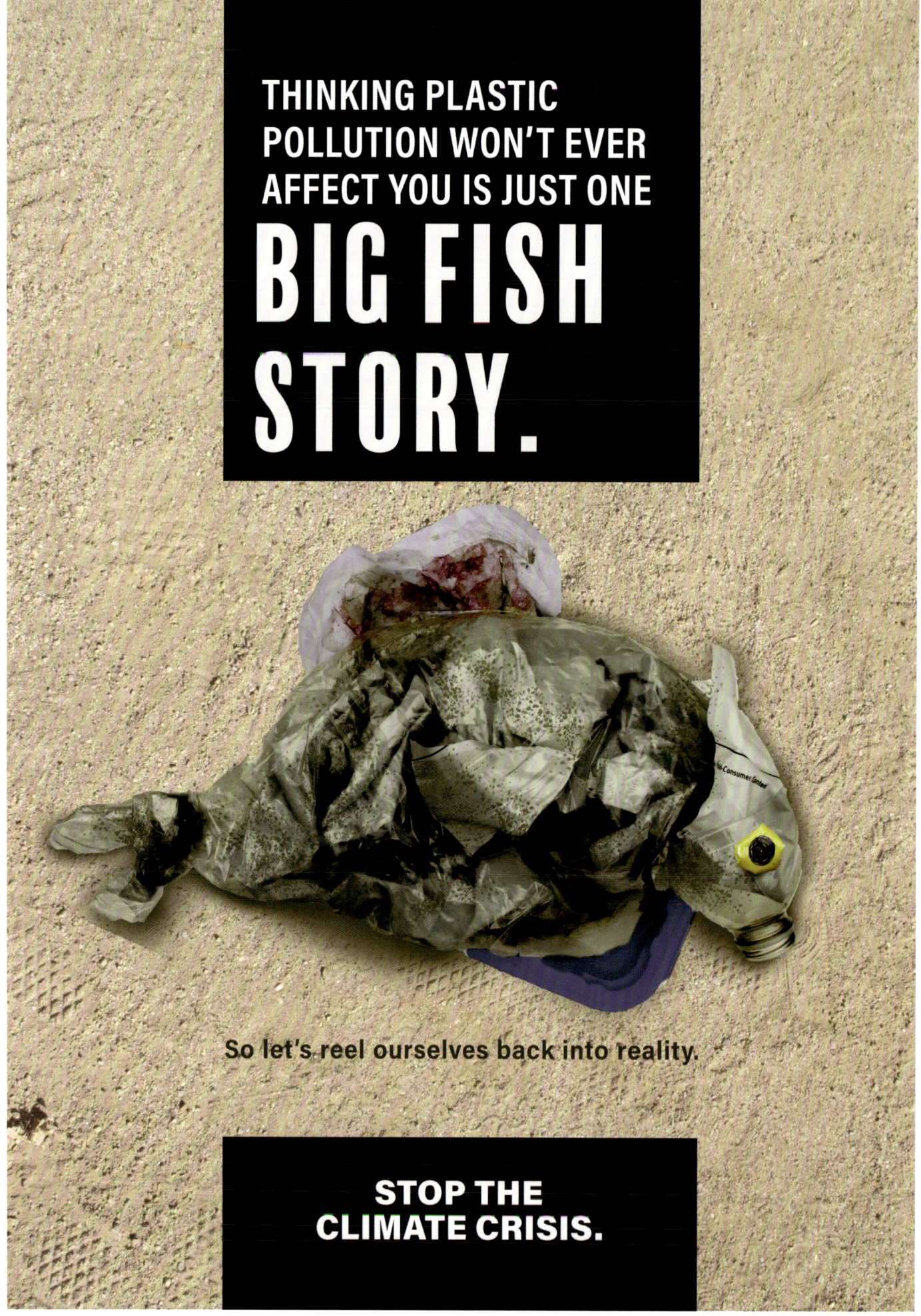

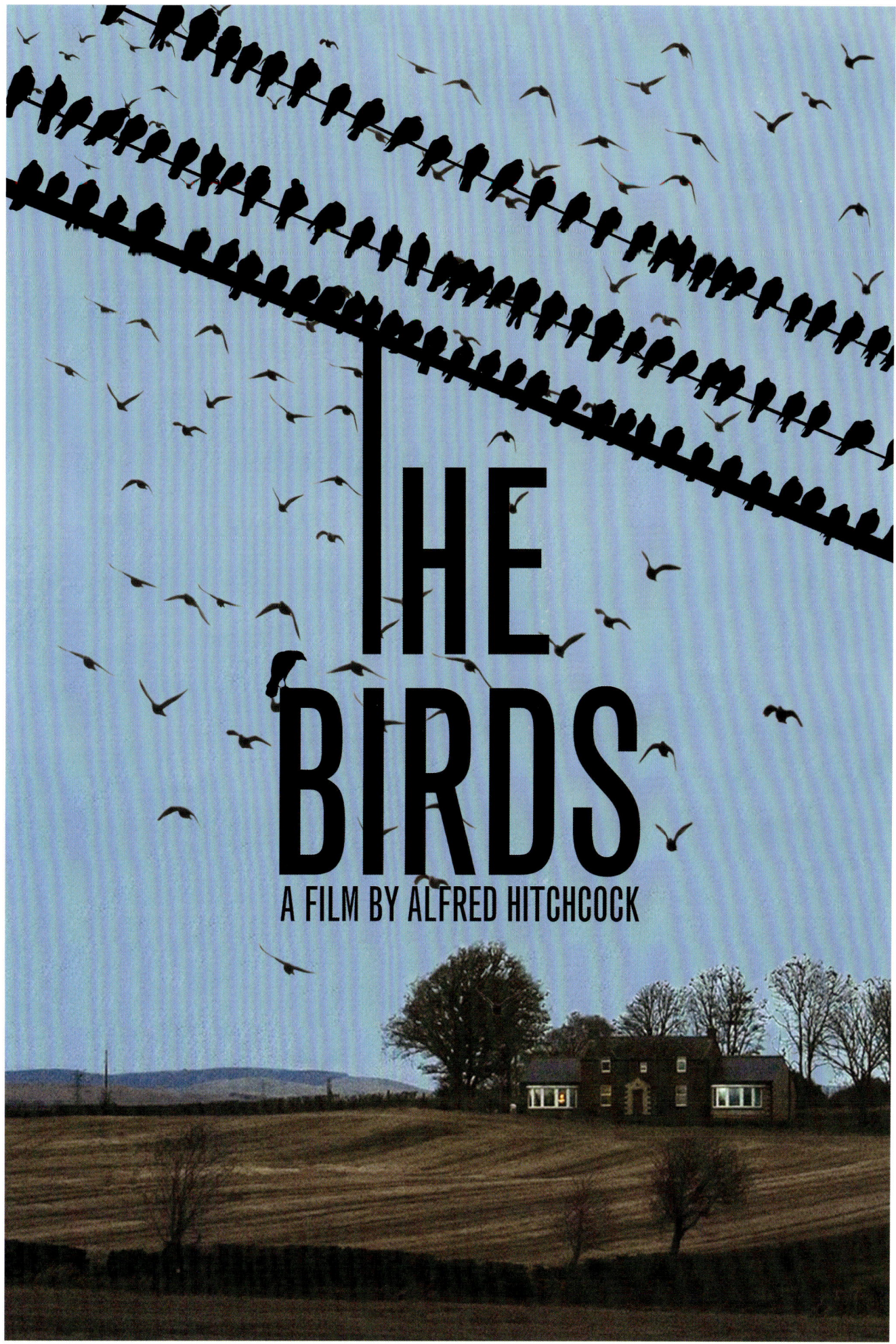

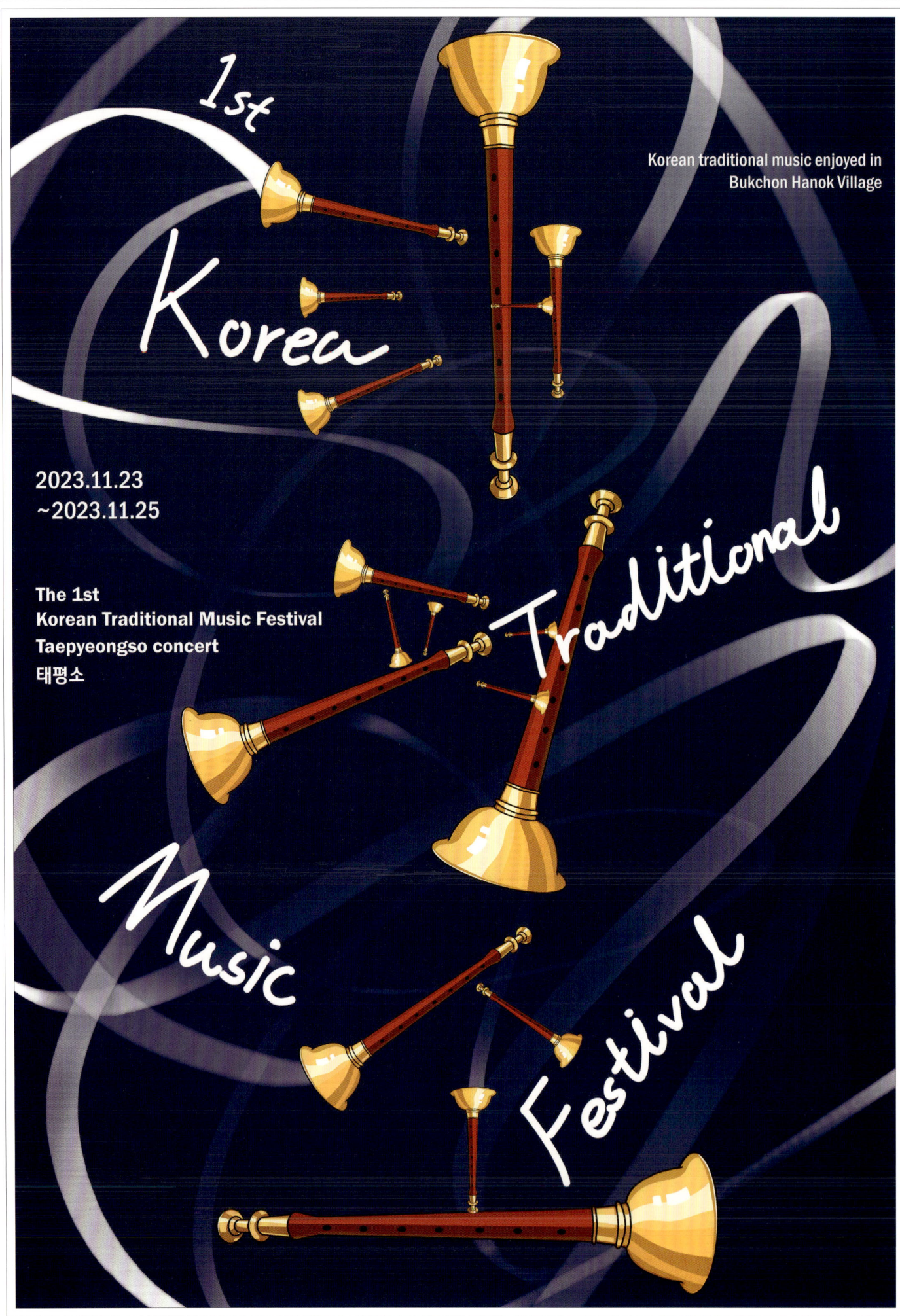

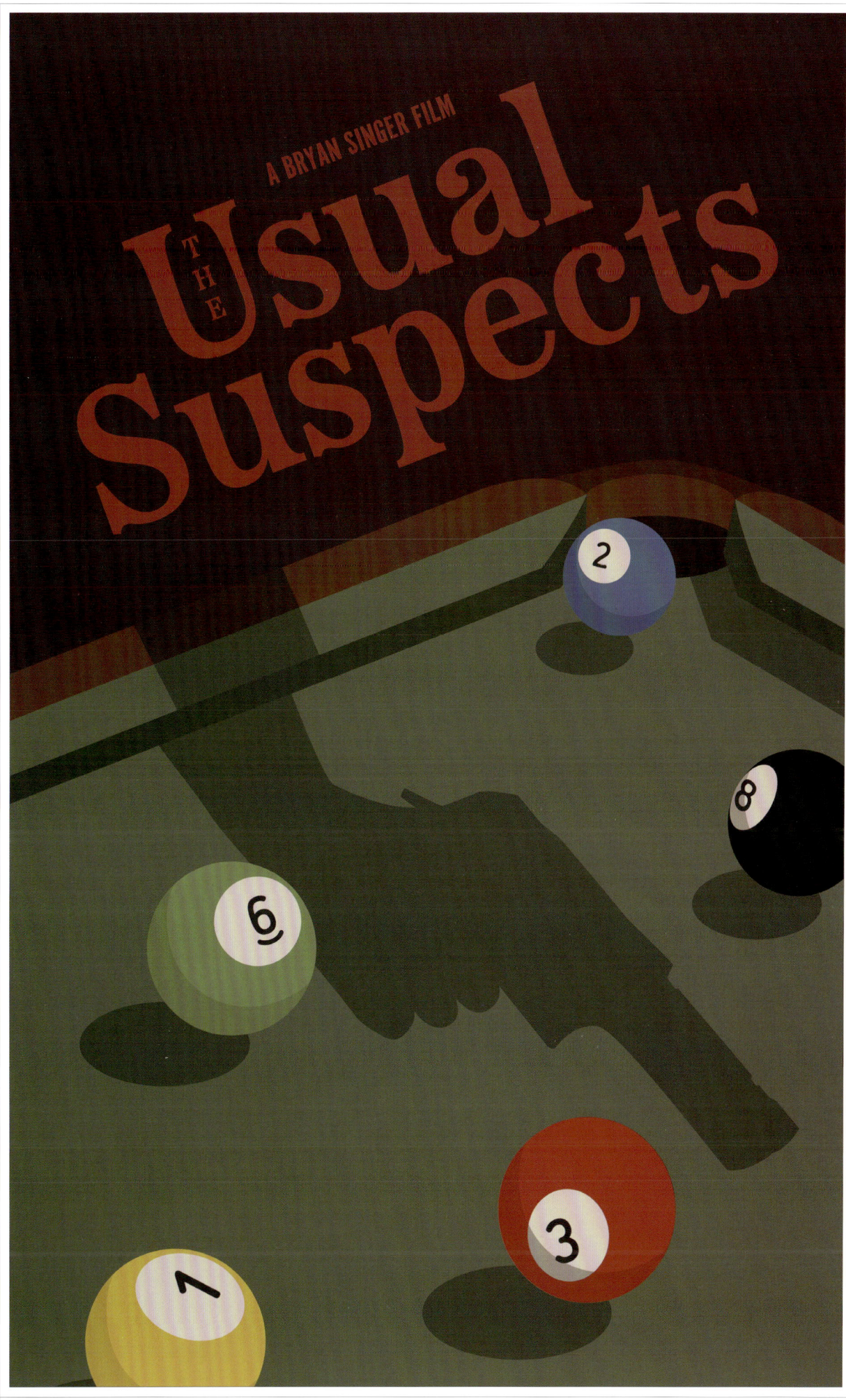

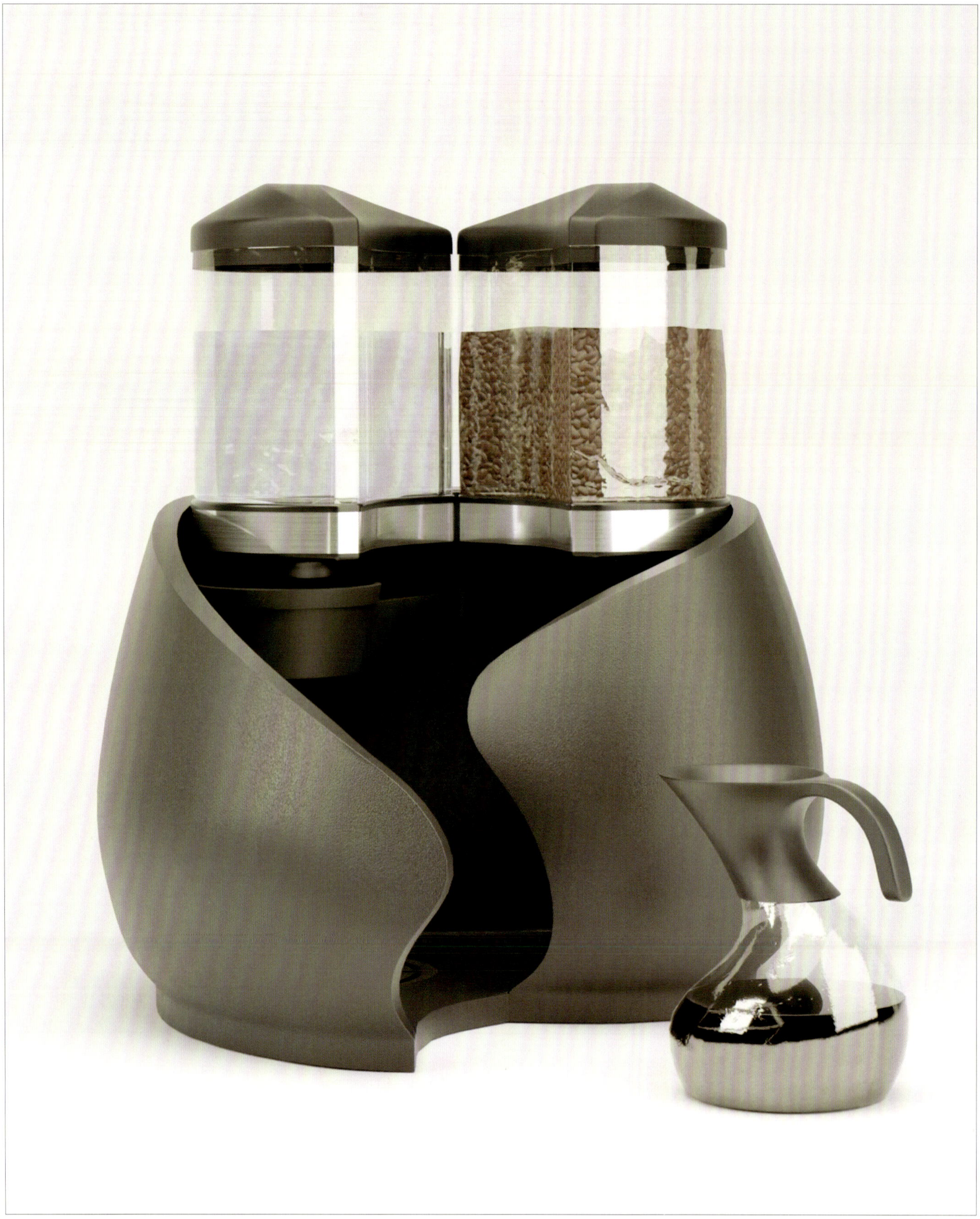

P240: Credit & Commentary **Student:** Bryan Robinson | **School:** M.AD School of Ideas Atlanta

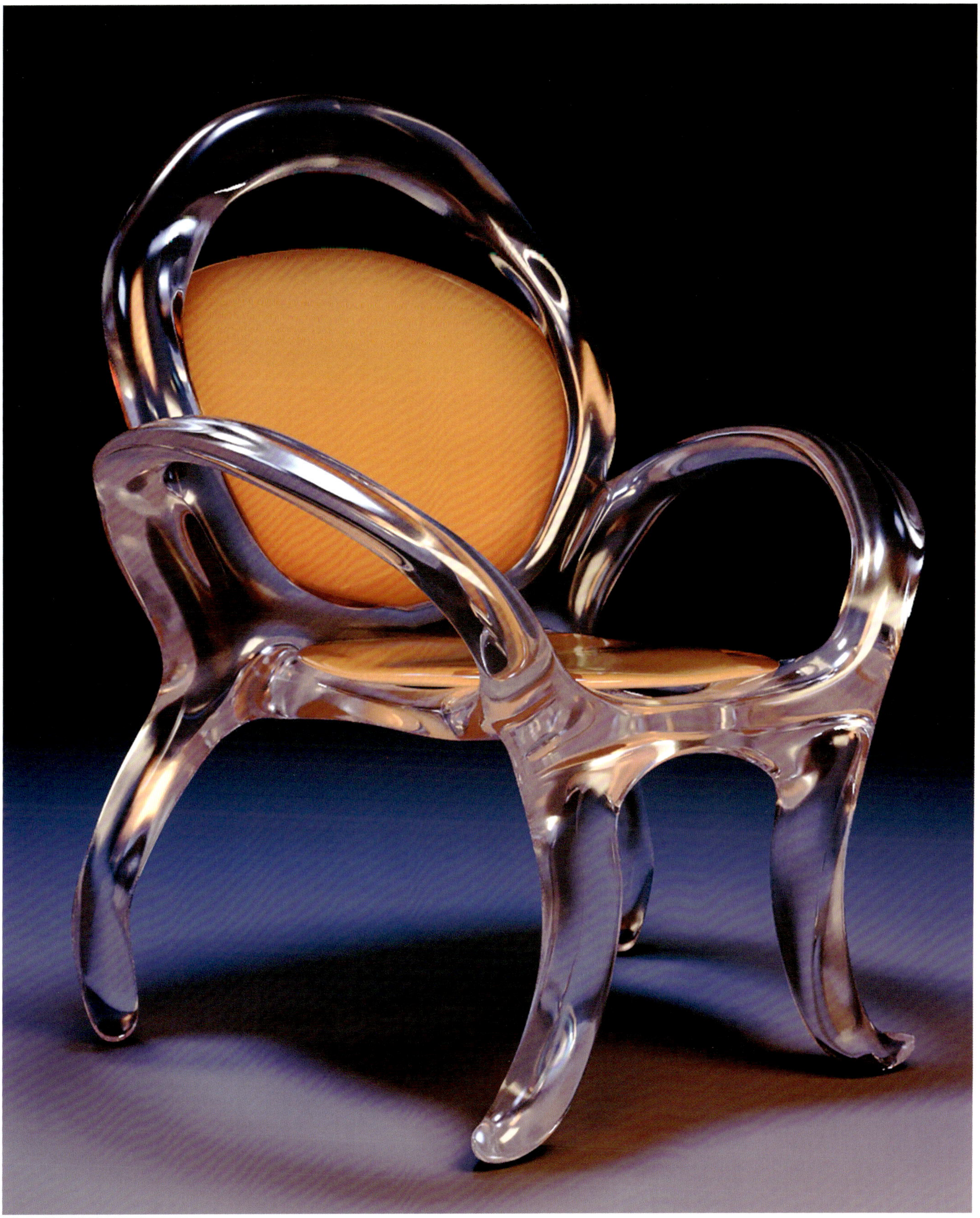

135 INSTRUCTOR **HANK RICHARDSON** GOLD

P240: Credit & Commentary   **Student:** Brianna Bowman | **School:** M.AD School of Ideas Atlanta

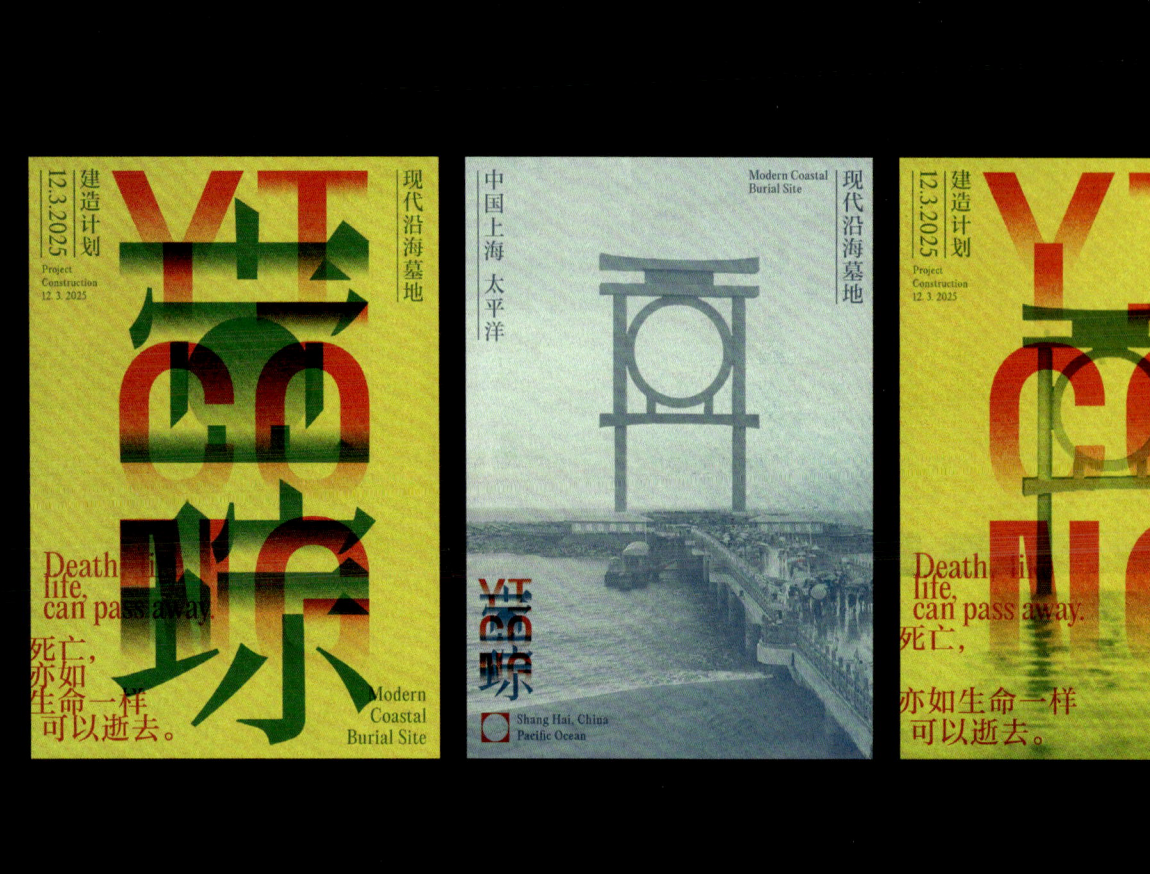
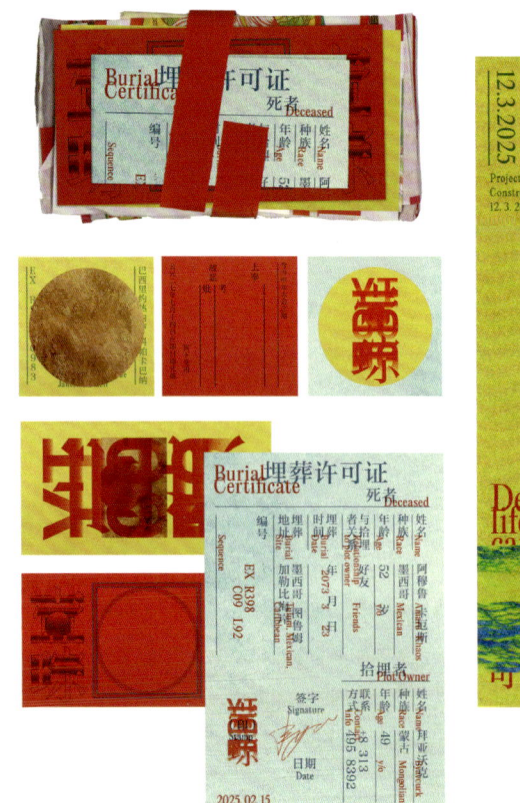
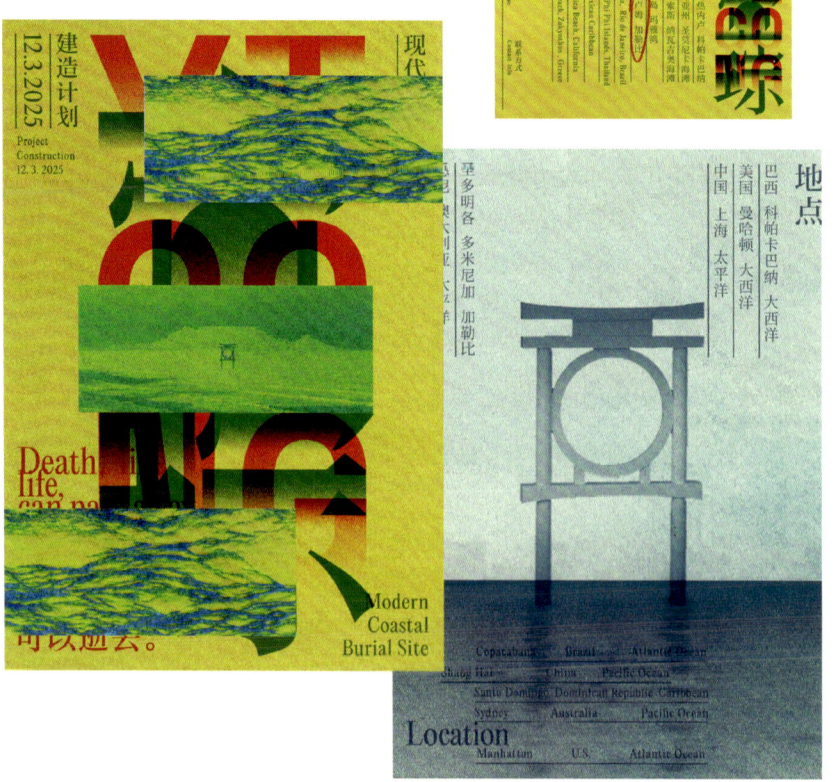

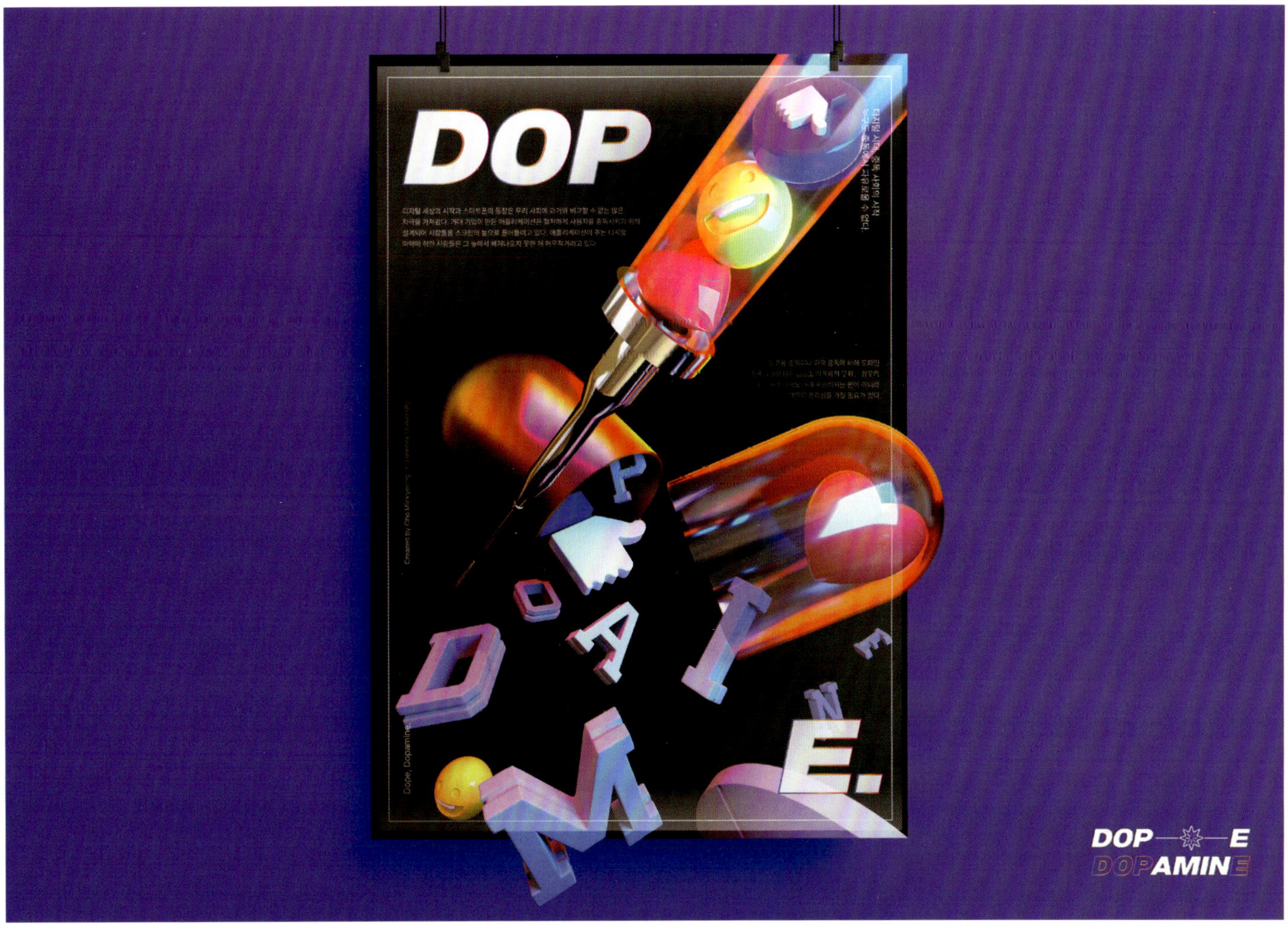

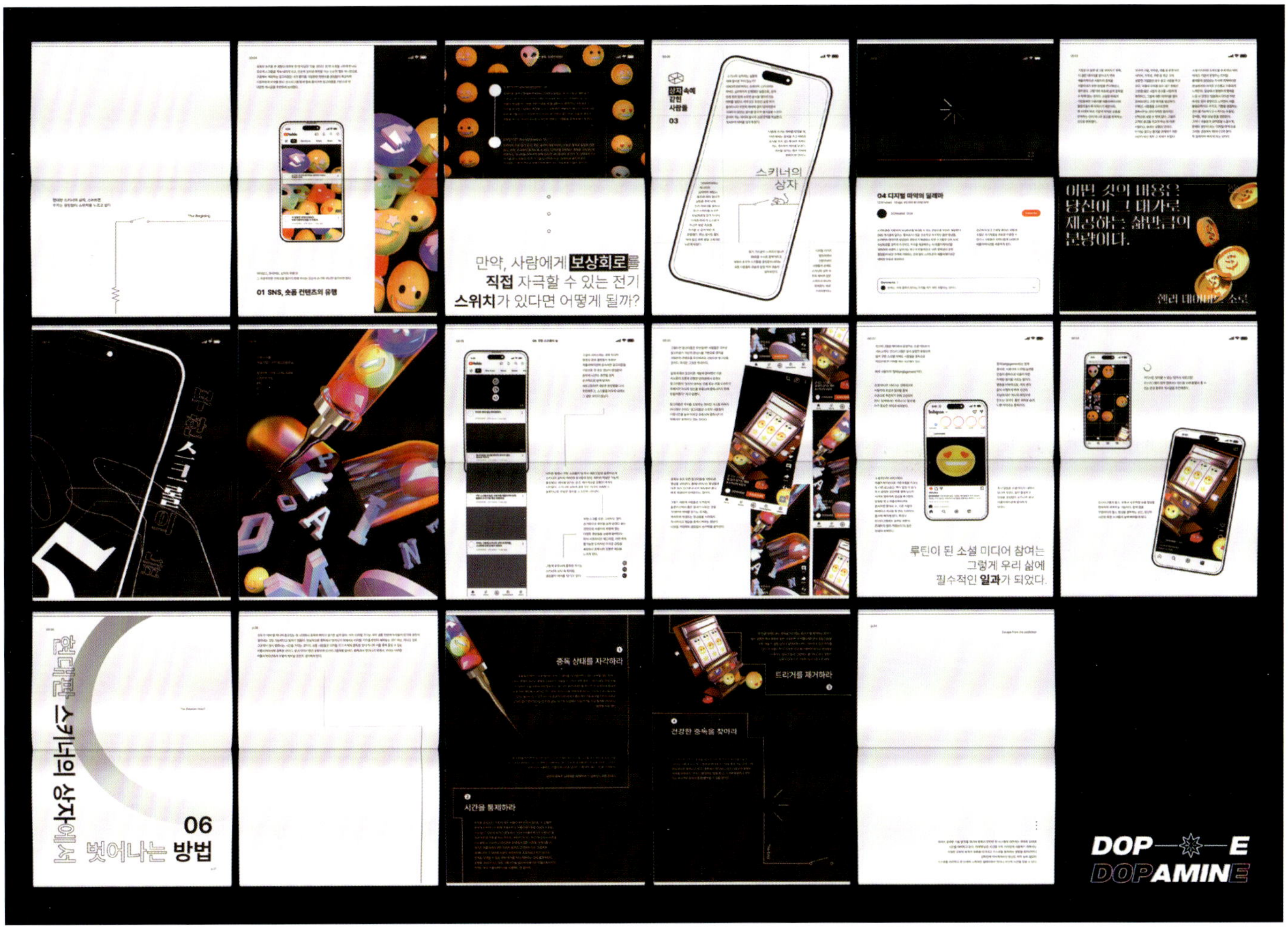

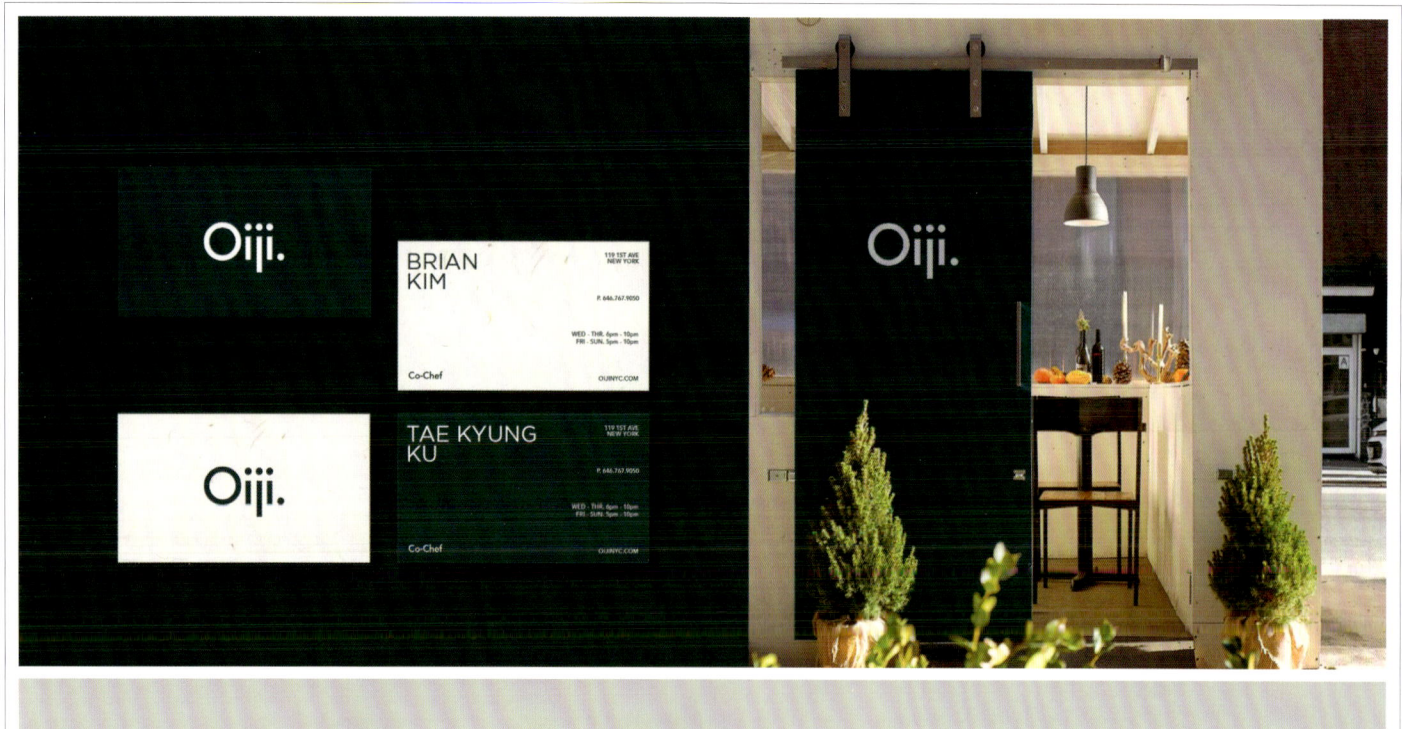
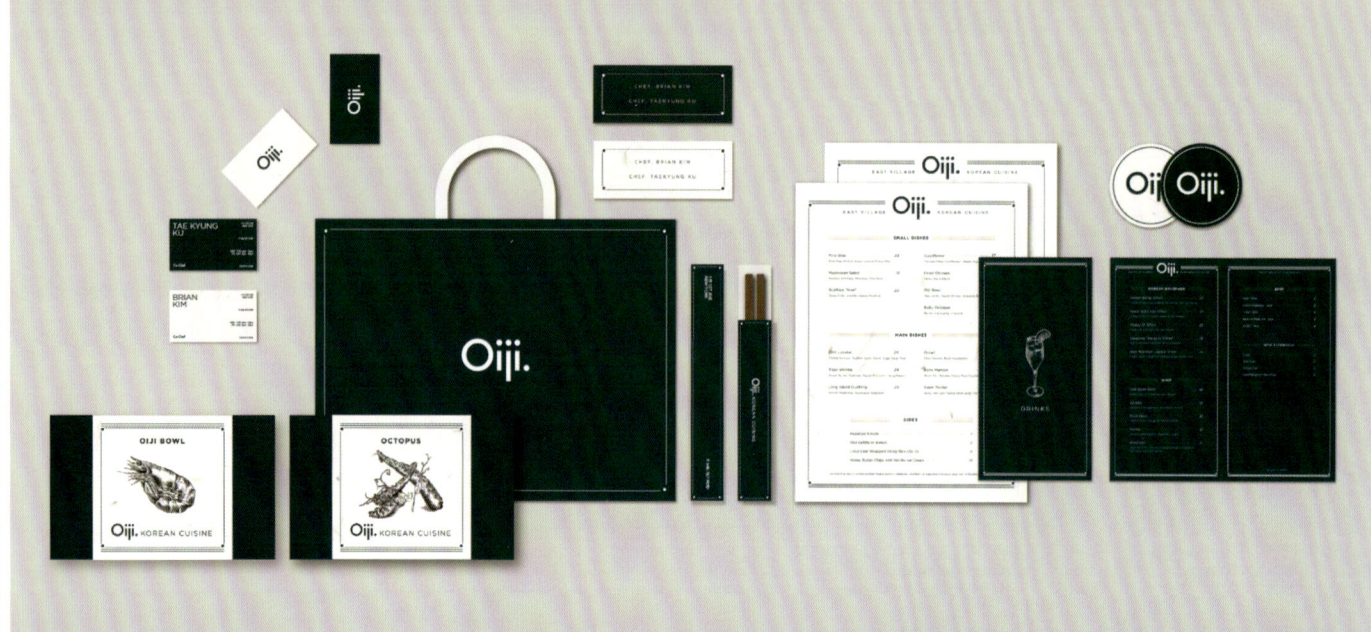
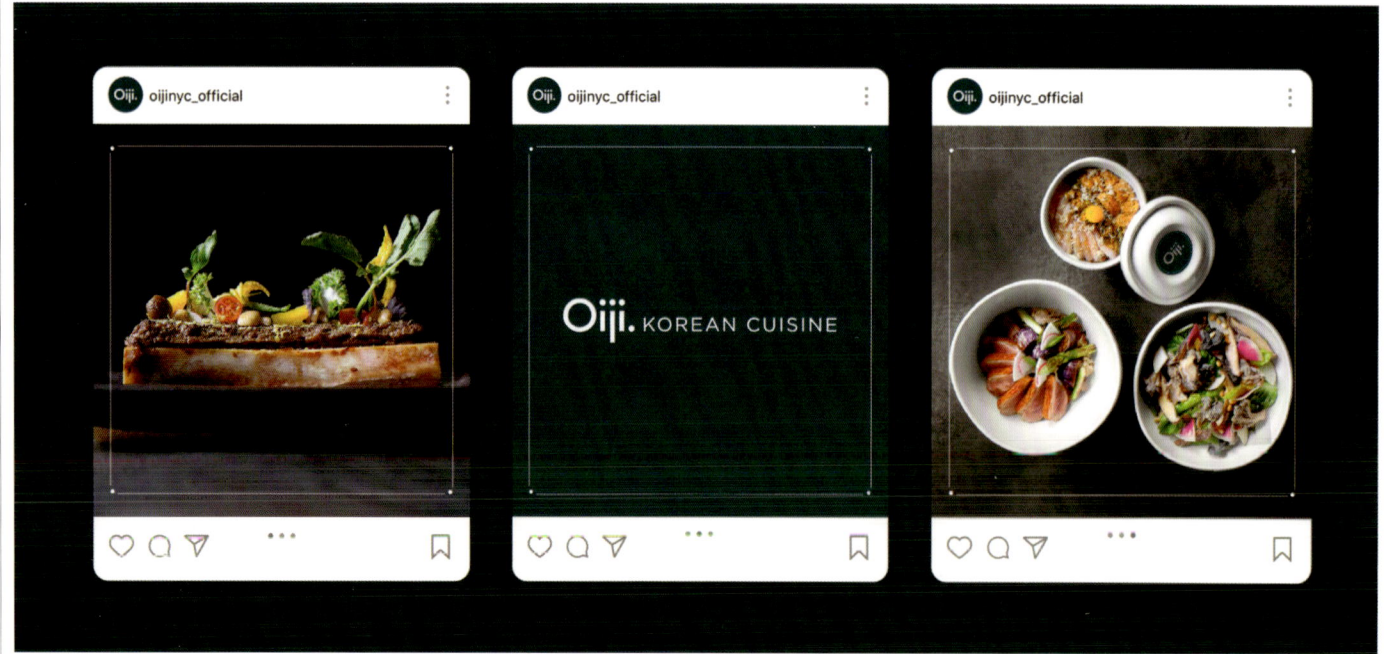

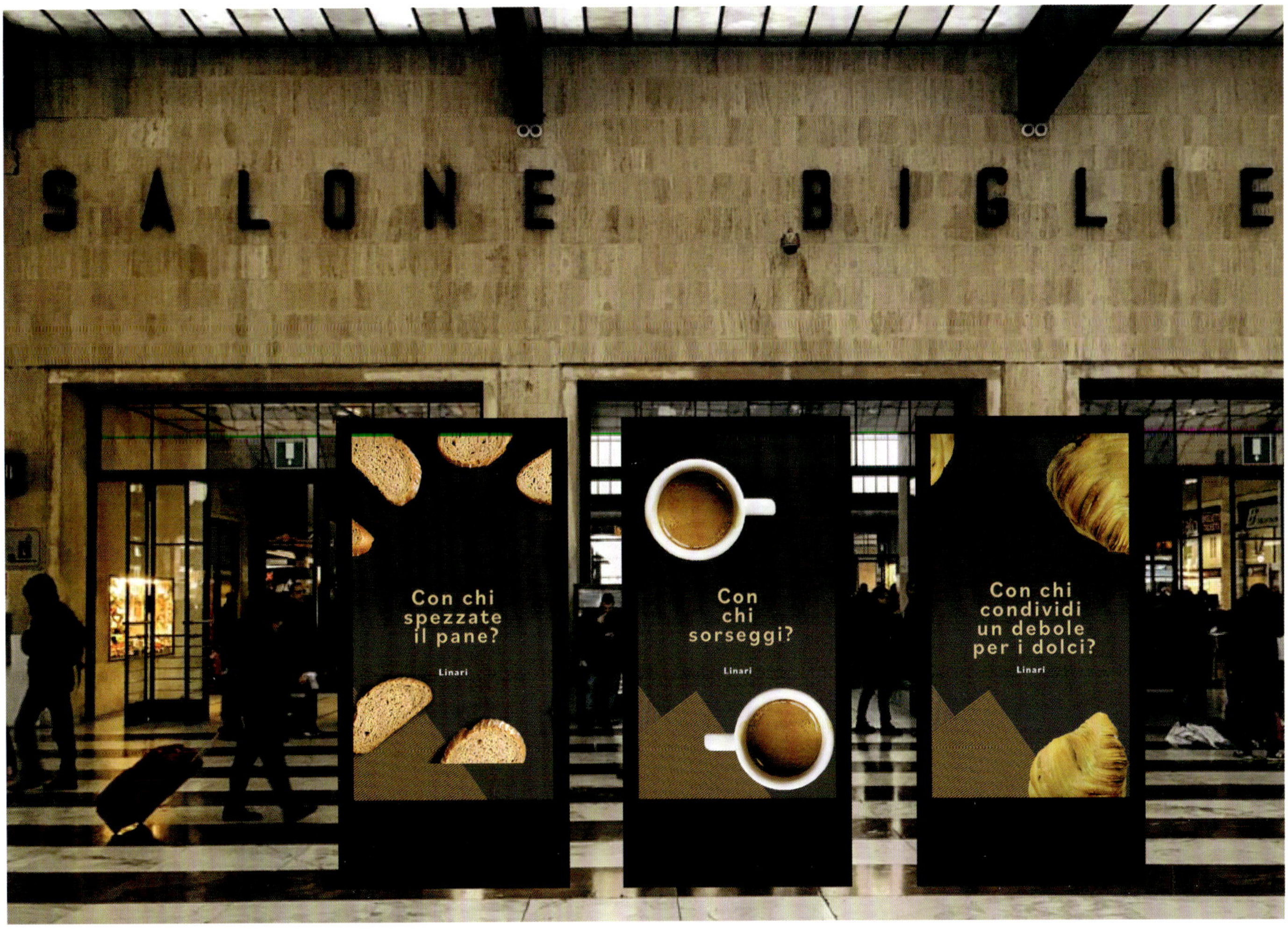

139 INSTRUCTOR VERONICA VAUGHN GOLD

CAFETTERIA

CAFFE	€ 0,50
CAFFE D'ORZA	€ 1,00
CAFFE LATTE	€ 1,50
CAFFE FREDDO	€ 1,20
CAPPUCCINO	€ 1,20
THÈ	€ 1,50
THÈ FREDDO	€ 1,80
CIOCCOLATA	€ 2,50

PASTICCERIA

VENTAGLIO	€ 1,80
CIAVATTONE	€ 2,00
UNGHERESE	€ 2,00
CROSTATINA	€ 2,00
OCCHIO DI BUE	€ 1,80
SFOGLIATELLA	€ 2,00
MIGNON ASSORTITI	€ 22,00 al Kg
PASTICCERIA DA TE	€ 22,00 al Kg
CROSTATA DI FRUTTA	€ 25,00 a; Kg

GASTRONOMIA

TRAMEZZINO	€ 2,00
MEDAGLIONE	€ 3,50
PIADINA	€ 3,50
TOAST	€ 3,00
PIZZA ROMANA	€ 3,50
PIZZETTA TONDA ROSSA	€ 0,90

LISTINO

PRIMO	€ 4,50	€ 4,50
SECONDO	€ 5,50	€ 5,50
INSALATE		€ 4,50
CONTORNO		€ 3,00
VERDURE MISTE		€ 13,00 al Kg
MACEDONIA		€ 2,00

Con chi spezzate il pane? *Linari*

Con chi sorseggi? *Linari*

Con chi condividi un debole per i dolci? *Linari*

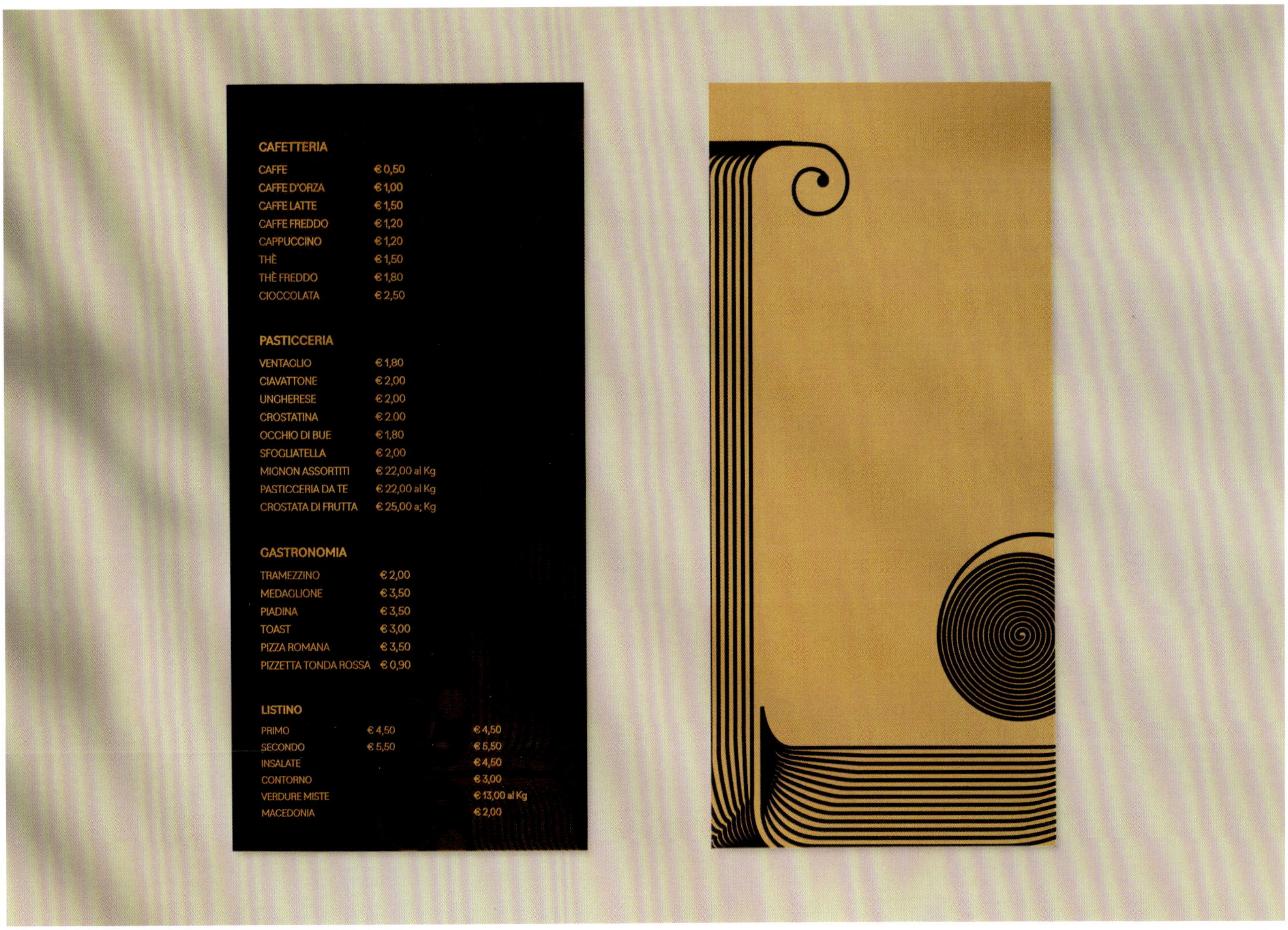

Student: Lexi Oliver | **School:** Texas A&M University-Commerce

Restaurant | Design

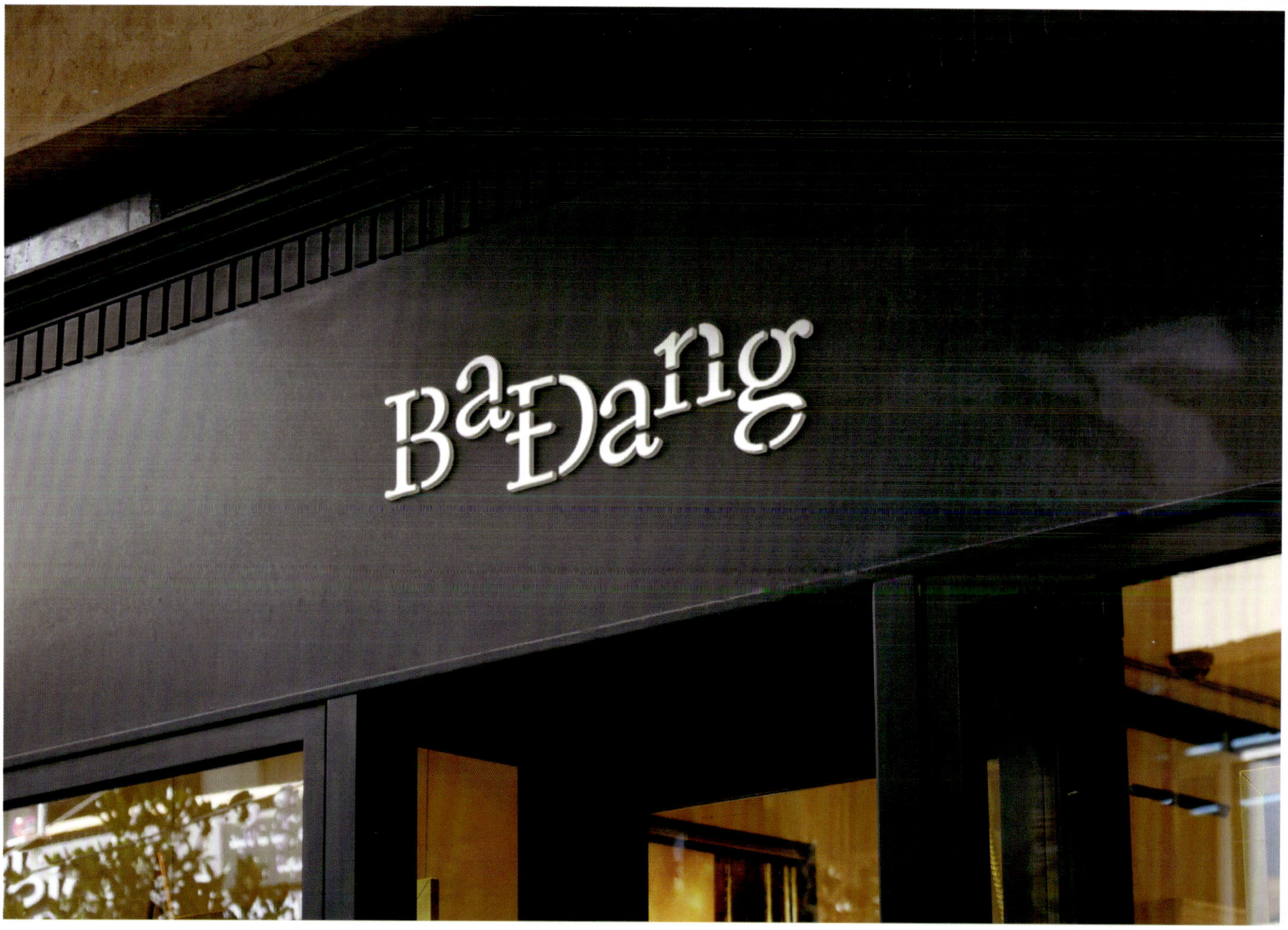

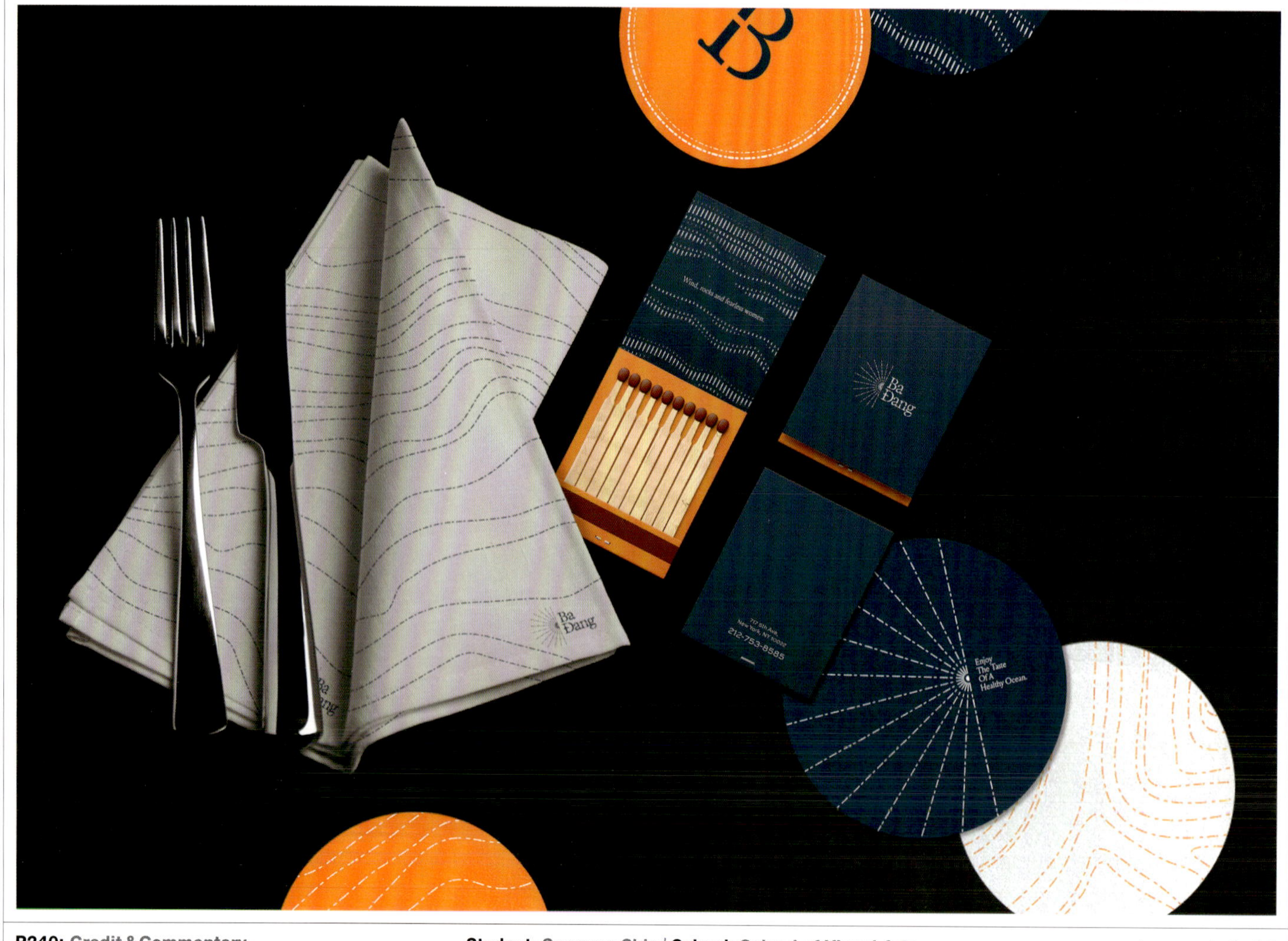

140 INSTRUCTOR **JUSTIN COLT** GOLD

P240: Credit & Commentary   **Student:** Sungeun Shin | **School:** School of Visual Arts   Images 1, 2 of 6

Design | Restaurant

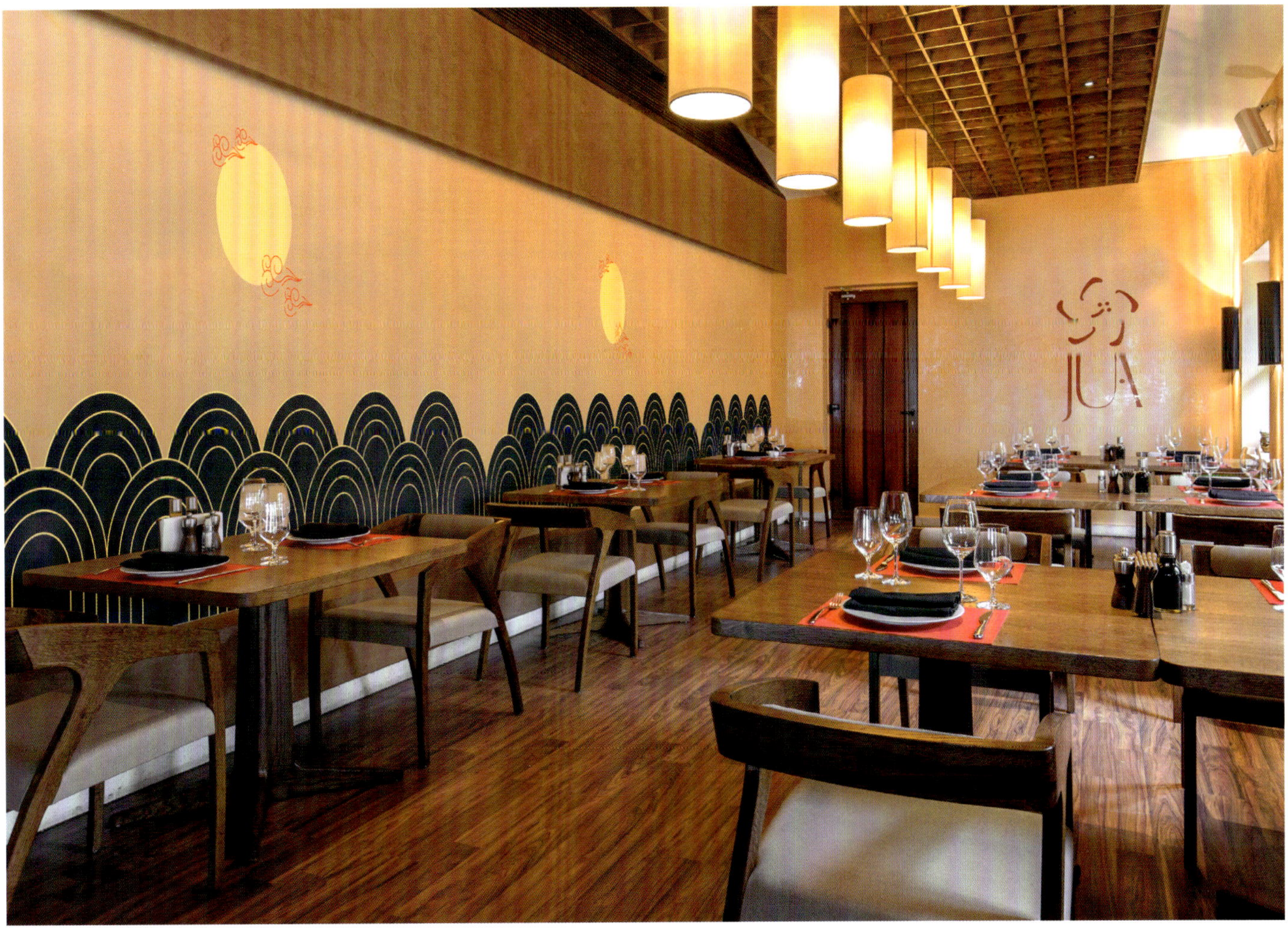

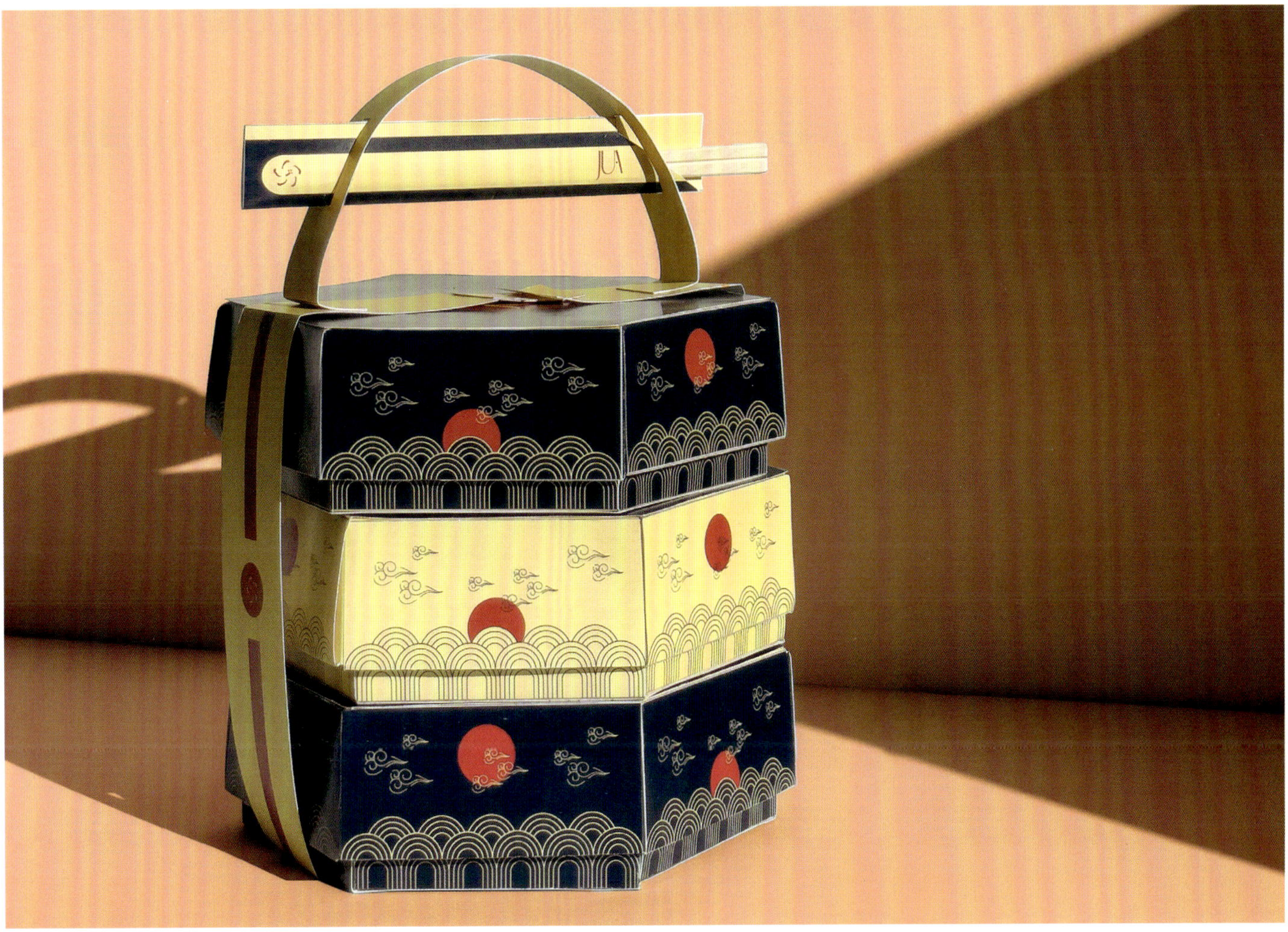

141 INSTRUCTOR **JON NEWMAN** GOLD

P241: Credit & Commentary   Student: Yoon-Gi Park | School: School of Visual Arts   Images 1, 2 of 7

Restaurant | Design

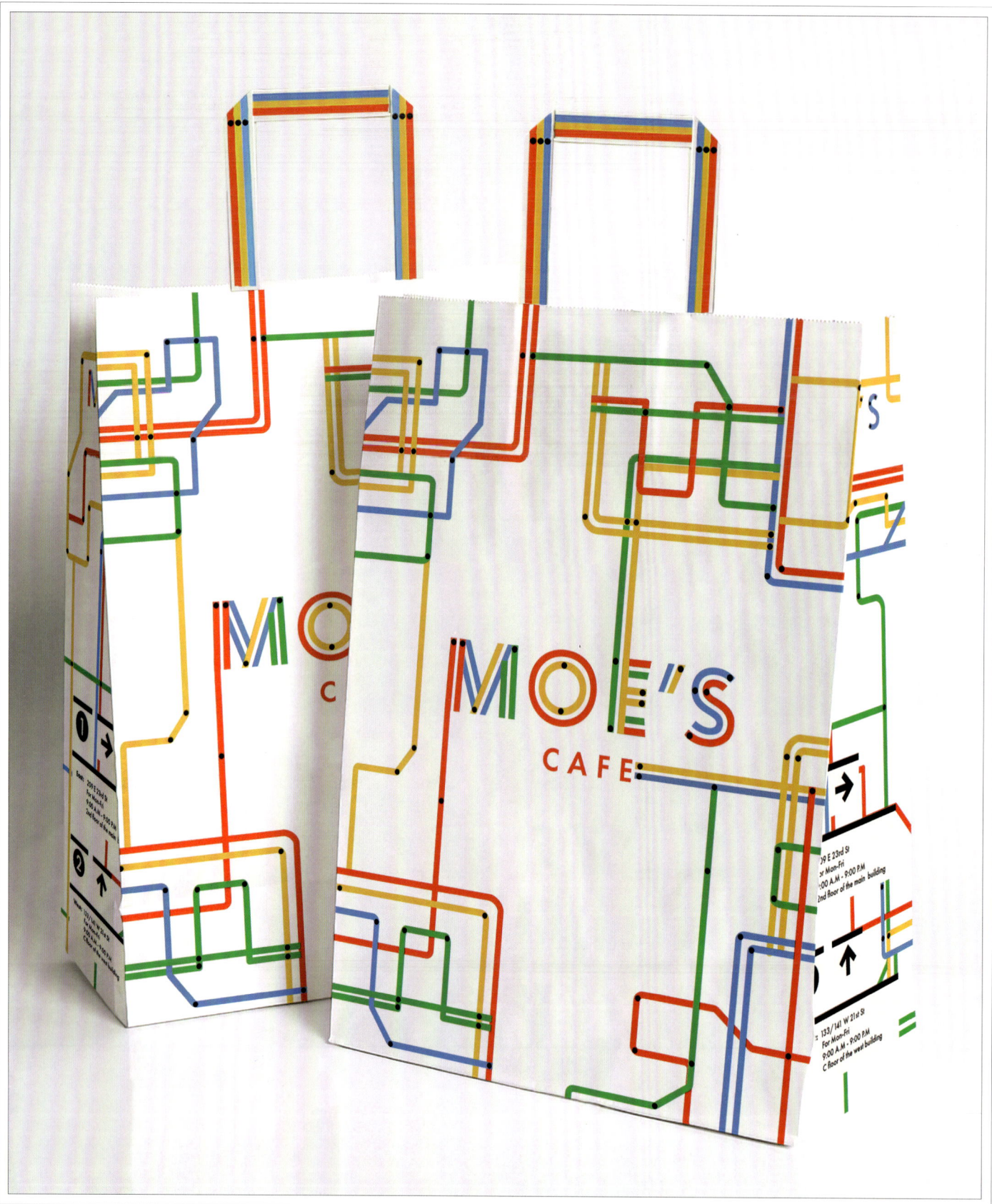

143 INSTRUCTOR **CHARLOTTE VON HARDENBURGH** GOLD

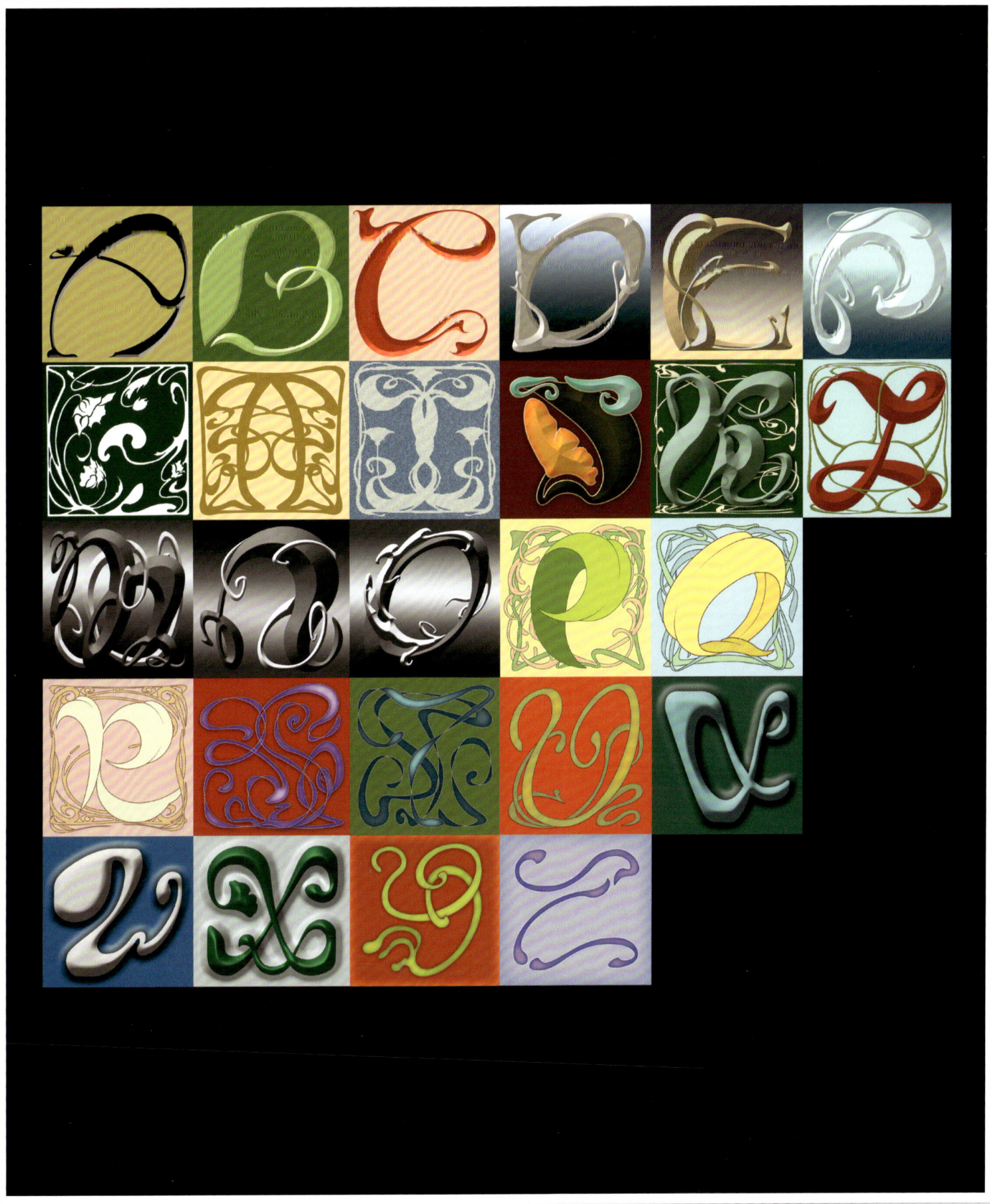

P241: Credit & Commentary   **Student:** Cynthia Huiwen Tan | **School:** Parsons School of Design

144 INSTRUCTOR **ZIPENG ZHU** GOLD

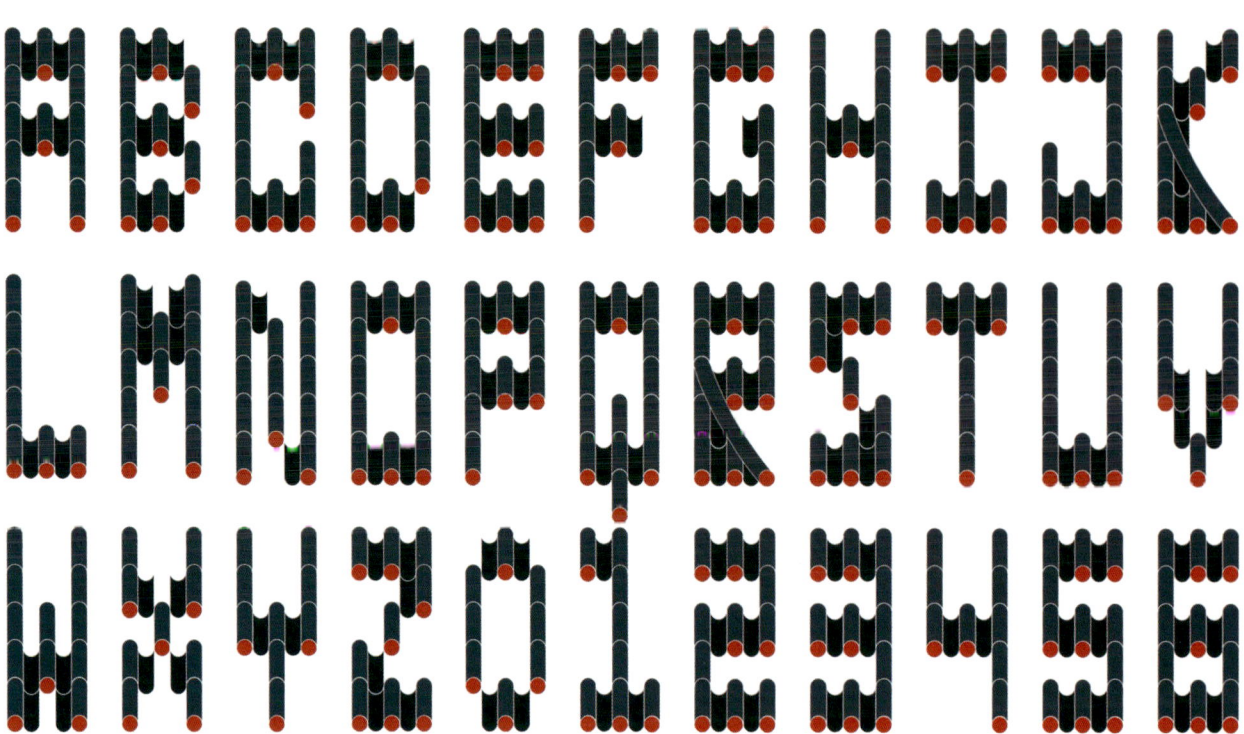

P241: Credit & Commentary | Student: Becky Baek | School: School of Visual Arts | Image 1 of 5

INSTRUCTOR **WILLIE IP** GOLD

P241: Credit & Commentary | Student: Sara Mehta | School: School of Visual Arts | Image 1 of 6

Design | Type Fonts A–Z

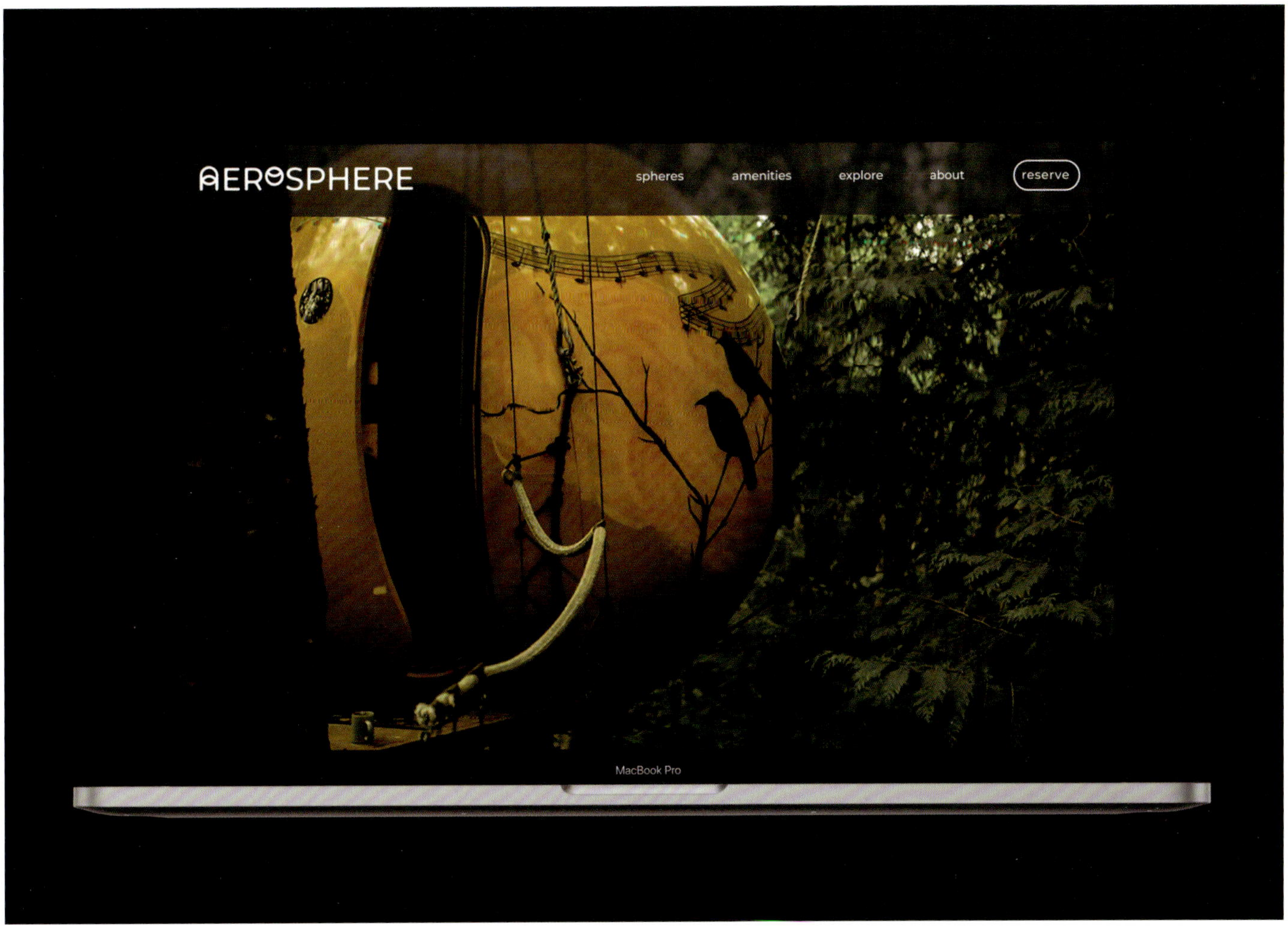

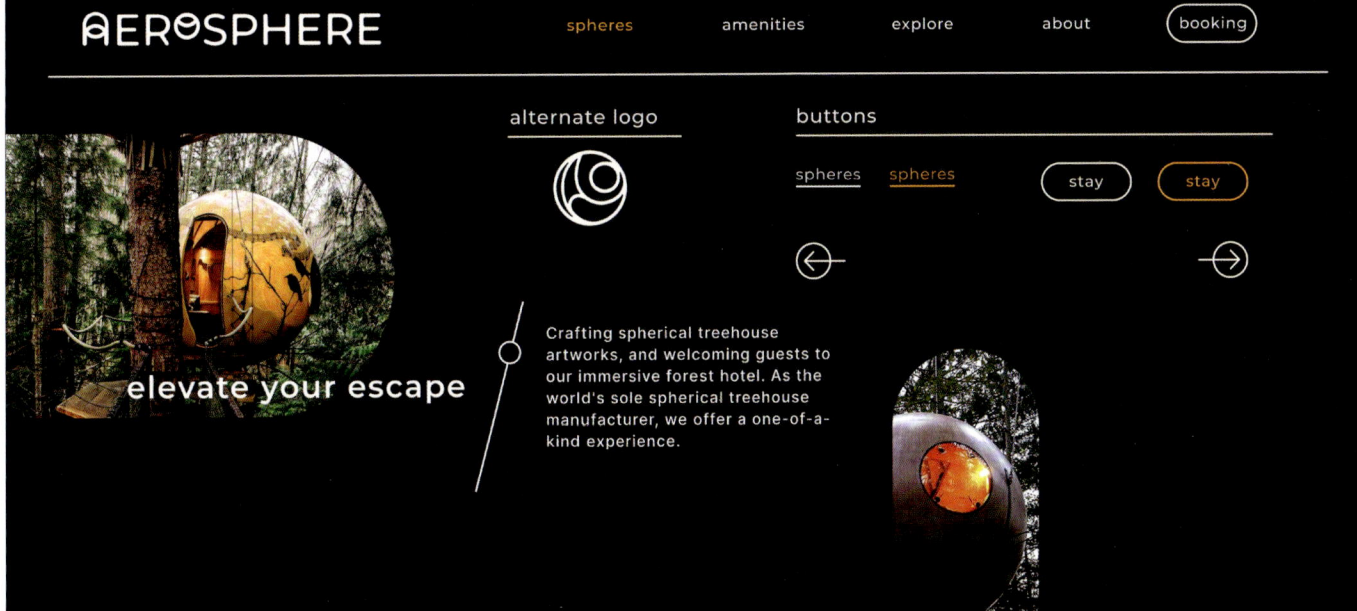

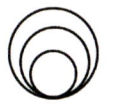  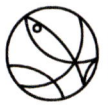 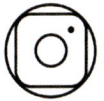

Design Silver Awards

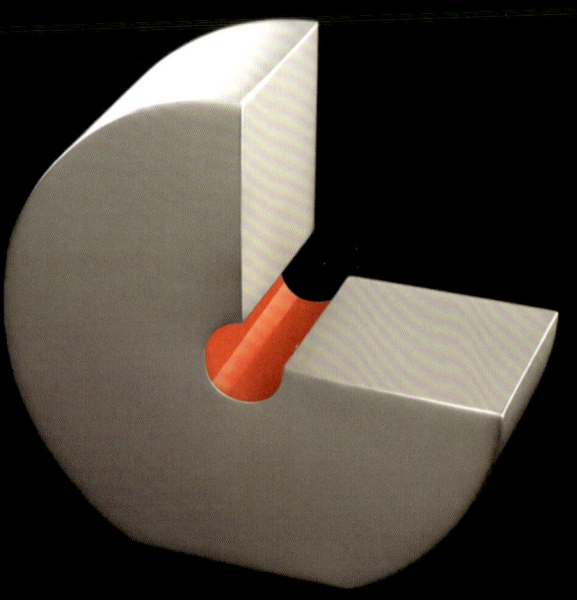

147 DESIGN SILVER

INSTRUCTORS **COURTNEY GOOCH, RORY SIMMS**

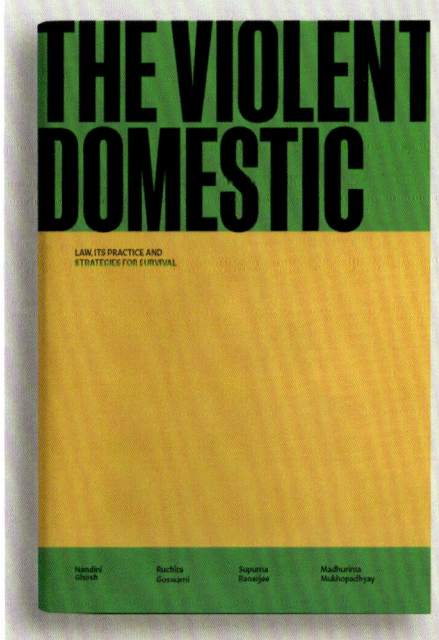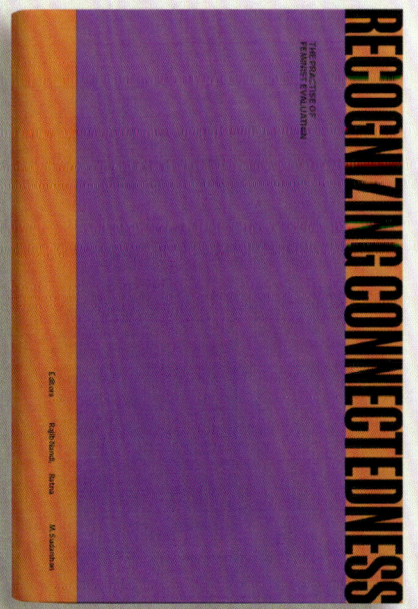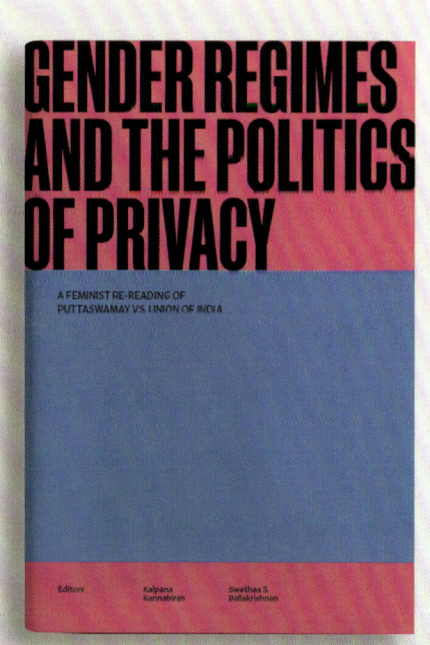

Student: Ariana Gupta | School: School of Visual Arts

INSTRUCTOR **JAN BALLARD**

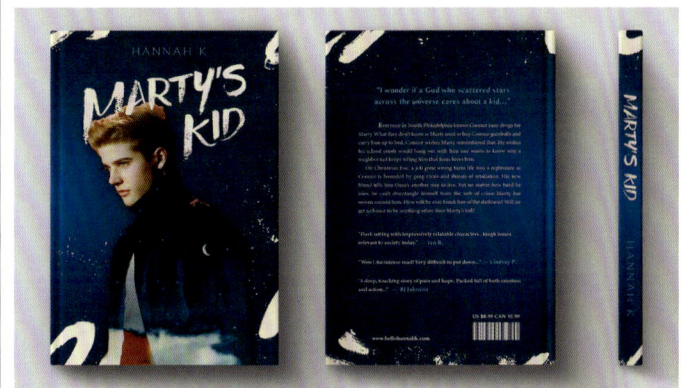

Student: Isabella Perez | School: Texas Christian University

INSTRUCTOR **MICHAEL NEAL**

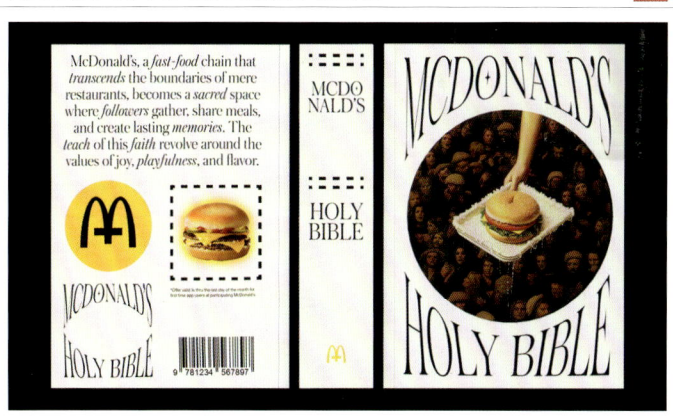

Student: Aoran Ma | School: ArtCenter College of Design

INST. **CONSTANTIN CHOPIN, SAMANTHA FLEMING**

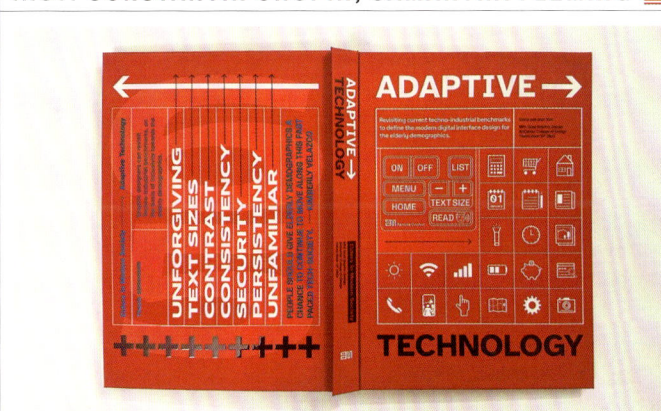

Student: Grace Kim | School: ArtCenter College of Design

INSTRUCTOR **JOSHUA EGE**

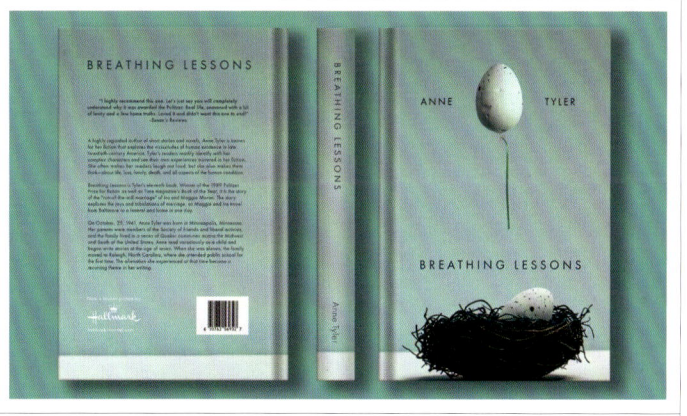

Student: Brett Roth | School: Texas A&M University-Commerce

Books | Design

148 DESIGN **SILVER**

INSTRUCTOR MAURIZIO MASI 🇺🇸

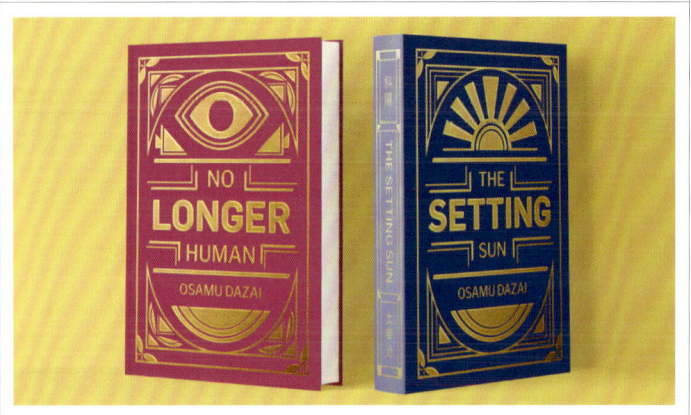

Student: Michelle Zhang | **School:** Lehigh University

INSTRUCTOR THERON MOORE 🇺🇸

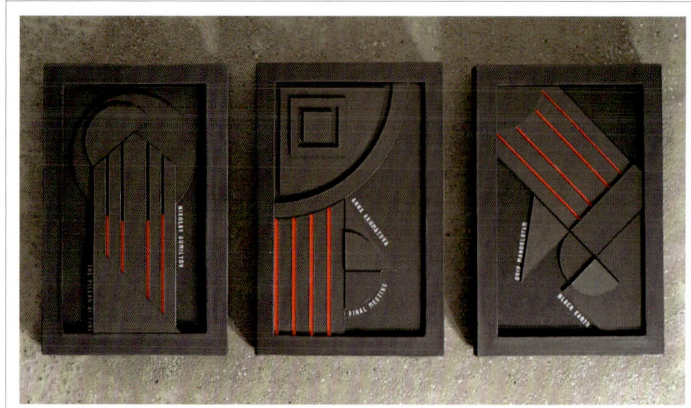

Student: Viktoriia Trapizonian | **School:** California State University, Fullerton

---

INSTRUCTOR THOMAS SCHARPF 🇺🇸

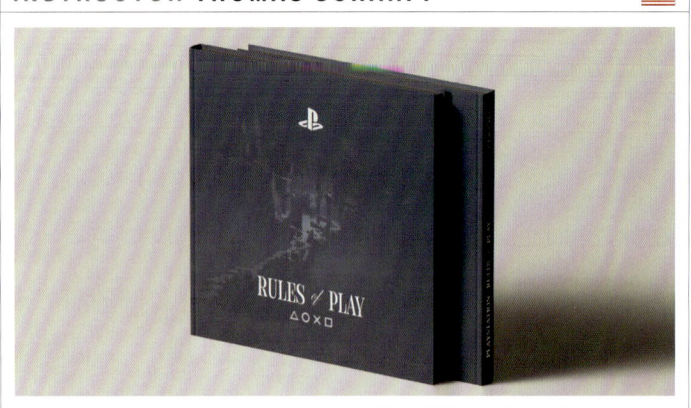

Students: Jade Chen, Jack DeMare
School: Virginia Commonwealth University, VCU Brandcenter

INSTRUCTOR STEPHEN ZHANG 🇺🇸

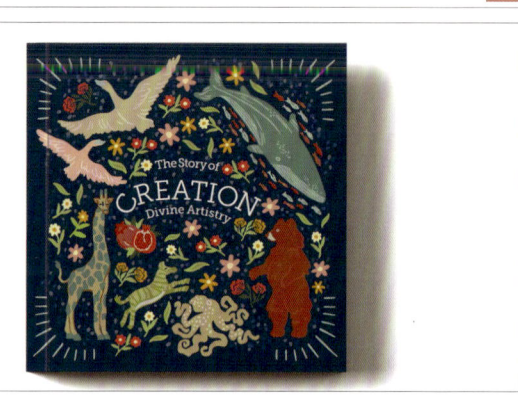

Student: Kyla Brown
School: University of North Texas

INSTRUCTOR LOUISE SANDHAUS 🇺🇸

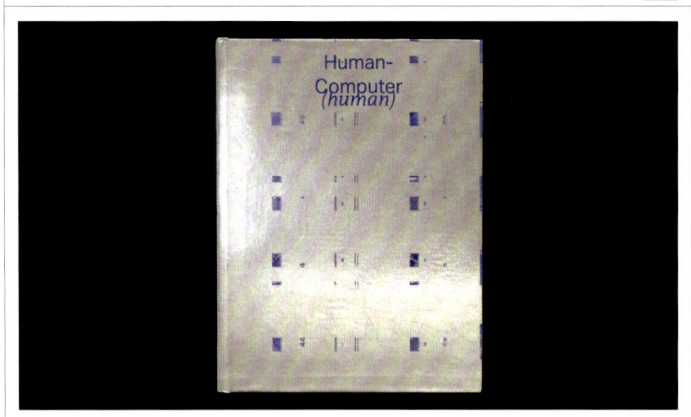

Student: Caihui Chen | **School:** California Institute of the Arts

---

INSTRUCTOR TRACEY SHIFFMAN 🇺🇸

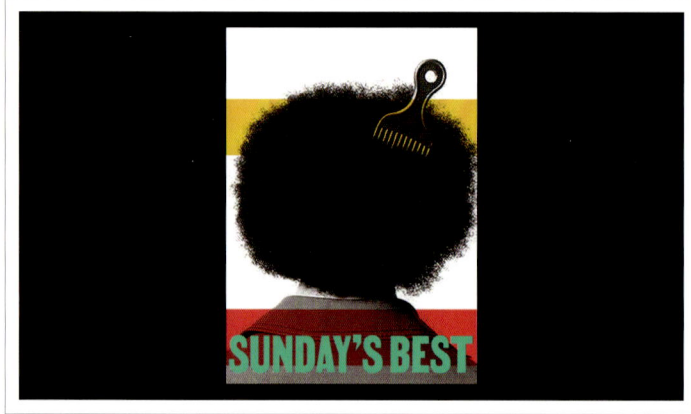

Student: Addis Ababa Barge | **School:** ArtCenter College of Design

---

INSTRUCTOR THERON MOORE 🇺🇸

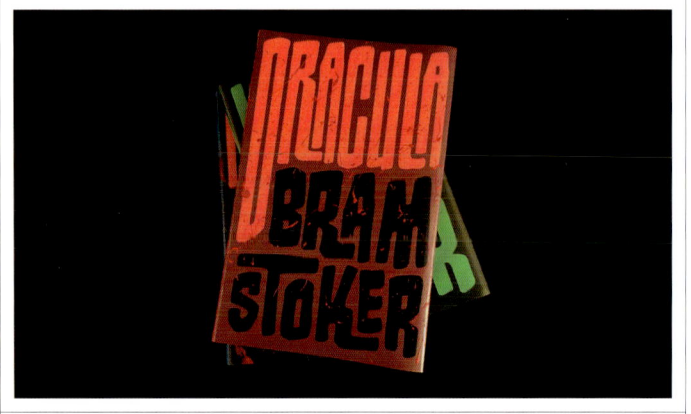

Student: Megan Cossins | **School:** California State University, Fullerton

---

INSTRUCTOR CHERI GRAY 🇺🇸

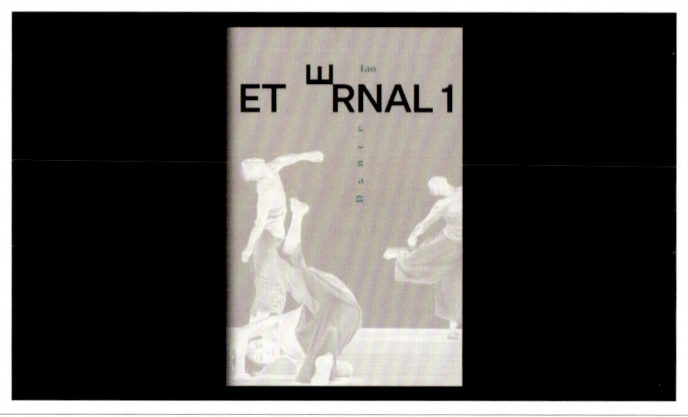

Student: Shuwen Ding | **School:** ArtCenter College of Design

Design | Books

149 DESIGN SILVER

INSTRUCTOR **UNATTRIBUTED**

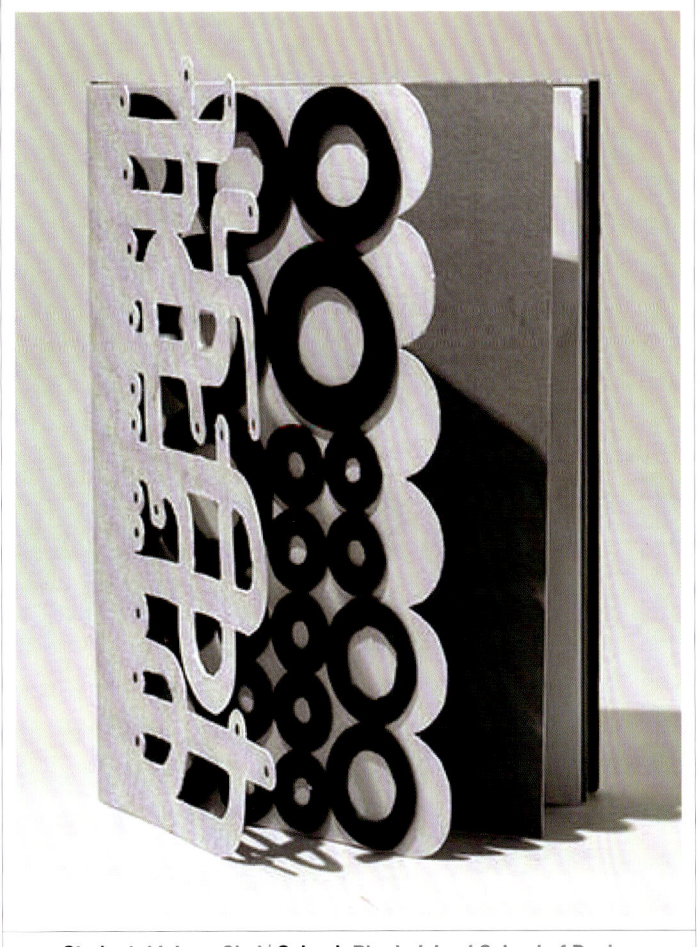

Student: Li June Choi | **School:** Rhode Island School of Design

INSTRUCTOR **HANK RICHARDSON**

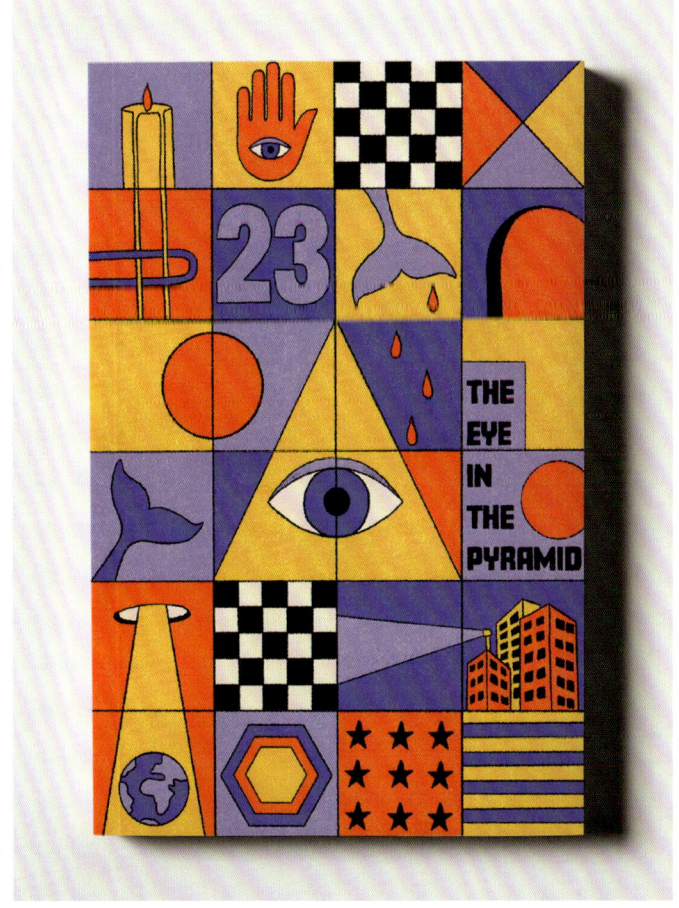

Student: Cassidy O'Connor | **School:** M.AD School of Ideas Atlanta

INSTRUCTOR **TRACEY SHIFFMAN**

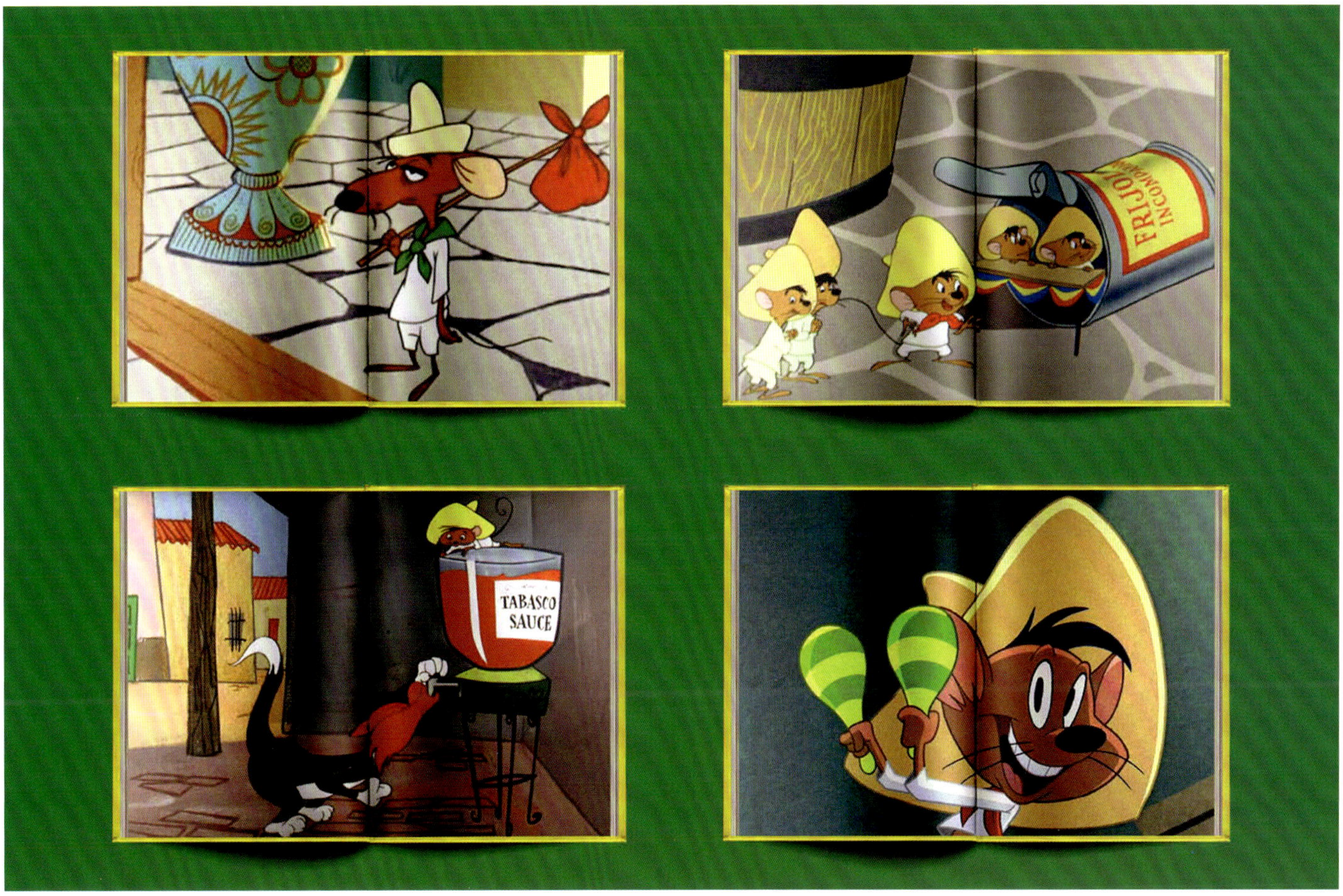

Student: Yvonne Ye | **School:** ArtCenter College of Design

Books | Design

150 DESIGN SILVER

INSTRUCTOR TRACEY SHIFFMAN

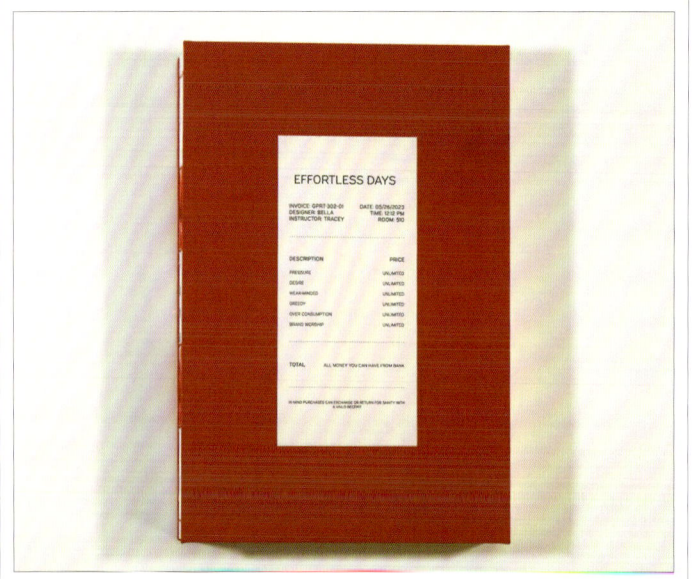

Student: Bella Wang | **School:** ArtCenter College of Design

INSTRUCTOR MAURIZIO MASI

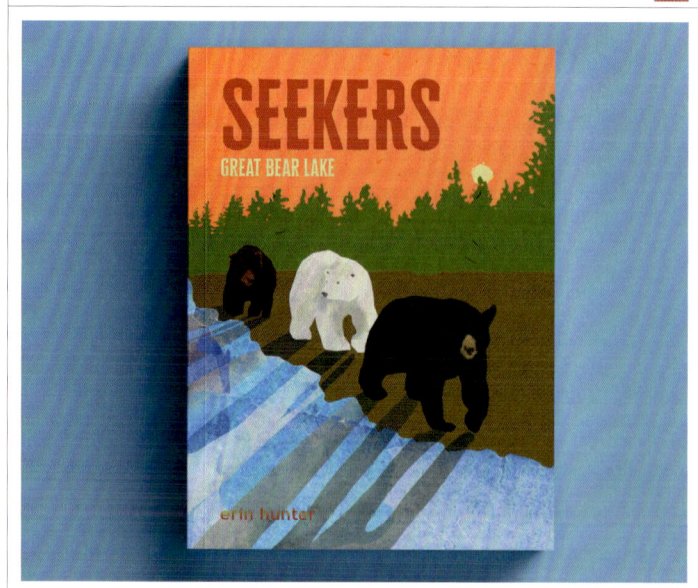

Student: Aviela Maynard | **School:** Lehigh University

INSTRUCTOR HANK RICHARDSON

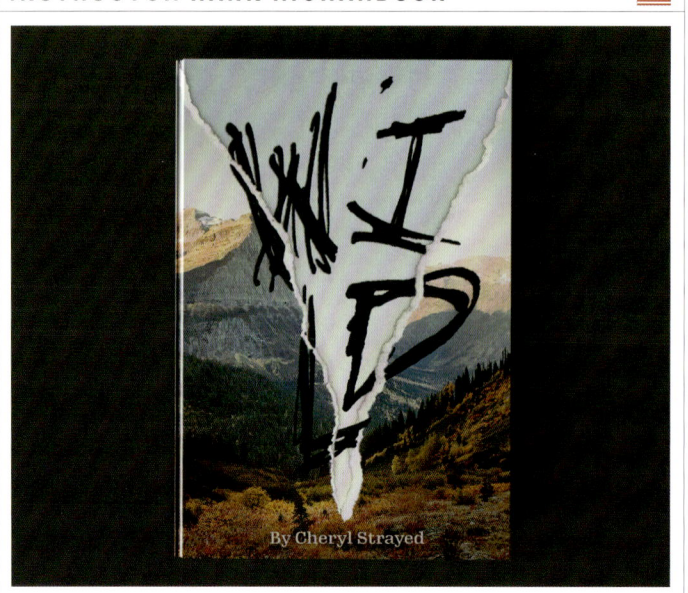

Student: Jamie Jason | **School:** M.AD School of Ideas Atlanta

INSTRUCTOR TRACEY SHIFFMAN

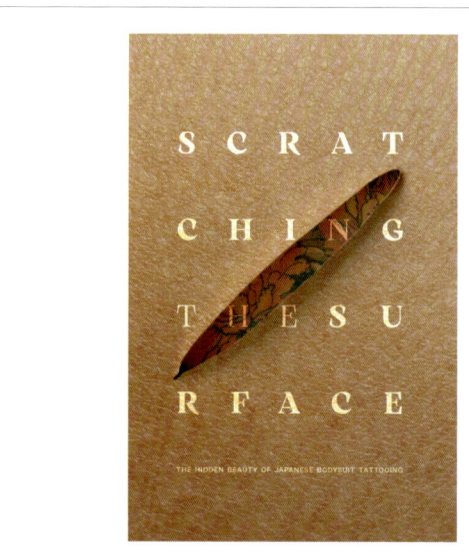

Student: Kyoko Takahashi | **School:** ArtCenter College of Design

INSTRUCTOR JIMENA GAMIO VALDIVIESO

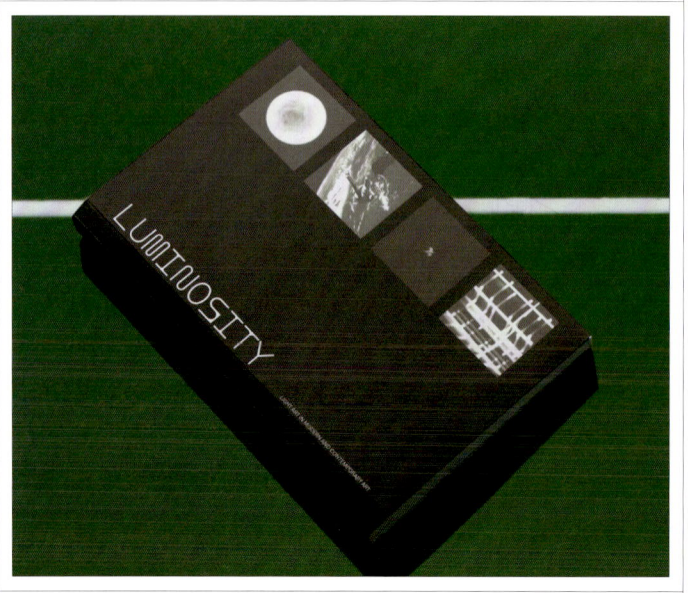

Student: Sydney Lee | **School:** ArtCenter College of Design

INSTRUCTORS TYLER COMRIE, ALEX MERTO

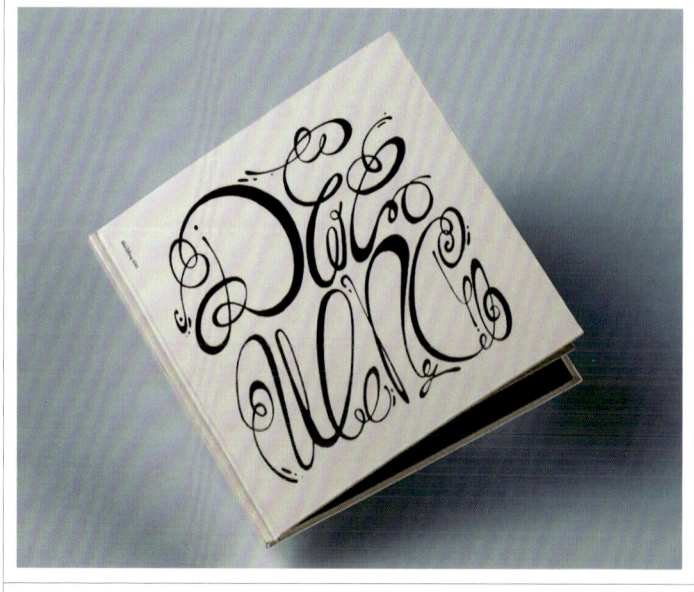

Student: Charlotte Grimm | **School:** School of Visual Arts

Design | Books

151 DESIGN SILVER

INSTRUCTOR **MATTHEW LENNING**

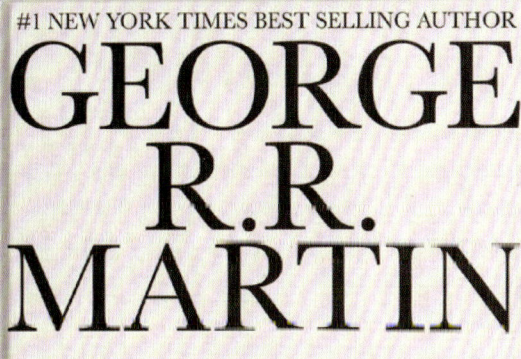

Student: Lela Fand | School: School of Visual Arts

INSTRUCTOR **STEPHEN ZHANG**

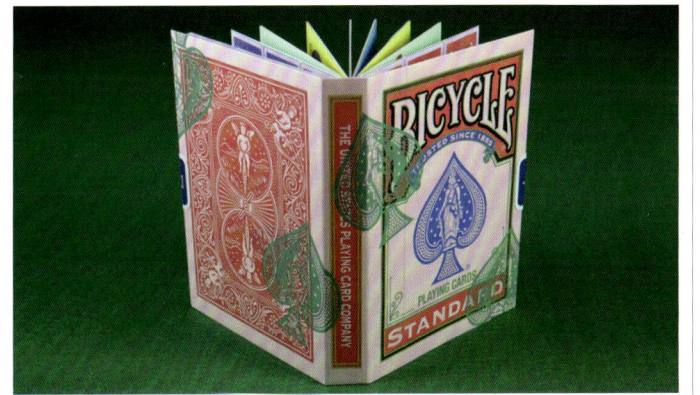

Student: Maxwell Pius | School: University of North Texas

INSTRUCTOR **HANK RICHARDSON**

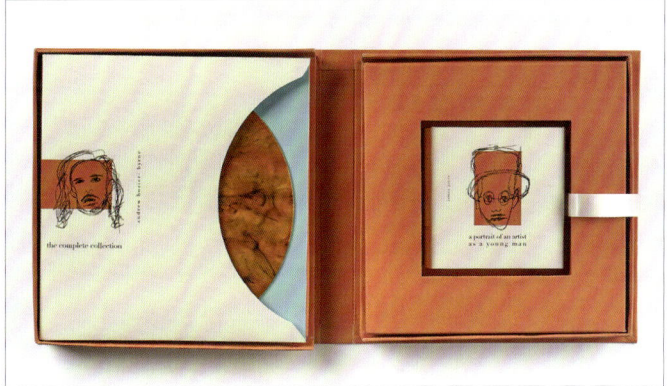

Student: Catarina Sterlacci | School: M.AD School of Ideas Atlanta

INSTRUCTOR **STEPHEN ZHANG**

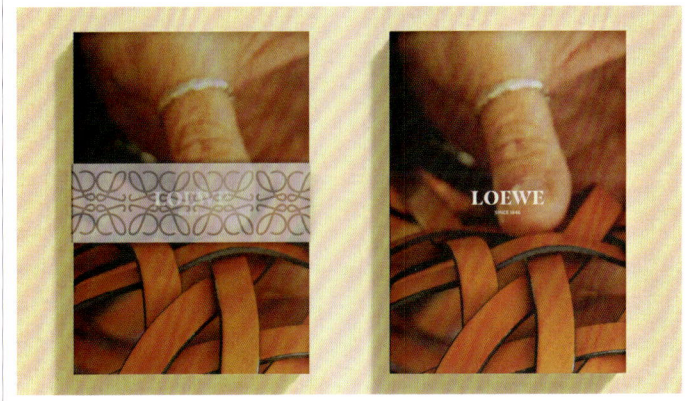

Student: Rachel Blow | School: University of North Texas

INSTRUCTOR **THERON MOORE**

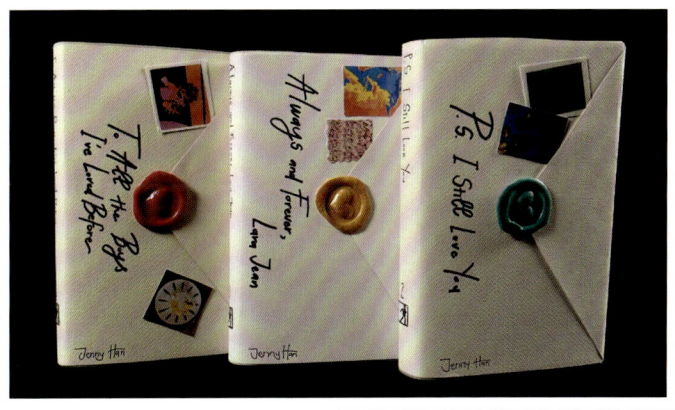

Student: Khoa Nguyen | School: California State University, Fullerton

152 DESIGN SILVER

INSTRUCTOR DOMINIQUE WALKER 🇨🇦

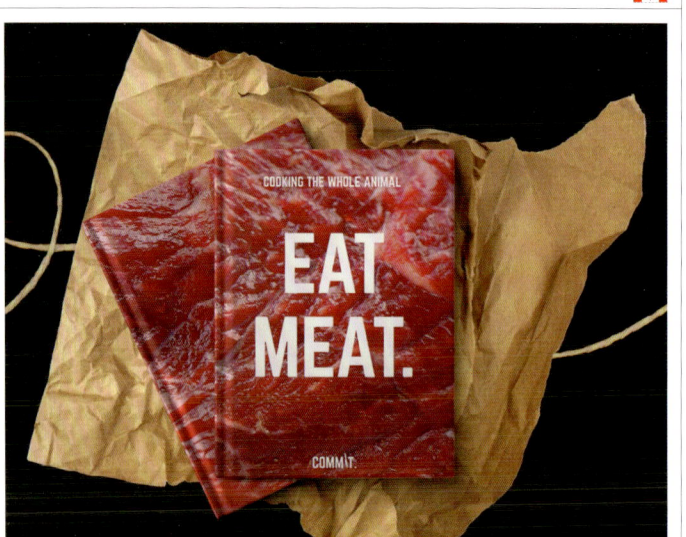

Student: Natasha Lee | **School:** Capilano University

INSTRUCTOR DOUG THOMAS 🇺🇸

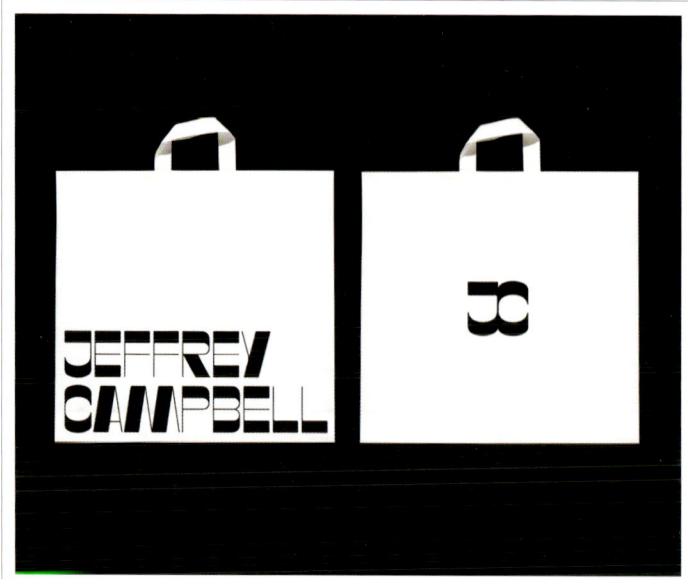

Student: Ellie Burrows | **School:** Brigham Young University

INSTRUCTOR SIMON JOHNSTON 🇺🇸

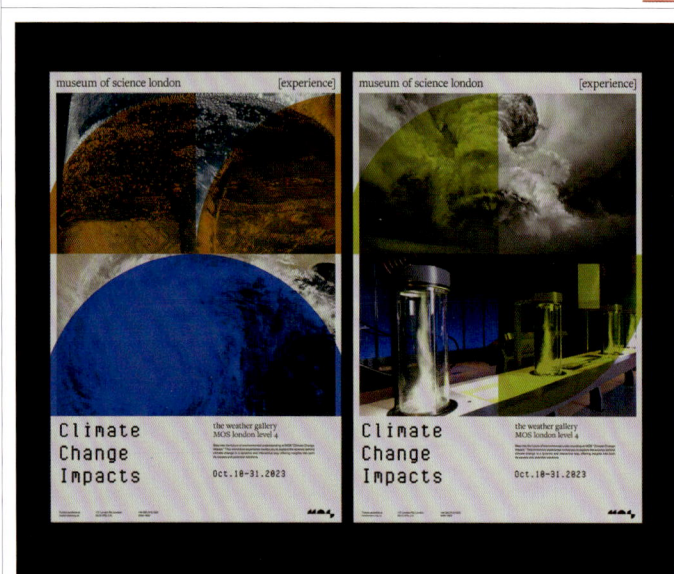

Student: Jaiwon Lee | **School:** ArtCenter College of Design

INSTRUCTOR JOSEPH HAN 🇺🇸

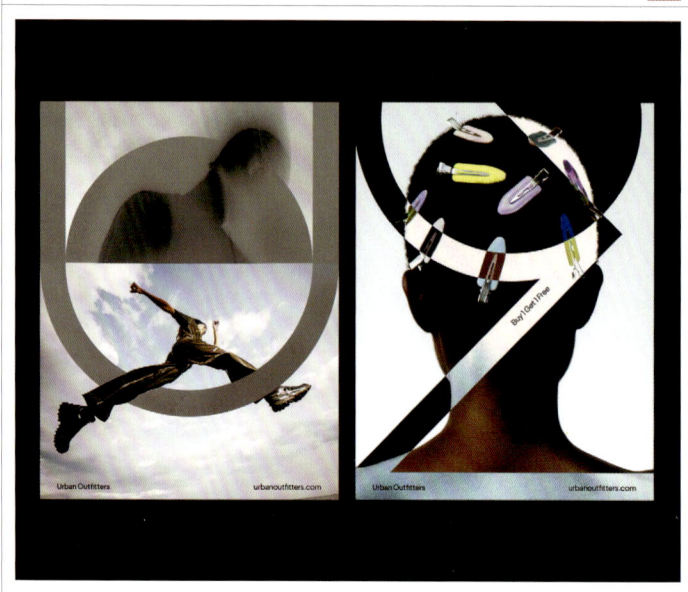

Student: Huu Minh Pham | **School:** School of Visual Arts

INSTRUCTOR ANNIE HUANG LUCK 🇺🇸

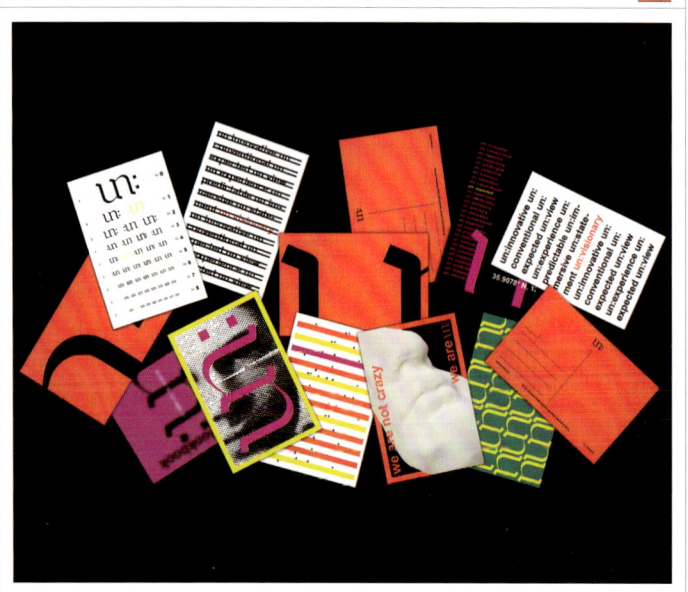

Student: Minsik Nam | **School:** ArtCenter College of Design

INSTRUCTOR JUSTIN COLT 🇺🇸

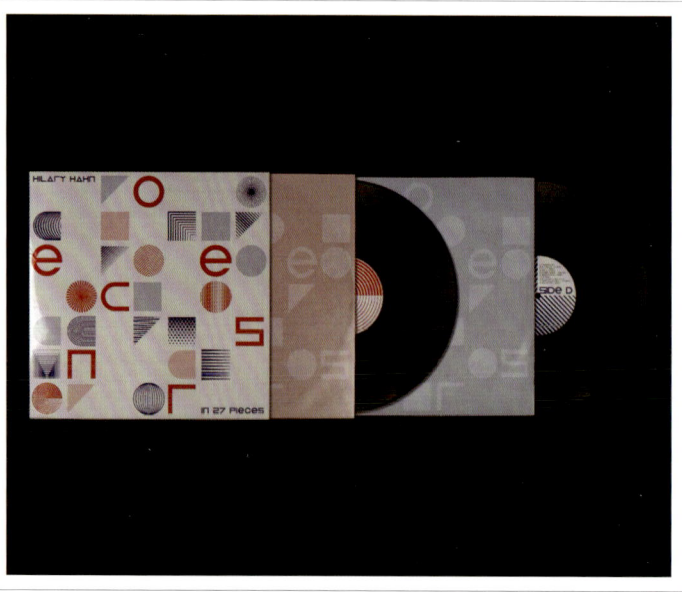

Student: Younghyun Kim | **School:** School of Visual Arts

Design | Branding

153 DESIGN SILVER

INSTRUCTOR SIMON JOHNSTON

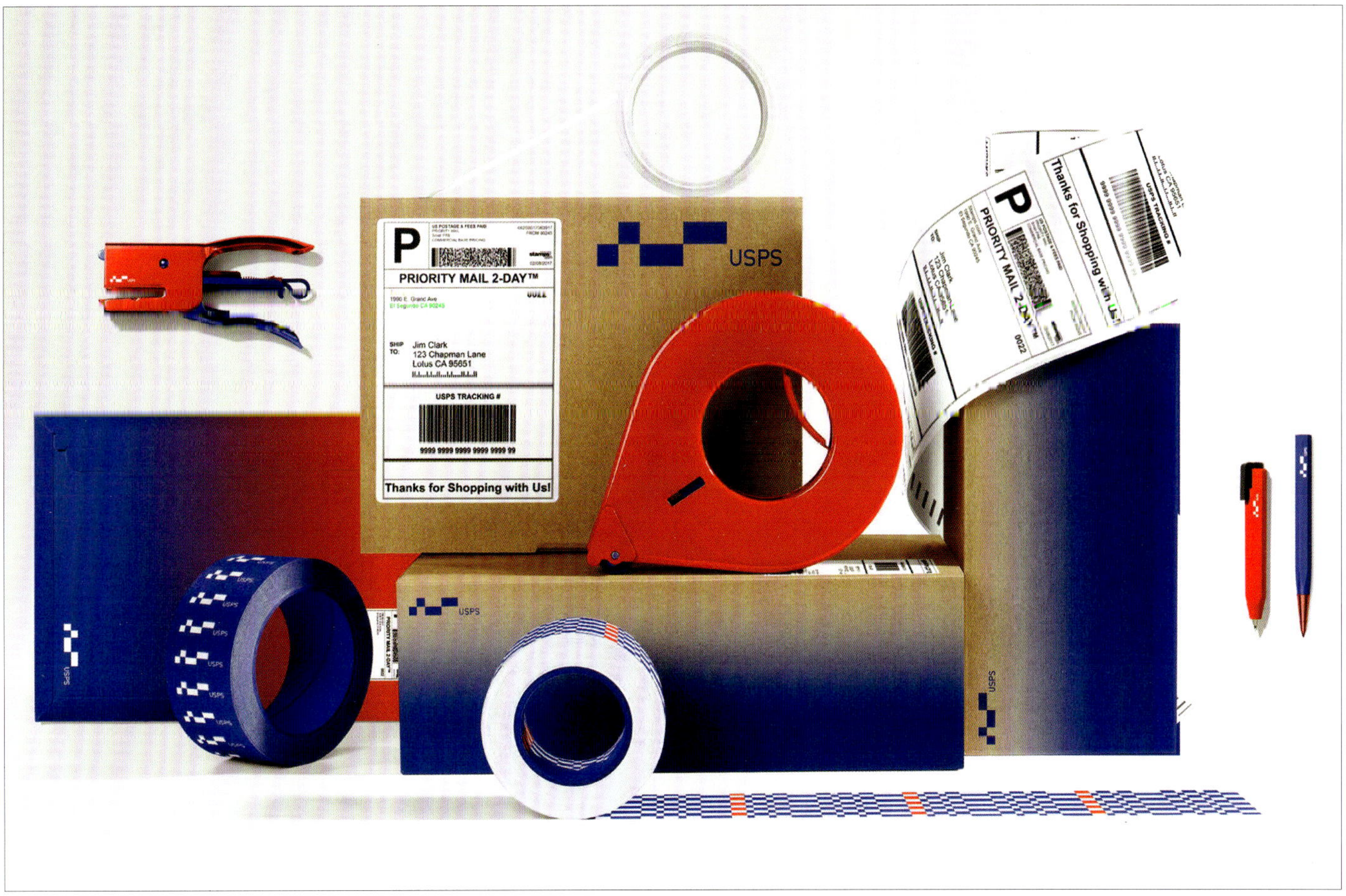

Student: Heejai Park | **School:** ArtCenter College of Design

INSTRUCTOR CHARLES LIN

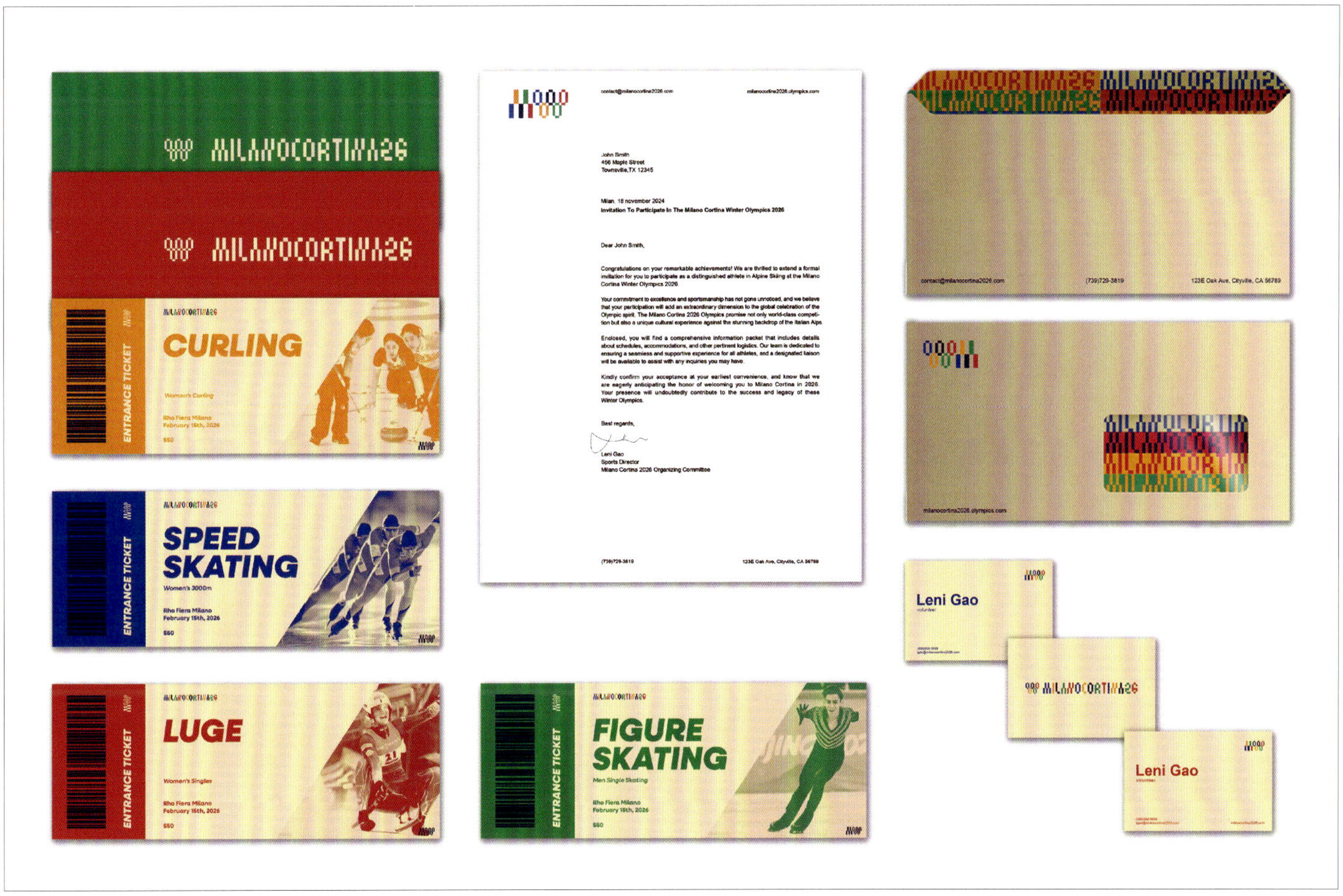

Student: Leni Gao | **School:** ArtCenter College of Design

154 DESIGN SILVER

INSTRUCTOR BILL GALYEAN
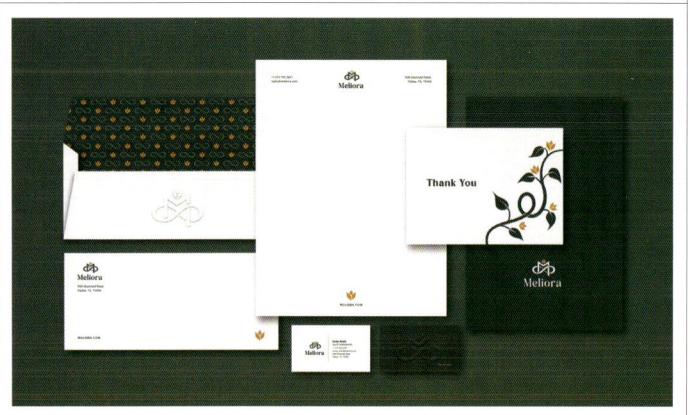
Student: Isabella Baker | **School:** Texas Christian University

INSTRUCTOR GERARDO HERRERA
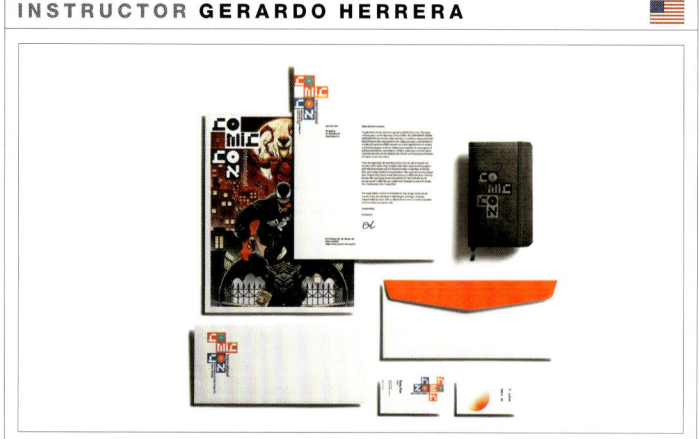
Student: Orlando Li | **School:** ArtCenter College of Design

INSTRUCTOR PETER AHLBERG
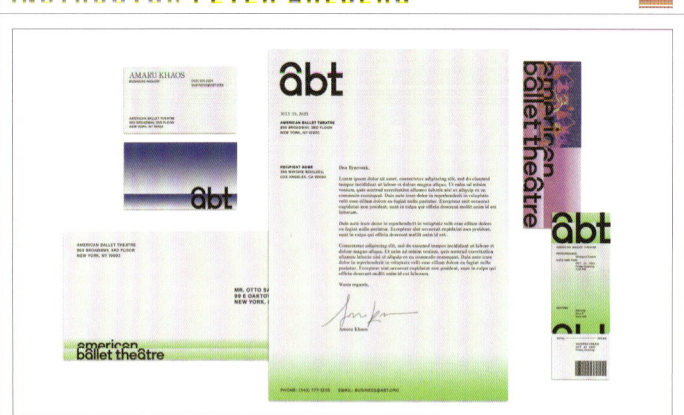
Student: Alicia Liu | **School:** School of Visual Arts

INSTRUCTOR SIMON JOHNSTON
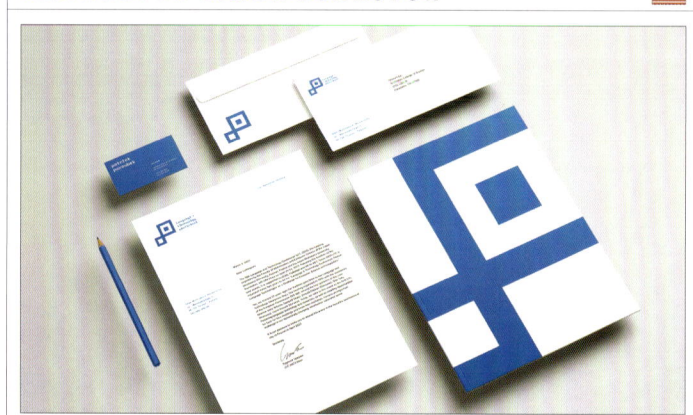
Student: Mishen Liu | **School:** ArtCenter College of Design

INSTRUCTOR GENARO SOLIS RIVERO
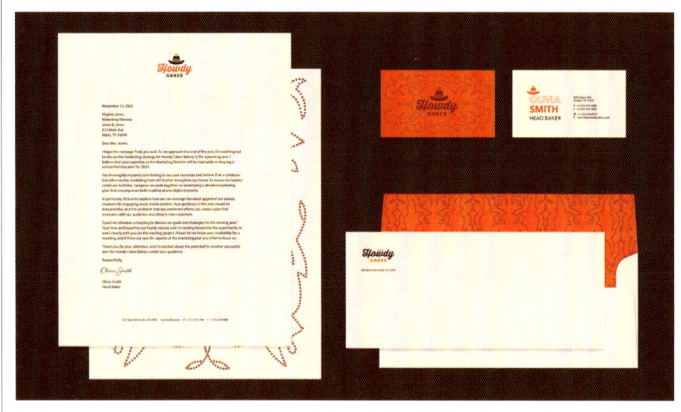
Student: Kate Sudderth | **School:** Baylor University

INSTRUCTOR ERIC BAKER
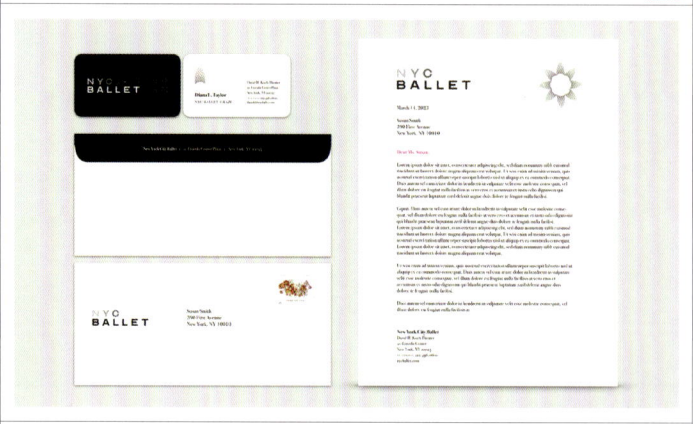
Student: Jiyeon Kim | **School:** School of Visual Arts

INSTRUCTOR GERARDO HERRERA
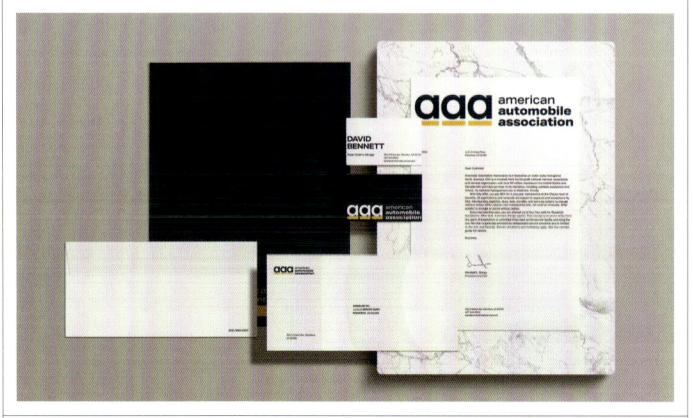
Student: Shengjie Wu | **School:** ArtCenter College of Design

INSTRUCTOR BILL GAYLEAN
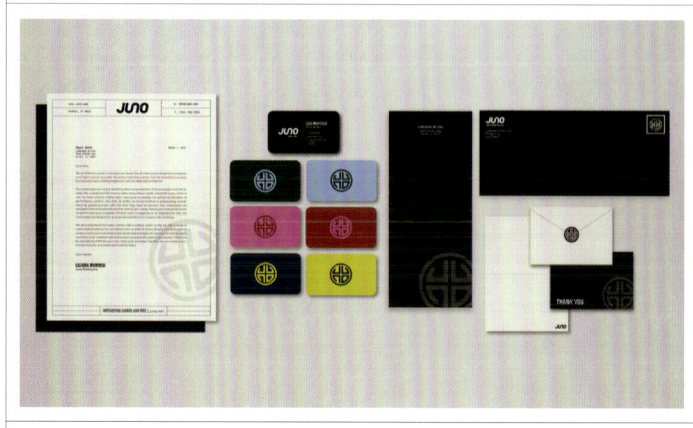
Student: Corinne Green | **School:** Texas Christian University

Design | Branding

155 DESIGN SILVER

INSTRUCTOR BRAD BARTLETT
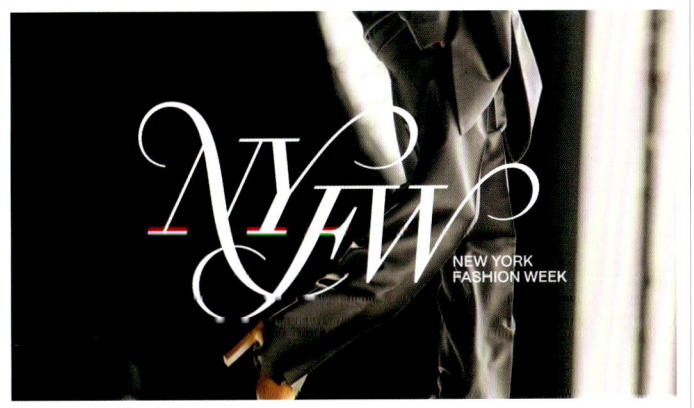
Student: Lilian Pham | **School:** ArtCenter College of Design

INSTRUCTOR HANK RICHARDSON
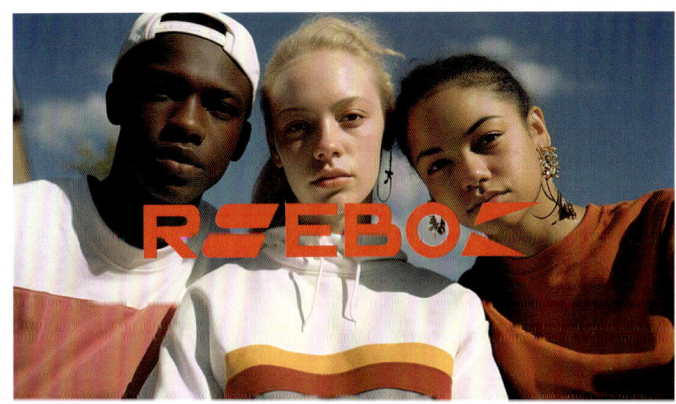
Student: Anna LeBer | **School:** M.AD School of Ideas Atlanta

INSTRUCTOR SIMON JOHNSTON
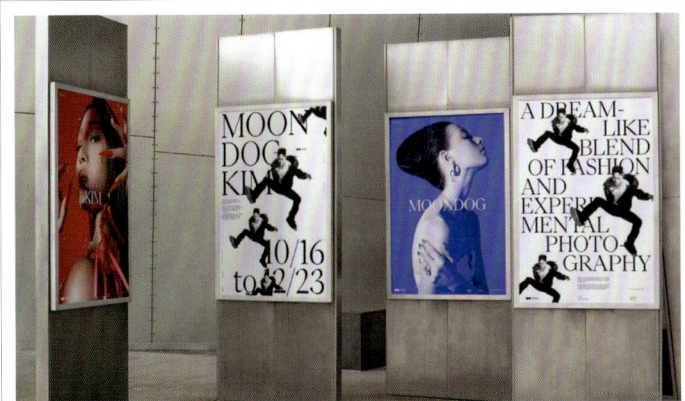
Student: Alan Xu | **School:** ArtCenter College of Design

INSTRUCTOR BEN DOLEZAL
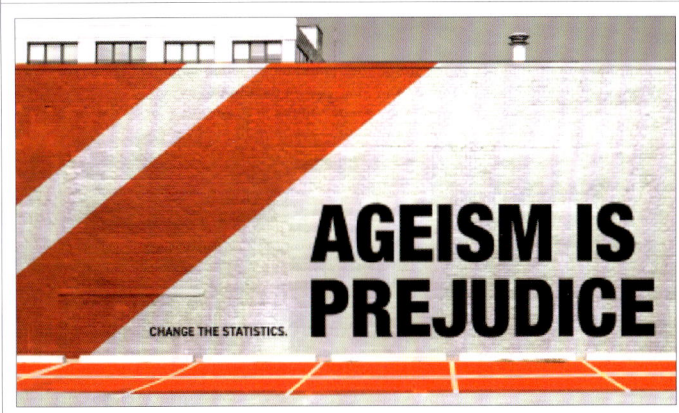
Student: Emily Brown | **School:** University of Texas at Arlington

INSTRUCTOR DOUGLAS MAY
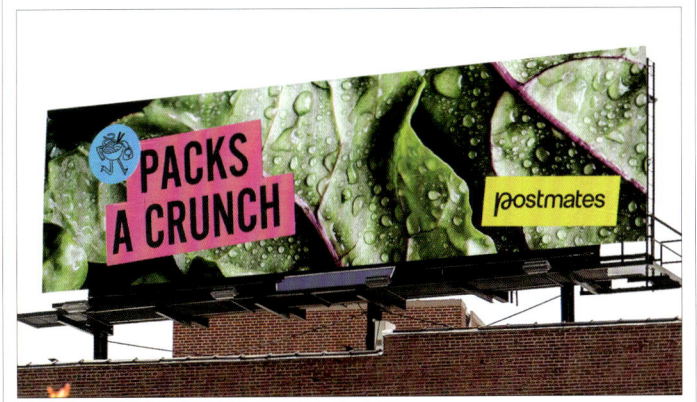
Student: Maeci Ray | **School:** University of North Texas

INSTRUCTOR CHARLES LIN
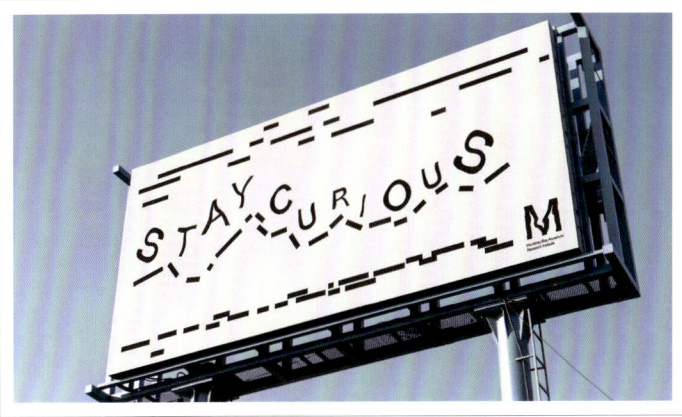
Student: Meiyun Chen | **School:** ArtCenter College of Design

INSTRUCTOR MING TAI
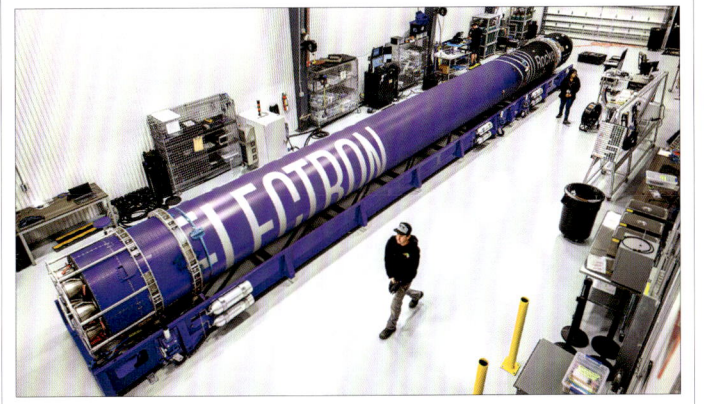
Student: Hanson Ma | **School:** ArtCenter College of Design

INSTRUCTOR DOUGLAS MAY
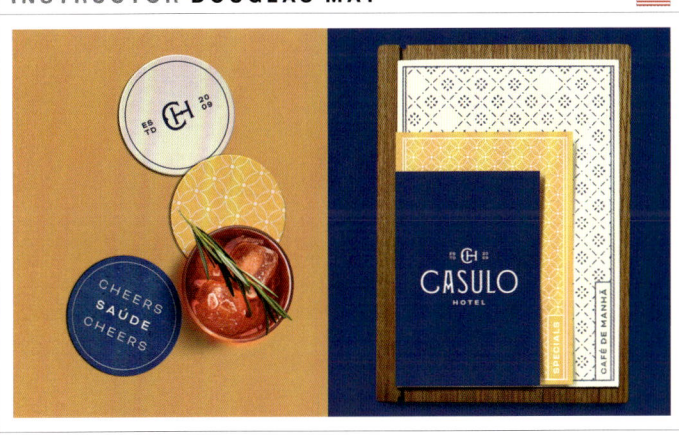
Student: Jordan Heath | **School:** University of North Texas

Branding | Design

156 DESIGN SILVER

INSTRUCTOR LINDA REYNOLDS 🇺🇸

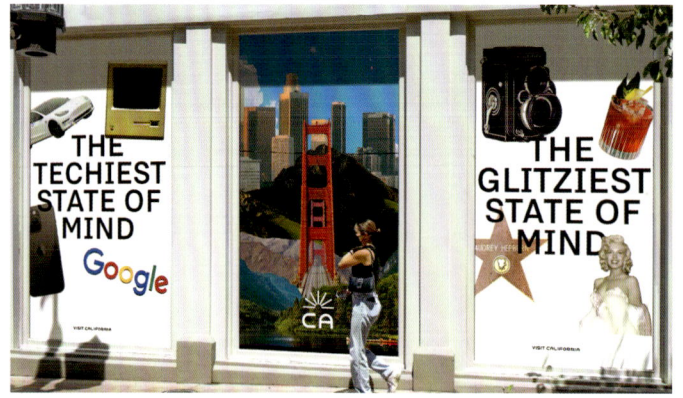

Student: Hannah Javadi | **School:** Brigham Young University

INSTRUCTOR ERIC BAKER 🇺🇸

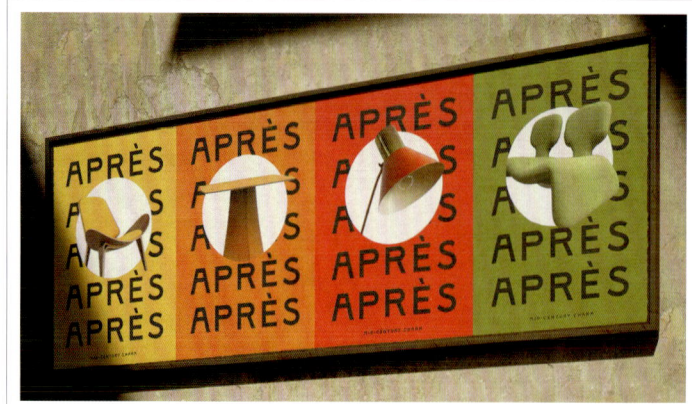

Student: Claudia Curbelo | **School:** School of Visual Arts

INSTRUCTOR MICHAEL KONETZKA 🇺🇸

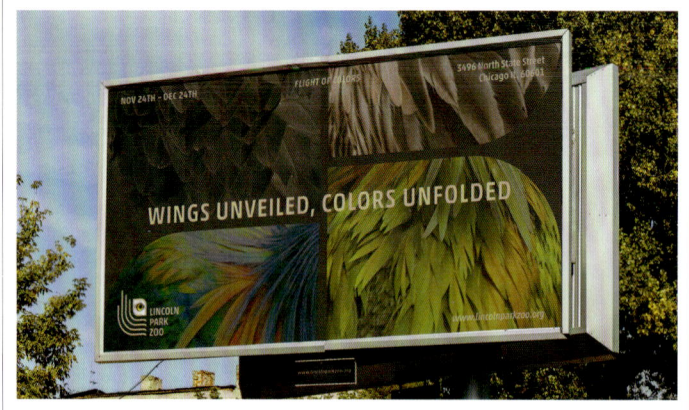

Student: Xiaoqi Shang | **School:** School of the Art Institute of Chicago

INSTRUCTOR CINDY BUCKLEY KOREN 🇺🇸

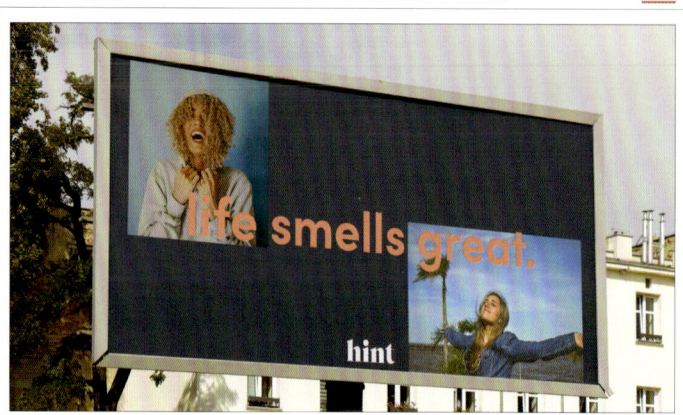

Student: Jonathan Lin | **School:** Pratt Institute

INSTRUCTOR ELAINE ALDERETTE 🇺🇸

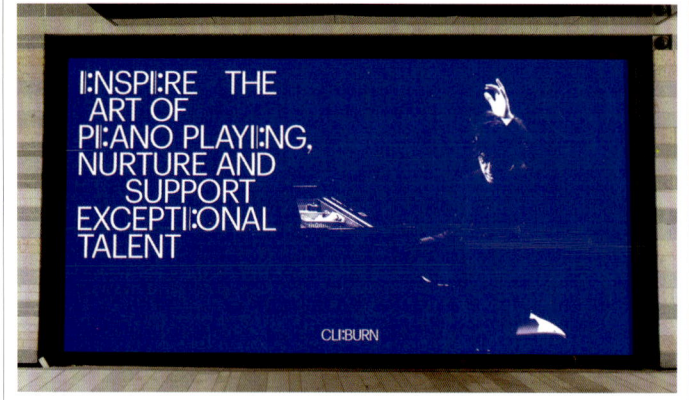

Student: Esther Yeseul Lee | **School:** ArtCenter College of Design

INSTRUCTOR JOANA PEREIRA 🇬🇧

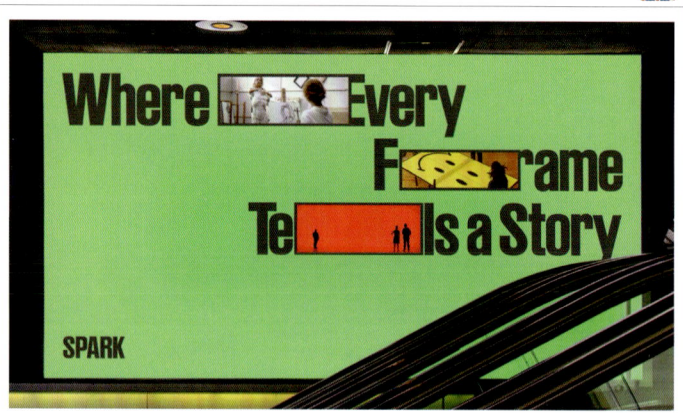

Student: Wenbin Sun | **School:** University of the Arts London

INSTRUCTOR PEDRO MENDES 🇺🇸

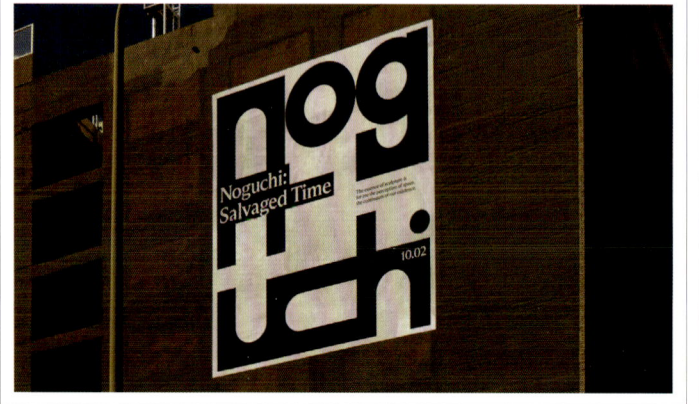

Student: Doah Kwon | **School:** School of Visual Arts

INSTRUCTOR LUIS BRAVO 🇺🇸

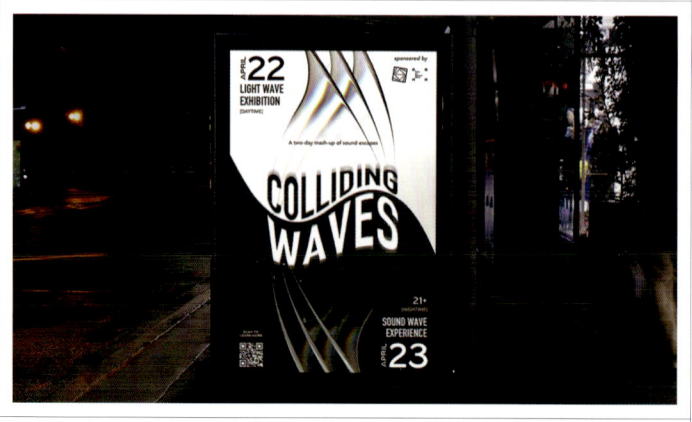

Student: Michele Mardorf | **School:** M.AD School of Ideas

Design | Branding

157 DESIGN SILVER

INSTRUCTOR SIMON JOHNSTON

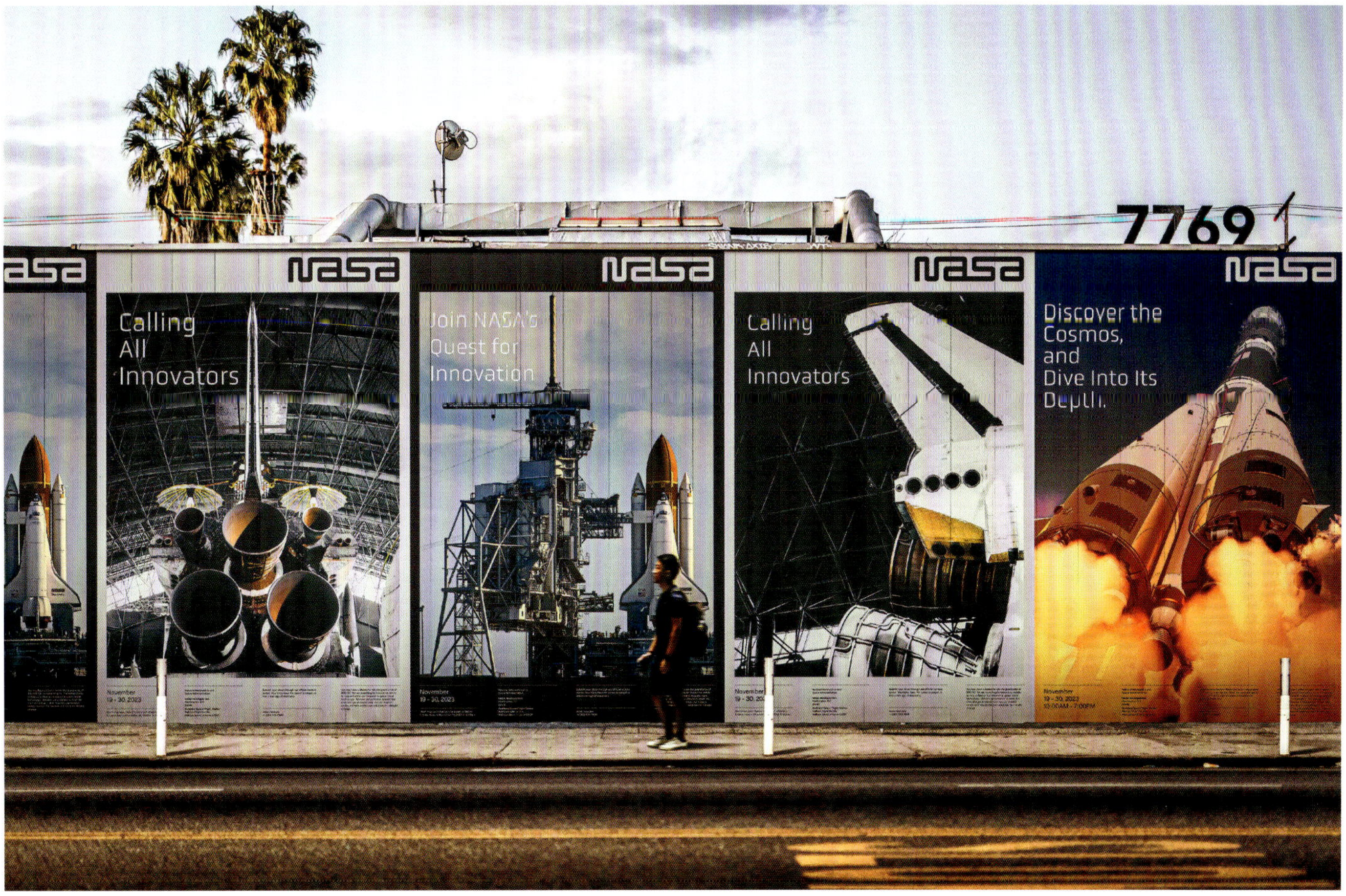

Student: Elaine Gong | School: ArtCenter College of Design

INSTRUCTOR MING TAI

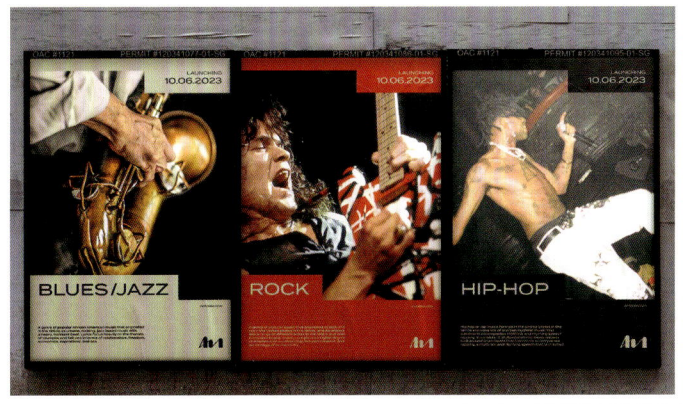

Student: Jiani Hong | School: ArtCenter College of Design

INSTRUCTOR SIMON JOHNSTON

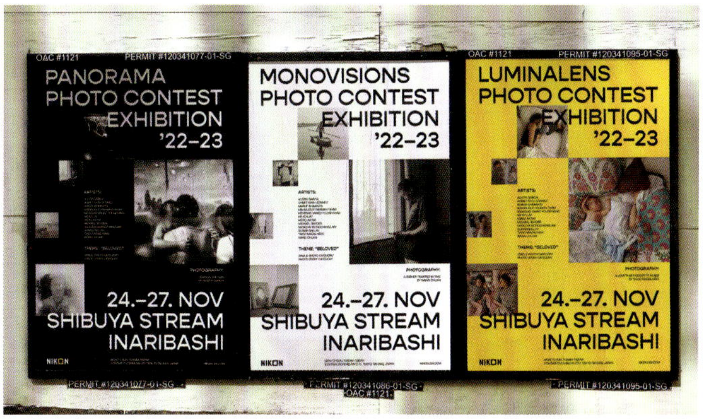

Student: Kissa Angjaya | School: ArtCenter College of Design

INSTRUCTOR SIMON JOHNSTON

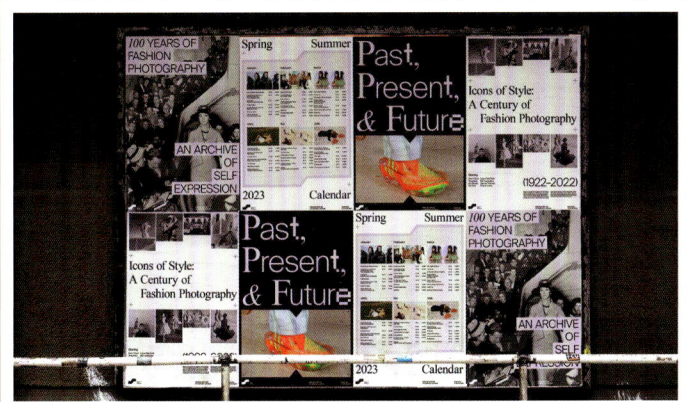

Student: Ruby Minhyoung Kim | School: ArtCenter College of Design

INSTRUCTOR ANDREA TRABUCCO-CAMPOS

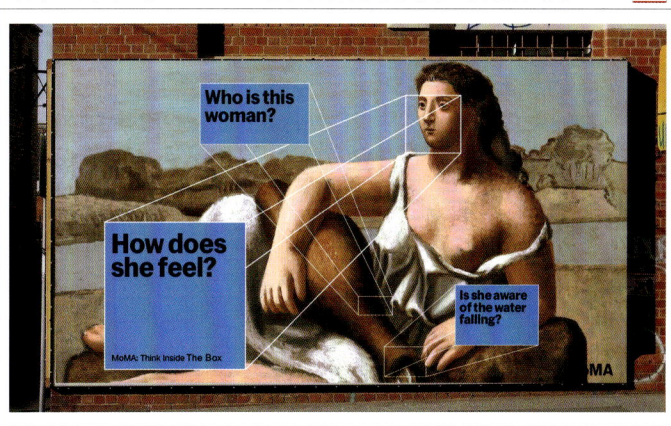

Student: Doyeon Kim | School: School of Visual Arts

Branding | Design

158 DESIGN SILVER

INSTRUCTOR KATHI ZSOLT

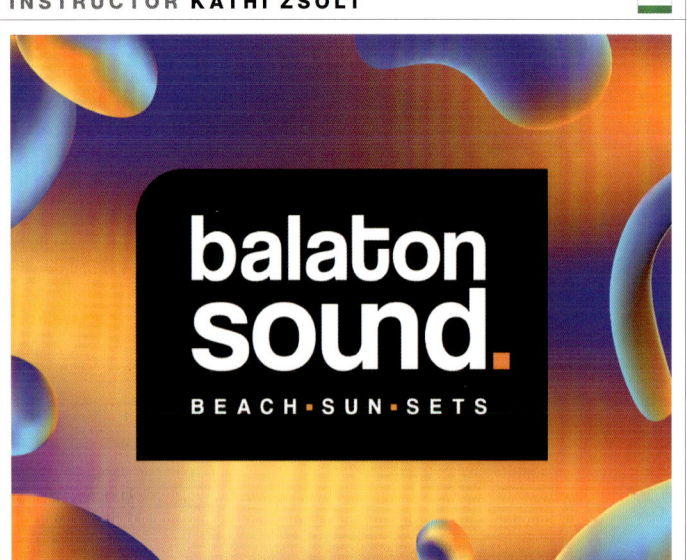

Student: Anastasia Charalambous | **School:** KREA Design School

INSTRUCTOR ANGAD SINGH

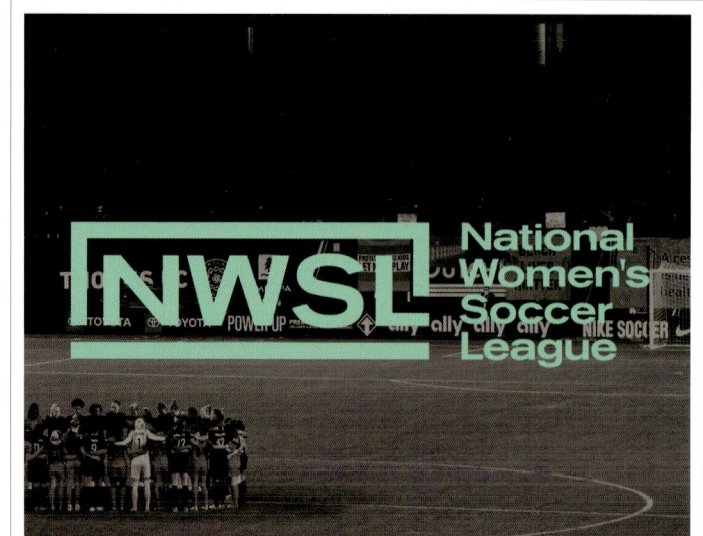

Student: Brian White | **School:** ArtCenter College of Design

INSTRUCTOR NICOLE ZIZILA

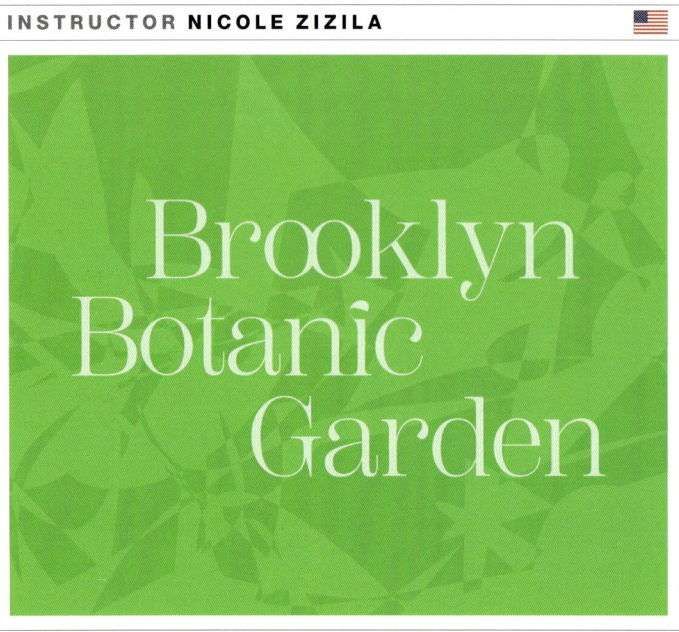

Student: Yong Han Shin | **School:** Fashion Institute of Technology

INSTRUCTOR NICOLE ZIZILA

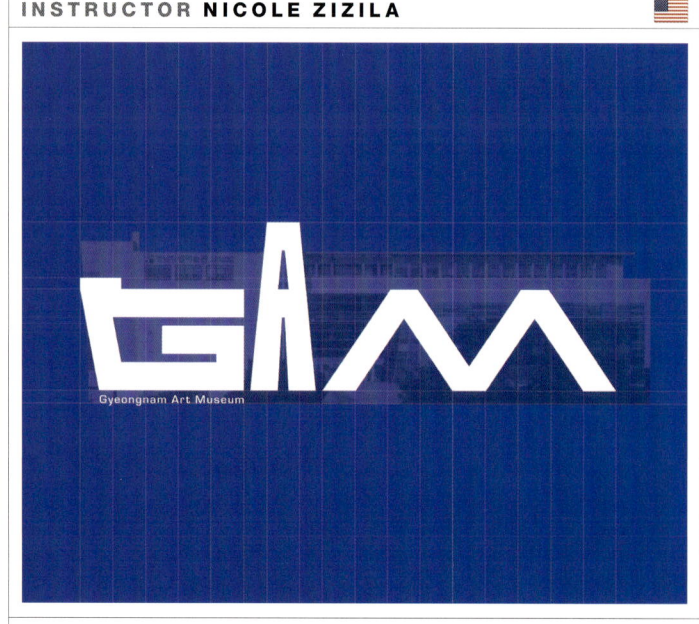

Student: Yong Han Shin | **School:** Fashion Institute of Technology

INSTRUCTOR HANK RICHARDSON

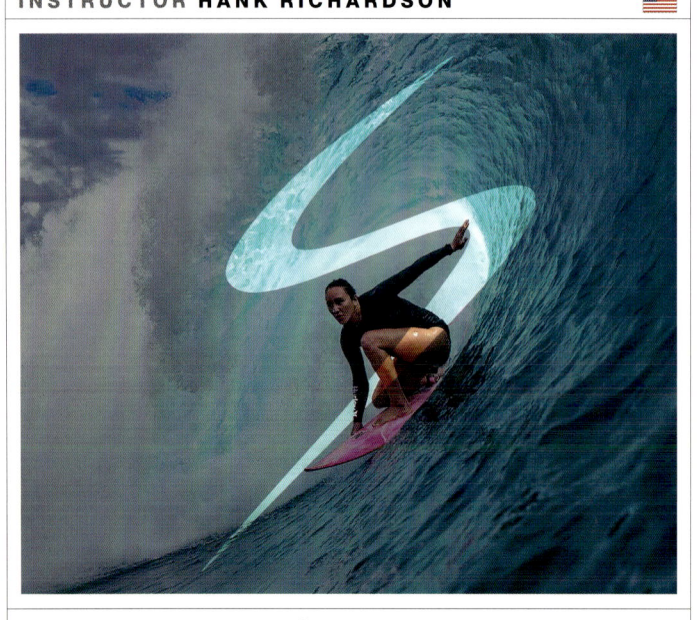

Student: Catarina Sterlacci | **School:** M.AD School of Ideas Atlanta

INSTRUCTORS JEFF DAVIS, WILLIAM MEEK

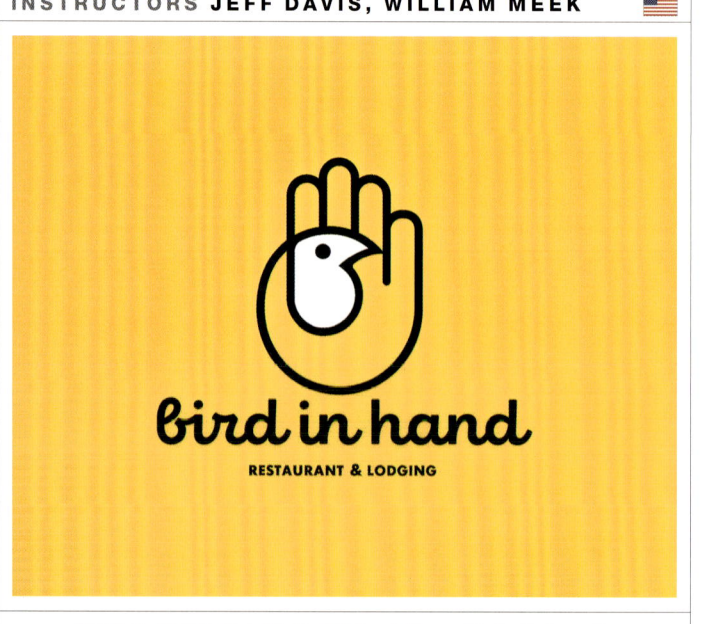

Student: Kelsie Brouillette | **School:** Texas State University

Design | Branding

159 DESIGN SILVER

INSTRUCTOR STEPHEN ZHANG 🇺🇸

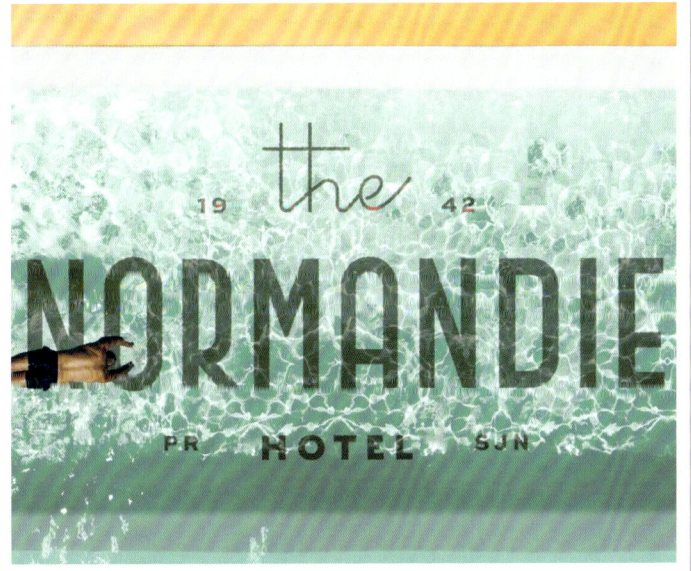

Student: Mariangelis Pagan | **School:** University of North Texas

INSTRUCTOR HANK RICHARDSON 🇺🇸

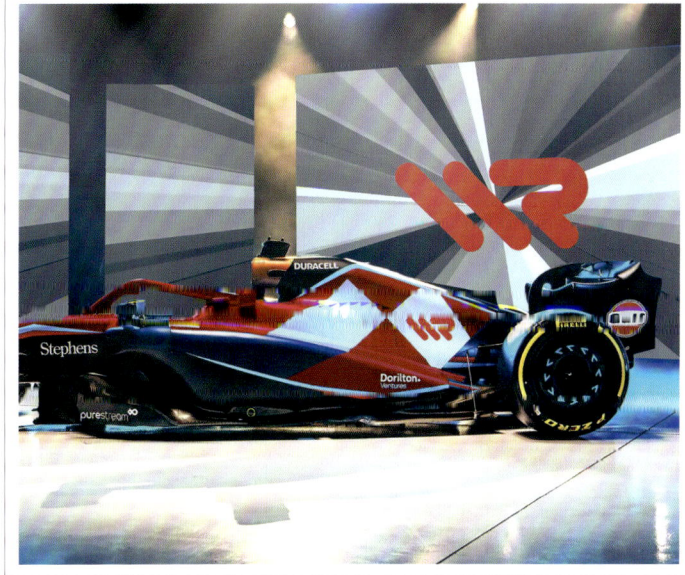

Student: Reagan Williams | **School:** M.AD School of Ideas Atlanta

INSTRUCTOR GENARO SOLIS RIVERO 🇺🇸

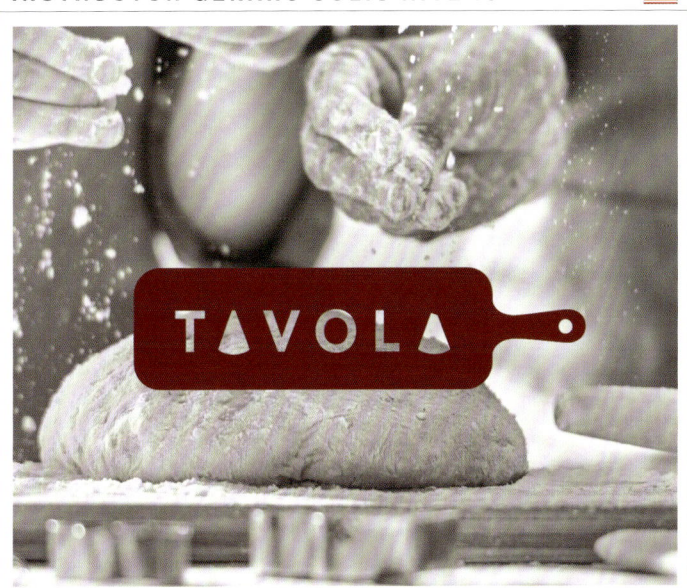

Student: Brooke Sockwell | **School:** Baylor University

INSTRUCTOR JUSTIN COLT 🇺🇸

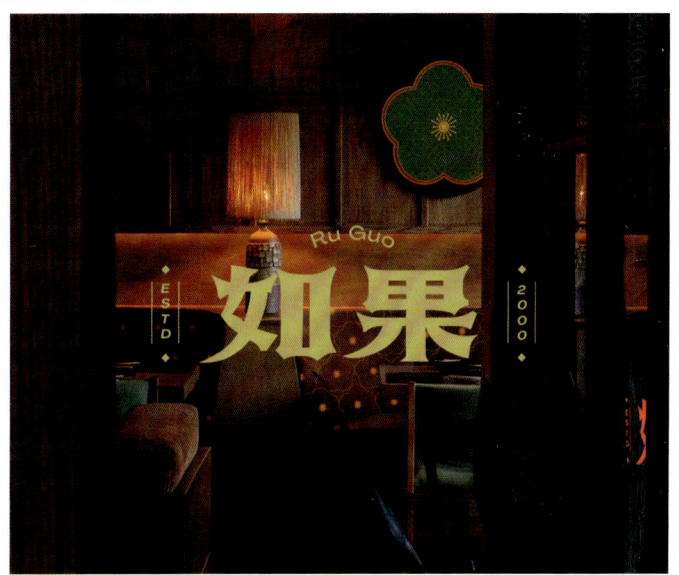

Student: Tzu-Chieh (Kate) Wu | **School:** School of Visual Arts

INSTRUCTORS SHIRLEEN LAVALAIS, MILES MAZZIE 🇺🇸

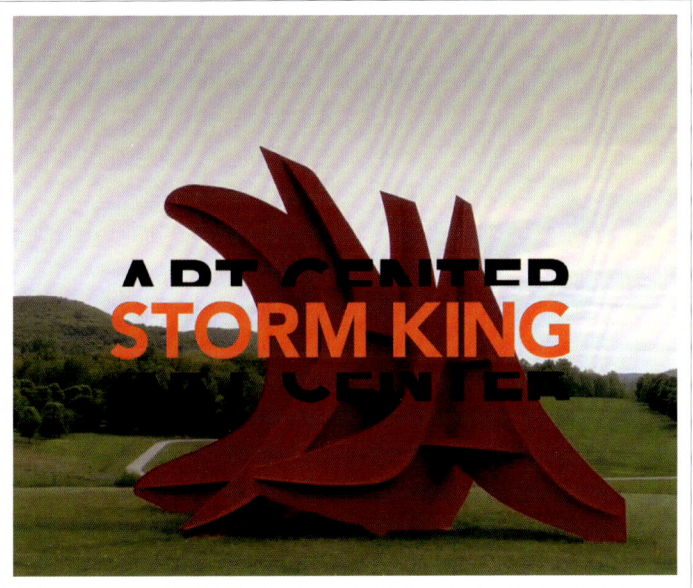

Student: Sydney Lee | **School:** ArtCenter College of Design

INSTRUCTOR SCOTTY REIFSNYDER 🇺🇸

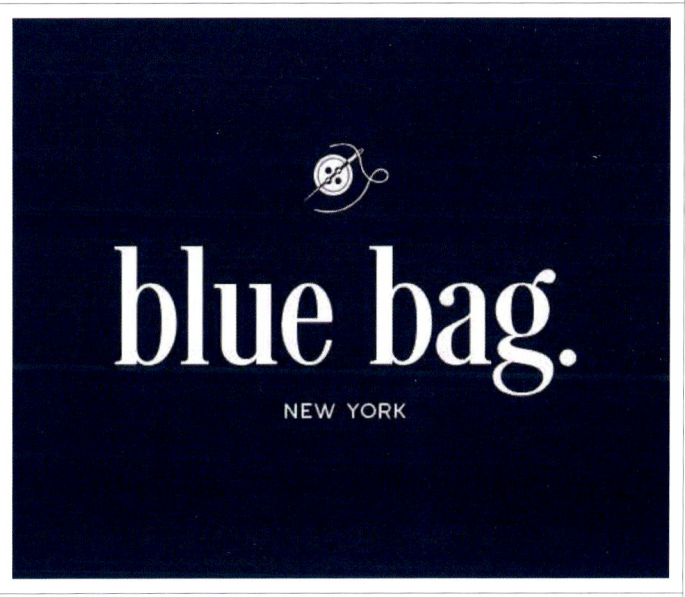

Student: Madison Kalbach | **School:** West Chester University

Branding | Design

160 DESIGN SILVER

INSTRUCTOR ELAINE ALDERETTE 🇺🇸

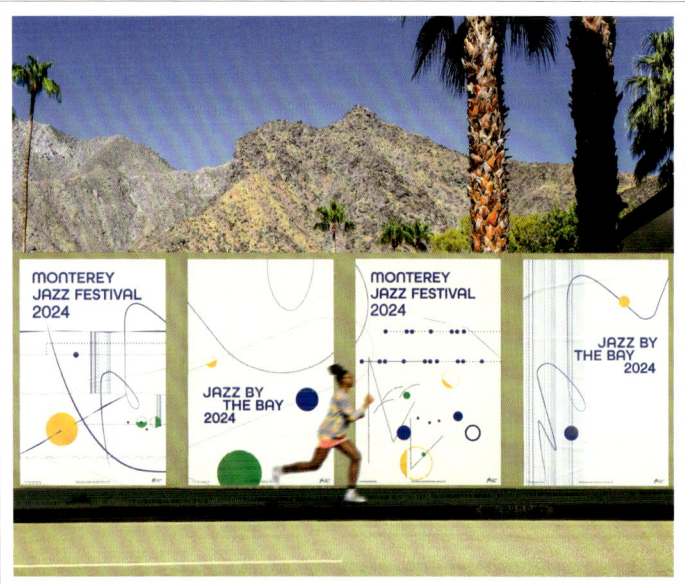

Student: Elaine Lee | **School:** ArtCenter College of Design

INSTRUCTOR BRAD BARTLETT 🇺🇸

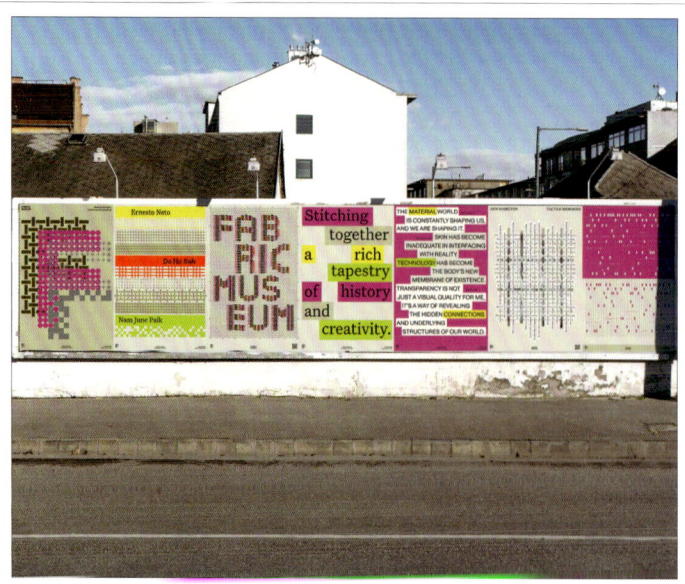

Student: Jocelyn Ziying Zhao | **School:** ArtCenter College of Design

INSTRUCTOR EMILY BURNS 🇺🇸

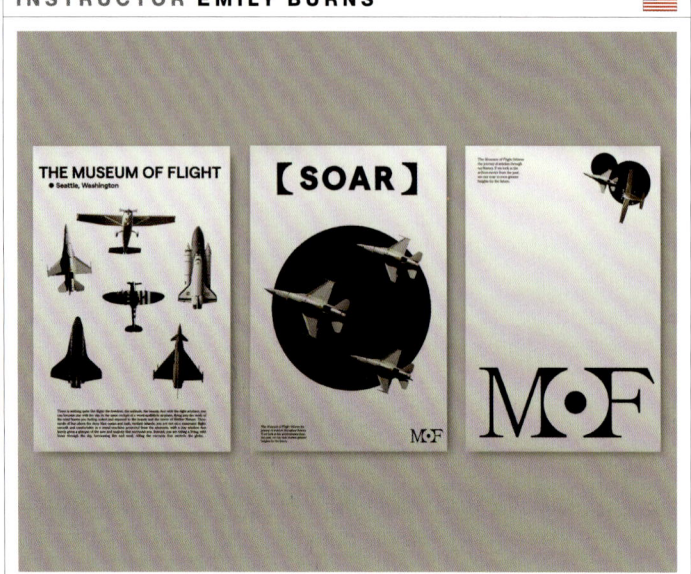

Students: Colette Albertson, Emma Cohen, Madison Laufer, Will Welsh
School: Pennsylvania State University

INSTRUCTOR PEDRO MENDES 🇺🇸

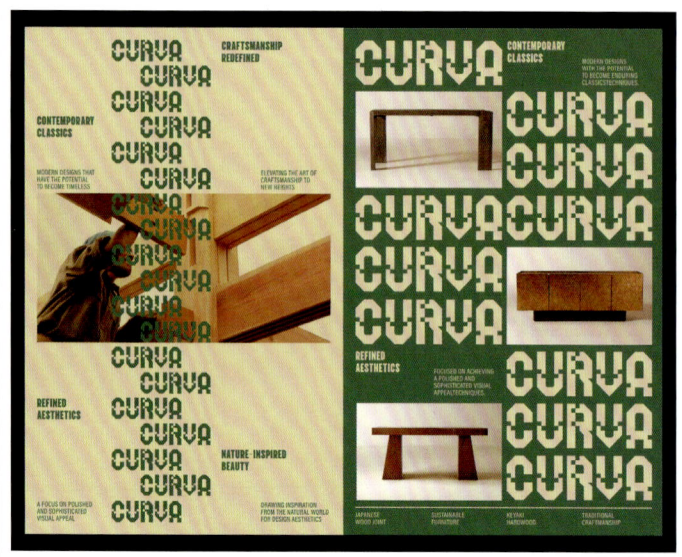

Student: Seongyun Park
School: School of Visual Arts

INSTRUCTOR KAREN WATKINS 🇺🇸

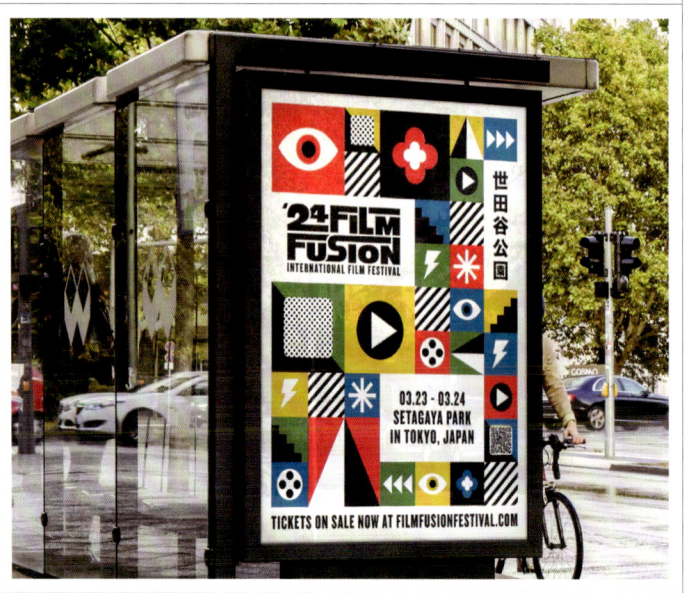

Student: Morgan Strusallen | **School:** West Chester University

INSTRUCTOR ERIC BAKER 🇺🇸

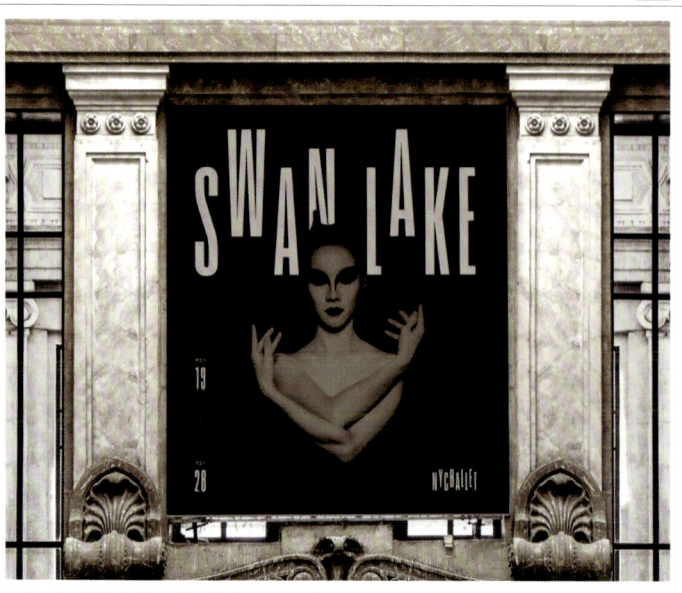

Student: Yixuan Wang | **School:** School of Visual Arts

Design | Branding

161 DESIGN SILVER

INSTRUCTOR BRAD BARTLETT

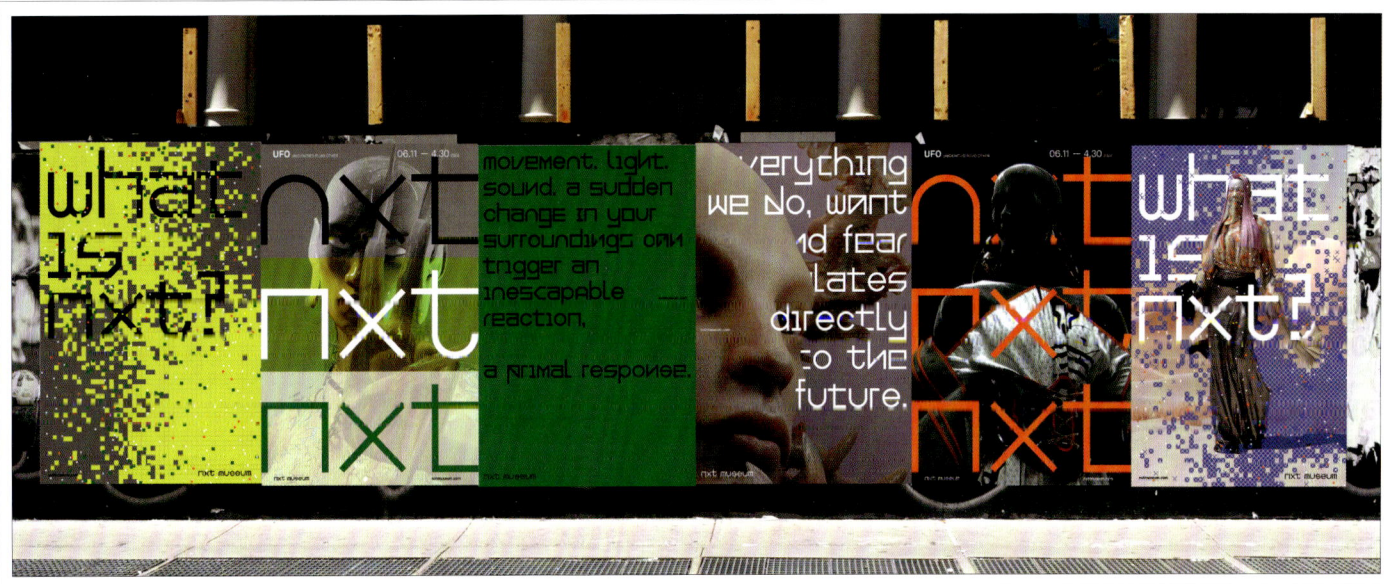

Student: Lillian Zhang | **School:** ArtCenter College of Design

INSTRUCTOR ELAINE ALDERETTE

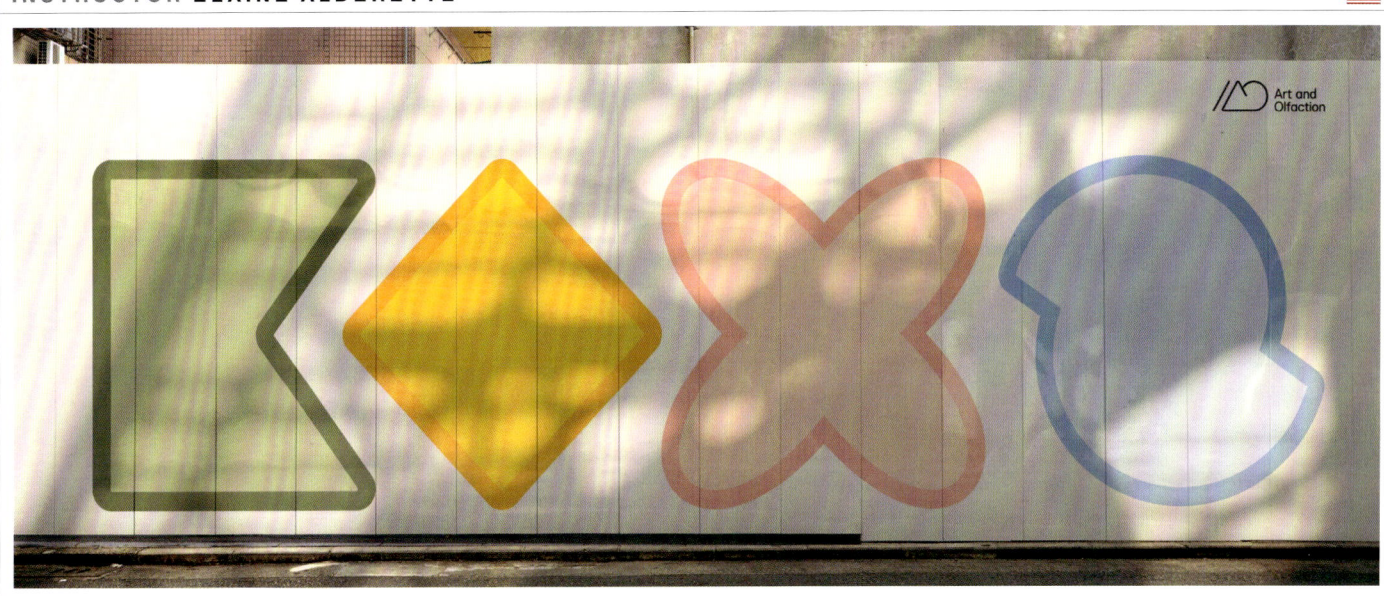

Student: Joonhee Park | **School:** ArtCenter College of Design

INSTRUCTOR STEPHEN SERRATO

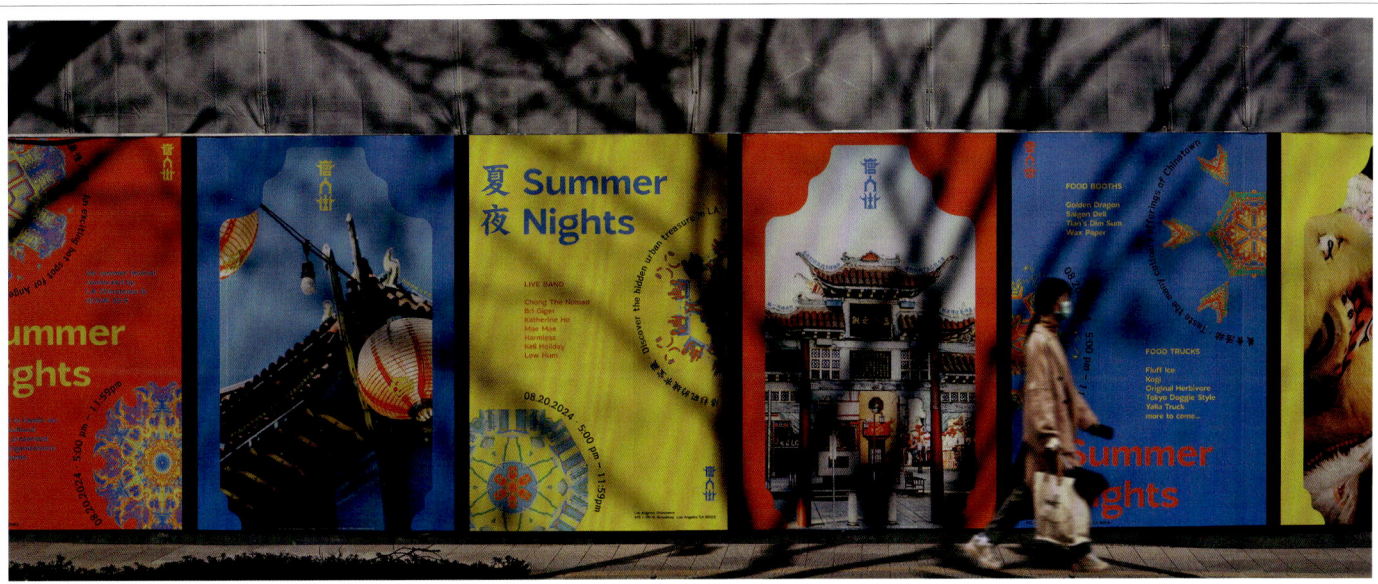

Student: Zifei Ding | **School:** ArtCenter College of Design

Branding | Design

162 DESIGN SILVER

INSTRUCTOR UNATTRIBUTED 🇨🇦
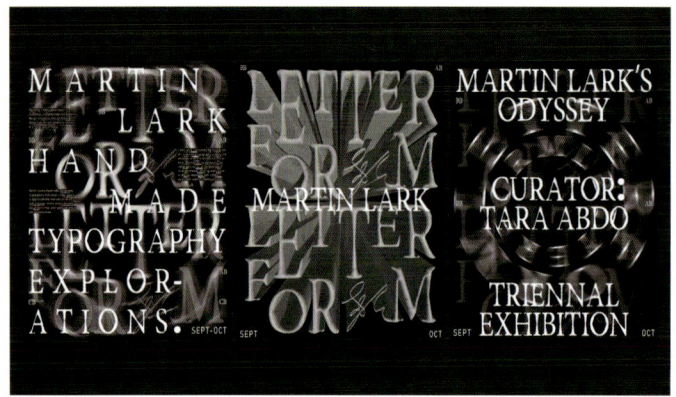
Student: Pantea Kouhpayeh | **School:** George Brown College

INSTRUCTOR BRAD BARTLETT 🇺🇸
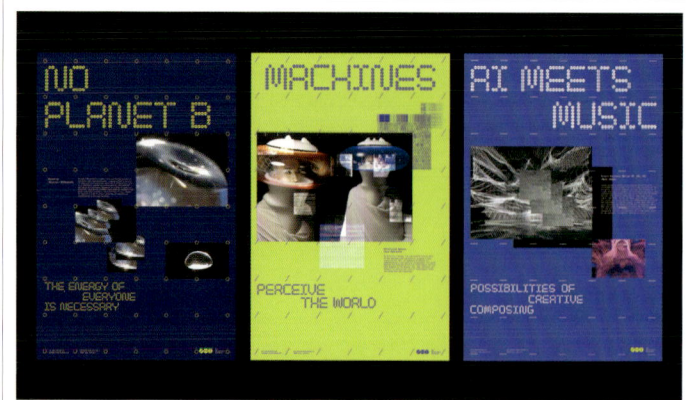
Student: Soomin Jeon | **School:** ArtCenter College of Design

INSTRUCTOR GERARDO HERRERA 🇺🇸
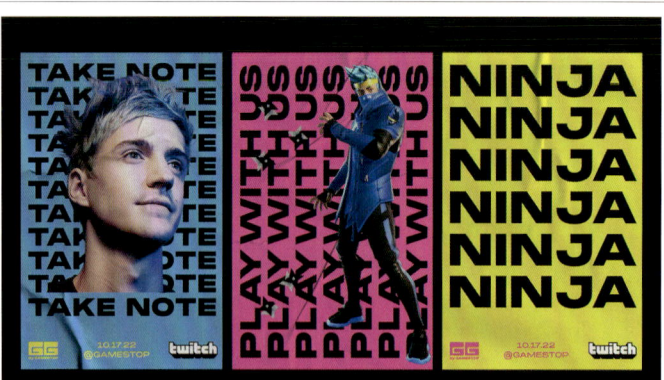
Student: Glenn Ryan | **School:** ArtCenter College of Design

INSTRUCTOR BRAD BARTLETT 🇺🇸
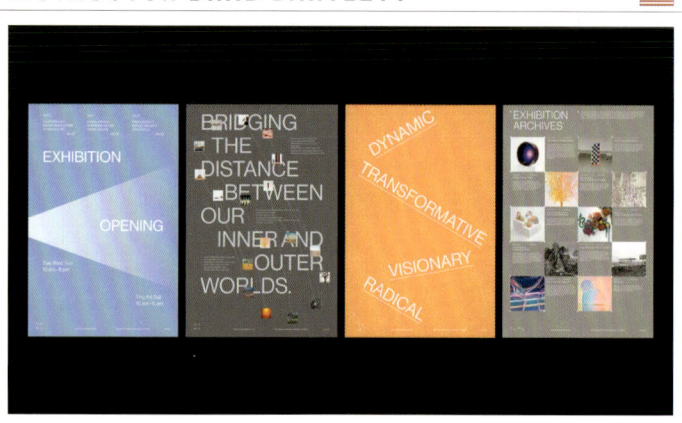
Student: Esther Yang | **School:** ArtCenter College of Design

INSTRUCTOR PEDRO MENDES 🇺🇸
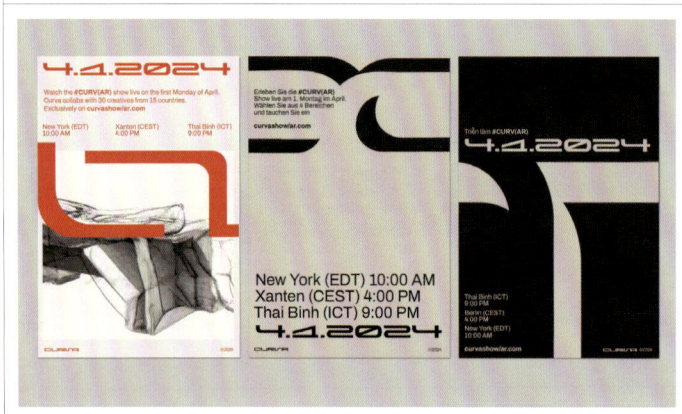
Student: Huu Minh Pham | **School:** School of Visual Arts

INSTRUCTOR ANDREA TRABUCCO-CAMPOS 🇺🇸
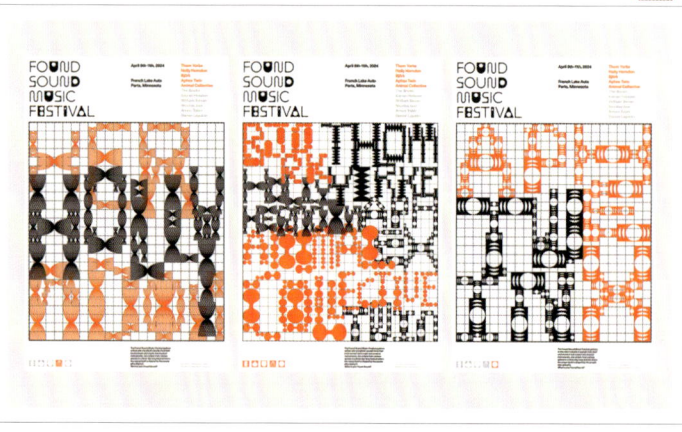
Student: Don Park | **School:** School of Visual Arts

INSTRUCTOR JOSEPH NEWTON 🇺🇸
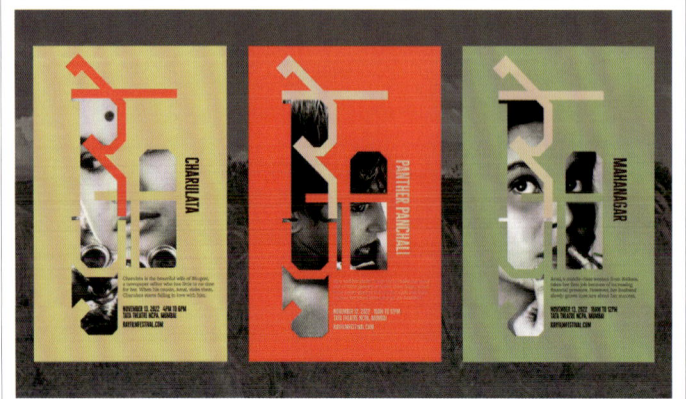
Student: Sara Mehta | **School:** School of Visual Arts

INSTRUCTOR BRAD BARTLETT 🇺🇸
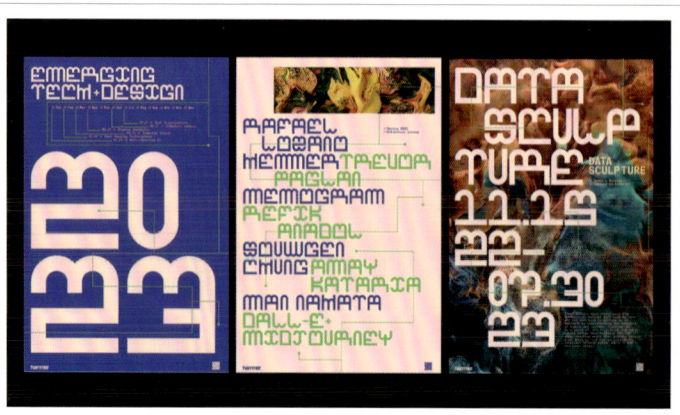
Student: Leonel Guardado | **School:** ArtCenter College of Design

Design | Branding

163 DESIGN SILVER

INSTRUCTORS RORY SIMMS, COURTNEY GOOCH

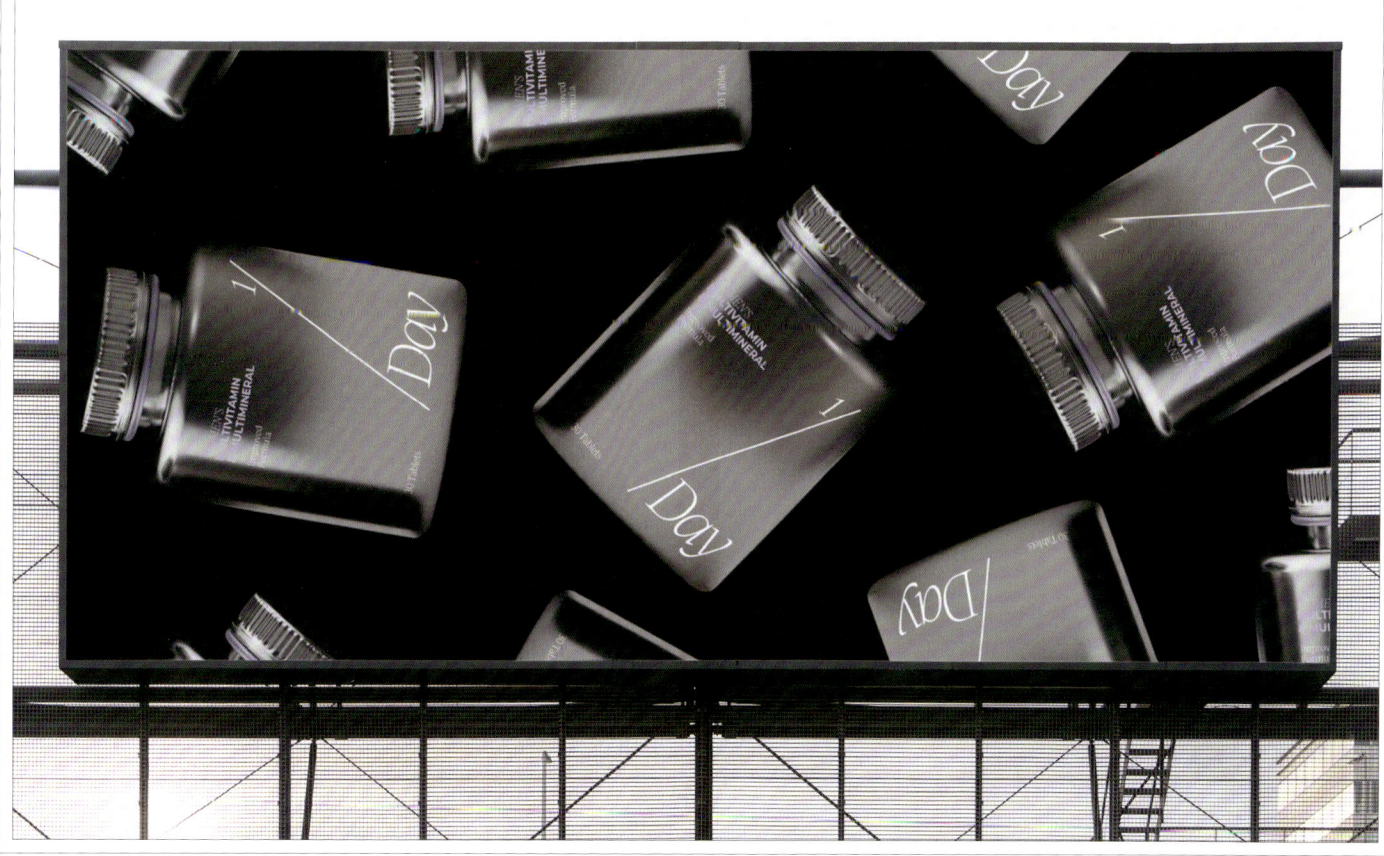

Student: Yaxin Zou | **School:** School of Visual Arts

INSTRUCTOR SIMON JOHNSTON

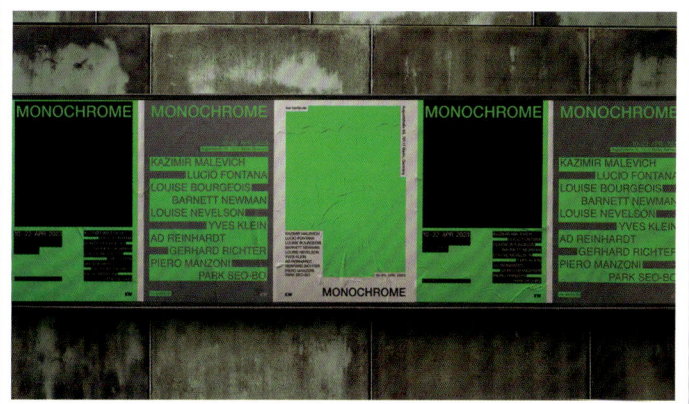

Student: Sydney Lee | **School:** ArtCenter College of Design

INSTRUCTOR RICHARD ROSE

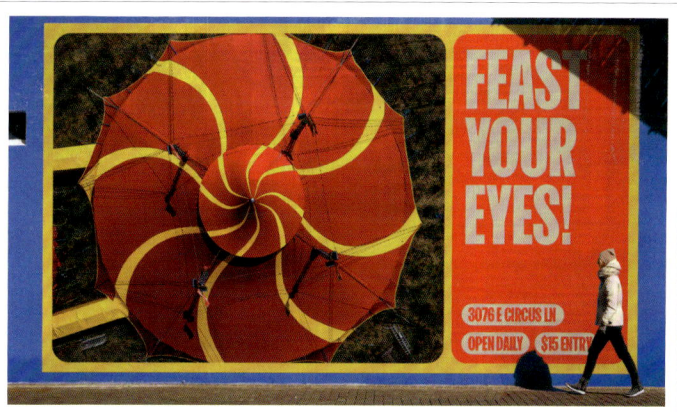

Student: Jacob Hwan Lee | **School:** Rhode Island School of Design

INSTRUCTOR PEDRO MENDES

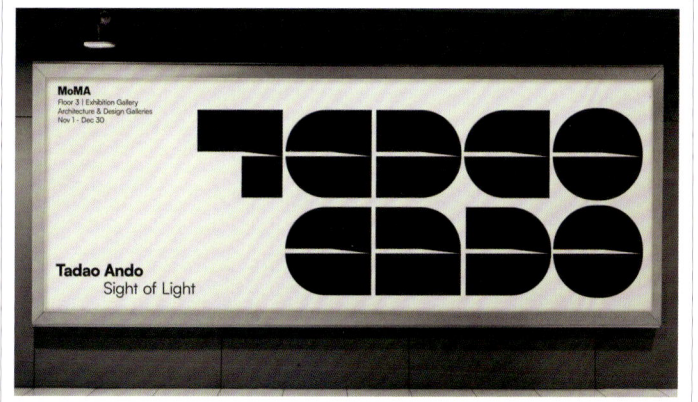

Student: Huu Minh Pham | **School:** School of Visual Arts

INSTRUCTOR TERESA TREVINO

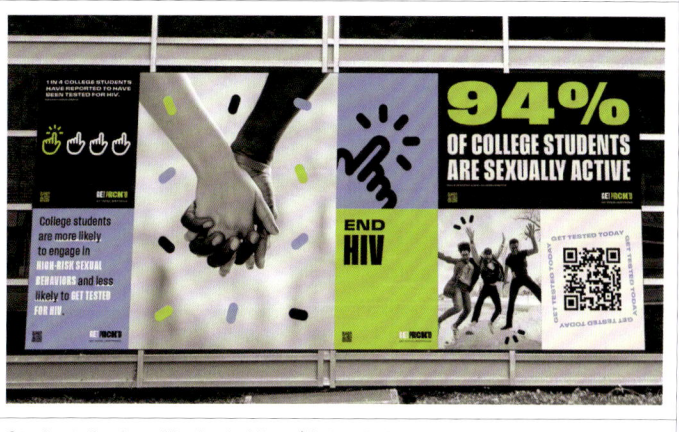

Student: Rozlynn Macbeth Olivas | **School:** University of the Incarnate Word

Branding | Design

164 DESIGN SILVER

INSTRUCTOR ANGAD SINGH

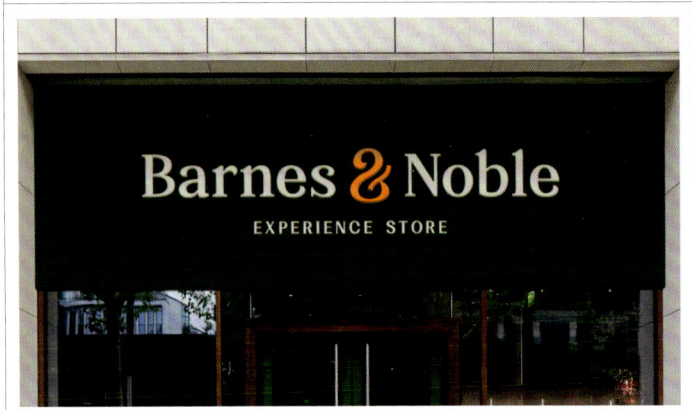

Student: Handanu Ardhata | **School:** ArtCenter College of Design

INSTRUCTOR GERARDO HERRERA

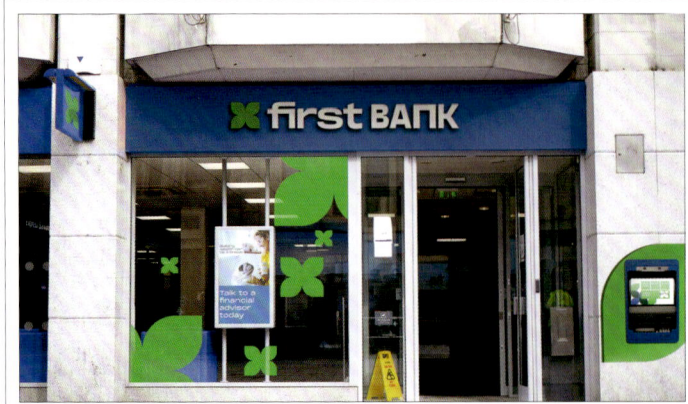

Student: Jamal Abdullahi | **School:** ArtCenter College of Design

INSTRUCTOR DARÁZS BÓDOG

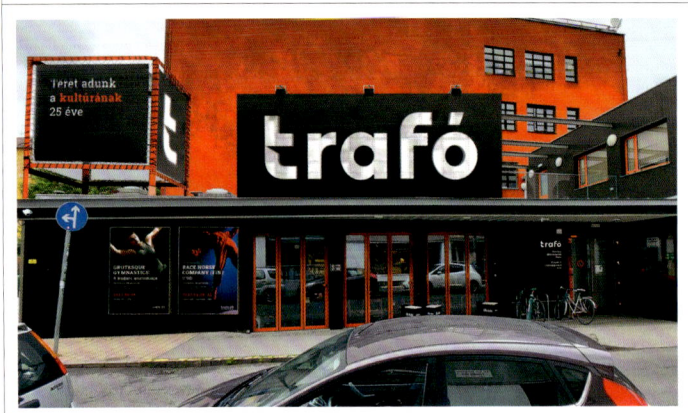

Student: Laár Ambrus | **School:** KREA Design School

INSTRUCTOR DAVID ELIZALDE

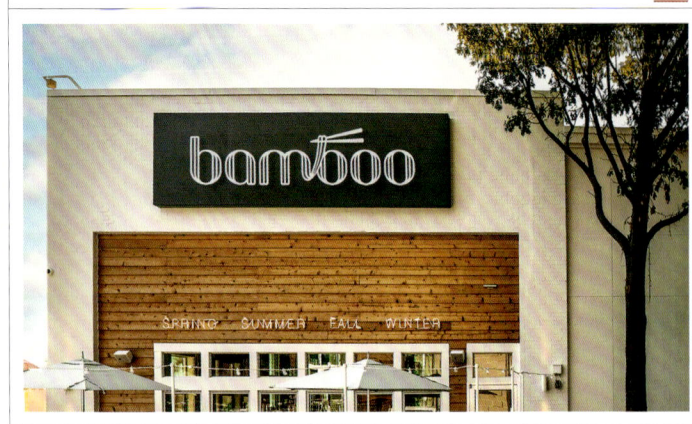

Student: Kien Nguyen | **School:** Texas Christian University

INST. NGUYEN TRI PHUONG DONG, LE PHUONG HIEU

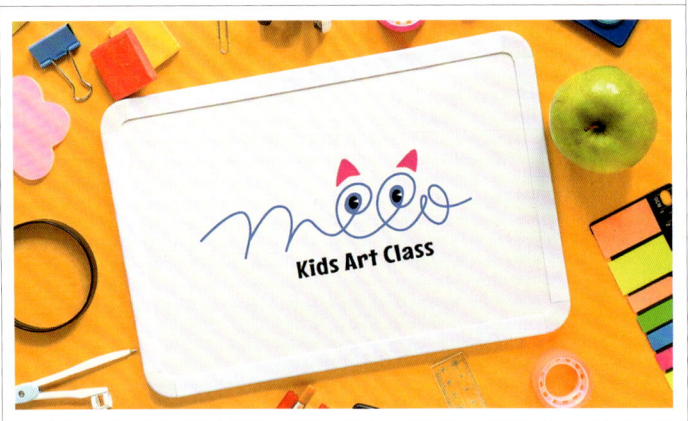

Student: Tran Uyen Nhi | **School:** Duy Tan University

INSTRUCTOR NGUYEN TRI PHUONG DONG

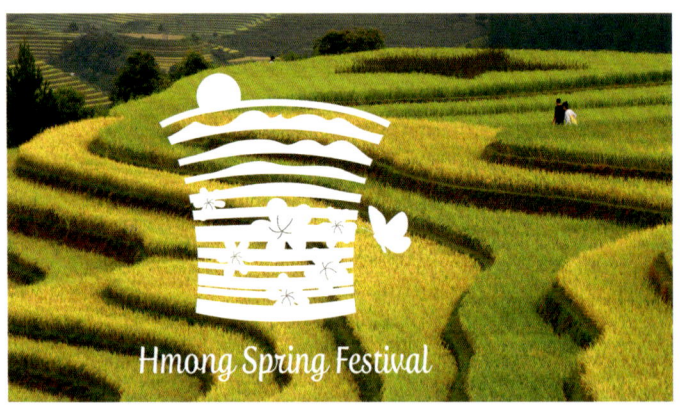

Student: Vo Ky Bao Ngoc | **School:** Duy Tan University

INSTRUCTOR TRYSH WAHLIG

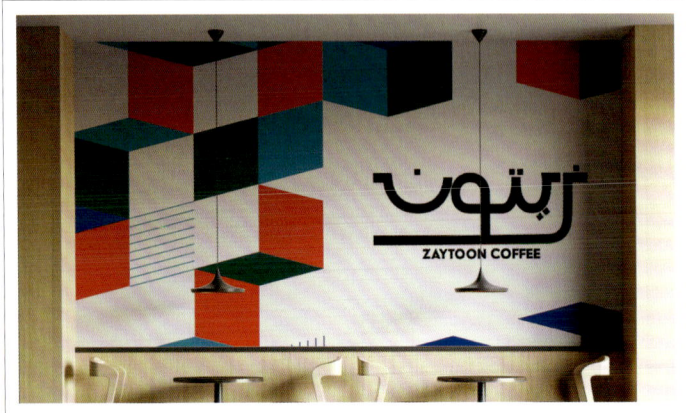

Student: Judie Haidar | **School:** University of Louisville

INSTRUCTOR NGUYEN TRI PHUONG DONG

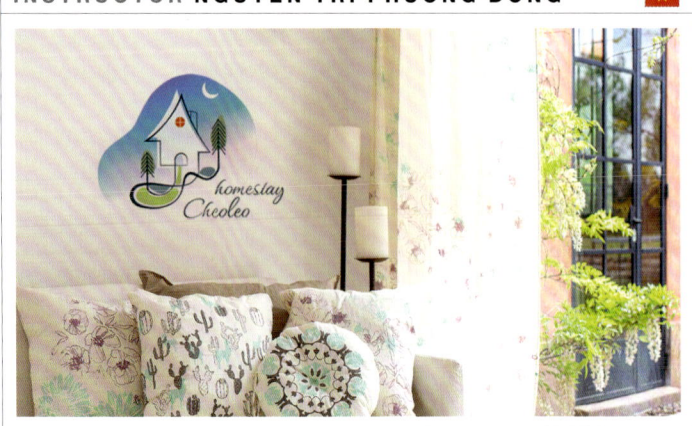

Student: Ngo Chau Vy | **School:** Duy Tan University

Design | Branding

165 DESIGN SILVER

INSTRUCTOR DOUGLAS MAY
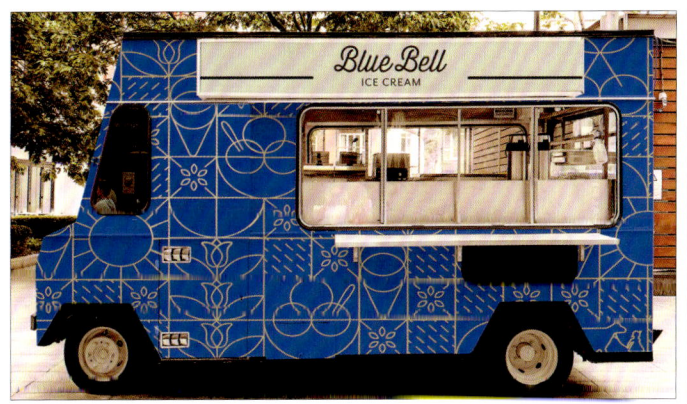
Student: Annika Snow | **School:** University of North Texas

INSTRUCTOR HYUNG JOO KIM
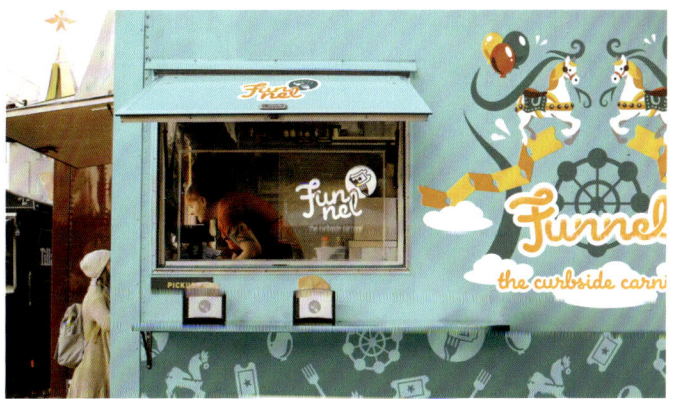
Student: Courtney Kurtz | **School:** Purdue University

INSTRUCTOR DOUGLAS MAY
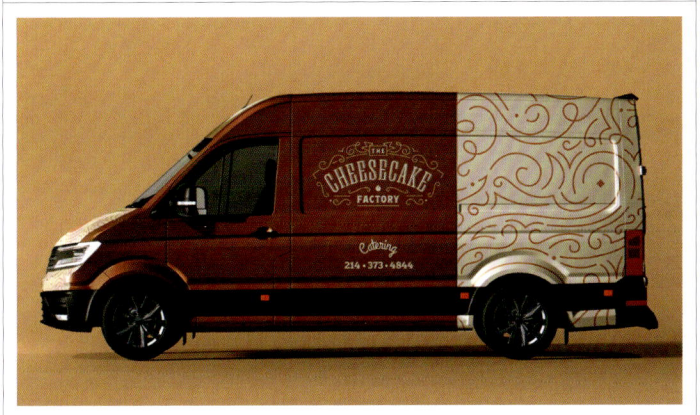
Student: Paige Sanders | **School:** University of North Texas

INSTRUCTOR SCOTTY REIFSNYDER
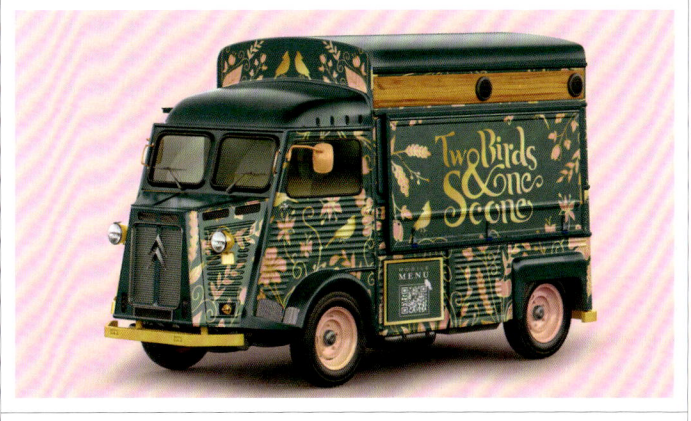
Student: Abby Gerber | **School:** West Chester University

INSTRUCTOR DOUGLAS MAY
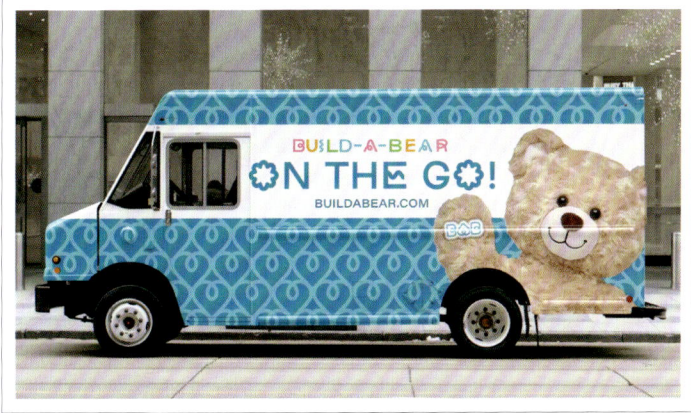
Student: Lauren Clark | **School:** University of North Texas

INSTRUCTOR HYUNG JOO KIM
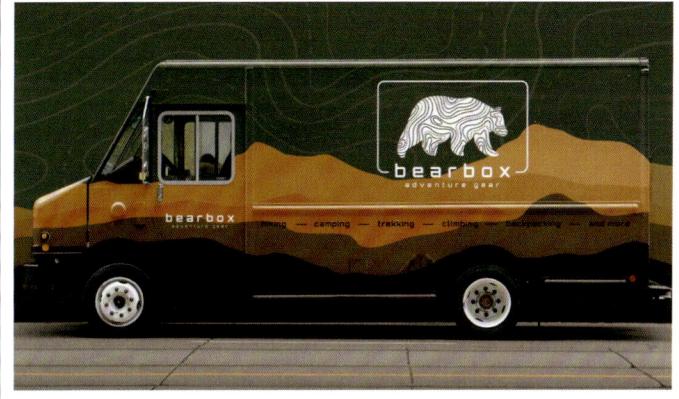
Student: Julie Haseman | **School:** Purdue University

INSTRUCTOR HYUNG JOO KIM
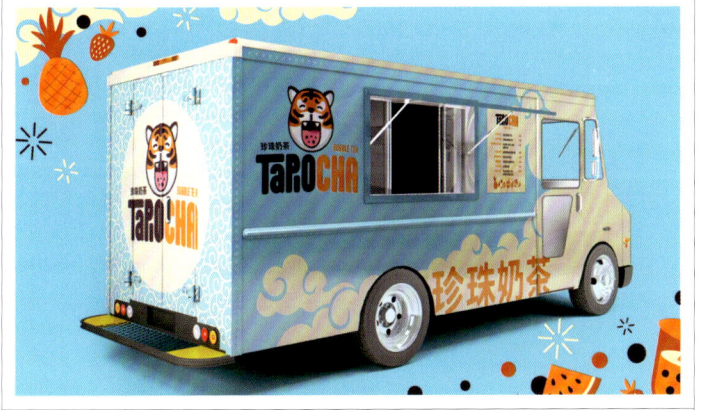
Student: Evan Olinger | **School:** Purdue University

INSTRUCTOR DOUGLAS MAY
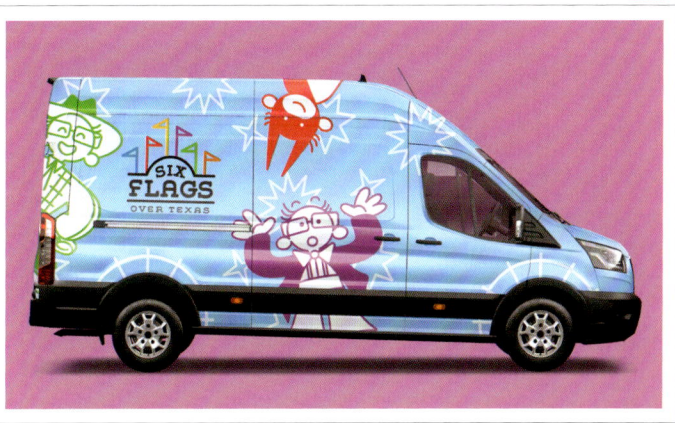
Student: Macy Belton | **School:** University of North Texas

Branding | Design

166 DESIGN SILVER

INSTRUCTOR GERARDO HERRERA

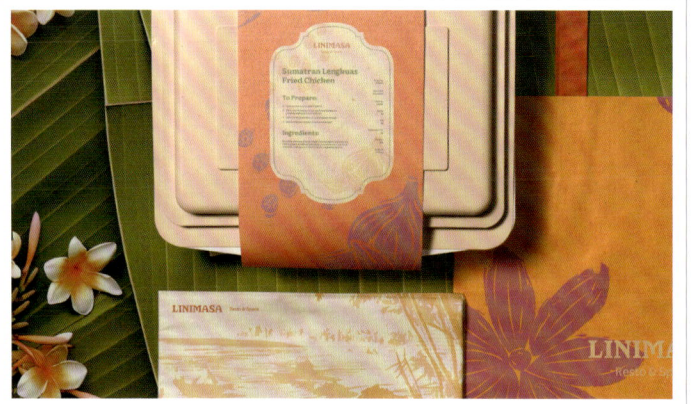

Student: Handanu Ardhata | School: ArtCenter College of Design

INSTRUCTOR JON NEWMAN

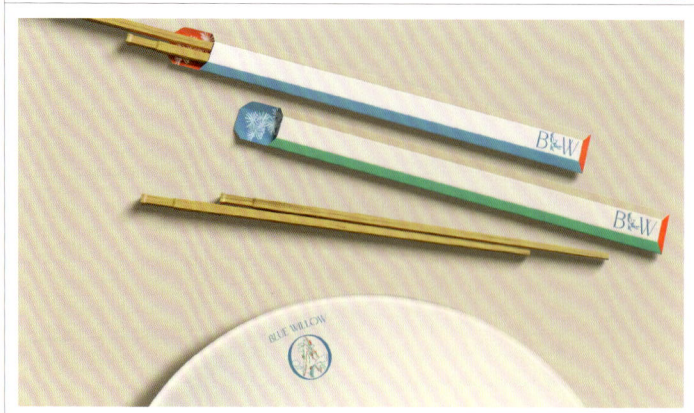

Student: Yubin Won | School: School of Visual Arts

INSTRUCTOR STEPHEN ZHANG

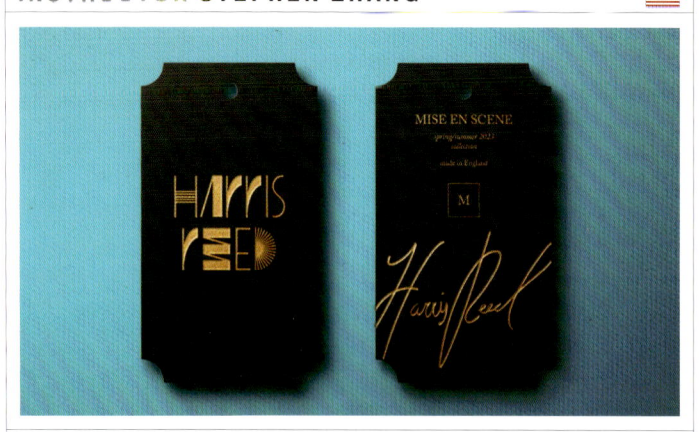

Student: Sabrina Franco Barrera | School: University of North Texas

INSTRUCTOR DOUG THOMAS

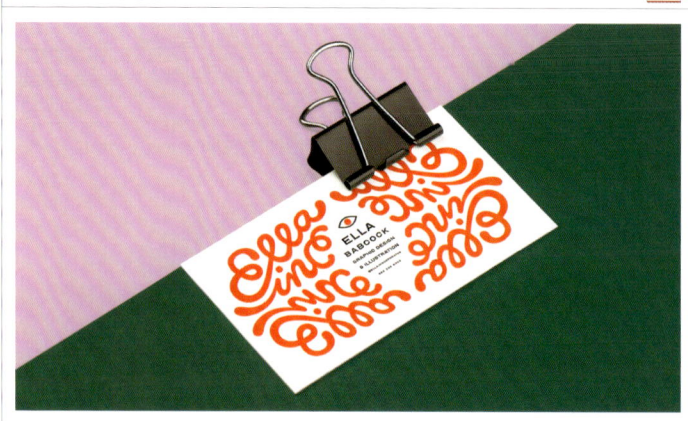

Student: Ella Babcock | School: Brigham Young University

INSTRUCTOR JENNY KOWALSKI

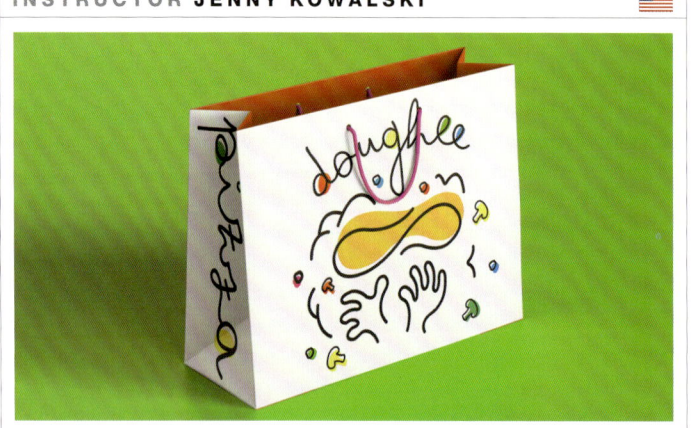

Student: Xinni Hong | School: Lehigh University

INSTRUCTOR KELLY HOLOHAN

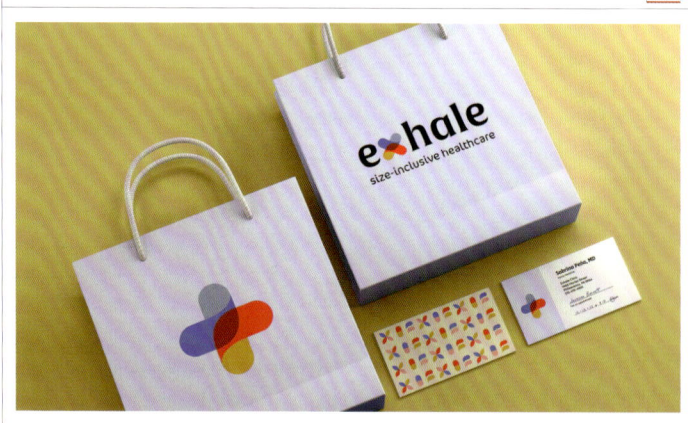

Student: MeiLi Carling | School: Temple University

INSTRUCTOR NGUYEN TRI PHUONG DONG

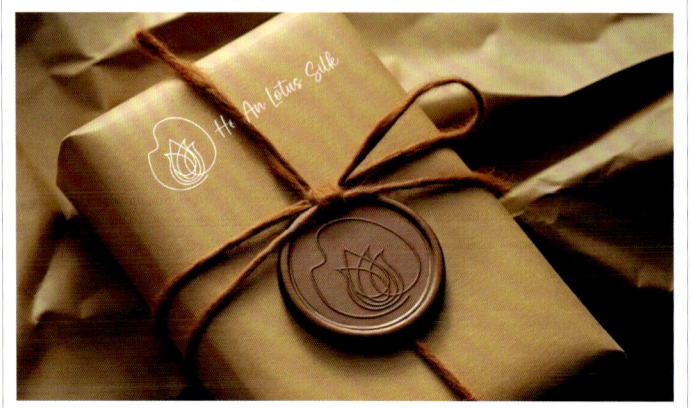

Student: Nguyen Thi My Linh | School: Duy Tan University

INSTRUCTOR JOSHUA EGE

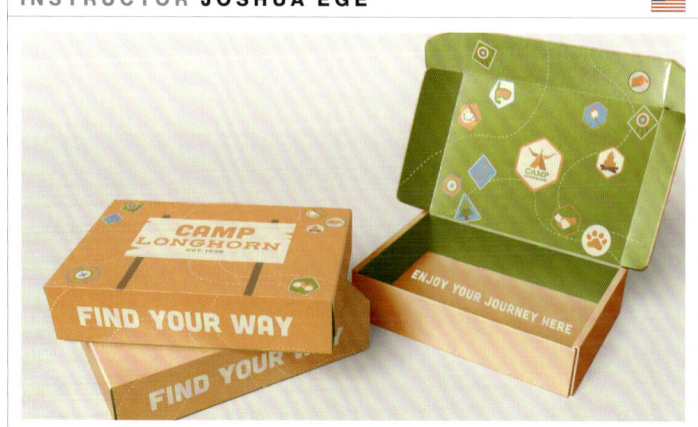

Student: Jackelyn De Lara | School: Texas A&M University-Commerce

Design | Branding

167 DESIGN SILVER

INSTRUCTOR HANK RICHARDSON

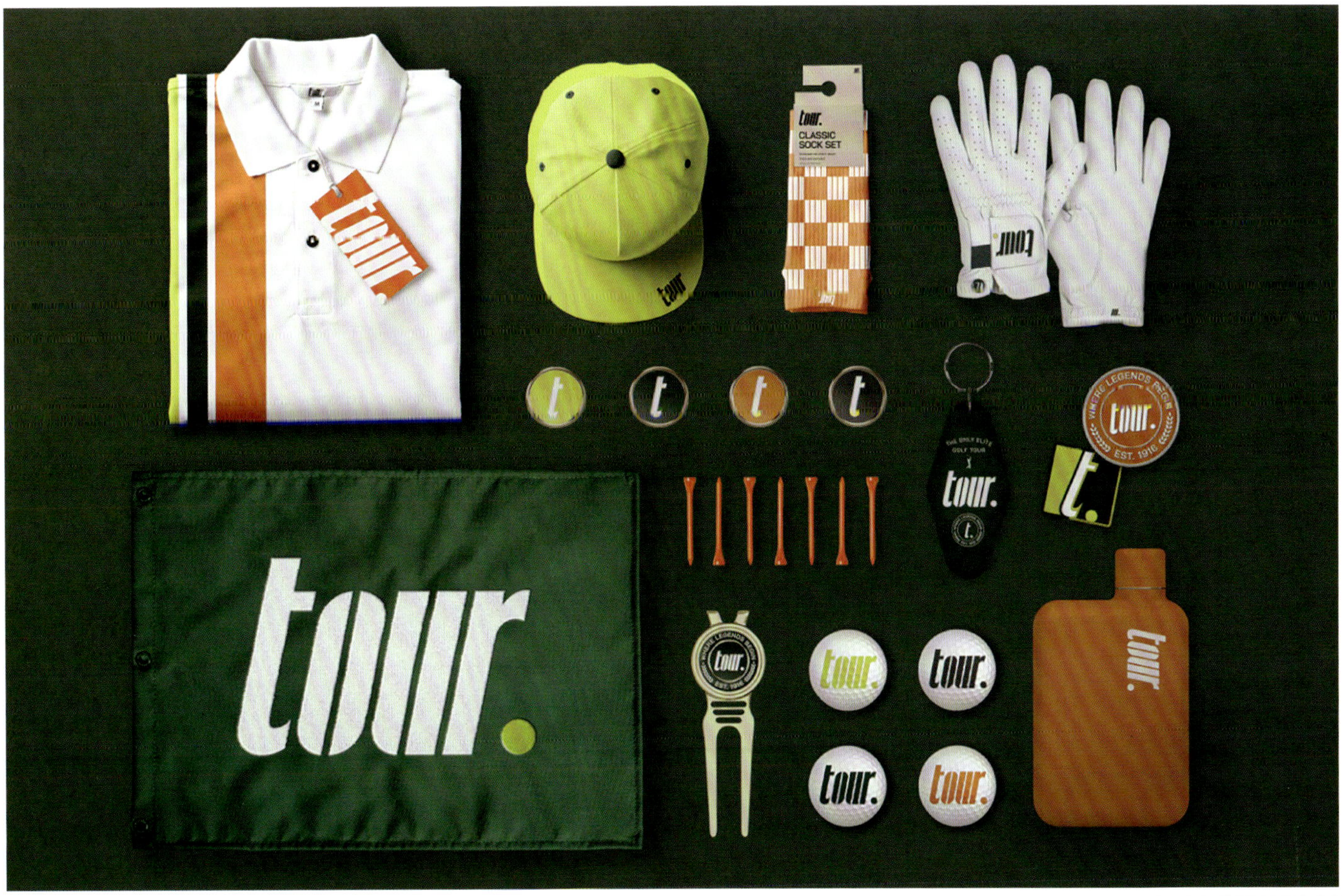

Student: Jamie Jason | **School:** M.AD School of Ideas Atlanta

INSTRUCTOR ANNE JORDAN

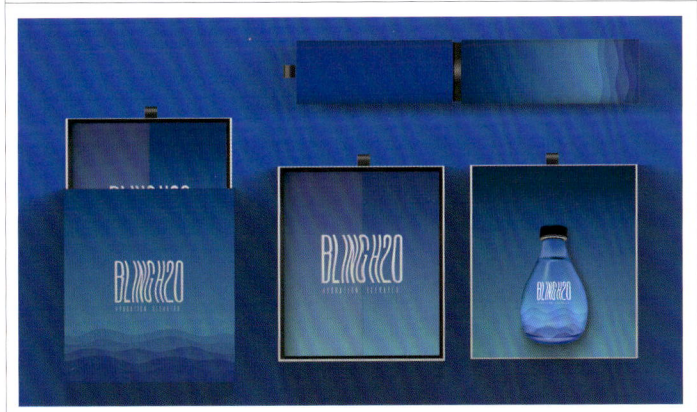

Student: Eshaan Sojatia | **School:** Rochester Institute of Technology

INSTRUCTOR PETER AHLBERG

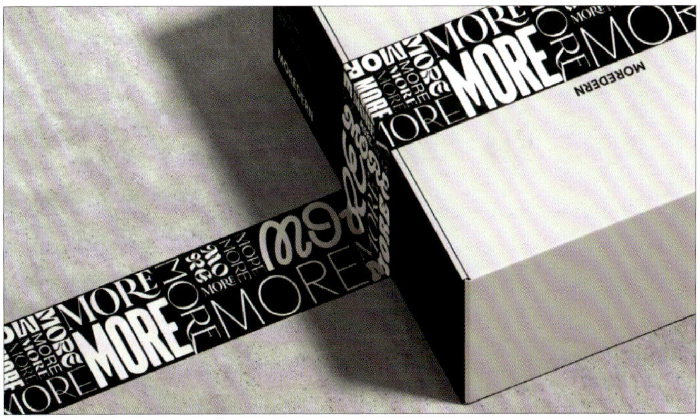

Student: Yuan Chen | **School:** School of Visual Arts

INSTRUCTOR RICH TU

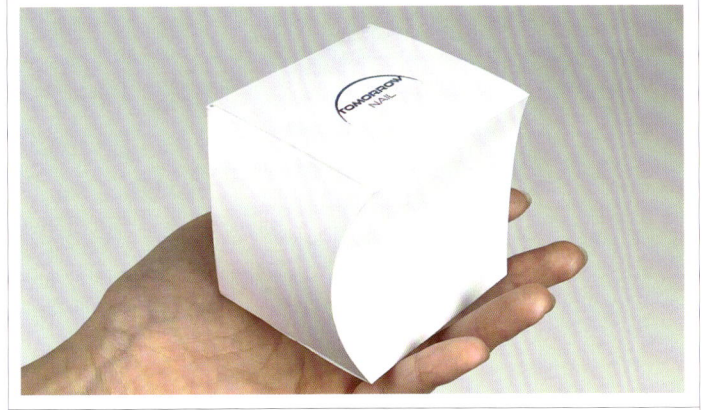

Student: Dong Hyun Kim | **School:** School of Visual Arts

INSTRUCTOR RICH TU

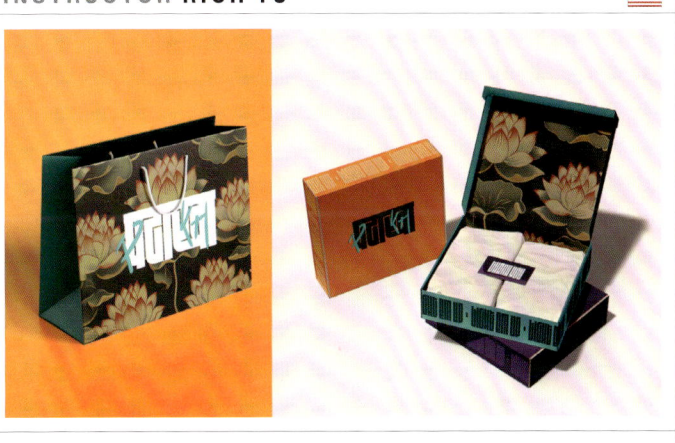

Student: Sara Mehta | **School:** School of Visual Arts

Branding | Design

168 DESIGN SILVER

INSTRUCTOR JAN BALLARD 🇺🇸

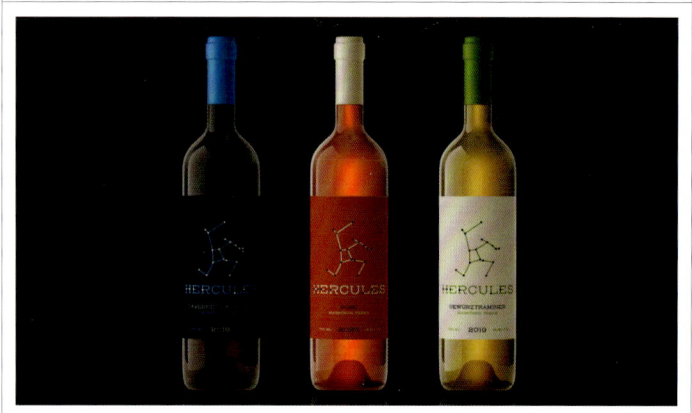

Student: Lucia Canseco | **School:** Texas Christian University

INSTRUCTOR DOMINIQUE WALKER 🇨🇦

Student: Celina Zhong | **School:** Capilano University

INSTRUCTOR WILLIAM MEEK 🇺🇸

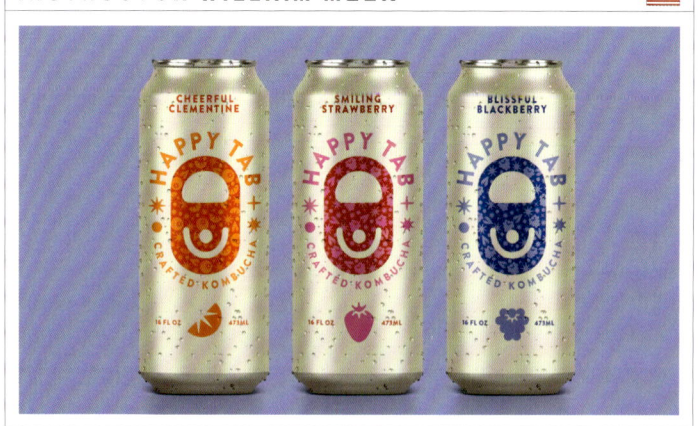

Student: Fallon Russell | **School:** Texas State University

INSTRUCTOR DOUGLAS MAY 🇺🇸

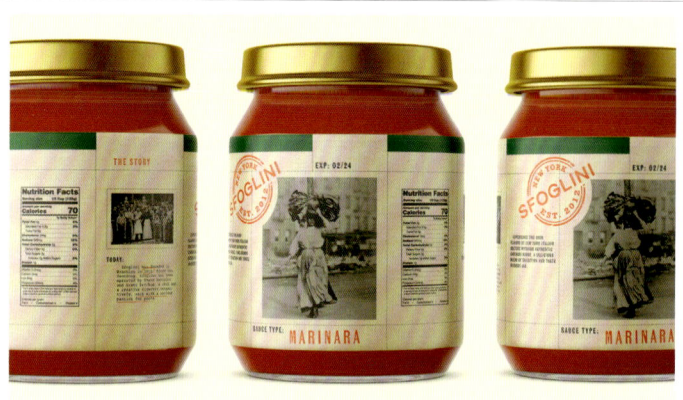

Student: Kara McKintosh | **School:** University of North Texas

INSTRUCTOR DOUGLAS MAY 🇺🇸

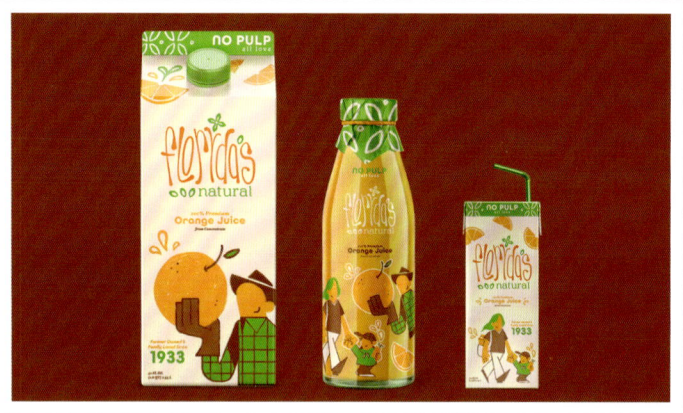

Student: Macy Belton | **School:** University of North Texas

INSTRUCTOR DOMINIQUE WALKER 🇨🇦

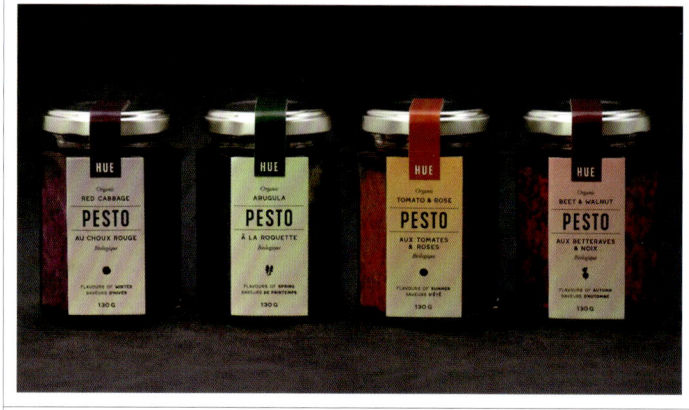

Student: Anais Bayle | **School:** Capilano University

INST. NGUYEN TRI PHUONG DONG, HOANG VIET QUOC 🇻🇳

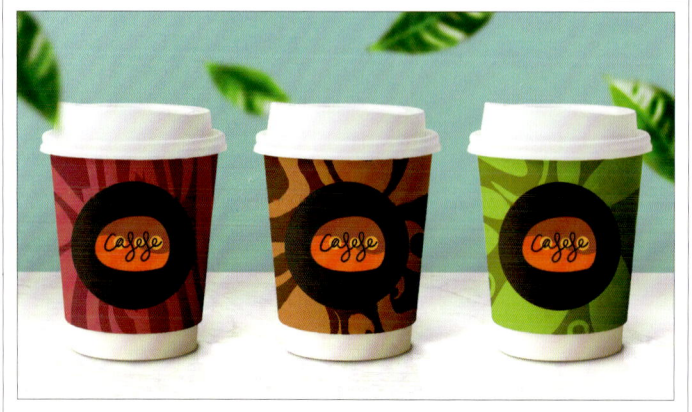

Student: Le Van Dung | **School:** Duy Tan University

INSTRUCTOR NGUYEN TRI PHUONG DONG 🇻🇳

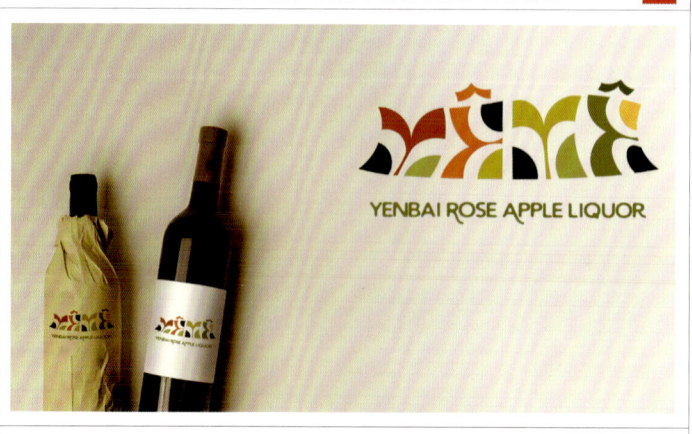

Student: Tran Vu Quynh Thi | **School:** Duy Tan University

Design | Branding

169 DESIGN SILVER

INSTRUCTOR JENNY KOWALSKI 🇺🇸

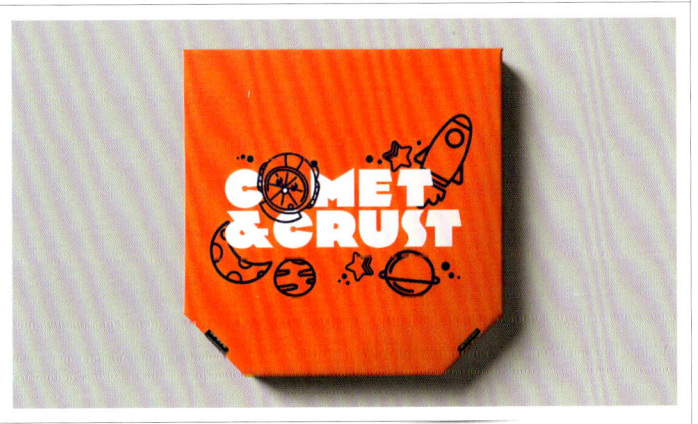

Student: Angelique Honca | **School:** Lehigh University

INSTRUCTORS MIKAELA BUCK, JEFF DAVIS 🇺🇸

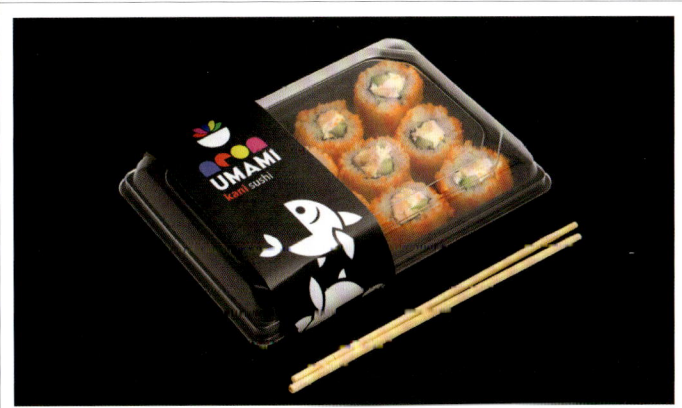

Student: Elmo Chavez | **School:** Texas State University

INSTRUCTOR NGUYEN TRI PHUONG DONG 🇻🇳

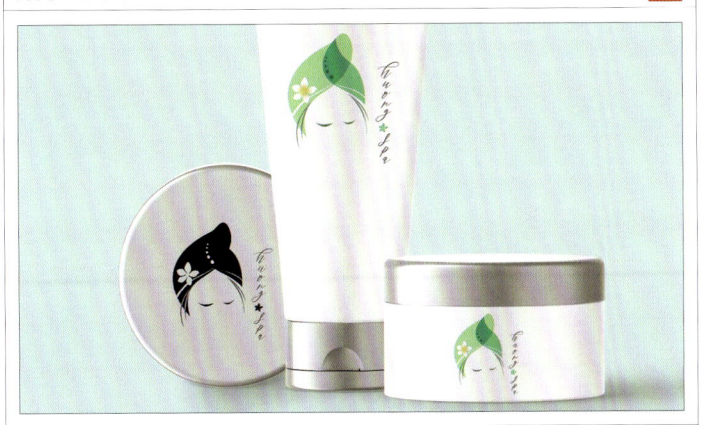

Student: Nguyen Thi Hoang Yen | **School:** Duy Tan University

INSTRUCTOR JOSHUA EGE 🇺🇸

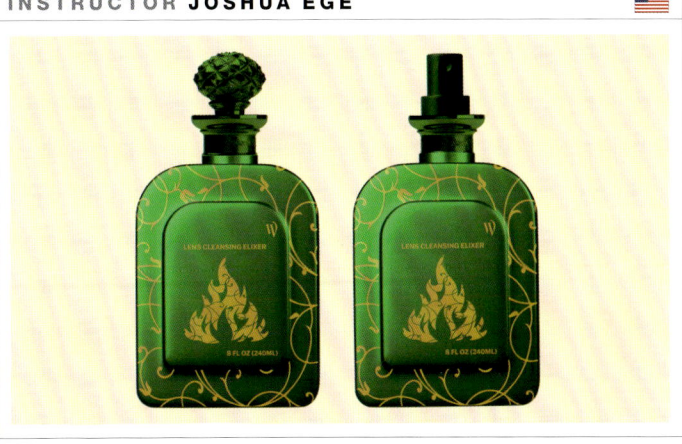

Student: Kiara Gomez | **School:** Texas A&M University-Commerce

INSTRUCTOR EMILY CARLSON 🇺🇸

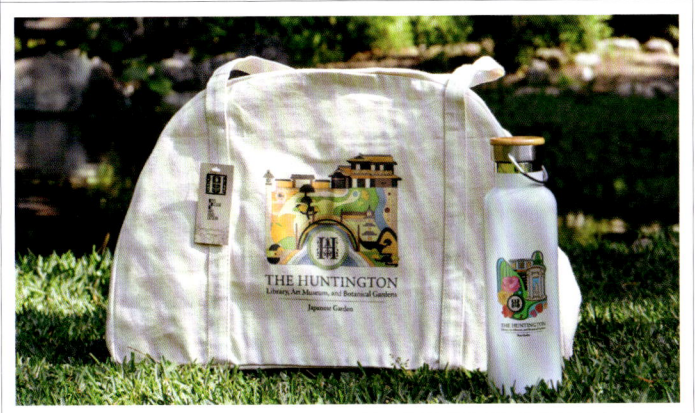

Student: Charlie Utter | **School:** Otis College of Art & Design

INSTRUCTOR ANNE JORDAN 🇺🇸

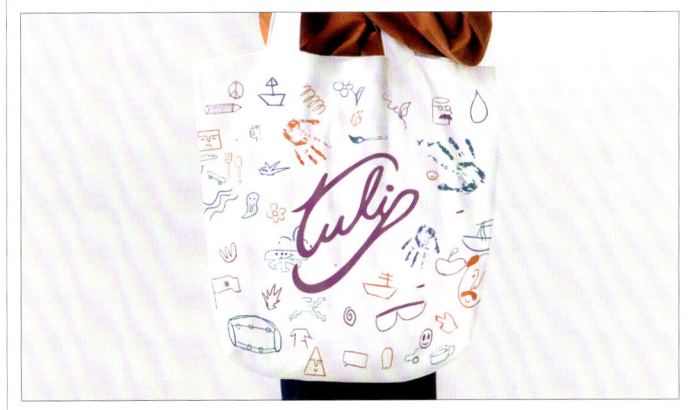

Student: Pranjal Sawai | **School:** Rochester Institute of Technology

INSTRUCTOR TRYSH WAHLIG 🇺🇸

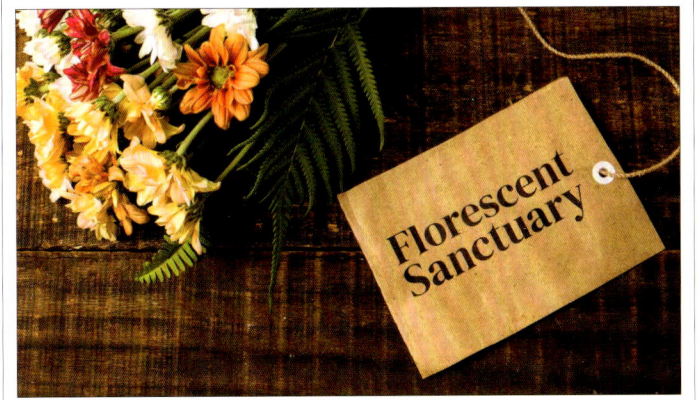

Student: Alyssa De Jesus | **School:** University of Louisville

INSTRUCTORS JEFF DAVIS, WILLIAM MEEK 🇺🇸

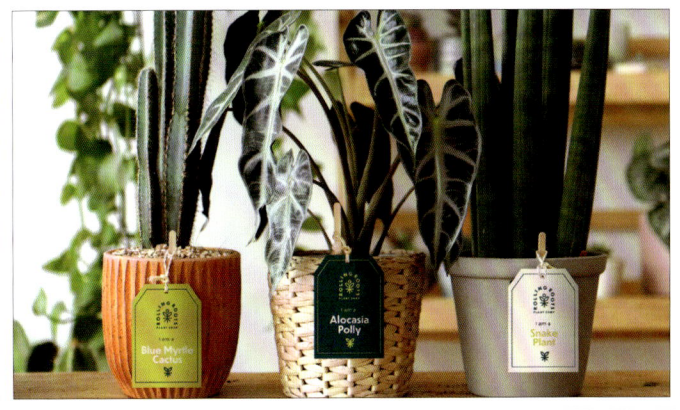

Student: Kelsie Brouillette | **School:** Texas State University

Branding | Design

170 DESIGN SILVER

INSTRUCTOR CHERYL SAVALA 🇺🇸

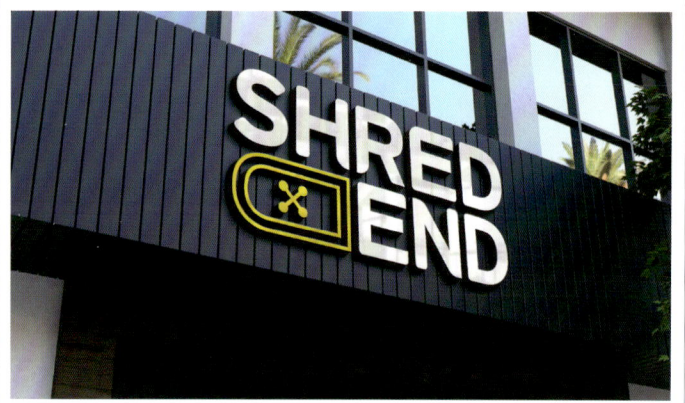

Student: Bryce Verti | **School:** California State University, Fullerton

INSTRUCTOR DOUGLAS MAY 🇺🇸

Student: Cuinn Cornwell | **School:** University of North Texas

INST. NGUYEN TRI PHUONG DONG, LE PHUONG HIEU 🇻🇳

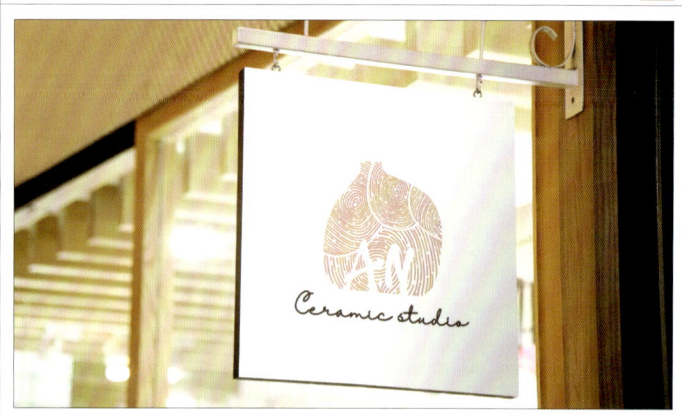

Student: Nguyen Ha Uyen | **School:** Duy Tan University

INSTRUCTOR DOUG THOMAS 🇺🇸

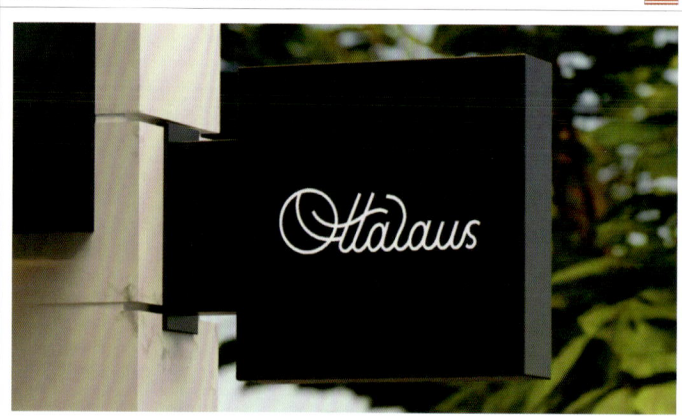

Student: Hannah Javadi | **School:** Brigham Young University

INST. NGUYEN TRI PHUONG DONG, HOANG VIET QUOC 🇻🇳

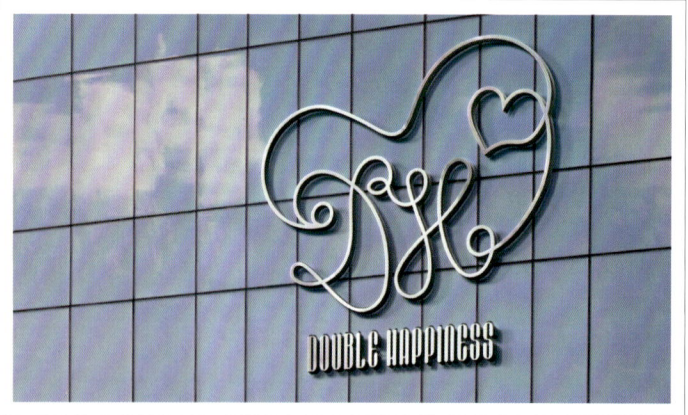

Student: Nguyen Thanh Thao | **School:** Duy Tan University

INSTRUCTOR DOUGLAS MAY 🇺🇸

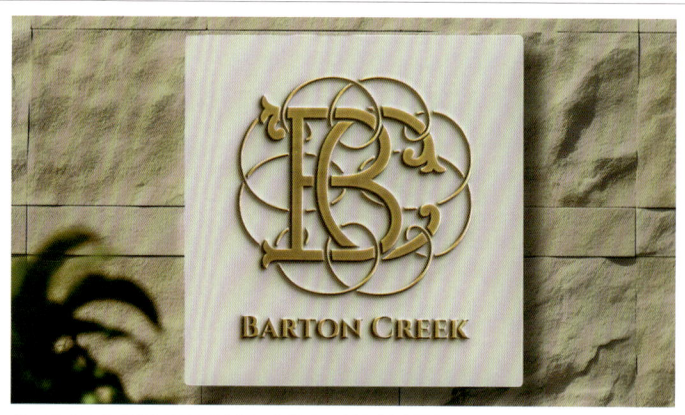

Student: Annika Snow | **School:** University of North Texas

INSTRUCTOR LINDA REYNOLDS 🇺🇸

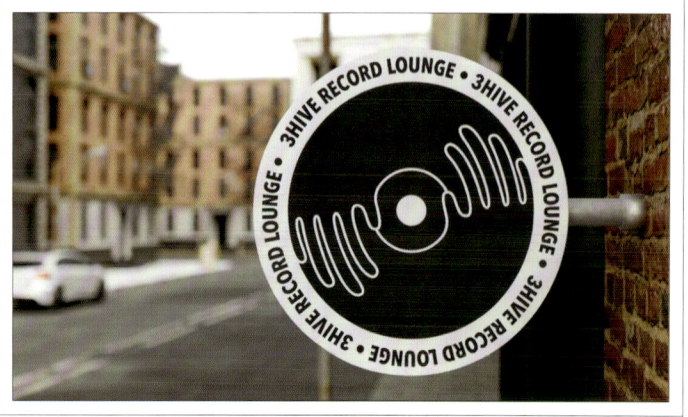

Student: Kiera Helquist | **School:** Brigham Young University

INSTRUCTOR NGUYEN TRI PHUONG DONG 🇻🇳

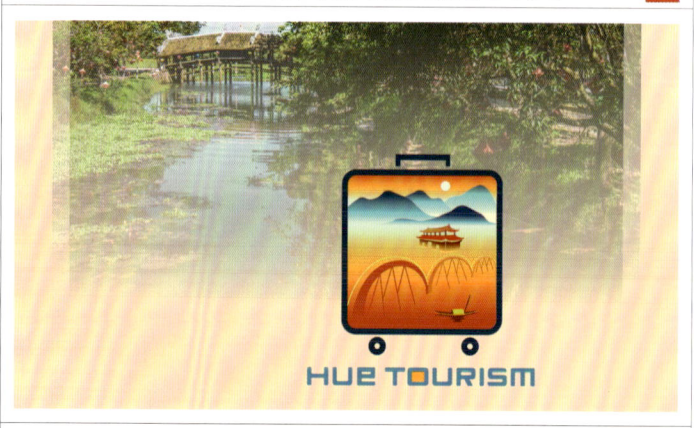

Student: Ho Thi Thu Thao | **School:** Duy Tan University

Design | Branding

171 DESIGN SILVER

INST. ANNABELLE RADFORD
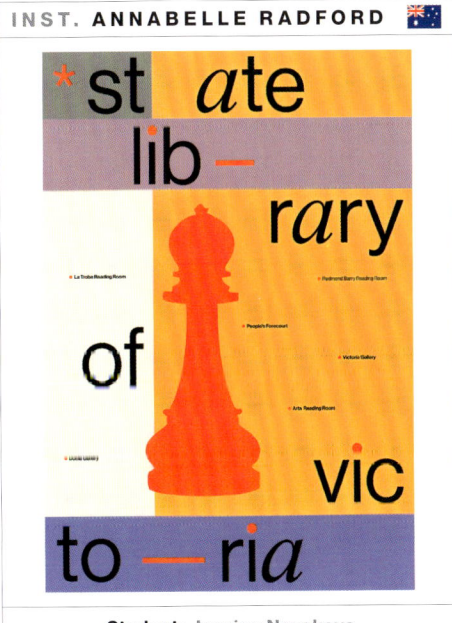
Student: Jessica Novakova
School: Swinburne University of Technology

INSTRUCTOR ANNE JORDAN
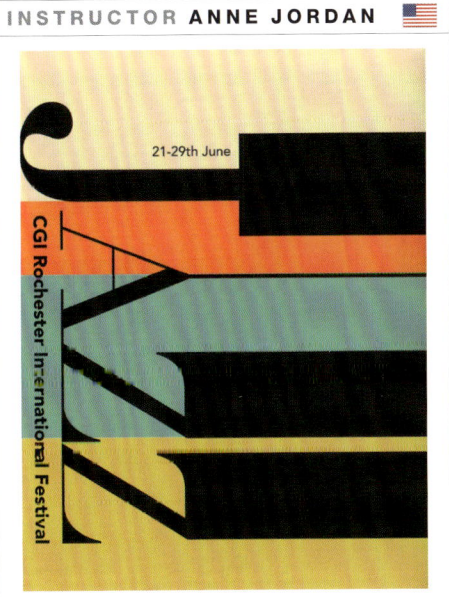
Student: Pranjal Sawai
School: Rochester Institute of Technology

INSTRUCTOR CLAUDIA STRONG
Student: Alexandra Ryberg Gonzalez
School: Syracuse University, The Newhouse School

INSTRUCTORS ERIC KARNES, MARK WILLIE
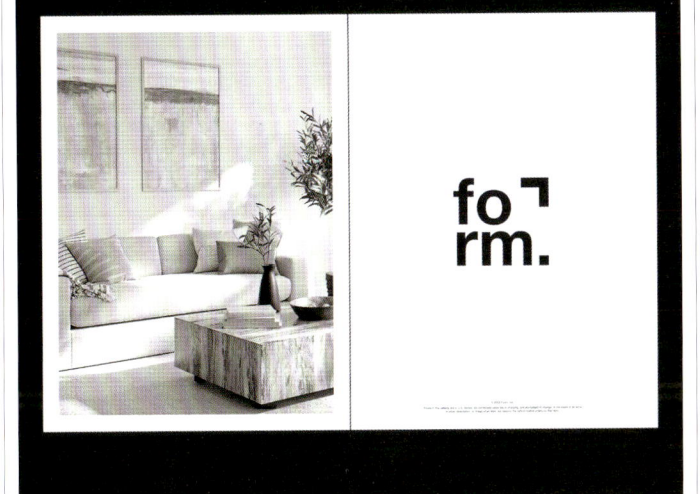
Student: Fiona Tran | **School:** Drexel University

INSTRUCTOR JUAN ESCALANTE
Student: Sophia Nguyen | **School:** California State University, Fullerton

INSTRUCTORS YASMIN GIBSON, COLIN FRAZER
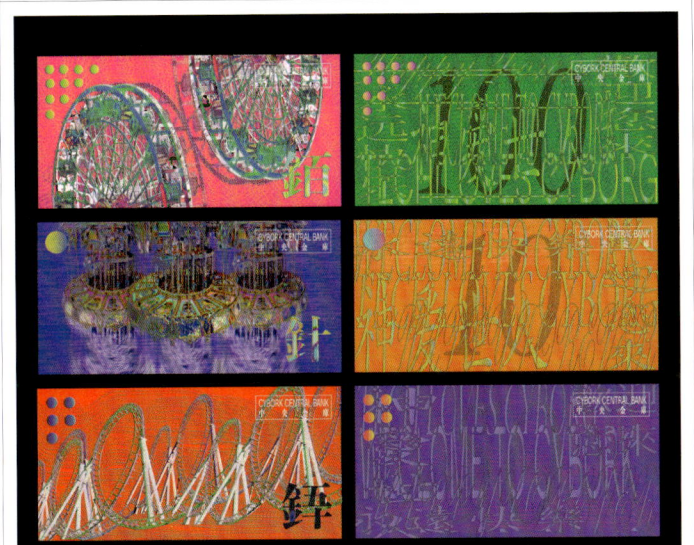
Student: Silei Fu | **School:** California Institute of the Arts

INSTRUCTOR UNATTRIBUTED
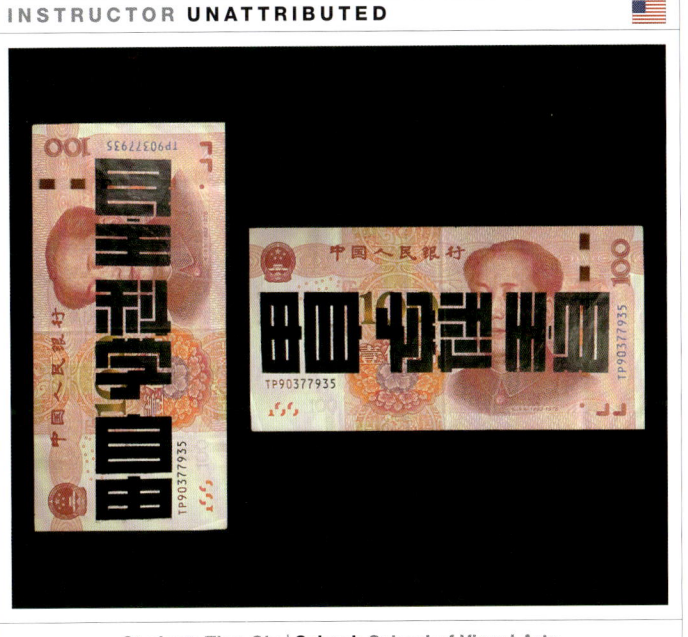
Student: Tian Qin | **School:** School of Visual Arts

Brochures, Cards, Catalogs, CD / DVD, Currency Design | Design

172 DESIGN SILVER

INSTRUCTOR **PETER AHLBERG**

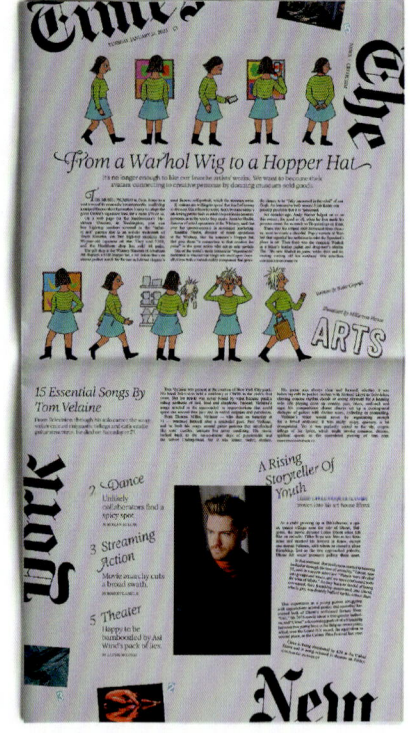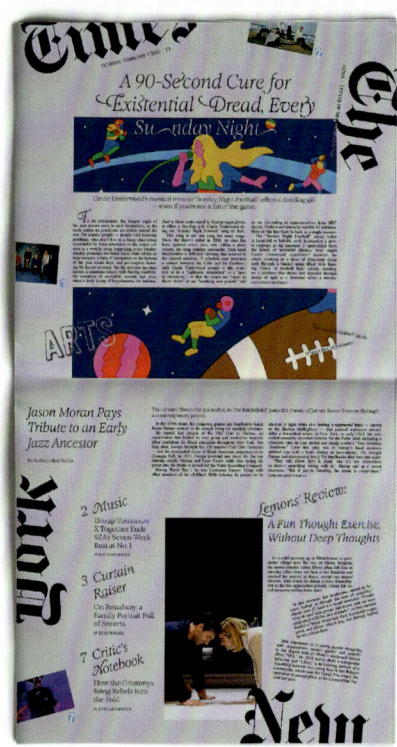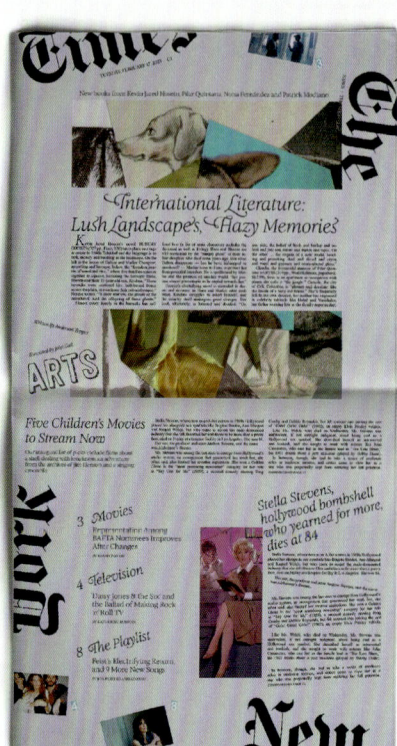

Student: Keumbie Hwang | **School:** School of Visual Arts

INSTRUCTOR **WARREN LEHRER**

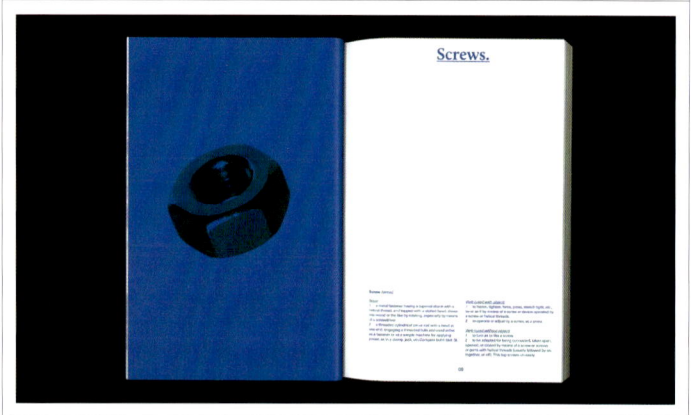

Student: Jiyoung Kim | **School:** School of Visual Arts

INSTRUCTOR **DEBRA BISHOP**

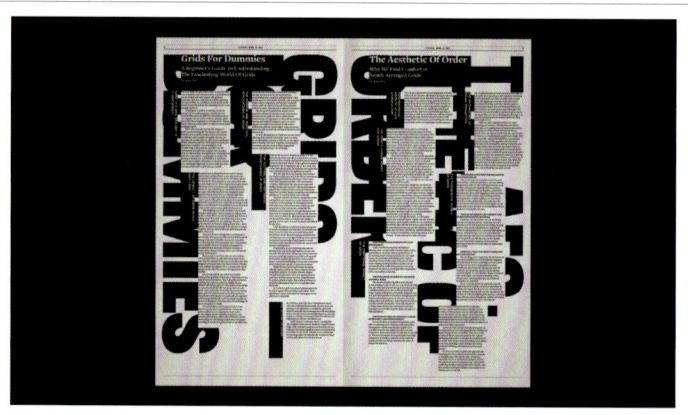

Student: Jiyoung Kim | **School:** School of Visual Arts

INSTRUCTOR **PEDRO MENDES**

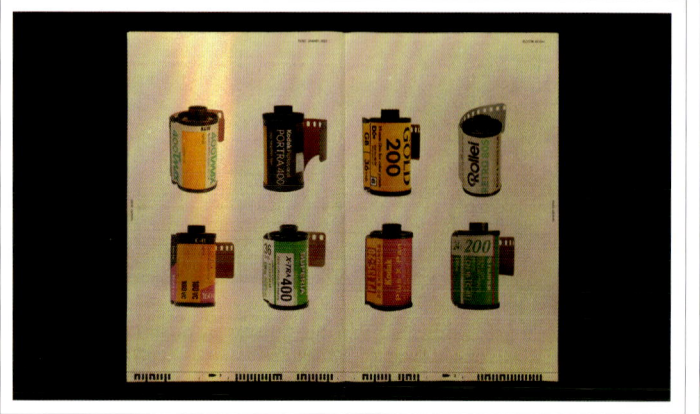

Student: Doyeon Kim | **School:** School of Visual Arts

INSTRUCTOR **PEDRO MENDES**

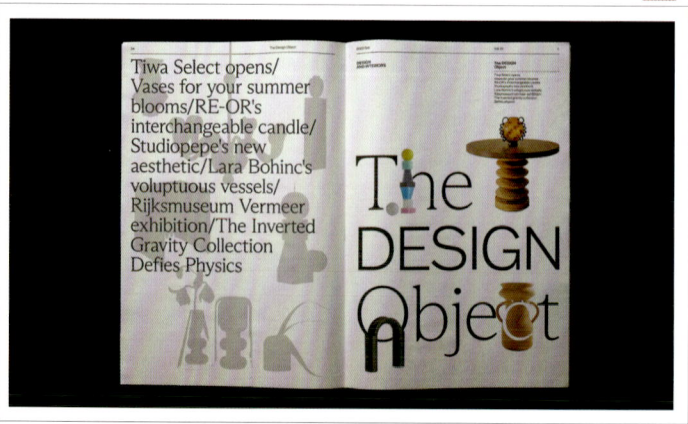

Student: Suin Choi | **School:** School of Visual Arts

Design | Editorial

173 DESIGN SILVER

INSTRUCTOR **ERIC GILLETT**

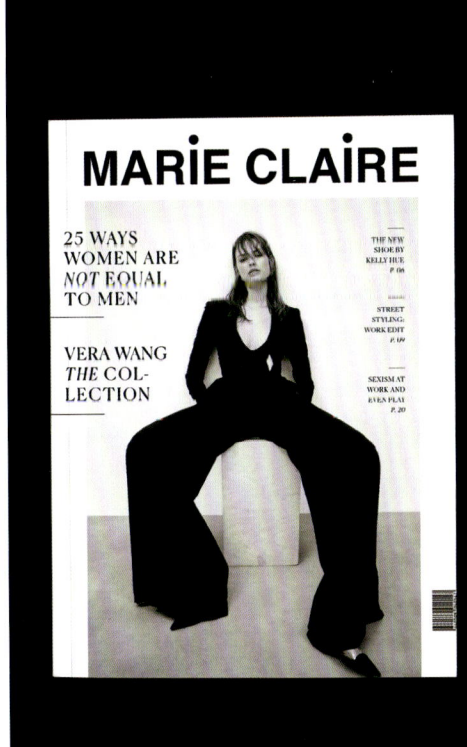
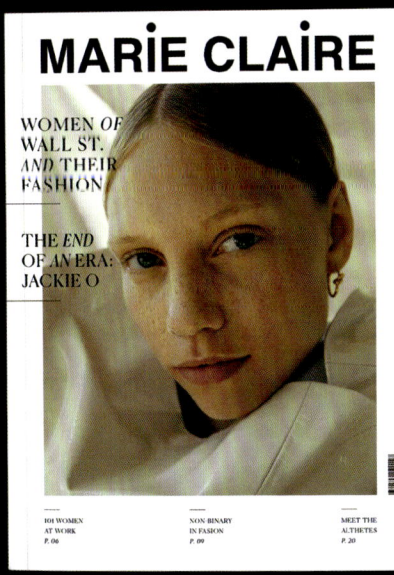
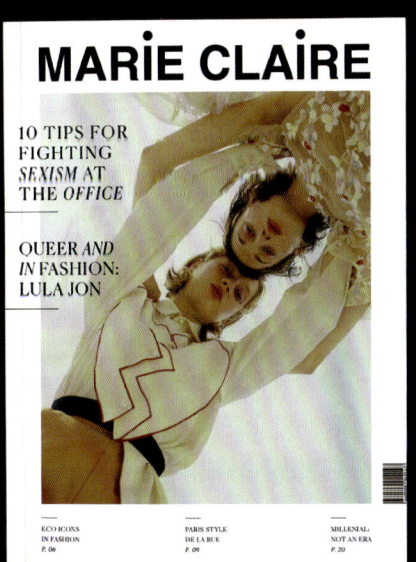

Student: Caitlin Ballantyne | **School:** Brigham Young University

INSTRUCTOR **NANCY CAMPBELL**

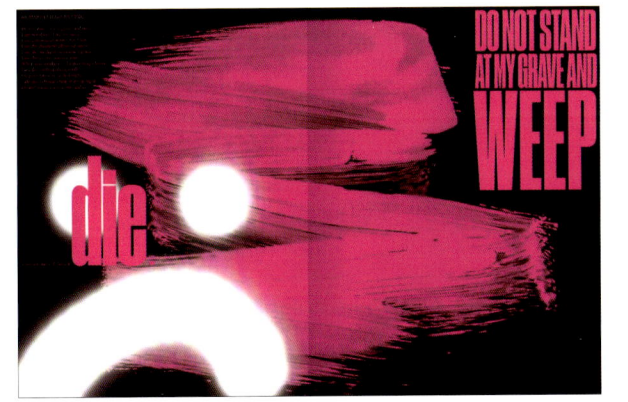

Student: Carlos DeLeon | **School:** Kean University

INSTRUCTOR **NATHAN SAVAGE**

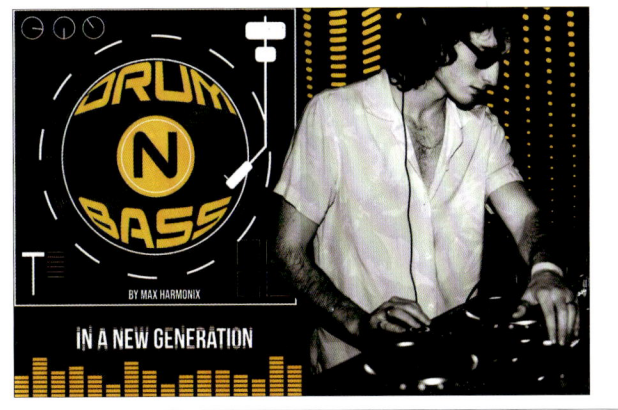

Student: Cole Popejoy | **School:** Portland Community College

INSTRUCTOR **NATHAN SAVAGE**

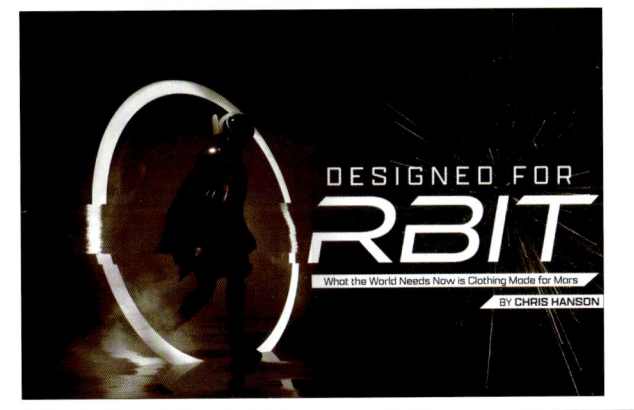

Student: Sara Rosario | **School:** Portland Community College

INSTRUCTOR **HANK RICHARDSON**

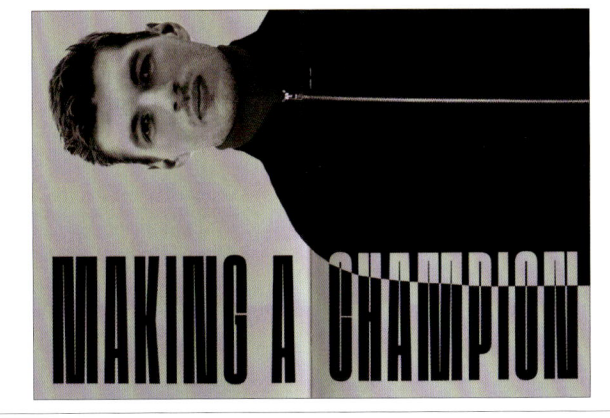

Student: Reagan Williams | **School:** M.AD School of Ideas Atlanta

Editorial | Design

174 DESIGN SILVER

INSTRUCTOR NATHAN SAVAGE 🇺🇸

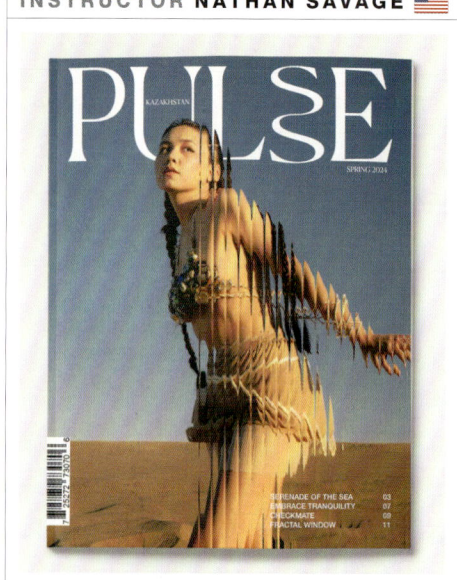

Student: Michael Madrid
School: Portland Community College

INSTRUCTOR TAYLOR SHIPTON 🇺🇸

Student: Gabrielle Harris
School: Pennsylvania State University

INSTRUCTOR ANNE JORDAN 🇺🇸

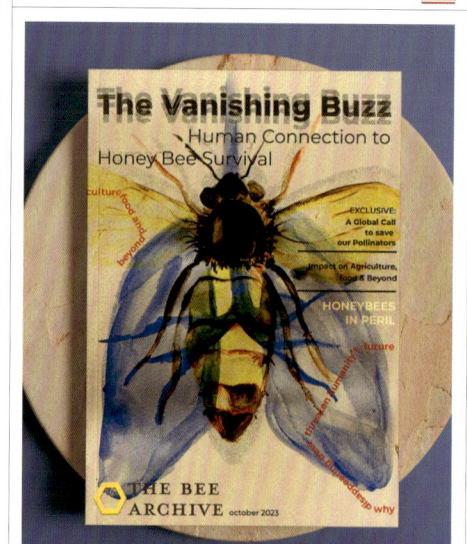

Student: Aditi Singh
School: Rochester Institute of Technology

INSTRUCTOR ERIC GILLETT 🇺🇸

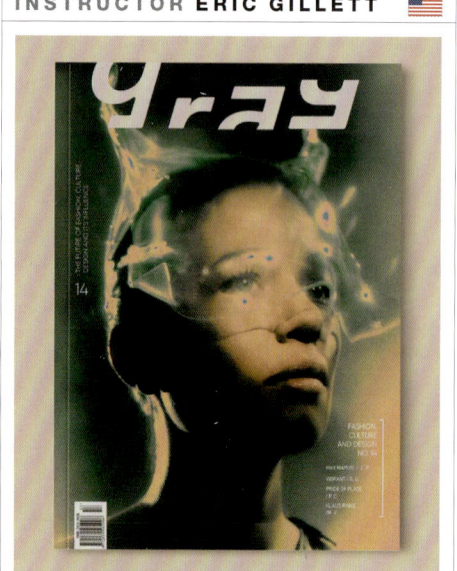

Student: Sophie Baddley
School: Brigham Young University

INSTRUCTOR EMILY BURNS 🇺🇸

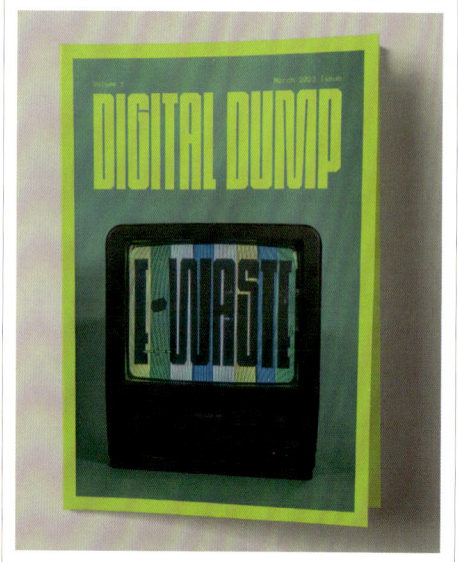

Student: Wyatt Poorman
School: Pennsylvania State University

INSTRUCTOR HANK RICHARDSON 🇺🇸

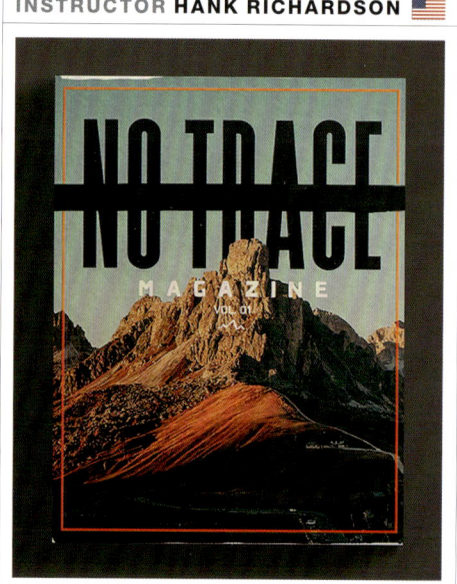

Student: Jamie Jason
School: M.AD School of Ideas Atlanta

INSTRUCTOR TAYLOR SHIPTON 🇺🇸

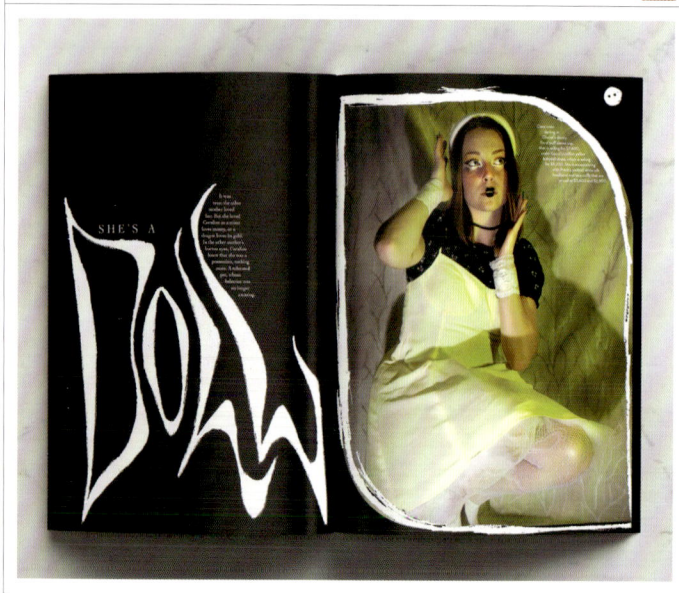

Student: Kathryn Gross | **School:** Pennsylvania State University

INSTRUCTOR JOHN KUDOS 🇺🇸

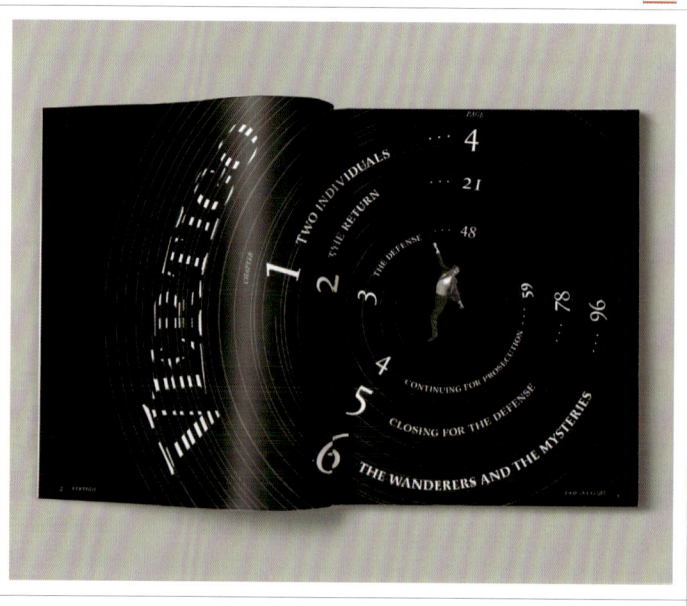

Student: Yubin Won | **School:** School of Visual Arts

Design | Editorial

175 DESIGN SILVER

INST. KAREN WATKINS, HEIDI HAYOUNG LEE

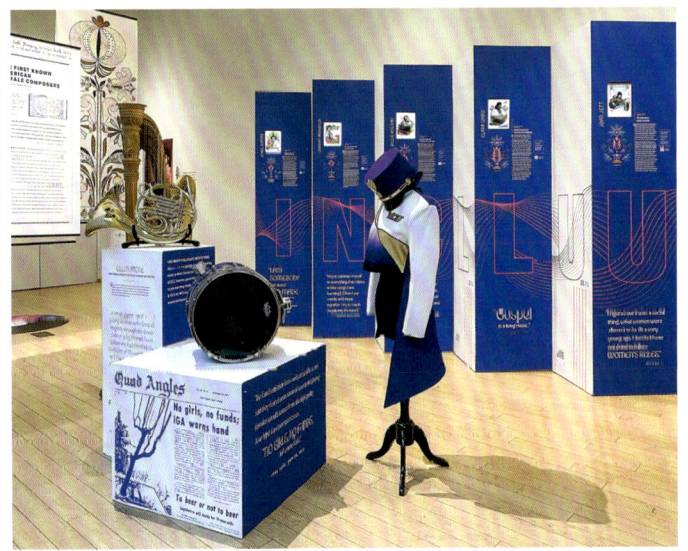

Students: Meredith DiPietro, Olivia Dreon, Emily Simon, Alyssa Crognale, Braydon Yearicks, Noah Burns | **School:** West Chester University

INSTRUCTOR KAREN WATKINS

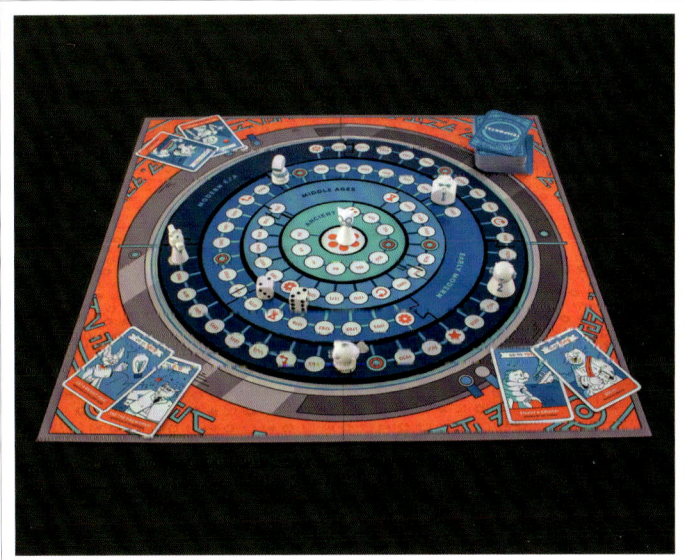

Student: Colleen Grant
School: West Chester University

INSTRUCTOR ALISA ZAMIR

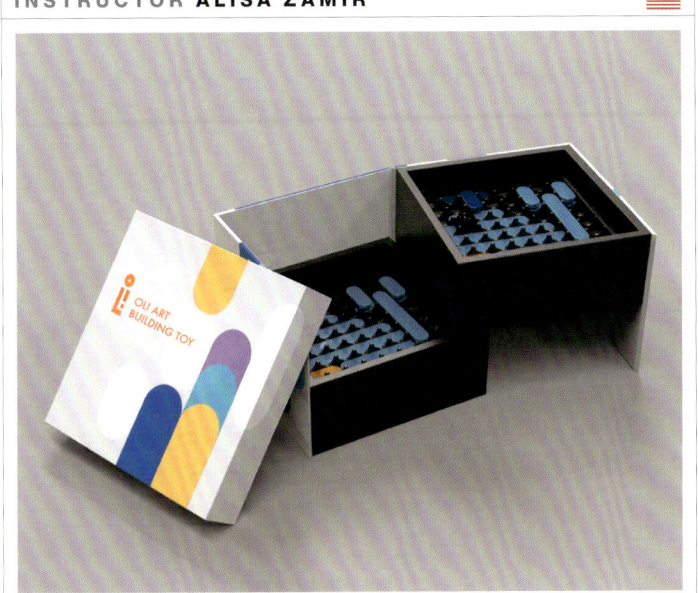

Student: Wen-Chi Hsueh | **School:** Pratt Institute

INSTRUCTOR WHITNEY HOLDEN

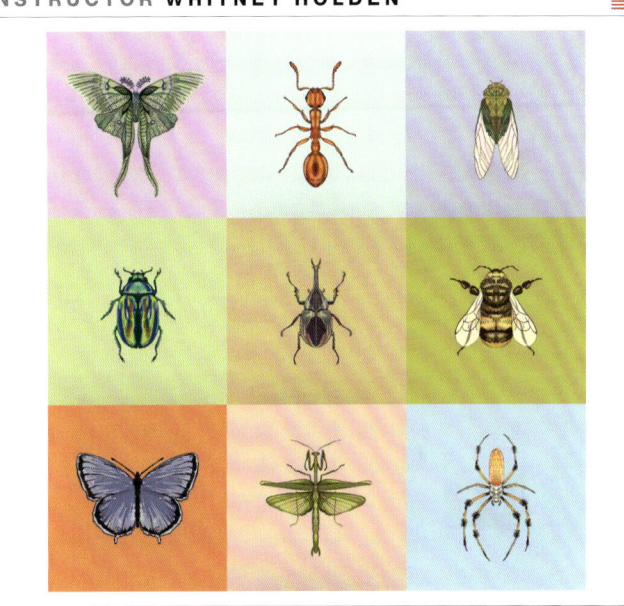

Student: Maeci Ray | **School:** University of North Texas

INSTRUCTOR VALERIE POBJOY

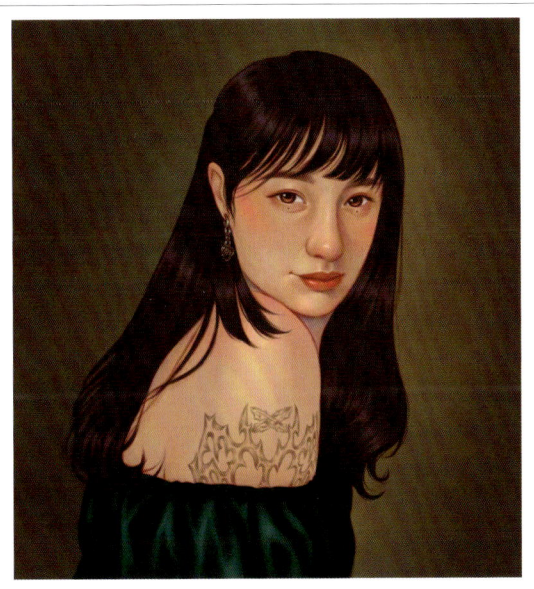

Student: Jess Martinez | **School:** ArtCenter College of Design

INSTRUCTOR SARAH VACCARIELLO

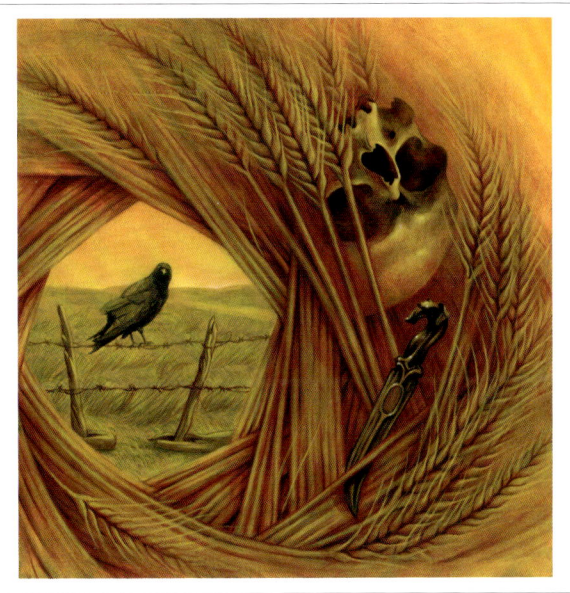

Student: Ariel Miner | **School:** School of Visual Arts

176 DESIGN SILVER

INSTRUCTOR LISK FENG 🇺🇸

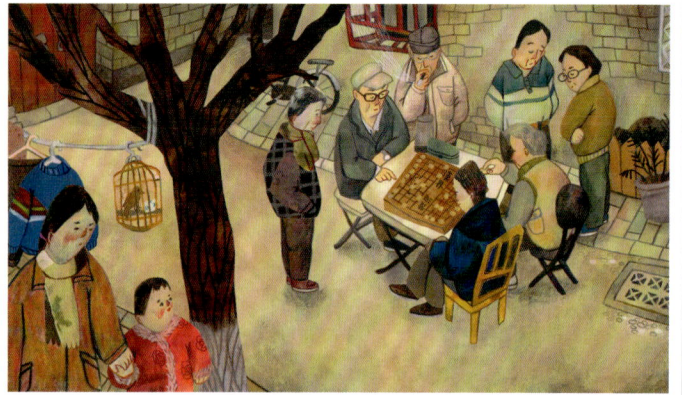

Student: Huilin Gui | **School:** School of Visual Arts

INSTRUCTOR DOUG SALATI 🇺🇸

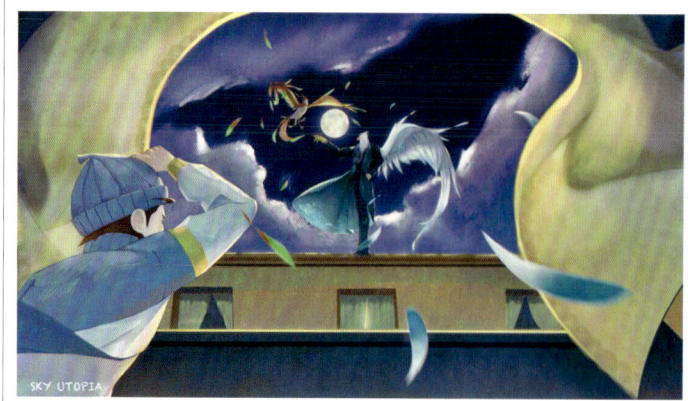

Student: Yijiang Dong | **School:** School of Visual Arts

INSTRUCTOR ANTHONY MACBAIN 🇺🇸

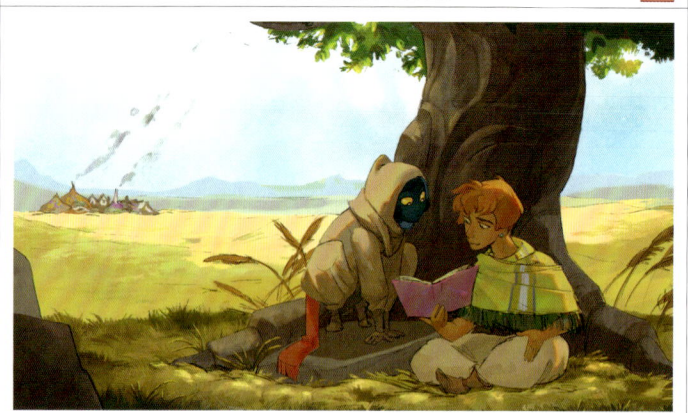

Student: Alana Green | **School:** School of Visual Arts

INSTRUCTOR STEVE BRODNER 🇺🇸

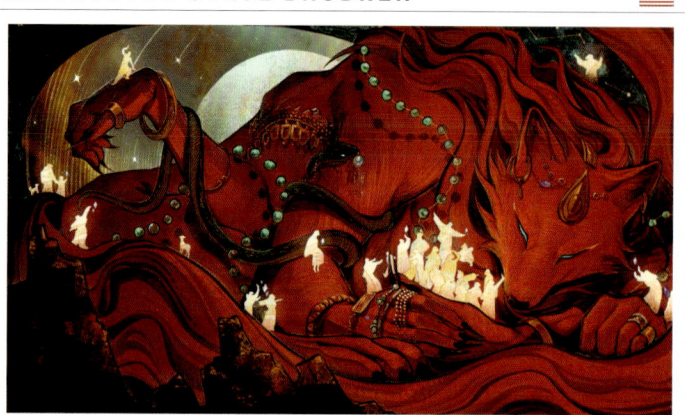

Student: Rongzhang Ye | **School:** School of Visual Arts

INSTRUCTOR LISK FENG 🇺🇸

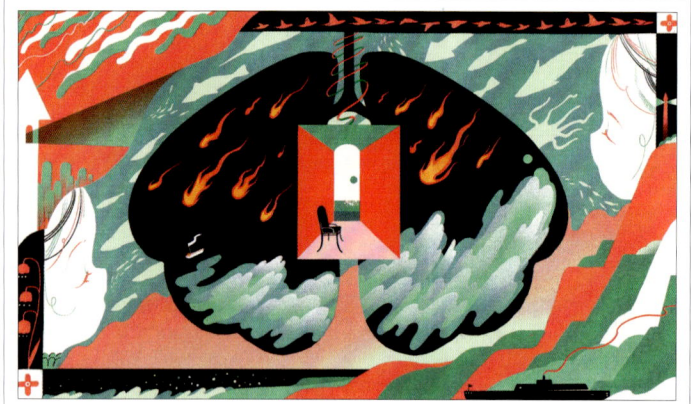

Student: Yawen Hu | **School:** School of Visual Arts

INSTRUCTOR LILY PADULA 🇺🇸

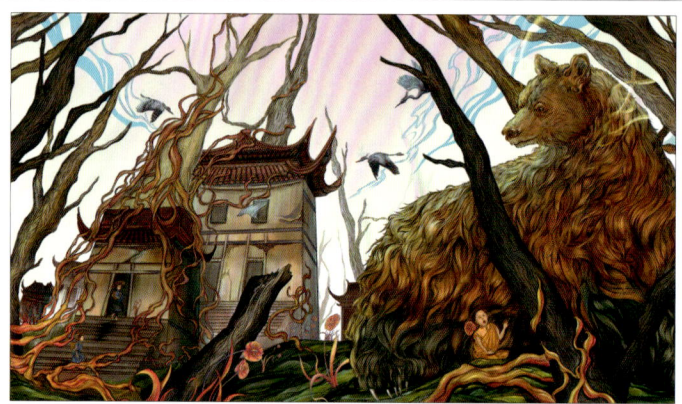

Student: Yi Chen | **School:** School of Visual Arts

INSTRUCTOR VIKTOR KOEN 🇺🇸

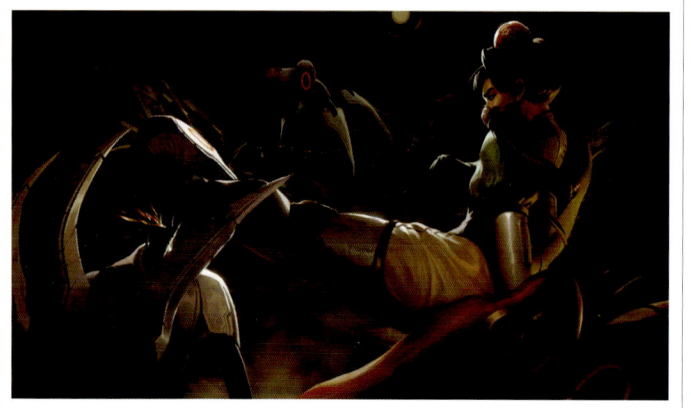

Student: Ting En Chou | **School:** School of Visual Arts

INSTRUCTOR LISK FENG 🇺🇸

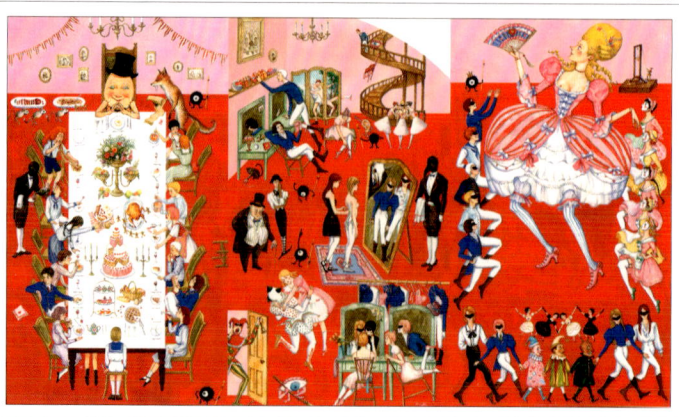

Student: Yunyao Chen | **School:** School of Visual Arts

Design | Illustration

177 DESIGN SILVER

INSTRUCTOR MATT ROTA 🇺🇸

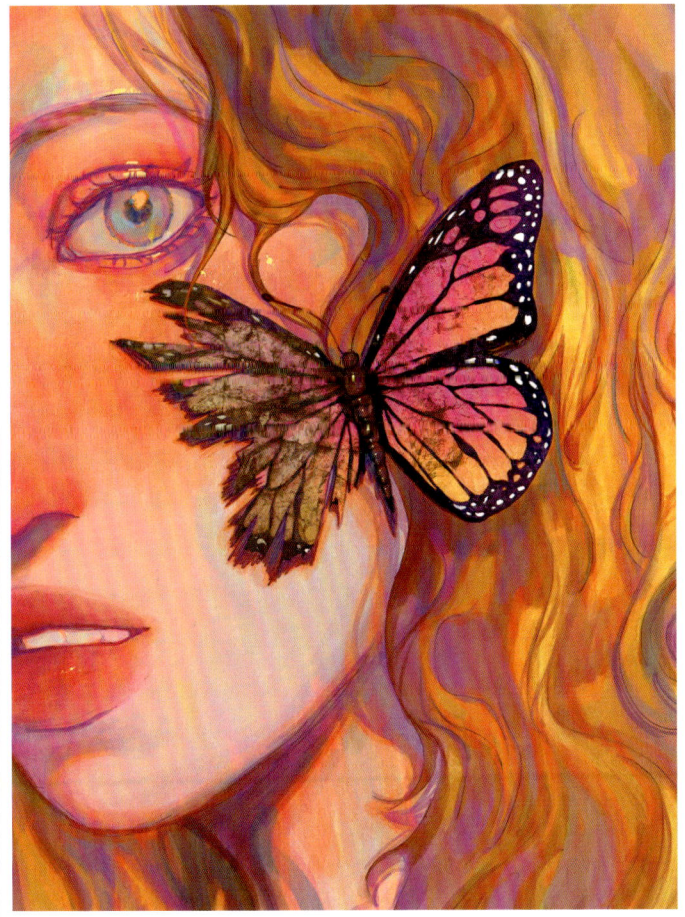

Student: Chalzea Xu | **School:** School of Visual Arts

INSTRUCTOR DILLON CARSON 🇺🇸

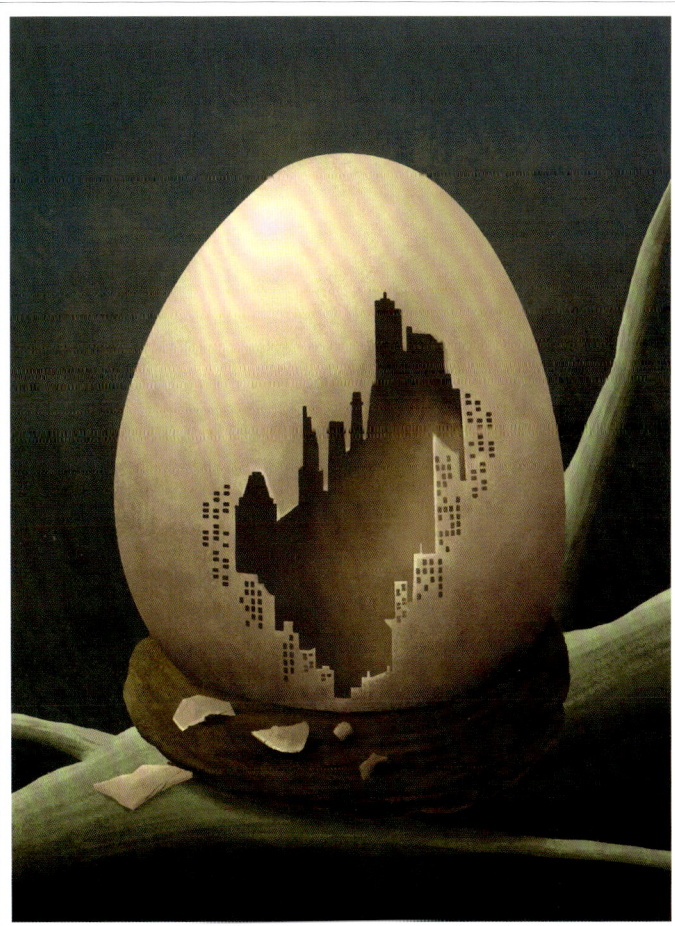

Student: Alicia Cheng | **School:** ArtCenter College of Design

INSTRUCTOR JIM SALVATI 🇺🇸

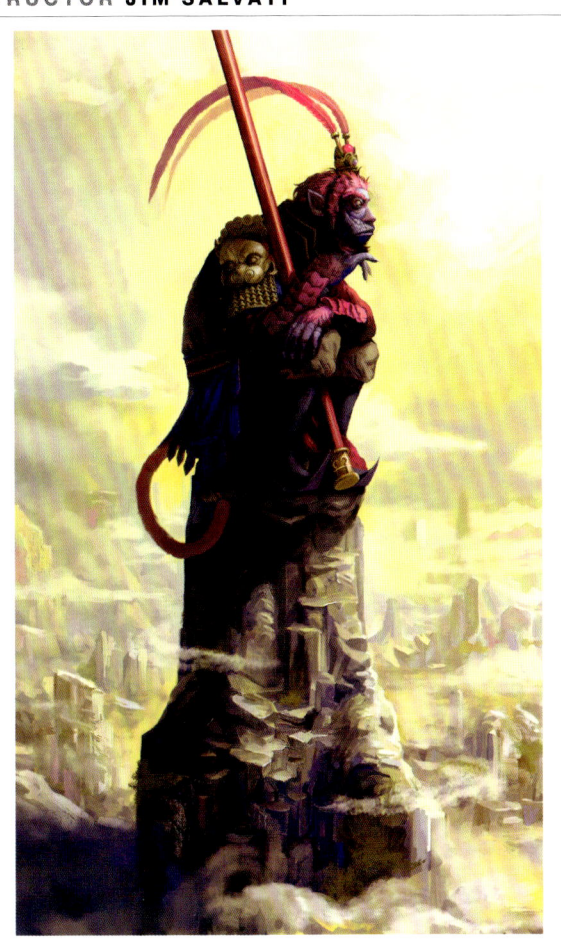

Student: Timothy Yan | **School:** ArtCenter College of Design

INSTRUCTOR JIM SALVATI 🇺🇸

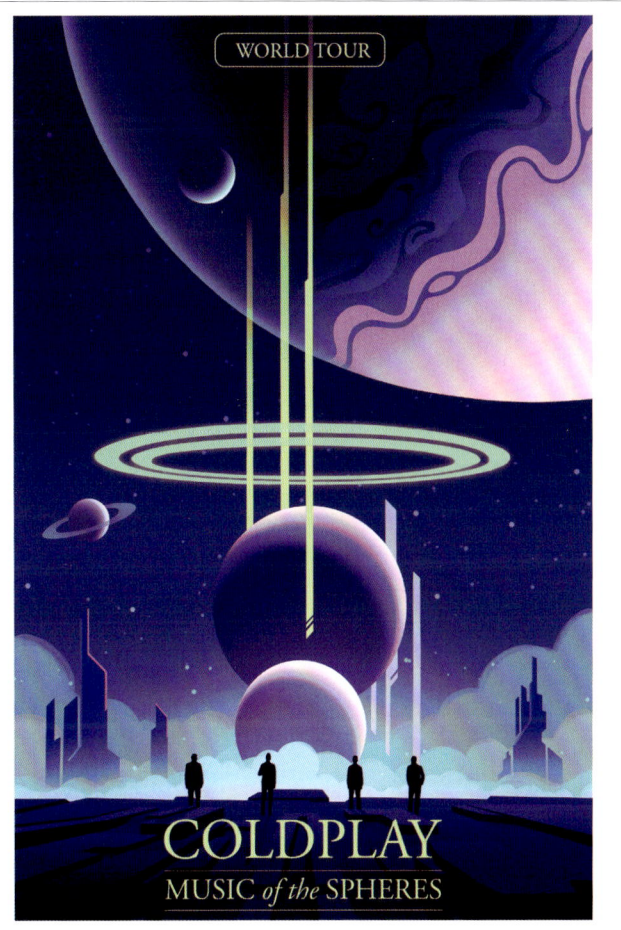

Student: Rain Gao | **School:** ArtCenter College of Design

178 DESIGN SILVER

INSTRUCTOR **LISK FENG** 🇺🇸	INSTRUCTOR **STEPHEN ZHANG** 🇺🇸	INST. **YUKO SHIMIZU, SAM WEBER** 🇺🇸
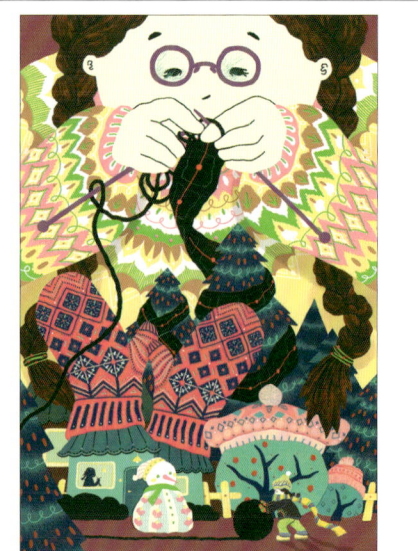		
Student: Letao Sun **School:** School of Visual Arts	**Student:** Emma Ortiz **School:** University of North Texas	**Student:** Mifei Zhou **School:** School of Visual Arts
INSTRUCTOR **JIM SALVATI** 🇺🇸	INSTRUCTOR **PAUL ROGERS** 🇺🇸	INST. **YUKO SHIMIZU, SAM WEBER** 🇺🇸
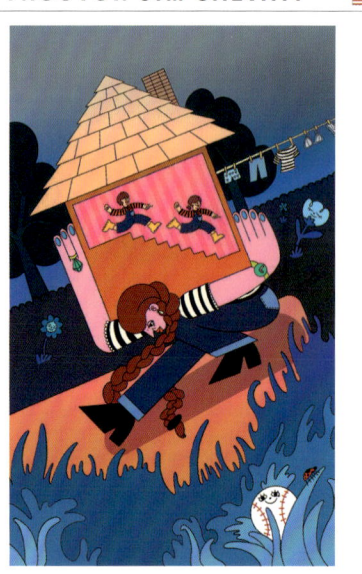	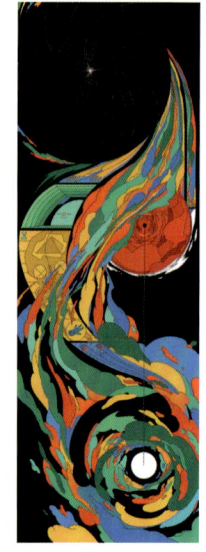	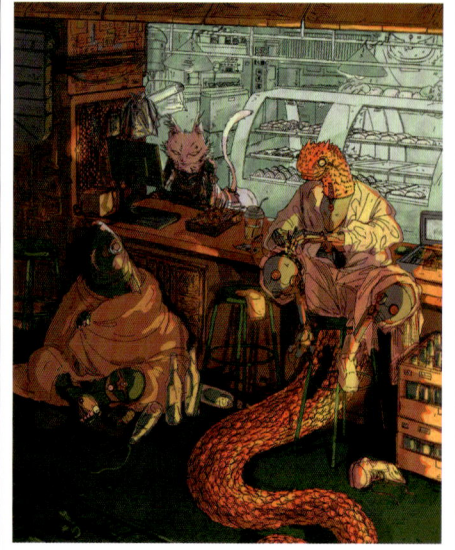
Student: Ciara Hart **School:** ArtCenter College of Design	**Student:** Jerilyn Lee **School:** ArtCenter College of Design	**Student:** Yuzhuan Zhou **School:** School of Visual Arts
INSTRUCTOR **STEVE BRODNER** 🇺🇸	INSTRUCTOR **JENSINE ECKWELL** 🇺🇸	INSTRUCTOR **JIM SALVATI** 🇺🇸
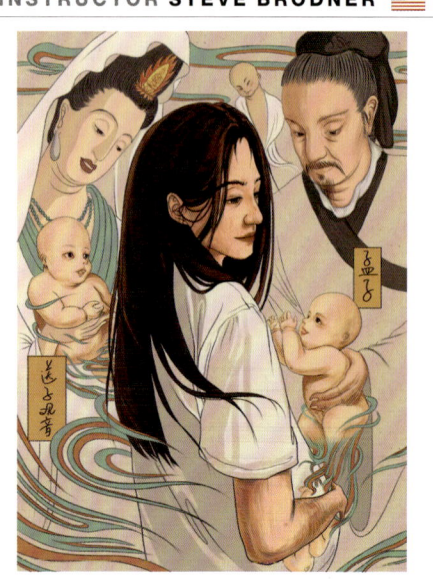	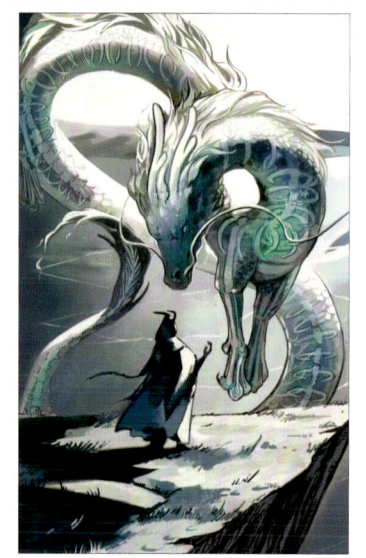	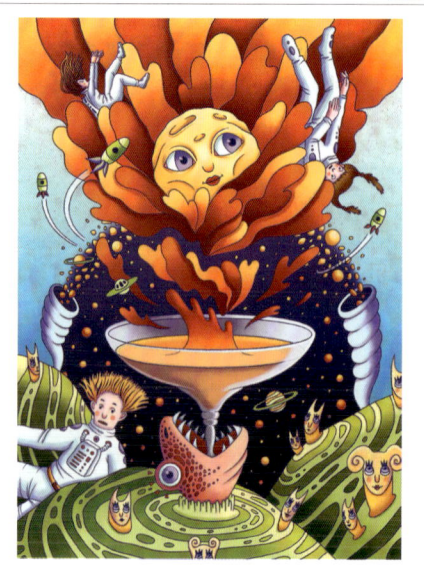
Student: Xin Huang **School:** School of Visual Arts	**Student:** Jingyao He **School:** School of Visual Arts	**Student:** Jiyun Choi **School:** ArtCenter College of Design

Design | Illustration

179 DESIGN SILVER

INSTRUCTOR SUSANNA COFFEY
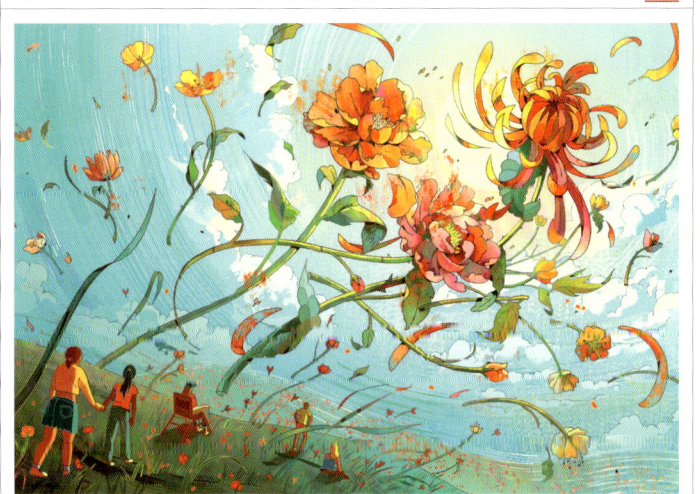
Student: Taylor Yingshi | **School:** Columbia University

INSTRUCTOR ARA DEVEJIAN
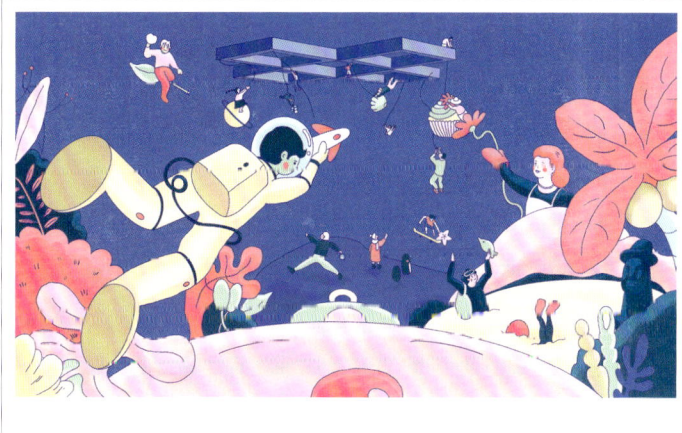
Student: Elaine Lee | **School:** ArtCenter College of Design

INSTRUCTOR ANTHONY MACBAIN
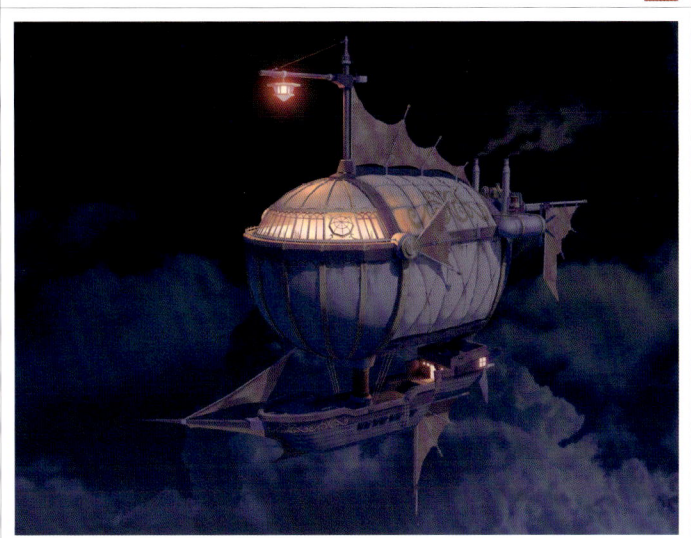
Student: Yinghao Lin | **School:** School of Visual Arts

INSTRUCTOR LISK FENG
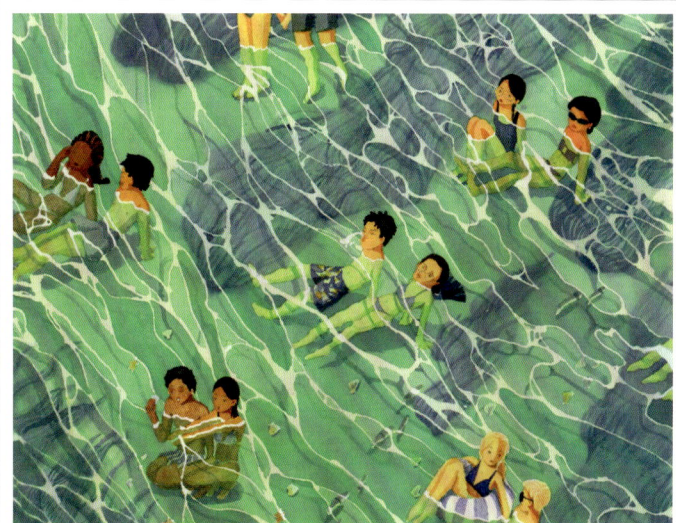
Student: Songer Yang | **School:** School of Visual Arts

INSTRUCTOR JOSH COCHRAN
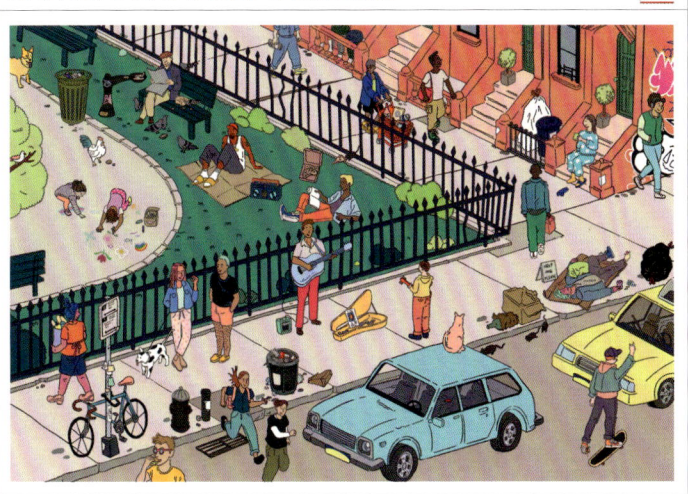
Student: Estelle Ha | **School:** School of Visual Arts

INSTRUCTOR JOSH COCHRAN
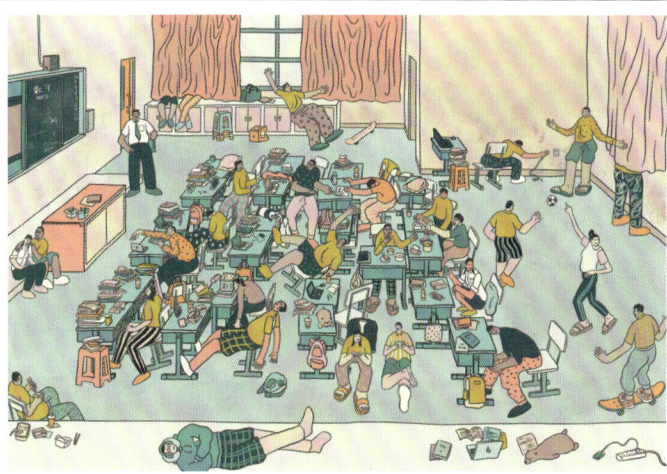
Student: Zhanhao Liang | **School:** School of Visual Arts

Illustration | Design

180 DESIGN SILVER

INST. BRIAN REA, PAUL ROGERS 🇺🇸
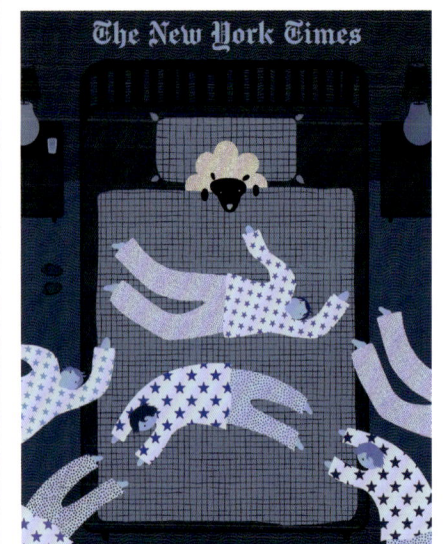
Student: Maria Dzulfayan
School: ArtCenter College of Design

INST. BRIAN REA, PAUL ROGERS 🇺🇸
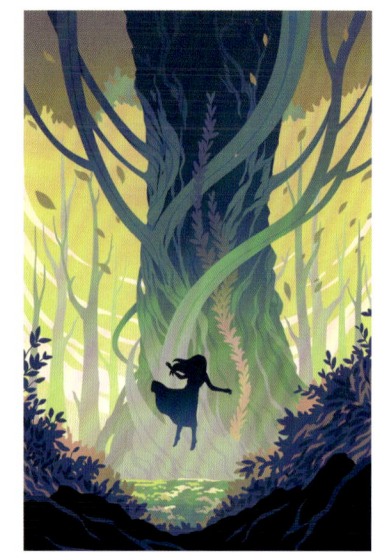
Student: Maria Dzulfayan
School: ArtCenter College of Design

INSTRUCTOR JOSH COCHRAN 🇺🇸
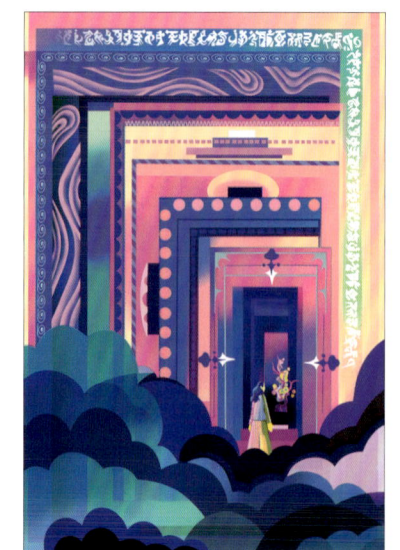
Student: Jiaxi Chen
School: School of Visual Arts

INST. YUKO SHIMIZU, MATT ROTA 🇺🇸
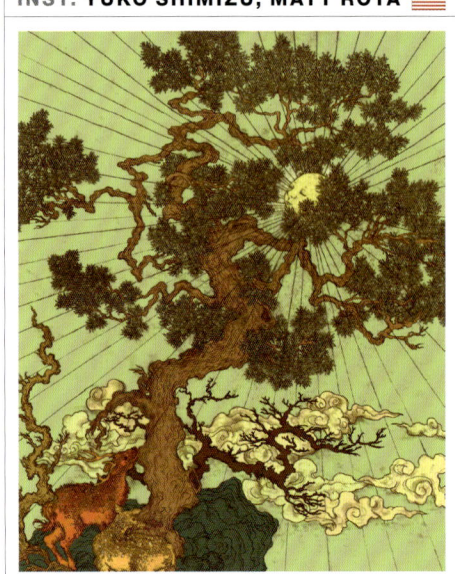
Student: Scarlet Ding
School: School of Visual Arts

INSTRUCTOR DOUG SALATI 🇺🇸
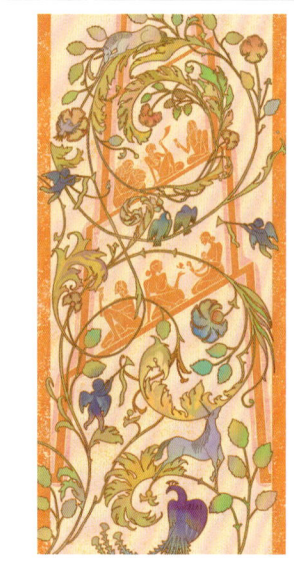
Student: Xiaohan Guo
School: School of Visual Arts

INSTRUCTOR DOUG SALATI 🇺🇸
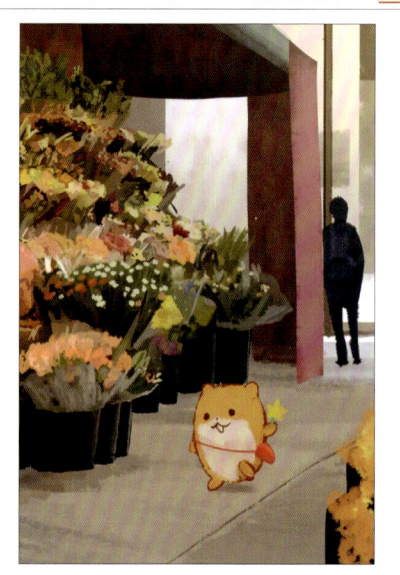
Student: Lauren Giancola
School: School of Visual Arts

INSTRUCTOR JIM SALVATI 🇺🇸
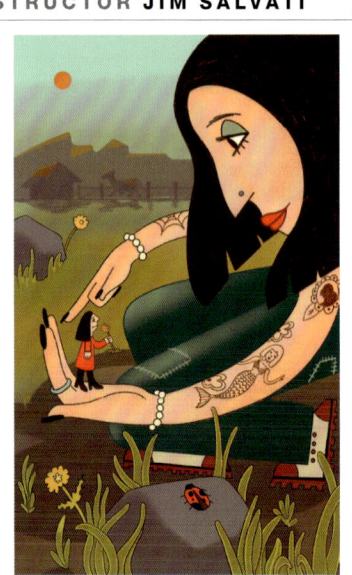
Student: Ciara Hart
School: ArtCenter College of Design

INSTRUCTOR JENSINE ECKWELL 🇺🇸
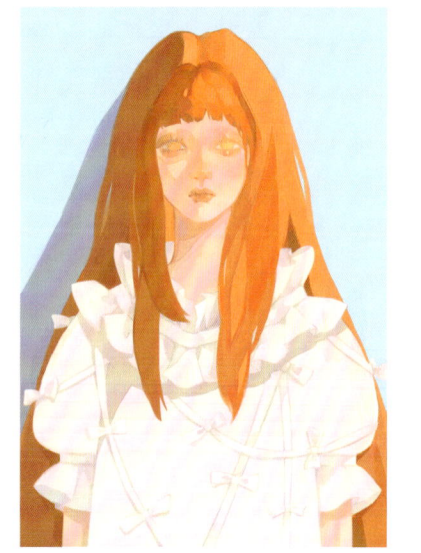
Student: Wenjun Shao
School: School of Visual Arts

INST. YUKO SHIMIZU, SAM WEBER 🇺🇸
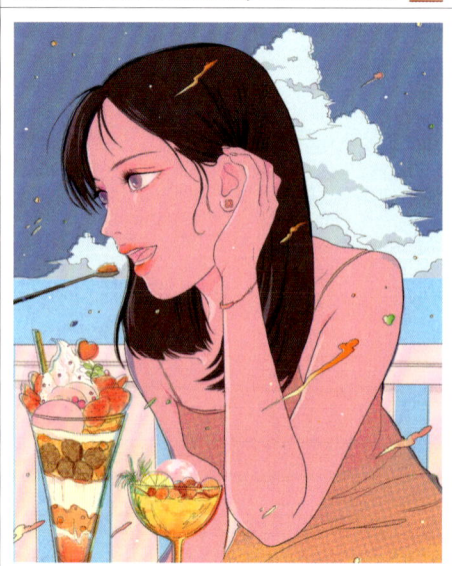
Student: Mika Ichikawa
School: School of Visual Arts

Design | Illustration

181 DESIGN SILVER

INSTRUCTORS YUKO SHIMIZU, SAM WEBER

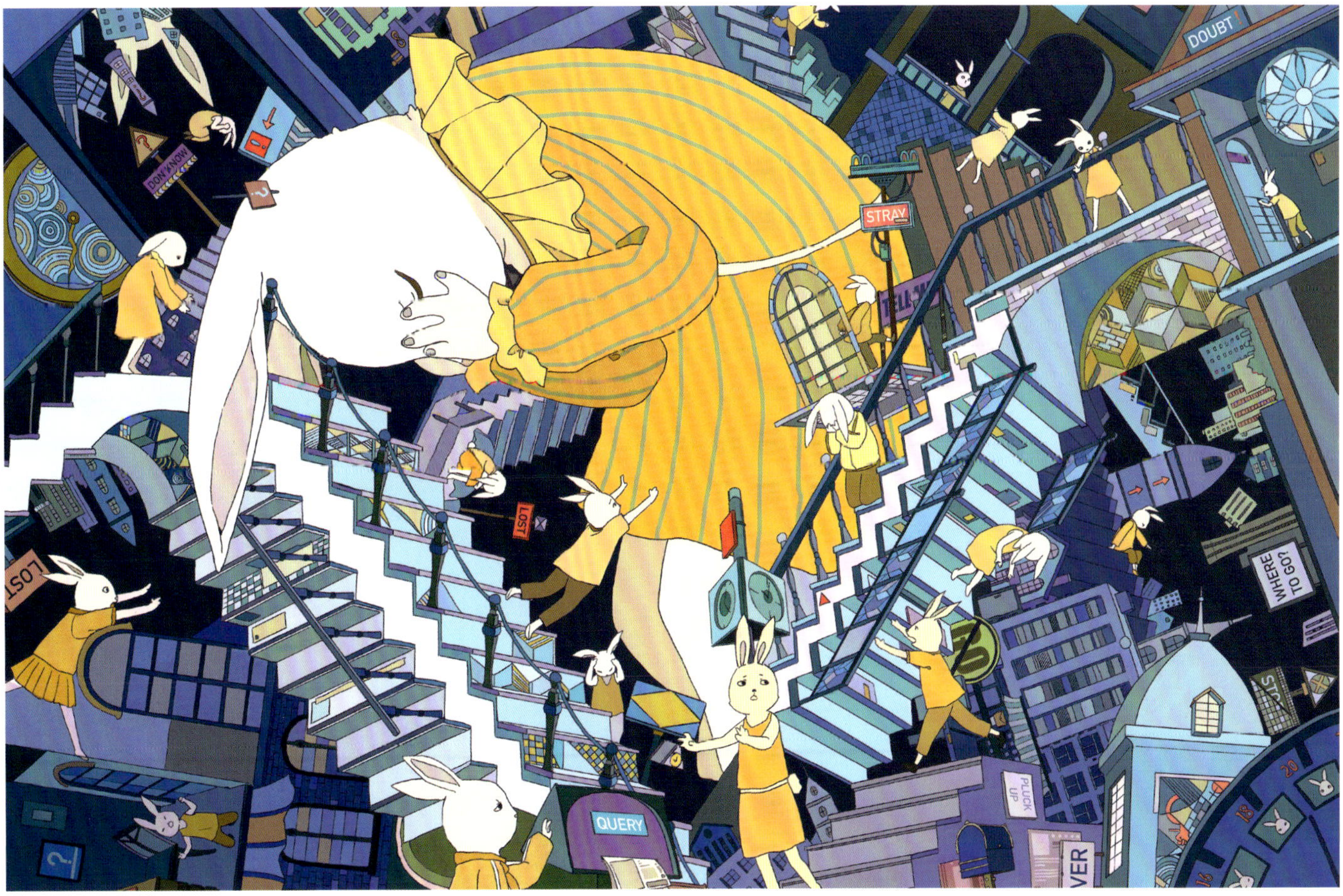

Student: Yilin Zhu | **School:** School of Visual Arts

INSTRUCTOR STEVE BRODNER

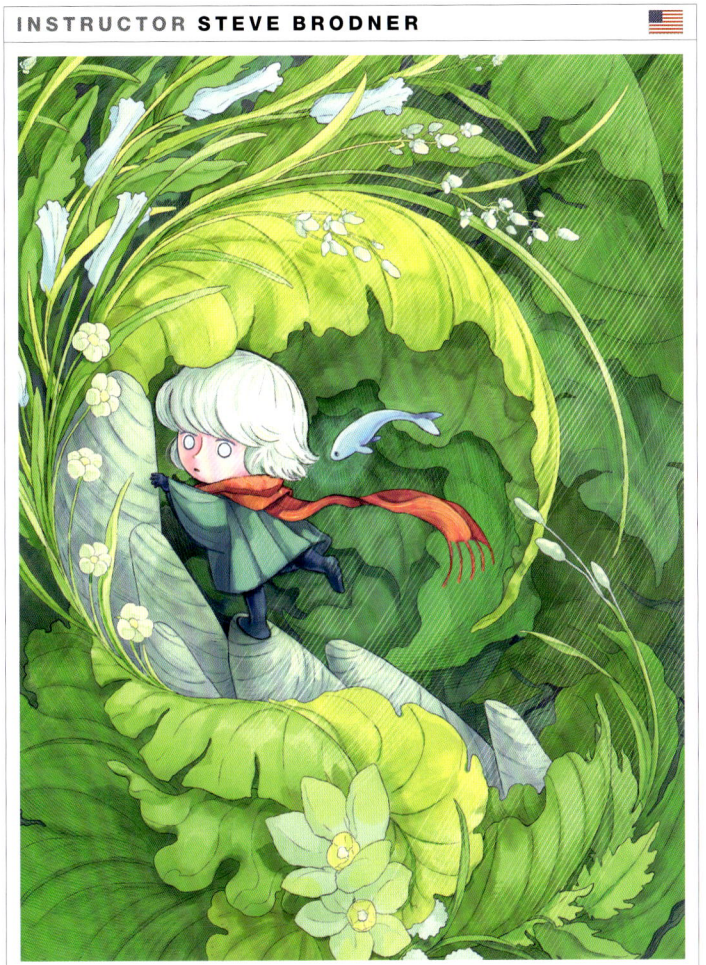

Student: Sirui Zou | **School:** School of Visual Arts

INSTRUCTORS MATT ROTA, YUKO SHIMIZU

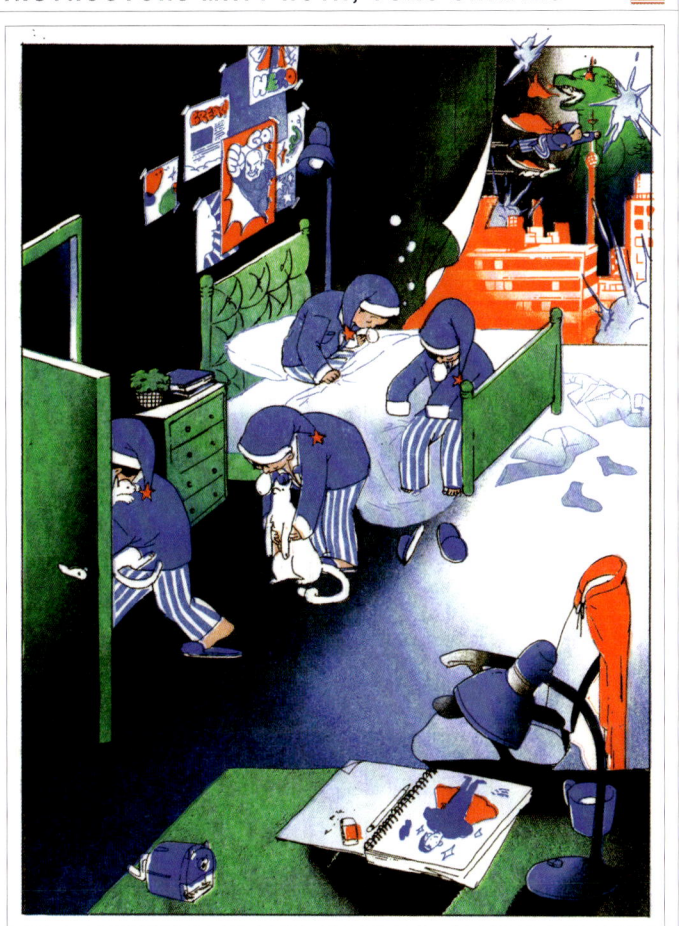

Student: Zhehao Wu | **School:** School of Visual Arts

182 DESIGN SILVER

INSTRUCTOR **UNATTRIBUTED** 🇪🇸
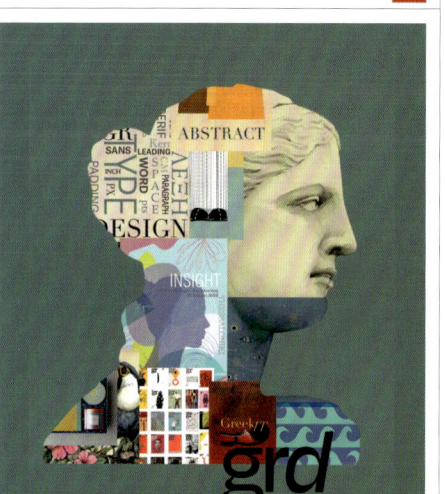
Student: Valia Papadopoulou | **School:** LABASAD Barcelona School of Arts & Design

INSTRUCTOR **BEN DOLEZAL** 🇺🇸
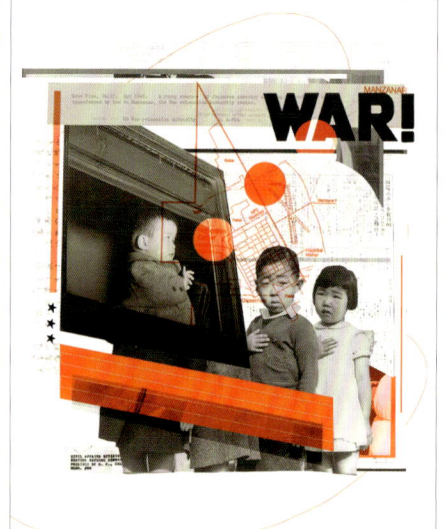
Student: Emily Brown
School: University of Texas at Arlington

INSTRUCTOR **JIM SALVATI** 🇺🇸
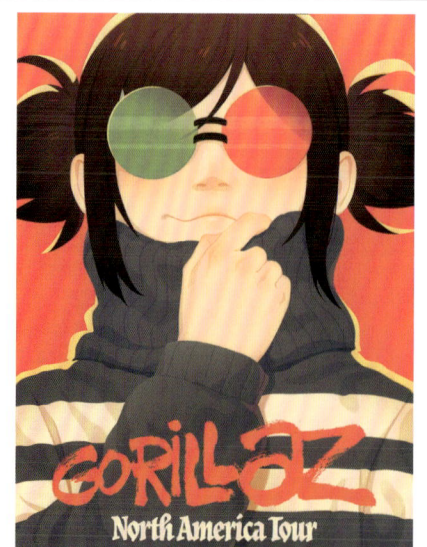
Student: Rain Gao
School: ArtCenter College of Design

INSTRUCTOR **ROBERT CLAYTON** 🇺🇸
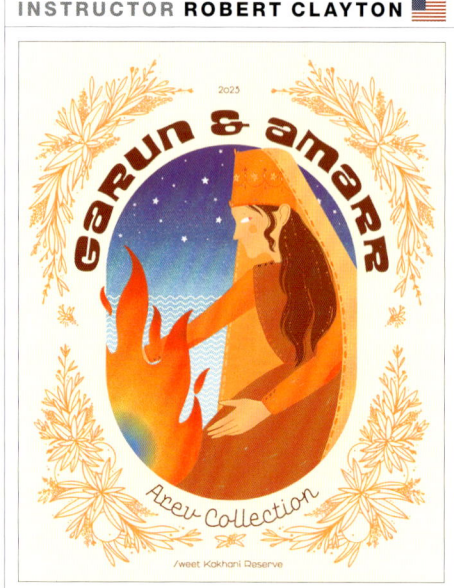
Student: Maria Dzulfayan
School: ArtCenter College of Design

INSTRUCTOR **JIM SALVATI** 🇺🇸
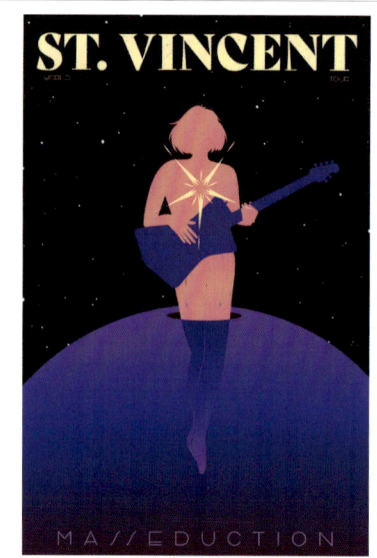
Student: Maria Dzulfayan
School: ArtCenter College of Design

INSTRUCTOR **STEPHEN ZHANG** 🇺🇸
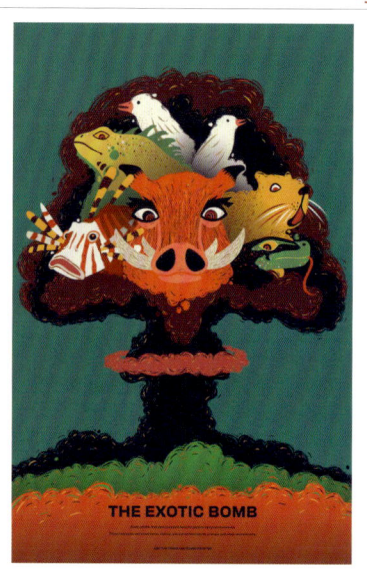
Student: Rebecca Dugan
School: University of North Texas

INSTRUCTOR **DAVID ELIZALDE** 🇺🇸
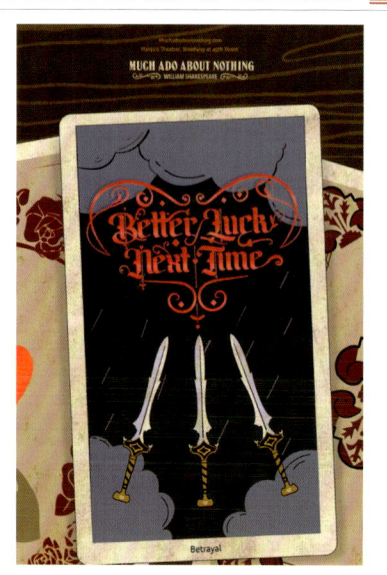
Student: Nho Hieu Kien Nguyen
School: Texas Christian University

INSTRUCTOR **WILLIE BARONET** 🇺🇸
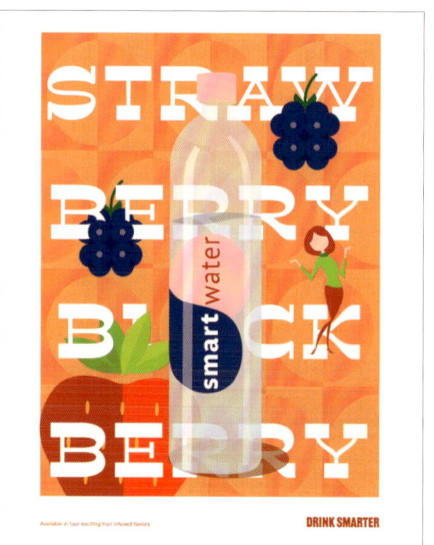
Students: Juan Silva, Delaney Gendron
School: Southern Methodist University

INSTRUCTOR **ADAM ROSS** 🇺🇸
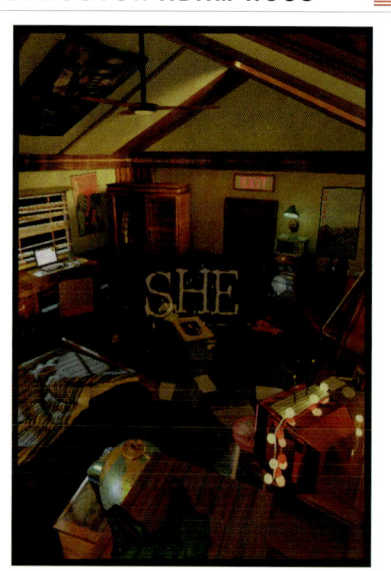
Student: Asha Seabron
School: ArtCenter College of Design

Design | Illustration

183 DESIGN SILVER

INSTRUCTOR VIRGINIA GREEN 🇺🇸

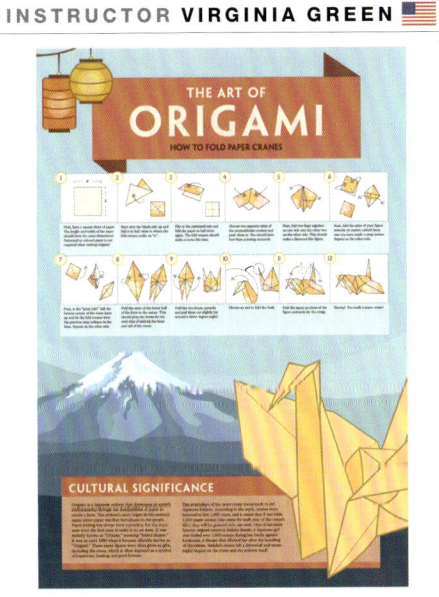

Student: Abigail Sanders
School: Baylor University

INSTRUCTOR NEETA VERMA 🇺🇸

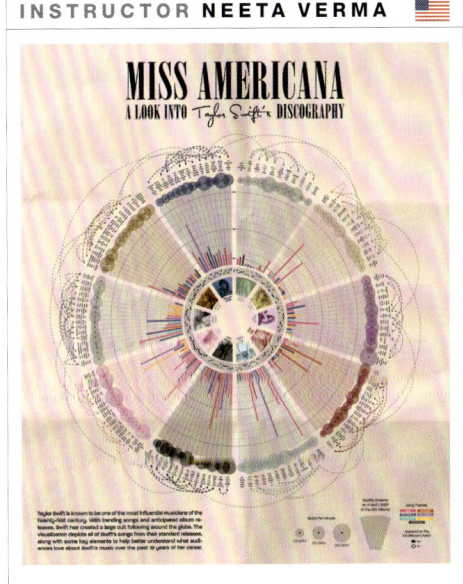

Students: Sophia Ochoa, Suhyeon Yi
School: University of Notre Dame

INSTRUCTOR VIRGINIA GREEN 🇺🇸

Student: Abigail Murschell
School: Baylor University

INSTRUCTOR DARREN WILSON 🇨🇦

Student: Minjoo Kim | **School:** York University

INSTRUCTOR DOUG THOMAS 🇺🇸

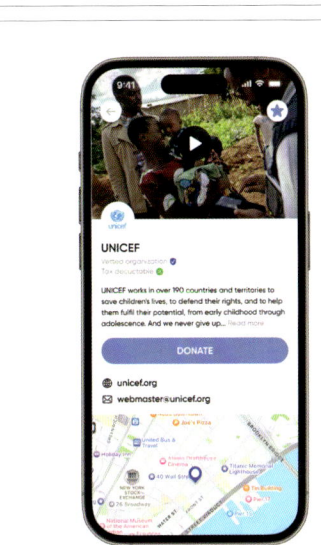

Student: Brett Hilton | **School:** Brigham Young University

INSTRUCTOR BILL GALYEAN 🇺🇸

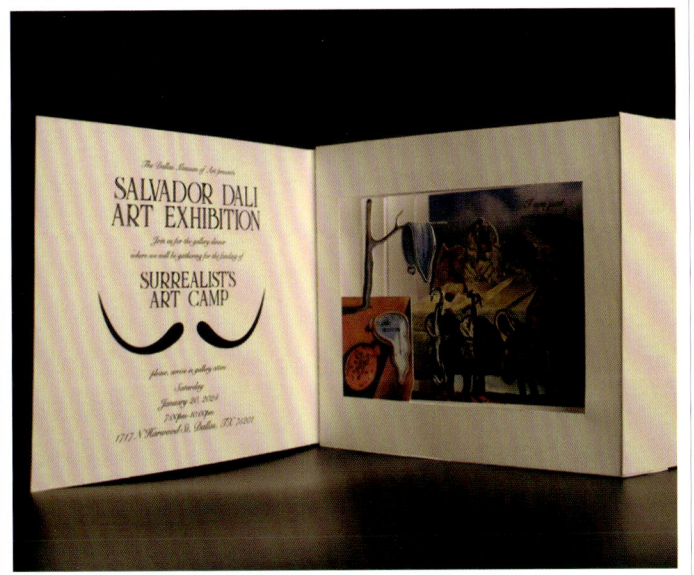

Student: Alexandra Tice | **School:** Texas Christian University

INSTRUCTOR DEJAN MRAOVIĆ 🇺🇸

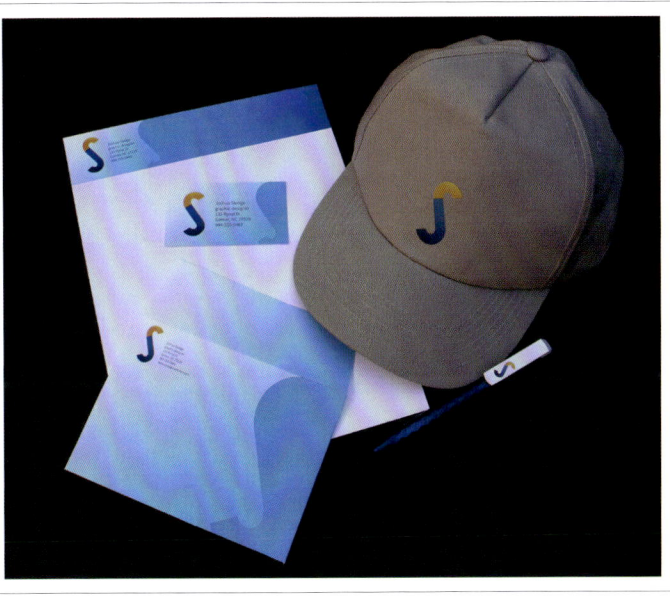

Student: Joshua Sledge | **School:** Campbell University

Infographic, Interaction Design, Invitation, Letterhead | Design

INSTRUCTOR JOSHUA EGE 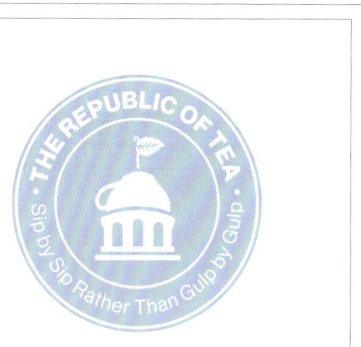 Student: Mariana Santana School: Texas A&M University-Commerce	**INSTRUCTOR UNATTRIBUTED** 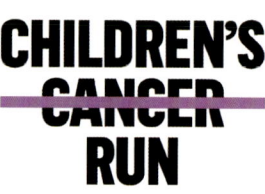 Student: Hieu Vo | School: University of Architecture Ho Chi Minh City	**INSTRUCTOR NATHAN SAVAGE** 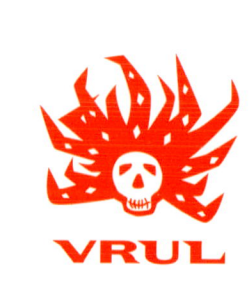 Student: Grey Shawger School: Portland Community College
INSTRUCTOR MARK BRINKMAN 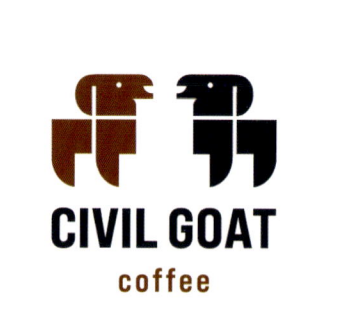 Student: Travis Crawford School: Texas State University	**INSTRUCTOR WILLIE BARONET** 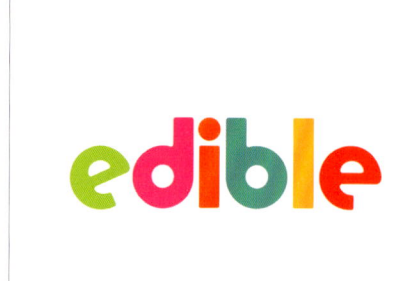 Student: Savanna Hodes School: Southern Methodist University	**INSTRUCTOR WILLIE BARONET** 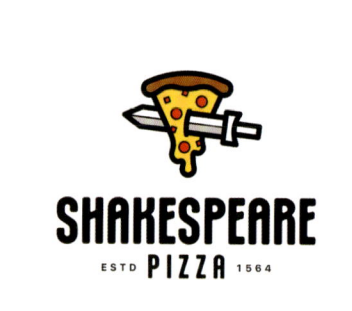 Student: Ethan Jones School: Southern Methodist University
INSTRUCTOR DOUGLAS MAY 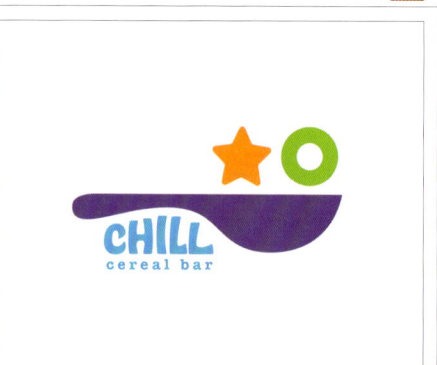 Student: Rylee Armstrong School: University of North Texas	**INSTRUCTOR MARK BRINKMAN** 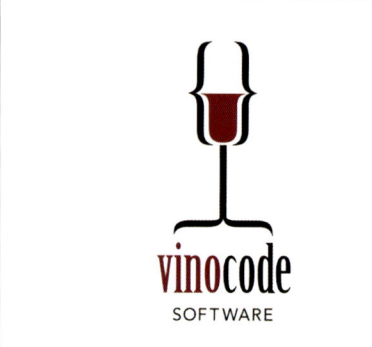 Student: Travis Crawford School: Texas State University	**INSTRUCTOR LINDA REYNOLDS** 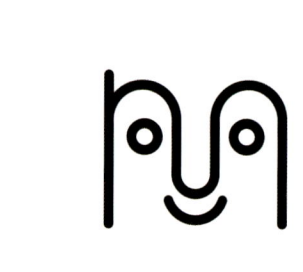 Student: Sophie Houghton School: Brigham Young University
INSTRUCTOR DEVON WARD 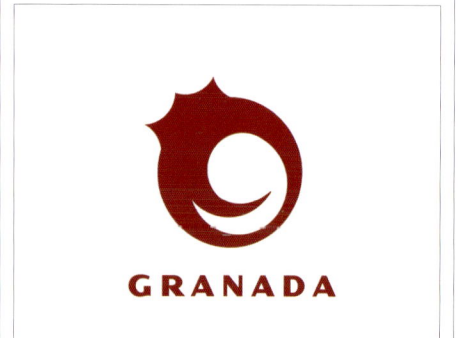 Student: Lavens Maginnis School: Auburn University	**INST. GENARO SOLIS RIVERO** 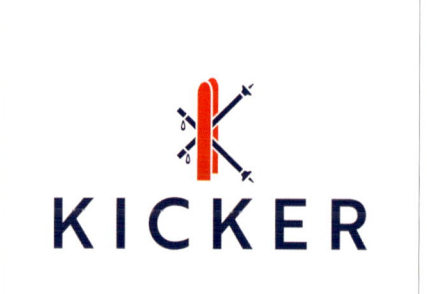 Student: Virginia Herschend School: Baylor University	**INSTRUCTOR MARK BRINKMAN** 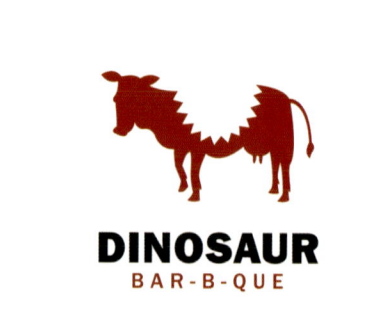 Student: Mason Havard School: Texas State University

185 DESIGN SILVER

INSTRUCTOR MARK BRINKMAN 🇺🇸	**INST. GENARO SOLIS RIVERO** 🇺🇸	**INSTRUCTOR JEFF DAVIS** 🇺🇸
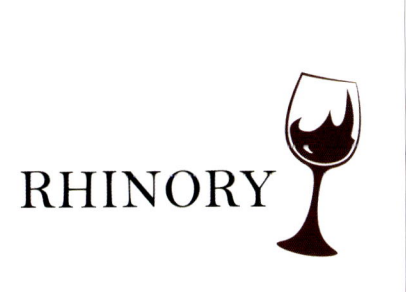	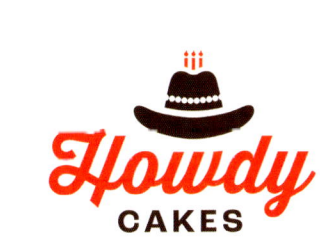	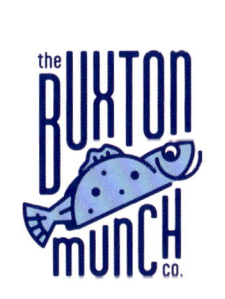
Student: Tessa Shellenberger **School:** Texas State University	**Student:** Kate Sudderth **School:** Baylor University	**Student:** Logan Dorsey **School:** Texas State University
INSTRUCTOR MARK BRINKMAN 🇺🇸	**INSTRUCTOR MARK BRINKMAN** 🇺🇸	**INSTRUCTOR MARK BRINKMAN** 🇺🇸
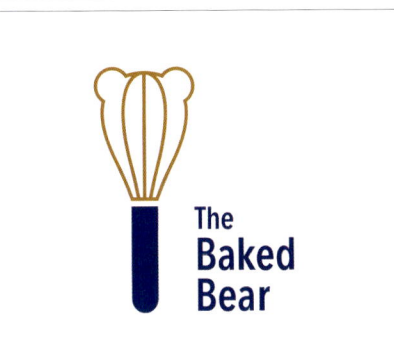	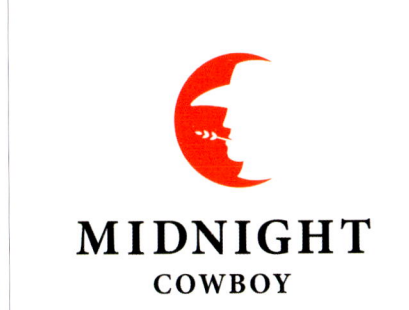	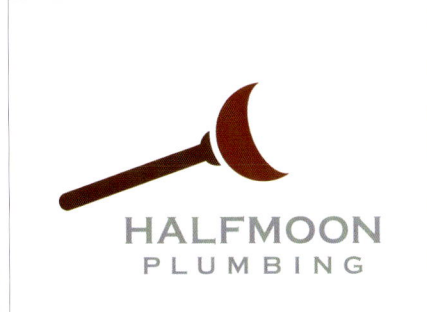
Student: Mandy Czyz **School:** Texas State University	**Student:** Travis Crawford **School:** Texas State University	**Student:** Tessa Shellenberger **School:** Texas State University
INSTRUCTOR JEFF DAVIS 🇺🇸	**INSTRUCTOR WILLIAM MEEK** 🇺🇸	**INST. GENARO SOLIS RIVERO** 🇺🇸
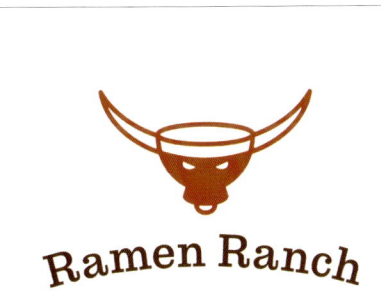	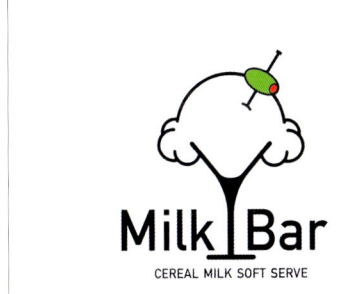	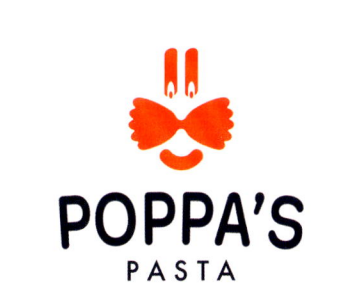
Student: Nick Voss **School:** Texas State University	**Student:** Mallory Randolph **School:** Texas State University	**Student:** Abriella Patti **School:** Baylor University
INST. DORIS PALMEROS-MCMANUS 🇺🇸	**INSTRUCTOR MARK BRINKMAN** 🇺🇸	**INSTRUCTOR MARK BRINKMAN** 🇺🇸
	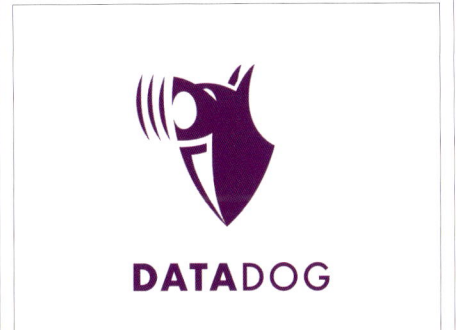	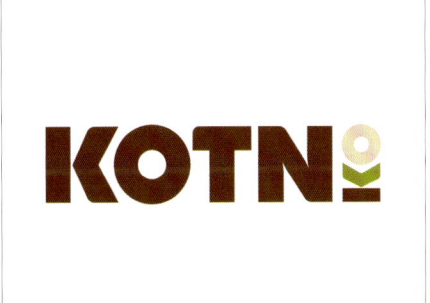
Student: Rozlynn Macbeth Olivas **School:** University of the Incarnate Word	**Student:** Travis Crawford **School:** Texas State University	**Student:** Yasseen Cherif Elassar **School:** Texas State University

Logo | Design

INSTRUCTOR WILLIE BARONET 🇺🇸 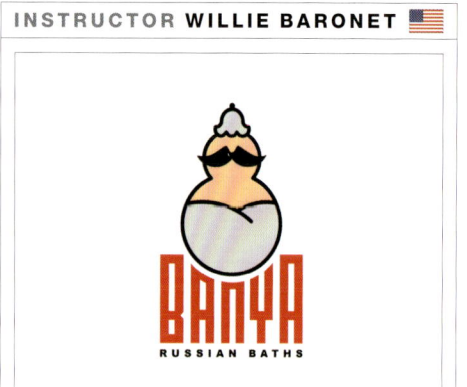 **Student:** Savanna Hodes **School:** Southern Methodist University	**INSTRUCTOR HANK RICHARDSON** 🇺🇸 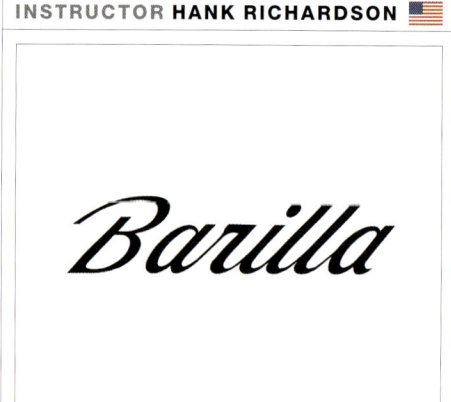 **Student:** Nic De La Hoz **School:** M.AD School of Ideas Atlanta	**INSTRUCTOR DOUGLAS MAY** 🇺🇸 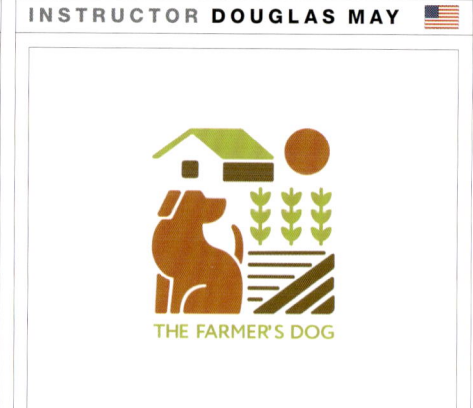 **Student:** Annika Snow **School:** University of North Texas
INSTRUCTOR ANNE JORDAN 🇺🇸 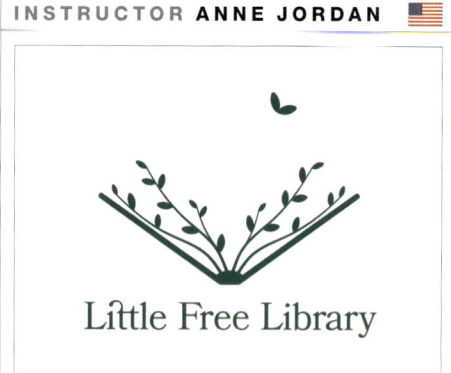 **Student:** Rachel Seaton **School:** Rochester Institute of Technology	**INSTRUCTOR WILLIE BARONET** 🇺🇸 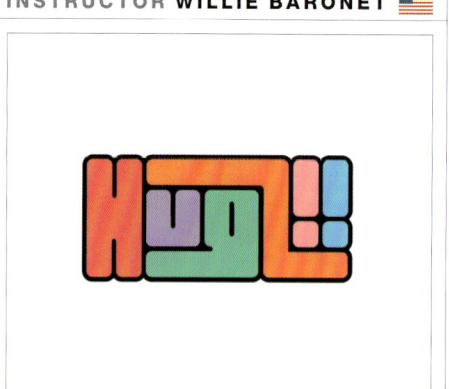 **Student:** Savanna Hodes **School:** Southern Methodist University	**INSTRUCTOR MARK BRINKMAN** 🇺🇸 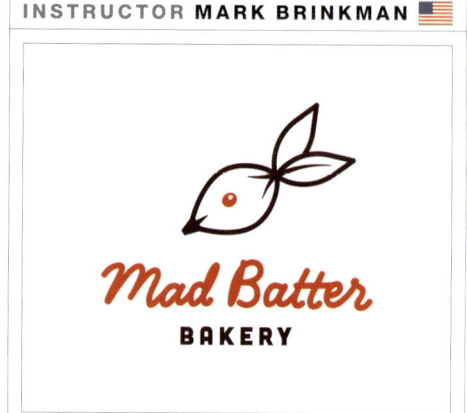 **Student:** Miles Skonberg **School:** Texas State University
INST. TRI P. D. NGUYEN, LE T. TRI 🇻🇳 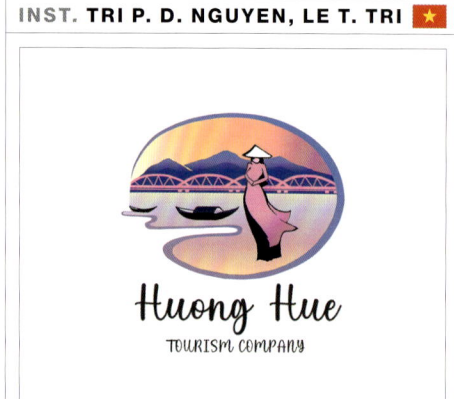 **Student:** Phan Le Binh Nguyen **School:** Duy Tan University	**INSTRUCTOR MARK BRINKMAN** 🇺🇸 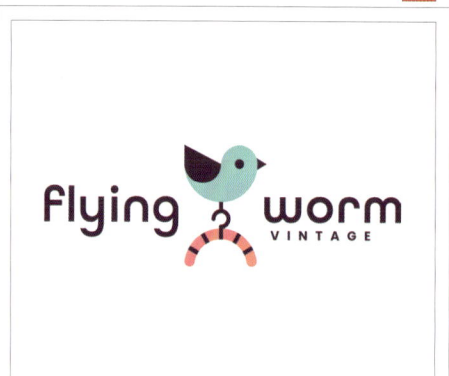 **Student:** Miles Skonberg **School:** Texas State University	**INSTRUCTOR DOUGLAS MAY** 🇺🇸 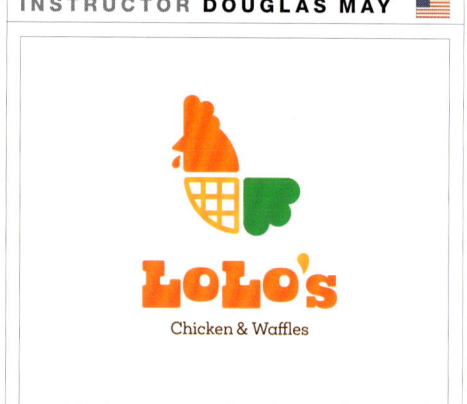 **Student:** Jalon Isabell **School:** University of North Texas
INST. GENARO SOLIS RIVERO 🇺🇸 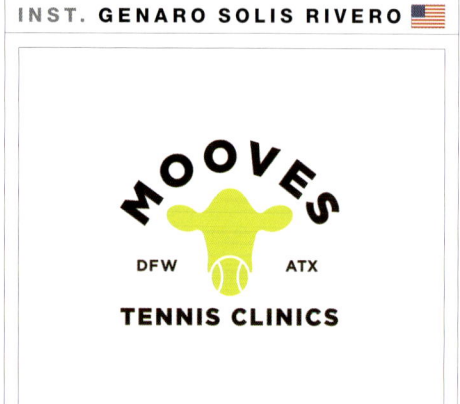 **Student:** Abriella Patti **School:** Baylor University	**INSTRUCTOR DEVON WARD** 🇺🇸 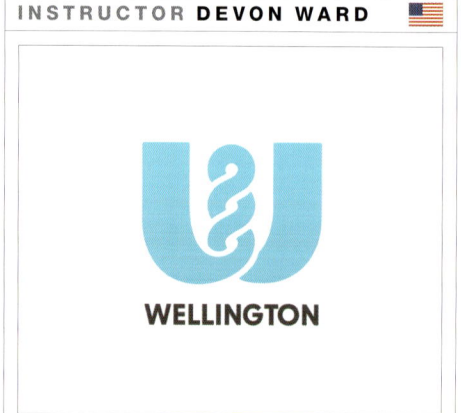 **Student:** Cole Sibley **School:** Auburn University	**INSTRUCTOR JEFF DAVIS** 🇺🇸 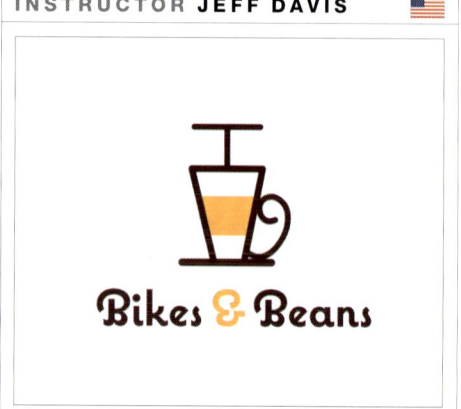 **Student:** Emma Brown **School:** Texas State University

187 DESIGN SILVER

INST. GENARO SOLIS RIVERO 🇺🇸	**INSTRUCTOR LEILA SINGLETON** 🇨🇦	**INST. A. BUCK, M. BRINKMAN** 🇺🇸
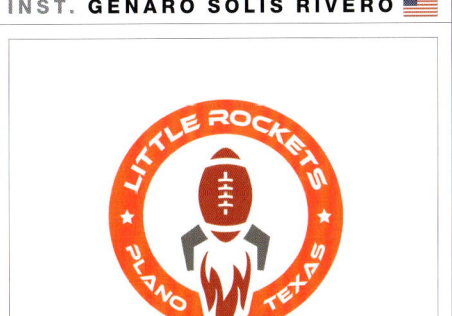	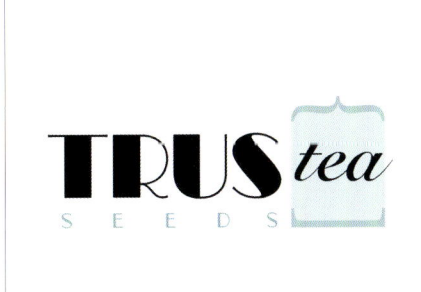	
Student: Kate Sudderth **School:** Baylor University	**Student:** Dia Pauls-Caruso **School:** InFocus Film School	**Student:** Olivia Espiritu **School:** Texas State University
INSTRUCTOR WILLIE BARONET 🇺🇸	**INST. JEFF BLEITZ, LISA WILLARD** 🇺🇸	**INSTRUCTOR DOUGLAS MAY** 🇺🇸
	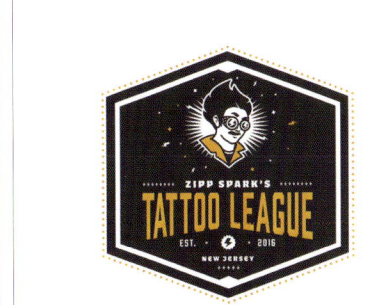	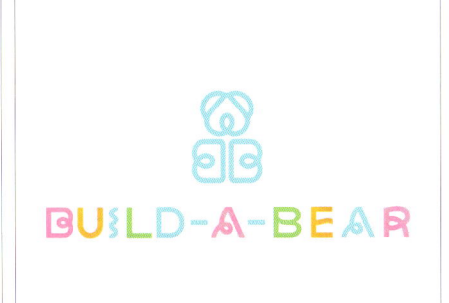
Student: Savanna Hodes **School:** Southern Methodist University	**Student:** Ivy Jenkins **School:** Ringling College of Art & Design	**Student:** Lauren Clark **School:** University of North Texas
INST. JEFF BLEITZ, LISA WILLARD 🇺🇸	**INSTRUCTOR LISA WILLARD** 🇺🇸	**INSTRUCTOR JOSHUA EGE** 🇺🇸
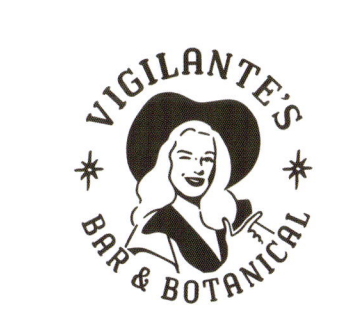	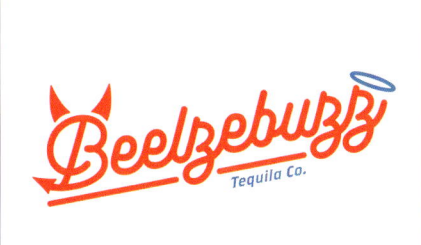	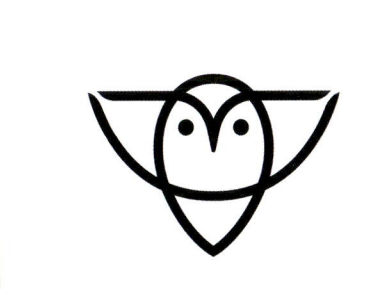
Student: Samantha Mandato **School:** Ringling College of Art & Design	**Student:** Danie Mainou **School:** Ringling College of Art & Design	**Student:** Abigail Killough **School:** Texas A&M University-Commerce
INSTRUCTOR DOUGLAS MAY 🇺🇸	**INST. GENARO SOLIS RIVERO** 🇺🇸	**INST. GENARO SOLIS RIVERO** 🇺🇸
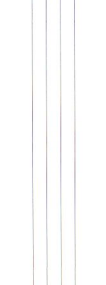	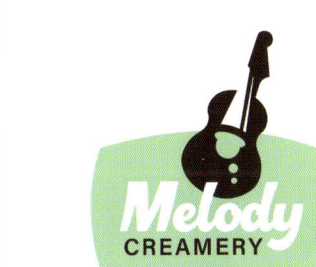	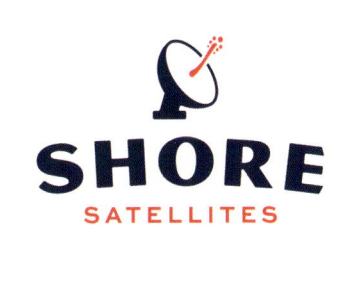
Student: Jazmine Garcia **School:** University of North Texas	**Student:** Brooke Sockwell **School:** Baylor University	**Student:** Virginia Herschend **School:** Baylor University

Logo | Design

188 DESIGN SILVER

INSTRUCTOR MARK BRINKMAN

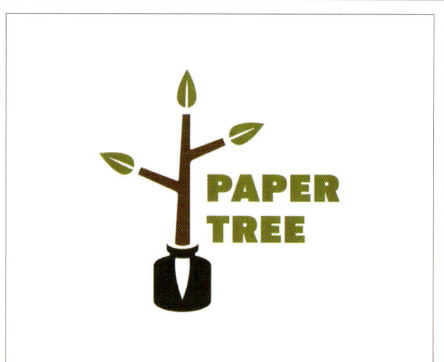

Student: Travis Crawford
School: Texas State University

INSTRUCTOR JEFF DAVIS

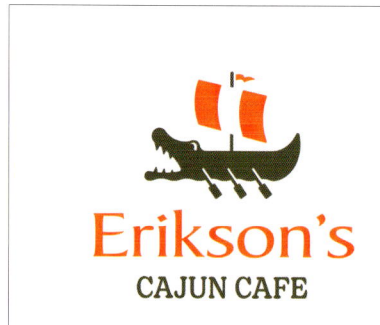

Student: Nick Voss
School: Texas State University

INST. BRIANA NICOLE JUAREZ

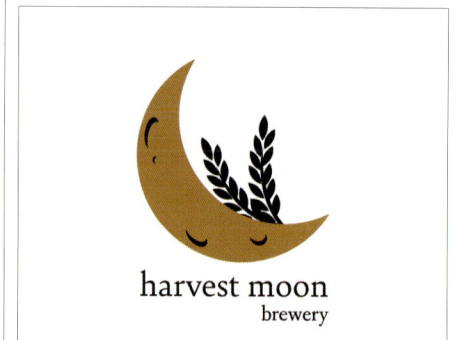

Student: Sarah Ortiz
School: Texas State University

INSTRUCTOR JEFF DAVIS

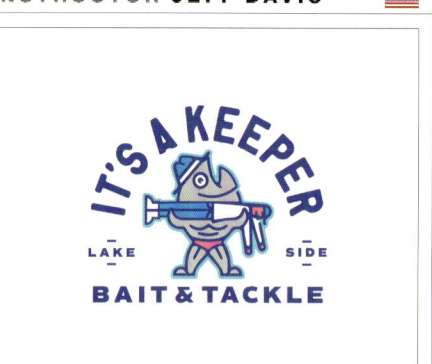

Student: Emily Palau
School: Texas State University

INST. JEFF BLEITZ, LISA WILLARD

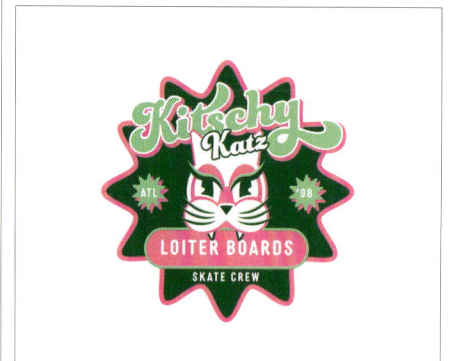

Student: Bella Thompson
School: Ringling College of Art & Design

INSTRUCTOR MARK BRINKMAN

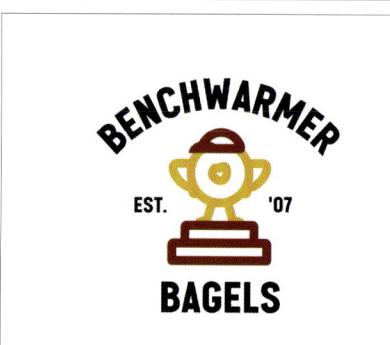

Student: Tessa Shellenberger
School: Texas State University

INSTRUCTOR MARK BRINKMAN

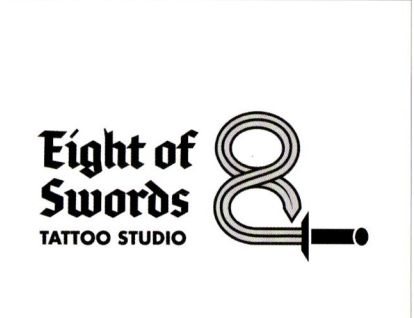

Student: Hannah Twining
School: Texas State University

INSTRUCTOR WILLIAM MEEK

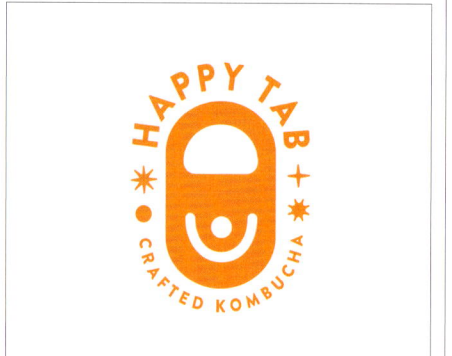

Student: Fallon Russell
School: Texas State University

INSTRUCTOR MARK BRINKMAN

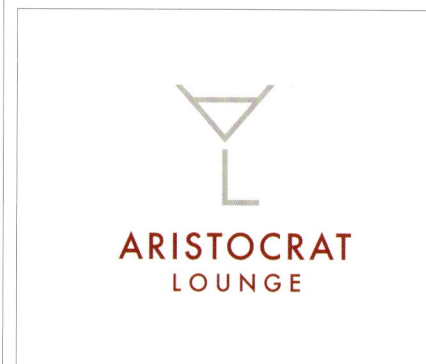

Student: Riley Ramsower
School: Texas State University

INST. GENARO SOLIS RIVERO

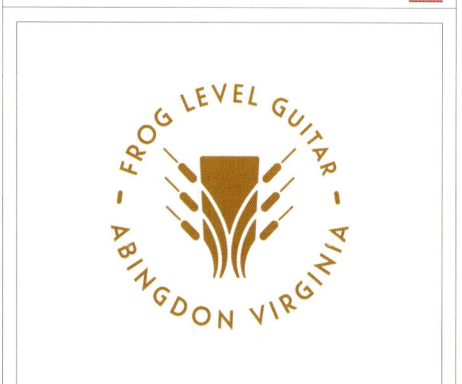

Student: Nick Voss
School: Texas State University

INSTRUCTOR NATHAN SAVAGE

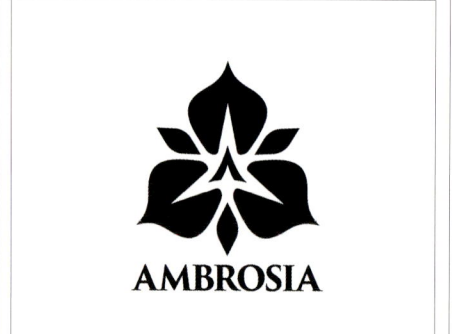

Student: Alyah Ibrahim
School: Portland Community College

INSTRUCTOR MARK BRINKMAN

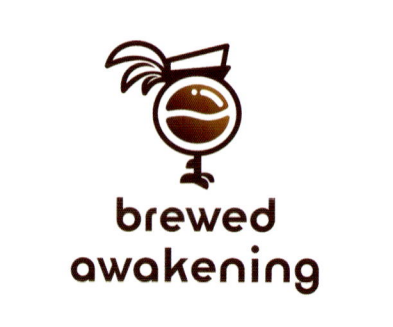

Student: Jeanette Deegear
School: Texas State University

Design | Logo

189 DESIGN SILVER

INSTRUCTOR JUSTIN COLT 🇺🇸

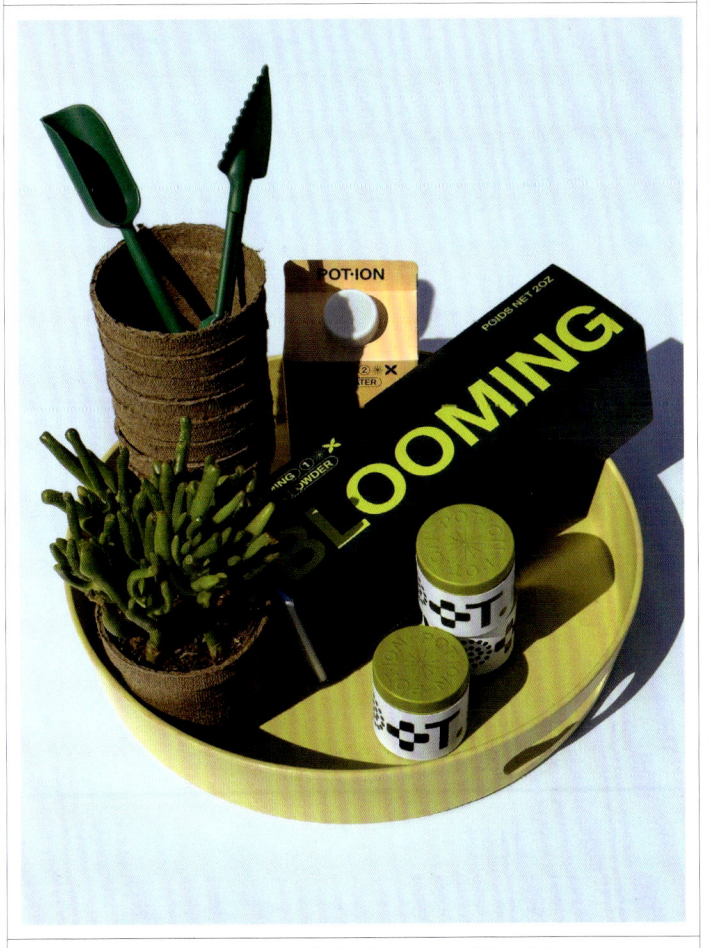

Student: Mina Son | **School:** School of Visual Arts

INSTRUCTORS ANDREW GIBBS, JESSICA DESEO 🇺🇸

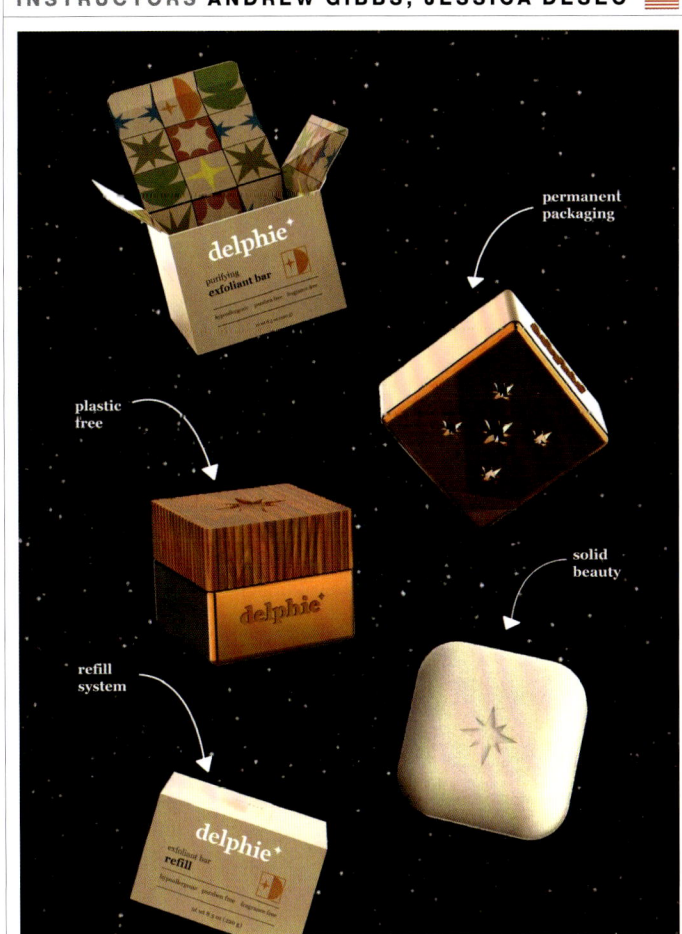

Student: Maggie Morton | **School:** ArtCenter College of Design

INSTRUCTORS DONG-JOO PARK, SEUNG-MIN HAN 🇰🇷

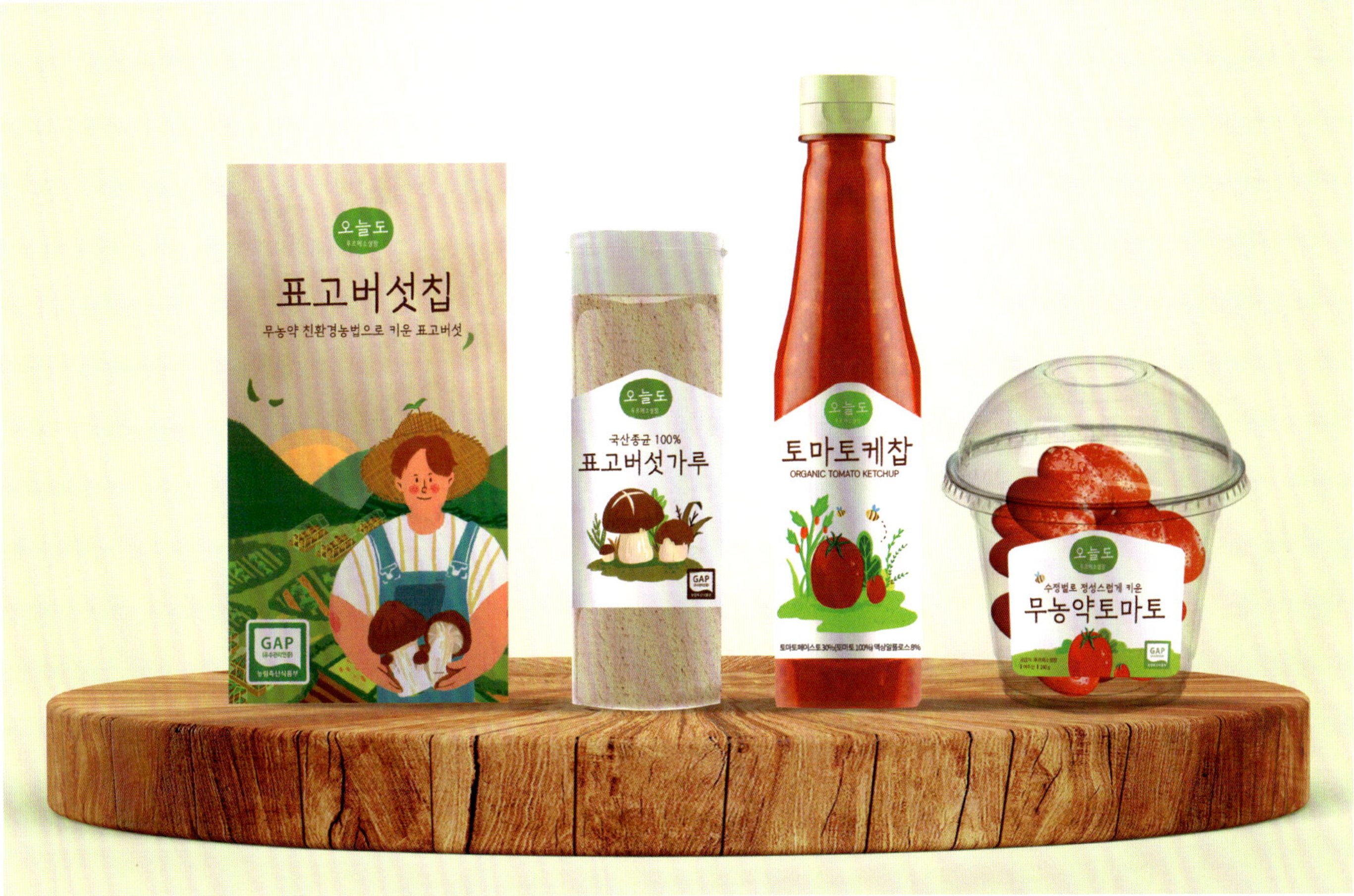

Student: Su-Min Ga | **School:** Hansung University, Design & Arts Institute

Packaging | Design

190 DESIGN SILVER

INSTRUCTOR JUSTIN COLT

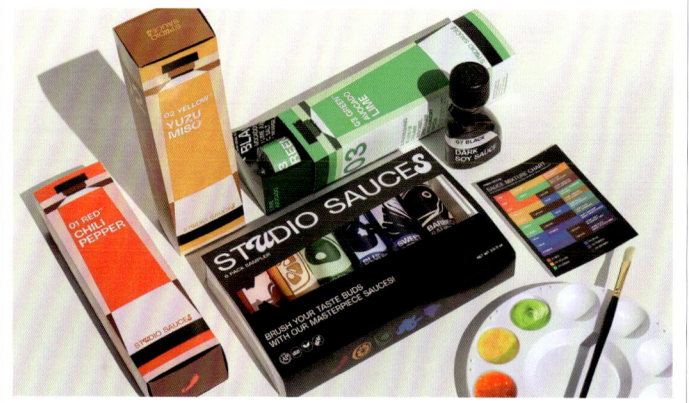

Student: Jiyoon Kim | School: School of Visual Arts

INSTRUCTOR GERARDO HERRERA

Student: Georgina Kurnia | School: ArtCenter College of Design

INSTRUCTOR CARSON AHLMAN

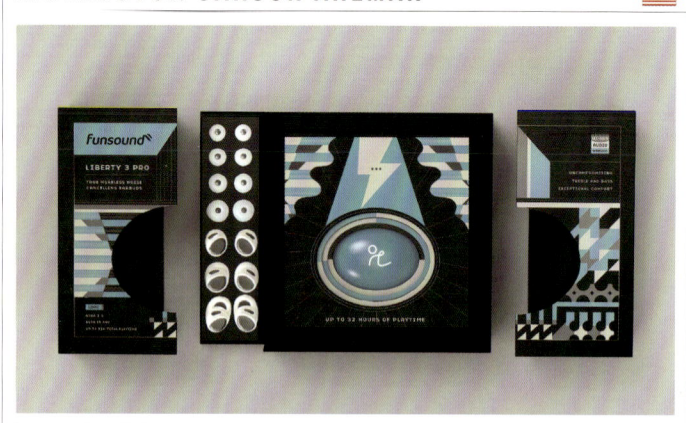

Student: Wen-Chi Hsueh | School: Pratt Institute

INSTRUCTOR THERON MOORE

Student: Leann So | School: California State University, Fullerton

INSTRUCTOR THERON MOORE

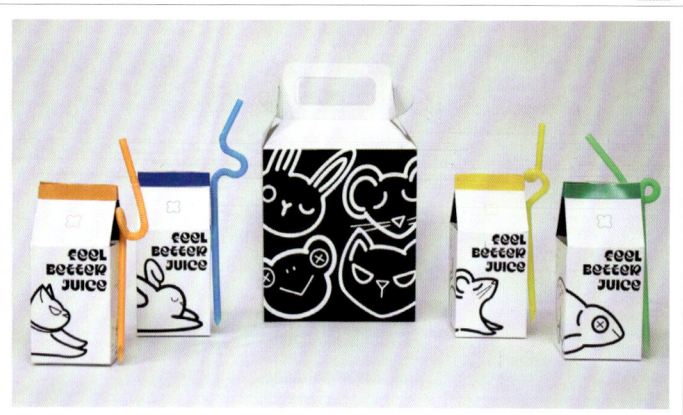

Student: Claudia Chacon | School: California State University, Fullerton

INSTRUCTOR UNATTRIBUTED

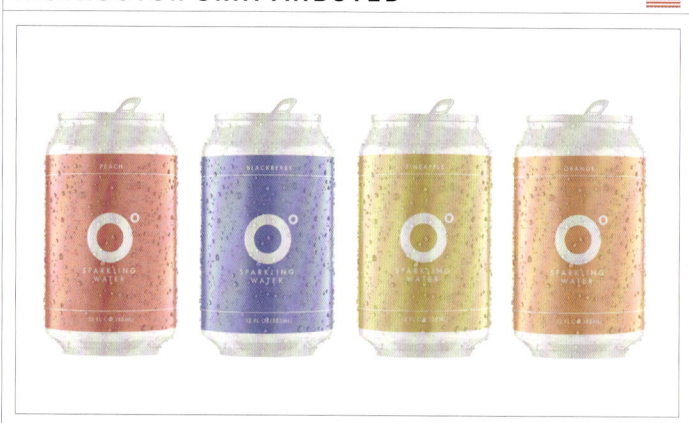

Student: Yiwei Cheng | School: School of Visual Arts

INSTRUCTOR LINDA REYNOLDS

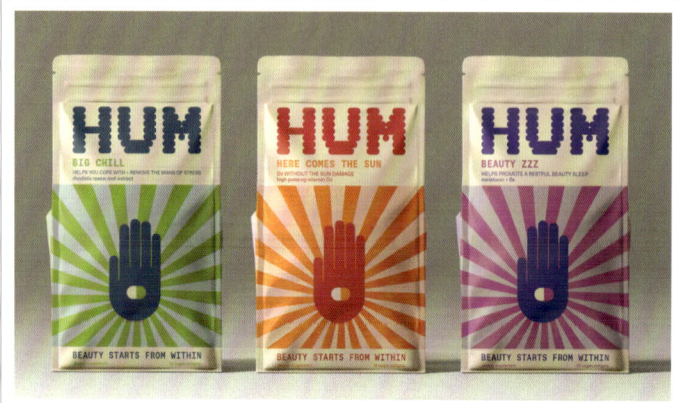

Student: Kate Holmes | School: Brigham Young University

INSTRUCTOR THERON MOORE

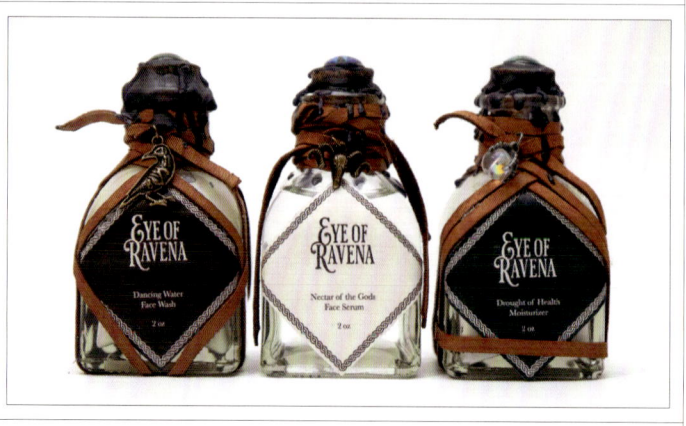

Student: Anna Whitelaw | School: California State University, Fullerton

Design | Packaging

191 DESIGN SILVER

INSTRUCTOR MONICA SCHLAUG

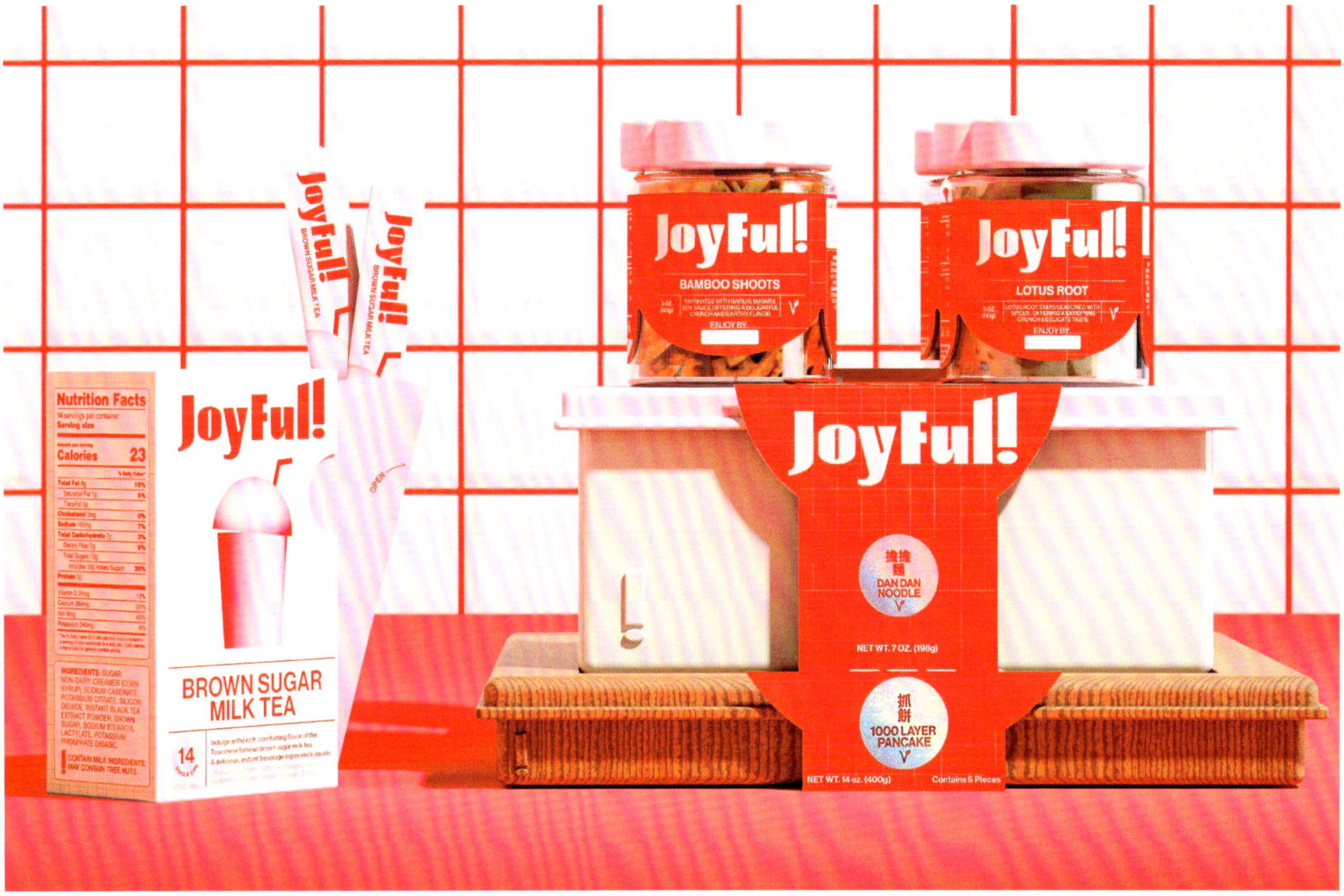

Student: Genie Wu | School: ArtCenter College of Design

INSTRUCTOR ABBY GUIDO

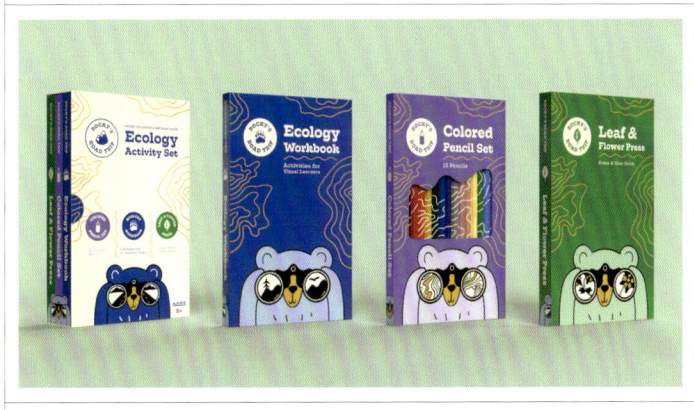

Student: MeiLi Carling
School: Temple University, Tyler School of Art & Architecture

INSTRUCTOR YVONNE CAO

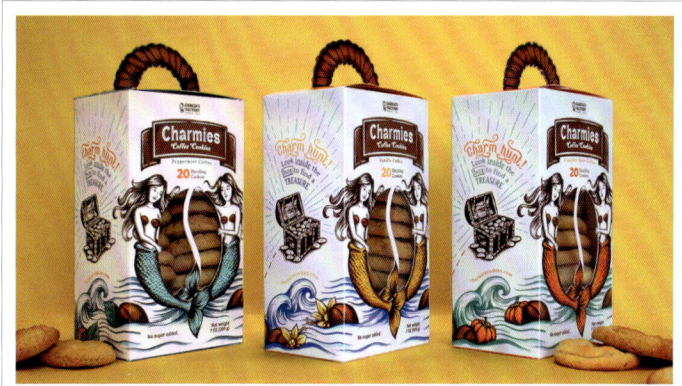

Student: Isabella Baker
School: Texas Christian University

INSTRUCTOR MONICA SCHLAUG

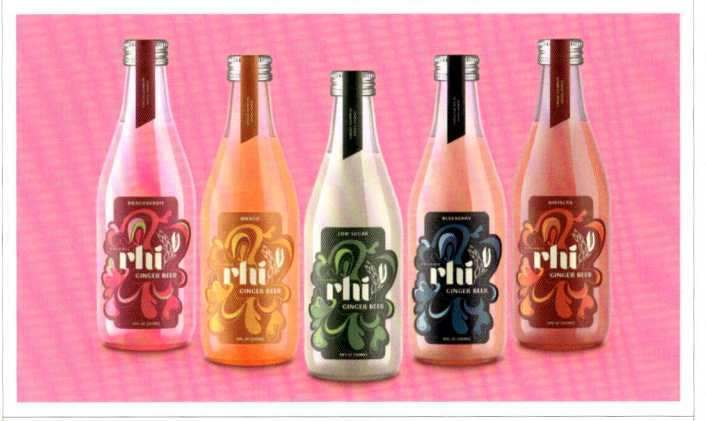

Student: Lauren Aquino | School: ArtCenter College of Design

INSTRUCTOR GERARDO HERRERA

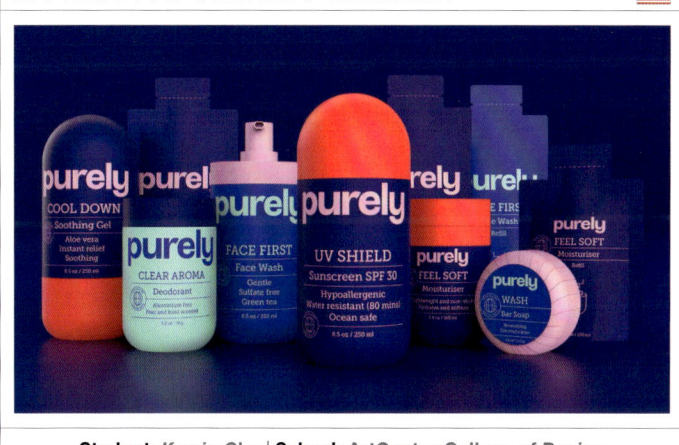

Student: Kerrie Chu | School: ArtCenter College of Design

Packaging | Design

192 DESIGN SILVER

INSTRUCTOR THERON MOORE 🇺🇸

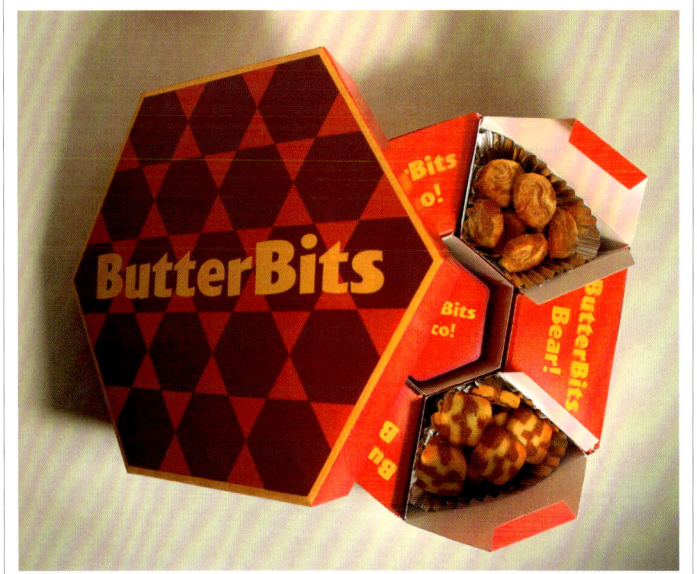

Student: Mia Lin | **School:** California State University, Fullerton

INSTRUCTOR DOUGLAS MAY 🇺🇸

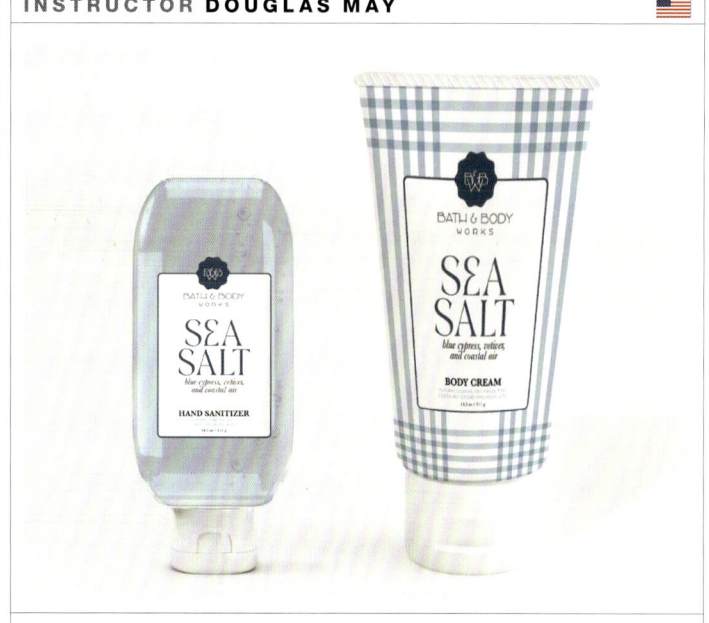

Student: Lauren Clark | **School:** University of North Texas

INSTRUCTOR DAVID BECK 🇺🇸

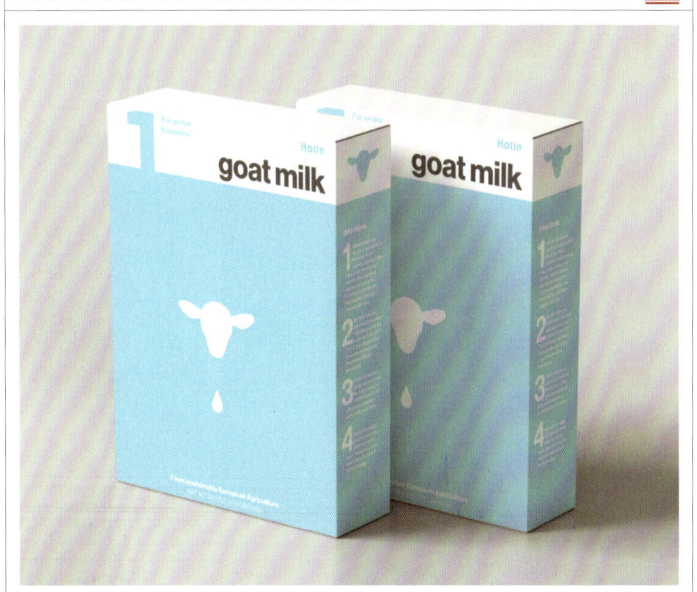

Student: Elisabeth Vaughn | **School:** Texas A&M University-Commerce

INSTRUCTOR ERIC BAKER 🇺🇸

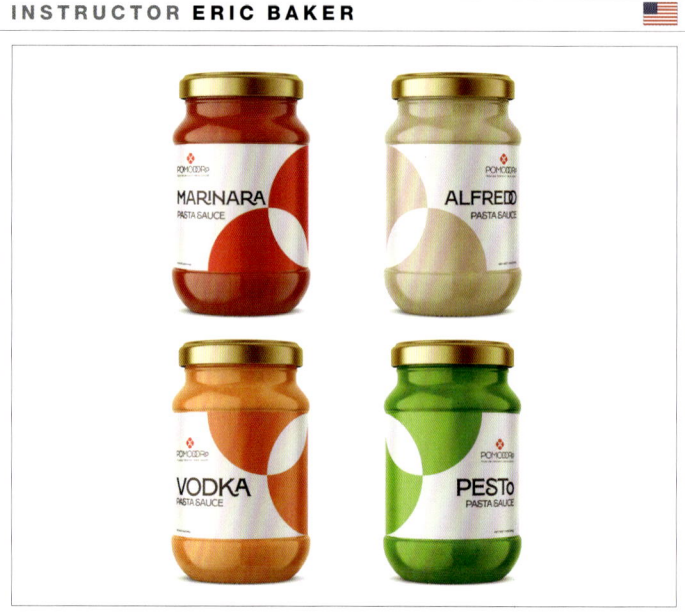

Student: Minsu Seo | **School:** School of Visual Arts

INSTRUCTOR THERON MOORE 🇺🇸

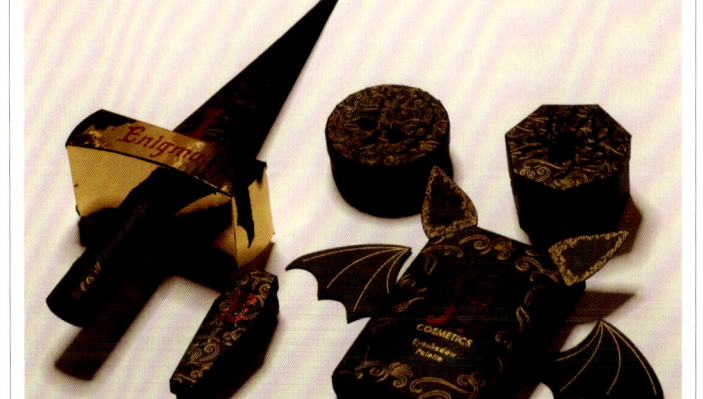

Student: Reilly Hew | **School:** California State University, Fullerton

INSTRUCTOR YVONNE CAO 🇺🇸

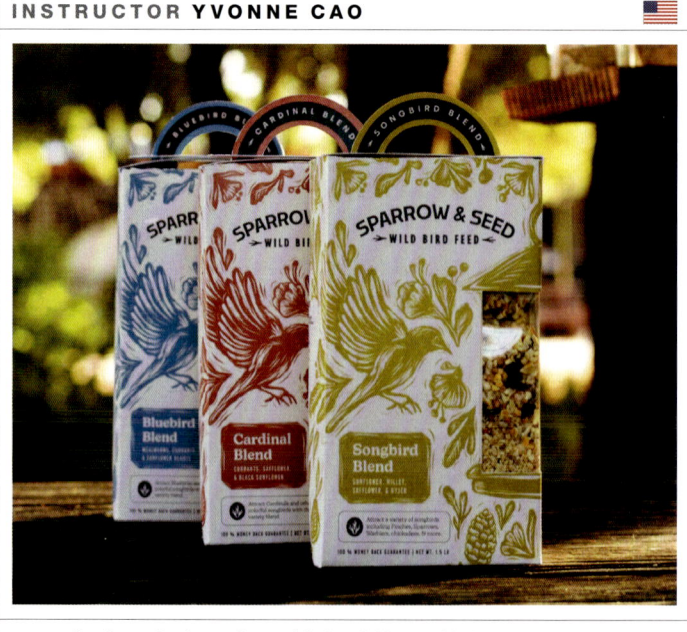

Student: Corinne Green | **School:** Texas Christian University

Design | Packaging

193 DESIGN SILVER

INSTRUCTOR HANK RICHARDSON 🇺🇸

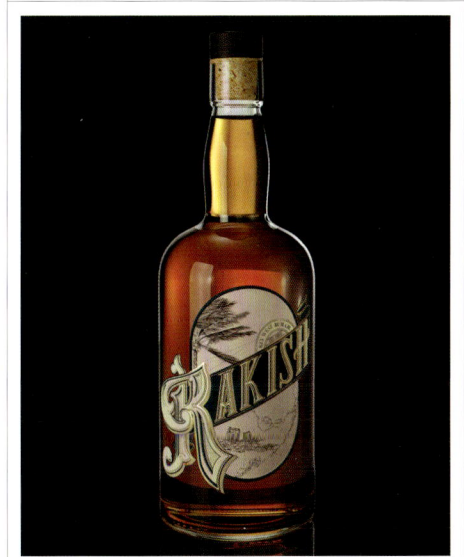

Student: Jamie Jason
School: M.AD School of Ideas Atlanta

INSTRUCTOR THERON MOORE 🇺🇸

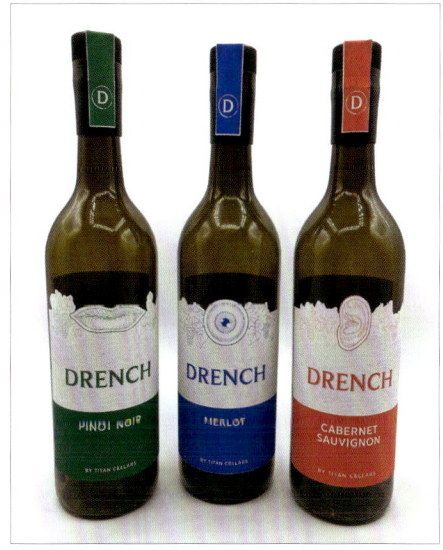

Student: Sang Nguyen
School: California State University, Fullerton

INSTRUCTOR ABBY GUIDO 🇺🇸

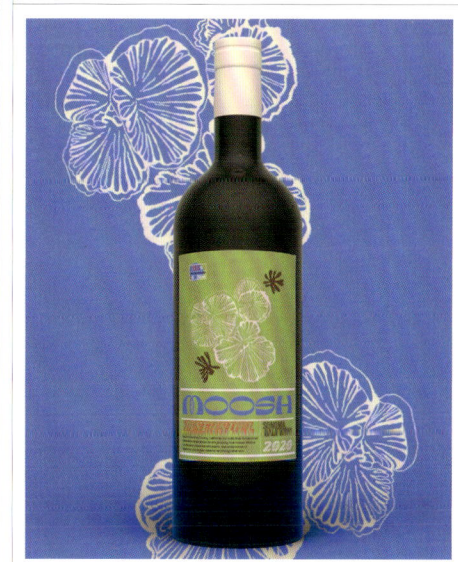

Student: Jillian Villafuerte | **School:** Temple University, Tyler School of Art & Architecture

INSTRUCTOR THERON MOORE 🇺🇸

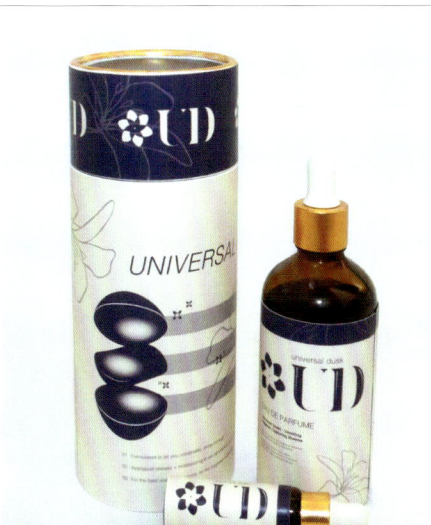

Student: Larisa Benguhe
School: California State University, Fullerton

INSTRUCTOR YVONNE CAO 🇺🇸

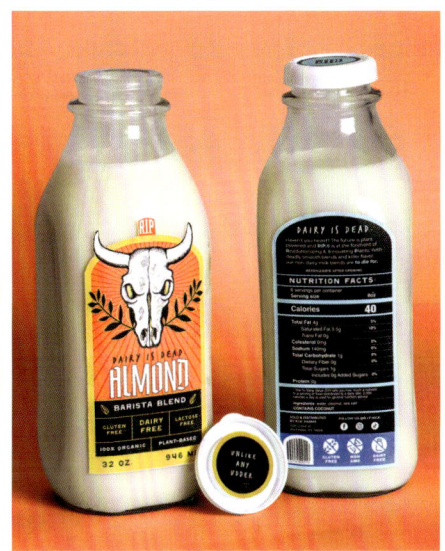

Student: Ellie Gonyea
School: Texas Christian University

INSTRUCTOR MONICA SCHLAUG 🇺🇸

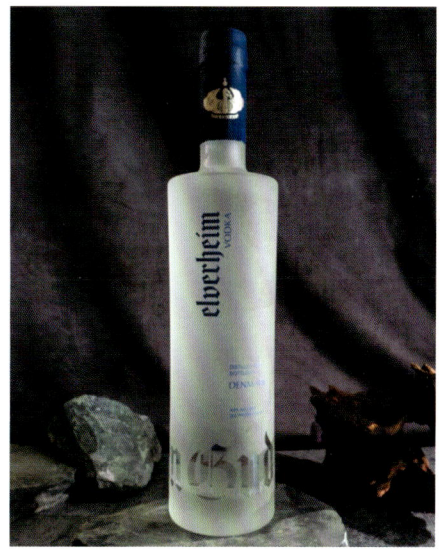

Student: Jonathan Kusnadi
School: ArtCenter College of Design

INSTRUCTOR BRIAN BOYD 🇺🇸

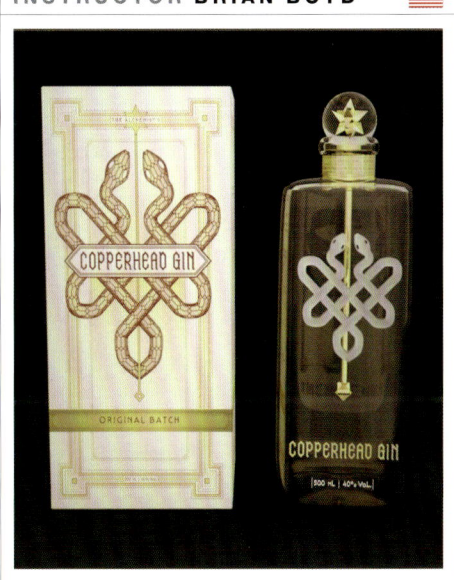

Student: Hannah Burke
School: University of North Texas

INSTRUCTOR YVONNE CAO 🇺🇸

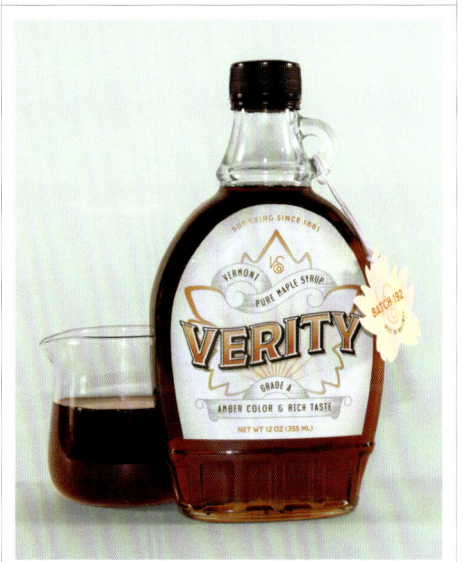

Student: Rebecca Richard
School: Texas Christian University

INSTRUCTOR ABBY GUIDO 🇺🇸

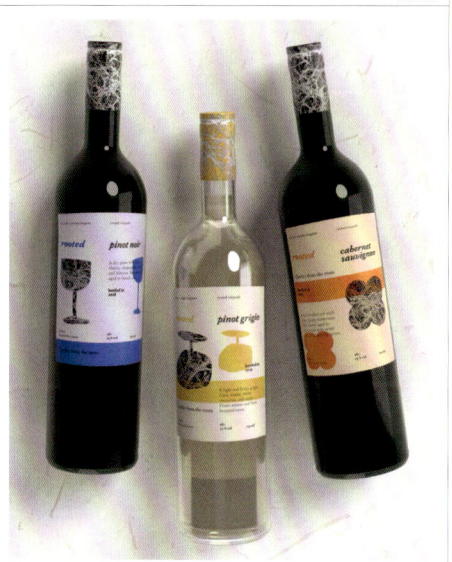

Student: Seth Dubrosky | **School:** Temple University, Tyler School of Art & Architecture

194 DESIGN SILVER

INSTRUCTOR THERON MOORE

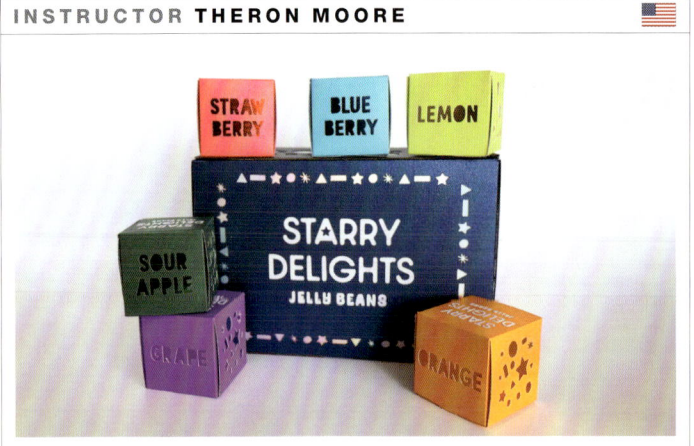

Student: Jennifer Cuevas | **School:** California State University, Fullerton

INSTRUCTOR LI ZHANG

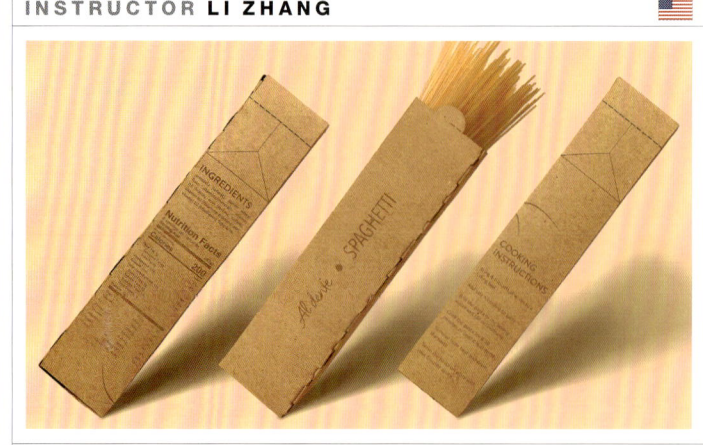

Student: Daniel Lu | **School:** Purdue University

INSTRUCTOR THERON MOORE

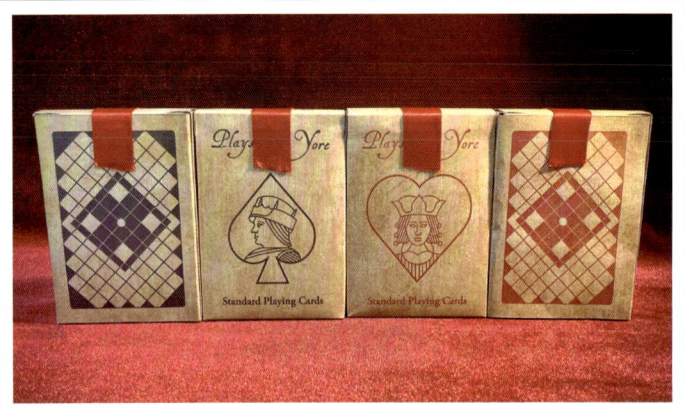

Student: Derek Daproza | **School:** California State University, Fullerton

INSTRUCTOR THERON MOORE

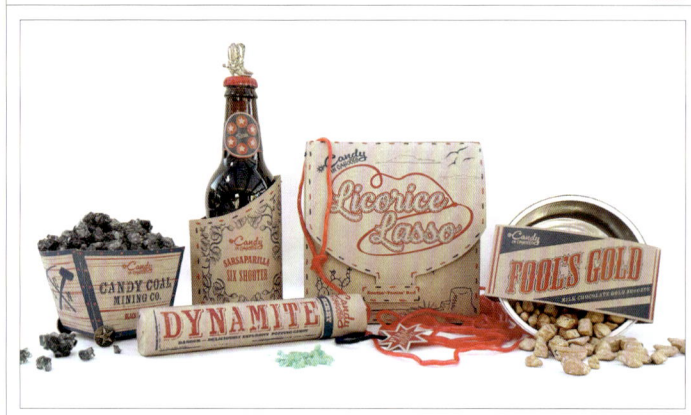

Student: Paige Garcia | **School:** California State University, Fullerton

INSTRUCTOR JUSTIN COLT

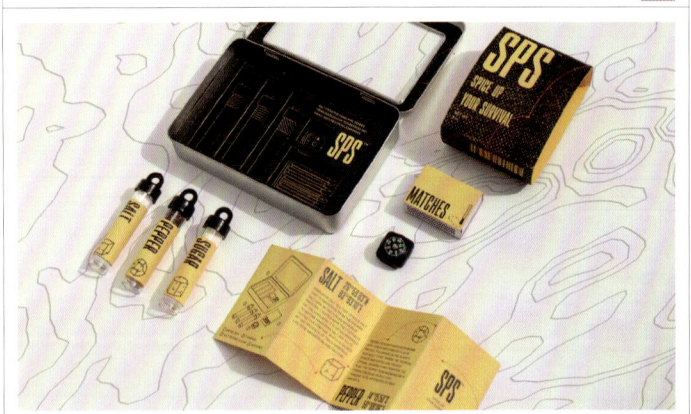

Student: Younghyun Kim | **School:** School of Visual Arts

INSTRUCTOR ELLIOTT WALKER

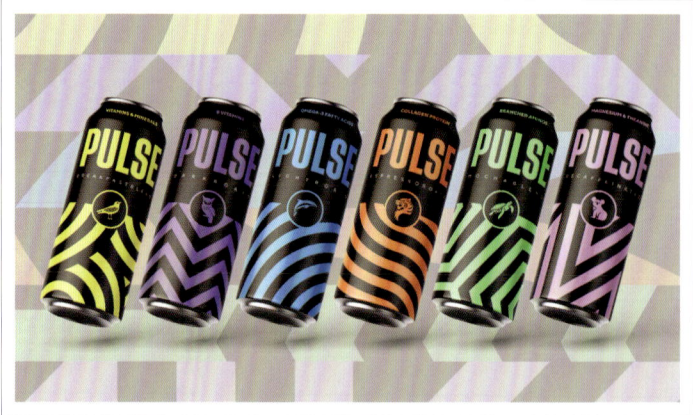

Student: Jung Youn Kim | **School:** School of Visual Arts

INSTRUCTOR GERARDO HERRERA

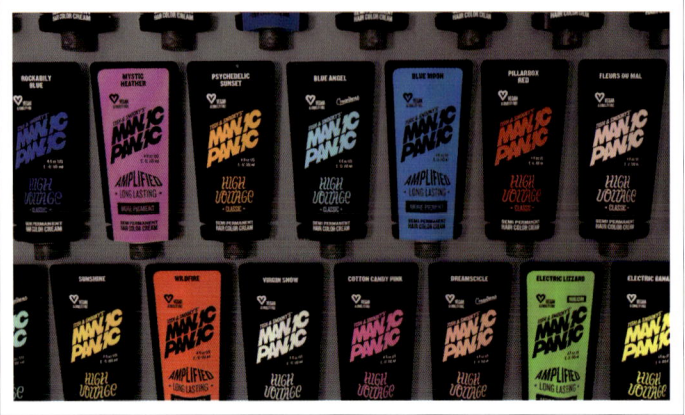

Student: Ana Vazquez | **School:** ArtCenter College of Design

INSTRUCTOR JOSEPH NEWTON

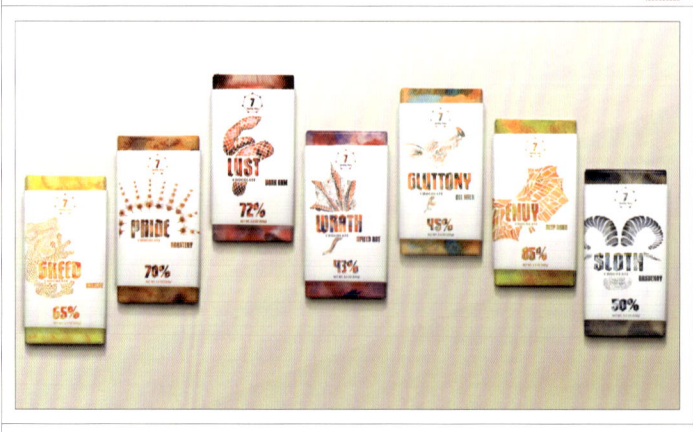

Student: Yubin Won | **School:** School of Visual Arts

Design | Packaging

195 DESIGN SILVER

INSTRUCTOR THERON MOORE

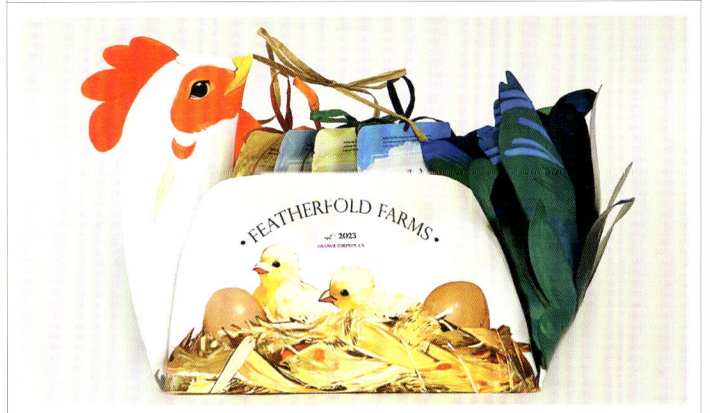

Student: Elena Germann | **School:** California State University, Fullerton

INSTRUCTOR JESSE WARNE

Student: Emma Minyard | **School:** University of Central Oklahoma

INSTRUCTOR LINDA REYNOLDS

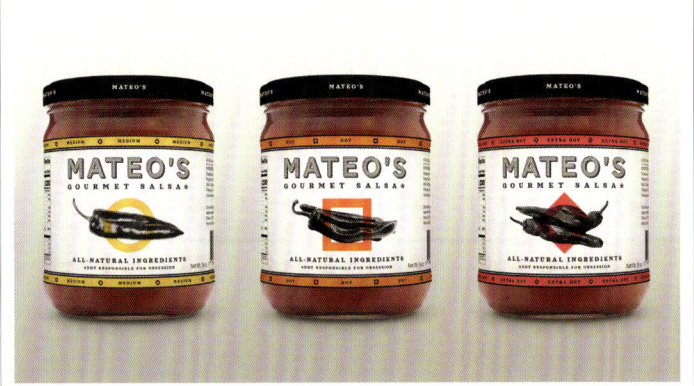

Student: Luke Miller | **School:** Brigham Young University

INSTRUCTOR THERON MOORE

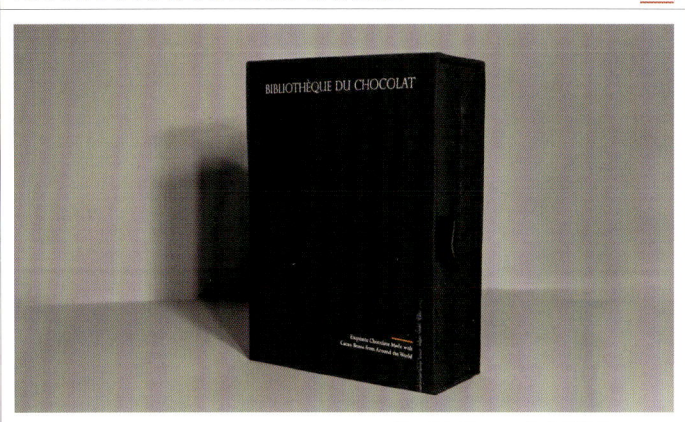

Student: Viktoriia Trapizonian | **School:** California State University, Fullerton

INSTRUCTOR DOUGLAS MAY

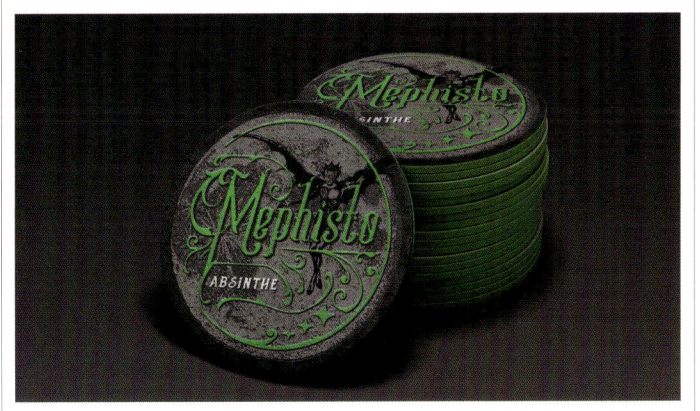

Student: Maxwell Pius | **School:** University of North Texas

INSTRUCTOR ERIC BAKER

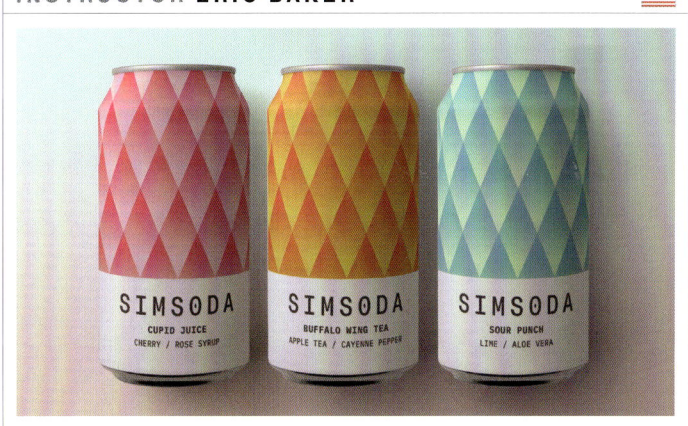

Student: Sijin Zhou | **School:** School of Visual Arts

INSTRUCTOR THERON MOORE

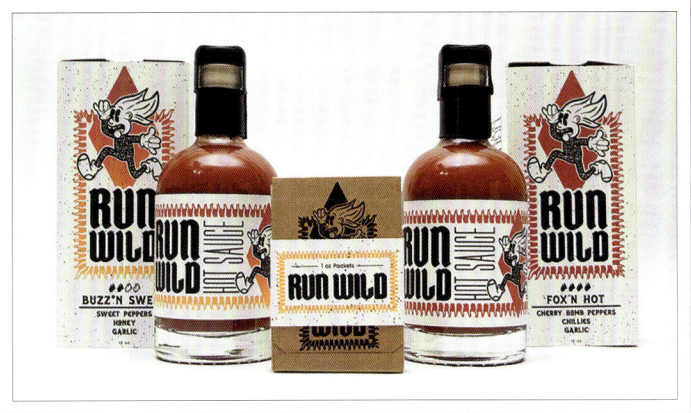

Student: Julieta Gazzoni | **School:** California State University, Fullerton

INSTRUCTOR YVONNE CAO

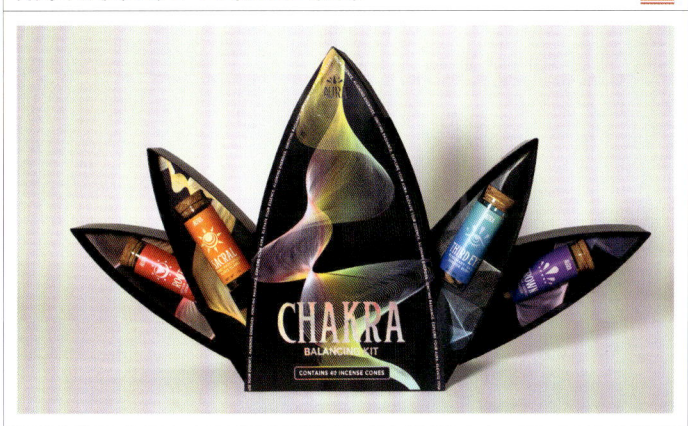

Student: Avery Kokinda | **School:** Texas Christian University

Packaging | Design

196 DESIGN SILVER

INST. CHEN JUNHONG, XIE SHENGMIN
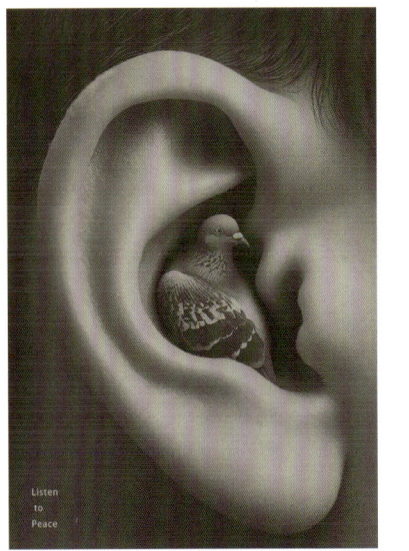
Student: Goyen Chen
School: Asia University

INSTRUCTOR CORY SAY
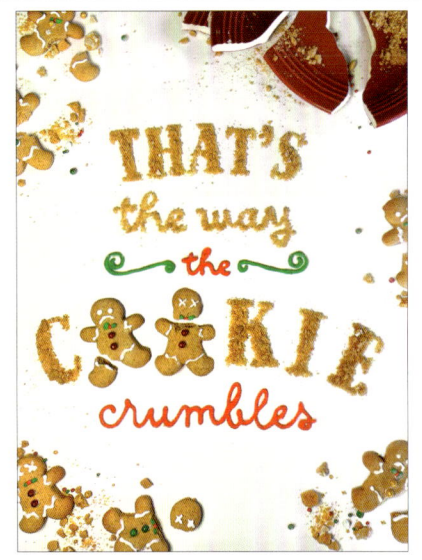
Student: Jackelyn De Lara
School: Texas A&M University-Commerce

INSTRUCTOR CHAD ANDERSON
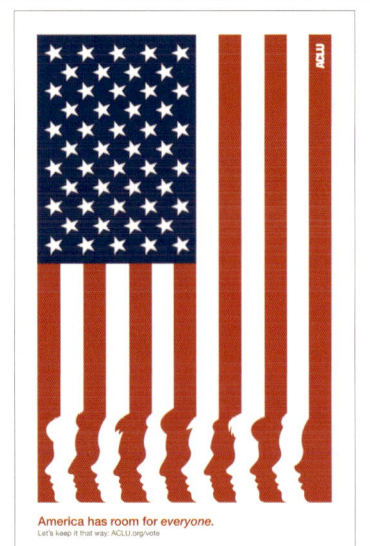
Student: Conner Gayda
School: Jacksonville State University

INSTRUCTOR JOSHUA EGE
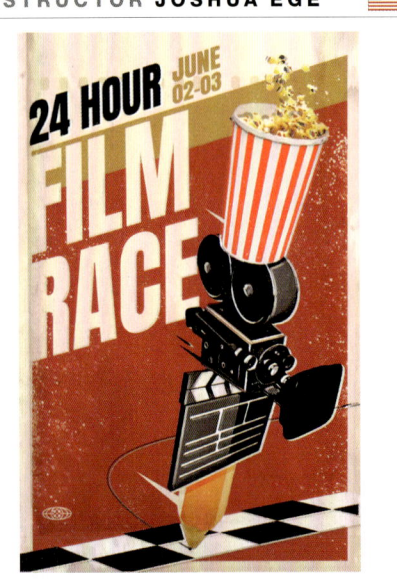
Student: David Ellis
School: Texas A&M University-Commerce

INST. DORIS PALMEROS-MCMANUS
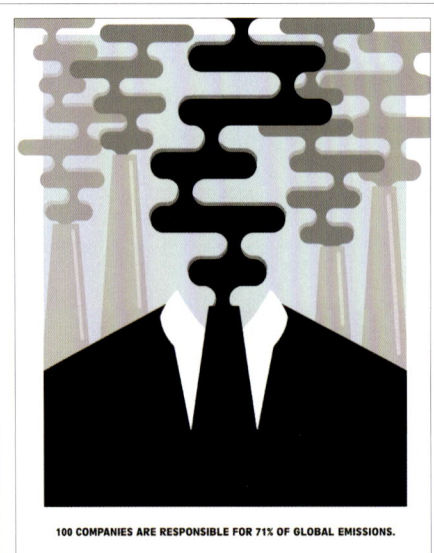
Student: Rozlynn Macbeth Olivas
School: University of the Incarnate Word

INSTRUCTOR NANCY CAMPBELL
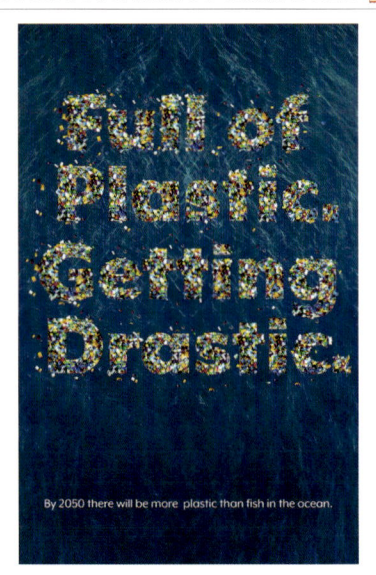
Student: Robert Tole
School: Kean University

INSTRUCTOR JOSHUA EGE
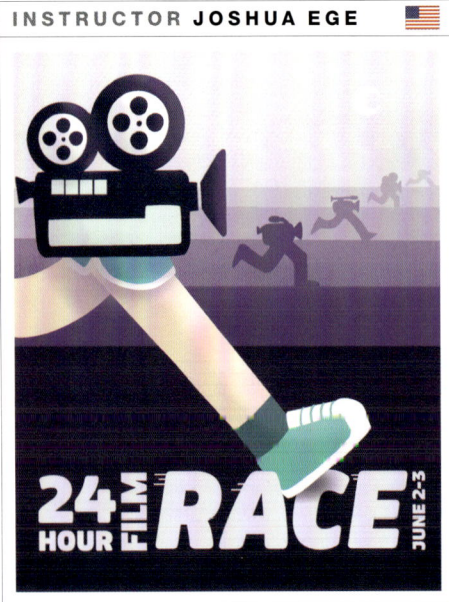
Student: Shyann Haught
School: Texas A&M University-Commerce

INSTRUCTOR DAVID TILLINGHAST
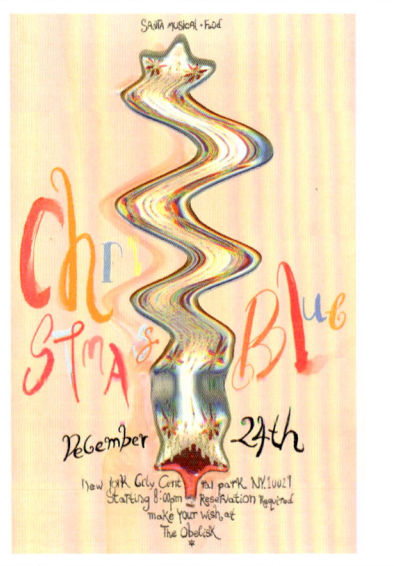
Student: Sizhe Wang
School: ArtCenter College of Design

INSTRUCTOR STEPHEN ZHANG
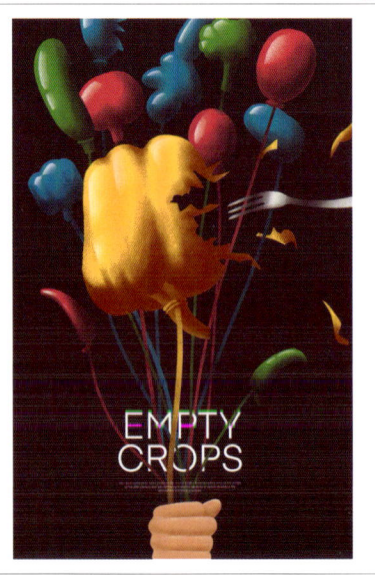
Student: Daniel Descamp
School: University of North Texas

Design | Poster

197 DESIGN SILVER

INSTRUCTORS DONG-JOO PARK, SEUNG-MIN HAN

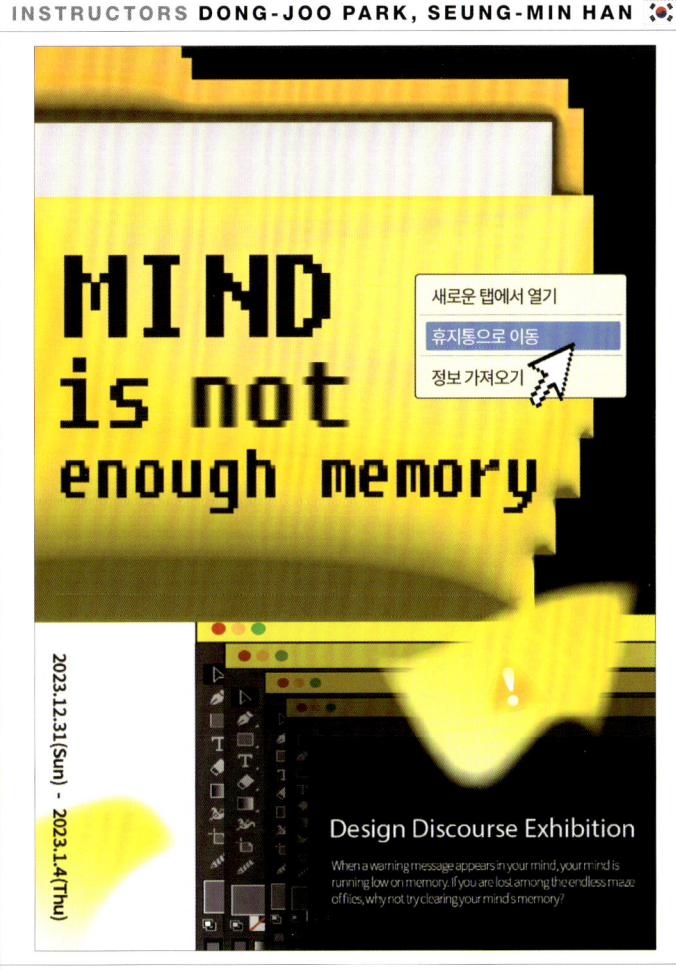

Student: Su-Min Ga | School: Hansung University, Design & Arts Institute

INSTRUCTOR JIM SALVATI

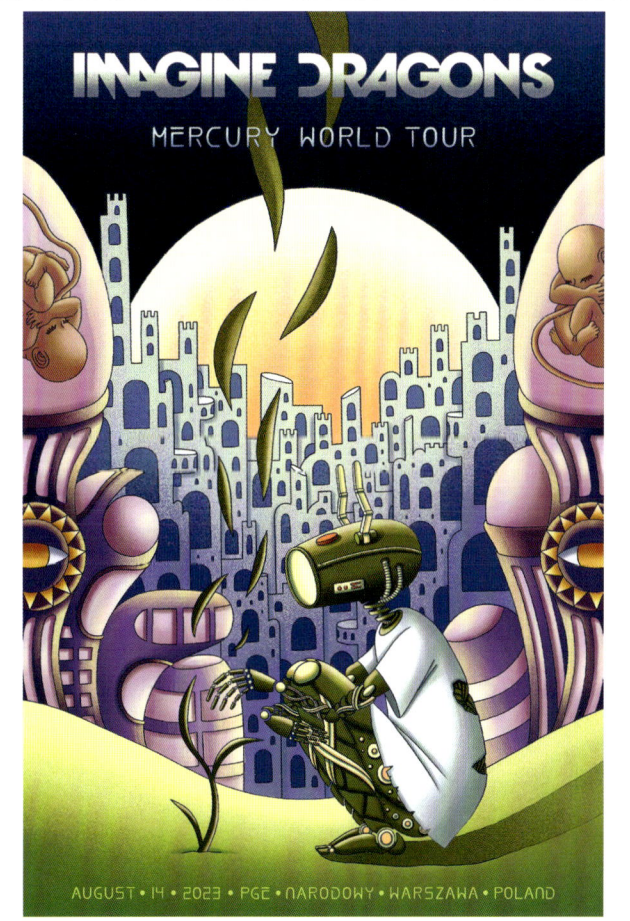

Student: Jiyun Choi | School: ArtCenter College of Design

INSTRUCTOR NANCY SKOLOS

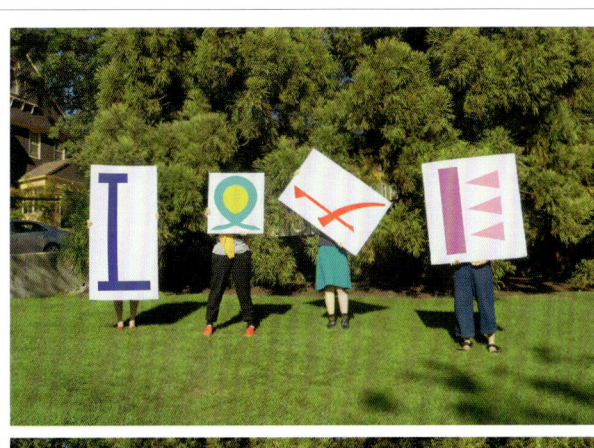

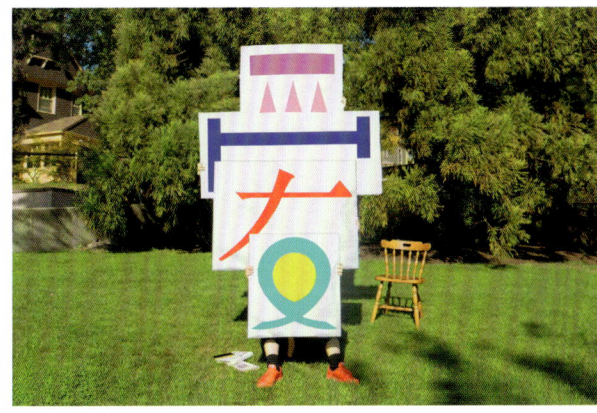

Student: Anita (Ningjing) Sun | School: Rhode Island School of Design

INSTRUCTOR SIMON JOHNSTON

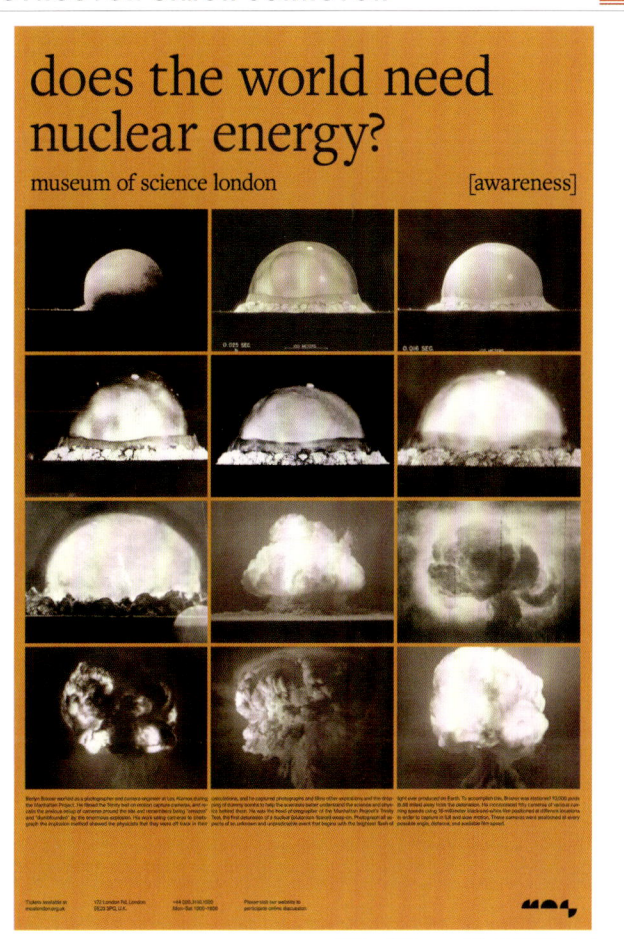

Student: Jaiwon Lee | School: ArtCenter College of Design

Poster | Design

198 DESIGN SILVER

INSTRUCTORS D. PARK, S. HAN 🇰🇷
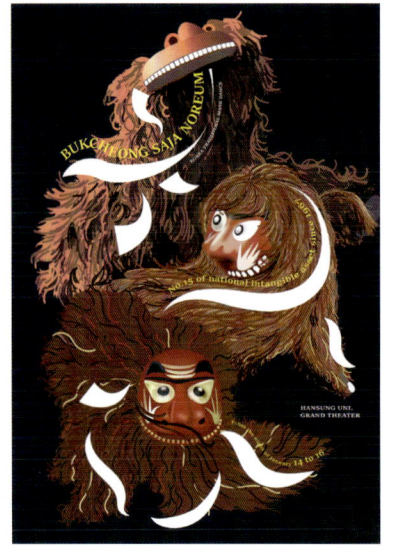
Student: Hyeon Seung Lee | **School:** Hansung University, Design & Arts Institute

INST. SANTIAGO CARRASQUILLA 🇺🇸
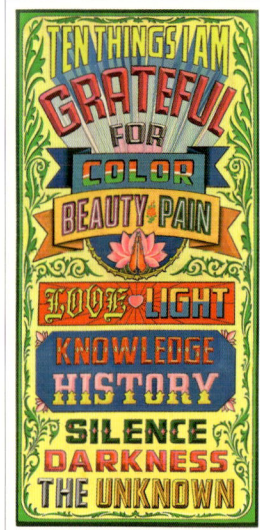
Student: Rabıya Gupta
School: School of Visual Arts

INSTRUCTOR HYOJUN SHIM 🇰🇷
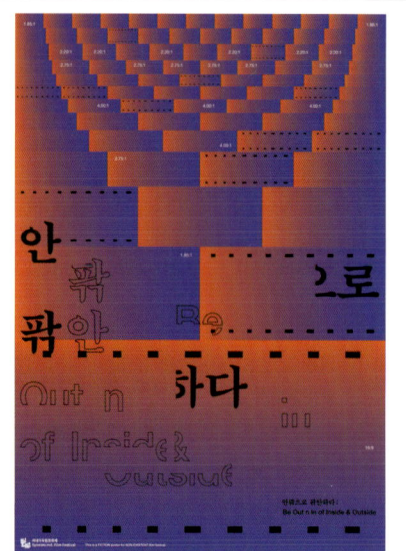
Student: Yeonjoo Jang
School: Dongduk Women's University

INSTRUCTOR NANCY CAMPBELL 🇺🇸
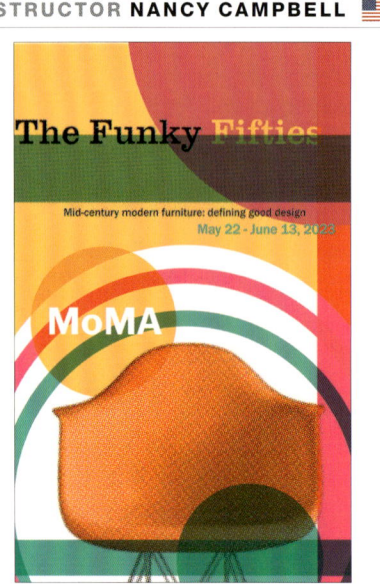
Student: Matthew Redzinski
School: Kean University

INST. ROSANA DURAN-GARIBI 🇺🇸
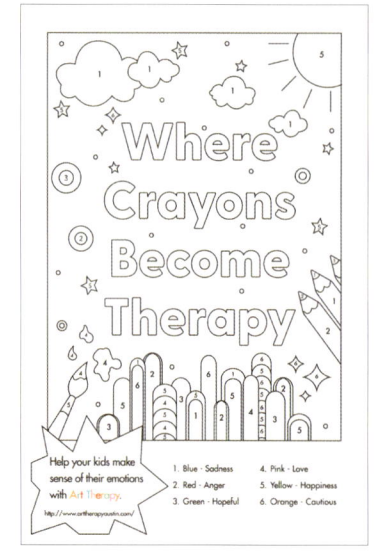
Student: Sarah Ortiz
School: Texas State University

INSTRUCTOR HYUNG JOO KIM 🇺🇸
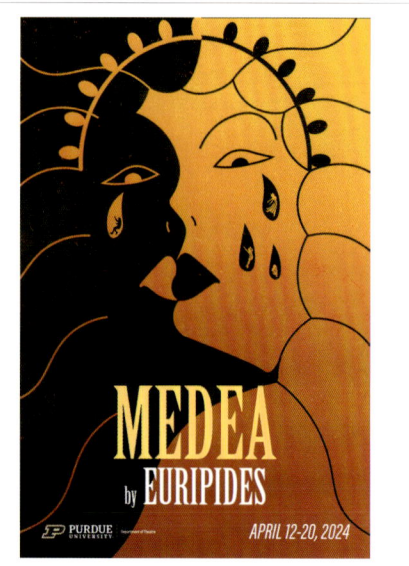
Student: Emily Bierma
School: Purdue University

INSTRUCTOR ANNE JORDAN 🇺🇸
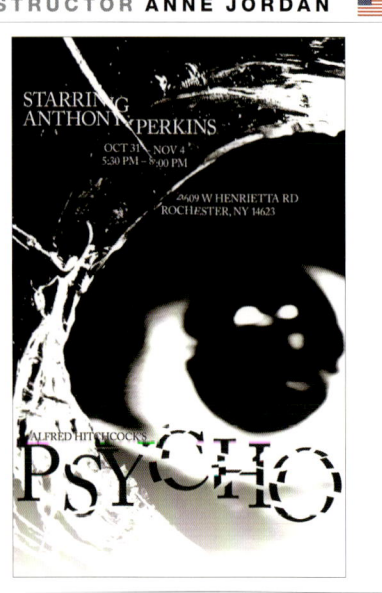
Student: Chris Dell'Aquila
School: Rochester Institute of Technology

INSTRUCTOR STEPHEN ZHANG 🇺🇸
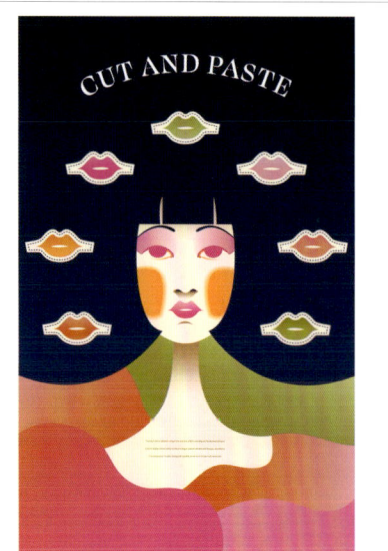
Student: Lee McClain
School: University of North Texas

INSTRUCTOR ANNE JORDAN 🇺🇸
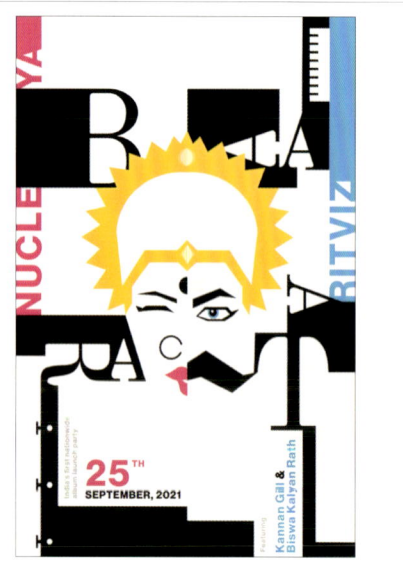
Student: Nagasai Vardhan Rao Sarvepalli
School: Rochester Institute of Technology

Design | Poster

199 DESIGN SILVER

INSTRUCTORS D. PARK, S. HAN

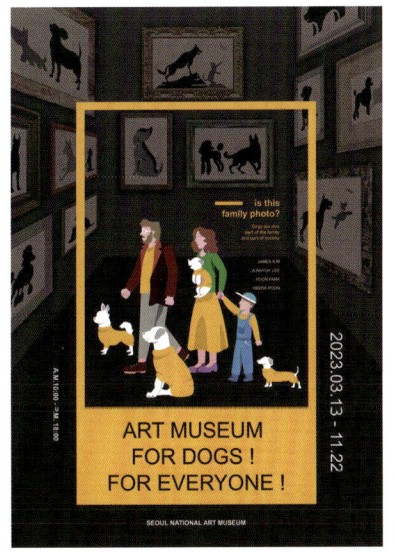

Student: Eungyeol Kim | School: Hansung University, Design & Arts Institute

INSTRUCTOR KATE CLAIR

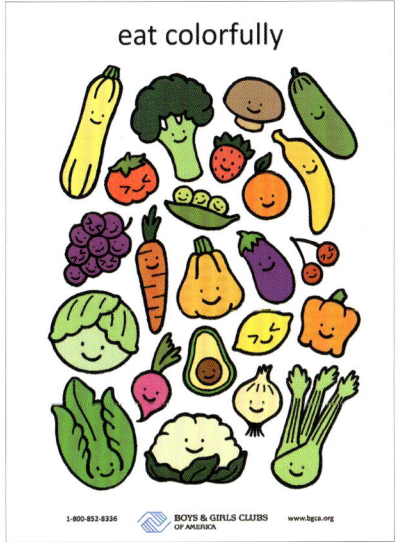

Student: Roseld Laguatan
School: Kutztown University

INSTRUCTORS D. PARK, S. HAN

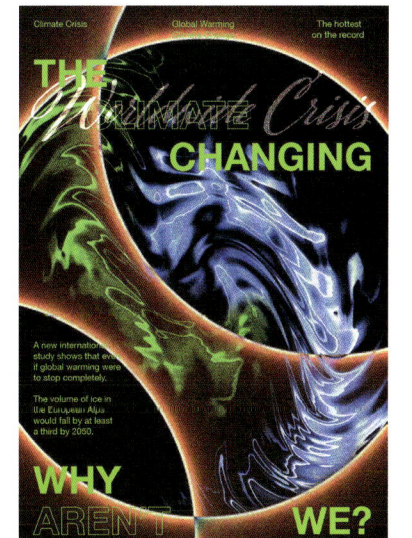

Student: Gyeongmin Park | School: Hansung University, Design & Arts Institute

INSTRUCTOR NANCY CAMPBELL

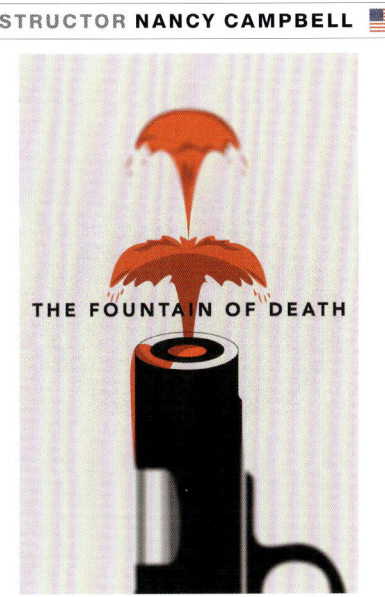

Student: Christopher Cruz
School: Kean University

INST. SCOTTY REIFSNYDER

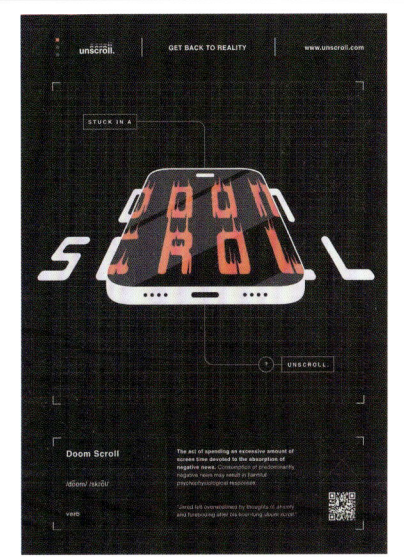

Student: Tully Ryan
School: West Chester University

INSTRUCTOR SOHEE KWON

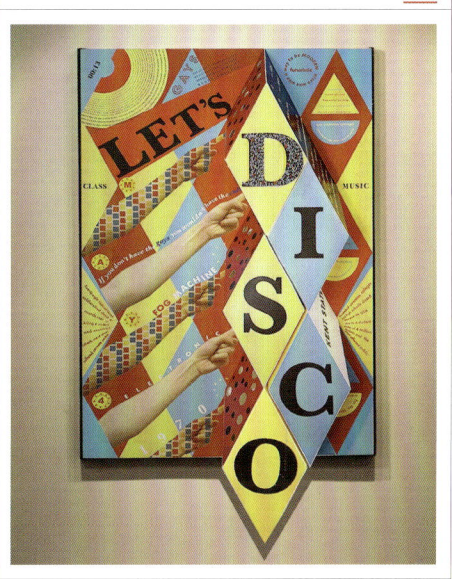

Student: Xuehui He
School: Savannah College of Art & Design

INSTRUCTORS DONG-JOO PARK, SEUNG-MIN HAN

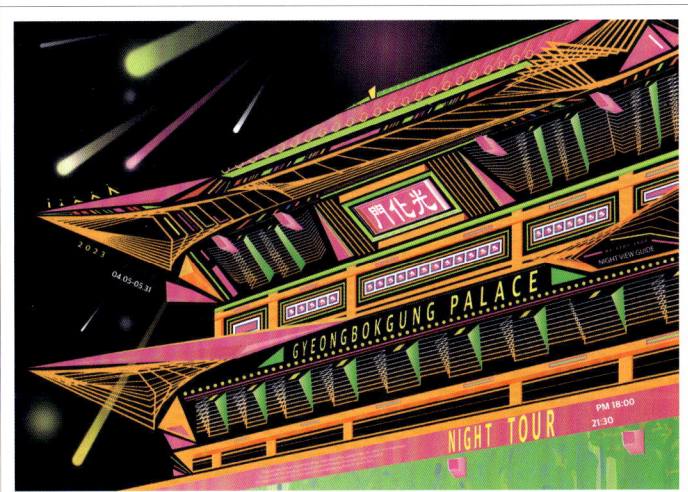

Student: Hwi-Seo Park
School: Hansung University, Design & Arts Institute

INSTRUCTOR HYUNG JOO KIM

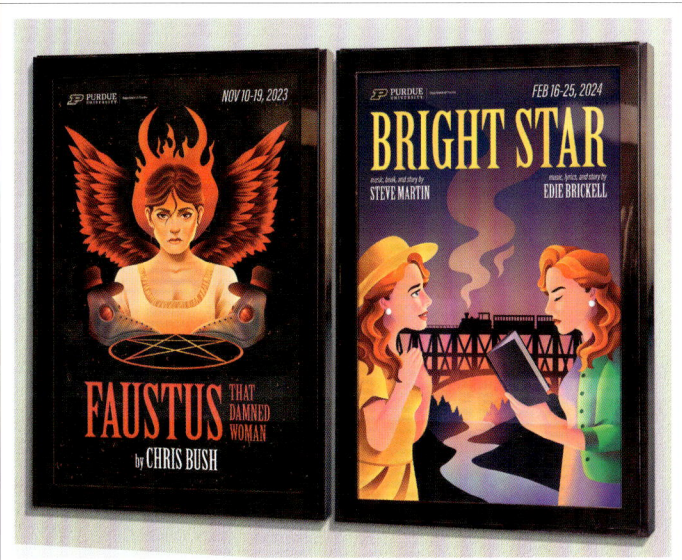

Student: Evan Olinger
School: Purdue University

Poster | Design

200 DESIGN SILVER

INSTRUCTOR BILL GALYEAN 🇺🇸

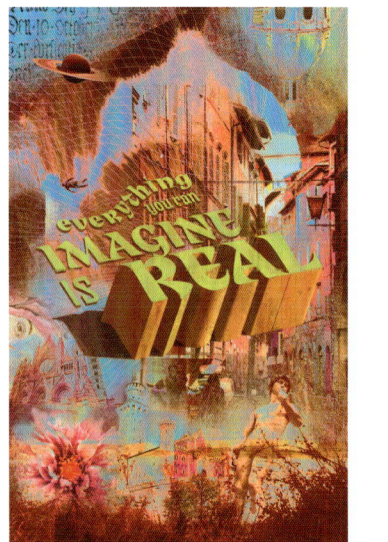

Student: Corinne Green
School: Texas Christian University

INST. HOON-DONG CHUNG 🇰🇷

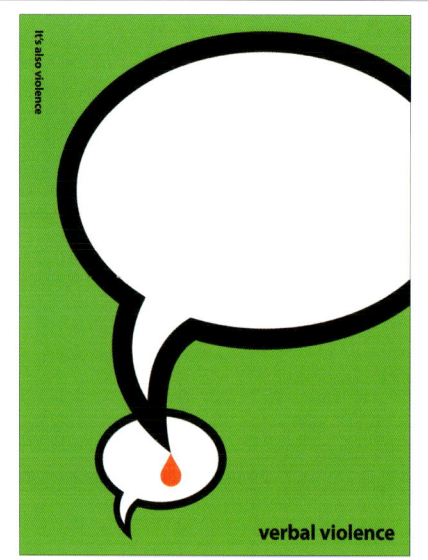

Student: Mingxing Zhang
School: Dankook University

INSTRUCTOR THERON MOORE 🇺🇸

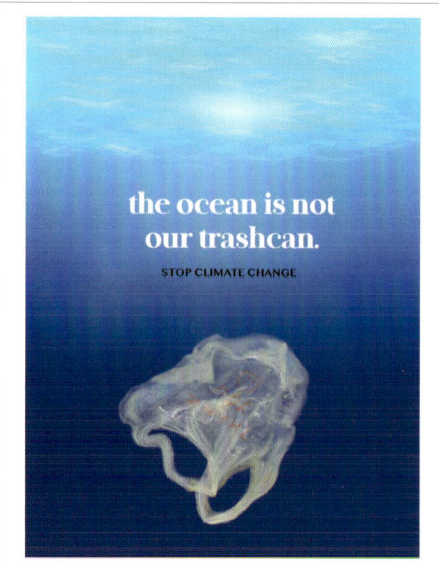

Student: Chelsea Alvarez
School: California State University, Fullerton

INSTRUCTOR TAYLOR SHIPTON 🇺🇸

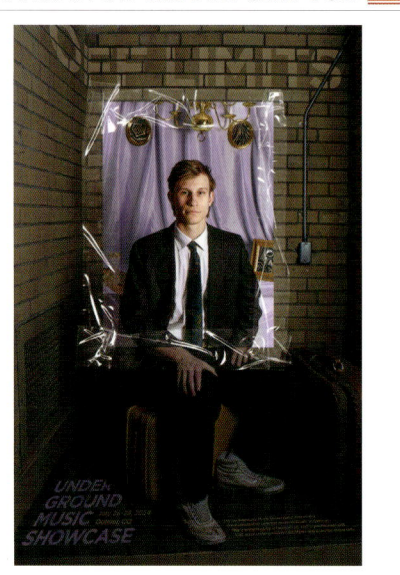

Students: Carson Schultz, Jessica Stencel
School: Pennsylvania State University

INSTRUCTOR NANCY CAMPBELL 🇺🇸

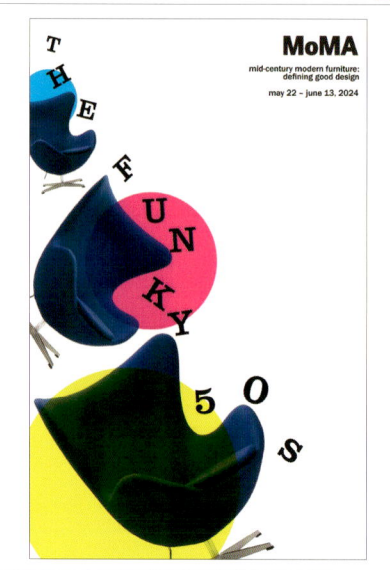

Student: Tracy Kwok
School: Kean University

INSTRUCTOR NANCY CAMPBELL 🇺🇸

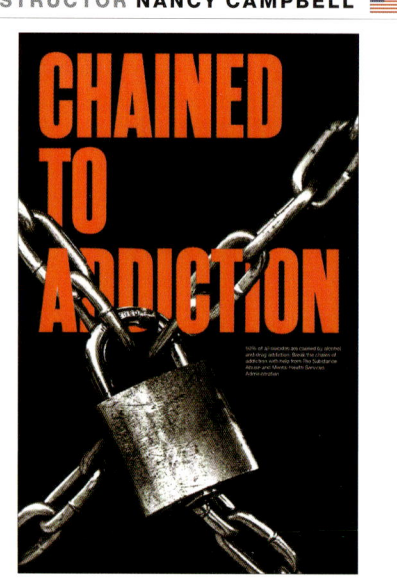

Student: Carlos DeLeon
School: Kean University

INST. HOON-DONG CHUNG 🇰🇷

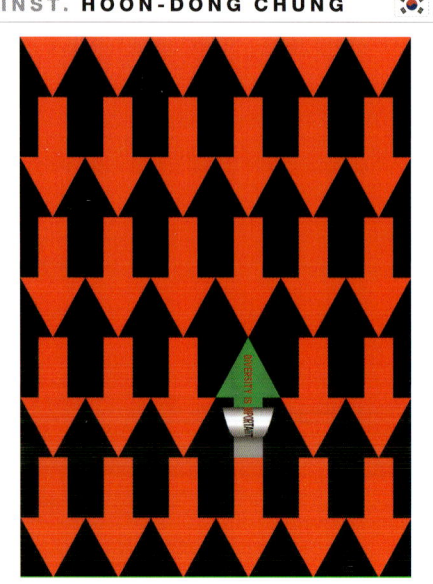

Student: Yanhua Li
School: Dankook University

INST. EUGENIUSZ SKORWIDER 🇵🇱

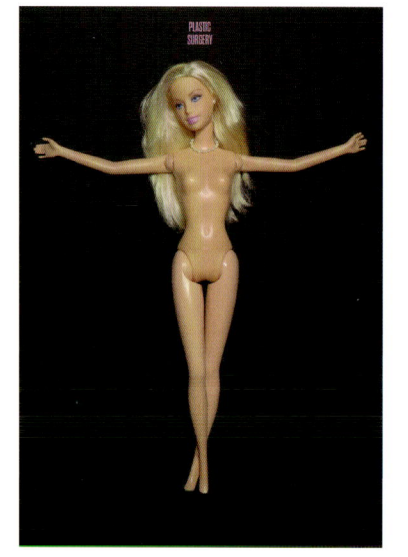

Student: Aleksandra Kortas
School: University of Arts Poznan

INSTRUCTOR PETER AHLBERG 🇺🇸

Student: Suin Choi
School: School of Visual Arts

Design | Poster

201 DESIGN SILVER

INSTRUCTOR REBEKAH ALBRECHT

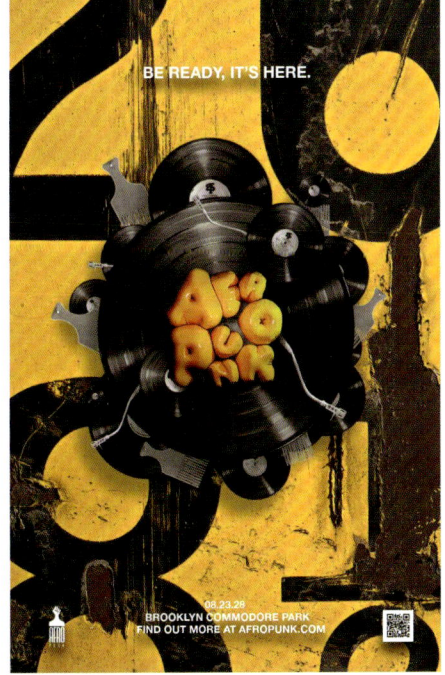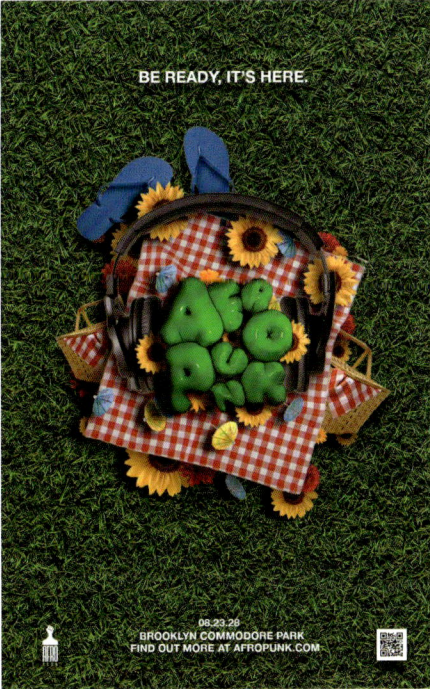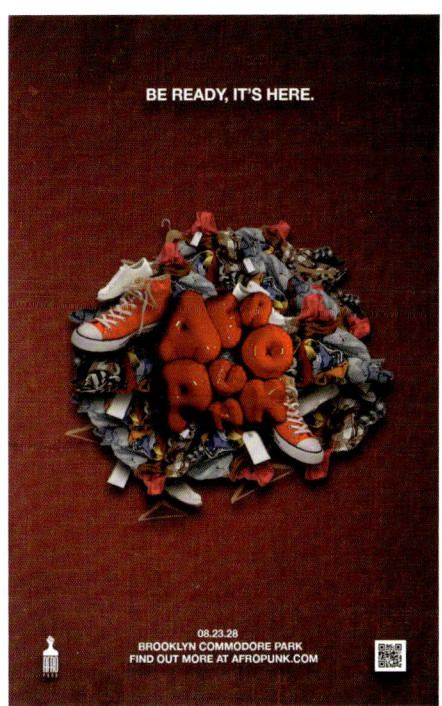

Student: Nya Durr | **School:** Woodbury University

INSTRUCTOR NATASHA JEN

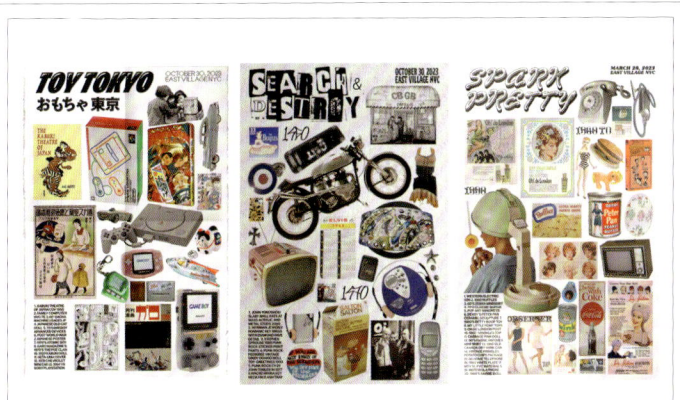

Student: Hyowon Kwon | **School:** School of Visual Arts

INSTRUCTOR NANCY SKOLOS

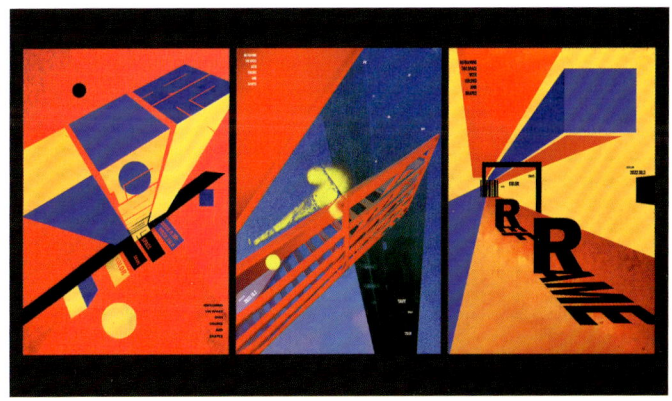

Student: Shuixin Wang | **School:** Rhode Island School of Design

INSTRUCTOR PETER AHLBERG

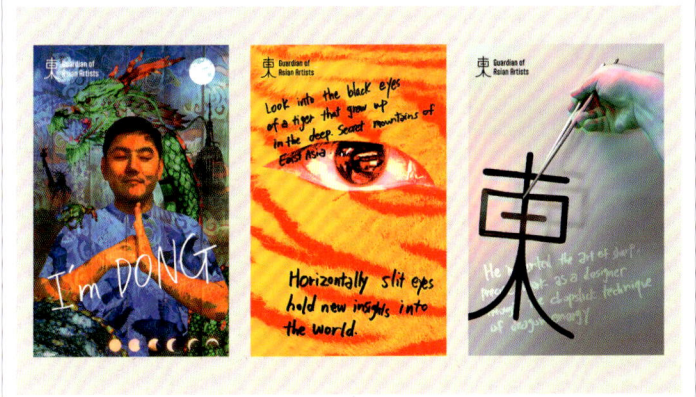

Student: Dong Hyun Kim | **School:** School of Visual Arts

INSTRUCTOR MEHRDAD SEDAGHAT BAGHBANI

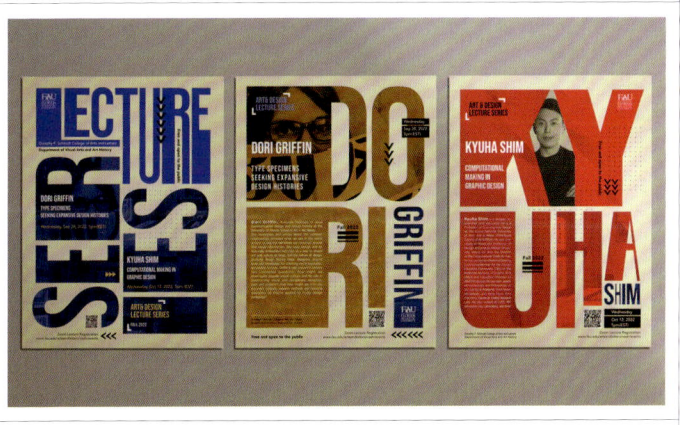

Student: Narges Panahandeh | **School:** Florida Atlantic University

Poster | Design

202 DESIGN SILVER

INSTRUCTOR HYOJUN SHIM
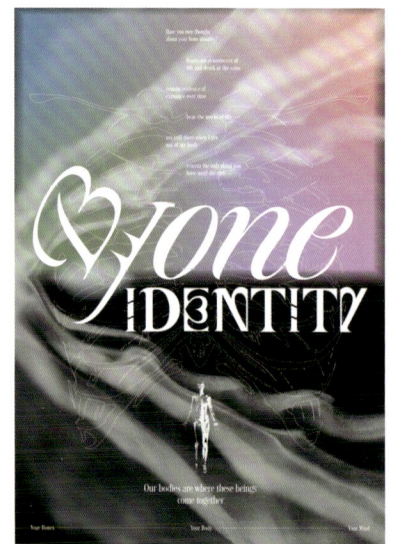
Student: Na Kyeong Yoon
School: Dongduk Women's University

INSTRUCTOR STEPHEN ZHANG
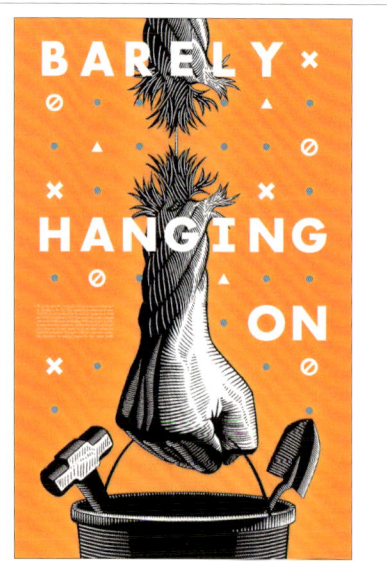
Student: Sean Howes
School: University of North Texas

INSTRUCTOR JIM SALVATI
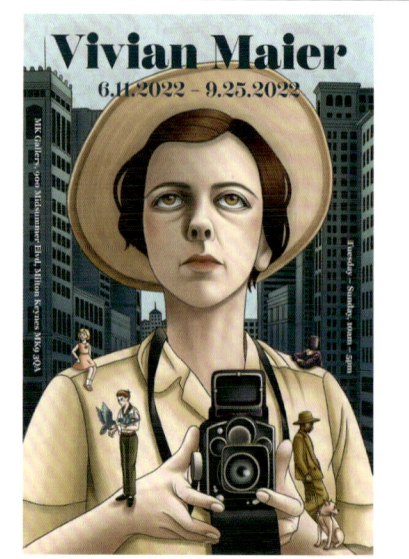
Student: Jiyun Choi
School: ArtCenter College of Design

INSTRUCTOR HYOJUN SHIM
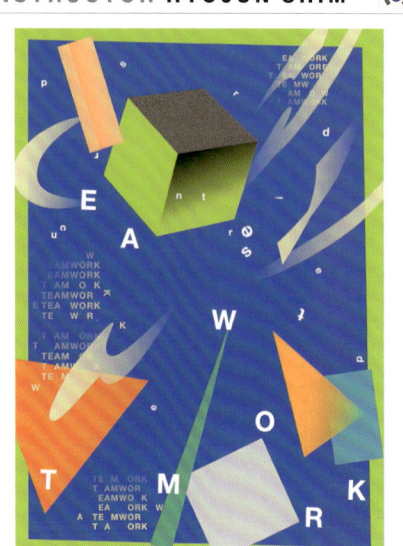
Student: Yena Shin
School: Dongduk Women's University

INSTRUCTOR ANNE JORDAN
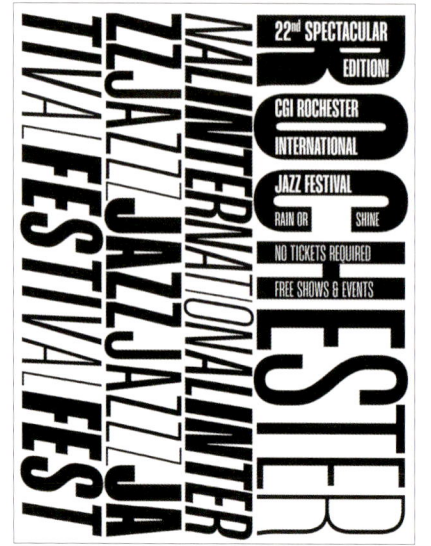
Student: Muhammad Tayyab Younas
School: Rochester Institute of Technology

INST. DOUGLAS RICCARDI
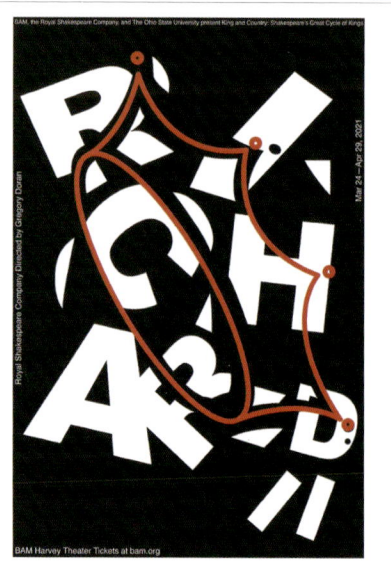
Student: Yawen Xiao
School: School of Visual Arts

INSTRUCTORS D. PARK, S. HAN
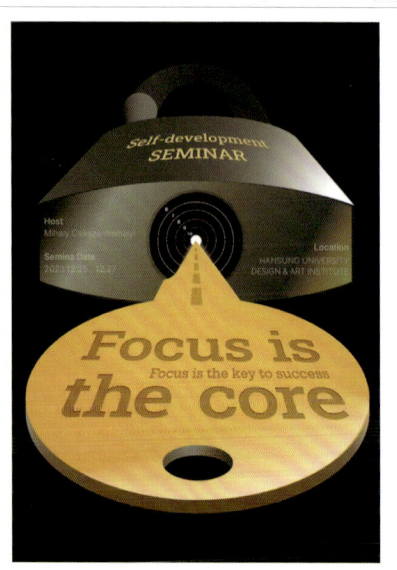
Student: Mi-Sun Park | **School:** Hansung University, Design & Arts Institute

INSTRUCTOR HYOJUN SHIM
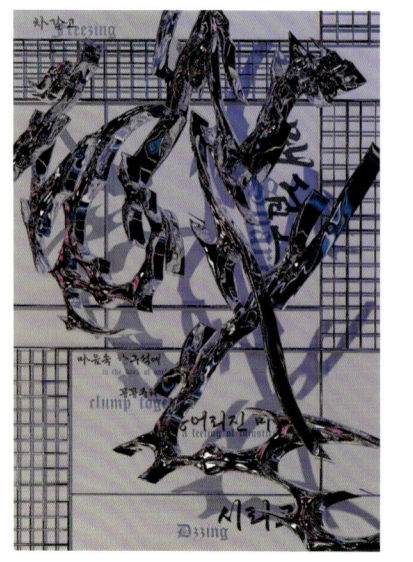
Student: Hyunju Lee
School: Dongduk Women's University

INSTRUCTOR EMILY BURNS
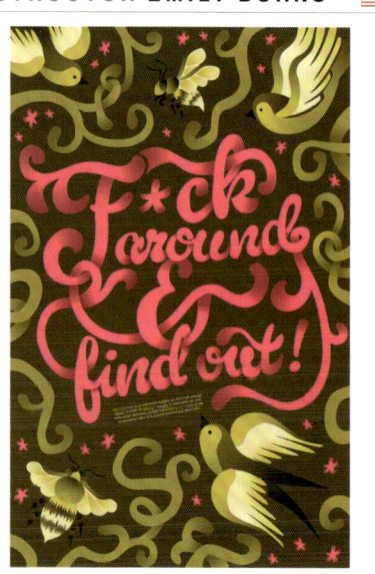
Student: Eden Balog
School: Pennsylvania State University

Design | Poster

203 DESIGN SILVER

INSTRUCTOR BRAD BARTLETT 🇺🇸

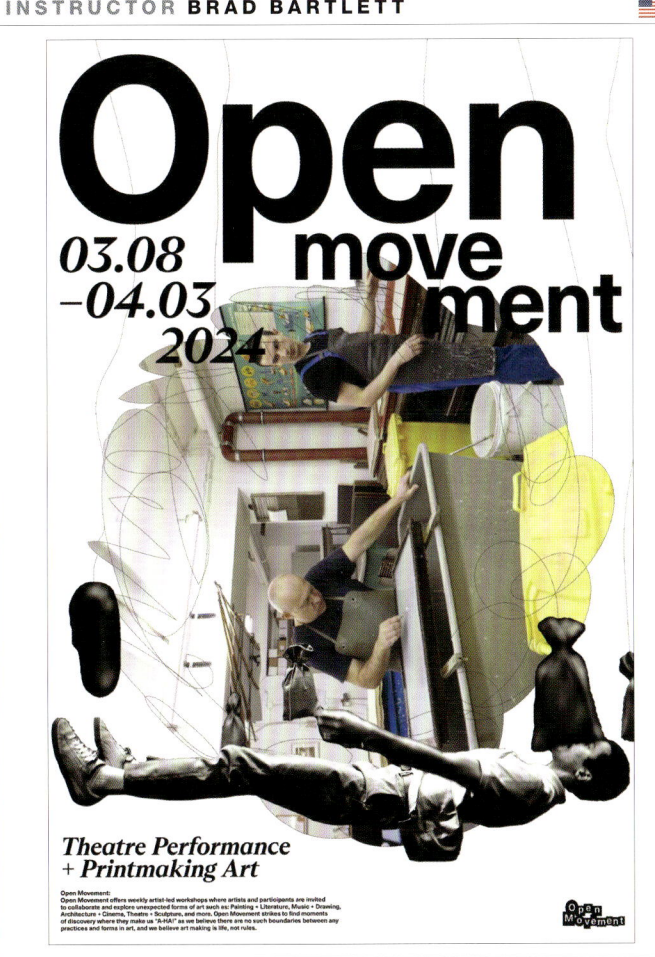

Student: Jaiwon Lee | School: ArtCenter College of Design

INSTRUCTOR HOON-DONG CHUNG 🇰🇷

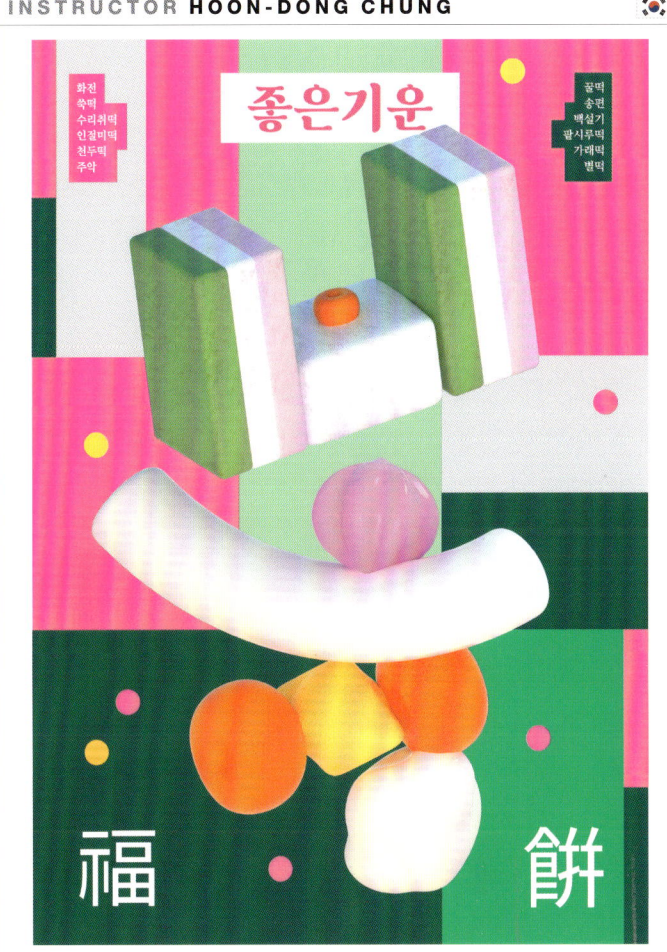

Student: Hyeon-Ha Jo | School: Dankook University

INSTRUCTORS DONG-JOO PARK, SEUNG-MIN HAN 🇰🇷

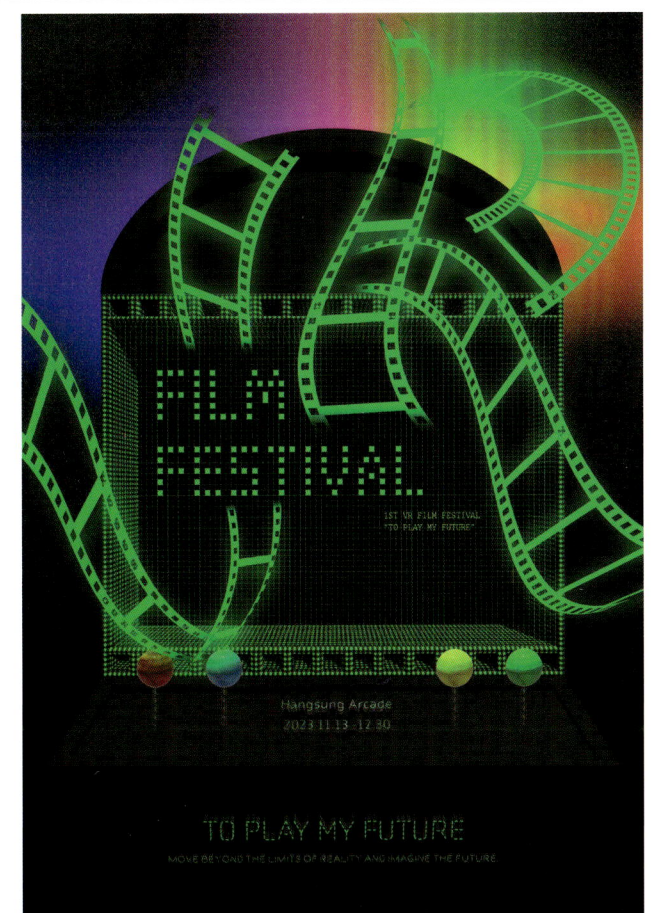

Student: Gang-Min Kim | School: Hansung University, Design & Arts Institute

INSTRUCTORS DONG-JOO PARK, SEUNG-MIN HAN 🇰🇷

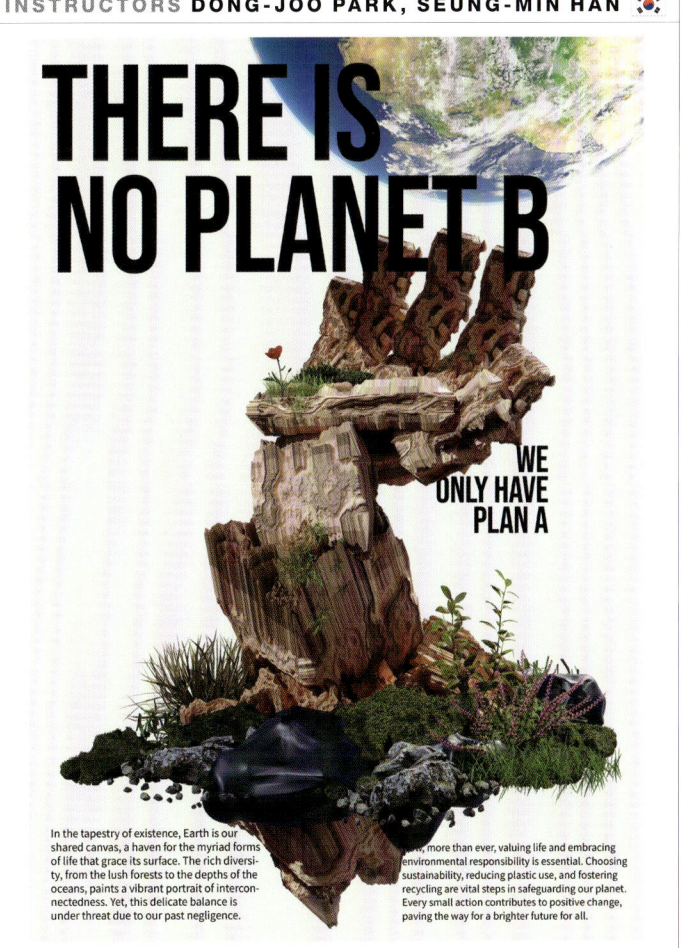

Student: Un-Hyeong Song | School: Hansung University, Design & Arts Institute

Poster | Design

204 DESIGN SILVER

INSTRUCTOR KAREN WATKINS

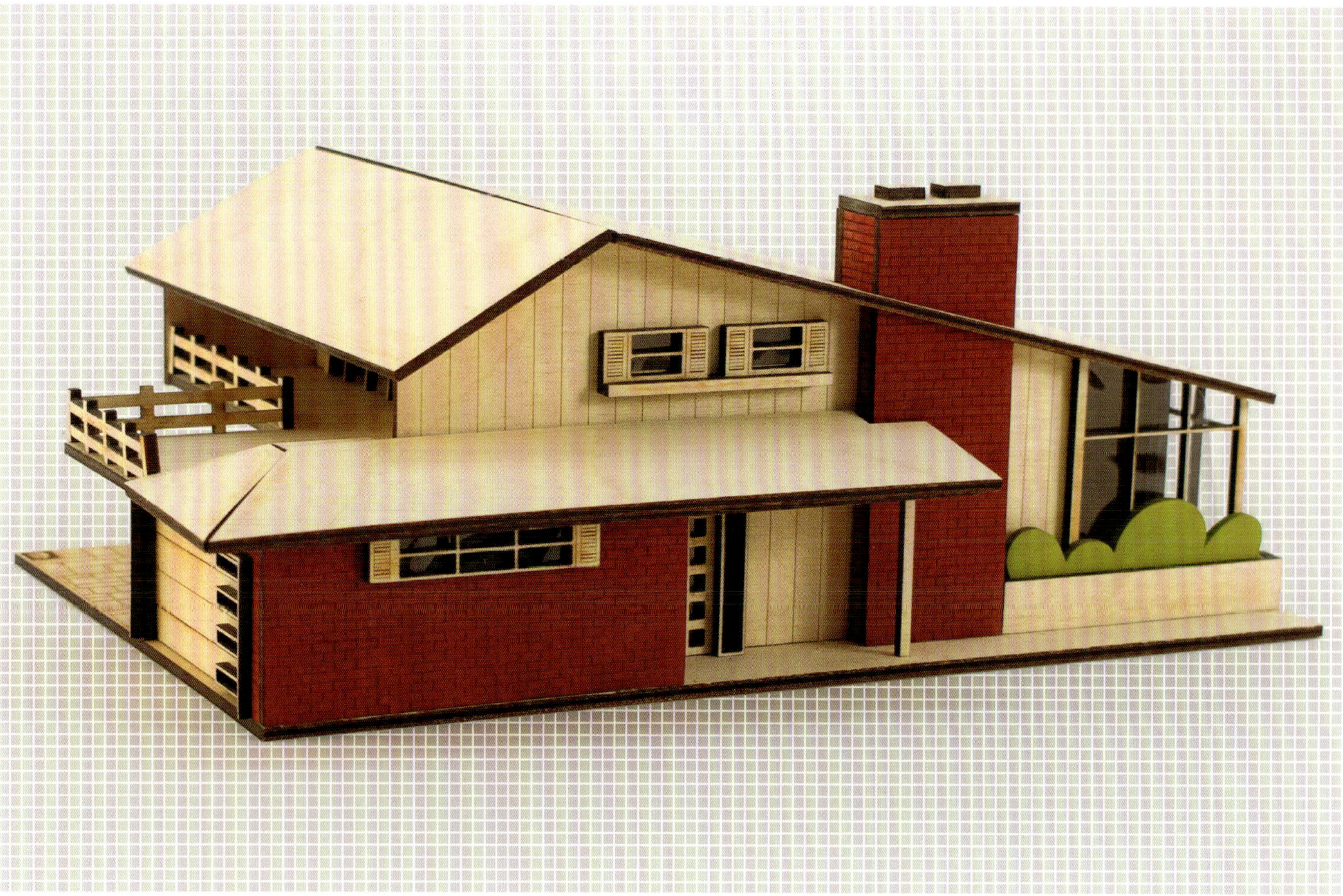

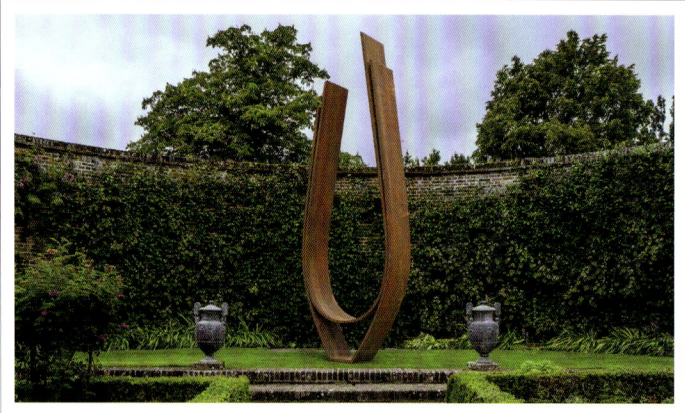

Student: Emily Simon | School: West Chester University

INSTRUCTOR HANK RICHARDSON

Student: Anna LeBer | School: M.AD School of Ideas Atlanta

INSTRUCTOR HANK RICHARDSON

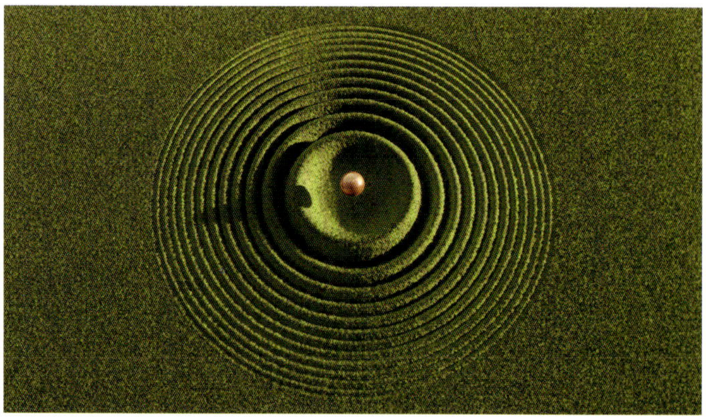

Student: Anna LeBer | School: M.AD School of Ideas Atlanta

INSTRUCTOR HANK RICHARDSON

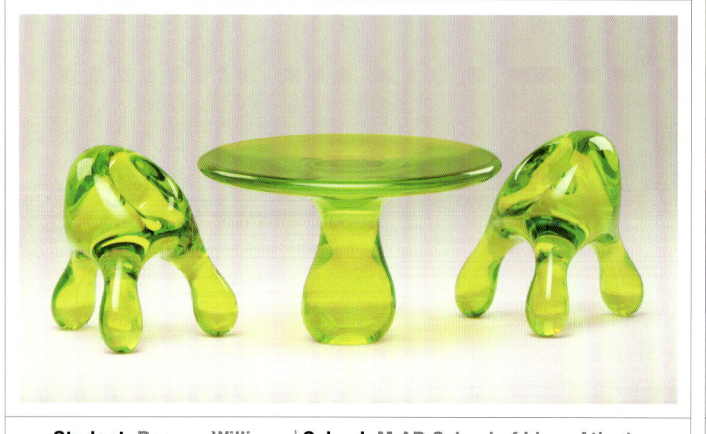

Student: Reagan Williams | School: M.AD School of Ideas Atlanta

INSTRUCTOR HANK RICHARDSON

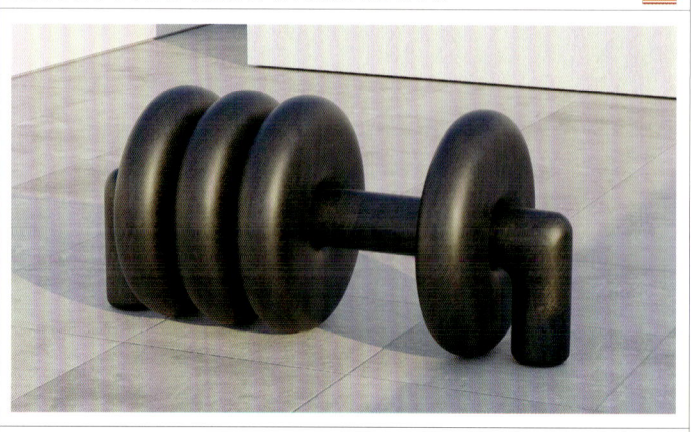

Student: Liza Langstaff | School: M.AD School of Ideas

Design | Product Design

205 DESIGN SILVER

INSTRUCTOR HANK RICHARDSON

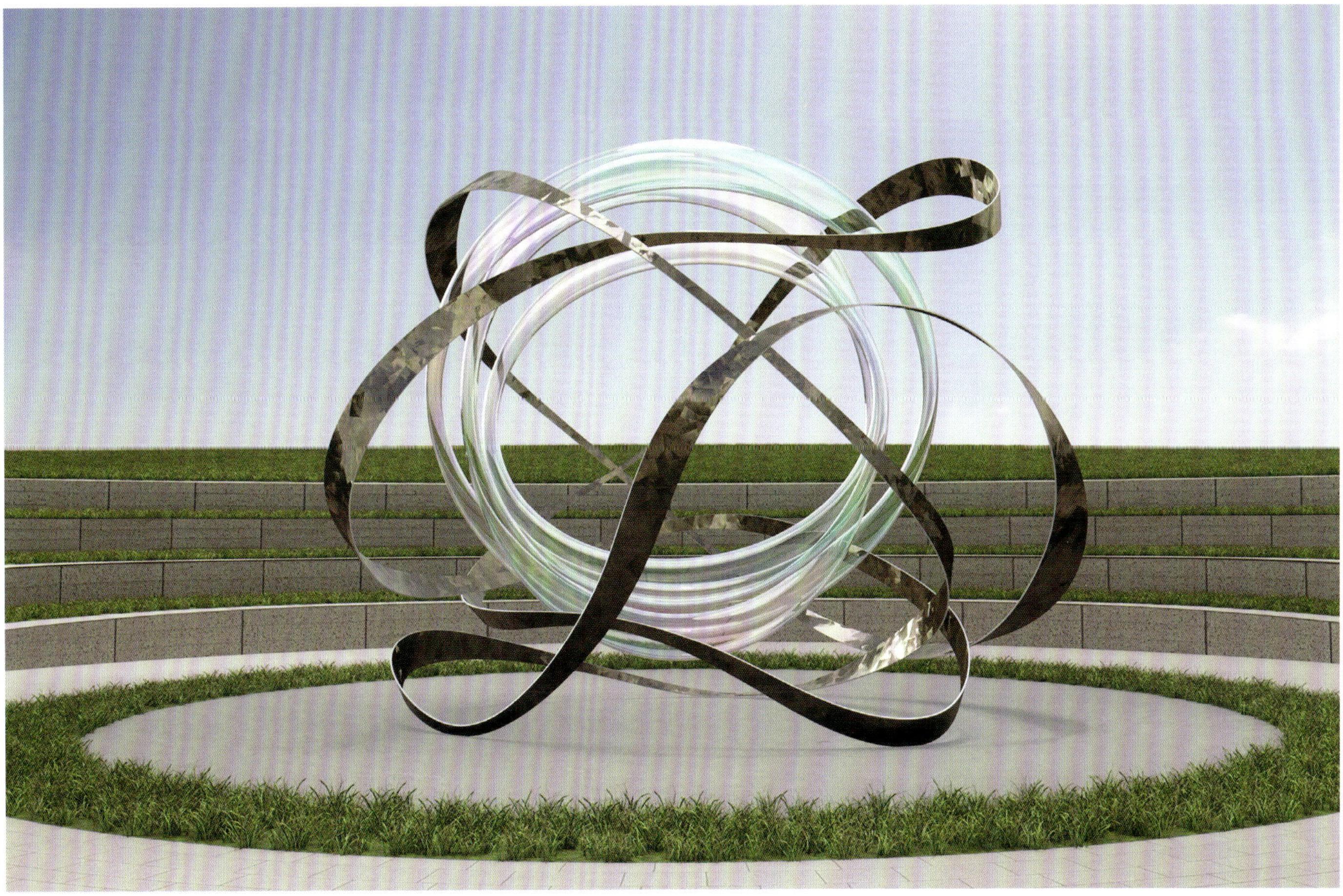

Student: Catarina Sterlacci | **School:** M.AD School of Ideas Atlanta

INSTRUCTOR HANK RICHARDSON

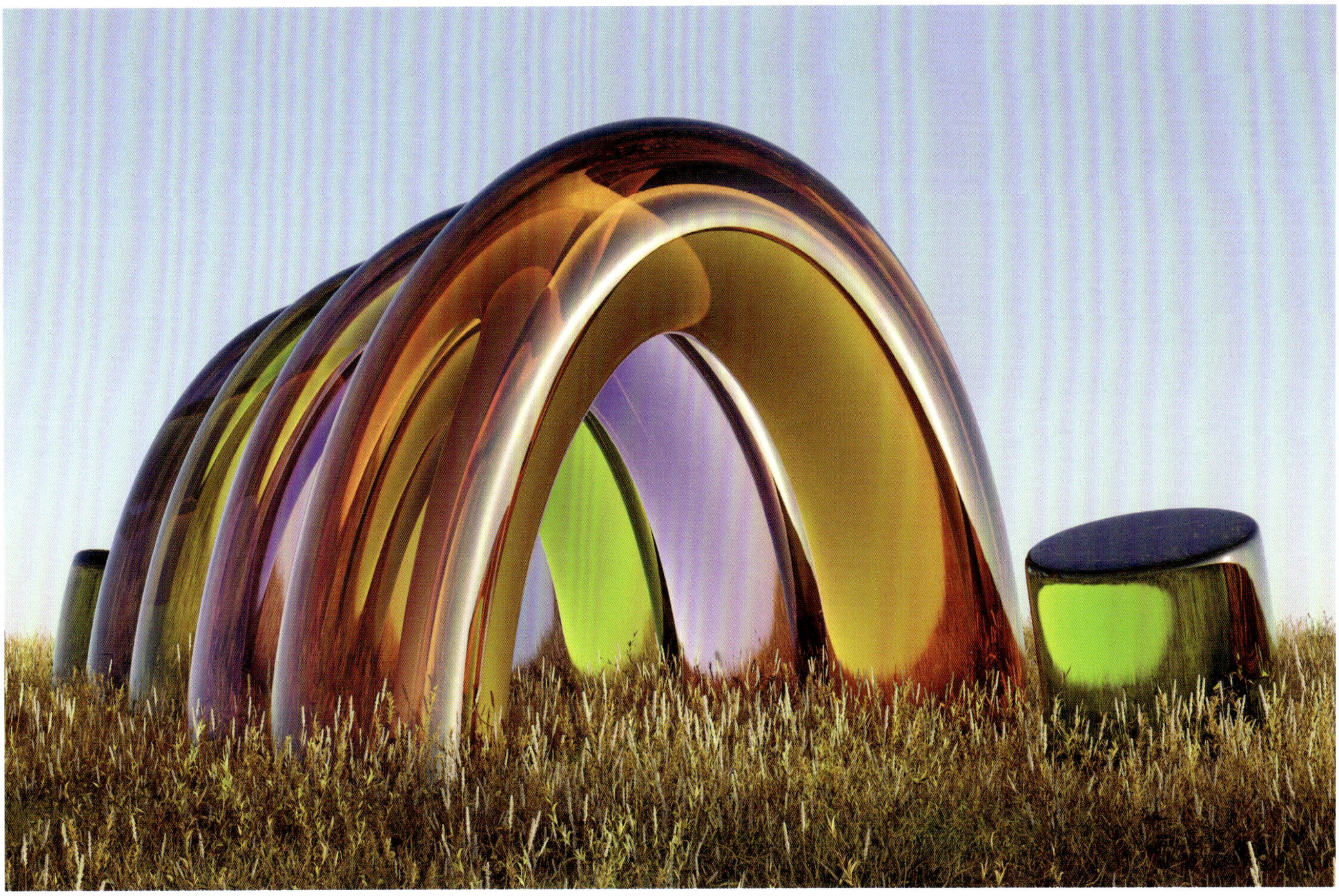

Student: Reagan Williams | **School:** M.AD School of Ideas Atlanta

Product Design | Design

206 DESIGN SILVER

INSTRUCTOR DUSTY CROCKER

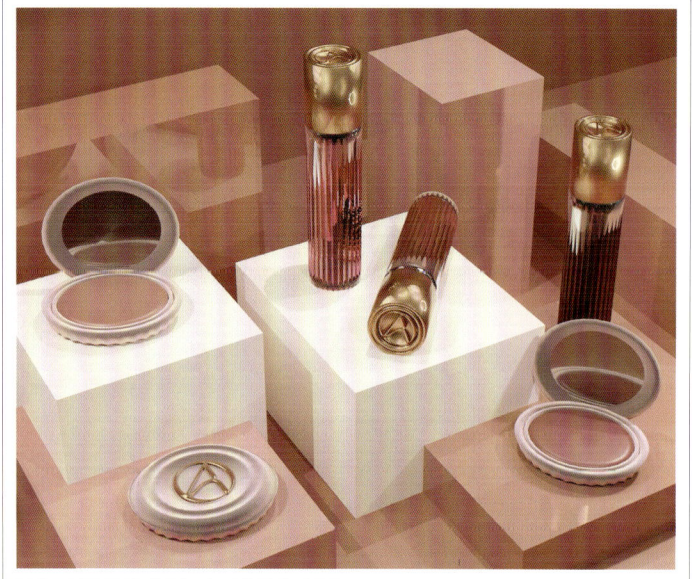

Student: Abigail Lund | **School:** Texas Christian University

INSTRUCTOR PETER AHLBERG

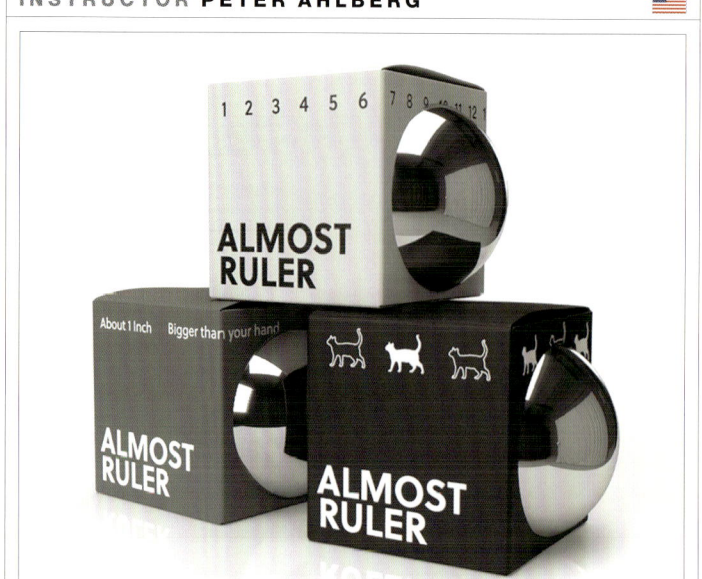

Student: Xiangyi Guo | **School:** School of Visual Arts

INSTRUCTOR HANK RICHARDSON

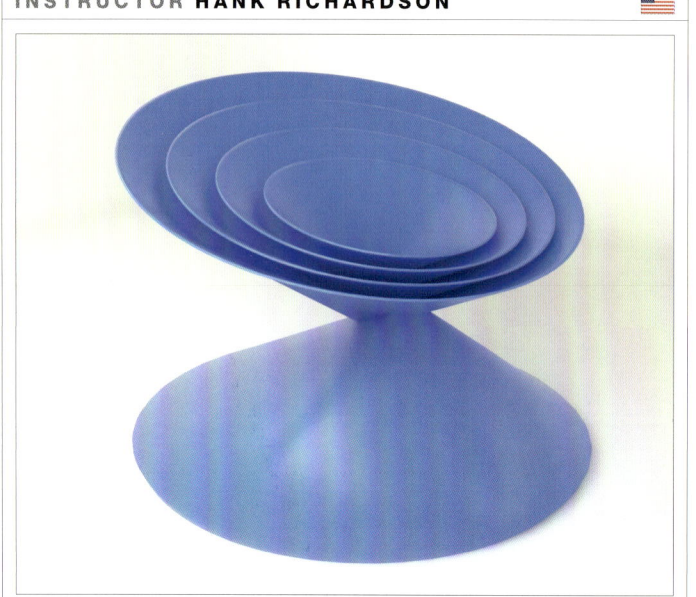

Student: Jonny Gleaton | **School:** M.AD School of Ideas Atlanta

INSTRUCTOR HANK RICHARDSON

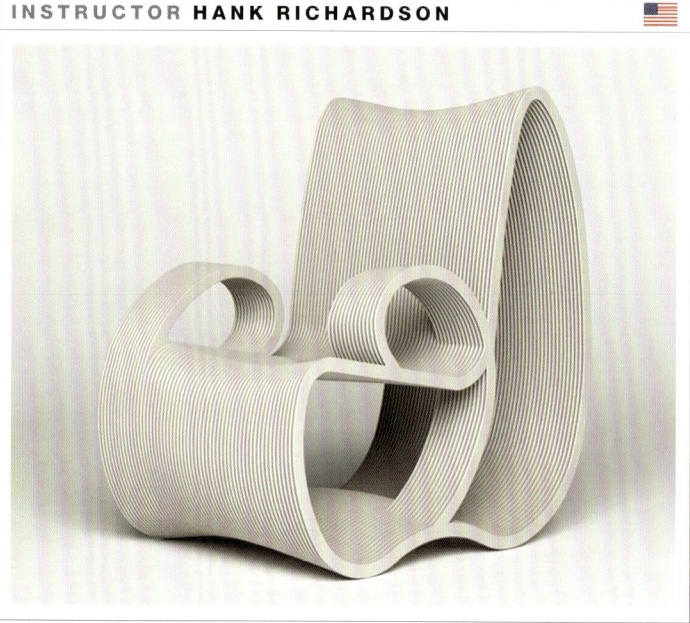

Student: Catarina Sterlacci | **School:** M.AD School of Ideas Atlanta

INSTRUCTOR HANK RICHARDSON

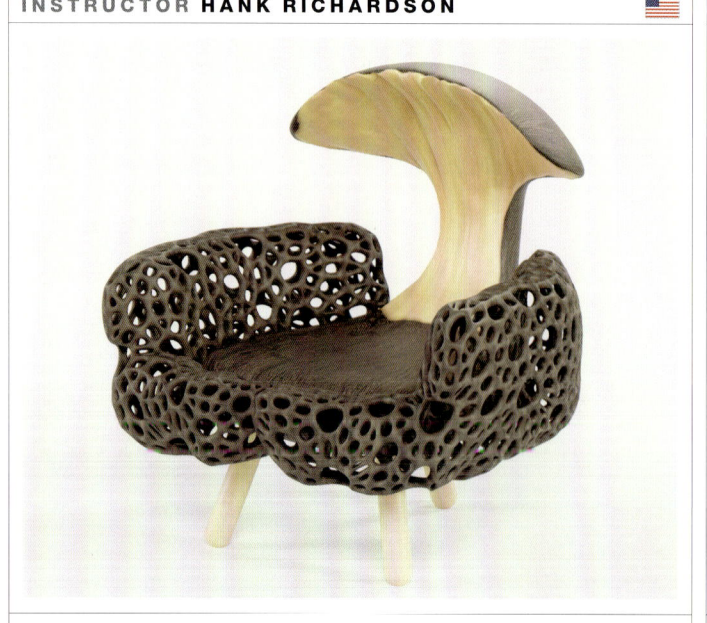

Student: Ramon Sanchez | **School:** M.AD School of Ideas Atlanta

INSTRUCTOR HANK RICHARDSON

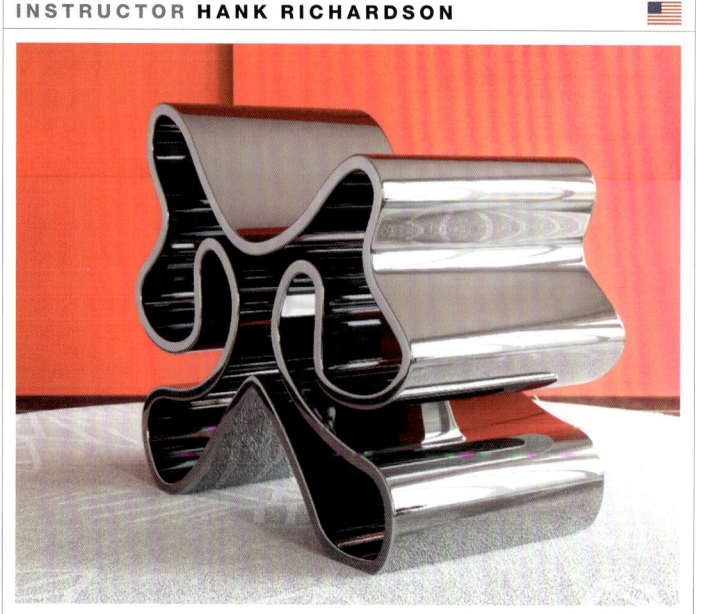

Student: Maya Givens | **School:** M.AD School of Ideas Atlanta

Design | Product Design

207 DESIGN SILVER

INSTRUCTOR HADAR KFIR

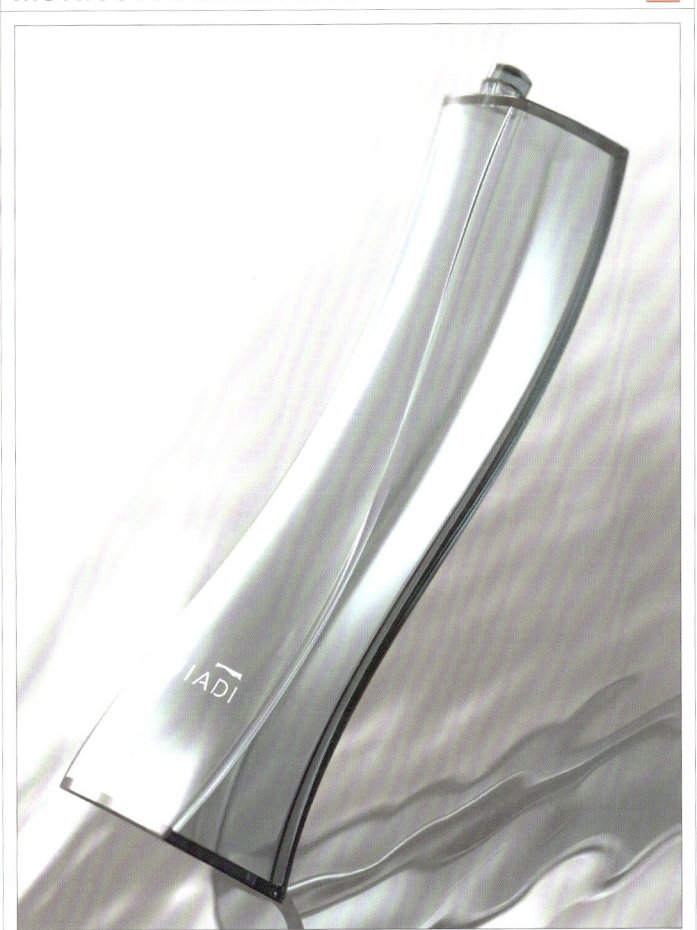

Student: Wen-Chi Hsueh | **School:** Pratt Institute

INSTRUCTOR UNATTRIBUTED

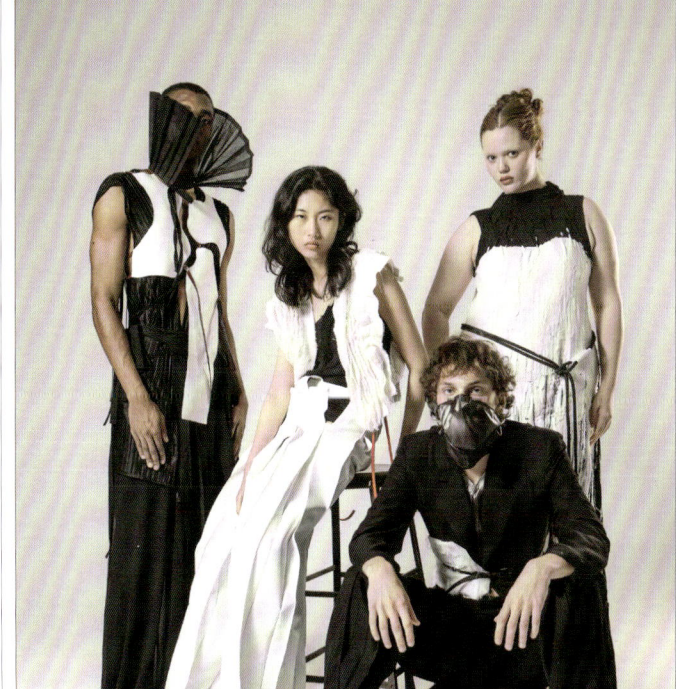

Student: Hyeonji Kim | **School:** Parsons School of Design

INSTRUCTOR UNATTRIBUTED

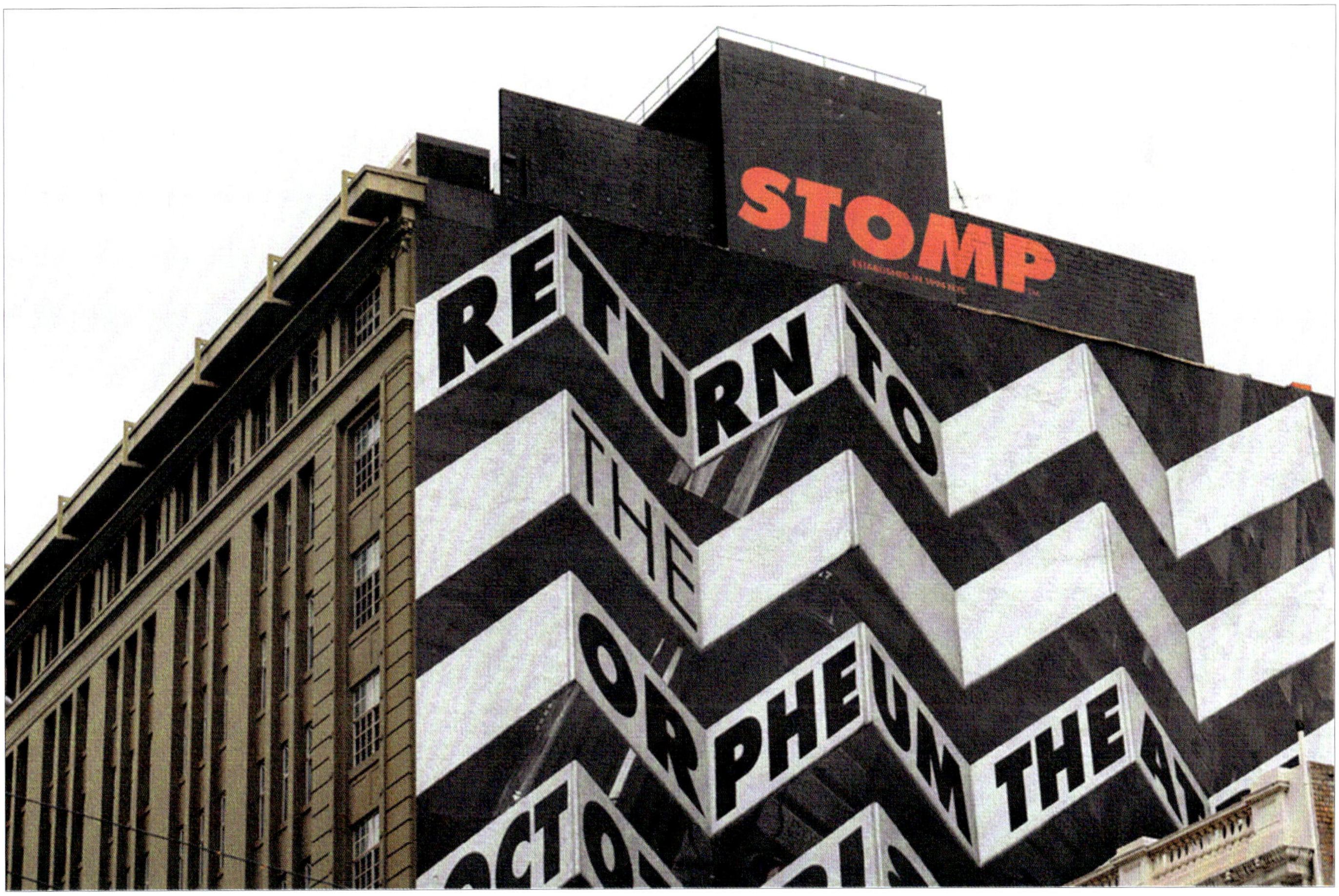

Student: Chuanyuan Lin | **School:** School of Visual Arts

Product Design, Promotion | Design

INSTRUCTOR MIA CULBERTSON

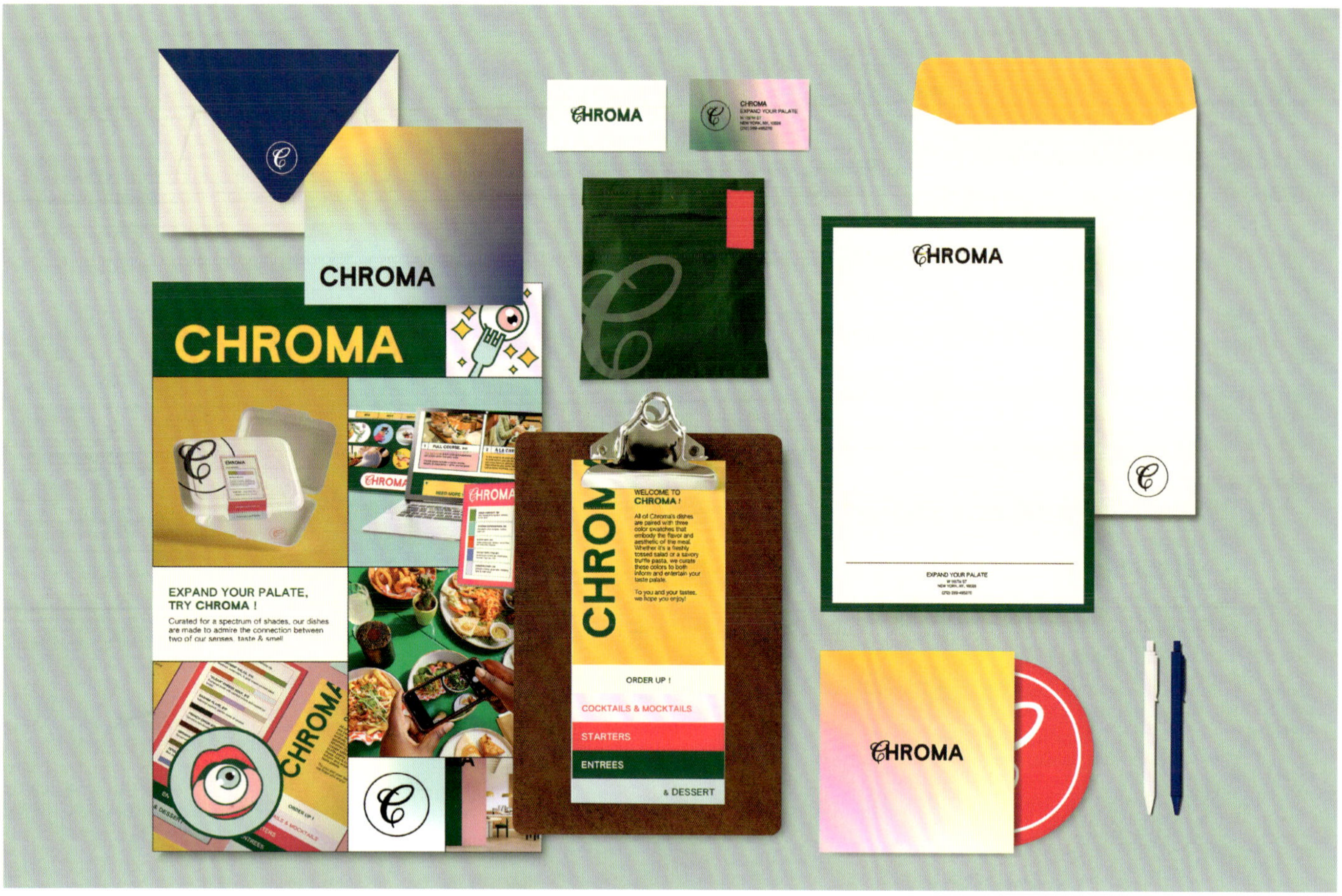

Student: Hunter Ruiz | **School:** Temple University, Tyler School of Art & Architecture

INSTRUCTOR KAREN WATKINS

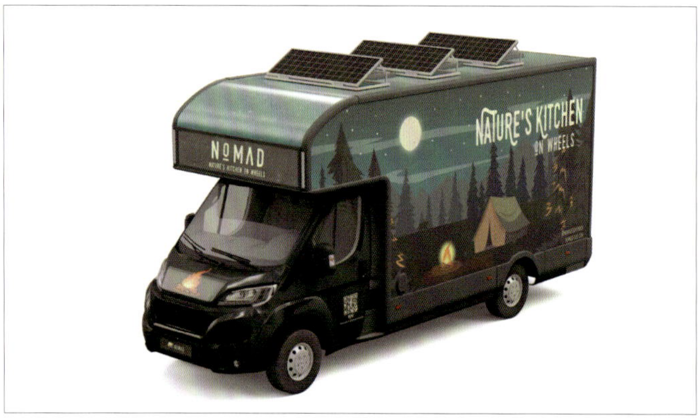

Student: Taylor Super | **School:** West Chester University

INSTRUCTOR KAREN WATKINS

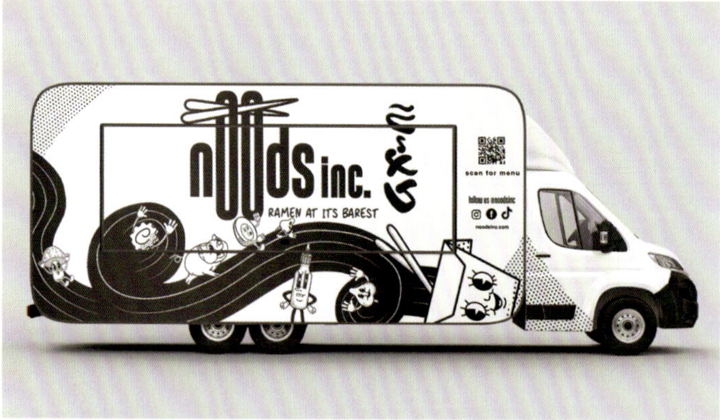

Student: Samuel McConnell | **School:** West Chester University

INSTRUCTOR JAN BALLARD

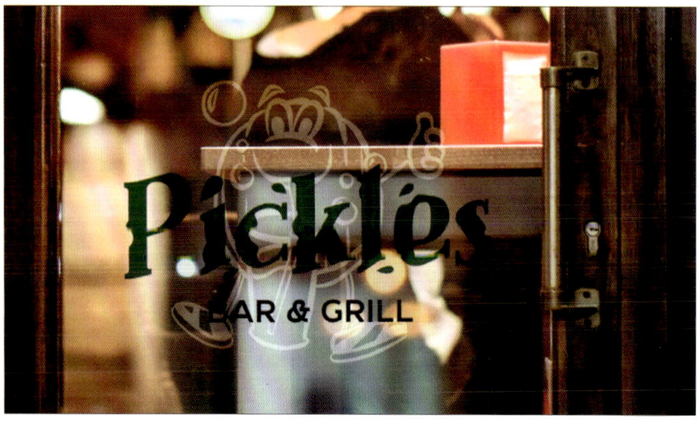

Student: Alexandra Tice | **School:** Texas Christian University

INSTRUCTOR HANK RICHARDSON

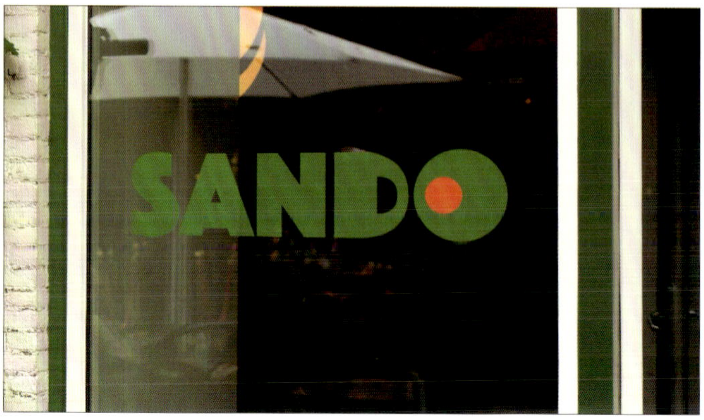

Student: Reagan Williams | **School:** M.AD School of Ideas Atlanta

209 DESIGN SILVER

INSTRUCTOR CLAUDIA STRONG

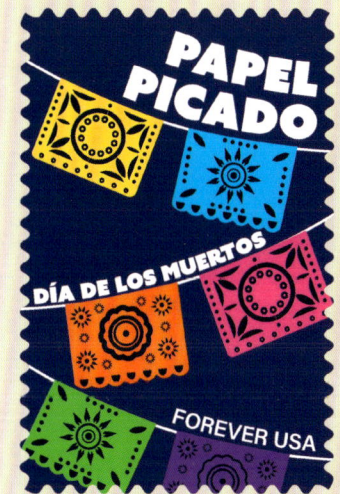 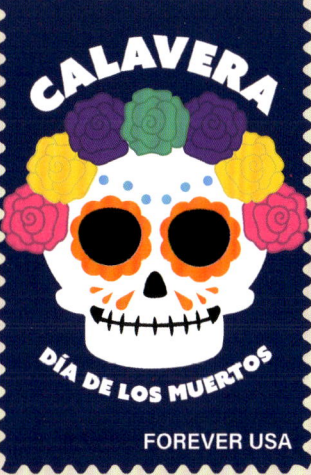 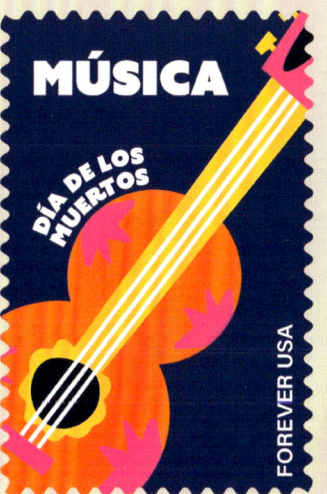 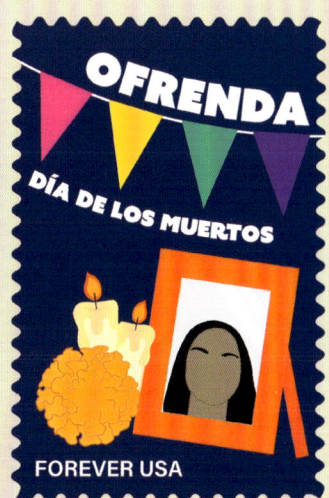

Student: Hailey Lawless | **School:** Syracuse University, The Newhouse School

INSTRUCTOR CLAUDIA STRONG

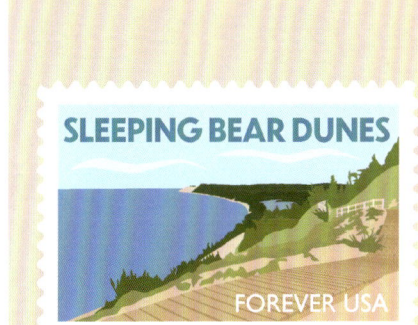 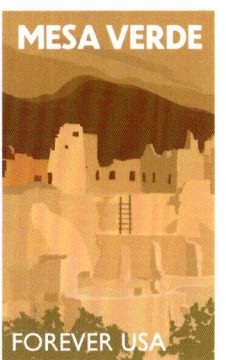 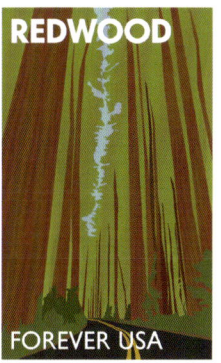 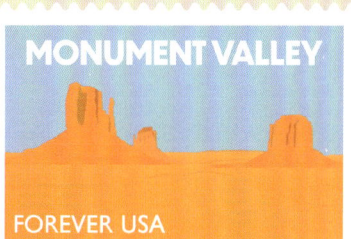

Student: Samantha Swiss | **School:** Syracuse University, The Newhouse School

INSTRUCTOR CLAUDIA STRONG

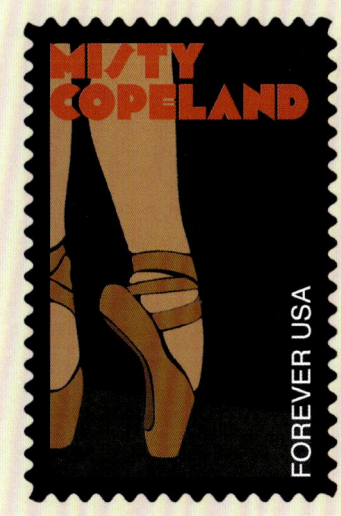 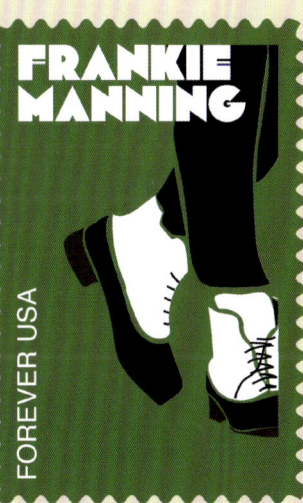 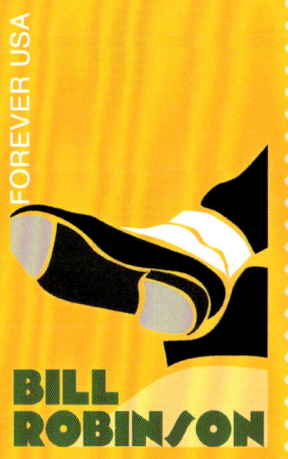 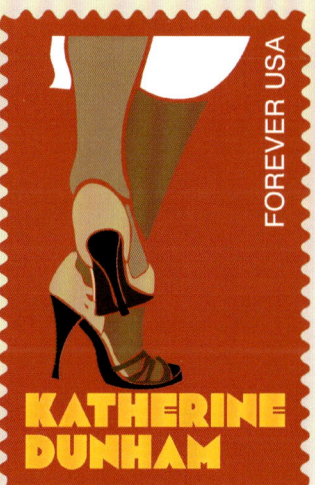

Student: Nicole Beaudet | **School:** Syracuse University, The Newhouse School

210 DESIGN SILVER

INSTRUCTOR DEJAN MRAOVIĆ

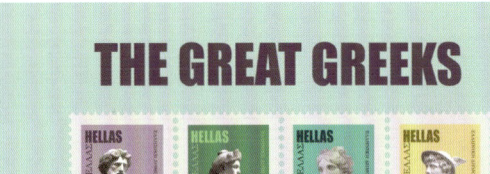

Student: Abigail Ellington | **School:** Campbell University

INSTRUCTOR HYUNG JOO KIM

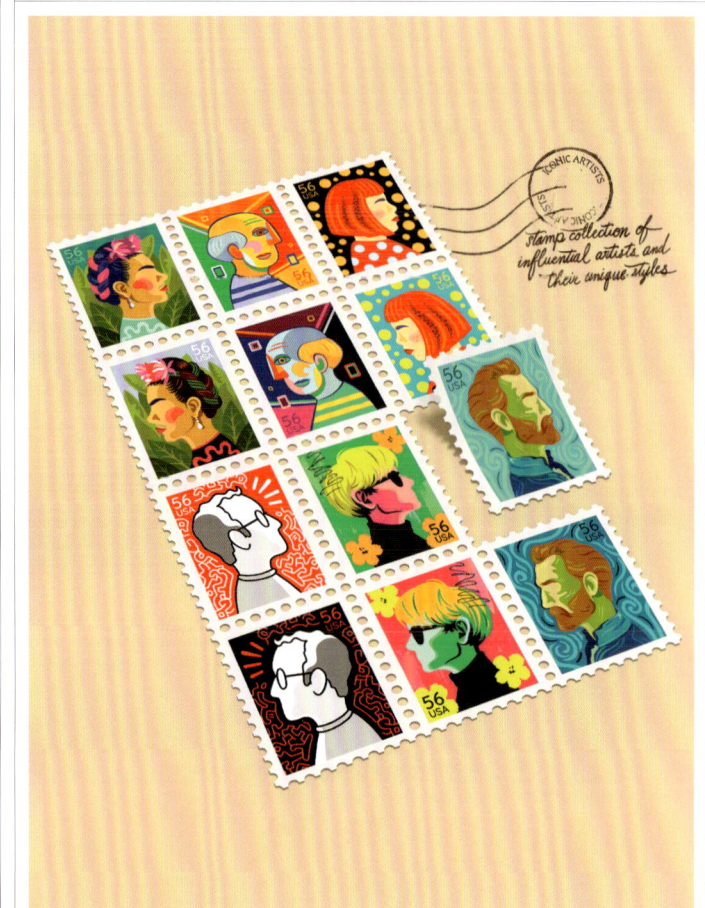

Student: Evan Olinger | **School:** Purdue University

INSTRUCTOR ZIPENG ZHU

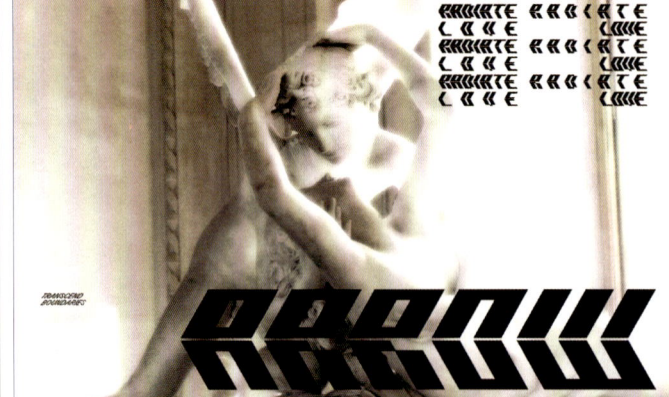

Student: Seongyun Park | **School:** School of Visual Arts

INSTRUCTOR UNATTRIBUTED

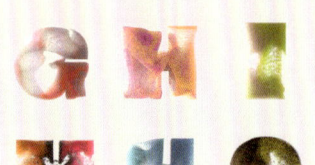

Student: Yun Shen (Angel) Liao | **School:** School of Visual Arts

211 DESIGN SILVER

INSTRUCTOR ZIPENG ZHU

Student: DeMia Courman
School: School of Visual Arts

INSTRUCTOR NATASHA JEN

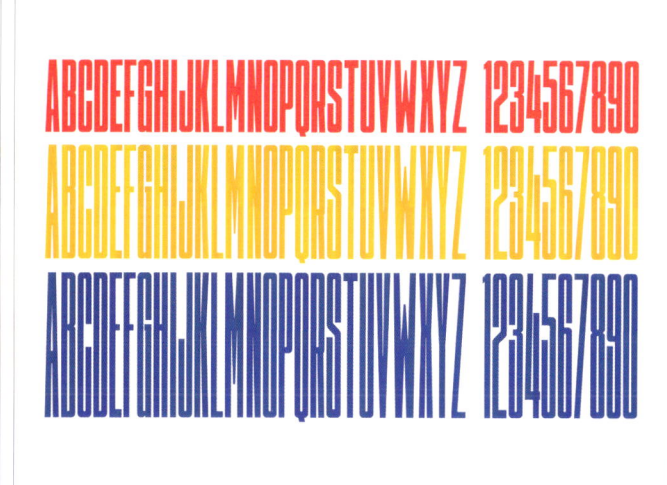

Student: Vasavi Bubna
School: School of Visual Arts

INSTRUCTOR RENÉE STEVENS

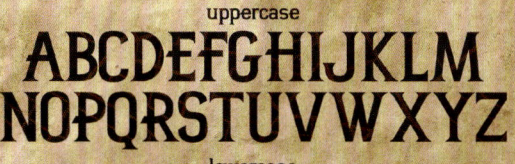

Student: Quinn Carletta
School: Syracuse University, The Newhouse School

INSTRUCTORS BILL MORAN, DEB LAWTON

Student: Natalie Mihal
School: University of Minnesota, Twin Cities

INSTRUCTORS KEN DEEGAN, BRANKICA HARVEY

Student: Alice Jung
School: School of Visual Arts

INSTRUCTOR RENÉE STEVENS

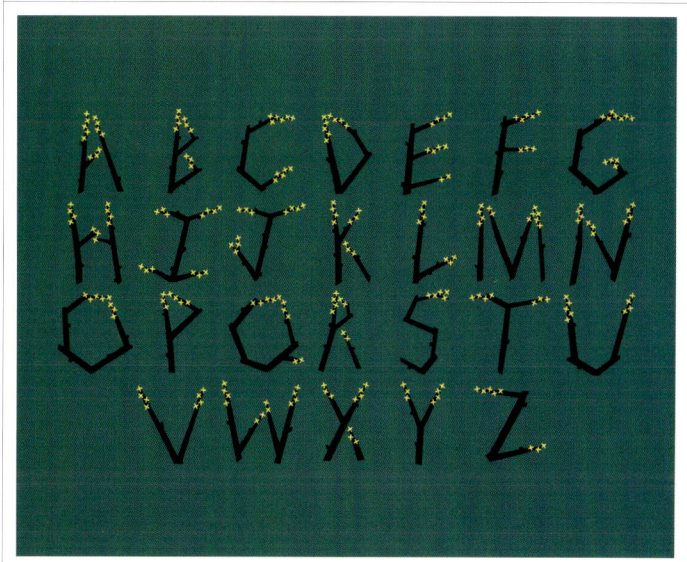

Student: Darren Cordoviz
School: Syracuse University, The Newhouse School

Type Fonts A-Z | Design

212 DESIGN SILVER

INSTRUCTOR GREG LINDY

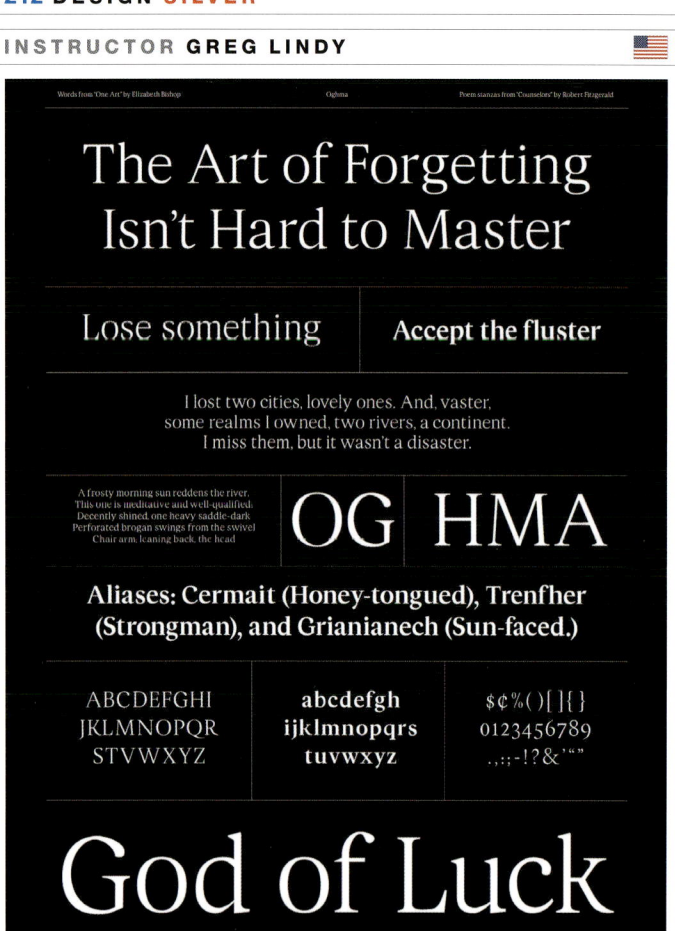

Student: Glenn Ryan | **School:** ArtCenter College of Design

INSTRUCTOR DAVID ELIZALDE

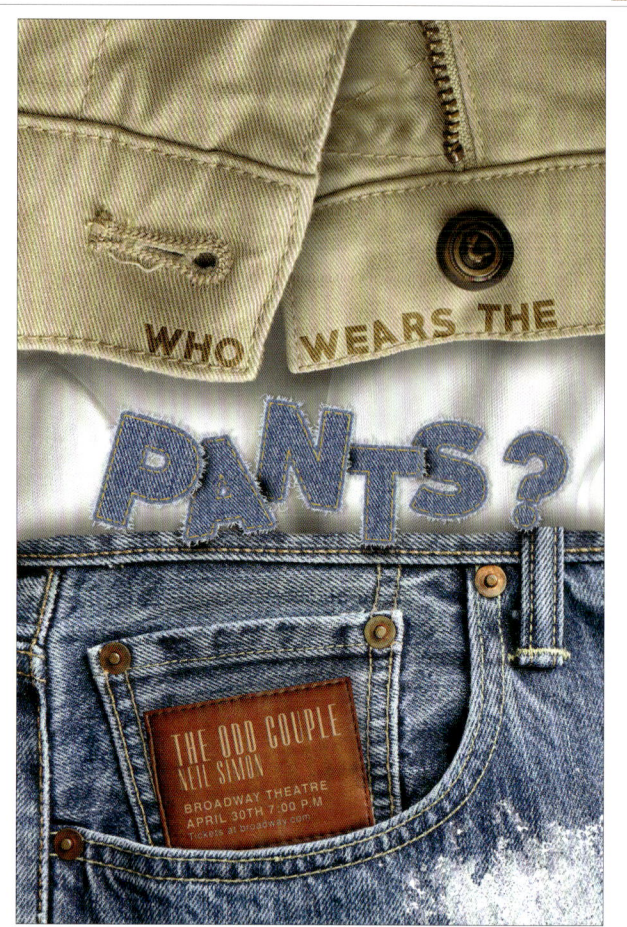

Student: Andy (Nhan) Nguyen | **School:** Texas Christian University

INSTRUCTOR MUHAMMAD RAHMAN

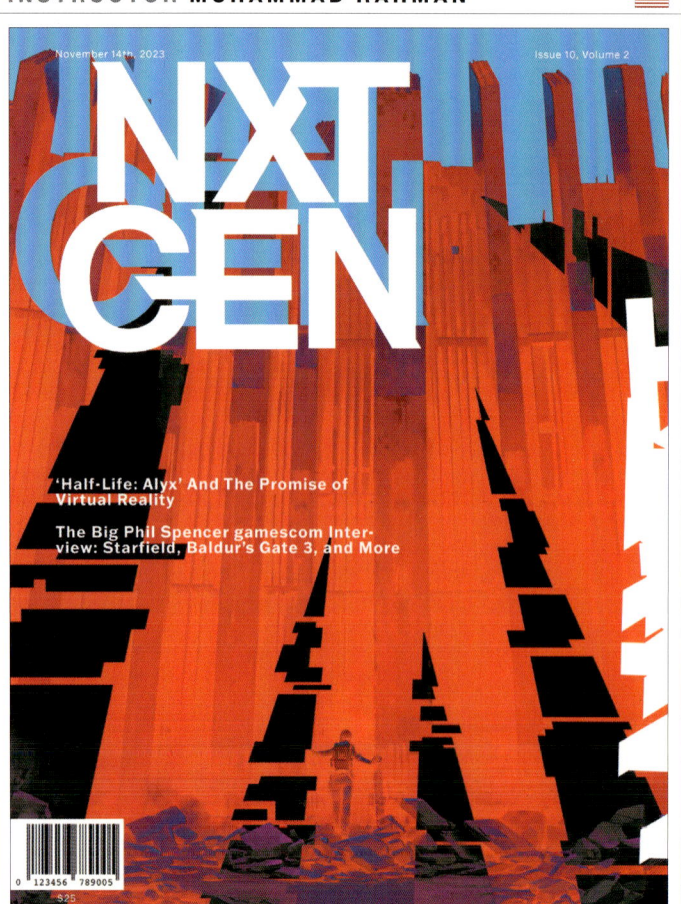

Student: Anya Bolton | **School:** University of Cincinnati DAAP, Myron E. Ullman Jr. School of Design

INSTRUCTOR LEWIS GLASER

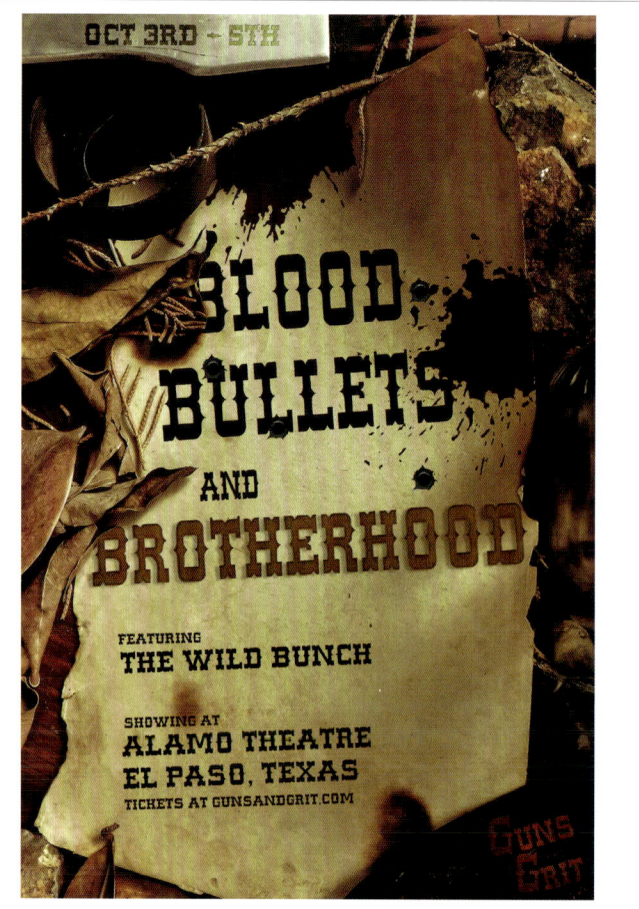

Student: Andy (Nhan) Nguyen
School: Texas Christian University

Design | Type Fonts A-Z, Typography

213 DESIGN SILVER

INSTRUCTOR SIMON JOHNSTON

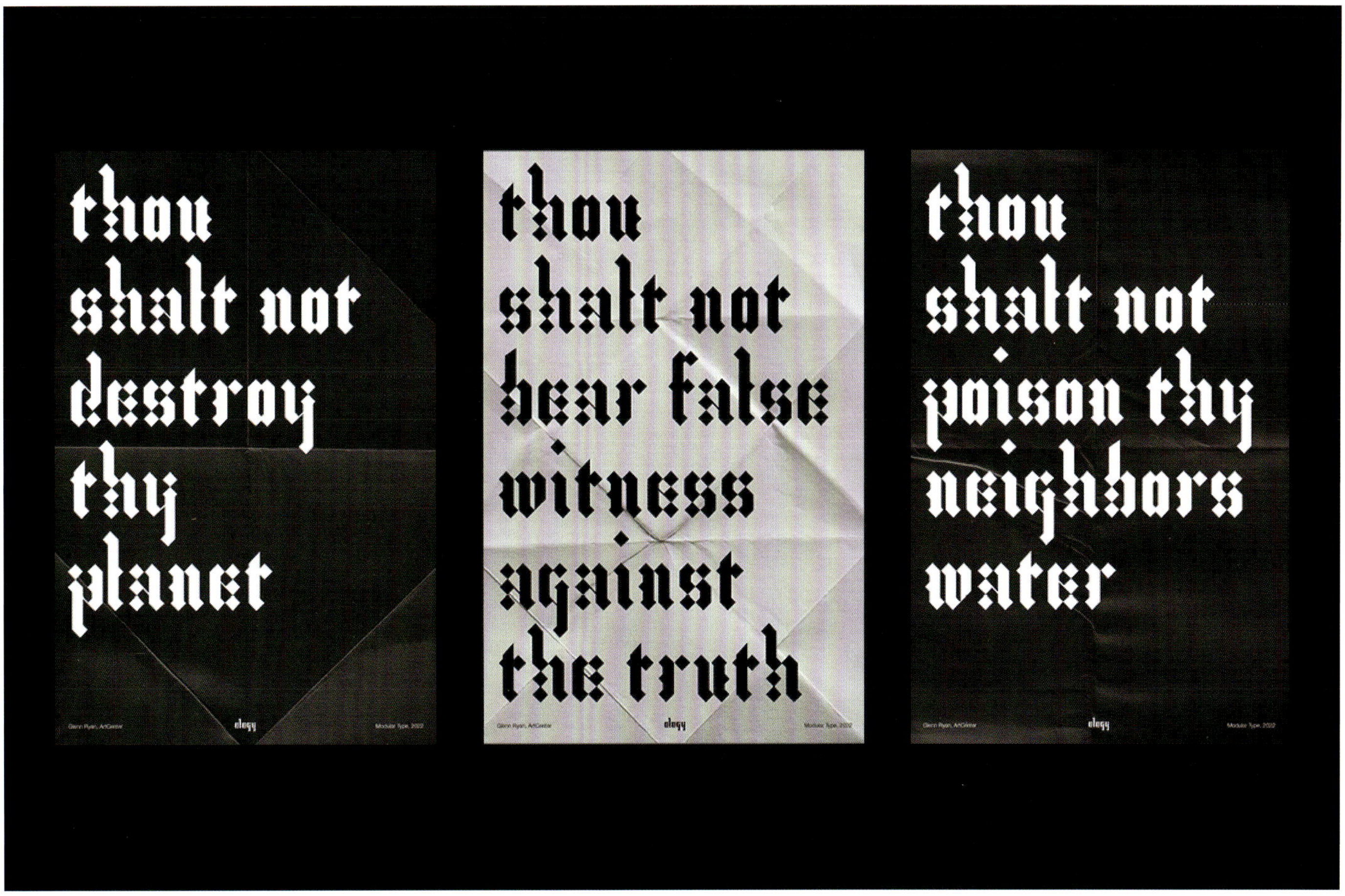

Student: Glenn Ryan | School: ArtCenter College of Design

INSTRUCTOR NATASHA JEN

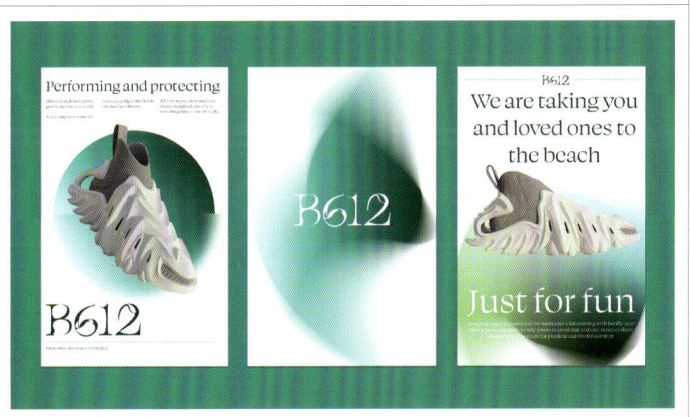

Student: Ipshita Krishan | School: School of Visual Arts

INSTRUCTORS KEN DEEGAN, BRANKICA HARVEY

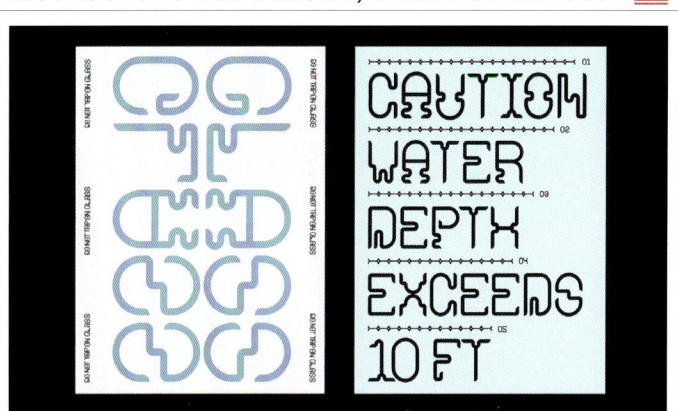

Student: Jennifer Han | School: School of Visual Arts

INSTRUCTOR ZIPENG ZHU

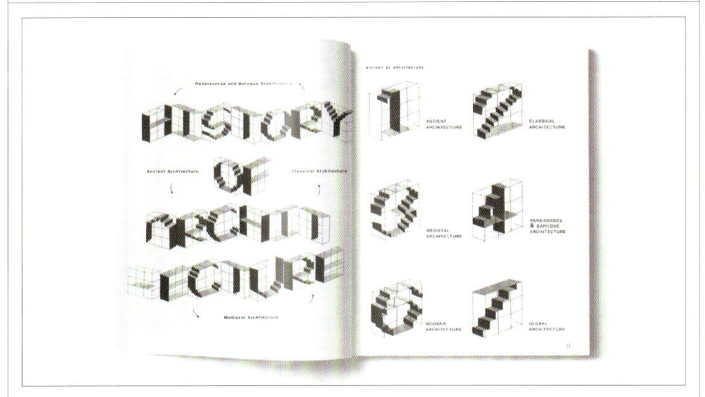

Student: Yubin Won
School: School of Visual Arts

INSTRUCTOR MUHAMMAD RAHMAN

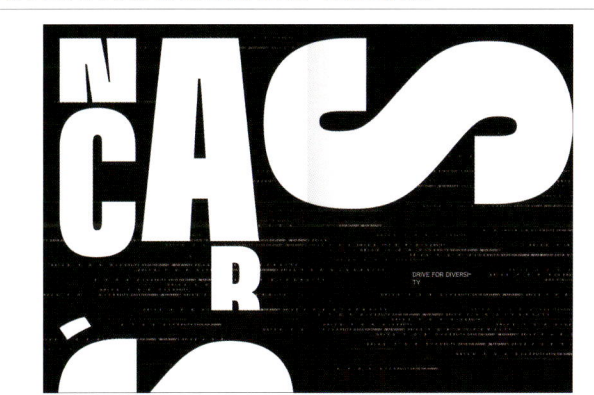

Student: Sophia Paroz | School: University of Cincinnati DAAP, Myron E. Ullman Jr. School of Design

Typography | Design

214 DESIGN SILVER

INSTRUCTOR JUSTIN COLT 🇺🇸

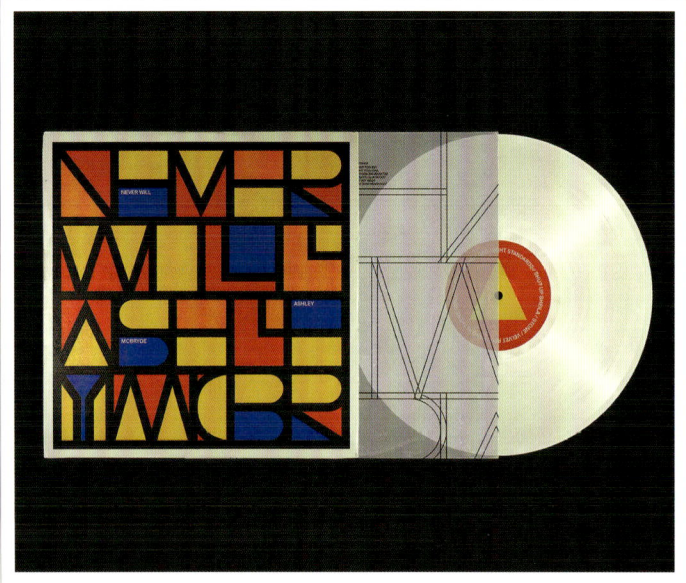

Student: Rabiya Gupta | **School:** School of Visual Arts

INSTRUCTOR SARAH WOOD 🇺🇸

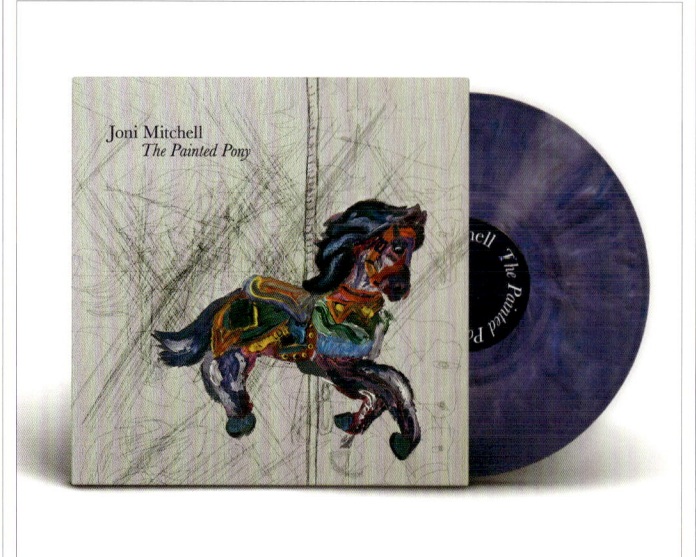

Student: Harper Herman | **School:** M.AD School of Ideas New York

INSTRUCTOR ANNE JORDAN 🇺🇸

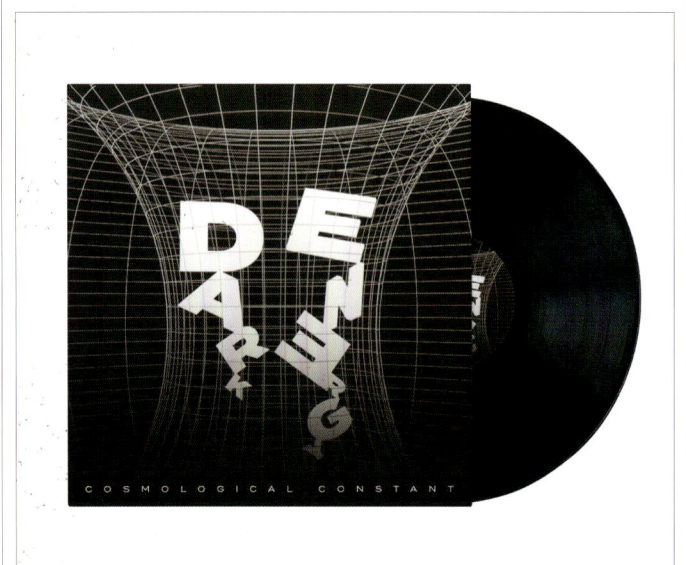

Student: Eshaan Sojatia | **School:** Rochester Institute of Technology

INSTRUCTOR PETER AHLBERG 🇺🇸

Student: Yubin Won | **School:** School of Visual Arts

INSTRUCTOR PETER AHLBERG 🇺🇸

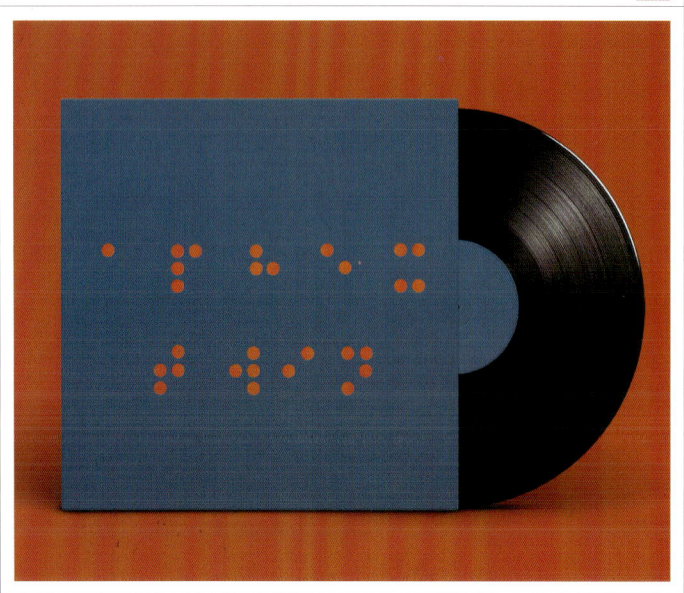

Student: Adya Jatia | **School:** School of Visual Arts

INSTRUCTOR SEAN ADAMS 🇺🇸

Student: Jo Iijima | **School:** ArtCenter College of Design

Design | Vinyl

215 DESIGN SILVER

INSTRUCTOR MAURIZIO MASI

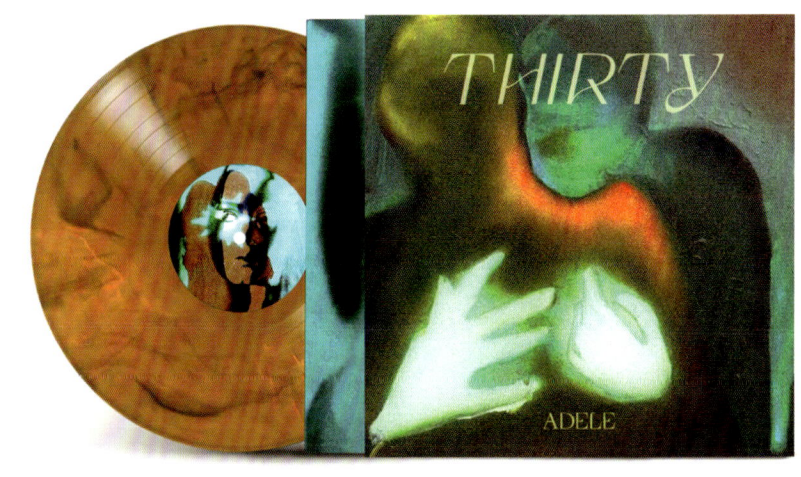
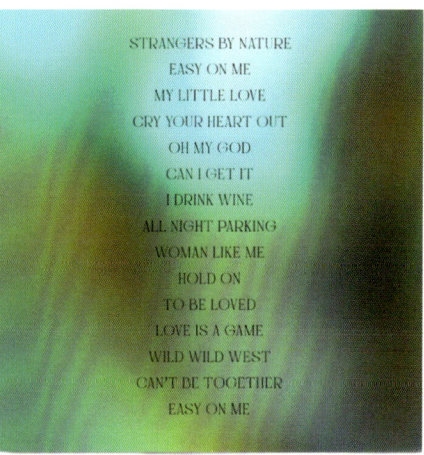

Student: Charlotte Cooper | **School:** Lehigh University

INSTRUCTOR MAURIZIO MASI

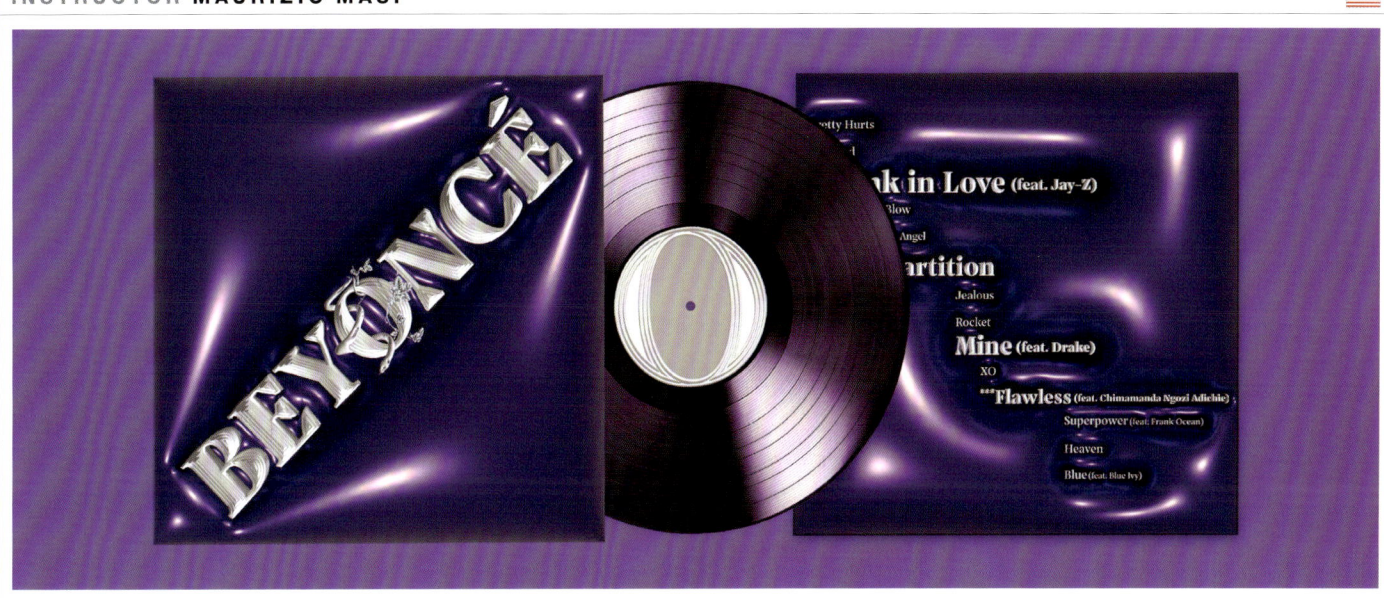

Student: Zoe LeiLi | **School:** Lehigh University

INSTRUCTOR PETER AHLBERG

Student: Keumbie Hwang | **School:** School of Visual Arts

Vinyl | Design

Design Film/Video

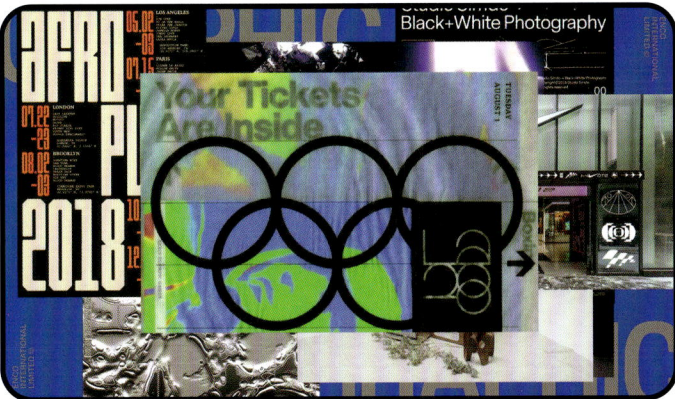
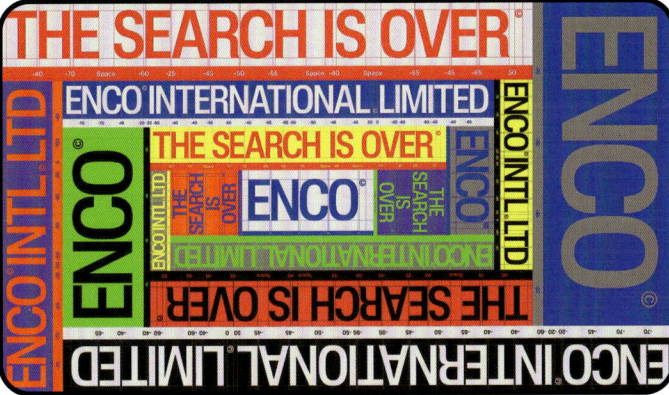
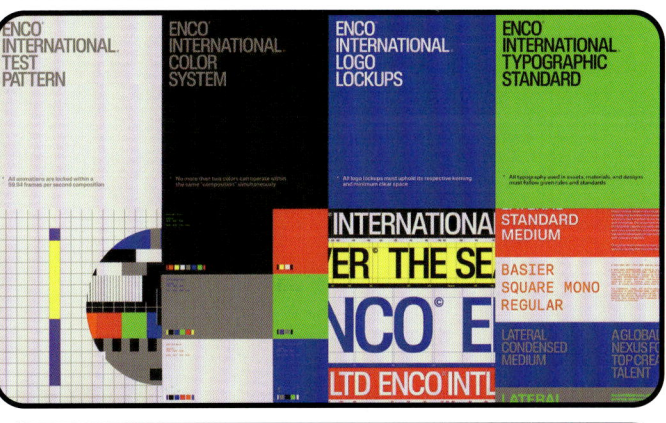
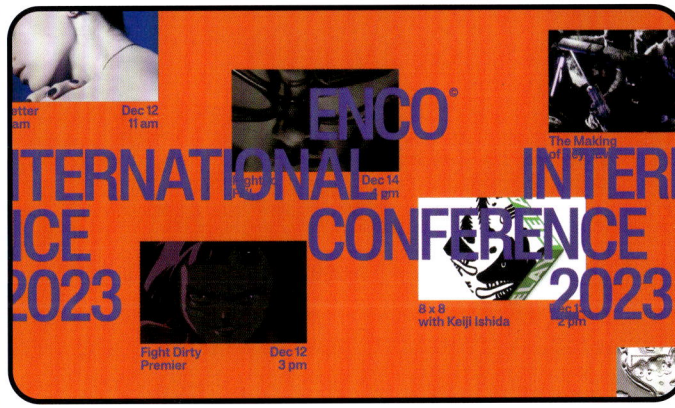
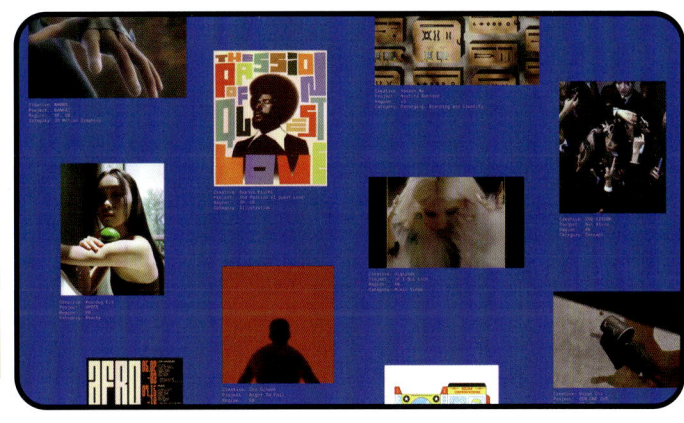

P247: Credit & Commentary   **Student:** Alan Xu | **School:** ArtCenter College of Design

Assignment: Rebrand an existing institution and showcase its new brand and identity through a 60 seconds or shorter motion montage.
Approach: The initial brand identity was inconsistent and lacked visual impact. The rebranding introduces a dynamic and engaging identity system.
Results: The project was a great success. Both my professor and classmates felt that the rebrand was able to breathe new life into ENCO.

Motion Graphics | Design Film/Video

218 DESIGN FILM/VIDEO GOLD

INSTRUCTOR RAPHAEL ZAMMIT

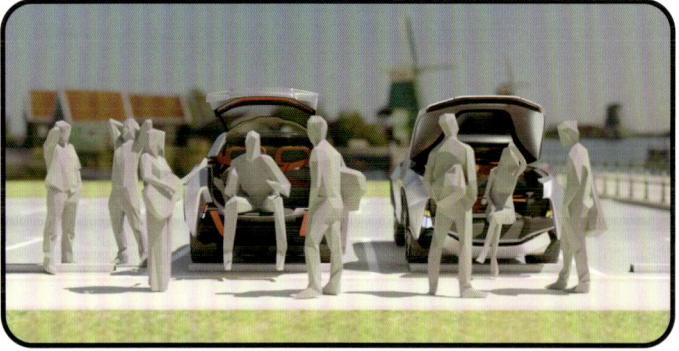
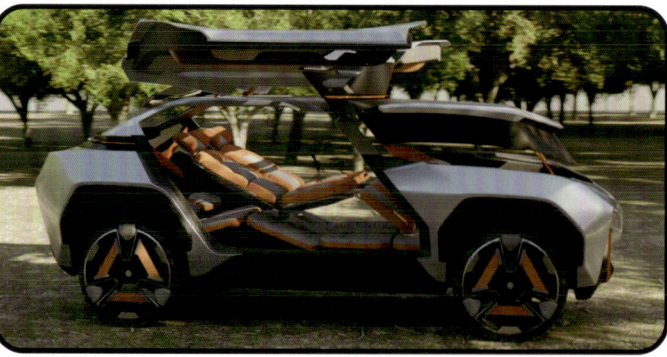

Student: Hung-Wei Lin
School: College for Creative Studies
P247: Credit & Commentary

INSTRUCTOR RAPHAEL ZAMMIT

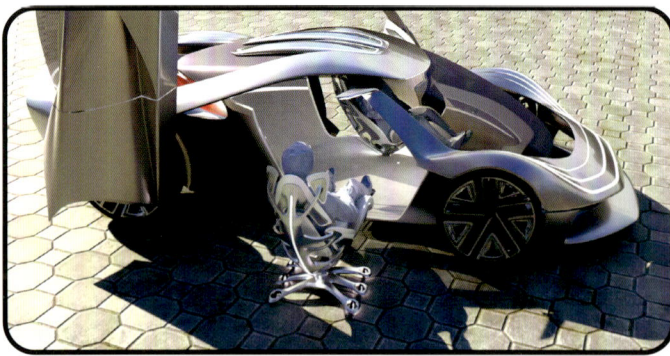
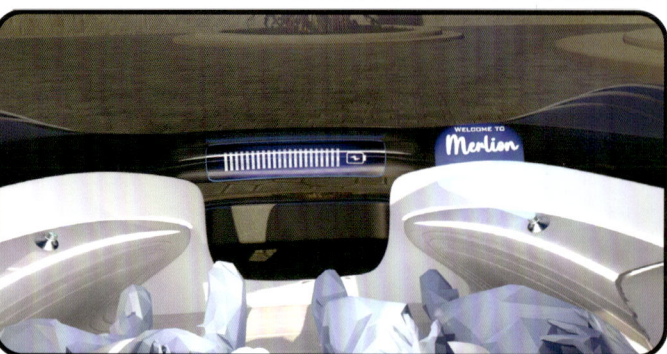

Student: James Shiels
School: College for Creative Studies
P247: Credit & Commentary

INSTRUCTOR MIGUEL LEE

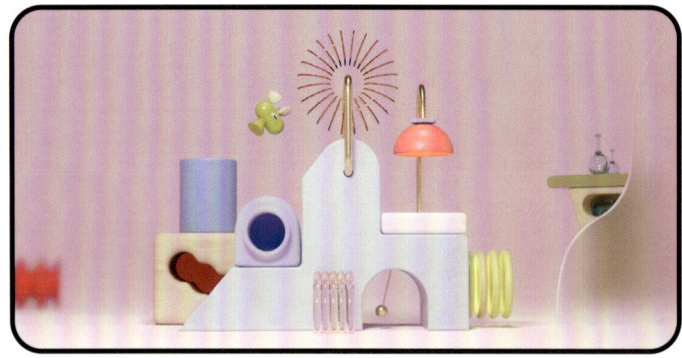
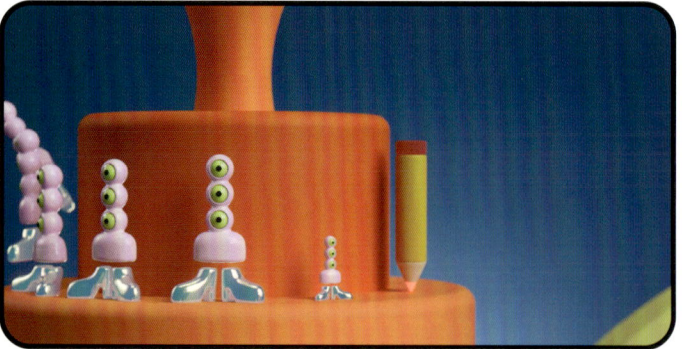

Student: Jamie Kim
School: ArtCenter College of Design
P247: Credit & Commentary

INSTRUCTOR NICOLE ZIZILA

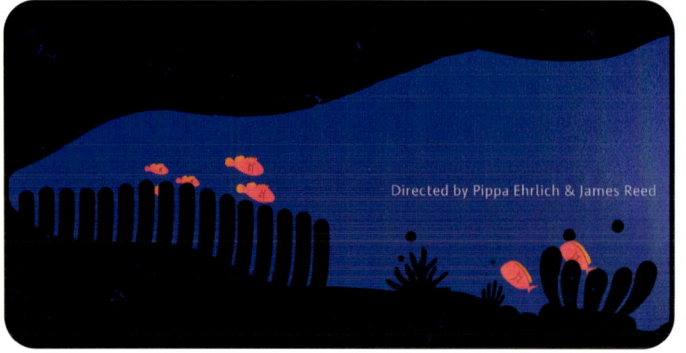
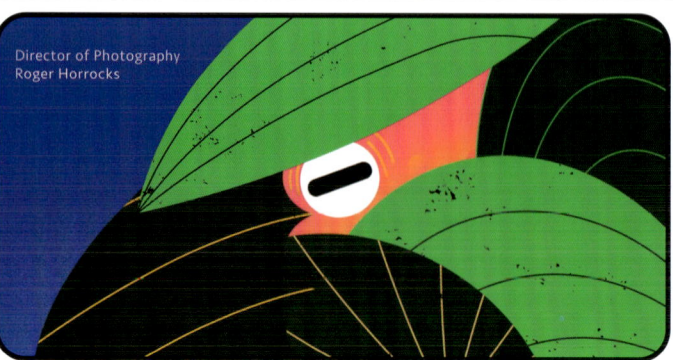

Student: Yong Han Shin
School: Fashion Institute of Technology
P247: Credit & Commentary

Design Film/Video | Film Title

219 DESIGN FILM/VIDEO GOLD

INSTRUCTOR YOSHIKO BURKE

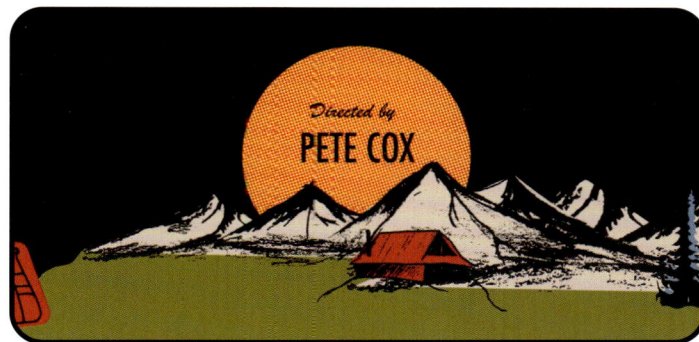
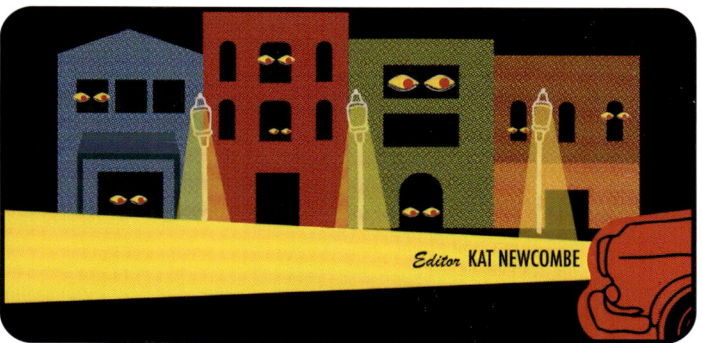

Student: Katherine Newcombe
School: University of Cincinnati DAAP, Myron E. Ullman Jr. School of Design
P247: Credit & Commentary

INSTRUCTOR MATT NORMAND

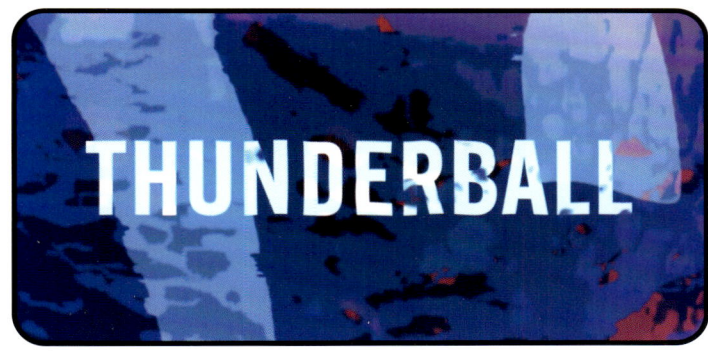
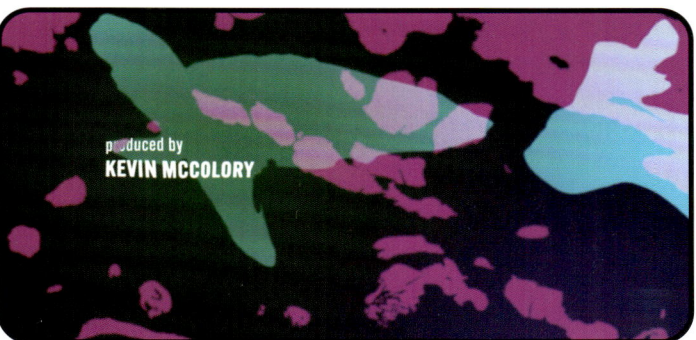

Student: Ella Balhoff
School: Loyola University New Orleans
P247: Credit & Commentary

INSTRUCTORS ROY TATUM, BRAD BARTLETT

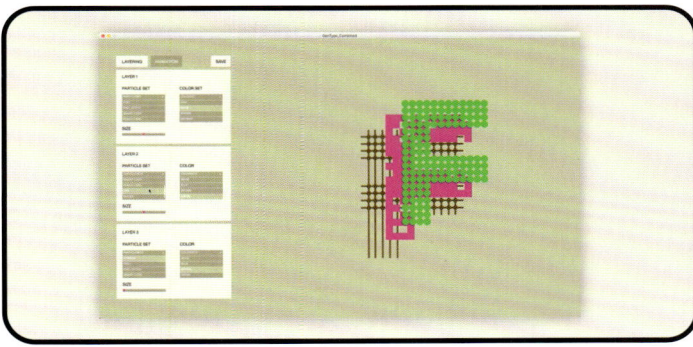
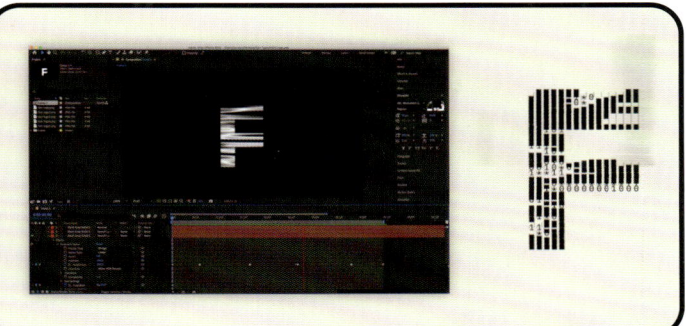

Student: Jocelyn Ziying Zhao
School: ArtCenter College of Design
P247: Credit & Commentary

INSTRUCTORS BRAD BARTLETT, IVAN CRUZ, MILES MAZZIE

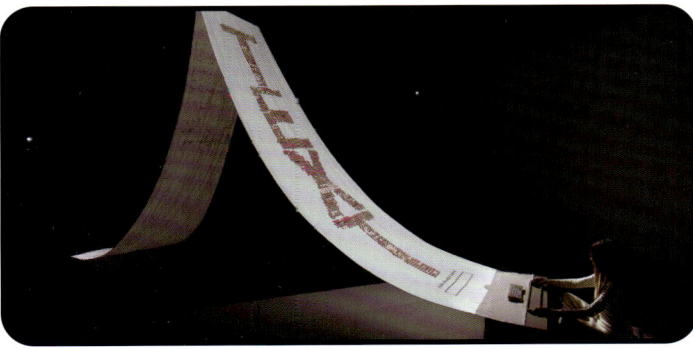
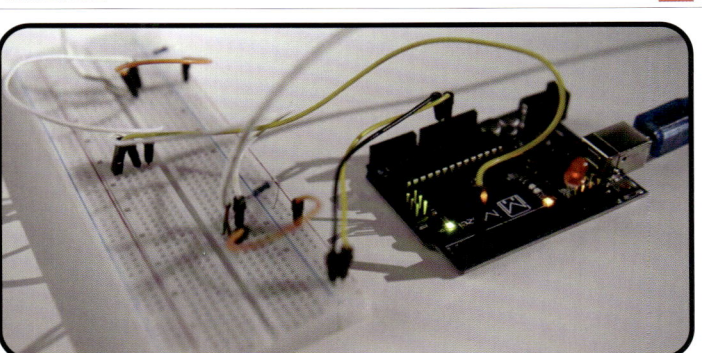

Student: Jocelyn Ziying Zhao
School: ArtCenter College of Design
P247: Credit & Commentary

Film Title, Interactive | Design Film/Video

220 DESIGN FILM/VIDEO GOLD

INSTRUCTOR MING TAI

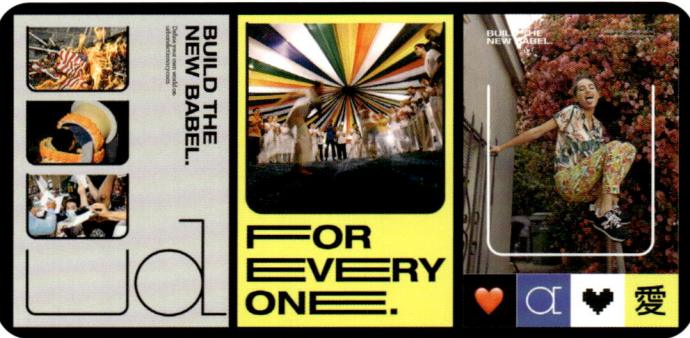

Student: Yuqin Ni
School: ArtCenter College of Design
P247: Credit & Commentary

INSTRUCTOR MING TAI

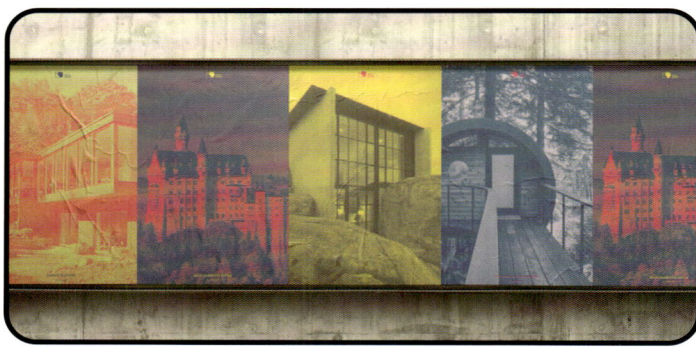
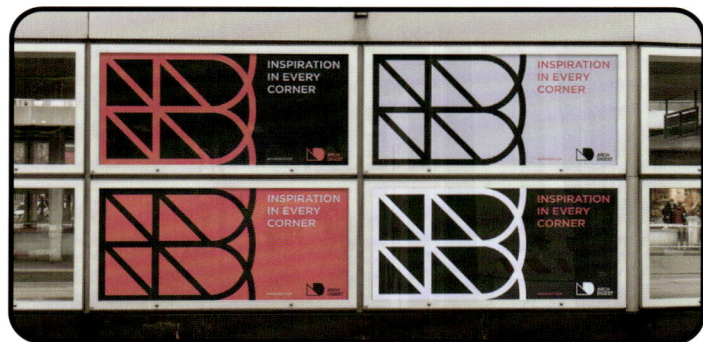

Student: Mishen Liu
School: ArtCenter College of Design
P247: Credit & Commentary

INSTRUCTOR JEREMY HOLMES

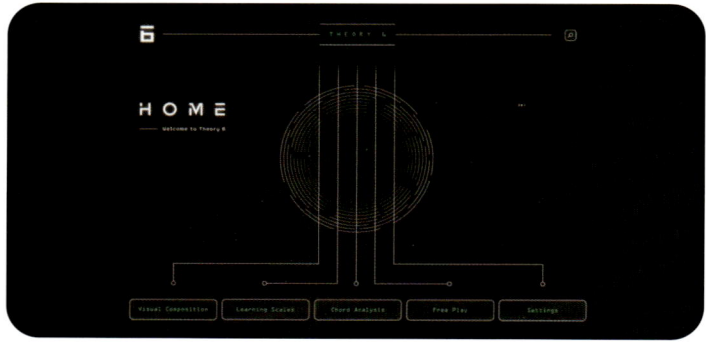
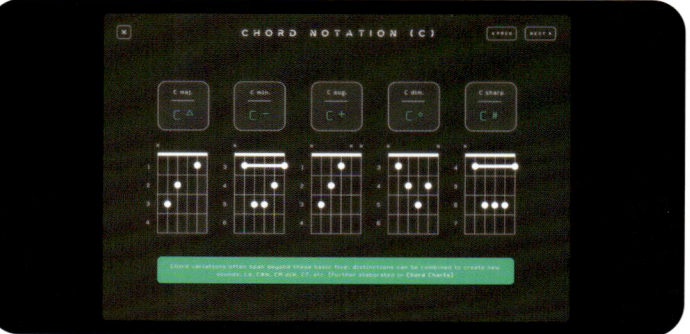

Student: Tully Ryan
School: West Chester University
P247: Credit & Commentary

INSTRUCTOR KAREN WATKINS

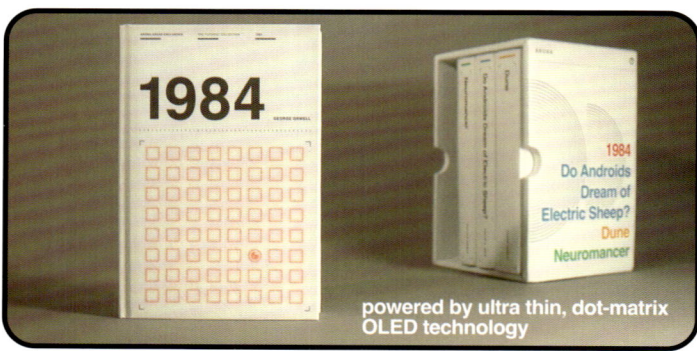
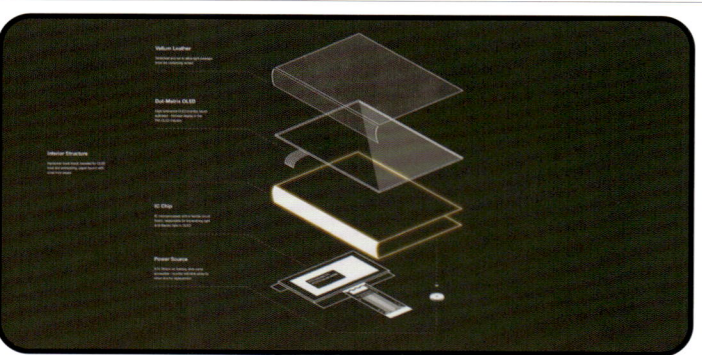

Student: Tully Ryan
School: West Chester University
P247: Credit & Commentary

Design Film/Video | Interactive

221 DESIGN FILM/VIDEO GOLD

INSTRUCTOR CHRISTIE SHIN

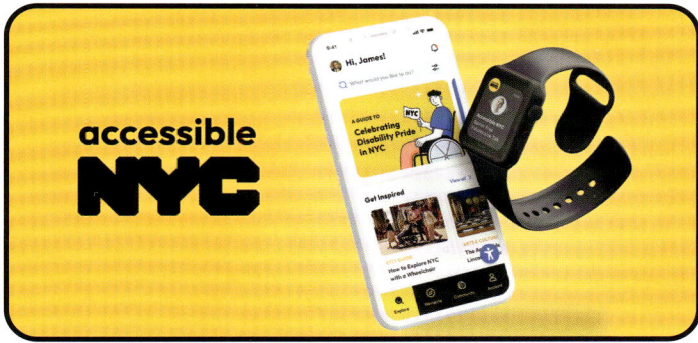
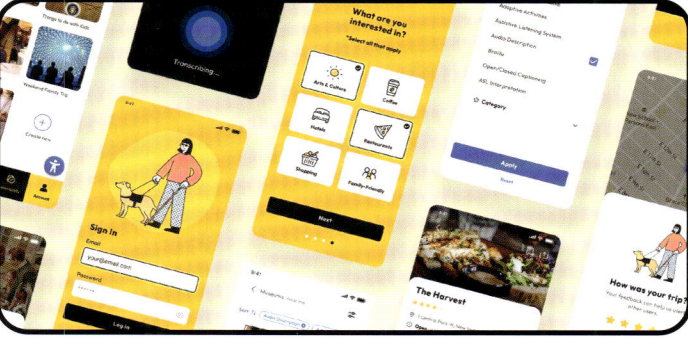

Students: Sara Park, Mariko Dreifuss, Yoojin Song
School: Fashion Institute of Technology
P247: Credit & Commentary

INSTRUCTOR ERIC GILLETT

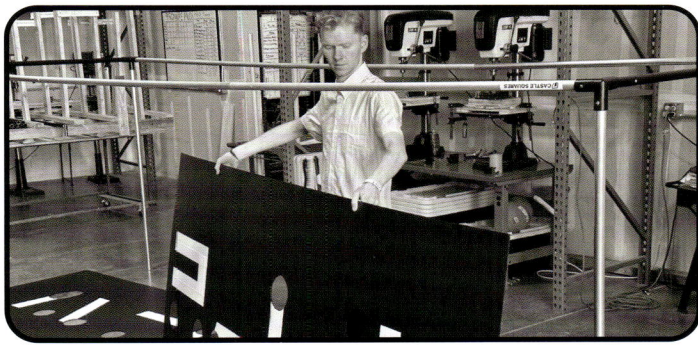
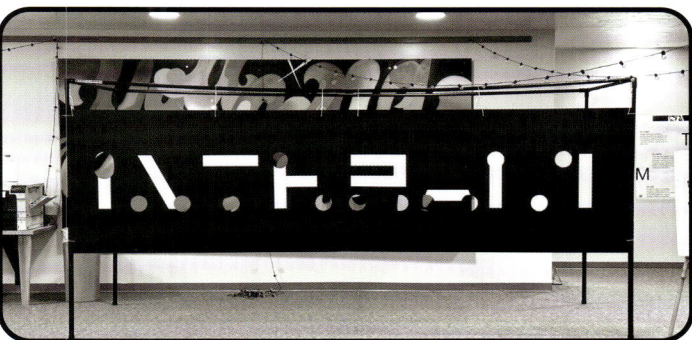

Student: Brett Hilton
School: Brigham Young University
P247: Credit & Commentary

INSTRUCTOR HOON-DONG CHUNG

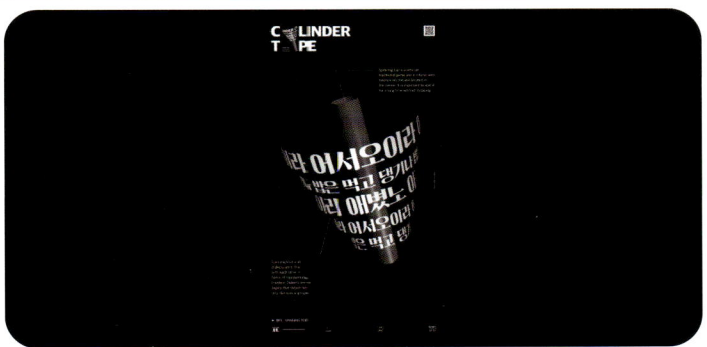
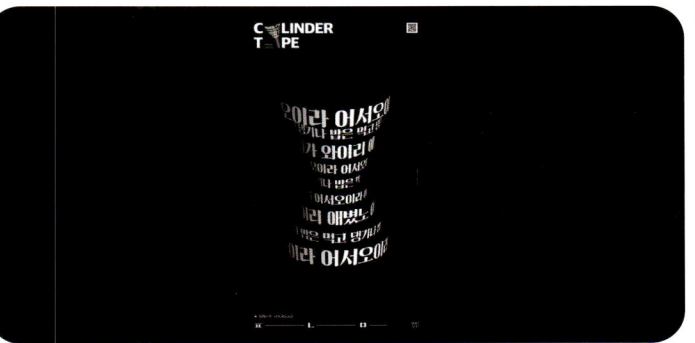

Student: Sumin Kwon
School: Dankook University
P247: Credit & Commentary

INSTRUCTOR HOON-DONG CHUNG

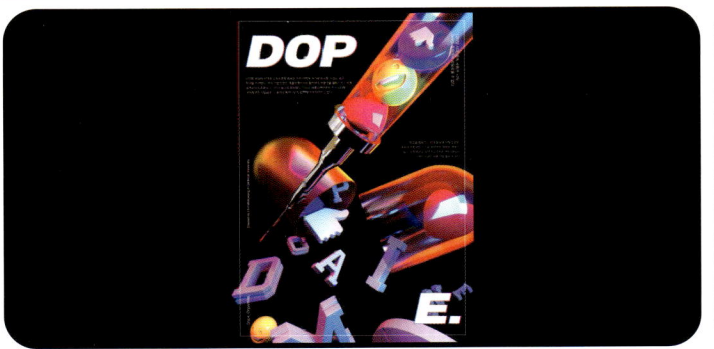
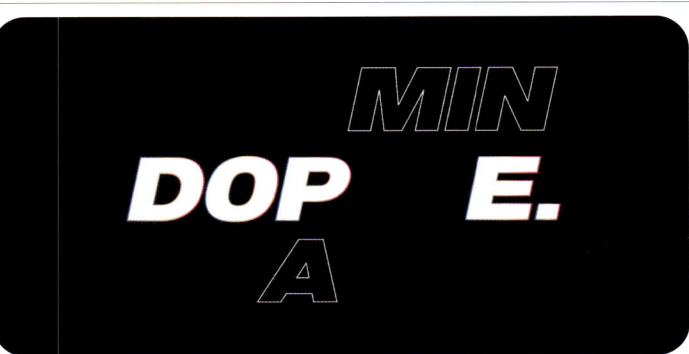

Student: Minkyeong Cho
School: Dankook University
P247: Credit & Commentary

222 DESIGN FILM/VIDEO GOLD

INSTRUCTOR **GREG LEE**

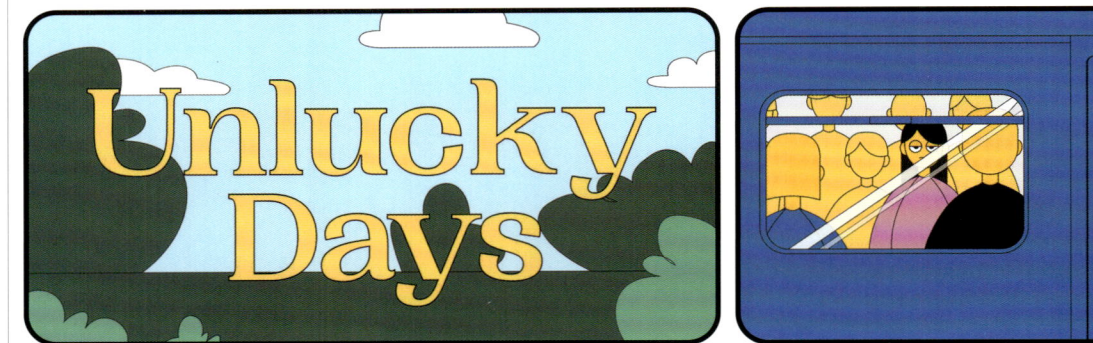
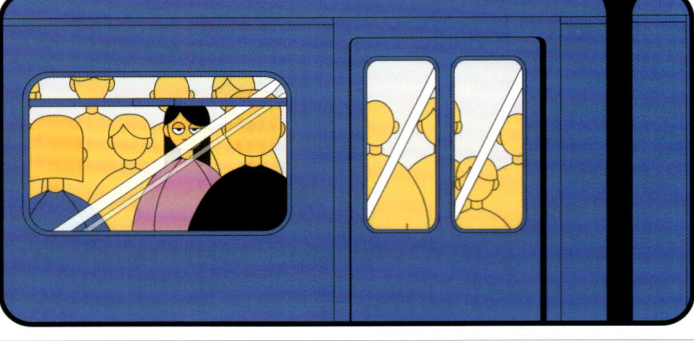

Student: Jennifer Han
School: School of Visual Arts
P248: Credit & Commentary

INSTRUCTOR **BRENT MCMAHAN**

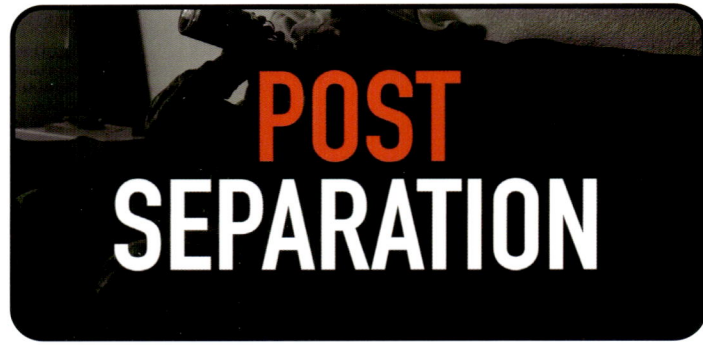
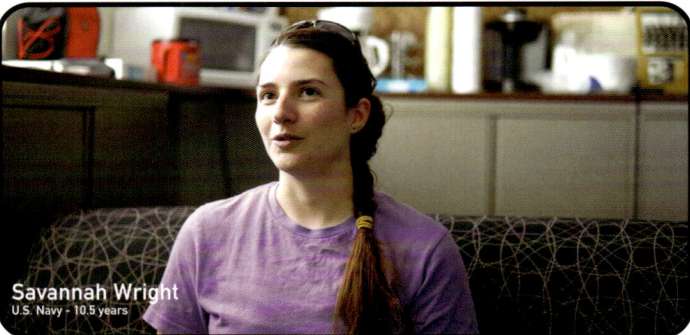

Student: Tyler Holloway
School: Texas A&M University-Commerce
P248: Credit & Commentary

INSTRUCTORS **GAEL TOWEY, STEPHEN DOYLE**

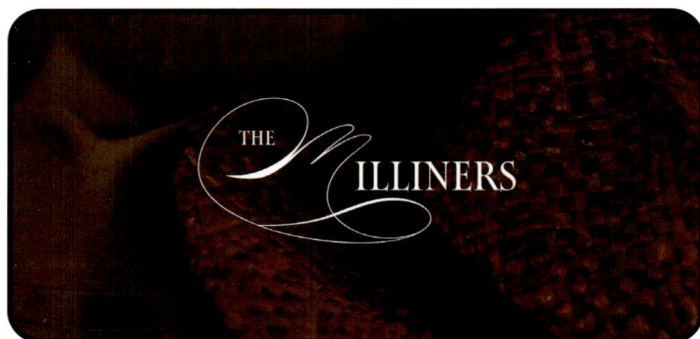
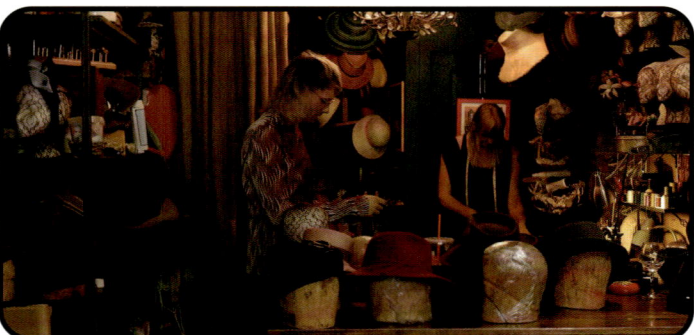

Student: Mingxin Cheng
School: School of Visual Arts
P248: Credit & Commentary

INSTRUCTOR **YOSHIKO BURKE**

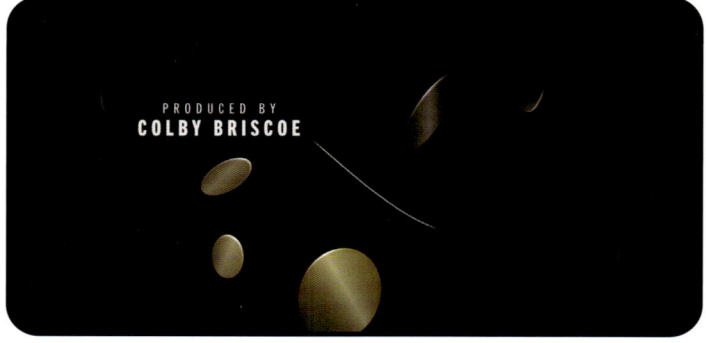
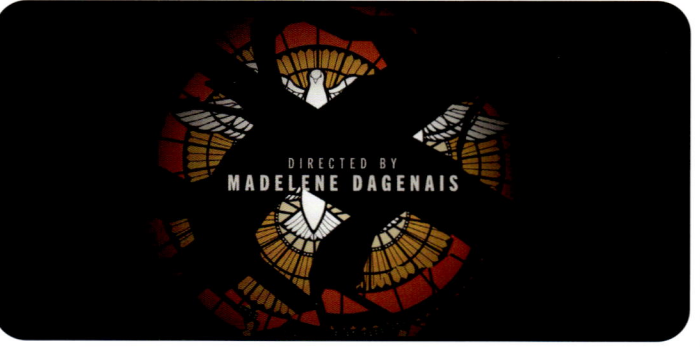

Student: Brady Rudisill
School: University of Cincinnati DAAP, Myron E. Ullman Jr. School of Design
P248: Credit & Commentary

Design Film/Video | Motion Graphics, Short Films, TV Titles

223 DESIGN FILM/VIDEO SILVER

INSTRUCTOR MIGUEL LEE 🇺🇸

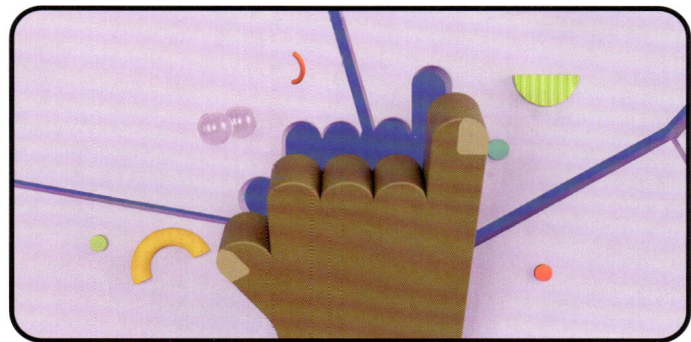

Student: Jamie Kim
School: ArtCenter College of Design

INSTRUCTOR JEFF GARLAND 🇺🇸

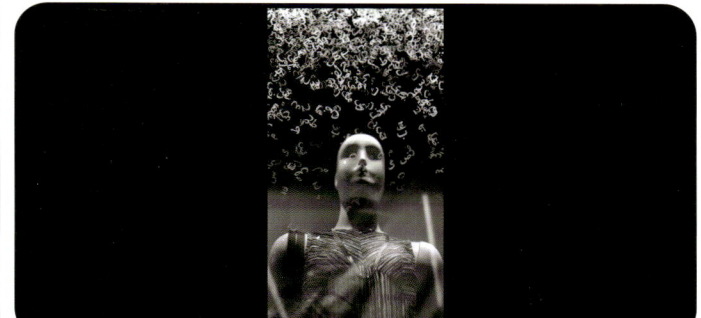

Student: Mona Gandomkar
School: Georgia Southern University

INSTRUCTOR ANDREJ KAMNIK 🇸🇮

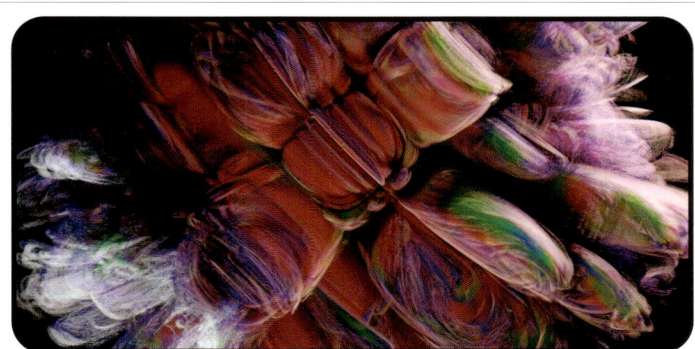

Student: Strahinja Jovanović
School: University of Ljubljana, Academy of Fine Arts & Design

INSTRUCTOR JEREMY HOLMES 🇺🇸

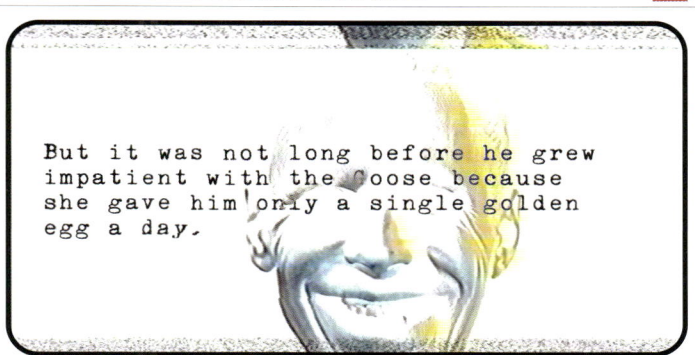

Student: Ryan McMullen
School: West Chester University

INSTRUCTOR HANK RICHARDSON 🇺🇸

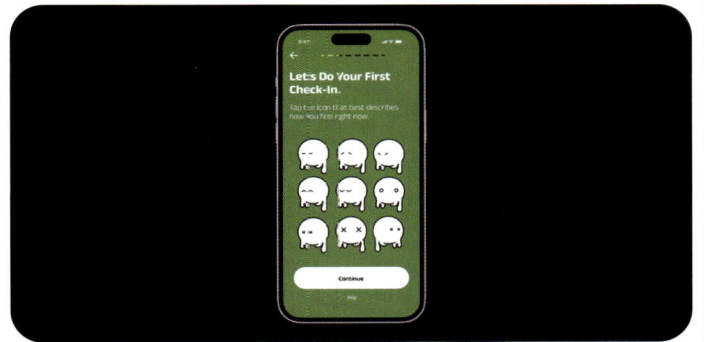

Student: Emily Jeffrey
School: M.AD School of Ideas Atlanta

INSTRUCTOR DAVID CONKLIN 🇺🇸

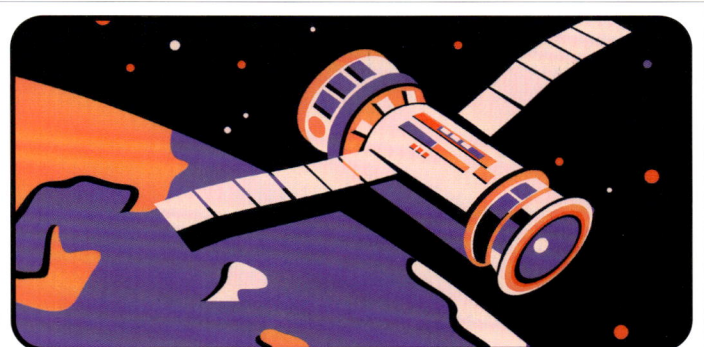

Student: Jiyoon Kim
School: School of Visual Arts

INSTRUCTOR DAVID WOLSKE 🇺🇸

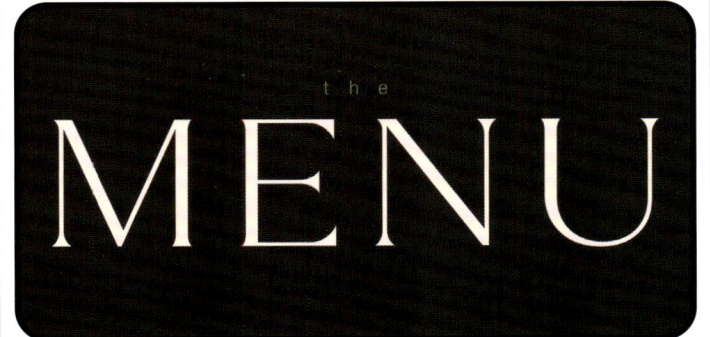

Student: Keaton Dillard
School: University of North Texas

INSTRUCTOR YOSHIKO BURKE 🇺🇸

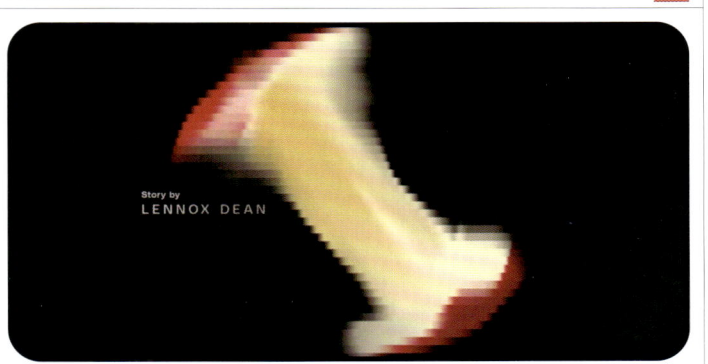

Student: Em Humphress
School: University of Cincinnati DAAP, Myron E. Ullman Jr. School of Design

Animation, Film Title | Design Film/Video

224 DESIGN FILM/VIDEO **SILVER**

INSTRUCTOR DAVID WOLSKE

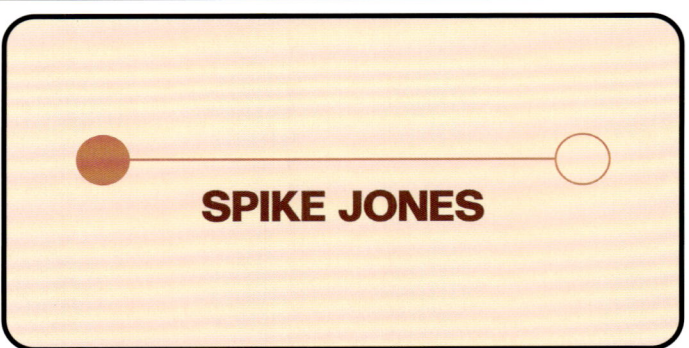

Student: Andrea Torrijos
School: University of North Texas

INSTRUCTOR MATT NORMAND

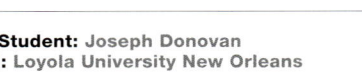

Student: Joseph Donovan
School: Loyola University New Orleans

INSTRUCTOR UNATTRIBUTED

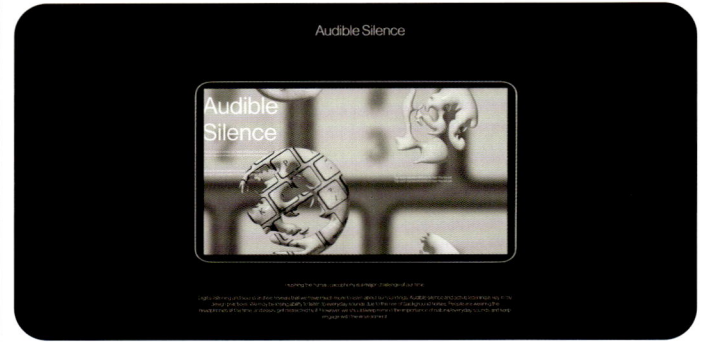

Student: Michelle Kim
School: Pratt Institute

INSTRUCTOR JEREMY HOLMES

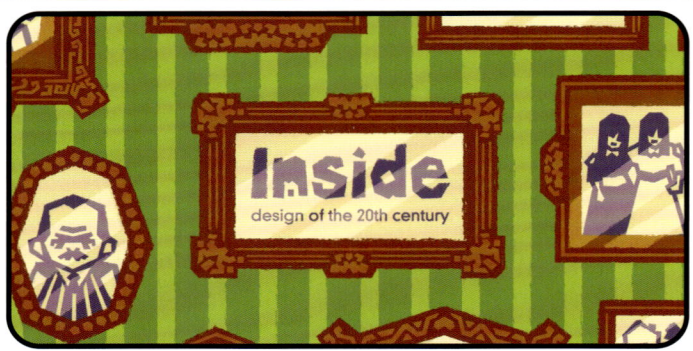

Student: Emily Simon
School: West Chester University

INSTRUCTOR YVONNE CAO

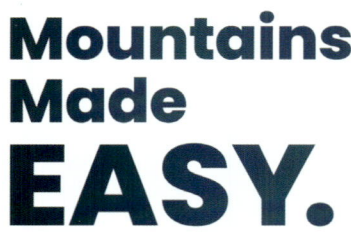

Student: Brooke Budde
School: Texas Christian University

INSTRUCTORS RANDY ELLES, JOSEPH STALUPPI

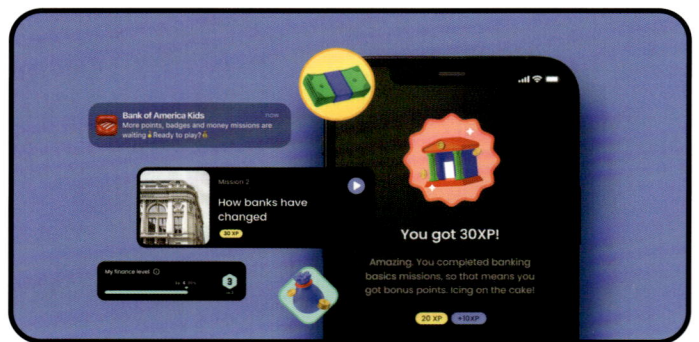

Student: Yoojin Song
School: Fashion Institute of Technology

INSTRUCTOR ALICE LEE

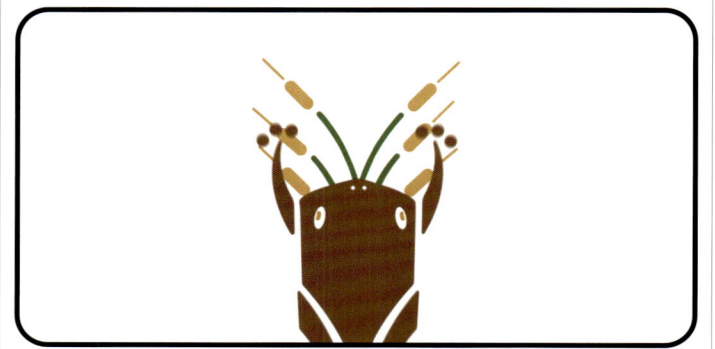

Student: Nick Voss
School: Texas State University

INSTRUCTOR RAPHAEL ZAMMIT

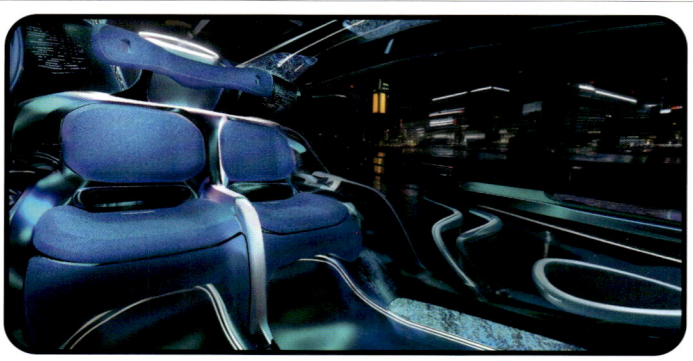

Student: Xuze Jin
School: College for Creative Studies

Design Film/Video | Film Title, Interactive, Logo Animation, Motion Graphics

225 DESIGN FILM/VIDEO SILVER

INSTRUCTOR ANDREA QUAM
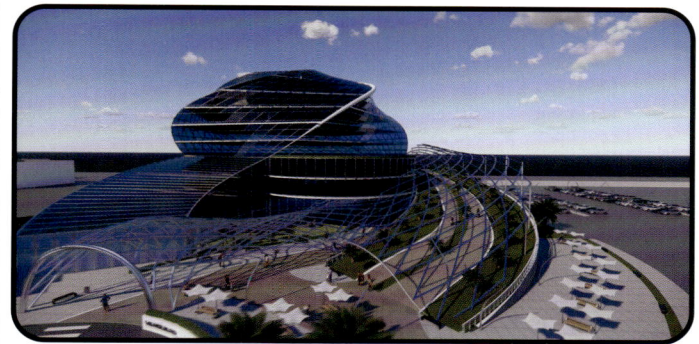
Student: Delaney Golden
School: Iowa State University

INSTRUCTOR DAVID CONKLIN
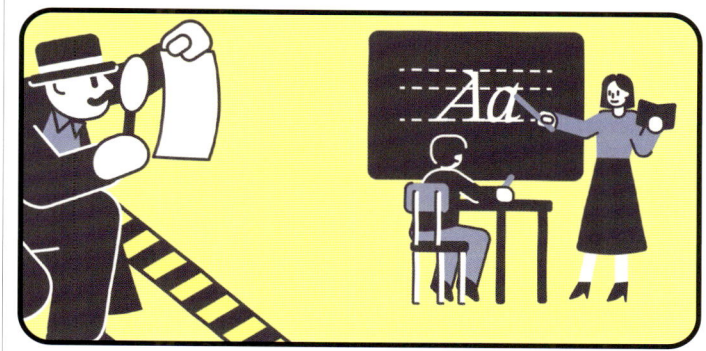
Student: Roy Kim
School: School of Visual Arts

INSTRUCTOR KAREN WATKINS
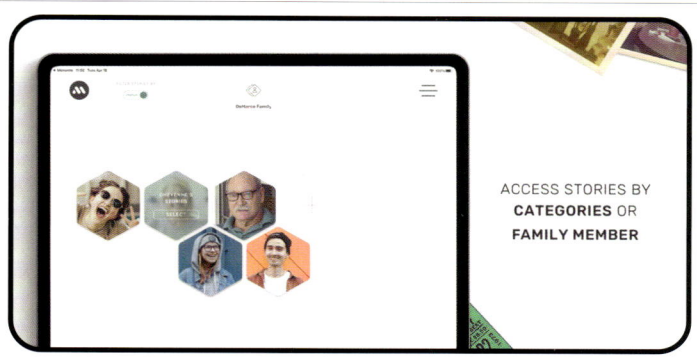
Student: Jimmy Hall
School: West Chester University

INSTRUCTOR LINDA REYNOLDS
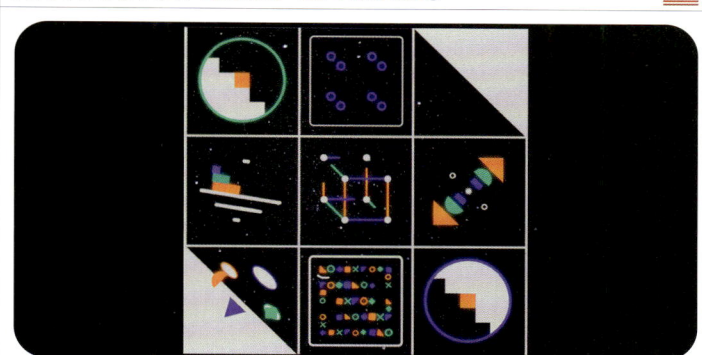
Student: Luke Miller
School: Brigham Young University

INSTRUCTOR GREG LEE
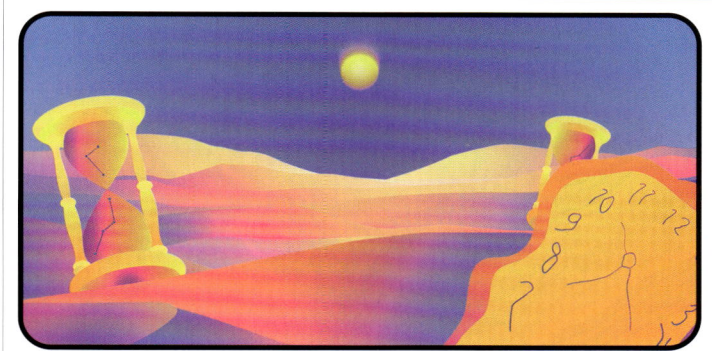
Student: Keumbie Hwang
School: School of Visual Arts

INSTRUCTOR HOON-DONG CHUNG
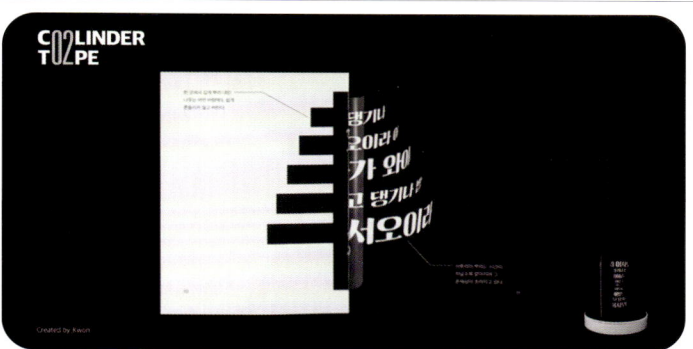
Student: Sumin Kwon
School: Dankook University

INSTRUCTOR DOUG THOMAS
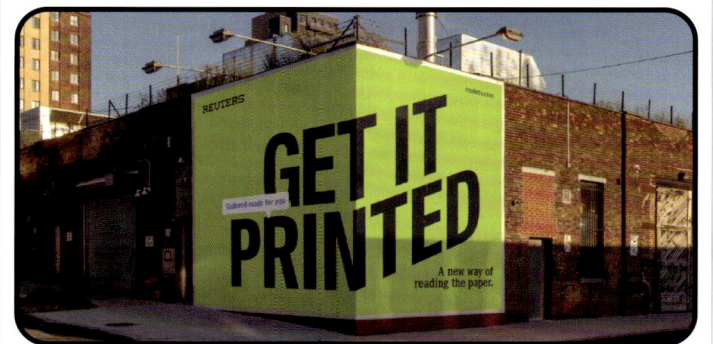
Student: Juan Pablo Gutierrez Hurtado
School: Brigham Young University

INSTRUCTOR GREG LEE
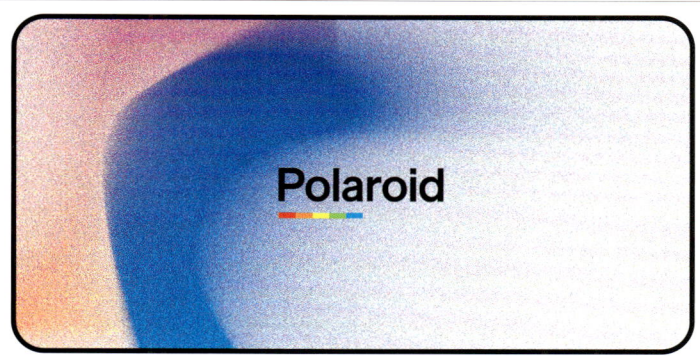
Student: Keumbie Hwang
School: School of Visual Arts

Motion Graphics | Design Film/Video

226 DESIGN FILM/VIDEO SILVER

INSTRUCTOR HANK RICHARDSON

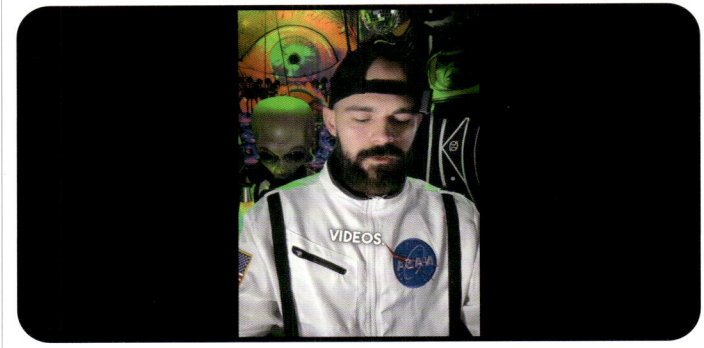

Student: Arthur Flaksman
School: M.AD School of Ideas Atlanta

INSTRUCTOR ANDREI DAN

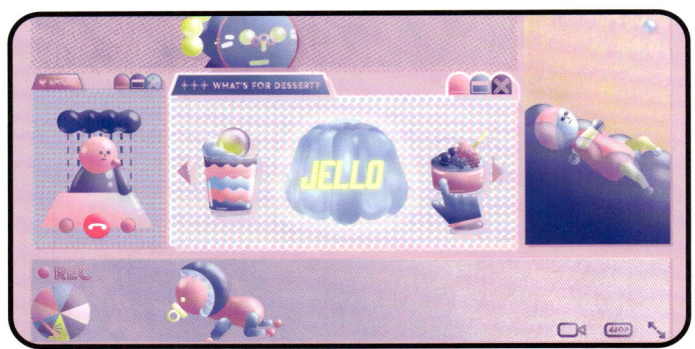

Student: Diexin Yu
School: School of Visual Arts

INSTRUCTOR LINDA REYNOLDS

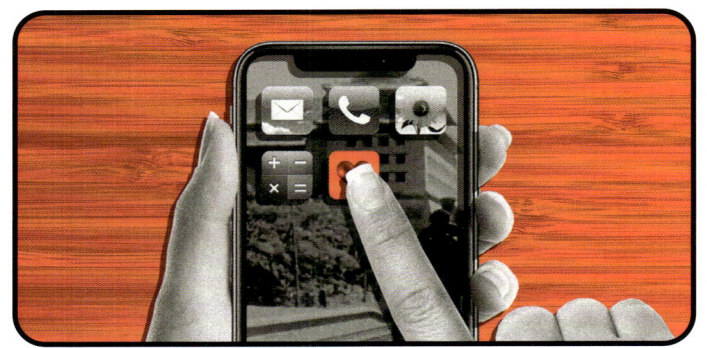

Student: Brett Hilton
School: Brigham Young University

INSTRUCTOR FAIYAZ JAFRI

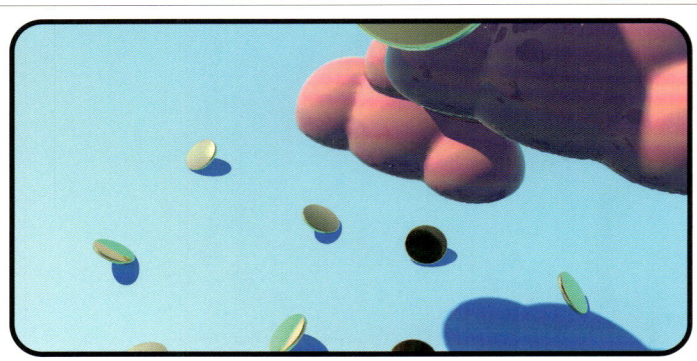

Student: Shristi Singh
School: Parsons School of Design

INSTRUCTORS BRAD BARTLETT, MILES MAZZIE

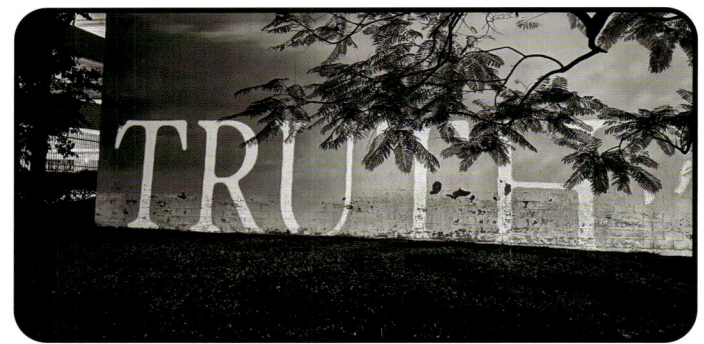

Student: Veronica Tsai
School: ArtCenter College of Design

INSTRUCTOR HANK RICHARDSON

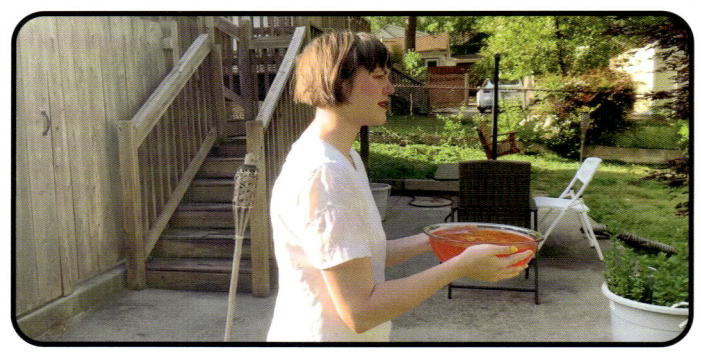

Student: Anna LeBer
School: M.AD School of Ideas Atlanta

INSTRUCTOR YOSHIKO BURKE

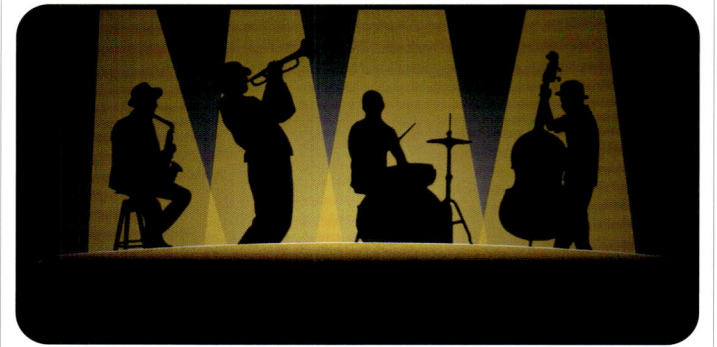

Student: Frankie Matthews
School: University of Cincinnati DAAP, Myron E. Ullman Jr. School of Design

INSTRUCTOR YOSHIKO BURKE

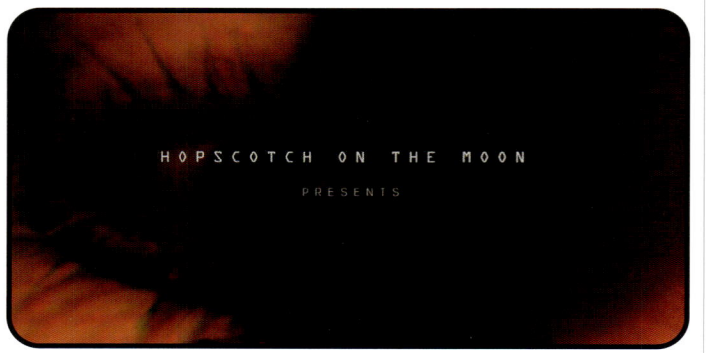

Student: Nova Ostermann
School: University of Cincinnati DAAP, Myron E. Ullman Jr. School of Design

Design Film/Video | Motion Graphics, Music Videos, Short Films, TV Titles

Photography Gold Awards

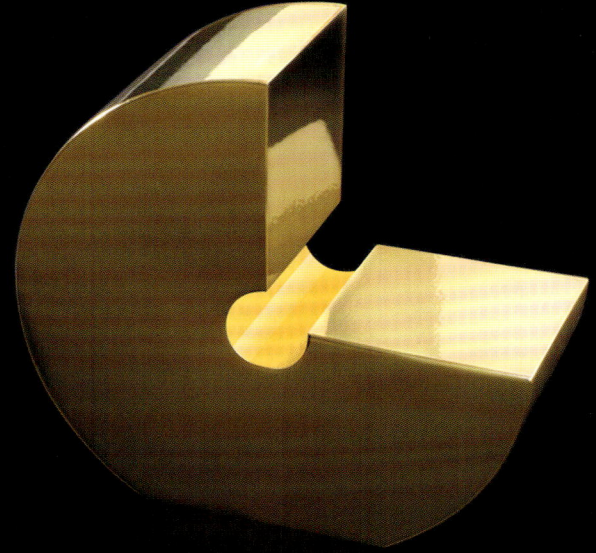

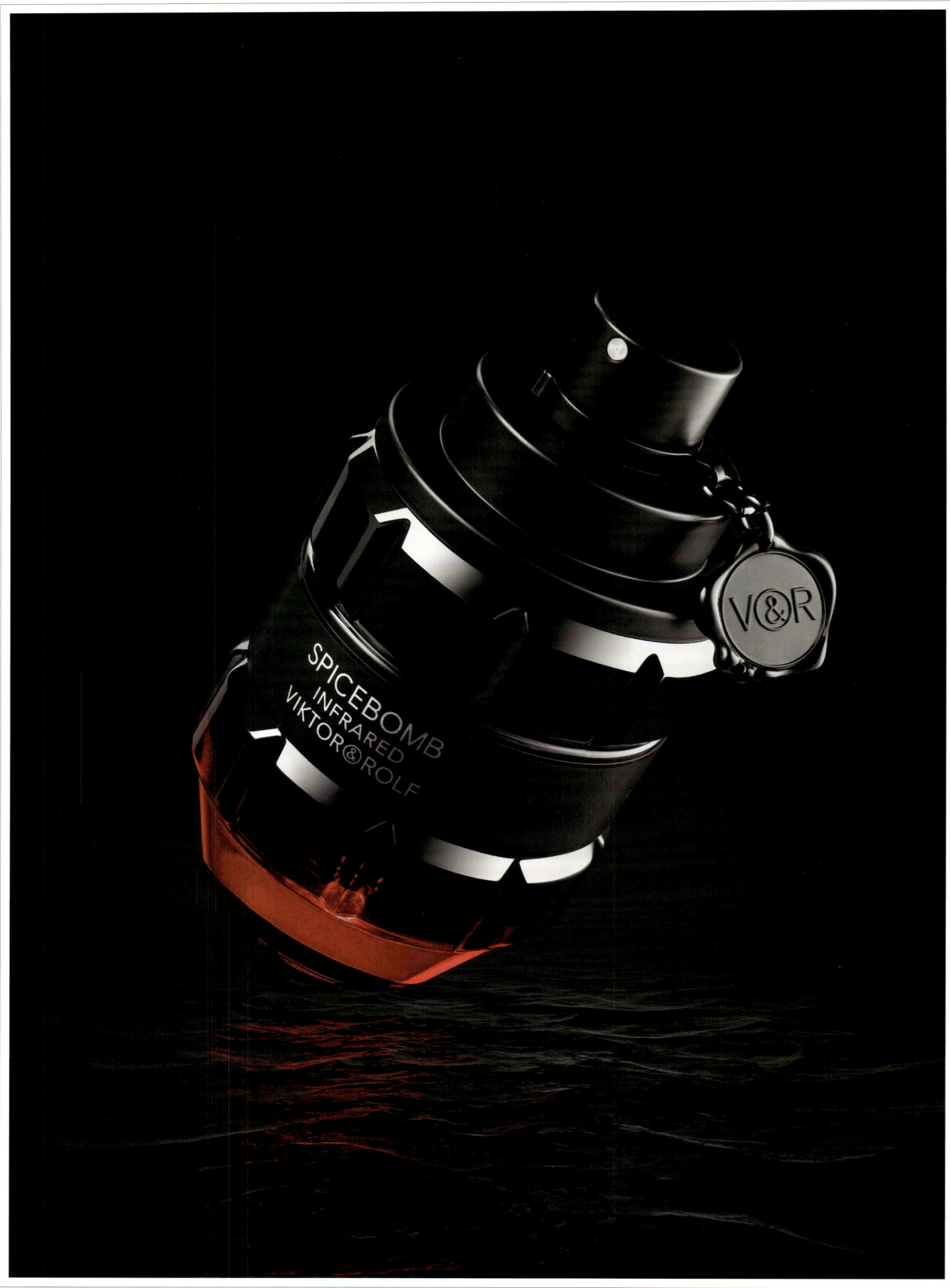

Photography Silver Awards

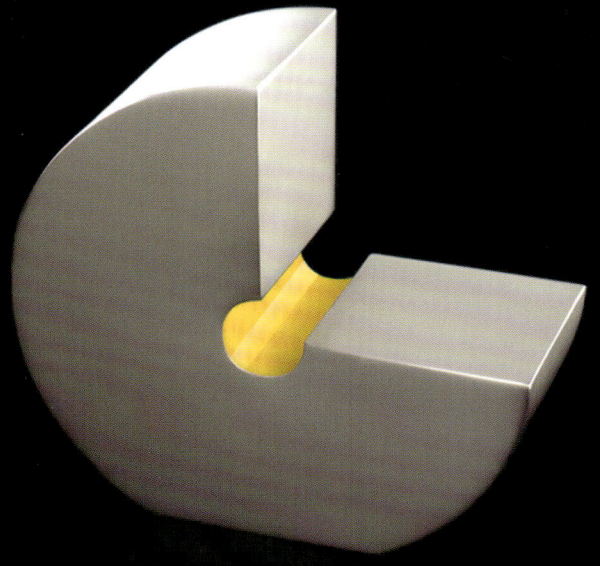

230 PHOTOGRAPHY SILVER

INSTRUCTOR DEJAN MRAOVIĆ

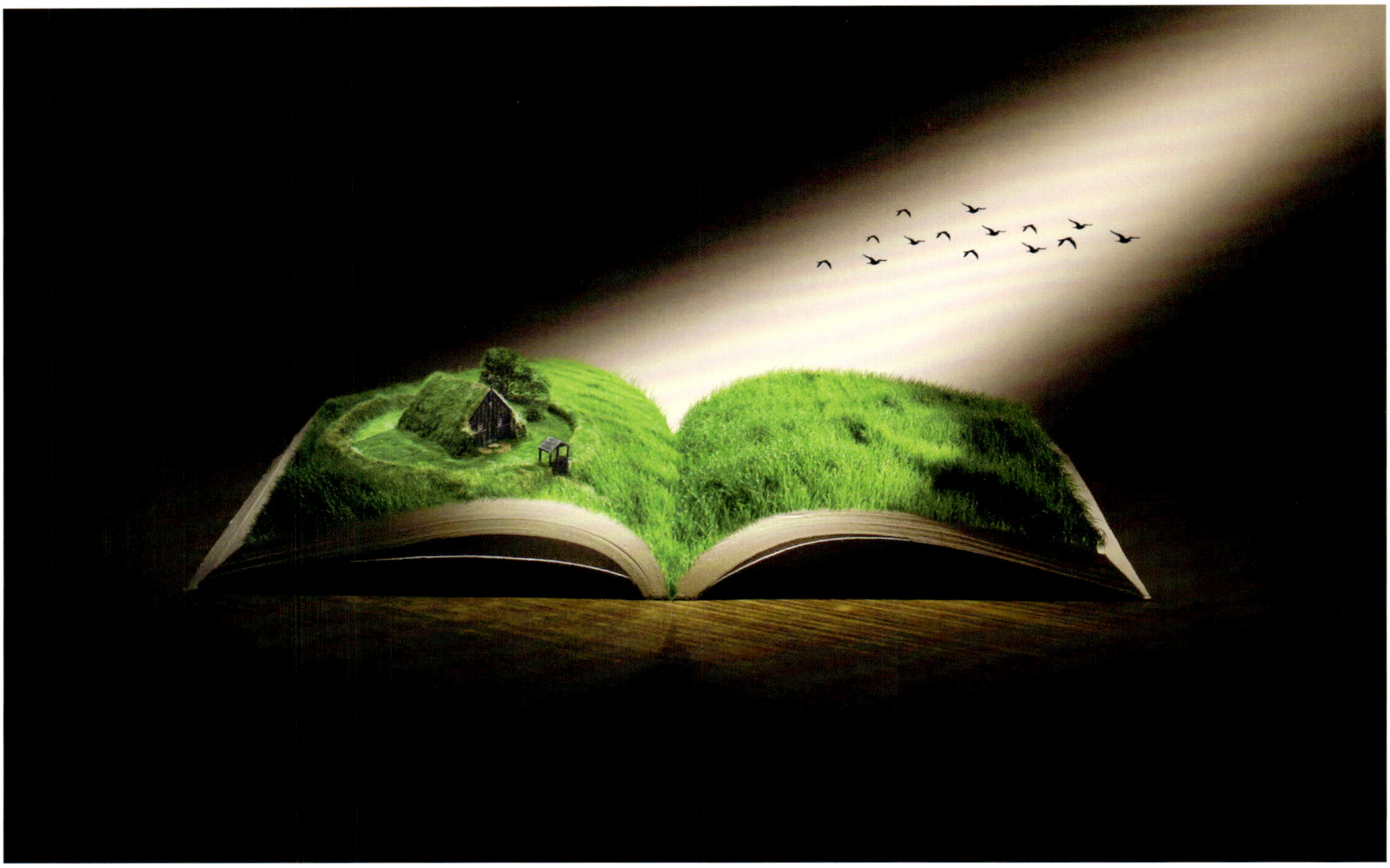

Student: Arianna Aguila | **School:** Campbell University

INSTRUCTOR KATHLEEN RICK

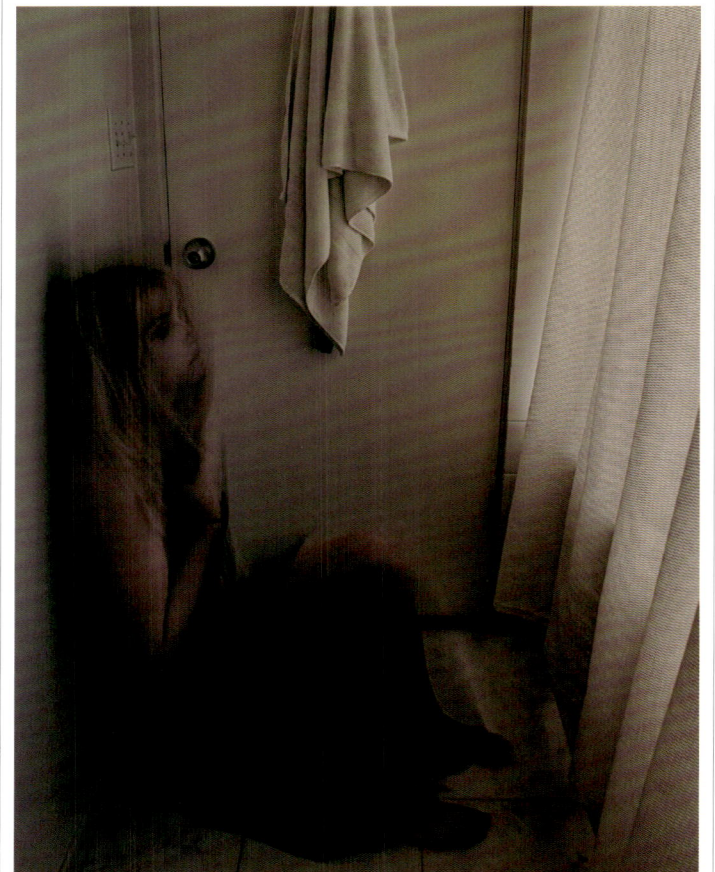

Student: Alexa Tusing | **School:** Portland Community College

INSTRUCTOR HANK RICHARDSON

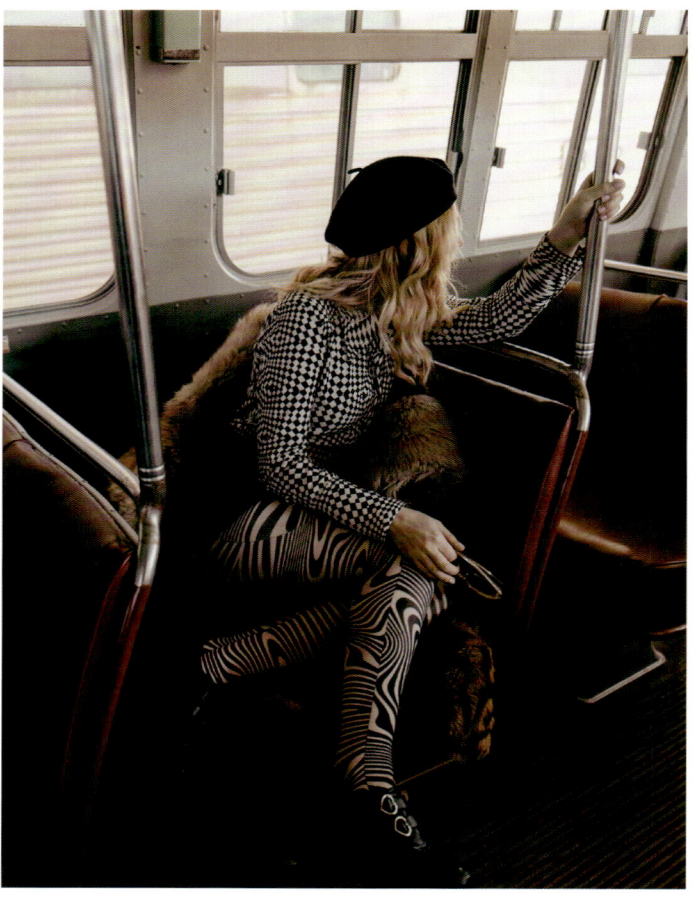

Student: Molly Jacobs | **School:** M.AD School of Ideas Atlanta

Photography | Digital Photography

INSTRUCTOR **KELLY LEWIS** 🇺🇸

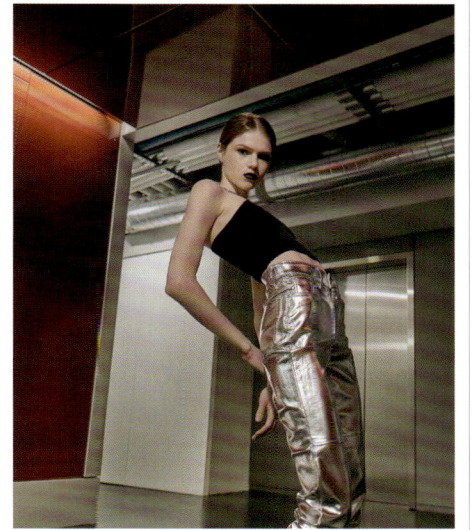

Student: Liv Donaldson
School: M.AD School of Ideas Atlanta

INSTRUCTOR **KELLY LEWIS** 🇺🇸

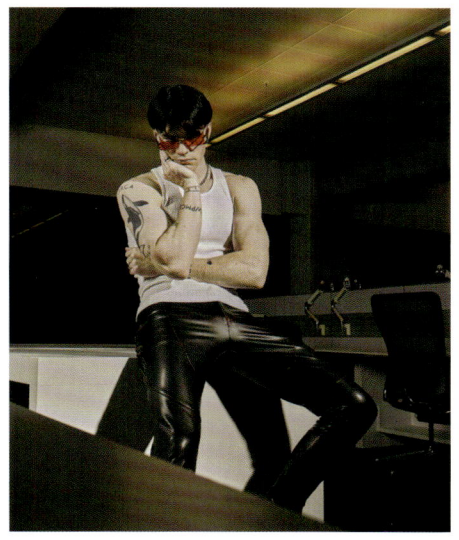

Student: Liv Donaldson
School: M.AD School of Ideas Atlanta

INSTRUCTOR **KELLY LEWIS** 🇺🇸

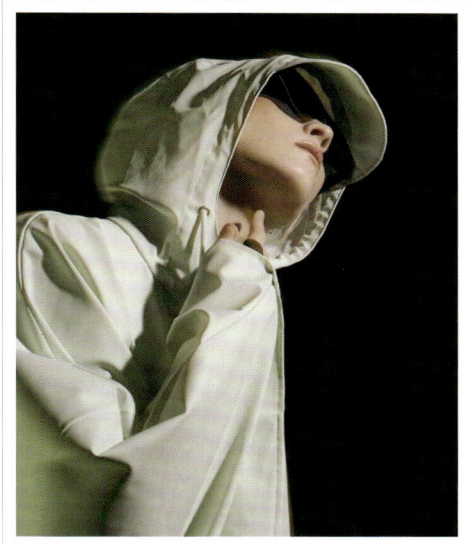

Student: Liv Donaldson
School: M.AD School of Ideas Atlanta

INSTRUCTOR **ARI SKIN** 🇺🇸

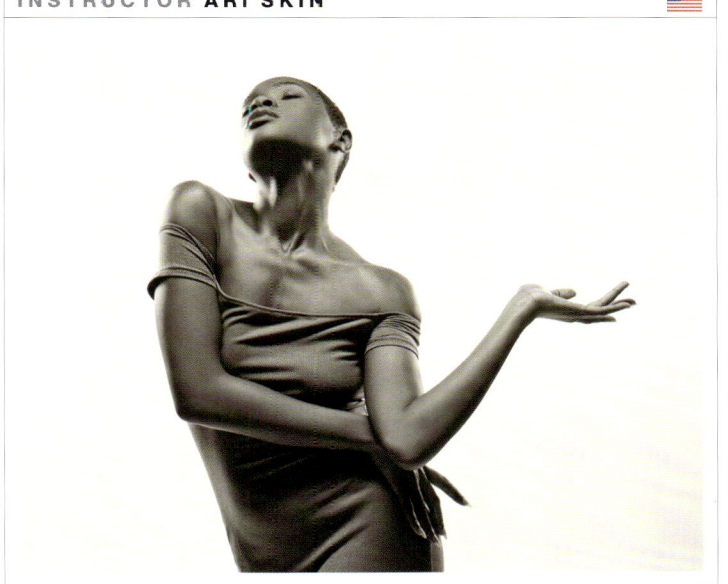

Student: Liv Donaldson | **School:** M.AD School of Ideas Atlanta

INSTRUCTOR **HANK RICHARDSON** 🇺🇸

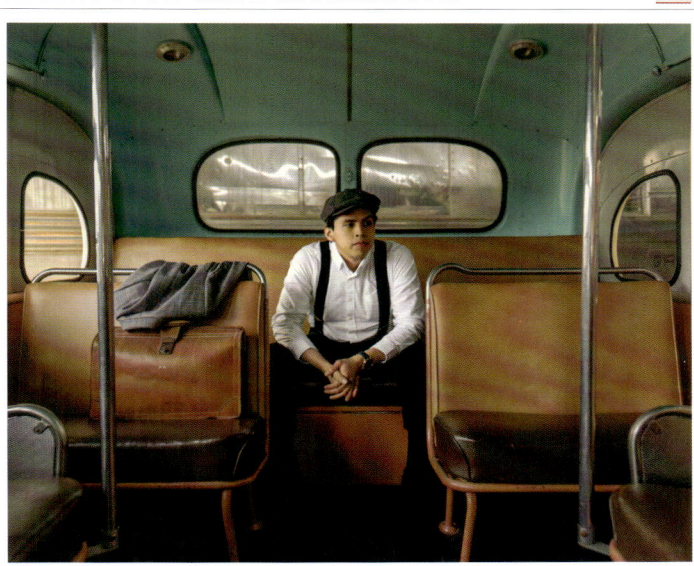

Student: Molly Jacobs | **School:** M.AD School of Ideas Atlanta

INSTRUCTOR **KELLY LEWIS** 🇺🇸

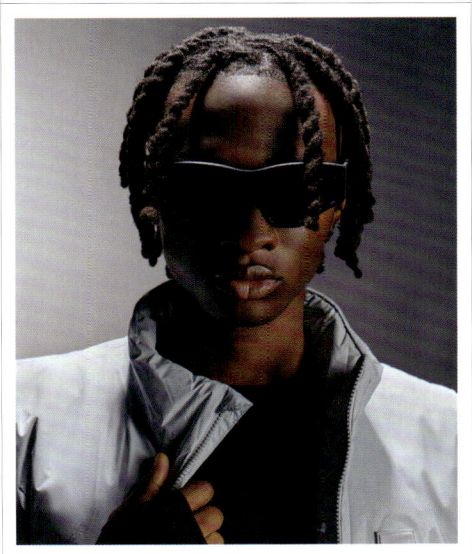

Student: Liv Donaldson
School: M.AD School of Ideas Atlanta

INST. **HILLARY KECKEISEN** 🇺🇸

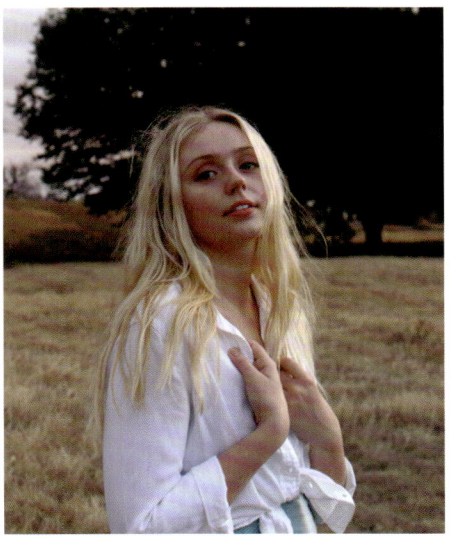

Student: Rebecca Richard
School: Texas Christian University

INSTRUCTOR **DUSTY CROCKER** 🇺🇸

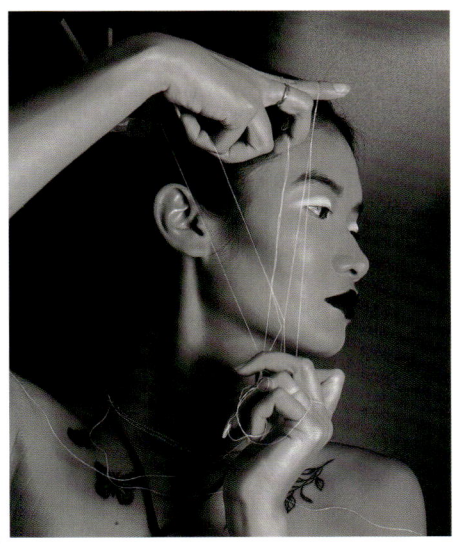

Student: Kien Nguyen
School: Texas Christian University

232 PHOTOGRAPHY SILVER

INSTRUCTOR DENIS GENDRON

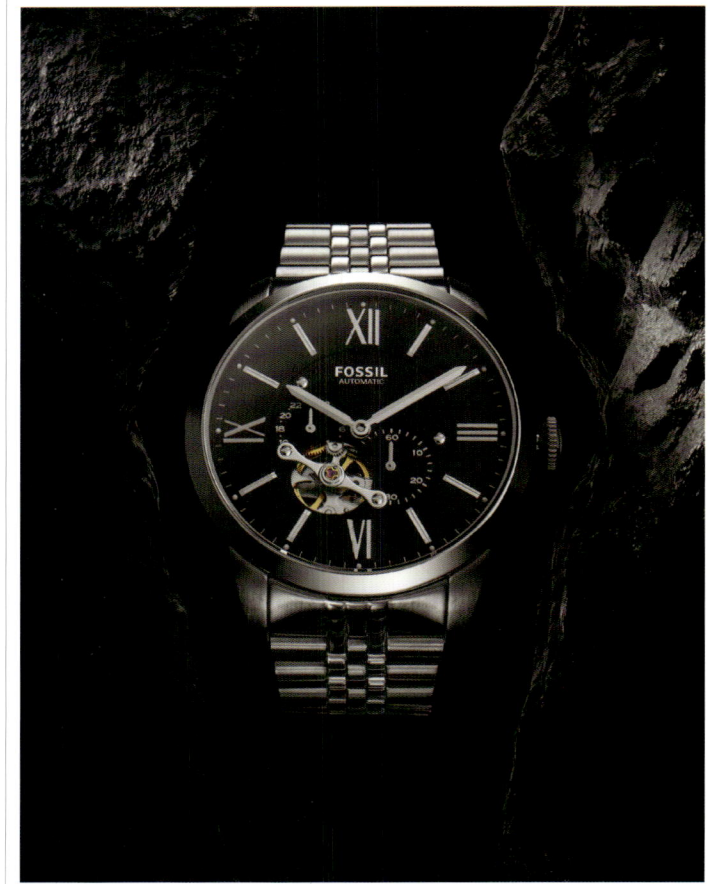

Student: Charchit Kant | **School:** Dawson College

INSTRUCTOR HILLARY KECKEISEN

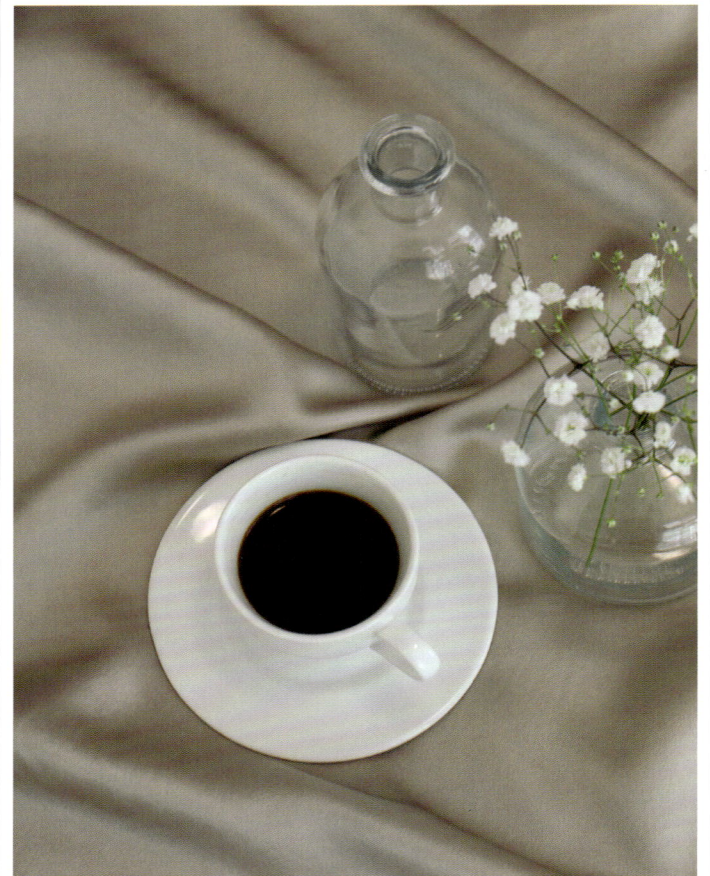

Student: Rebecca Richard | **School:** Texas Christian University

INSTRUCTOR DENIS GENDRON

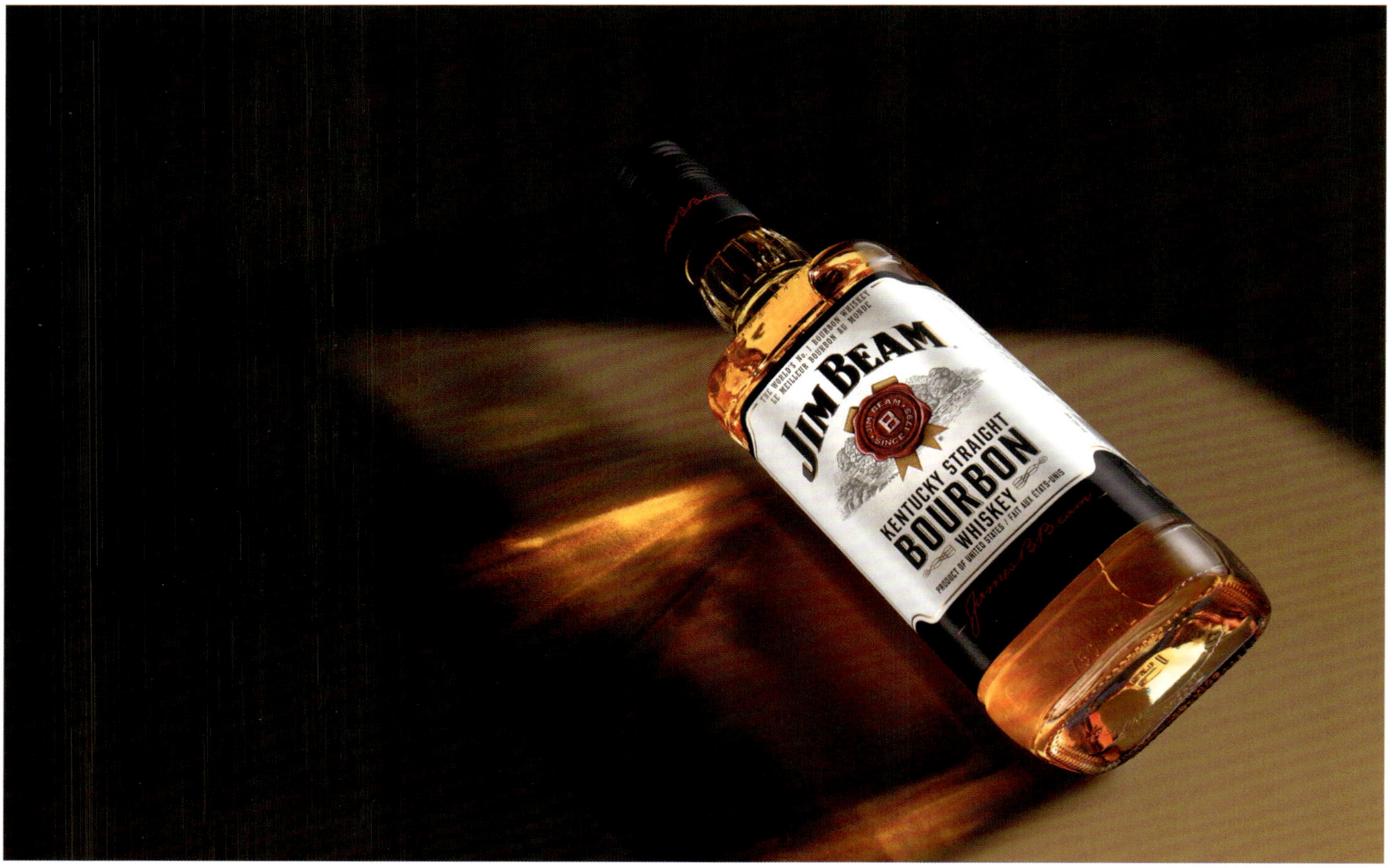

Student: Charchit Kant | **School:** Dawson College

Credits & Commentary

234 CREDITS & COMMENTARY

GOLD ADVERTISING WINNERS:

19 IT'S OBVIOUS. | School: Syracuse University, The Newhouse School
Instructor/Professor: Mel White | Students: Jenna Byers, Sophia Donio
Copywriter: Jenna Byers | Art Director: Sophia Donio
Assignment: Create a solution for Tile to explain how this product finds your lost items.
Approach: Through visual metaphor, Tile makes your lost object's whereabouts obvious.
Results: A visual print campaign that shows where you can find easy to lose objects.

20, 21 WEAR THE CHANGE | School: Syracuse University, The Newhouse School
Instructor/Professor: Kevin O'Neill | Student: Gabriella Enriquez
Assignment: Create a Print Ad to promote Gap's Washwell program.
Approach: Combine jeans with water to symbolize Gap's mission to be more sustainable.
Results: A unique graphic that visually combines jeans with water to raise awareness about Gap's water saving techniques.

22 OREOPHORIA | School: Southern Methodist University
Instructor/Professor: Willie Baronet | Students: Savanna Hodes, Maddie Otero
Assignment: Take 'Stay Playful' to a whole new level when you bite into Oreophoria, a place where you can let your sugar high run wild!
Approach: When we started the campaign, we noticed that they've been playing it safe for years. We knew we wanted to do something new, colorful, and exciting; something that exemplified their "stay playful" tagline. We started illustrating, using our childhood fantasies as inspiration and after a few rounds of thumbnails, Oreophoria was born.
Results: This is a student campaign, so we have not received any feedback from the client.

23 MIRACLE GROW | School: Texas State University
Instructor/Professor: William Meek | Student: Travis Crawford
Assignment: The Miracle Gro campaign is designed to visually encapsulate the transformative effect of Miracle Gro plant food. Our primary goal is to capture the imagination of our target demographic, and inspire them with the potential for change in their own green spaces.
Approach: My approach was rooted in the concept of transformation and developing a visual metaphor that would symbolize the impact of Miracle Gro on plants. To achieve this, I adopted a dualistic imagery strategy, using both Chat GPT and Photoshop.
Results: The project's visual narrative is one of stark transformation: a barren, lifeless scene on one side and a lush, vibrant garden on the other, all brought to life by Miracle Gro. The overarching objective is to reinforce brand recognition, affirm the product's position in the market, and ultimately drive sales.

24 SUNBURNS | School: M.AD School of Ideas
Instructor/Professor: Nour Da Silva | Student: Javier Forero
Assignment: According to the National Cancer Institute, sunscreen use is low among Americans. So, how can Coppertone remind people to use their product in a funny and visual way?
Approach: Although marine animals are not exposed to sunlight as much as we are, there are some species that do get in the sun from time to time, exposing themselves to UV rays. Thanks to these animals, Coppertone introduces a funny metaphor to remember to take care of our skin.

SILVER ADVERTISING WINNERS:

26 FORD TRANSIT - HOME AWAY FROM HOME | School: University of North Texas
Instructor/Professor: Douglas May | Student: Macy Belton

26 INFAMOUS LAST WORDS | School: Southern Methodist University
Instructor/Professor: Mark Allen | Student: Roshan Gupta

26 MAISON MARGIELA REPLICA FRAGRANCES
School: Southern Methodist University | Instructor/Professor: Willie Baronet
Students: Morgan Martinez, Delaney Gendron

26 AURORA | School: Texas Christian University
Instructor/Professor: Dusty Crocker | Student: Abigail Lund

26 DRUNK ELEPHANT | School: Southern Methodist University
Instructor/Professor: Willie Baronet | Students: Kaitlyn Blan, Caroline Davis

26 TO ME, WITH LOVE | School: Southern Methodist University
Instructor/Professor: Willie Baronet | Students: Roshan Gupta, Morgan Martinez
Photographer: Abbie Biegert | Model: Vivian Hynes

26 "EVERY MOVE" HOKA ADVERTISING CAMPAIGN
School: Texas Christian University | Instructor/Professor: Bill Galyean
Students: Isabella Pasino, Rebecca Richard, Rachel Stegall, Emma Wilkie
Image Sources: Bethany Perr, Anastasia Shuraeva, Tatiana Syrikova (Pexels)

26 L'ORÉAL SUBLIME BRONZE SELF-TANNER
School: Southern Methodist University | Instructor/Professor: Mark Allen
Students: Blake Lyster, Morgan Martinez

26 FOLGER'S COFFEE ESCALATOR MOCKUP | School: Baylor University
Instructor/Professor: Genaro Solis Rivero | Student: Abigail Sanders

27 SEEDLIP / NON-ALCOHOLIC SPIRIT | School: Southern Methodist University
Instructor/Professor: Mark Allen | Students: Emma Clarke, Callie Oden

27 LIQUID IV / GET MORE OUT OF YOUR WATER
School: Southern Methodist University | Instructor/Professor: Mark Allen
Students: Andrea Torroni, Nicole Zimmer

27 TOPO CHICO CAMPAIGN | School: University of North Texas
Instructor/Professor: Douglas May | Student: John Paul Nguyen

28 BAYLOR UNIVERSITY TRASH AWARENESS CAMPAIGN | School: Baylor University
Instructor/Professor: Genaro Solis Rivero | Student: Abigail Sanders

28 UNTWIST THE TRUTH | School: Capilano University
Instructor/Professor: Bracken Hanuse Corlett | Student: Anais Bayle
Designers: Ethan Woronko, Tiffany Zhong

28 YOU CAN'T TAKE IT BACK | School: Texas A&M University-Commerce
Instructor/Professor: Joshua Ege | Student: Jonathan Ramsingh
Illustrators: Diane Kim, Alex Martinez | Typesetter: Nikki Caballero

29 YOU CAN'T BEAT A SEARCH DOG
School: Syracuse University, The Newhouse School | Instructor/Professor: Mel White
Students: Lang Delapa, Katelyn Hughes | Art Director: Katelyn Hughes
Copywriter: Lang Delapa

29 FLOAT ABOVE | School: Syracuse University, The Newhouse School
Instructor/Professor: Mel White | Student: Meiling Xiong

29 DON'T ALSO LOSE YOUR HEAD
School: Syracuse University, The Newhouse School | Instructor/Professor: Mel White
Students: Destiny Erazo, Anastasia Svetlova | Art Director: Anastasia Svetlova

29 FEIT ELECTRIC CANCELED CAMPAIGN
School: Texas State University | Instructor/Professor: William Meek
Students: Logan Dorsey, Hannah Kim, Kaliah Orum-Harris

29 SWITCH THE SCENE | School: Syracuse University, The Newhouse School
Instructor/Professor: Mel White | Student: Anastasia Svetlova

29 AIRTAG & DEMENTIA | School: School of Visual Arts
Instructor/Professor: Able Parris | Student: Seongyun Park

30 DAFFODIL BOWLING EVENTS CAMPAIGN | School: Texas State University
Instructor/Professor: William Meek | Student: Briana Harris | Image Source: Adobe Stock

30 DECREASE FOOD WASTE CAMPAIGN | School: Pratt Institute
Instructor/Professor: Einat Lahat-Blum | Student: Saki Hinaga

30 GET BACK OUR ANIMALS | School: Syracuse University, The Newhouse School
Instructor/Professor: Mel White | Students: Ryan Garret Conner, Mackenzie Murphy
Art Director: Ryan Garret Conner | Copywriter: Mackenzie Murphy

31 WATER CAN'T WAIT | School: Syracuse University, The Newhouse School
Instructor/Professor: Mel White | Students: Alex Lund, Ava Schefren
Art Director: Ava Schefren | Copywriter: Alex Lund

31 THE BLUE JEANS BUOY | Schools: Hansung University, Design & Arts Institute, Kyung Hee University, Ewha Womans University, Methodist Theological University, Kyonggi University | Instructors/Professors: Dong-Joo Park, Seung-Min Han, Na-Min Kim
Students: Hyo-bin Park, Sae-Hee Jeong, Se-Young Lee, Eun-Hye Lee, Min-Jae Jung

31 JAPAN DRONE | School: Texas State University
Instructor/Professor: William Meek | Student: Travis Crawford

31 ZEN DRONES | School: Texas State University
Instructor/Professor: William Meek | Student: Tina Zurga

31 VITACO EDITORIAL ADVERTISING CAMPAIGN
School: Jacksonville State University | Instructor/Professor: Jamie Runnells
Student: Conner Gayda

31 INSOMNIA COOKIES / PERFECT PAIRINGS | School: Southern Methodist University
Instructor/Professor: Mark Allen | Student: Ross Yenerich

31 THE TRINKET TIN | School: Syracuse University, The Newhouse School
Instructors/Professors: Kevin O'Neill, Mel White | Student: Olivia Doe

31 I CAN'T BELIEVE IT'S NOT BUTTER / BUTTER BELIEVE IT CONSPIRACIES
School: Southern Methodist University | Instructor/Professor: Mark Allen
Students: Roshan Gupta, Maddie Otero

32 PROTEIN OREO | School: Belmont University, Watkins College of Art
Instructor/Professor: Doug Regen | Student: Caleigh Furyk

32 SISTER PIE AD | School: Texas State University
Instructor/Professor: Genaro Solis Rivero | Student: Veronica Jones

33 LOMA LINDA CHIK'N | School: University of North Texas
Instructor/Professor: Douglas May | Student: Craig Smith

33 DORITOS PRINT AND OUT-OF-HOME ADVERTISEMENT: DARE TO CRUNCH, DARE TO LIVE | School: Texas Christian University | Instructor/Professor: Dusty Crocker
Student: Nhi Vo | Additional Title: Midjourney

33 THE PATH TO THE END OF YOUR NIGHT
School: Syracuse University, The Newhouse School | Instructor/Professor: Mel White
Students: Marlana Bianchi, Lara Molinari | Copywriter: Brooke Hirsch

34 MOUNTAIN HOUSE CAMPING MEALS / ROUGH IT RIGHT
School: Southern Methodist University | Instructor/Professor: Mark Allen
Student: Emma Clarke

34 TRUTH INITIATIVE / ANTI-VAPING PSA | School: Southern Methodist University
Instructor/Professor: Mark Allen | Students: Spencer Hogan, Bella Mac, Allie Weinstein

34 ZILDJIAN CYMBALS | School: Southern Methodist University
Instructor/Professor: Willie Baronet | Students: Timmy Chae, Ethan Jones

35 FENDER / PROOF YOU PLAY | School: Southern Methodist University
Instructor/Professor: Mark Allen | Students: Helena Hargraves, Kailyn Sawhny

35 SKOUT'S HONOR PET ODOR ELIMINATOR | School: Southern Methodist University
Instructor/Professor: Mark Allen | Student: Helena Hargraves

35 ANY LENGTH | School: Syracuse University, The Newhouse School
Instructor/Professor: Mel White | Students: Yaoxinyu Guo, Noah Lourie
Art Director: Yaoxinyu Guo | Copywriter: Noah Lourie

35 MIRACLE GRO - MAGIC SPELLS NOT REQUIRED | School: Texas State University
Instructor/Professor: William Meek | Student: Jayden Wilson

35 SUPERGOOP ADVERTISING CAMPAIGN | School: Baylor University
Instructor/Professor: Genaro Solis Rivero | Student: Kennedy Walton

35 MIRACLEGRO GARDEN SOIL | School: Texas State University
Instructor/Professor: William Meek | Student: Tina Zurga

35 BIALETTI MOKA EXPRESS CAMPAIGN | School: University of North Texas
Instructor/Professor: Douglas May | Student: Macy McClish

35 MIRACLE-GRO | School: Texas State University
Instructor/Professor: William Meek | Student: Caroline Koi

36 UNDER ARMOUR HOVR SONIC SHOES | School: University of North Texas
Instructor/Professor: Douglas May | Student: Jordan Heath

36 GREENPAN CONSUMER AD CAMPAIGN | School: University of North Texas
Instructor/Professor: Douglas May | Student: Cuinn Cornwell
Photographer: Jim Zuckerman (Alamy)

36 THOROGOOD WORK BOOTS | School: University of North Texas
Instructor/Professor: Douglas May | Student: Emily Tran

36 HEINZ BLASTER BATTLE | School: School of Visual Arts
Instructor/Professor: Ryan Paulson | Student: Elyza Nachimson

36 STUF BY OREO | School: School of Visual Arts
Instructor/Professor: Dirk Kammerzell | Student: Elyza Nachimson

36 AS SHARP AS IT GETS | School: M.AD School of Ideas New York
Instructor/Professor: Villy Devlioti | Student: Yuchien Wang
Art Director: Dahlia Sevy

36 WHIFF OF TERROR | School: Syracuse University, The Newhouse School
Instructor/Professor: Mel White | Students: Marlana Bianchi, Lara Molinari
Art Director: Marlana Bianchi | Other Titles: Midjourney

37 TAKE A SAFER RIDE | School: Syracuse University, The Newhouse School
Instructor/Professor: Mel White | Student: Juliette Keller | Art Director: Juliette Keller

37 OUTLAND DENIM ADVERTISEMENT | School: University of North Texas
Instructor/Professor: Douglas May | Student: Maxwell Pius

37 AD CAMPAIGN SERIES PROMOTING THE AUSTRALIAN OPEN
School: Baylor University | Instructor/Professor: Genaro Solis Rivero
Student: Gabriel Powers

37 CONTROL YOURSELF | School: Syracuse University, The Newhouse School
Instructors/Professors: Kevin O'Neill, Mel White | Student: Emily Saad

38 RUNDERWEAR / ANTI-CHAFING SPORTS GEAR
School: Southern Methodist University
Instructor/Professor: Mark Allen | Student: Callie Oden

38 HIPCAMP / SEARCH FOR TENT CAMPING, RV PARKS, CABINS & GLAMPING
School: Southern Methodist University | Instructor/Professor: Mark Allen
Students: Tyler Chapman, Linh Vu

38 ALLIANZ TRAVEL INSURANCE / UNEXPECTED POSTCARDS
School: Southern Methodist University | Instructor/Professor: Mark Allen
Students: Hannah Jacobbe, Sydney Sam

39 EVITE / PUSH THE ENVELOPE | School: Southern Methodist University
Instructor/Professor: Willie Baronet | Students: Caroline Davis, Blake Lyster

39 FEEL THE HEAT | School: Syracuse University, The Newhouse School
Instructor/Professor: Kevin O'Neill | Students: Maggie Mallon, Meiling Xiong
Copywriter: Maggie Mallon

GOLD ADVERTISING FILM/VIDEO WINNERS:

41 NATIONAL GEOGRAPHIC BRAND EXTENSION | School: Texas Christian University
Instructor/Professor: Yvonne Cao | Student: Morgan Goerke
Assignment: Create a brand extension for any company. In choosing National Geographic, I wanted to expand the brand from publication and TV to providing outdoor gear so their audience could get out and explore the world they are learning about.
Approach: Utilizing National Geographic's infamous yellow rectangle logo, I created this idea of "Stepping outside of the yellow box." The goal was to inspire customers to take action and get outdoors, and not just read about the places they could be exploring. The social media advertisement series features three different outdoor activities where the subjects are actively moving out of the yellow box.
Results: This campaign was very successful.

41 1PASSWORD: BREAKUP WITH YOUR LAME PASSWORD
School: Southern Methodist University | Instructor/Professor: Mark Allen
Students: Roshan Gupta, Kayla Hanrahan
Approach: Easy people are like easy passwords. Make yourself less vulnerable with 1Password and use dual-key encryption that ensures your data is safe and secure.
Results: This campaign was accepted into my program's year-end Portfolio Night exhibition which is judged by creative professionals from around the country. It was also published on Ads of the World (part of the Clio network).

41 CARBON CYCLE | School: Syracuse University, The Newhouse School
Instructor/Professor: Mel White | Students: Dianna Higaki, Avery Schildhaus
Copywriter: Avery Schildhaus | Art Director: Dianna Higaki
Assignment: Show how Volvo can pioneer technology to make people feel aware of, and protected from, a safety issue. Here, the issue at hand is climate change.
Approach: Our goal was to turn apathy towards climate change into action by implementing the effects of climate change into something about which people are deeply passionate.
Results: To show the effects of climate change, insert environmental disasters into Mario Kart Tour through a new Carbon Cycle Cup, complete with remixed tracks and character karts.

41 MAPSAFER | School: Syracuse University, The Newhouse School
Instructor/Professor: Mel White | Students: Ava Schefren, Alex Lund
Copywriter: Alex Lund | Art Director: Ava Schefren
Assignment: Connect an audience of your choosing to a product or service from a global brand in a way that wasn't possible three years ago.
Approach: GPS software isn't updated, causing an incredible amount of preventable accidents. People are put in danger by the lack of map updating.
Results: Mass initiative to update GPS software using geotagging. People can photograph dangerous roads/blocked-off areas, use a geotag and this data will be reported to Apple Mps.

42 AMTRAK / SOMETIMES THE LONG WAY IS THE ONLY WAY
School: Southern Methodist University | Instructor/Professor: Mark Allen
Students: Timmy Chae, Blake Lyster
Assignment: Train travel is slow, less direct, and considered outdated. So how do you get Gen-Z and Millennials to consider it? Let's lean into the fact that train travel is slow because it offers a new, spacious, and scenic way to prioritize the journey, not just the destination.
Approach: We created an integrated cross-platform campaign starting with a commercial/online video to launch it. Since train travel is associated with unique sounds, we created the musical experience "Train Tracks." We created a Train Tracks Concert Series featuring popular music artists from specific regions of the country, intentionally paired with regional Amtrak routes. Amtrak would partner with well-known music producers and artists to incorporate actual train travel sounds into popular music tracks, then create Spotify playlists. Amtrak would also partner with ROKU to put a new train-travel spin on their horizontal scenery screensaver, paired with songs from the "Train Tracks" playlist.
Results: The campaign was accepted into my program's year-end Portfolio Night event.

42 BELIEVE ME
School: Syracuse University, The Newhouse School | Instructor/Professor: Mel White
Students: Alyssa Thompson, Juliette Keller, Maggie Mallon
Assignment: Connect an audience of your choosing to a product or service from a global brand in a way that wasn't possible three years ago. The global brand chosen was Dove.
Approach: Our audience was women, and we used the insight that a woman's pain isn't heard and taken seriously by doctors. AI is now capable of listening to conversations and coming up with a response in real time, so it would be able to identify when doctors gaslight or downplay symptoms during an appointment.
Results: Dove will release an app called "Believe Me", which uses ASR AI technology to listen to your doctor's appointments to identify dismissive statements and medical gaslighting before politely responding with suggestions for the doctor to give you a better diagnosis.

42 SAUCY SOUNDS | School: Syracuse University, The Newhouse School
Instructor/Professor: Mel White | Students: Remi Tsunoda, Avery Schildhaus
Copywriter: Avery Schildhaus | Art Director: Remi Tsunoda
Assignment: Encourage Gen Z to live their life in pleasure with Velveeta as their wingman.
Approach: There's just something so irresistibly tantalizing about the sound of cooking Velveeta mac 'n cheese. That's how we leveled up Velveeta from edible pleasure to audible pleasure.
Results: Integrated campaign featuring Velveeta-branded ASMR experiences placed as a restaurant, mobile app, erotic audio story, and phone booth.

42 OPEN AI / INNOVATION AT YOUR FINGERTIPS (3 SOCIAL VIDEOS END TO END)
School: Southern Methodist University | Instructor/Professor: Willie Baronet
Students: Timmy Chae, Savanna Hodes
Results: This campaign was accepted into my program's year-end Portfolio Night exhibition which is judged by creative professionals from around the country. It was also published on Ads of the World (part of the Clio network).

43 DIGITAL BLACKOUT | School: Syracuse University, The Newhouse School
Instructor/Professor: Mel White | Students: Brooke Hirsch, Charlotte Shea
Copywriter: Brooke Hirsch | Art Director: Charlotte Shea
Assignment: The average person doesn't realize the environmental impact of digital presence. All digital content, especially digital advertising, releases carbon into the atmosphere.
Approach: Do something radical. Cut Volvo's production of digital ads for a year. Release a minimally designed, low-carbon app that helps people track their own digital carbon footprint.
Results: By going digitally silent, Volvo's starting a global conversation about digital pollution. The social media buzz Volvo is getting is bigger than any digital campaign they could produce.

43 ALZHEIMER'S ASSOCIATION / WARNING SIGNS (3 COMMERCIALS END-TO-END) | School: Southern Methodist University
Instructor/Professor: Willie Baronet | Student: Maddie Otero
Assignment: When someone you know is diagnosed with Alzheimer's, it affects their life and yours. Oftentimes, the warning signs can be so small, they're hard to notice or identify.
Results: This campaign was accepted into my program's year-end Portfolio Night exhibition which is judged by creative professionals from around the country. It was also published on Ads of the World (part of the Clio network).

43 VOLVO LOW KEY | School: M.AD School of Ideas
Instructor/Professor: Hank Richardson | Student: Nikolas Sandevski
Copywriter: Lilly Graham | Art Director: Harper Herman | Strategy: Maria Rodriguez
Assignment: The brief, set by Volvo, was to create a technology that makes people safe. We pitched a device that can test for fentanyl.
Approach: Fentanyl is the leading cause of death among Americans ages 18-45. Most unknowingly ingest fentanyl when using other recreational drugs. Although test strips are accurate, efficacy relies entirely on user compliance. Our insight revealed that reaching for a test strip on the dance floor, or in a bathroom stall with your friends is bound to discourage people from using them. Solution: A low-key device that helps someone test for fentanyl.
Results: People in the healthcare industry are interested in making this tech come to life.

43 GOOGLE SWEET TOOTH | School: M.AD School of Ideas Toronto
Instructor/Professor: Vinay Parmar | Students: Kailin Zhang, Krishna Betai
Assignment: We were tasked to find a cause we genuinely cared about, and come up with an interactive idea to affect change for that cause, with the help of technology.
Approach: The news that one of my friends was diagnosed with pre-diabetes shook me. It turns out that 1 in 3 Americans are pre-diabetic, and more than 80% of them are unaware of it. We started thinking of ways to detect pre-diabetes which didn't involve finger-pricking or blood glucose tests. We stumbled upon Google's superior image-recognition technology, and harnessed Google software to come up with an app called "Google Sweet Tooth". When using it, you would point your smartphone camera at any product at the grocery store and see the amount of sugar in it. Healthier substitutes would then be suggested.
Results: Our instructor loved the idea, praising it for the cause it tackled.

SILVER ADVERTISING FILM/VIDEO WINNERS:

44 BARISTA BLENDS | School: School of the Art Institute of Chicago
Instructor/Professor: Priyoshi Kapur | Student: Liz Mathews

44 THE CLOTS MATTER | School: M.AD School of Ideas
Instructor/Professor: Hank Richardson | Student: Andrea Avila

44 JUST LET IT GO | School: Syracuse University, The Newhouse School
Instructor/Professor: Mel White | Students: Tori Aragi, Kayla Beck | Art Director: Tori Aragi

44 I CAN'T BELIEVE IT'S NOT BUTTER / BUTTER BELIEVE IT CONSPIRACIES (TV)
School: Southern Methodist University | Instructor/Professor: Mark Allen
Students: Roshan Gupta, Maddie Otero

44 BRAINFIT | School: M.AD School of Ideas | Instructor/Professor: Hank Richardson
Students: Marie Sophie Baier, Aïna Zaragoza Sostre | Art Director: Aïna Zaragoza Sostre
Copywriter: Daniel Iván Torres Almeida

44 QUIETON SLEEP EARBUDS: DREAM ON, SOUND OFF
School: Southern Methodist University | Instructor/Professor: Mark Allen
Students: Ethan Jones, Atenas Vijil

44 FAKE IT TILL YOU MAKE IT THERE
School: Syracuse University, The Newhouse School | Instructor/Professor: Mel White
Students: Meghan Gulley, Greta Hartwyk

44 SEX NEVER GETS OLD | School: M.AD School of Ideas
Instructor/Professor: Hank Richardson | Student: Marie Sophie Baier
Art Director: Lawren Elderkin | Copywriter: Kiah Kimpton

45 AT LEAST YOU'RE NOTHUNGOVER.
School: Syracuse University, The Newhouse School | Instructor/Professor: Mel White
Students: Jenna Byers, Sophia Donio | Art Director: Sophia Donio | Copywriter: Jenna Byers

45 ON THE LINE | School: Syracuse University, The Newhouse School
Instructor/Professor: Mel White | Students: Ryan Garret Conner, Mackenzie Murphy
Art Director: Ryan Garret Conner | Copywriter: Mackenzie Murphy

45 FTND / PULL BACK FROM PORN. | School: Southern Methodist University
Instructor/Professor: Mark Allen | Student: Tyler Chapman

45 NOTTOILET
School: M.AD School of Ideas New York | Instructor/Professor: Hank Richardson
Students: Philip Acierno, Harper Herman, Aleah Jones, Paige Shin

45 GET BACK OUR ANIMALS | School: Syracuse University, The Newhouse School
Instructor/Professor: Mel White | Students: Ryan Garret Conner, Mackenzie Murphy
Art Director: Ryan Garret Conner | Copywriter: Mackenzie Murphy

45 UNITE AMERICA / THE TWO-PARTY MATRIX (3 COMMERCIALS)
School: Southern Methodist University | Instructor/Professor: Mark Allen
Student: Morgan Martinez

45 PHONETIC JERSEYS | School: M.AD School of Ideas
Instructor/Professor: Hank Richardson | Students: Iuliana Vilcan, Javier Forero
Art Director: Javier Forero

45 SILENT SCROLL | School: Syracuse University, The Newhouse School
Instructor/Professor: Mel White | Students: Will Thorpe, Isabella Uribe
Art Director: Isabella Uribe | Copywriter: Will Thorpe

46 THE OTHER SIDE | School: Syracuse University, The Newhouse School
Instructor/Professor: Mel White | Students: Julia Gershowitz, Amina Shreve
Art Director: Amina Shreve | Copywriter: Julia Gershowitz

236 CREDITS&COMMENTARY

46 PENGUIN'S NEW CHAPTERS | School: Syracuse University, The Newhouse School
Instructor/Professor: Mel White | Students: Megan Adams, Dianna Higaki
Art Director: Dianna Higaki | Copywriter: Megan Adams

46 KRAFT MOOSIC FESTIVAL
School: M.AD School of Ideas New York | Instructor/Professor: Hank Richardson
Students: Philip Acierno, Harper Herman, Aleah Jones, Paige Shin

46 AI VS. AI | School: Syracuse University, The Newhouse School
Instructor/Professor: Mel White | Student: Brooke Hirsch

46 AVOIDABLE REALITY | School: Syracuse University, The Newhouse School
Instructor/Professor: Mel White | Students: Tori Aragi, Kayla Beck
Art Director: Tori Aragi | Copywriter: Kayla Beck | Other Titles: Midjourney

46 DON'T WORRY, DRIVE HAPPY | School: Syracuse University, The Newhouse School
Instructor/Professor: Mel White | Students: Julia Gershowitz, Amina Shreve
Art Director: Amina Shreve | Copywriter: Julia Gershowitz

46 EVA: AN AI FINANCIAL ADVISOR SPECIALIZED IN ADHD
School: M.AD School of Ideas Madrid
Instructors/Professors: Tim Dunn, Sara Boback, Marinette Fargo, Hatem El Akad
Students: Elena Fernández de Torres, Laila al-Kowatli, Ilu Shilpakar

46 AMERICAN MUSEUM OF NATURAL HISTORY MOTION POSTER
School: School of Visual Arts | Instructor/Professor: James Daher
Student: Dong Hyun Kim

PLATINUM DESIGN WINNERS:

50, 51 GLOW BOOK | School: School of Visual Arts
Instructor/Professor: Natasha Jen | Student: Hyowon Kwon
Assignment: GLOW is a book about fluorescence, a naturl phenomenon which has contributed to the advancement of science and technology and has served as a catalyst for the emergence of both art and science. The main purpose of the book is to celebrate the value and power of the color and to introduce the core logic of fluorescence. Each image serves to illustrate the common applications of fluorescent colors and represents distinct chapters.
Approach: By combining images and text, readers are granted comprehensive insight into the principles of fluorescence. To show the variety of usages of fluorescent colors, the editorial system is defined by each usage of fluorescence, which will be coded in RGB. Additionally, the black and white image, which was converted from the original image showing the value of fluorescence on the right side, contrasts and emphasizes the main message of the book.
Results: The book recognized that informative texts can be unfamiliar to people and may create a gap that discourages reading. Therefore, it attempted to create an appealing impression that would encourage people to easily access and appreciate fluorescence of nature.

52, 53 TIME AND SPACE | School: ArtCenter College of Design
Instructor/Professor: Stephen Serrato | Student: Heejai Park
Assignment: "Time and Space" is an exhibition that brings together 6 installation artists who have redefined the concept of time and space through their unique perspectives.
Approach: The exhibition and catalog design incorporated a rainbow gradient as a visual language to establish a sense of cohesion among six different artists within a single theme.

54, 55 KODAK | School: ArtCenter College of Design
Instructor/Professor: Simon Johnston | Student: Esther Yeseul Lee
Assignment: This identity system aims to modernize and reposition Kodak for a millennial audience while retaining its heritage.
Approach: The aspect ratio of the rectangle comes from a ratio of traditional photos. The logo is designed to be used as a container for images to showcase Kodak moments. Promotional Posters are designed to showcase photographers and the Kodak Moment campaign. To promote Kodak's new innovative digital printing technologies, pixel stretch treatments, and graphic movement of lines are used to convey the scanning process of photography.

56, 57 2023 STUDENT MAGAZINE | School: Portland Community College
Instructor/Professor: Nathan Savage | Student: Grace Howard
Assignment: We were tasked with creating a 12 page magazine with a front cover, two feature spreads, and at least one department page. The goal was to create visually engaging spreads that creatively combined typography and image, while also relaying needed information.
Approach: For our first feature spread, we were to choose any article headline and find creative solutions to illustrate it. I chose an article that talks about how jewelry designers are using their childhood toys for inspiration. I went found a toy bear and some costume jewelry, and photographed them. I then photographed my own jewelry in the shapes of letterforms. For another spread, I focused on the Icelandic icon, Björk. I found a photo series of hers where I was inspired by the mask she was wearing, and wanted to do a hand-drawn type to replicate it. To create a feeling of cohesion with the letterforms and spread, I chaotically arranged each letter behind Björk and did the same thing on the continuing spread. For the cover, I used the same photo of Björk and custom type, and chose a similar background color with a slight radial gradient. For the table of contents, I played around with a condensed, bold sans-serif. I broke the word into four lines and played with different angles and overlaps. I also angled the letters to go across the entire page and fit the departments into the title itself. For the first department page, I used a combination of halftones, electric colors and grunge fonts. I decided on the coloring for the editors note/masthead in a way that would blend with the neighboring department, but also stand on its own. For the final department, I tried fitting a lot of copy into a circle. To help the text flow better I opened up the circle to have the copy come out in some areas, while being constrained in others. Putting the accompanying photos into circles further adds to the breaks and harmony within the design.
Results: The complete magazine was met with an abundance of positive feedback from both my professors and my peers. I printed, cut and saddle stitched multiple copies at multiple sizes and handed them out to people in the program, as well as friends and family. I received an A on this project, with little revisions.

58 ANIMAL DESIGNS | School: ArtCenter College of Design
Instructors/Professors: David Tillinghast, Robert Clayton | Student: David J. Lee
Assignment: I used my favorite subject matter (animals) to create beautiful illustrations that could be applied to my brand identity as well as on products such as stationary, tote bags, stickers, and more. The illustrations showcase my ability to create well designed characters, compose color and apply my illustrations to real world products and job opportunities.
Approach: I started with a lot of research into the animal I was drawing. I then began sketching a variety of different poses and compositions. Then I moved on to a clean line drawing, color compositions and final rendering and application.
Results: My professors were pleased and suggested that I submit this into competitions.

59 JAPAN DRONE | School: Texas State University
Instructor/Professor: William Meek | Student: Brandy Compton
Assignment: The assignment was to create an illustration for Japan Drone 2025 that highlighted tradition and innovation.
Approach: The approach I took was to show a traditional geisha with a drone landing on her nose. The geisha is also adorned with drone hair accessories to symbolize the fusion of tradition and technology. Other modifications were made in Photoshop to execute my vision.
Results: The result is successful because the illustration merges both tradition & innovation and folds in a playful element that indicates fun.

60 GENERAL DYNAMICS POSTER | School: School of Visual Arts
Instructor/Professor: Natasha Jen | Student: Rachel Pan
Assignment: I designed an updated brand identity system for General Dynamics, an aerospace and defense corporation.
Approach: I was inspired by semiconductors as I wanted the brand identity to call back to the core of General Dynamics - technology and engineering.
Results: I updated the archaic design of General Dynamics' branding to reflect the company's work of new and innovative technology.

61 DEEP | School: Dongduk Women's University
Instructor/Professor: Hyojun Shim | Student: Sojung Won
Assignment: Anxiety about algorithms.
Approach: Algorithms is the technology which could be appreciative for someone, but a troubling experience for other. I aimed to convey the anxiety coming from the fact that the impact of algorithms can be either positive or negative. I wish to give an opportunity for introspection – to reconsider their influence on our lives, through this poster containing the feeling of confusion.
Results: I select the keyword, Deep, to express anxiety. The main color is dark blue that goes well with it. Also I made digital graphic image that stands for algorithm and added some noise in background for dizziness. Nobody knows where does it (spring) splashes, I used sparing as the main part and sprayed sticky liquid on it to express nasty feelings.

62 RENAISSANCE | School: Royal College of Art
Instructor/Professor: Billy Magbua | Student: Shahen Markarian
Assignment: In this project, I used AI to create only the background, and for the rest, chairs, and lights, color corrections I used the professional program Blender.
Approach: This project enabled me to showcase my prowess in translating historical inspiration into tangible art forms. The Renaissance-inspired flower chairs serve as a testament to my creativity, meticulous craftsmanship, and dedication to bridging the gap between eras. Through this labor of love, I pay homage to Siani Corvace's legacy while crafting a unique and captivating addition to the world of 3D design.
Results: At the heart of this endeavor are the exquisite flower chairs. These chairs stand as a testament to Corvace's profound influence, echoing his intricate detailing and visionary approach. By seamlessly weaving the essence of his designs into these chairs, I aimed to capture the essence of sophistication and timeless allure that defines his work.

63 AVE NITOR | School: Metropolitan State University of Denver
Instructor/Professor: Peter Bergman | Student: Courtney Meyer
Assignment: The assignment was to create a typeface as well as promote it. I wanted to create a typeface that emulated luxury and elegance. After a lot of revision, I brought all the letterforms into Glyphs which allowed for the proper finalization of my typeface. Then, the last step was to utilize this typeface in different mediums, such as a promotional poster.
Approach: Within my poster promotion, I wanted to emulate a vouge-esque visual to share the luxury, high-end aesthetic of the typeface while also displaying all the letterforms I made. To get the necessary picture, I conducted my own photoshoot. The name of the typeface is utilized as the "magazine" name while the rest of the letterforms are on display. Details of what the typeface is intended for as well as where to find it are also added to the poster.
Results: I physically produced the poster by printing it. It was displayed in the Communication Design department, for the class to critique as well as enjoy.

64, 65 AMERICAN BALLET THEATRE POSTER SERIES
School: School of Visual Arts | Instructor/Professor: Richard Mehl
Student: Dong Hyun Kim
Assignment: The tragic love stories of Swan Lake, Giselle, Romeo and Juliet was visualized through an unfinished heart-shaped type design. Through the design, I intend to show the delicate and strong energy of ballet dancers. When designing the type for Swan Lake, I worked with the shape of a swan. For Giselle's type shape, it has an intersecting detail representing the corset detail of Giselle's iconic ballet costume.
Approach: The most interesting thing about this series is the interpretation of three different ballet performances through type design. I went through several rounds of design, which were then reworked in Adobe Illustrator and Photoshop. Each type design seeks perfection through details inspired by the story's characters, costumes, and ballet dancers' movements.
Results: Working on this poster design gave me a stronger attachment and passion for typography. I was also recognized by SVA's chair, Gail Anderson, and my professor.

66, 67 GOLDFRAPP ALBUM PACKAGING | School: School of Visual Arts
Instructor/Professor: Justin Colt | Student: Rabiya Gupta
Assignment: Goldfrapp is an electronic music duo. I created covers for two of their albums. I wanted to experiment with hand lettering and create a custom type with a chrome texture, which the entire system is based on. I modified the secondary typeface I used and added flourishes to it to match my hand done lettering. I also worked on a cassette and tour posters.

GOLD DESIGN WINNERS:

69 TYPE SPECIMEN BOOKLET | School: School of Visual Arts
Instructor/Professor: Pedro Mendes | Student: Suin Choi
Assignment: Create a collection of type specimens based on foundational typefaces. This project needed to be a collection of books that should be developed systematically, making it look like part of a system while being slightly different. The differentiating elements should be informed by the typefaces.
Approach: I created a collection of type specimens booklets based on six foundational typefaces. It provides overall information about each typeface and designed every book to look like part of the system. Differentiating elements were placed in typeface and various color.

70 DRACULA | School: University of North Texas
Instructor/Professor: Whitney Holden | Student: Rebecca Dugan
Assignment: Redesign a classic book cover using only vector graphics.
Approach: The student references the major themes and symbolism in the book, combining imagery to create a cover that hints at major plot points without giving too much away.
Results: The end result is a cover that represents a 130-year-old story in a fresh way.

71 MURDER ON THE ORIENT EXPRESS BOOK COVER
School: University of North Texas | Instructor/Professor: Whitney Holden
Student: Rachel Felner
Assignment: For this project, students were assigned a well-known literature piece to design an original illustration-focused book cover.
Approach: When designing my book cover for Murder on the Orient Express I created a subtle design that references themes from the narrative, with attention paid to an accurate depiction of the original Orient Express from the 1930s.
Results: The final design includes enough detail to effectively communicate the key points of the story while leaving the mystery of the Orient Express within.

72 BOOK COVER SERIES REDESIGN | School: Lehigh University
Instructor/Professor: Maurizio Masi | Student: Zoe LeiLi
Assignment: The Book Cover Series Redesign project focuses on redesigning book covers.
Approach: To kickstart the creative process, I delved into the essence of the Tom Ripley series by immersing myself in excerpts from the books and watching the film adaptation, "The Talented Mr. Ripley" (1999). Then, I constructed a mood board, a mosaic of images and words reflecting the themes, as well as some simple sketches.

237 CREDITS&COMMENTARY

Results: The covers became a focal point of discussion, prompting classmates and my instructor to unravel the elements embedded within the artwork. The colors, placement, and portraits provided hints of the dangers and complexities inherent in the characters and plot.

73 ENOUGH IS A FEAST | School: M.AD School of Ideas Atlanta
Instructor/Professor: Hank Richardson | Student: Taylor Pirtle
Assignment: For this project we were asked to concept and design a cookbook, including the cover and 15-20 spreads, that demonstrated our ability to lay typography.
Approach: This cookbook is rooted in the wisdom of mindful eating and the Buddhist proverb "Enough is a Feast." Organized by seasons, it aligns with Ayurvedic principles, promoting harmony with the Earth's rhythms. The book serves as a guide to conscious living, encouraging a connection with nature and the appreciation of life's ever-changing tapestry.

74 BODEGA | School: School of Visual Arts
Instructor/Professor: Natasha Jen | Student: Hyowon Kwon
Assignment: BODEGA is a capsule hotel where you can travel back in time.
Approach: BODEGA was designed for people who are burned out and get stressed from modern society. People can experience a fantastic memory palace from it.
Results: The display typeface was inspired by the brain wave and sleeping capsule.

75 REFRAKT | School: ArtCenter College of Design
Instructor/Professor: Gerardo Herrera | Student: Jamal Abdullahi
Photographer: Carlijn Jacobs
Assignment: The jewelry industry suffers from a lack of representation, personalization, and innovation in sustainability. Refrakt is a brand for tastemakers, stylists, and creatives that serves as a solution to these problems without compromising design and luxury.
Approach: The concept is based on the concept of refraction. Refrakt's jewelry showcases the uniqueness of our identities. The custom logotype illustrates this concept as well. The typography choice in the project was DINPro, which reinforces the modularity and the raw materials of the jewelry. In order solve the lack of representation, inclusive imagery and messaging were used across brand platforms. To solidify the brand story, the brand comes in three lines: the convert+, adapt+, and the transmute+.
Results: After final presentations, I was notified of the realism of the branding as well as the positioning. In the US jewelry industry, there is a market size of $60 billion. After launch, there is a market opportunity of $2.25 billion of which I conservatively expect to reach to reach 30%. The market opportunity, design, and strategy make refrakt a strong choice for consumers looking for a breath of fresh air in jewelry.

76 GENERAL DYNAMICS BRAND IDENTITY | School: School of Visual Arts
Instructor/Professor: Natasha Jen | Student: Hyowon Kwon
Assignment: General Dynamics is a global aerospace and defense company, which engages in the provision of tanks, rockets, missiles, submarines, warships, and fighters.
Approach: General Dynamics' expansive potential prioritizes the importance of connections among its four main fields. A crane loop is used in various fields to connect and combine several different parts and can be viewed as the driving force behind the development of General Dynamics. The visual direction was created based on the key words "Recombination," "Connection," and "Engineered." The display typeface was inspired by the diagram of a crane.
Results: By interpreting the main idea metaphorically, using the connection between images and the display type, it visually shows the core idea beyond imagination and the stereotypes that people have about the defense company.

77 NOGUCHI MUSEUM BRANDING | School: School of Visual Arts
Instructor/Professor: Joseph Han | Student: Zedan Peng
Assignment: The assignment is to design a new branding system for the Noguchi Museum.
Approach: From the air, the museum is missing the upper left corner. The Carving behavior also shows in Noguchi's sculptures, so I decided to visualize this "lack of corner" feature.
Results: A set of typefaces that lack one corner was designed based on the carving edges, symbolizing Noguchi's sculptures.

78 INNERCITY ARTS | School: ArtCenter College of Design
Instructor/Professor: Stephen Serrato | Student: Genie Wu
Assignment: InnerCity Arts empowering Los Angeles children, teens and the community through the transformational power of the arts. The mission is to engage young people in the creative process in order to shape a society of creative, confident, and collaborative individuals.
Approach: The new logo highlights the community's structural unity, symbolizing individuals coming together and fostering a more creative environment for both children and juniors.

79 TENON | School: School of Visual Arts
Instructor/Professor: Eric Baker | Student: Jialu Xu
Assignment: Tenon is a furniture company, where tradition meets modernity. Our pieces are handcrafted by skilled artisans who use the tenon technique to create furniture. Each piece is made from high-quality materials and is designed to last for generations.
Approach: I love traditional handcraft techniques for furniture, so I looked deeper into them.
Results: Research and having a concept-based design is important.

80 INTERNATIONAL SPY MUSEUM | School: School of Visual Arts
Instructors/Professors: Courtney Gooch, Rory Simms | Student: Ray Chang
Assignment: The International Spy Museum is an independent non-profit museum that documents the techniques, history, and role of espionage. The rebrand is inspired by blacked-out text found in redacted files. This motif is then translated into various aspects of the museum's identity, creating the world of mystery and secrecy that espionage is known for.

81 PACIFIC AQUARIUM BRANDING | School: ArtCenter College of Design
Instructors/Professors: Brad Bartlett, Ming Tai | Student: Yuqin Ni
Assignment: In this project, I did the branding for the Pacific Aquarium.
Approach: When people think of aquarium design, they tend to imagine friendly and playful identities geared towards families and children. However, my goal was to capture the more dreamy, poetic, musical, and elegant atmosphere of the place. Pacific Aquarium is a window to the underwater garden, unlimited imagination, and a song of the ocean.

82 B612 BRAND & TYPE IDENTITY | School: School of Visual Arts
Instructor/Professor: Natasha Jen | Student: Mina Son
Assignment: B612 is a fictional sneakers brand with the theme of Coexistence of Contrast.
Approach: I captured the contrast between ancient Roman architecture aesthetics and the products of modern technology in a new typeface, 'B612.' It has a difference in thickness, rounding, and sharp corners, but their harmony is recreated into beauty.
Results: The characteristics of the typeface became the basis of the visual system and were applied to a shoebox, status, and spatial design.

83 UNION SQUARE PARK | School: School of Visual Arts
Instructor/Professor: Eric Baker | Student: So Yeon Park
Assignment: The project is to rebrand Union Square Park in New York City.
Approach: This park connected not only past and present but also connected a lot of people with various events, such as green markets or protests. My design intends to show this function of Union Square Park. The logo symbol represents not just the bird's view of the park shape, but also the link shape that connects all together.
Results: Logo symbols are simple and timeless. In addition, the branding system also works with all kinds of events in Union Square Park.

84 GENERAL DYNAMICS BRANDING | School: School of Visual Arts
Instructor/Professor: Natasha Jen | Student: Rachel Pan
Assignment: I designed an updated brand identity system for General Dynamics, an aerospace and defense corporation.
Approach: I was inspired by semiconductors as I wanted the brand identity to call back to the core of General Dynamics - technology and engineering.
Results: With this rebrand, I reflected on General Dynamics' dedication to innovation and precision by creating a more delicate and intricate design system.

85 CAS (CALIFORNIA ACADEMY OF SCIENCES) REBRAND
School: ArtCenter College of Design | Instructor/Professor: Brad Bartlett
Student: Jo Iijima
Assignment: This is a rebrand project for CAS (California Academy of Sciences).
Approach: In highlighting the significance of sustainable architecture at CAS, the custom typeface "CAS Ultra" is inspired by the iconic hill-shaped "living roof" designed by Renzo Piano. The interconnected hills also represent a genome pattern shown in the ID collaterals.
Results: The project was well received by professors and peers.

86 MUSENIA | School: ArtCenter College of Design
Instructor/Professor: Carolina Trigo | Student: Yaheng Li
Assignment: I wanted to offer greater access to artwork by lowering entry barriers. This gateway could be a community for those who collect and invest in art. For those who want to purchase pricier pieces but can't afford to do so, "Musenia" provides the option of becoming a shareholder with an app and a UX/UI programming website for artwork trading. Musenia (Greek goddess of art plus "ia", which means "a piece of land for artworks") is a place a land, a community, and a marketplace for people who love arts or investments.

87 ALLIANCE OF AGING RESEARCH | School: School of Visual Arts
Instructor/Professor: Joseph Han | Student: Hannah YinTian Lee
Assignment: An identity refresh for the Alliance of Aging Research to reposition and change the negative stigma around the concept of aging.

88 PARIS GAMING EXPO BRANDING SYSTEM | School: Texas State University
Instructor/Professor: William Meek | Student: Nick Voss
Image Sources: Photo of Event at Night, Danny Howe, Under the Unsplash License, Photo of a Paris Concert, Wikidomebb, Edits were made to the two stage televisions, Under the the Creative Commons Attribution-Share Alike 4.0 International license: https://creativecommons.org/licenses/by-sa/4.0/deed.en., Facebook and Instagram Icons, Feather Icons, Under the MIT License., Photo of the Louvre Interior, DAT VO, Under the Unsplash License., Photo of Eiffel Tower at Night, Spencer Davis, Under Pexels Free to Use License., Photo of the Arch de Triomphe, Arthur Humeau, Under the Unsplash License., Map of Paris Streets, OpenStreetMap, Under the Open Data Commons Open Database License (ODbL) by the OpenStreetMap Foundation (OSMF).
Assignment: The goal of this project was to expand a previously created logo into a complete branded system. Logos not sourced from existing companies had to be re-designed to fit an existing company or become mock proposals for a new company.
Approach: I started researching Paris and other pre-existing gaming festivals. I learned about Paris Games Week, but my research identified a unique niche that justifies a new festival. The Paris Gaming Expo could be the world's first city-wide gaming and city tour festival. Participants would gain access to locations, shows, and transportation across the city, and the festival itself would take place at theaters, parks, and convention centers. To establish the brand, aspects of technology and gaming was merged with the culturally rich Paris identity.
Results: The project was positively received by the class and faculty.

89 CHARLOTTE STINGERS | School: University of North Texas
Instructor/Professor: Gus Granger | Student: John Paul Nguyen
Assignment: The objective was to introduce the Charlotte Stingers, a new XFL team, into the league and seamlessly integrate it into the city's dynamic sports landscape. The scope of the project includes the design of the main logo, branding materials, and team collateral.
Approach: The design choices involve a color scheme inspired by the stinger bee, along with unique symbolic elements designed to resonate with the Queen City.
Results: The versatility of the design ensures the effective implementation of the logo and coherent styling across various platforms.

90 MICROGREENS CALENDAR
School: University of Ljubljana, Academy of Fine Arts & Design
Instructors/Professors: Eduard Čehovin, Radovan Jenko | Student: Strahinja Jovanović
Photographer: Žiga Gorišek
Assignment: This is a 3D calendar where each month has different microgreens that can be grown. The user is not just using the calendar but also learning about plants and making a mini garden. The vases are 3D printed and parametrically designed to fit the plant. As in nature, the calendar is created as a cycle; at the end of the year, a user can reuse the whole design product and repeat the planting process.
Approach: I investigated the connection of the calendar and nature, then created a calendar where plants could be nurtured and grown. I chose microgreens that can be easily grown, fulfill the calendar's use, and create a garden that shows us what time is in a new perspective.
Results: The project was exhibited on Academy of Fine Arts and Design, showing great potential to new ways of understanding of what calendar can be.

91 METAMORPHOSIS LOOKBOOK FOR DIOR'S CRUISE 2024
School: University of North Texas | Instructor/Professor: Stephen Zhang
Student: Marilyn Garcia
Assignment: Design a publication such as a brandbook, catalog, or lookbook. I created a lookbook of Dior's Cruise 2024 collection, which is inspired by Frida Kahlo. It aims to capture her colorful style while incorporating elements of traditional Mexican craftsmanship.
Approach: The lookbook incorporates design elements that reflect Frida's aesthetic. This approach pay homages to Frida's legacy while linking Dior's creativity and craftsmanship.
Results: The final iteration of "Metamorphosis" presents the inspiration of Frida Kahlo on Dior's Cruise 2024 collection through the usage of typography, image placement, and color.

92 ANNIHILATION | School: ArtCenter College of Design
Instructor/Professor: Jim Salvati | Student: Rain Gao

93 THE SLOW RUSH | School: ArtCenter College of Design
Instructor/Professor: Jim Salvati | Student: Maria Dzulfayan
Assignment: The objective for this project was to design a tour poster.
Approach: "The Slow Rush" by Tame Impala focuses on the concept of time. I designed poster that included time-related elements and incorporates an element of breathlessness. This helps establish a connection between time and catching one's breath.
Results: The poster received very positive feedback. Many enjoyed how the imagery went with the theme of the album.

94 FIG | School: ArtCenter College of Design
Instructor/Professor: Adam Ross | Student: Jess Martinez
Assignment: This piece was part of a series based on fruits and flora with the theme of Georgian jewelry. I created multiple portraits with jewelry that took inspiration from the 1700s.
Approach: I researched jewelry pieces I liked and set to design them to fit alongside the portrait and the fruit, in this case, being a fig. This series was an A-Z series and this piece was F for Fig.
Results: I created an intricate and texturized portrait with jewelry I wish existed in real life.

238 CREDITS&COMMENTARY

95 THE LURE | School: School of Visual Arts
Instructor/Professor: Josh Cochran | Student: Jenna Park

96 PADDYSNOW | School: School of Visual Arts
Instructor/Professor: Anthony Macbain | Student: Yiwen You

97 METROPOLITAN DIARY | School: School of Visual Arts
Instructor/Professor: Lily Padula | Student: Samantha Wang

98 ALLPA FARMS IDENTITY | School: Ringling College of Art & Design
Instructors/Professors: Jeff Bleitz, Lisa Willard | Student: Bella Race
Assignment: Identity design for an alpaca farm in Ollantaytambo, Peru.
Approach: The Allpa Farms logo captures the rustic and kind-hearted atmosphere of the farm, while paying homage to the historic significance of alpacas in Inca culture.

98 BEERHIVE PUB | School: Texas State University
Instructor/Professor: Mark Brinkman | Student: Danielle Stowe
Assignment: Design a logo for "Beerhive Pub." The logo should encapsulate the pub's friendly atmosphere while incorporating elements related to beer.
Approach: My approach centered on seamlessly integrating key elements of the establishment. I opted for a cohesive design that combined a beer barrel with the concept of a hive and bee. To enhance the impact, I selected a brown and yellow color palette. This deliberate color selection contributes to the overall unity of the logo, successfully marrying the dual concepts of beer and hive into a visually compelling and memorable symbol for Beerhive Pub.
Results: I received recognition from my professor and a good grade.

98 MAPLE RIDGE WOODWORKS LOGO | School: Jacksonville State University
Instructor/Professor: Chad Anderson | Student: Conner Gayda
Assignment: Maple Ridge Woodworks is a woodworking shop located in Alabama. The shop's owner requested a logo that referenced woodworking and his military background.
Approach: I created a badge-style logo that references military patches. The badge is shaped like the blade of a miter saw and a monogram of the shop's initials (MR) rest inside of it. The monogram's distinct line work implies the active spinning motion of the miter saw blade.
Results: The client was thrilled. He especially appreciated the "spinning" monogram detail.

98 LOGO | School: Texas State University
Instructor/Professor: Mark Brinkman | Student: Courtney Acevedo
Assignment: Create a logo for a company of our choice real or imagined. I 'created' my company Groovy Jams, which is a line of jams named after famous fruit-themed bands/songs.
Approach: When brainstorming different solutions, I found the treble clef contains shapes that mimic the letters G and J. I began playing with how to blend the two elements together.
Results: The G is the central body of the treble clef and the J creates the bottom hooked part of the clef. I also took some creative liberties with the top section of the treble clef which I made mimic the shape of a leaf since they are fruit jams.

98 CEREAL KILLERZ | School: Texas State University
Instructor/Professor: Mark Brinkman | Student: Aliya Ibarra
Assignment: The assignment was to redesign a logo for an existing company in America. I decided to create a logo for a company called Cereal Killerz.
Approach: I began brainstorming ideas for a new and fun logo. I began with thumbnails, then progressed to various digital roughs, and in the end I created the finished product shown.
Results: The logo successfully depicts a fun play on the brand's name.

99 ELECTRIC CAROUSEL LETTERMARK | School: Texas A&M University-Commerce
Instructor/Professor: Joshua Ege | Student: Michael Tucker
Assignment: The goal was to infuse a sense of joy and wonder into the brand, creating a vibrant and playful experience for customers with a new lettermark.
Approach: Crafting Electric Carousel was a vibrant journey, fueled by playful colors and imaginative concepts. Infusing the unicorn and carousel into the lettermark was pivotal—it's an invitation to experience the joy and magic of the brand at a simple first glance.
Results: Electric Carousel's branding and lettermark was met with positivity. My professor applauded the seamless synergy between the name and the vibrant visuals.

99 CHARLOTTE STINGERS | School: University of North Texas
Instructor/Professor: Gus Granger | Student: John Paul Nguyen
Assignment: The objective was to introduce the Charlotte Stingers, a new XFL team, into the league and seamlessly integrate it into the city's dynamic sports landscape. The scope of the project includes the design of the main logo, branding materials, and team collateral.
Approach: The design choices involve a color scheme inspired by the stinger bee, along with unique symbolic elements designed to resonate with the Queen City.
Results: The versatility of the design ensures the effective implementation of the logo and coherent styling across various platforms.

99 "BT", A PERSONAL TYPOGRAPHIC LOGO (MONOGRAM), 2023
School: Campbell University | Instructor/Professor: Dejan Mraović
Student: Breonna Tolson-Tucker
Assignment: Create a personal logo with the initials of our name.
Approach: I put most of the emphasis on the letter 'B.' My goal was to keep my design simple yet regal, and convey a sense of professionalism and elegance. I wanted the correlation of the letters to represent my aspirations toward creating positive business relationships.
Results: I accomplished something that represents me as a creative person. I feel that my elegance, professionalism, and love for simplicity are well exemplified in the logo.

100 MOE'S CAFE | School: School of Visual Arts
Instructor/Professor: Joseph Newton | Student: Yubin Won
Assignment: The goal of this project was to redesign a school cafe in SVA called Moe's Cafe. They serve quick meals for busy students but lacked a strong and cohesive brand identity.
Approach: Since SVA is such a diverse school, I got inspired by the New York subway, from the idea that everybody comes from different countries and gather in Moe's.
Results: Students from SVA enjoyed the brand concept that it mimics the subway vibe but also mentioned that it wasn't so obvious and gave a lot of good feedbacks.

100 SILVA AURI LOGO | School: Southern Methodist University
Instructor/Professor: Willie Baronet | Student: Juan Silva
Assignment: Silva Auri is a start up ready to wear apparel line that brings romanticism in the modern age. Inspired by vintage florals and romantic gestures, Silva Auri's main goal is to share a piece of elegance with every stitch.
Approach: The creative process entail taking inspiration from the luxury fashion industry and graphic elements to create a logo that is timeless and delicate.
Results: Since this is an original brand concept, there has not been feedback from the public.

100 CONSUMER ELECTRONICS SHOW LOGO | School: InFocus Film School
Instructor/Professor: Leila Singleton | Student: Darlington Ilukhor
Assignment: Students were tasked with designing a two-color logo for a conference of their choice. This student selected the Consumer Electronics Show, known popularly as CES.
Approach: The bespoke lettering is made from power cords, underscoring the focus of the conference. The alternating colors and positioning of the plugs lend movement to the design.
Results: The logo was successfully integrated into a larger identity project that was voted best in the class by the student's peers.

101 HI-WIRE BREWING LOGO | School: University of North Texas
Instructor/Professor: Douglas May | Student: Felicia Tshimanga
Assignment: I was tasked to rebrand Hi-Wire Brewing.
Approach: I created a logo that tied into the circus big top identity they created. I then created a narrative of a circus bear on a unicycle holding a beer. I wanted the logo to relate to their core belief of being playful while designing a sophisticated mark for the company.
Results: I created a fun and whimsical logo that captures their beliefs.

101 TNT'S CUSTOM SCREEN PRINTING LOGO REDESIGN
School: University of North Texas | Instructor/Professor: Douglas May
Student: Macy Belton
Assignment: Redesign the logo for TNT's Custom Screen Printing.
Approach: I landed on the idea of a squeegee with the handle being an actual stick of TNT. I explored gritty and stencil typography and was able to simplify the name to just TNT's. I emphasized the energy and the brand's hard-core messaging with the added flames on the TNT stick and movement of ink out of the squeegee.
Results: By creating a force connection between the screen printing squeegee and physical TNT, it speaks more to the bombastic, messy, and energetic nature of screen printing.

101 PENGUIN POTTERY TRADEMARK | School: Texas State University
Instructor/Professor: William Meek | Student: Emily Anne Chu
Assignment: Create a logo for Penguin Foot Pottery.
Approach: I chose to combine the likeness of a penguin with a vase, with the vase creating the form of the penguin's stomach. For the colors, I chose to keep the penguin iblack and white. For the beak, I used a terracotta color inspired by the color of clay before firing.
Results: This project was a success. Part of this project was to contact the business owners to ask if they want to purchase the logo. I have yet to do this but I plan to at a later date.

102 HOCUS POCUS | School: Texas State University
Instructor/Professor: Mark Brinkman | Student: Hannah Twining
Assignment: Create a logo that portrays the name of our chosen company.
Approach: The logo combines a record and a cauldron in a simple yet readable way. The logotype is combined with the emblem to further symbolize a bubbling, steaming cauldron.
Results: I'm happy with this logo, and it was well received by my professor and my peers.

102 BIG APPLE SCOOTER TRADEMARK | School: Texas State University
Instructor/Professor: William Meek | Student: Emily Anne Chu
Assignment: Creat a logo for Big Apple Scooter located in NYC.
Approach: Inspired by the vespa scooter, I chose to represent this scooter head on, made it bright red, and combined the headlight with an apple to represent the "big apple" that is NYC.
Results: I got full marks for this project. Another optional part of the project was to contact the business and offer to sell the logo, which I plan to do so.

102 WALRUS & CARPENTER | School: Texas State University
Instructor/Professor: Mark Brinkman | Student: Brandy Compton
Assignment: Create a logo for Walrus & Carpenter, an oyster bar in Seattle.
Approach: The logo combines a walrus with a carpenter's handscrew wood clamp, resulting in a playful character with many branding applications.
Results: The logo was met with positive reviews from both faculty and classmates alike. They described the logo as playful yet elegant, versatile, and simple.

102 WORLD ARCHERY | School: University of North Texas
Instructor/Professor: Douglas May | Student: Jalon Isabell
Assignment: Create a new logo for the World Archery Federation.
Approach: I wanted to elevate the logo to be in line with other sports federations. I did so by using the motif of an arrowhead and bow to create A and W letterforms in the logo. The color scheme reflects the familiar palette seen in archery targets to complete the concept.
Results: The project received positive feedback in class.

102 SQUID INK SUSHI BAR | School: Texas State University
Instructor/Professor: Mark Brinkman | Student: Sam Roberts
Assignment: Explore company names and make/redesign a logo for one. The goal was to focus on the design process and create a visually appealing logo that was successful in the concept and communication, the layout, and lastly the execution and craftsmanship.
Approach: I evoked a sushi roll by designing the inner part to resemble a squid through the use of various-sized circles. I wanted to integrate the "ink" motif by fashioning the sushi roll's wrap to resemble an ink stroke. I also opted for a typeface with an inked appearance.
Results: When designing multiple thumbnails and presenting my concepts to the class, I was able to narrow down my selections to one logo, culminating in the final design.

103 BEAR'S SMOKEHOUSE AND BBQ | School: University of North Texas
Instructor/Professor: Douglas May | Student: Rachel Blow
Assignment: The project's goal revolved around rebranding Bear's Smokehouse and BBQ, a restaurant located in North Carolina and Connecticut that serves premium barbecue.
Approach: Creating a new identity required a thorough research process. This resulted in a mnemonic device that is recognizable, friendly, but strong.
Results: The final logo was well received by the student's instructor and peers.

103 MARBLE GEMSTONE GIFT HAT SHOP | School: Duy Tan University
Instructor/Professor: Nguyen Tri Phuong Dong | Student: Doan Van Huan
Assignment: About 200 years ago, King Minh Mang named a cluster of five mountains in central Vietnam "Ngu Hanh Son." The logo features five colorful conical hats against the traditional orange color background of the ancient walls of Hoi An, symbolizing the five mountains and representing the traditional of Vietnamese women. It tells a concise story of local culture, and the gift shop product's diversity.

103 NALGENE LOGO | School: University of North Texas
Instructor/Professor: Douglas May | Student: Macy McClish
Assignment: Create a new identity for Nalgene, an outdoor water bottle brand.
Approach: The iconic silhouette of the original Nalgene water bottle honors the history and the vision of the brand along with emphasizing their distinction from competitors.
Results: The logo is successful because it visualizes Nalgene's defining attribute and their consistency for their product and their customers.

104 BAMBOO SLIPS LIQUOR | School: School of the Art Institute of Chicago
Instructor/Professor: Unattributed | Student: Qianying Niu
Assignment: The design of Bamboo Slips Liquor is based on two motifs: the bamboo slips used to document and spread Chinese cultur. Second, the liquor requires years to distill, echoing the ancient philosophy that rewards come with patience.
Approach: This design centers around "Zen," using black as the main color. The package uses bamboo slips as material. Inside is a Chinese poem, "The Decree of Wine." The design blends a reading experience with the liquor, uncovering a story which blooms with every sip.
Results: This is the first Chinese liquor to use a non-label design. All the materials are sustainable and reusable. Blending bamboo slips, calligraphy, and carefully orchestrated bottle shape, the design brings back both reading and drinking cultures central to Asian people.

105 BELLE STARR | School: M.AD School of Ideas Atlanta
Instructor/Professor: Hank Richardson | Student: Anna LeBer

239 CREDITS&COMMENTARY

Approach: Belle Starr was the Outlaw Queen of Kentucky. Known for her sleek style, Belle lived life passionately, entangled in romances with Wild West figures. This whiskey embodies Belle's spirit—bold yet refined, with a sharp-shooting essence and a touch of sophistication.

106 NIGHTINGALE | School: M.AD School of Ideas Atlanta
Instructor/Professor: Hank Richardson | Student: Catarina Sterlacci

107 AEITHALÍS MASTIC LIQUEUR | School: Texas Christian University
Instructor/Professor: Yvonne Cao | Student: Corinne Green
Assignment: Create a bottle design for a liquid of my choice. I landed on the unique Mastic Liqueur made from the resin of the Mastic tree on the island of Chios.
Approach: I did extensive research to create my brand. I then designed an illustration for the front label with patterns inspired by ancient etchings from the villages where artisans harvest mastic resin. The logo combines traditional motifs with the iconic teardrop shape of dripping resin. The teardrops form a flower symbol, connecting the geometric style back to its natural roots. Aeithalis is Greek for "Evergreen" relating to both the evergreen Mastic tree and the continuation of the tradition of distilling Mastiha.
Results: This project cohesively blends elements of the culture and architecture of Chios with a strong brand identity, type-setting, and illustration.

108 SUPERB | School: School of Visual Arts
Instructor/Professor: Justin Colt | Student: Sungeun Shin
Assignment: We were randomly assigned both a category of packaging and a conceptual theme. I combined both of these requirements to create a unique packaging system.
Approach: SUPERB is a dried goods package that embodies superfoods with a futuristic concept. The packaging design is inspired by a fun tradition at the Kennedy Space Center where beans were enjoyed as a reward for a successful shuttle launch. The copywriting comes in a weird but beautiful neon color and emphasizes that beans are a superfood. Beans are also easy to grow, So, I added a growing kit in the package.
Results: The professor was pleased with the progress made and the outcome of the assignment.

109 LURE TIN FISH | School: M.AD School of Ideas Atlanta
Instructor/Professor: Hank Richardson | Student: Reagan Williams
Assignment: Lure is a modern tin fish brand designed for a Gen-Z audience. The packaging is both sleek and portable, aligning with the lifestyle of contemporary consumers. Committed to sustainability, Lure provides responsibly sourced seafood in eco-conscious materials.

110 DAVINES OI | School: Brigham Young University
Instructor/Professor: Linda Reynolds | Student: Kate Holmes
Assignment: To design a packaging system for a line of haircare products.
Approach: Davines, an Italy-based haircare company, is committed to doing their best through beauty and ethics. I wanted my packaging system to display these qualities.
Results: This project was nominated by Professors to be submitted because of its success in creating a visual system that differentiates but unites all the products in the line.

111 BAOBAB COLLECTION REBRAND | School: ArtCenter College of Design
Instructor/Professor: Gerardo Herrera | Student: Jocelyn Ziying Zhao
Assignment: The Baobab Collection lacked a distinctive brand narrative, an iconic identity, and diverse product offerings. Drawing inspiration from the baobab tree trunk's hollows, the 'Heart of Baobab' collection emphasizes the tree's resilient spirit by showcasing the hollow in its glass form, transcending from scented candles to diffusers, essential oils, and room sprays.
Approach: The design weaves the cavity theme into the packaging and across the whole product line. The logo is also inspired by the baobab tree. Color-coded packaging represents top note, heart note, and base note for easy identification and enhanced brand recognition. The design emphasizes an enriched tactile experience and rapid narrative comprehension. Initiated by pressing the die-cut hole at the bottom, customers can pull out the product nestled within a recycled paper pulp insert. The final act involves peeling off the seed paper label.

112 TWININGS TEA PACKAGING REDESIGN | School: School of Visual Arts
Instructor/Professor: Peter Ahlberg | Student: Jiayi Meng
Assignment: Refresh the packaging of English breakfast tea and infuse new life into the brand while maintaining a sense of tradition and familiarity.
Approach: I maintained the original color palette but introduced a vintage pattern to add a modern yet classic appeal.
Results: The success of this redesign would be measured by its ability to rejuvenate the brand's image, increase consumer engagement, and potentially boost sales.

113 SIXTH STREET'S TEQUILA | School: Texas Christian University
Instructor/Professor: Yvonne Cao | Student: Isabella Baker
Assignment: The goal was to create a new branding and packaging for an existing bottle. This should be followed by at least one extension of the brand.
Approach: During my research, I found that Austin is known as "The live music capital of the world." I thought there was potential to position this brand as "THE TEQUILA" of Austin. I used Sixth Street in the name because this is where most of the bars in Austin are located. The icon consists of a guitar pick with an agave leaf. I also used a guitar-shaped bottle. The style is bold and uses musical note patterns to soften the rock vibes and to be more inclusive of other music styles. I used holographic and fluorescent vinyl to create contrast and transmit the electrifying energy of music.
Results: The following was stated by my professor Yvonne; "You've truly excelled with the 6th Street spirit concept. The harmony between the bottle shape and the concept is remarkable, and your choice of materials was perfect. The intricate pattern contains numerous details, yet the label information remains impeccably organized and easy to follow."

114 DUNNELL'S CIGAR HOUSE | School: ArtCenter College of Design
Instructor/Professor: Dan Hoy | Student: Brian White
Assignment: Dunnells Cigar House is a conceptual members-only cigar and whiskey club located in Newport Beach, California. Captain Samuel S. Dunnells was an instrumental character in the development of Newport, and surrounding areas of Orange County, California. The project itself is a "welcome package" for new members. As a high-end club, it was important that the packaging was on par with high-end execution and material. The interior boxes are made with a 1-ply chipboard and wrapped with a specialty soft-touch coated paper, while the larger kit was created with 2-ply chipboard, wrapped in a specialty leather-like paper.
Approach: Newport Beach gave the identity a lot of unique characteristics to pull inspiration from. None more so than the color palette. The dark natural greens, the light sandstone/beige, and the bright orange are all inspired by the area. The orange is also reflective of the bright glow of a lit Cuban cigar. The typography and the bottle is inspired by old, wooden cargo crates. The hero script and simple san serif pairing is directly related to those crates. The bottle itself uses the necessary legal copy as a visual element, rather than a secondary thought. The single color illustration of Capt. Dunnells himself also expresses the nostalgic nature of the brand's roots.
Results: The project's success was immediate clear. For the last 3 months it has been featured in the ArtCenter Student Gallery, and will remain there for the rest of the year.

115 MOON RISE SEAFOOD ALASKAN GIFT SET
School: California State University, Fullerton | Instructor/Professor: Theron Moore
Student: Natalie Quiros
Assignment: This project entails the invention of a packaging system for an original product line with various components, or a grouping of products that relate to one another in some way. The problem must be clearly defined by establishing the verbal context, and there should be an interesting and relevant idea in place that addresses both the functional considerations and the visual opportunities in response to the established problem.
Approach: The product line is named Moon Rise Seafood Alaskan Fish Gift Set, and is intended as a souvenir for tourists to buy when they visit Alaska. It features sustainably sourced fish and caviar. The wooden fish skeleton basket was designed to be functional packaging that also served as an eye-catching display piece. The tin cans' illustrations are minimalistic, mimicking the design of the fish skeleton head. The outer packaging features the brand's blue palette paired with wooden textures, contrasting with the bright, color-coded can labels within.
Results: The wrapped fish skeleton packaging system makes this gift set functional by keeping the cans sealed inside and easy to carry with the dorsal fin handle. The skeleton also makes the gift set a visually interesting display piece for customers.

116 AIR SHOES PACKAGING | School: Pratt Institute
Instructor/Professor: Hadar Kfir | Student: Wen-Chi Hsueh
Assignment: The packaging design for "Air Shoes" combines cutting-edge innovation with an otherworldly sense of freedom and lightness.
Approach: The packaging mirrors the streamlined contours and dynamic lines of a spaceship in flight. The sleek lines create a sense of forward momentum, echoing the wearer's experience of propulsion and speed. Just like a spaceship defies gravity, the Air Shoes defy the norms of traditional footwear. The packaging communicates a promise of unburdened movement, urging the consumer to imagine a sensation of weightlessness and liberation.
Results: The packaging is not just protective but serves as a prelude to the sensory experience that awaits the consumer. Opening the packaging is akin to unlocking the doors of a spacecraft, further emphasizing the journey that awaits the wearer.

117 HORSEPOWER COLD BREW COFFEE | School: School of Visual Arts
Instructor/Professor: Justin Colt | Student: Vasavi Bubna
Assignment: Just like a car's engine would seize up without motor oil, many people cannot make it through the day without their caffeine fix. Inspired by vintage motor oil cans, Horsepower Cold Brew Coffee depicts coffee like a fuel for humans.
Approach: Coffee, for many, feels like 'pouring fuel into the engine.' The hand-lettering quality in vintage packaging type inspired the brand's logo. The ratios on each package represent the roast and brew intensity, just like motor oil has mixing ratios on the front of their tins.
Results: The packaging illicits the feeling of oil tin cans, making the audience stop and look closer. The packaging meshed the conceptual theme with the product cohesively.

118 ESSENTIAL OIL NATURAL PACKAGING
School: Budapest Metropolitan University | Instructor/Professor: Judit Tóth
Student: Ágota Habony | Photo Retouching: Erzsébet Jámbor
Assignment: Design a new, natural packaging for a chosen Hungarian essential oil manufacturing company with three distinct scents, alongside reimagining the company's logo. My choice fell on a company named Herby's, who are dedicated to the production of 100% pure essential oils and place special emphasis on manufacturing BIO products.
Approach: The logo uses the original "Herby's" logo while deliberately directing attention. I created a printable handmade paper for the external packaging. Additionally, I hand-drew all the packaging illustrations and added leaf prints inside. I categorized the company's marketed essential oils for different age groups, each represented by a distinct package. The autumn package has oils intended for middle-aged and elderly individuals. A similar packaging concept could be applied for summer (young adults) and spring (teenagers).
Results: My professors were very satisfied with the result.

119 HNY TEA PACKAGING | School: California State University, Fullerton
Instructor/Professor: Theron Moore | Student: Dasia Williams
Assignment: This project involves creating a packaging system for a diverse product line. The challenge is to invent a product line name, establish verbal context, and define the problem clearly. The design, material choices, creative approach, and decisions about form and function are open-ended. The key requirement is complexity, with a minimum of five distinct pieces in the package. The goal is to address both functional considerations and visual opportunities in response to the established problem.
Approach: "Hny," a tea brand that infuses honey directly into raw tea leaves. With a focus on convenience and affordability, Hny targets adults who are regular tea consumers. The process of creating this product was conducting research, brainstorming and streamlining ideas, and executing it using a wide range of materials.
Results: This project received an "A" grade and led to many personal developments as a designer. The process taught me the importance of combining creativity with practical solutions, understanding consumer needs, and creating a diverse brand that resonates with a audience.

120 HELP ME | School: Dankook University
Instructor/Professor: Hoon-Dong Chung | Student: Yongfeng Liu
Assignment: I wanted to emphasize the seriousness of marine pollution through the combination of fish and PET bottles.
Approach: By combining fish and PET bottles, I aimed for a symbolic and ambiguous approach.

121 ARTIFICIAL NATURE | School: Dongduk Women's University
Instructor/Professor: Hyojun Shim | Student: Hyeyoung Seo
Assignment: Mankind can imitate nature, but does not follow its organicity. People have lived in nature, yet have the power to destroy it, and they should take care not to. A world where the only nature left is formed of artificial materials expresses 'Artificial Nature.'
Approach: Artificial flowers, trees, and stones were produced to visualize the paradoxical aspect of humanity that lives in the natural order but at the same time destroys nature. Through this, the value of nature is newly established and destruction of the natural environment is suggested.
Results: This poster was displayed at the school and was shown to many people. It gathered a lot of reactions from the people and received good reviews from them.

122 THE PLIGHTS OF WOMEN | School: Rhode Island School of Design
Instructor/Professor: Nancy Skolos | Student: Shuixin Wang
Assignment: Violence and discrimination against women is a historical and universal plight. It transcends boundaries, affecting women around the world. Inspired by these sobering realities, I wanted to use graphic design as a tool to evoke thought and instigate change.
Approach: In these posters, I utilized the symbolism of a red moon or red shapes to represent women. The moon is often associated with femininity in many cultures, while the color red has become a symbol for women, and the tragically violent situations they often encounter. The imagery used is mostly derived from photographs taken around campus, a subtle reminder that these horrifying scenarios can occur anywhere, even in places familiar to us.
Results: This work has perfectly conveyed my intention and garnered widespread acclaim.

123 OPEN MOVEMENT POSTER | School: ArtCenter College of Design
Instructor/Professor: Brad Bartlett | Student: Jaiwon Lee
Assignment: "Open Movement" is a series of weekly artist-led workshops at Performance Space New York, where artists and participants come together to collaborate and venture into unconventional artistic expressions like: Choreography + Neo-Classical Ballet, Printmaking + Theatre Performance, Painting + Literature, and more.
Approach: The poster conveys the concept of collaboration and synergy by overlaying patterns created from the logo, which consists of rhythmic geometric shapes.
Results: The poster celebrates the collaboration of artists in an unconventional manner, celebrating art beyond traditional boundaries.

240 CREDITS&COMMENTARY

124 FILM POSTER: A CLOCKWORK ORANGE | School: Lehigh University
Instructor/Professor: Maurizio Masi | Student: Savannah Thomas
Assignment: I aimed to craft a film poster embodying the peculiar and unsettling nuances of the 1971 dystopian movie, A Clockwork Orange. Amidst a plethora of existing designs, my priority was to ensure mine stood out as uniquely original and avant-garde.
Approach: Embracing a less-than-sober state enhanced the creative process for this particular project. I generated numerous ideas, sketched out abstract concepts, and deciphered them the following morning to recreate the fever-dream experience of watching the film.
Results: After refining my creative process, I arrived at a singular design that effectively encapsulated the eye-catching yet unsettling elements of Ludovico's Technique depicted in the movie. Unanimously praised by peers, professors, and roommates, it proved to be a captivating representation that faithfully conveyed the film's iconic elements.

125 STREET POETS POSTER | School: ArtCenter College of Design
Instructor/Professor: Stephen Serrato | Student: Jaiwon Lee
Assignment: Street Poets is a non-profit organization in L.A. that invites schools, youths on probation, and adults to make and share poetry and music to build community and express themselves. The poster promotes their community event, "Hula Hula."
Approach: The poster showcases identity system that drew inspiration from the varied languages and typography found on street signs in Los Angeles. The combination of colors and typefaces conveys the city's diversity and the expressive voices of poetry.
Results: The poster displays Street Poet's mission and the healing power of poetry.

126 TRASH - CLIMATE CHANGE POSTER
School: California State University, Fullerton | Instructor/Professor: Theron Moore
Student: Matthew Tweedie
Assignment: My goal was to design a poster that shows the climate change problem. That one problem has to do with the enormous amount of trash that covers our land and sea.
Approach: My creative process for this project included finding trash all around my neighborhood, which was not difficult—then taking that trash to create my typography that allowed me to spell out the words on the poster.

127 PARIS AIR SHOW 2025 POSTER | School: Texas State University
Instructor/Professor: William Meek | Student: Emily Anne Chu
Assignment: Create a promotional poster for the 2025 Paris Air Show. My goal was to make my poster look at first glance like birds were flying around the Eiffel Tower. I hoped to make the birds just as recognizable as planes as I could to make the audience take another look.
Approach: The Paris Air Show celebrates all things aeronautics. Birds also fall into the category of aeronautics. For this reason, I wanted to put planes around the Eiffel Tower in a way that made them look like birds flocking at first glance. I first started by finding a high-quality photo of the Eiffel Tower, as well as several images of various types of planes. I then downsized the planes to make them bird-sized and placed them around the Eiffel Tower in a flocking formation. I chose to let the poster speak for itself and not include a headline.
Results: I think this project was a success. Most people when asked identified the planes as birds first like intended. The only thing I would maybe change is researching bird formations further to make the planes more convincingly look like birds.

128 THE COOPER UNION 3 POSTER SERIES | School: School of Visual Arts
Instructor/Professor: Peter Ahlberg | Student: Sang Eun Chae
Assignment: A series of 3 posters for the Fall 2023 Cooper Union Lectures and Events at The Irwin S. Chanin School of Architecture.
Approach: Designing structural posters inspired by architectural schools and their box-shaped logos. I propose a dynamic and organized layout based on the title and content of each poster on a grid of hexahedrons.
Results: The process of creating a three-dimensional and structural poster in a plane using only text was a process to overcome the limitations of space.

129 STRANGE CREATURES OF THE WEST WOODLANDS
School: Belmont University, Watkins College of Art | Instructor/Professor: Lauren Lowen
Student: Marina Ibrahim | Poster Size: 18 x 24in
Assignment: The assignment was to make a scientific poster of made-up creatures that you would find in a video game or animated show (such as Avatar the Last Airbender). The goal was to make interesting creatures and fit them together in a way that was harmonious.
Approach: I chose a region/terrain to unify the animals and played off of their existing traits to transform them to either better aid them and/or make them seem more mystical.
Results: Overall, the project succeeded in its objectives and form.

130 PLASTIC POLLUTION AWARENESS (POSTER SERIES)
School: California State University, Fullerton | Instructor/Professor: Theron Moore
Student: Christine Rodriguez
Assignment: For many years, scientists have been publicly reporting about climate change. Many huge corporations are major contributors and turn a blind eye towards this topic. A good portion of the public does not know how much they pollute or know if the companies they are buying from engage in environmentally sustainable manufacturing practices. This project criticizes the mass consumption of plastic. My intention was to go a step further beyond the cautionary tale of plastic ending up in the ocean. I created an alternate reality of an everyday item that you would see at the market to make it uncomfortable to look at. The tone is oddly eccentric to make this topic approachable, and yet ominous and uncomfortable.
Approach: Originally, this project was focused on criticizing fast fashion. Fast fashion is the mass production of trending fashion styles that mainly involve materials that require a lot of important resources to create. Producing fast fashion and washing clothes made with plastic materials allow mini plastic particles into the ocean and in our drinking water. Throughout my process, it became more broad than solely focusing on fast fashion. The message transformed into communicating plastic pollution awareness.
Results: My mentor was proud of the journey I went through with this project. He gave me feedback while I interpreted his words and brought something new for critique every week. He always encouraged to create something that would change the way a viewer would interpret something. At the end of four weeks, this is what the idea was finalized into.

131 THE BIRDS | School: Kean University
Instructor/Professor: Nancy Campbell | Student: Samantha Caban
Assignment: The assignment was to create a poster for a classic movie.
Approach: Samantha chose to illustrate The Birds by Alfred Hitchcock using the top of the T to create an electrical wire filled with birds that will attack people.
Results: The class thought the design was very interesting and clever.

132 KOREA TRADITIONAL MUSIC FESTIVAL
School: Hansung University, Design & Arts Institute
Instructors/Professors: Dong-Joo Park, Seung-Min Han | Student: Kyeong Joo Choi
Assignment: This is a festival poster to promote the Taepyeongso, a traditional Korean musical instrument. It is often used in marching songs because of its loud and morale-boosting tone. It was also used in agricultural music to create excitement. In addition, the Taepyeongso can also express a sense of loss and mourning.The Tae Pyeongso Festival is a festival where you can feel emotions of 'excitement' and 'sadness'. Through this festival, we hope that people will become interested in the Taepyeongso and Korean traditional music.
Approach: We focused on "excitement" by emphasizing the Korean emotions of "excitement" and "han." First, I designed the typography using the taepyeongso as inspiration. The Taepyeongso has a wide range of high and low pitches, so I used white lines to represent this sound. The white lines also symbolizes the Korean sangmo dance (the taepyeongso is an instrument used in the sangmo dance). The colors were inspired by the Korean colors of Obangsang, and we wanted to use traditional colors to showcase the charm of Korea.

133 FILM POSTER: THE USUAL SUSPECTS | School: Lehigh University
Instructor/Professor: Maurizio Masi | Student: Emma Valle
Assignment: Recreate a movie poster from a film on a list of cult classics. My parents helped me pick the movie and I took note of scenes and images that they, as viewers who had seen the movie before, and myself, a new viewer, found important.
Approach: I started my creative process by picking out scenes and images from the film that were engaging and thought-provoking. I originally wanted to use symbolism to capture the twist in the movie and had a few drafts centered around the big reveal, but I found that some scenes were able to capture the intensity of the movie more clearly in a single poster.

134 EUCLID COFFEE MAKER | School: M.AD School of Ideas Atlanta
Instructor/Professor: Hank Richardson | Student: Bryan Robinson
Assignment: Redesign a product to solve a problem that exists with its current design.
Approach: My approach was centered around people not knowing how much coffee grounds and/or water to add to their coffee machine when they make a pot. The key is to have a ratio of 1:17, coffee to water. Since this ratio is key, I used the Golden Ratio as my design inspiration and named it after Euclid's Mathematics. The user can swivel the brew basket from side to side grinding the coffee directly into the filter. A scale built into the brew basket measures the grounds and then disperses the perfect 1:17 ratio of water to have the perfect pot of coffee regardless of how much coffee is in the brew basket.

135 CHAIR - TRANSPARENCY | School: M.AD School of Ideas Atlanta
Instructor/Professor: Hank Richardson | Student: Brianna Bowman
Assignment: "From a random drawing of two graphic styles, spanning a timeline from 1847 through 2023, each selected by you from a blind drawing, research and prepare a written 1 page brief on the background of the styles. Based upon your research of the period, interpret, plan, and construct a chair. As you begin your design, consider how you are employing a historical comparison, taking into account that the transition of such a comparison might employ a different set of values than what was the manifesto of the original movement. You will need to unite contemporary influences of culture, taking into consideration social and economic climates of today. Look for the relationship of revivalism, however remember your design ultimate will not look anything like your period. The design of your Chair should reflect Modernist principles of both form and function."
Approach: The 'graphic style' that initially inspired my Chair was postmodernism. Postmodern style often relied on the fusion of diverse influences and mediums, especially those which may initially seem incompatible. In doing so, this style challenged both designers and viewers to question traditional practices and established norms. My chair embodies a celebration of individuality and an invitation to be boldly, authentically oneself. The transparent glass frame symbolizes the courage to navigate the world with full-hearted transparency, shameless and barefaced, while the vibrant red center serves as a display of inner boldness. Deliberately shaped with inward-curving arms, the shape of the frame mirrors the warmth of a self-embrace, providing the user with a sense of comfort and acceptance.

136 YI CONG | School: School of Visual Arts
Instructor/Professor: Peter Ahlberg | Student: Alicia Liu
Assignment: Yi Cong is a series of installations that are designed nearby beaches and oceans as a way to utilize the space for climate resilience infrastructure. They are designed to deteriorate naturally. The concept focuses on the dematerialization and decay aspect of life.

137 DOPE, DOPAMINE | School: Dankook University
Instructor/Professor: Hoon-Dong Chung | Student: Minkyeong Cho
Assignment: Short-form videos such as YouTube Shorts and Instagram Reels have gained tremendous popularity. These formats create a swamp of infinite scrolling, making it difficult for users to escape. Moreover, application addiction is meticulously designed, utilizing features such as 'likes' or 'push notifications' as triggers for application addiction. This project was conceived to raise awareness about dopamine addiction caused by such applications.
Approach: While there is general caution against dopamine addiction from alcohol, drugs, and gambling, there is less awareness about dopamine addiction from applications. Drawing parallels with drug and gambling addiction, the aim was to highlight the dangers of application addiction. To maximize impact, vivid colors were chosen. I also visually represented the dangers of dopamine addiction using an unconventional format with 3D types.
Results: The work was exhibited at the graduation exhibition and garnered significant attention. Viewers were intrigued by posters and compilations composed of vibrant emoji colors, providing everyone who saw it with time to contemplate the issue of application addiction.

138 OIJI | School: School of Visual Arts
Instructor/Professor: Jon Newman | Student: Jae Ho Yi
Assignment: Oiji is a restaurant pursuing a creative contemporary Korean dining experience composed uniquely for NYC.
Approach: One of the most important elements of branding is the logo, so I tried to find the right one. Then I bring identities from the mood of the restaurant and the cultural element.
Results: After finishing the project, I contacted Chef Brian to inquire about the possibility of taking a photoshoot at his restaurant. He agreed, allowing me to visit and capture images for my project. This experience was valuable and expanded my role as a designer, shifting from sitting at a desk to actively engaging with people who might benefit from my design.

139 LINARI PASTICCERIA | School: Texas A&M University-Commerce
Instructor/Professor: Veronica Vaughn | Student: Lexi Oliver
Assignment: Research and rebrand an existing Italian bakery. Create a brand logo/logotype that is distinctive and memorable. Translate the visual identity effectively across branded material.
Approach: Linari Pasticceria is a bakery based in Rome, Italy. It has your everyday stop and go pastries as well as substantial catering services. My concept was to lean into the sophistication of catering and place it into the fast pace life of this Italian city. The solution being high contrast brand colors and strong but elegant line work.
Results: After critiques and grading, Professor Vaughn thought I had earned a high B. The piece was later selected by the panel of lead teachers and director to be submitted into shows.

140 BADANG | School: School of Visual Arts
Instructor/Professor: Justin Colt | Student: Sungeun Shin
Assignment: Designing an identity for a restaurant is a unique challenge. Many different components needs to be carefully considered. All need to work harmoniously, and reflect the overall feeling of the restaurant. Perhaps this is why 9 in 10 restaurants fail. The type of restaurant, theme, location and overall concept were up to us.
Approach: Haenyeo are female free-divers who sell freshly caught seafood from Jeju Island directly in local markets to make a living. Badang is a high-end restaurant known for its highly specialized customer service and a spirit of fearlessness and passion inspired by the Haenyeo. Discover Jeju Island's untamed beauty and savor the ocean's bounty with the Jeju Haenyeo. The textures of rock and wind was used as graphic materials. I used a dashed line to reflect the characteristics of Jeju Island's basalt stones, which have many holes. The elongated straight line in the logo symbolizes the bravery of female free divers.
Results: I designed a unique restaurant in New York City, resulting in a successful project.

241 CREDITS & COMMENTARY

141 JUA RESTAURANT REBRANDING | School: School of Visual Arts
Instructor/Professor: Jon Newman | Student: Yoon-Gi Park
Assignment: Jua is a fine dining restaurant that specializes in Korean cuisine. For the rebranding, I wanted to reflect the restaurant's sophisticated atmosphere and its contemporary dishes. Additionally, I wanted to create a take-out packaging that recognized Korea's traditional culture while also giving the design a modern application.
Approach: While designing the logo, I conducted extensive research into Korean design elements, particularly drawing inspiration from traditional patterns. Subsequently, a more profound investigation led me to discover the hibiscus flower, which stands as Korea's national emblem. Embracing this symbol not only paid homage to Korea's heritage but also seamlessly aligned with the restaurant's culinary concept. Furthermore, the choice of a primary color palette was derived from the hues prevalent in traditional Korean architecture. The packaging design took inspiration from Korea's historical three-tiered lunch boxes, distinguished by intricate surface patterns. The patterns on the packaging were inspired by the brush strokes found in traditional Korean paintings portraying majestic mountains.
Results: The project was positively received by classmates and my professor.

142 MOE'S CAFE | School: School of Visual Arts
Instructor/Professor: Joseph Newton | Student: Yubin Won
Assignment: The goal was to redesign a school cafe in SVA called Moe's Cafe. Moe's Cafe serves quick meals for busy students but lacked strong and cohesive brand identity.
Approach: Since SVA is such a diverse school, I got inspired by the New York subway, from the idea that everybody comes from different countries and gather in Moe's.
Results: Students from SVA enjoyed the brand concept that it mimics the subway vibe but also mentioned that it wasn't so obvious and gave a lot of good feedbacks.

143 NEUVEAU A TO Z | School: Parsons School of Design
Instructor/Professor: Charlotte Von Hardenburgh | Student: Cynthia Huiwen Tan
Assignment: This is experimental typeface inspired by Hector Guimard and art nouveau.
Approach: As part of the 36 Days of Type challenge, the entire typeface takes an abstract visual approach inspired by the Art Nouveau movement in France. From its colors to shapes to texture rendering, it mimics the fluidity and elegance from the movement.

144 GIWA | School: School of Visual Arts
Instructor/Professor: Zipeng Zhu | Student: Becky Baek
Assignment: Giwa is a buildable custom typeface named after the traditional roof construction of Korean architecture.
Approach: The motivation for creating Giwa was to design a typeface that connects to my cultural heritage. Giwa is named after the roof-tiling method used in traditional Korean architecture. The repeated patterns and construction of the tiles inspired me to create a buildable typeface using a consistent grid system.
Results: The Giwa typeface visually connects the Korean cultural background and the practical, buildable grid system.

144 SHARD TYPEFACE | School: School of Visual Arts
Instructor/Professor: Willie Ip | Student: Sara Mehta
Assignment: Shard is a bold and contemporary typeface that stands out with its unique design. This sans serif font is characterized by its high contrast and geometric shapes. The typeface is made up of three shapes: a square, a rectangle, and a rhombus. Each letter is constructed using a combination of these shapes, resulting in a distinctive look and feel.
Approach: Process started by sketching out letter forms on a grid. Learning the anatomy of a letter was the main purpose of this project. I gave myself three shapes to play with and used the shapes to create the typeface in Latin as well as Devanagri characters.
Results: It was so rewarding to see how three simple shapes can be used to create so many different letters. It was also interesting to see how it could apply to different languages.

145 AEROSPHERES WEBSITE
School: University of North Texas | Instructor/Professor: Whitney Holden
Students: Ylliana Larsen, Aurora Schafer, Daniel Mejia, Lauren Hinson
Assignment: Rebrand and website design for Free Spirit Spheres, a unique glamping destination in Canada known for its one-of-a-kind spherical treehouses.
Approach: The team researched the industry, created user personas and re-imagined the content and information architecture of the site for a better user experience. The website was inspired by the spherical architecture and tranquil nature of the location.
Results: The final website is a contemporary approach, with content significantly curated from the original site. The user interface was refined, and photography became the most important tool for communicating the uniqueness of the accommodations.

SILVER DESIGN WINNERS:

147 ZUBAAN BOOK COVER | School: School of Visual Arts
Instructors/Professors: Courtney Gooch, Rory Simms | Student: Ariana Gupta

147 MARTY'S KID (BOOK COVER) | School: Texas Christian University
Instructor/Professor: Jan Ballard | Student: Isabella Perez
Author: Hannah K. Johnson | Photographer: CJ Johnson

147 MCDONALD'S HOLY BIBLE | School: ArtCenter College of Design
Instructor/Professor: Michael Neal | Student: Aoran Ma | Other: AI-Generated Imagery

147 ELDERS IN MODERN SOCIETY | School: ArtCenter College of Design
Instructors/Professors: Constantin Chopin, Samantha Fleming | Student: Grace Kim

147 BREATHING LESSONS BOOK COVER | School: Texas A&M University-Commerce
Instructor/Professor: Joshua Ege | Student: Brett Roth

148 BOOK COVER SERIES REDESIGN | School: Lehigh University
Instructor/Professor: Maurizio Masi | Student: Michelle Zhang

148 SOVIET POETRY BOOK COLLECTION
School: California State University, Fullerton | Instructor/Professor: Theron Moore
Student: Viktoriia Trapizonian

148 PLAYSTATION - BRAND BOOK
School: Virginia Commonwealth University, VCU Brandcenter
Instructor/Professor: Thomas Scharpf | Students: Jade Chen, Jack DeMare

148 THE STORY OF CREATION DIVINE ARTISTRY | School: University of North Texas
Instructor/Professor: Stephen Zhang | Student: Kyla Brown

148 HUMAN-COMPUTER (HUMAN) | School: California Institute of the Arts
Instructor/Professor: Louise Sandhaus | Student: Caihui Chen

148 SUNDAY'S BEST: HOW BLACK PEOPLE USED FASHION AS PROTEST & HOW IT INFLUENCED A CULTURAL SHIFT | School: ArtCenter College of Design
Instructor/Professor: Tracey Shiffman | Student: Addis Ababa Barge
Printer: NonStop Printing

148 HORROR THROUGH TIME | School: California State University, Fullerton
Instructor/Professor: Theron Moore | Student: Megan Cossins

148 ETERNAL 1 | School: ArtCenter College of Design
Instructor/Professor: Cheri Gray | Student: Shuwen Ding

149 CIRCULAR BOOK DESIGN COVER | School: Rhode Island School of Design
Instructor/Professor: Unattributed | Student: Li June Choi

149 ILLUMINATUS | School: M.AD School of Ideas Atlanta
Instructor/Professor: Hank Richardson | Student: Cassidy O'Connor

149 ¡ARRIBA ARRIBA! ¡ANDALE ANDALE! | School: ArtCenter College of Design
Instructor/Professor: Tracey Shiffman | Student: Yvonne Ye

150 EFFORTLESS DAYS: CONSUMING AND ITS RELATIONSHIP TO PERSONAL VALUE | School: ArtCenter College of Design
Instructor/Professor: Tracey Shiffman | Student: Bella Wang

150 BOOK COVER SERIES REDESIGN | School: Lehigh University
Instructor/Professor: Maurizio Masi | Student: Aviela Maynard

150 WILD | School: M.AD School of Ideas Atlanta
Instructor/Professor: Hank Richardson | Student: Jamie Jason

150 SCRATCHING THE SURFACE: THE HIDDEN BEAUTY OF JAPANESE BODYSUIT TATTOOING | School: ArtCenter College of Design
Instructor/Professor: Tracey Shiffman | Student: Kyoko Takahashi

150 LUMINOSITY | School: ArtCenter College of Design
Instructor/Professor: Jimena Gamio Valdivieso | Student: Sydney Lee

150 DEE DUM: DISNEY 100 | School: School of Visual Arts
Instructors/Professors: Tyler Comrie, Alex Merto | Student: Charlotte Grimm

151 A SONG OF ICE AND FIRE BOOK REDESIGN | School: School of Visual Arts
Instructor/Professor: Matthew Lenning | Student: Lela Fand

151 BICYCLE BRAND CAPABILITY BOOK | School: University of North Texas
Instructor/Professor: Stephen Zhang | Student: Maxwell Pius

151 ART FROM ART | School: M.AD School of Ideas Atlanta
Instructor/Professor: Hank Richardson | Student: Catarina Sterlacci

151 LOEWE BRAND BOOK | School: University of North Texas
Instructor/Professor: Stephen Zhang | Student: Rachel Blow

151 TO ALL THE BOYS I'VE LOVED BEFORE BOOK COVERS & JACKETS REDESIGN | School: California State University, Fullerton
Instructor/Professor: Theron Moore | Student: Khoa Nguyen

152 COMMIT OFFAL MEATS | School: Capilano University
Instructor/Professor: Dominique Walker | Student: Natasha Lee

152 JEFFREY CAMPBELL | School: Brigham Young University
Instructor/Professor: Doug Thomas | Student: Ellie Burrows

152 MUSEUM OF SCIENCE LONDON | School: ArtCenter College of Design
Instructor/Professor: Simon Johnston | Student: Jaiwon Lee

152 URBAN OUTFITTERS REDESIGN | School: School of Visual Arts
Instructor/Professor: Joseph Han | Student: Huu Minh Pham

152 UN: | School: ArtCenter College of Design
Instructor/Professor: Annie Huang Luck | Student: Minsik Nam

152 HILARY HAHN ALBUM BRANDING | School: School of Visual Arts
Instructor/Professor: Justin Colt | Student: Younghyun Kim

153 USPS REBRANDING | School: ArtCenter College of Design
Instructor/Professor: Simon Johnston | Student: Heejai Park

153 MILANO CORTINA 2026 WINTER OLYMPICS REBRANDING
School: ArtCenter College of Design | Instructor/Professor: Charles Lin
Student: Leni Gao

154 MELIORA | School: Texas Christian University
Instructor/Professor: Bill Galyean | Student: Isabella Baker

154 SAN DIEGO COMIC-CON REBRAND | School: ArtCenter College of Design
Instructor/Professor: Gerardo Herrera | Student: Orlando Li

154 AMERICAN BALLET THEATRE REBRANDING | School: School of Visual Arts
Instructor/Professor: Peter Ahlberg | Student: Alicia Liu

154 LANGUAGE + TECHNOLOGY CONFERENCE | School: ArtCenter College of Design
Instructor/Professor: Simon Johnston | Student: Mishen Liu

154 HOWDY CAKES BRANDING SYSTEM | School: Baylor University
Instructor/Professor: Genaro Solis Rivero | Student: Kate Sudderth

154 NYC BALLET REBRAND | School: School of Visual Arts
Instructor/Professor: Eric Baker | Student: Jiyeon Kim

154 TRIPLE A REBRAND | School: ArtCenter College of Design
Instructor/Professor: Gerardo Herrera | Student: Shengjie Wu

154 JUNO MOTORCYCLES | School: Texas Christian University
Instructor/Professor: Bill Gaylean | Student: Corinne Green

155 NEW YORK FASHION WEEK | School: ArtCenter College of Design
Instructor/Professor: Brad Bartlett | Student: Lilian Pham

155 REEBOK | School: M.AD School of Ideas Atlanta
Instructor/Professor: Hank Richardson | Student: Anna LeBer

155 MUSEUM OF CONTEMPORARY PHOTOGRAPHY
School: ArtCenter College of Design
Instructor/Professor: Simon Johnston | Student: Alan Xu

155 ANTI-AGEISM CAMPAIGN | School: University of Texas at Arlington
Instructor/Professor: Ben Dolezal | Student: Emily Brown

155 POSTMATES | School: University of North Texas
Instructor/Professor: Douglas May | Student: Maeci Ray

155 MBARI | School: ArtCenter College of Design
Instructor/Professor: Charles Lin | Student: Meiyun Chen

155 ROCKET LAB REDESIGN | School: ArtCenter College of Design
Instructor/Professor: Ming Tai | Student: Hanson Ma

155 CASULO HOTEL | School: University of North Texas
Instructor/Professor: Douglas May | Student: Jordan Heath

156 VISIT CALIFORNIA | School: Brigham Young University
Instructor/Professor: Linda Reynolds | Student: Hannah Javadi

242 CREDITS & COMMENTARY

156 APRÈS FURNITURE | School: School of Visual Arts
Instructor/Professor: Eric Baker | Student: Claudia Curbelo

156 LINCOLN PARK ZOO REBRAND | School: School of the Art Institute of Chicago
Instructor/Professor: Michael Konetzka | Student: Xiaoqi Shang

156 HINT - BRAND IDENTITY | School: Pratt Institute
Instructor/Professor: Cindy Buckley Koren | Student: Jonathan Lin

156 THE CLIBURN | School: ArtCenter College of Design
Instructor/Professor: Elaine Alderette | Student: Esther Yeseul Lee

156 SPARK | School: University of the Arts London
Instructor/Professor: Joana Pereira | Student: Wenbin Sun

156 NOGUCHI MUSEUM BRAND IDENTITY | School: School of Visual Arts
Instructor/Professor: Pedro Mendes | Student: Doah Kwon

156 COLLIDING WAVES: MUSIC FESTIVAL BRANDING | School: M.AD School of Ideas
Instructor/Professor: Luis Bravo | Student: Michele Mardorf

157 NASA REBRAND | School: ArtCenter College of Design
Instructor/Professor: Simon Johnston | Student: Elaine Gong
Photographers: Terence Burke, Meriç Dağlı, Joe Han, Tengyart
Photo Editor: Benjamin Recino | Image Sources: done4today, Tryfonov - stock.adobe.com

157 AMOEBA MUSIC REBRAND | School: ArtCenter College of Design
Instructor/Professor: Ming Tai | Student: Jiani Hong

157 NIKON (RE)BRAND IDENTITY SYSTEM | School: ArtCenter College of Design
Instructor/Professor: Simon Johnston | Student: Kissa Angjaya
Photographers: Henri-Carter Bresson, Wang Chuan, Austin Garcia, Tiago Magalhães, Irving Penn, Steven Sebring, Hiroshi Sugimoto | Typefaces: BC Novatica, Gopher

157 MUSEUM OF FASHION PHOTOGRAPHY | School: ArtCenter College of Design
Instructor/Professor: Simon Johnston | Student: Ruby Minhyoung Kim

157 MOMA FALL CAMPAIGN | School: School of Visual Arts
Instructor/Professor: Andrea Trabucco-Campos | Student: Doyeon Kim

158 VISUAL IDENTITY MAKEOVER OF BALATON SOUND MUSIC FESTIVAL
School: KREA Design School | Instructor/Professor: Kathi Zsolt
Student: Anastasia Charalambous

158 NATIONAL WOMEN'S SOCCER LEAGUE | School: ArtCenter College of Design
Instructor/Professor: Angad Singh | Student: Brian White

158 BROOKLYN BOTANIC GARDEN | School: Fashion Institute of Technology
Instructor/Professor: Nicole Zizila | Student: Yong Han Shin

158 GYEONGNAM ART MUSEUM | School: Fashion Institute of Technology
Instructor/Professor: Nicole Zizila | Student: Yong Han Shin

158 ISA | School: M.AD School of Ideas Atlanta
Instructor/Professor: Hank Richardson | Student: Catarina Sterlacci

158 BIRD-IN-HAND BRAND PITCH DECK | School: Texas State University
Instructors/Professors: Jeff Davis, William Meek | Student: Kelsie Brouillette

159 NORMANDIE HOTEL BRANDING | School: University of North Texas
Instructor/Professor: Stephen Zhang | Student: Mariangelis Pagan

159 WILLIAMS RACING | School: M.AD School of Ideas Atlanta
Instructor/Professor: Hank Richardson | Student: Reagan Williams

159 TAVOLA BRANDING SYSTEM | School: Baylor University
Instructor/Professor: Genaro Solis Rivero | Student: Brooke Sockwell

159 RU GUO - RESTAURANT IDENTITY | School: School of Visual Arts
Instructor/Professor: Justin Colt | Student: Tzu-Chieh (Kate) Wu

159 STORM KING ART CENTER | School: ArtCenter College of Design
Instructors/Professors: Shirleen Lavalais, Miles Mazzie | Student: Sydney Lee

159 BLUE BAG | School: West Chester University
Instructor/Professor: Scotty Reifsnyder | Student: Madison Kalbach

160 MONTEREY JAZZ FESTIVAL | School: ArtCenter College of Design
Instructor/Professor: Elaine Alderette | Student: Elaine Lee

160 FABRIC MUSEUM | School: ArtCenter College of Design
Instructor/Professor: Brad Bartlett | Student: Jocelyn Ziying Zhao

160 MUSEUM OF FLIGHT BRANDING
School: Pennsylvania State University | Instructor/Professor: Emily Burns
Students: Colette Albertson, Emma Cohen, Madison Laufer, Will Welsh

160 CURVA BRANDING | School: School of Visual Arts
Instructor/Professor: Pedro Mendes | Student: Seongyun Park

160 FILM FUSION FILM FESTIVAL | School: West Chester University
Instructor/Professor: Karen Watkins | Student: Morgan Strusallen

160 REBRANDING OF NEW YORK CITY BALLET | School: School of Visual Arts
Instructor/Professor: Eric Baker | Student: Yixuan Wang

161 NXT MUSEUM | School: ArtCenter College of Design
Instructor/Professor: Brad Bartlett | Student: Lillian Zhang

161 INSTITUTE FOR ART AND OLFACTION | School: ArtCenter College of Design
Instructor/Professor: Elaine Alderette | Student: Joonhee Park

161 LA CHINATOWN REBRANDING PROJECT | School: ArtCenter College of Design
Instructor/Professor: Stephen Serrato | Student: Zifei Ding

162 LETTERFORM ARCHIVE | School: George Brown College
Instructor/Professor: Unattributed | Student: Pantea Kouhpayeh

162 ARS ELECTRONICA INSTITUTE | School: ArtCenter College of Design
Instructor/Professor: Brad Bartlett | Student: Soomin Jeon

162 GG BY GAMESTOP | School: ArtCenter College of Design
Instructor/Professor: Gerardo Herrera | Student: Glenn Ryan

162 OCMA | School: ArtCenter College of Design
Instructor/Professor: Brad Bartlett | Student: Esther Yang

162 CURVA BRAND IDENTITY | School: School of Visual Arts
Instructor/Professor: Pedro Mendes | Student: Huu Minh Pham

162 FOUND SOUND MUSIC FESTIVAL | School: School of Visual Arts
Instructor/Professor: Andrea Trabucco-Campos | Student: Don Park

162 RAY FILM FESTIVAL | School: School of Visual Arts
Instructor/Professor: Joseph Newton | Student: Sara Mehta

162 HAMMER MUSEUM | School: ArtCenter College of Design
Instructor/Professor: Brad Bartlett | Student: Leonel Guardado

163 ONE A DAY HEALTH CARE | School: School of Visual Arts
Instructors/Professors: Rory Simms, Courtney Gooch | Student: Yaxin Zou

163 MONOCHROME | School: ArtCenter College of Design
Instructor/Professor: Simon Johnston | Student: Sydney Lee

163 CIRCUS HALL OF FAME | School: Rhode Island School of Design
Instructor/Professor: Richard Rose | Student: Jacob Hwan Lee

163 TADAO ANDO EXHIBITION | School: School of Visual Arts
Instructor/Professor: Pedro Mendes | Student: Huu Minh Pham

163 GET PRICK'D | School: University of the Incarnate Word
Instructor/Professor: Teresa Trevino | Student: Rozlynn Macbeth Olivas

164 BARNES & NOBLE REBRANDING | School: ArtCenter College of Design
Instructor/Professor: Angad Singh | Student: Handanu Ardhata

164 FIRST BANK | School: ArtCenter College of Design
Instructor/Professor: Gerardo Herrera | Student: Jamal Abdullahi

164 RENEWED CORPORATE IDENTITY OF TRAFÓ HOUSE OF CONTEMPORARY ARTS | School: KREA Design School | Instructor/Professor: Darázs Bódog
Student: Laár Ambrus

164 BAMBOO RESTAURANT | School: Texas Christian University
Instructor/Professor: David Elizalde | Student: Kien Nguyen

164 KIDS ART CLASS | School: Duy Tan University
Instructors/Professors: Nguyen Tri Phuong Dong, Le Phuong Hieu
Student: Tran Uyen Nhi

164 HMONG SPRING FESTIVAL | School: Duy Tan University
Instructor/Professor: Nguyen Tri Phuong Dong | Student: Vo Ky Bao Ngoc

164 ZAYTOON, A SYRIAN COFFEE HOUSE | School: University of Louisville
Instructor/Professor: Trysh Wahlig | Student: Judie Haidar

164 CHEOLEO HOMESTAY | School: Duy Tan University
Instructor/Professor: Nguyen Tri Phuong Dong | Student: Ngo Chau Vy

165 BLUE BELL ICE CREAM BRANDING PROGRAM
School: University of North Texas | Instructor/Professor: Douglas May
Student: Annika Snow

165 FUNNEL | School: Purdue University
Instructor/Professor: Hyung Joo Kim | Student: Courtney Kurtz

165 CHEESECAKE FACTORY BRANDING | School: University of North Texas
Instructor/Professor: Douglas May | Student: Paige Sanders

165 TWO BIRDS & ONE SCONE FOOD TRUCK | School: West Chester University
Instructor/Professor: Scotty Reifsnyder | Student: Abby Gerber

165 BUILD-A-BEAR | School: University of North Texas
Instructor/Professor: Douglas May | Student: Lauren Clark

165 BEARBOX ADVENTURE GEAR BRAND PROPOSAL | School: Purdue University
Instructor/Professor: Hyung Joo Kim | Student: Julie Haseman

165 TAPIOCHA BUBBLE TEA BRANDING CONCEPT | School: Purdue University
Instructor/Professor: Hyung Joo Kim | Student: Evan Olinger

165 SIX FLAGS CAMPAIGN | School: University of North Texas
Instructor/Professor: Douglas May | Student: Macy Belton

166 LINIMASA RESTO & SPACE | School: ArtCenter College of Design
Instructor/Professor: Gerardo Herrera | Student: Handanu Ardhata

166 BLUE WILLOW RESTAURANT BRANDING | School: School of Visual Arts
Instructor/Professor: Jon Newman | Student: Yubin Won

166 HARRIS REED BRANDING CAMPAIGN | School: University of North Texas
Instructor/Professor: Stephen Zhang | Student: Sabrina Franco Barrera

166 ELLA.INCORPORATED PERSONAL BRAND | School: Brigham Young University
Instructor/Professor: Doug Thomas | Student: Ella Babcock

166 DOUGHEE PIZZA | School: Lehigh University
Instructor/Professor: Jenny Kowalski | Student: Xinni Hong

166 EXHALE: SIZE-INCLUSIVE HEALTHCARE | School: Temple University
Instructor/Professor: Kelly Holohan | Student: MeiLi Carling
Photography Sources: Allgo, Disabled and Here, Michael Poley, Pexels, SELF Magazine, Shoog McDaniel, Vice Gender Spectrum Collection, #WOCinTech Chat

166 HOI AN LOTUS SILK | School: Duy Tan University
Instructor/Professor: Nguyen Tri Phuong Dong | Student: Nguyen Thi My Linh

166 CAMP LONGHORN
School: Texas A&M University-Commerce | Instructor/Professor: Joshua Ege
Student: Jackelyn De Lara | Image Sources: Mego-studio, #416836844; Oleg R, #618181668; x10, #591171246 (Adobe Stock)

167 TOUR. | School: M.AD School of Ideas Atlanta
Instructor/Professor: Hank Richardson | Student: Jamie Jason

167 BLING H2O | School: Rochester Institute of Technology
Instructor/Professor: Anne Jordan | Student: Eshaan Sojatia

167 MOREDERN: STREETWEAR BRAND FOR ENTHUSIASTS OF MODERN FURNITURE DESIGN AND GRAPHIC ART | School: School of Visual Arts
Instructor/Professor: Peter Ahlberg | Student: Yuan Chen

167 NAIL QR CODE BRANDING | School: School of Visual Arts
Instructor/Professor: Rich Tu | Student: Dong Hyun Kim | Other: AI

167 PATAKHA FASHION BRAND | School: School of Visual Arts
Instructor/Professor: Rich Tu | Student: Sara Mehta

168 HERCULES WINE | School: Texas Christian University
Instructor/Professor: Jan Ballard | Student: Lucia Canseco

168 SOYA VEGAN FUSION | School: Capilano University
Instructor/Professor: Dominique Walker | Student: Celina Zhong

243 CREDITS & COMMENTARY

168 HAPPY TAB KOMBUCHA | School: Texas State University
Instructor/Professor: William Meek | Student: Fallon Russell | Other: Unsplash

168 SFOGLINI PASTA BRAND CAMPAIGN | School: University of North Texas
Instructor/Professor: Douglas May | Student: Kara McKintosh

168 FLORIDA'S NATURAL | School: University of North Texas
Instructor/Professor: Douglas May | Student: Macy Belton

168 HUE SEASONAL EATING | School: Capilano University
Instructor/Professor: Dominique Walker | Student: Anais Bayle

168 CAFEFE (SHOP) | School: Duy Tan University
Instructors/Professors: Nguyen Tri Phuong Dong, Hoang Viet Quoc
Student: Le Van Dung

168 MEME YENBAI ROSE APPLE LIQUOR | School: Duy Tan University
Instructor/Professor: Nguyen Tri Phuong Dong | Student: Tran Vu Quynh Thi
Photographers: VTV News, Communist Party of Vietnam Online Newspaper

169 COMET AND CRUST | School: Lehigh University
Instructor/Professor: Jenny Kowalski | Student: Angelique Ronca

169 NEON UMAMI | School: Texas State University
Instructors/Professors: Mikaela Buck, Jeff Davis | Student: Elmo Chavez

169 HUONG SPA | School: Duy Tan University
Instructor/Professor: Nguyen Tri Phuong Dong | Student: Nguyen Thi Hoang Yen

169 WICKED VISION BRANDING | School: Texas A&M University-Commerce
Instructor/Professor: Joshua Ege | Student: Kiara Gomez

169 RETAIL LINE FOR THE HUNTINGTON | School: Otis College of Art & Design
Instructor/Professor: Emily Carlson | Student: Charlie Utter
Art Directors: Robert Creighton, Rebecca Todd

169 TULIP PAINTS REBRANDING | School: Rochester Institute of Technology
Instructor/Professor: Anne Jordan | Student: Pranjal Sawai

169 FLORESCENT SANCTUARY: A COMMUNITY-BASED FLOWER SHOP
School: University of Louisville | Instructor/Professor: Trysh Wahlig
Student: Alyssa De Jesus

169 ROLLING ROOTS PLANT SHOP: BRAND PITCH DECK
School: Texas State University | Instructors/Professors: Jeff Davis, William Meek
Student: Kelsie Brouillette

170 SHRED END SKATE AND APPAREL - BRANDING
School: California State University, Fullerton | Instructor/Professor: Cheryl Savala
Student: Bryce Verti

170 MOVIE TAVERN REBRAND CAMPAIGN
School: University of North Texas | Instructor/Professor: Douglas May
Student: Cuinn Cornwell | Photography Sources: kiwihug (Unsplash), Jason Lung (Unsplash), Pixabay (Pexels) | Model Makers: mrmockup.com, Tinydesignr, Victor Ketom (Behance), Vitaliy Kolomiets (Dribble)

170 AN CERAMIC STUDIO | School: Duy Tan University
Instructors/Professors: Nguyen Tri Phuong Dong, Le Phuong Hieu
Student: Nguyen Ha Uyen

170 OTTALAUS SALON | School: Brigham Young University
Instructor/Professor: Doug Thomas | Student: Hannah Javadi

170 DOUBLE HAPPINESS WEDDING BRIDAL SHOP | School: Duy Tan University
Instructors/Professors: Nguyen Tri Phuong Dong, Hoang Viet Quoc
Student: Nguyen Thanh Thao

170 BARTON CREEK RESORT AND COUNTRY CLUB
School: University of North Texas | Instructor/Professor: Douglas May
Student: Annika Snow

170 3HIVE RECORD LOUNGE | School: Brigham Young University
Instructor/Professor: Linda Reynolds | Student: Kiera Helquist

170 HUE TOURISM | School: Duy Tan University
Instructor/Professor: Nguyen Tri Phuong Dong | Student: Ho Thi Thu Thao

171 STATE LIBRARY OF VICTORIA TOURIST GUIDE
School: Swinburne University of Technology | Instructor/Professor: Annabelle Radford
Student: Jessica Novakova

171 JAZZ POSTER BY PRANJAL | School: Rochester Institute of Technology
Instructor/Professor: Anne Jordan | Student: Pranjal Sawai

171 LOTERIA: MEXICAN BINGO
School: Syracuse University, The Newhouse School
Instructor/Professor: Claudia Strong   Student: Alexandra Ryberg Gonzalez

171 FORM | School: Drexel University
Instructors/Professors: Eric Karnes, Mark Willie | Student: Fiona Tran

171 CD DESIGN OF EURO BEATS | School: California State University, Fullerton
Instructor/Professor: Juan Escalante | Student: Sophia Nguyen

171 CYBORK CURRENCY | School: California Institute of the Arts
Instructors/Professors: Yasmin Gibson, Colin Frazer | Student: Silei Fu

171 DEMOCRACY SCIENCE FREEDOM | School: School of Visual Arts
Instructor/Professor: Unattributed | Student: Tian Qin

172 THE NEW YORK TIMES REDESIGN | School: School of Visual Arts
Instructor/Professor: Peter Ahlberg | Student: Keumbie Hwang

172 SCREWY BOOK | School: School of Visual Arts
Instructor/Professor: Warren Lehrer | Student: Jiyoung Kim

172 THE GRID: NEWSPAPER | School: School of Visual Arts
Instructor/Professor: Debra Bishop | Student: Jiyoung Kim

172 DAMAGED GOODS | School: School of Visual Arts
Instructor/Professor: Pedro Mendes | Student: Doyeon Kim

172 THE DESIGN OBJECT | School: School of Visual Arts
Instructor/Professor: Pedro Mendes | Student: Suin Choi

173 MARIE CLAIRE MAGAZINE REBRAND | School: Brigham Young University
Instructor/Professor: Eric Gillett | Student: Caitlin Ballantyne

173 DO NOT STAND AT MY GRAVE AND WEEP | School: Kean University
Instructor/Professor: Nancy Campbell | Student: Carlos DeLeon

173 DRUM 'N' BASS IN A NEW GENERATION
School: Portland Community College | Instructor/Professor: Nathan Savage
Student: Cole Popejoy

173 DESIGNED FOR ORBIT | School: Portland Community College
Instructor/Professor: Nathan Savage | Student: Sara Rosario
Digital Artist: James Thew | Photographer: Casey Horner

173 THE PIT | School: M.AD School of Ideas Atlanta
Instructor/Professor: Hank Richardson | Student: Reagan Williams

174 PULSE MAGAZINE | School: Portland Community College
Instructor/Professor: Nathan Savage | Student: Michael Madrid

174 BEWITCHED MAGAZINE | School: Pennsylvania State University
Instructor/Professor: Taylor Shipton | Student: Gabrielle Harris

174 THE VANISHING BUZZ | School: Rochester Institute of Technology
Instructor/Professor: Anne Jordan | Student: Aditi Singh

174 GRAY MAGAZINE | School: Brigham Young University
Instructor/Professor: Eric Gillett | Student: Sophie Baddley

174 DIGITAL DUMP SUSTAINABLE QUARTERLY
School: Pennsylvania State University | Instructor/Professor: Emily Burns
Student: Wyatt Poorman

174 NO TRACE MAGAZINE | School: M.AD School of Ideas Atlanta
Instructor/Professor: Hank Richardson | Student: Jamie Jason

174 SEWN MAGAZINE | School: Pennsylvania State University
Instructor/Professor: Taylor Shipton | Student: Kathryn Gross

174 VERTIGO NOVEL DESIGN | School: School of Visual Arts
Instructor/Professor: John Kudos | Student: Yubin Won

175 WOMEN ON RECORD: MUSIC VANGUARDS OF PENNSYLVANIA
School: West Chester University | Instructors/Professors: Karen Watkins, Heidi Hayoung Lee | Students: Meredith DiPietro, Olivia Dreon, Emily Simon, Alyssa Crognale, Braydon Yearicks, Noah Burns | Creative Director: Karen Watkins
Content Strategist: Heidi Hayoung Lee | Fabricator: Thomas Haughey

175 TEMPORTAL | School: West Chester University
Instructor/Professor: Karen Watkins | Student: Colleen Grant

175 OLI ART BUILDING TOY | School: Pratt Institute
Instructor/Professor: Alisa Zamir | Student: Wen-Chi Hsueh

175 A BRIEF INQUIRY INTO INTERESTING BUGS
School: University of North Texas | Instructor/Professor: Whitney Holden
Student: Maeci Ray

175 YVE | School: ArtCenter College of Design
Instructor/Professor: Valerie Pobjoy | Student: Jess Martinez

175 CLOSE TO DAWN | School: School of Visual Arts
Instructor/Professor: Sarah Vaccariello | Student: Ariel Miner

176 UNTITLED | School: School of Visual Arts
Instructor/Professor: Lisk Feng | Student: Huilin Gui

176 JOURNEY TO SKY UTOPIA | School: School of Visual Arts
Instructor/Professor: Doug Salati | Student: Yijiang Dong

176 SUPERPARADISE | School: School of Visual Arts
Instructor/Professor: Anthony Macbain | Student: Alana Green

176 WOLF | School: School of Visual Arts
Instructor/Professor: Steve Brodner | Student: Rongzhang Ye

176 LIFE IS LIKE SUMMER FLOWERS | School: School of Visual Arts
Instructor/Professor: Lisk Feng | Student: Yawen Hu

176 PEACH GARDEN | School: School of Visual Arts
Instructor/Professor: Lily Padula | Student: Yi Chen

176 ORBITER | School: School of Visual Arts
Instructor/Professor: Viktor Koen | Student: Ting En Chou

176 FIESTA | School: School of Visual Arts
Instructor/Professor: Lisk Feng | Student: Yunyao Chen

177 SERIES OF PORTRAIT | School: School of Visual Arts
Instructor/Professor: Matt Rota | Student: Chalzea Xu

177 THE CRACK ON EARTH | School: ArtCenter College of Design
Instructor/Professor: Dillon Carson | Student: Alicia Cheng

177 THE MONKEY KING | School: ArtCenter College of Design
Instructor/Professor: Jim Salvati | Student: Timothy Yan

177 MUSIC OF THE SPHERES | School: ArtCenter College of Design
Instructor/Professor: Jim Salvati | Student: Rain Gao

178 OBSESSIONS | School: School of Visual Arts
Instructor/Professor: Lisk Feng | Student: Letao Sun

178 IN MEXICO, THE POTTERS OF MATA ORTIZ KEEP TRADITION ALIVE
School: University of North Texas | Instructor/Professor: Stephen Zhang
Student: Emma Ortiz

178 RECONCILIATION | School: School of Visual Arts
Instructors/Professors: Yuko Shimizu, Sam Weber | Student: Mifei Zhou

178 A MOTHER'S STRENGTH | School: ArtCenter College of Design
Instructor/Professor: Jim Salvati | Student: Ciara Hart

178 BLACK HOLES | School: ArtCenter College of Design
Instructor/Professor: Paul Rogers | Student: Jerilyn Lee

178 CONSCIOUSNESS | School: School of Visual Arts
Instructors/Professors: Yuko Shimizu, Sam Weber | Student: Yuzhuan Zhou

178 UNTITLED | School: School of Visual Arts
Instructor/Professor: Steve Brodner | Student: Xin Huang

178 SEALED CRESCENT | School: School of Visual Arts
Instructor/Professor: Jensine Eckwell | Student: Jingyao He

178 CHAMPAGNE SUPERNOVA | School: ArtCenter College of Design
Instructor/Professor: Jim Salvati | Student: Jiyun Choi

244 CREDITS & COMMENTARY

179 FLEETING PETALS | School: Columbia University
Instructor/Professor: Susanna Coffey | Student: Taylor Yingshi

179 DROPBOX: COLLABORATE WITH EASE
School: ArtCenter College of Design | Instructor/Professor: Ara Devejian
Student: Elaine Lee

179 STEAMPUNK MAGIC | School: School of Visual Arts
Instructor/Professor: Anthony Macbain | Student: Yinghao Lin

179 GROUPISM | School: School of Visual Arts
Instructor/Professor: Lisk Feng | Student: Songer Yang

179 HELLO, STRANGER! | School: School of Visual Arts
Instructor/Professor: Josh Cochran | Student: Estelle Ha

179 城市浮乐园 CITY PLAYGROUND | School: School of Visual Arts
Instructor/Professor: Josh Cochran | Student: Zhanhao Liang

180 COUNTING MEN | School: ArtCenter College of Design
Instructors/Professors: Brian Rea, Paul Rogers | Student: Maria Dzulfayan

180 COUNTING MEN | School: ArtCenter College of Design
Instructors/Professors: Brian Rea, Paul Rogers | Student: Maria Dzulfayan

180 JOURNEY | School: School of Visual Arts
Instructor/Professor: Josh Cochran | Student: Jiaxi Chen

180 ONTOLOGY OF EXISTENCE | School: School of Visual Arts
Instructor/Professor: Yuko Shimizu, Matt Rota | Student: Scarlet Ding

180 FANTASY SCROLLS | School: School of Visual Arts
Instructor/Professor: Doug Salati | Student: Xiaohan Guo

180 HAM'S DAY OFF | School: School of Visual Arts
Instructor/Professor: Doug Salati | Student: Lauren Giancola

180 DEAR INNER CHILD, | School: ArtCenter College of Design
Instructor/Professor: Jim Salvati | Student: Ciara Hart

180 LUAN XU | School: School of Visual Arts
Instructor/Professor: Jensine Eckwell | Student: Wenjun Shao

180 INTO THE WORLD OF JOY | School: School of Visual Arts
Instructors/Professors: Yuko Shimizu, Sam Weber | Student: Mika Ichikawa

181 YELL WITHOUT VOICE | School: School of Visual Arts
Instructors/Professors: Yuko Shimizu, Sam Weber | Student: Yilin Zhu

181 TRAVELING | School: School of Visual Arts
Instructor/Professor: Steve Brodner | Student: Sirui Zou

181 FURRY COMPANIONS | School: School of Visual Arts
Instructors/Professors: Matt Rota, Yuko Shimizu | Student: Zhehao Wu

182 MIGHTY APHRODITE | School: LABASAD Barcelona School of Arts & Design
Instructor/Professor: Unattributed | Student: Valia Papadopoulou
Illustrator: Valia Papadopoulou | Designer: Valia Papadopoulou

182 JAPANESE INTERNMENT | School: University of Texas at Arlington
Instructor/Professor: Ben Dolezal | Student: Emily Brown

182 GORILLAZ | School: ArtCenter College of Design
Instructor/Professor: Jim Salvati | Student: Rain Gao

182 GARUN & AMARR, ARMENIAN WINE COLLECTION
School: ArtCenter College of Design | Instructor/Professor: Robert Clayton
Student: Maria Dzulfayan

182 MALSEDUCTION | School: ArtCenter College of Design
Instructor/Professor: Jim Salvati | Student: Maria Dzulfayan

182 THE EXOTIC BOMB | School: University of North Texas
Instructor/Professor: Stephen Zhang | Student: Rebecca Dugan

182 PLAY POSTER | School: Texas Christian University
Instructor/Professor: David Elizalde | Student: Nho Hieu Kien Nguyen

182 SMARTWATER | School: Southern Methodist University
Instructor/Professor: Willie Baronet | Students: Juan Silva, Delaney Gendron

182 POSTER DESIGNS MADE WITH BLENDER, PHOTOSHOP, AND ILLUSTRATOR
School: ArtCenter College of Design | Instructor/Professor: Adam Ross
Student: Asha Seabron

183 HOW TO FOLD ORIGAMI CRANES | School: Baylor University
Instructor/Professor: Virginia Green | Student: Abigail Sanders

183 MISS AMERICANA: A LOOK INTO TAYLOR SWIFT'S DISCOGRAPHY
School: University of Notre Dame | Instructor/Professor: Neeta Verma
Students: Sophia Ochoa, Suhyeon Yi | Illustrators: Sophia Ochoa, Suhyeon Yi
Designers: Sophia Ochoa, Suhyeon Yi | Creative Team: Sophia Ochoa, Suhyeon Yi

183 BASICS OF QUADBALL | School: Baylor University
Instructor/Professor: Virginia Green | Student: Abigail Murschell

183 NECESSITY OF COMPLETING PRIMARY EDUCATION RATE
School: York University | Instructor/Professor: Darren Wilson | Student: Minjoo Kim

183 CHARITEASE | School: Brigham Young University
Instructor/Professor: Doug Thomas | Student: Brett Hilton

183 SALVADOR DALI BENEFIT INVITATION | School: Texas Christian University
Instructor/Professor: Bill Galyean | Student: Alexandra Tice

183 "JS", PERSONAL BRAND | School: Campbell University
Instructor/Professor: Dejan Mraović | Student: Joshua Sledge
Photographer: Dejan Mraović

184 LOGO FOR THE REPUBLIC OF TEA | School: Texas A&M University-Commerce
Instructor/Professor: Joshua Ege | Student: Mariana Santana

184 CHILDREN'S RUN | School: University of Architecture Ho Chi Minh City
Instructor/Professor: Unattributed | Student: Hieu Vo | Design Lead: Tien Nguyen
Designer: Hieu Vo | Creative Director: Joshua Breidenbach | Agency: Rice

184 VRUL | School: Portland Community College
Instructor/Professor: Nathan Savage | Student: Grey Shawger

184 CIVIL GOAT COFFEE | School: Texas State University
Instructor/Professor: Mark Brinkman | Student: Travis Crawford

184 EDIBLE ARRANGEMENTS | School: Southern Methodist University
Instructor/Professor: Willie Baronet | Student: Savanna Hodes

184 SHAKESPEARE PIZZA LOGO | School: Southern Methodist University
Instructor/Professor: Willie Baronet | Student: Ethan Jones

184 CHILL CEREAL BAR LOGO | School: University of North Texas
Instructor/Professor: Douglas May | Student: Rylee Armstrong

184 VINO CODE | School: Texas State University
Instructor/Professor: Mark Brinkman | Student: Travis Crawford

184 CONCEPTUAL LETTERMARK | School: Brigham Young University
Instructor/Professor: Linda Reynolds | Student: Sophie Houghton

184 GRANADA, SPAIN LOGO | School: Auburn University
Instructor/Professor: Devon Ward | Student: Lavens Maginnis

184 KICKER IDENTITY | School: Baylor University
Instructor/Professor: Genaro Solis Rivero | Student: Virginia Herschend

184 DINOSAUR BAR-B-QUE ALTERNATE LOGO | School: Texas State University
Instructor/Professor: Mark Brinkman | Student: Mason Havard

185 RHINORY | School: Texas State University
Instructor/Professor: Mark Brinkman | Student: Tessa Shellenberger

185 HOWDY CAKES LOGO | School: Baylor University
Instructor/Professor: Genaro Solis Rivero | Student: Kate Sudderth

185 BUXTON MUNCH LOGO | School: Texas State University
Instructor/Professor: Jeff Davis | Student: Logan Dorsey

185 THE BAKED BEAR LOGO | School: Texas State University
Instructor/Professor: Mark Brinkman | Student: Mandy Czyz

185 MIDNIGHT COWBOY | School: Texas State University
Instructor/Professor: Mark Brinkman | Student: Travis Crawford

185 HALFMOON PLUMBING | School: Texas State University
Instructor/Professor: Mark Brinkman | Student: Tessa Shellenberger

185 RAMEN RANCH LOGO | School: Texas State University
Instructor/Professor: Jeff Davis | Student: Nick Voss

185 LOGO | School: Texas State University
Instructor/Professor: William Meek | Student: Mallory Randolph

185 POPPA'S PASTA LOGO | School: Baylor University
Instructor/Professor: Genaro Solis Rivero | Student: Abriella Patti

185 PROPER TWEETMENT LOGO | School: University of the Incarnate Word
Instructor/Professor: Doris Palmeros-McManus | Student: Rozlynn Macbeth Olivas

185 DATA DOG | School: Texas State University
Instructor/Professor: Mark Brinkman | Student: Travis Crawford

185 KOTN | School: Texas State University
Instructor/Professor: Mark Brinkman | Student: Yasseen Cherif Elassar

186 BANYA | School: Southern Methodist University
Instructor/Professor: Willie Baronet | Student: Savanna Hodes

186 BARILLA LOGO | School: M.AD School of Ideas Atlanta
Instructor/Professor: Hank Richardson | Student: Nic De La Hoz

186 THE FARMER'S DOG LOGO | School: University of North Texas
Instructor/Professor: Douglas May | Student: Annika Snow

186 LITTLE FREE LIBRARY | School: Rochester Institute of Technology
Instructor/Professor: Anne Jordan | Student: Rachel Seaton

186 GIVE HUGZ STUFFED ANIMALS | School: Southern Methodist University
Instructor/Professor: Willie Baronet | Student: Savanna Hodes

186 MAD BATTER BAKERY LOGO | School: Texas State University
Instructor/Professor: Mark Brinkman | Student: Miles Skonberg

186 HUONG HUE TOURISM COMPANY | School: Duy Tan University
Instructors/Professors: Nguyen Tri Phuong Dong, Le Thanh Tri
Student: Phan Le Binh Nguyen

186 FLYING WORM VINTAGE LOGO | School: Texas State University
Instructor/Professor: Mark Brinkman | Student: Miles Skonberg

186 LOLO'S CHICKEN & WAFFLES | School: University of North Texas
Instructor/Professor: Douglas May | Student: Jalon Isabell

186 MOOVES LOGO | School: Baylor University
Instructor/Professor: Genaro Solis Rivero | Student: Abriella Patti

186 WELLINGTON, NEW ZEALAND LOGO | School: Auburn University
Instructor/Professor: Devon Ward | Student: Cole Sibley

186 BIKES AND BEANS | School: Texas State University
Instructor/Professor: Jeff Davis | Student: Emma Brown

187 LITTLE ROCKETS LOGO | School: Baylor University
Instructor/Professor: Genaro Solis Rivero | Student: Kate Sudderth

187 TRUSTEA SEEDS LOGO | School: InFocus Film School
Instructor/Professor: Leila Singleton | Student: Dia Pauls-Caruso

187 THE BIG STORE | School: Texas State University
Instructors/Professors: Austin Buck, Mark Brinkman | Student: Olivia Espiritu

187 THE WOODS | School: Southern Methodist University
Instructor/Professor: Willie Baronet | Student: Savanna Hodes

187 ZIPP SPARK'S TATTO LEAGUE | School: Ringling College of Art & Design
Instructors/Professors: Jeff Bleitz, Lisa Willard | Student: Ivy Jenkins

187 BUILD-A-BEAR | School: University of North Texas
Instructor/Professor: Douglas May | Student: Lauren Clark

187 VIGILANTE'S BAR & BOTANICAL | School: Ringling College of Art & Design
Instructors/Professors: Jeff Bleitz, Lisa Willard | Student: Samantha Mandato

187 BEELZEBUZZ TEQUILA CO. LOGO
School: Ringling College of Art & Design | Instructor/Professor: Lisa Willard
Student: Danie Mainou

245 CREDITS & COMMENTARY

187 EARLY BIRDS & NIGHT OWLS LOGO | School: Texas A&M University-Commerce
Instructor/Professor: Joshua Ege | Student: Abigail Killough

187 STUMPY'S HATCHET HOUSE | School: University of North Texas
Instructor/Professor: Douglas May | Student: Jazmine Garcia

187 MELODY CREAMERY LOGO | School: Baylor University
Instructor/Professor: Genaro Solis Rivero | Student: Brooke Sockwell

187 SHORE SATELLITES IDENTITY | School: Baylor University
Instructor/Professor: Genaro Solis Rivero | Student: Virginia Herschend

188 PAPER TREE | School: Texas State University
Instructor/Professor: Mark Brinkman | Student: Travis Crawford

188 ERIKSON'S CAJUN CAFE LOGO | School: Texas State University
Instructor/Professor: Jeff Davis | Student: Nick Voss

188 HARVEST MOON BREWERY | School: Texas State University
Instructor/Professor: Briana Nicole Juarez | Student: Sarah Ortiz

188 IT'S A KEEPER, BAIT & TACKLE | School: Texas State University
Instructor/Professor: Jeff Davis | Student: Emily Palau

188 KITSCHY KATZ LOITER BOARDS | School: Ringling College of Art & Design
Instructors/Professors: Jeff Bleitz, Lisa Willard | Student: Bella Thompson

188 BENCHWARMER BAGELS | School: Texas State University
Instructor/Professor: Mark Brinkman | Student: Tessa Shellenberger

188 EIGHT OF SWORDS | School: Texas State University
Instructor/Professor: Mark Brinkman | Student: Hannah Twining

188 HAPPY TAB KOMBUCHA | School: Texas State University
Instructor/Professor: William Meek | Student: Fallon Russell

188 ARISTOCRAT LOUNGE | School: Texas State University
Instructor/Professor: Mark Brinkman | Student: Riley Ramsower

188 FROG LEVEL GUITAR LOGO | School: Texas State University
Instructor/Professor: Genaro Solis Rivero | Student: Nick Voss

188 "AMBROSIA" LOGO | School: Portland Community College
Instructor/Professor: Nathan Savage | Student: Alyah Ibrahim

188 BREWED AWAKENING | School: Texas State University
Instructor/Professor: Mark Brinkman | Student: Jeanette Deegear

189 POT.ION PACKAGING DESIGN | School: School of Visual Arts
Instructor/Professor: Justin Colt | Student: Mina Son

189 DELPHIE SKINCARE – EQUATE REBRAND | School: ArtCenter College of Design
Instructors/Professors: Andrew Gibbs, Jessica Deseo | Student: Maggie Morton

189 PURME SOCIAL FARM | School: Hansung University, Design & Arts Institute
Instructors/Professors: Dong-Joo Park, Seung-Min Han | Student: Su-Min Ga

190 STUDIO SAUCES | School: School of Visual Arts
Instructor/Professor: Justin Colt | Student: Jiyoon Kim

190 EARTHBATH REBRAND | School: ArtCenter College of Design
Instructor/Professor: Gerardo Herrera | Student: Georgina Kurnia

190 FUNSOUND EARPHONE | School: Pratt Institute
Instructor/Professor: Carson Ahlman | Student: Wen-Chi Hsueh

190 PASTA PASTO | School: California State University, Fullerton
Instructor/Professor: Theron Moore | Student: Leann So

190 FEEL BETTER JUICE | School: California State University, Fullerton
Instructor/Professor: Theron Moore | Student: Claudia Chacon

190 "O" SPARKLING WATER | School: School of Visual Arts
Instructor/Professor: Unattributed | Student: Yiwei Cheng

190 HUM NUTRITION | School: Brigham Young University
Instructor/Professor: Linda Reynolds | Student: Kate Holmes

190 EYE OF RAVENA PACKAGING DESIGN
School: California State University, Fullerton
Instructor/Professor: Theron Moore | Student: Anna Whitelaw

191 JOYFUL! | School: ArtCenter College of Design
Instructor/Professor: Monica Schlaug | Student: Genie Wu

191 ROCKY'S ROAD TRIP | School: Temple University, Tyler School of Art & Architecture
Instructor/Professor: Abby Guido | Student: MeiLi Carling

191 CHARMIES COFFEE COOKIES | School: Texas Christian University
Instructor/Professor: Yvonne Cao | Student: Isabella Baker

191 RHI GINGER BEER | School: ArtCenter College of Design
Instructor/Professor: Monica Schlaug | Student: Lauren Aquino

191 PURELY | School: ArtCenter College of Design
Instructor/Professor: Gerardo Herrera | Student: Kerrie Chu

192 BUTTERBITS | School: California State University, Fullerton
Instructor/Professor: Theron Moore | Student: Mia Lin

192 BATH & BODY WORKS PACKAGING SYSTEM | School: University of North Texas
Instructor/Professor: Douglas May | Student: Lauren Clark

192 HOLLE BABY FORMULA PACKAGING | School: Texas A&M University-Commerce
Instructor/Professor: David Beck | Student: Elisabeth Vaughn

192 POMODORO | School: School of Visual Arts
Instructor/Professor: Eric Baker | Student: Minsu Seo

192 ENIGMA COSMETICS | School: California State University, Fullerton
Instructor/Professor: Theron Moore | Student: Reilly Hew

192 SPARROW & SEED | School: Texas Christian University
Instructor/Professor: Yvonne Cao | Student: Corinne Green

193 RAKISH RUM | School: M.AD School of Ideas Atlanta
Instructor/Professor: Hank Richardson | Student: Jamie Jason

193 PRODUCT PACKAGING LINE - DRENCH
School: California State University, Fullerton
Instructor/Professor: Theron Moore | Student: Sang Nguyen

193 MOOSH | School: Temple University, Tyler School of Art & Architecture
Instructor/Professor: Abby Guido | Student: Jillian Villafuerte

193 PERFUME LINE (UNIVERSAL DUSK) PACKAGING DESIGN
School: California State University, Fullerton
Instructor/Professor: Theron Moore | Student: Larisa Benguhe

193 R.I.P. ALTERNATIVE MILK | School: Texas Christian University
Instructor/Professor: Yvonne Cao | Student: Ellie Gonyea

193 ELVERHEIM VODKA | School: ArtCenter College of Design
Instructor/Professor: Monica Schlaug | Student: Jonathan Kusnadi

193 COPPERHEAD GIN | School: University of North Texas
Instructor/Professor: Brian Boyd | Student: Hannah Burke

193 VERITY SYRUP CO. PACKAGE DESIGN | School: Texas Christian University
Instructor/Professor: Yvonne Cao | Student: Rebecca Richard

193 ROOTED | School: Temple University, Tyler School of Art & Architecture
Instructor/Professor: Abby Guido | Student: Seth Dubrosky

194 STARRY DELIGHTS JELLY BEANS
School: California State University, Fullerton | Instructor/Professor: Theron Moore
Student: Jennifer Cuevas

194 AL DENTE - NO INK, NO GLUE, NO PLASTIC | School: Purdue University
Instructor/Professor: Li Zhang | Student: Daniel Lu

194 PLAYS OF YORE | School: California State University, Fullerton
Instructor/Professor: Theron Moore | Student: Derek Daproza

194 CANDY IN CAHOOTS | School: California State University, Fullerton
Instructor/Professor: Theron Moore | Student: Paige Garcia

194 SPS PACKAGING | School: School of Visual Arts
Instructor/Professor: Justin Colt | Student: Younghyun Kim

194 PULSE PRODUCT AND PACKAGING DESIGN | School: School of Visual Arts
Instructor/Professor: Elliott Walker | Student: Jung Youn Kim

194 MANIC PANIC | School: ArtCenter College of Design
Instructor/Professor: Gerardo Herrera | Student: Ana Vazquez

194 7 DEADLY SINS | School: School of Visual Arts
Instructor/Professor: Joseph Newton | Student: Yubin Won

195 CALIFORNIA STATE UNIVERSITY, FULLERTON
School: California State University, Fullerton
Instructor/Professor: Theron Moore | Student: Elena Germann

195 ARBOR PERFUME | School: University of Central Oklahoma
Instructor/Professor: Jesse Warne | Student: Emma Minyard

195 MATEO'S SALSA PACKAGING | School: Brigham Young University
Instructor/Professor: Linda Reynolds | Student: Luke Miller

195 BIBLIOTHÈQUE DU CHOCOLAT | School: California State University, Fullerton
Instructor/Professor: Theron Moore | Student: Viktoriia Trapizonian

195 MEPHISTO ABSINTHE PACKAGING | School: University of North Texas
Instructor/Professor: Douglas May | Student: Maxwell Pius

195 SIMSODA PACKAGE DESIGN | School: School of Visual Arts
Instructor/Professor: Eric Baker | Student: Sijin Zhou

195 RUN WILD HOT SAUCE | School: California State University, Fullerton
Instructor/Professor: Theron Moore | Student: Julieta Gazzoni

195 AURA INCENSE | School: Texas Christian University
Instructor/Professor: Yvonne Cao | Student: Avery Kokinda

196 LISTEN TO PEACE | School: Asia University
Instructors/Professors: Chen Junhong, Xie Shengmin | Student: Goyen Chen

196 THAT'S THE WAY THE COOKIE CRUMBLES
School: Texas A&M University-Commerce | Instructor/Professor: Cory Say
Student: Jackelyn De Lara

196 "AMERICA HAS ROOM FOR EVERYONE" ACLU POSTER
School: Jacksonville State University | Instructor/Professor: Chad Anderson
Student: Conner Gayda

196 "24 HOUR FILM RACE" POSTER | School: Texas A&M University-Commerce
Instructor/Professor: Joshua Ege | Student: David Ellis

196 POLLUTION POSTER | School: University of the Incarnate Word
Instructor/Professor: Doris Palmeros-McManus | Student: Rozlynn Macbeth Olivas

196 FULL OF PLASTIC. GETTING DRASTIC. | School: Kean University
Instructor/Professor: Nancy Campbell | Student: Robert Tole

196 24 HOUR FILM RACE | School: Texas A&M University-Commerce
Instructor/Professor: Joshua Ege | Student: Shyann Haught

196 BLUE CHRISTMAS FESTIVAL | School: ArtCenter College of Design
Instructor/Professor: David Tillinghast | Student: Sizhe Wang

196 EMPTY CROPS | School: University of North Texas
Instructor/Professor: Stephen Zhang | Student: Daniel Descamp

197 MIND IS NOT ENOUGH MEMORY
School: Hansung University, Design & Arts Institute
Instructors/Professors: Dong-Joo Park, Seung-Min Han | Student: Su-Min Ga

197 MERCURY WORLD TOUR | School: ArtCenter College of Design
Instructor/Professor: Jim Salvati | Student: Jiyun Choi

197 LOVE POSTER | School: Rhode Island School of Design
Instructor/Professor: Nancy Skolos | Student: Anita (Ningjing) Sun

197 MUSEUM OF SCIENCE LONDON AWARENESS POSTER
School: ArtCenter College of Design | Instructor/Professor: Simon Johnston
Student: Jaiwon Lee

198 BUKCHEONG SAJA NOREUM (LION MASK DANCE OF BUKCHEONG)
School: Hansung University, Design & Arts Institute
Instructors/Professors: Dong-Joo Park, Seung-Min Han | Student: Hyeon Seung Lee

198 TEN THINGS I'M GRATEFUL FOR | School: School of Visual Arts
Instructor/Professor: Santiago Carrasquilla | Student: Rabiya Gupta

246 CREDITS & COMMENTARY

198 BE OUT 'N IN OF INSIDE & OUTSIDE | School: Dongduk Women's University
Instructor/Professor: Hyojun Shim | Student: Yeonjoo Jang

198 THE FUNKY FIFTIES | School: Kean University
Instructor/Professor: Nancy Campbell | Student: Matthew Redzinski

198 WHERE CRAYONS BECOME THERAPY | School: Texas State University
Instructor/Professor: Rosana Duran-Garibi | Student: Sarah Ortiz

198 PURDUE THEATER DEPARTMENT 2023 POSTERS
School: Purdue University | Instructor/Professor: Hyung Joo Kim | Student: Emily Bierma

198 PSYCHO REDESIGN | School: Rochester Institute of Technology
Instructor/Professor: Anne Jordan | Student: Chris Dell'Aquila

198 CUT AND PASTE | School: University of North Texas
Instructor/Professor: Stephen Zhang | Student: Lee McClain

198 BAARAAT ALBUM LAUNCH POSTER | School: Rochester Institute of Technology
Instructor/Professor: Anne Jordan | Student: Nagasai Vardhan Rao Sarvepalli

199 ART MUSEUM FOR DOG! FOR EVERYONE!
School: Hansung University, Design & Arts Institute
Instructors/Professors: Dong-Joo Park, Seung-Min Han | Student: Eungyeol Kim

199 HEALTH AND SAFETY POSTERS FOR BOYS AND GIRLS CLUBS OF AMERICA
School: Kutztown University | Instructor/Professor: Kate Clair | Student: Roseld Laguatan

199 THERE IS NO PLANET B | School: Hansung University, Design & Arts Institute
Instructors/Professors: Dong-Joo Park, Seung-Min Han | Student: Gyeongmin Park

199 THE FOUNTAIN OF DEATH | School: Kean University
Instructor/Professor: Nancy Campbell | Student: Christopher Cruz

199 UNSCROLL: ANTI SOCIAL MEDIA AWARENESS CAMPAIGN
School: West Chester University | Instructor/Professor: Scotty Reifsnyder
Student: Tully Ryan

199 LET'S DISCO | School: Savannah College of Art & Design
Instructor/Professor: Sohee Kwon | Student: Xuehui He

199 2023 GYEONGBOKGUNG PALACE NIGHTTIME SPECIAL VIEWING EVENT POSTER | School: Hansung University, Design & Arts Institute
Instructors/Professors: Dong-Joo Park, Seung-Min Han | Student: Hwi-Seo Park

199 PURDUE UNIVERSITY THEATRE POSTERS | School: Purdue University
Instructor/Professor: Hyung Joo Kim | Student: Evan Olinger

200 EVERYTHING YOU CAN IMAGINE IS REAL | School: Texas Christian University
Instructor/Professor: Bill Galyean | Student: Corinne Green

200 VERBAL VIOLENCE | School: Dankook University
Instructor/Professor: Hoon-Dong Chung | Student: Mingxing Zhang

200 CLIMATE CHANGE POSTERS | School: California State University, Fullerton
Instructor/Professor: Theron Moore | Student: Chelsea Alvarez

200 OFF LIMITS POSTER | School: Pennsylvania State University
Instructor/Professor: Taylor Shipton | Students: Carson Schultz, Jessica Stencel

200 THE FUNKY 50S | School: Kean University
Instructor/Professor: Nancy Campbell | Student: Tracy Kwok

200 CHAINED TO ADDICTION | School: Kean University
Instructor/Professor: Nancy Campbell | Student: Carlos DeLeon

200 DIVERSITY IS IMPORTANT | School: Dankook University
Instructor/Professor: Hoon-Dong Chung | Student: Yanhua Li

200 PLASTIC SURGERY | School: University of Arts Poznan
Instructor/Professor: Eugeniusz Skorwider | Student: Aleksandra Kortas

200 BLANK CITY POSTER | School: School of Visual Arts
Instructor/Professor: Peter Ahlberg | Student: Suin Choi

201 AFROPUNK FESTIVAL POSTERS | School: Woodbury University
Instructor/Professor: Rebekah Albrecht | Student: Nya Durr

201 EAST VILLAGE NEIGHBORHOOD GUIDE | School: School of Visual Arts
Instructor/Professor: Natasha Jen | Student: Hyowon Kwon

201 REFRAMING THE SPACE WITH COLORS AND SHAPES
School: Rhode Island School of Design | Instructor/Professor: Nancy Skolos
Student: Shuixin Wang

201 GUARDIAN OF ASIAN ARTISTS | School: School of Visual Arts
Instructor/Professor: Peter Ahlberg | Student: Dong Hyun Kim

201 FAU LECTURE SERIES | School: Florida Atlantic University
Instructor/Professor: Mehrdad Sedaghat Baghbani | Student: Narges Panahandeh

202 BONE IDENTITY | School: Dongduk Women's University
Instructor/Professor: Hyojun Shim | Student: Na Kyeong Yoon

202 BEARLY HANGING ON | School: University of North Texas
Instructor/Professor: Stephen Zhang | Student: Sean Howes

202 VIVIAN MAIER | School: ArtCenter College of Design
Instructor/Professor: Jim Salvati | Student: Jiyun Choi

202 CROWD | School: Dongduk Women's University
Instructor/Professor: Hyojun Shim | Student: Yena Shin

202 ROCHESTER JAZZ FESTIVAL | School: Rochester Institute of Technology
Instructor/Professor: Anne Jordan | Student: Muhammad Tayyab Younas

202 SHAKESPEARE POSTER | School: School of Visual Arts
Instructor/Professor: Douglas Riccardi | Student: Yawen Xiao

202 SELF-DEVELOPMENT SEMINAR POSTER
School: Hansung University, Design & Arts Institute
Instructors/Professors: Dong-Joo Park, Seung-Min Han | Student: Mi-Sun Park

202 MODERN HAN | School: Dongduk Women's University
Instructor/Professor: Hyojun Shim | Student: Hyunju Lee

202 SOCIAL IMPACT POSTER | School: Pennsylvania State University
Instructor/Professor: Emily Burns | Student: Eden Balog

203 OPEN MOVEMENT POSTER | School: ArtCenter College of Design
Instructor/Professor: Brad Bartlett | Student: Jaiwon Lee

203 BOKTTEOK | School: Dankook University
Instructor/Professor: Hoon-Dong Chung | Student: Hyeon-Ha Jo

203 VR FILM FESTIVAL | School: Hansung University, Design & Arts Institute
Instructors/Professors: Dong-Joo Park, Seung-Min Han | Student: Gang-Min Kim

203 THERE IS NO PLANET B | School: Hansung University, Design & Arts Institute
Instructors/Professors: Dong-Joo Park, Seung-Min Han | Student: Un-Hyeong Song

204 KIT HOUSE KIT | School: West Chester University
Instructor/Professor: Karen Watkins | Student: Emily Simon

204 PLACE | School: M.AD School of Ideas Atlanta
Instructor/Professor: Hank Richardson | Student: Anna LeBer

204 TOMBSTONE | School: M.AD School of Ideas Atlanta
Instructor/Professor: Hank Richardson | Student: Anna LeBer

204 CHAIR - TRANSCEND | School: M.AD School of Ideas Atlanta
Instructor/Professor: Hank Richardson | Student: Reagan Williams

204 CHAIR PROJECT | School: M.AD School of Ideas
Instructor/Professor: Hank Richardson | Student: Liza Langstaff

205 EQUANIMITY | School: M.AD School of Ideas Atlanta
Instructor/Professor: Hank Richardson | Student: Catarina Sterlacci

205 LUMINOUS PASSAGE | School: M.AD School of Ideas Atlanta
Instructor/Professor: Hank Richardson | Student: Reagan Williams

206 AURORA | School: Texas Christian University
Instructor/Professor: Dusty Crocker | Student: Abigail Lund

206 ALMOST RULER | School: School of Visual Arts
Instructor/Professor: Peter Ahlberg | Student: Xiangyi Guo

206 CHAIR - TSEVA | School: M.AD School of Ideas Atlanta
Instructor/Professor: Hank Richardson | Student: Jonny Gleaton

206 ETERNAL | School: M.AD School of Ideas Atlanta
Instructor/Professor: Hank Richardson | Student: Catarina Sterlacci

206 MUSHROOM CHAIR | School: M.AD School of Ideas Atlanta
Instructor/Professor: Hank Richardson | Student: Ramon Sanchez

206 CHAIR | School: M.AD School of Ideas Atlanta
Instructor/Professor: Hank Richardson | Student: Maya Givens

207 JIADI PERFUME | School: Pratt Institute
Instructor/Professor: Hadar Kfir | Student: Wen-Chi Hsueh

207 SURVEILLANCE AND PERCEPTION | School: Parsons School of Design
Instructor/Professor: Unattributed | Student: Hyeonji Kim | Designer: Hyeonji Kim
Photographer: Jin Hyun | Photographer's Assistant: Heather Moon
Models: Calder Anderson, Austin, Finley Dahl, Alina Yiyuan Zhang

207 ELEVATING EVERYDAY SOUNDS | School: School of Visual Arts
Instructor/Professor: Unattributed | Student: Chuanyuan Lin

208 CHROMA | School: Temple University, Tyler School of Art & Architecture
Instructor/Professor: Mia Culbertson | Student: Hunter Ruiz

208 NOMAD | School: West Chester University
Instructor/Professor: Karen Watkins | Student: Taylor Super

208 NOODS | School: West Chester University
Instructor/Professor: Karen Watkins | Student: Samuel McConnell

208 PICKLES BAR & GRILL RESTAURANT | School: Texas Christian University
Instructor/Professor: Jan Ballard | Student: Alexandra Tice

208 SANDO SANDWICH SHOP | School: M.AD School of Ideas Atlanta
Instructor/Professor: Hank Richardson | Student: Reagan Williams

209 DIA DE LOS MUERTOS | School: Syracuse University, The Newhouse School
Instructor/Professor: Claudia Strong | Student: Hailey Lawless

209 PRESERVING THE PAST, PROTECTING THE FUTURE
School: Syracuse University, The Newhouse School
Instructor/Professor: Claudia Strong | Student: Samantha Swiss

209 BLACK HISTORY THROUGH DANCE
School: Syracuse University, The Newhouse School
Instructor/Professor: Claudia Strong | Student: Nicole Beaudet

210 "THE GREAT GREEKS" - A SERIES OF FOUR POSTAGE STAMPS AND FOUR COMMEMORATIVE ENVELOPES | School: Campbell University
Instructor/Professor: Dejan Mraović | Student: Abigail Ellington

210 ICONIC ARTISTS STAMP COLLECTION | School: Purdue University
Instructor/Professor: Hyung Joo Kim | Student: Evan Olinger

210 CUPID TYPEFACE | School: School of Visual Arts
Instructor/Professor: Zipeng Zhu | Student: Seongyun Park

210 36 DAYS OF TYPE | School: School of Visual Arts
Instructor/Professor: Unattributed | Student: Yun Shen (Angel) Liao

211 A (SPEC)IMEN OF TYPE | School: School of Visual Arts
Instructor/Professor: Zipeng Zhu | Student: DeMia Courman

211 B612 SNEAKERS TYPE IDENTITY | School: School of Visual Arts
Instructor/Professor: Natasha Jen | Student: Vasavi Bubna

211 SNYDER SERIF ORIGINAL TYPEFACE
School: Syracuse University, The Newhouse School
Instructor/Professor: Renée Stevens | Student: Quinn Carletta

211 FORSYTHIA | School: University of Minnesota, Twin Cities
Instructors/Professors: Bill Moran, Deb Lawton | Student: Natalie Mihal

211 LINKS TYPEFACE | School: School of Visual Arts
Instructors/Professors: Ken Deegan, Brankica Harvey | Student: Alice Jung

211 VERGE ORIGINAL TYPEFACE
School: Syracuse University, The Newhouse School
Instructor/Professor: Renée Stevens | Student: Darren Cordoviz

212 OGHMA | School: ArtCenter College of Design
Instructor/Professor: Greg Lindy | Student: Glenn Ryan

247 CREDITS & COMMENTARY

212 THE ODD COUPLE PLAY POSTER | School: Texas Christian University
Instructor/Professor: David Elizalde | Student: Andy (Nhan) Nguyen

212 NXTGEN PUBLICATION
School: University of Cincinnati DAAP, Myron E. Ullman Jr. School of Design
Instructor/Professor: Muhammad Rahman | Student: Anya Bolton

212 BLOOD, BULLETS, AND BROTHERHOOD - MOVIE POSTER "THE WILD BUNCH" | School: Texas Christian University
Instructor/Professor: Lewis Glaser | Student: Andy (Nhan) Nguyen

213 ELEGY | School: ArtCenter College of Design
Instructor/Professor: Simon Johnston | Student: Glenn Ryan

213 B612, SHOES FOR THE BEACH | School: School of Visual Arts
Instructor/Professor: Natasha Jen | Student: Ipshita Krishan

213 JELLYFISH TYPEFACE | School: School of Visual Arts
Instructors/Professors: Ken Deegan, Brankica Harvey
Student: Jennifer Han

213 BUILD CUSTOM TYPOGRAPHY | School: School of Visual Arts
Instructor/Professor: Zipeng Zhu | Student: Yubin Won

213 SKRT PUBLICATION
School: University of Cincinnati DAAP, Myron E. Ullman Jr. School of Design
Instructor/Professor: Muhammad Rahman | Student: Sophia Paroz

214 NEVER WILL ALBUM PACKAGING | School: School of Visual Arts
Instructor/Professor: Justin Colt | Student: Rabiya Gupta

214 JONI MITCHELL "THE PAINTED PONY"
School: M.AD School of Ideas New York | Instructor/Professor: Sarah Wood
Student: Harper Herman

214 DARK ENERGY | School: Rochester Institute of Technology
Instructor/Professor: Anne Jordan | Student: Eshaan Sojatia

214 VINYL FOR HOON-HEE JUNG | School: School of Visual Arts
Instructor/Professor: Peter Ahlberg | Student: Yubin Won

214 APHEX TWIN - VINYL DESIGN | School: School of Visual Arts
Instructor/Professor: Peter Ahlberg | Student: Adya Jatia

214 KING GNU "ASURA" VINYL DESIGN | School: ArtCenter College of Design
Instructor/Professor: Sean Adams | Student: Jo Iijima

215 MUSIC ALBUM DESIGN: LP VINYL | School: Lehigh University
Instructor/Professor: Maurizio Masi | Student: Charlotte Cooper

215 MUSIC ALBUM DESIGN: LP VINYL | School: Lehigh University
Instructor/Professor: Maurizio Masi | Student: Zoe LeiLi

215 APHEX TWIN'S SELECTED AMBIENT WORKS | School: School of Visual Arts
Instructor/Professor: Peter Ahlberg | Student: Keumbie Hwang

PLATINUM DESIGN FILM/VIDEO WINNERS:

217 ENCO INTERNATIONAL LIMITED BRAND MONTAGE
School: ArtCenter College of Design | Instructor/Professor: Ming Tai | Student: Alan Xu
Assignment: The objective of this project is to rebrand an existing institution and showcasing its new brand and identity through a 60 seconds or shorter motion montage.
Approach: The initial brand identity of was not effectively conveying the organization's fundamental values and services. The rebranding solves that problem by introducing a dynamic and engaging identity system. It features a versatile and adaptable color palette, a robust and uniform typographic approach, and crisp, attention-grabbing motion elements.
Results: Project was a great success. Both my professor and fellow classmates felt that the rebrand was able to breathe new life into "ENCO INTERNATIONAL LIMITED."

GOLD DESIGN FILM/VIDEO WINNERS:

218 PROJECT AMSTERDAM - ONE MORE MILE | School: College for Creative Studies
Instructor/Professor: Raphael Zammit | Student: Hung-Wei Lin
Assignment: A concept vehicle designed for Amsterdam in 2040 that can be privately owned or used for shared mobility purposes. This design helps people reach areas that can't be visited by current public transportation systems and provides living functions within the cabin. The exterior and interior show the taste of Amsterdam.
Approach: Started by sketching on paper, then modeling in 3D, and animating in Blender.
Results: As a first-year graduate transportation design studio work, it shows more profound design research and thinking process on the designated topic at a master student level. The final video demonstrates the overall performance of the taste of car styling, the sense of color and material, and is able to structure and frame all the information in a video format.

218 SINGAPORE MERLION | School: College for Creative Studies
Instructor/Professor: Raphael Zammit | Student: James Shiels
Assignment: By 2040, Singapore will come to dominate the global health sphere. With rapid growth in the healthcare industry, insurance companies have prospered, enabling Singapore's leading health insurance company to venture into the mobility sphere. Singapore Merlion is the most exclusive subscription service available, offering a dynamic and expressive form of transport to the less-abled.
Approach: Sketch, Photoshop, Alias, Blender, Premiere Pro.

218 SUPERNATURAL LAB | School: ArtCenter College of Design
Instructor/Professor: Miguel Lee | Student: Jamie Kim
Assignment: Create a triptych motion piece that explores three different ideas centered around one motif. By traveling through abstract spaces with elements of teleportation, transformation, and creation, this piece showcases a unifying theme of the supernatural.
Approach: I started with character sketches and a storyboard. I then built out the scenes in 3D, experimenting with lighting, texture, and camera settings. Abstract, fantastical transitions were used to travel through the scenes and emphasize the whimsical tone of this piece.

218 TITLE SEQUENCE OF MY OCTOPUS TEACHER
School: Fashion Institute of Technology | Instructor/Professor: Nicole Zizila
Student: Yong Han Shin
Assignment: Brooklyn Botanic Garden is a small natural sanctuary in NYC. I redesigned their visual identity to create a trendy mood and promote the garden better.

219 SOMETHING IN THE SHADOWS
School: University of Cincinnati DAAP, Myron E. Ullman Jr. School of Design
Instructor/Professor: Yoshiko Burke | Student: Katherine Newcombe
Assignment: Create a title sequence for a hypothetical movie, TV show, or online series.
Approach: A dark comedy mystery about a retired psychologist who arrives in a small Pacific Northwest town. He is haunted by dark secrets, and settling into the new town, he discovers secrets about the people who reside in it. Halftone's illustrative style was created to mimic the retro setting. Brighter colors are used to highlight importance. The halftone effect and type choice create a 60s feel. The music used is Crosby, Stills & Nash's "Long Time Gone."

Results: The purpose of the title sequence is to build suspense and curiosity while also establishing the overall mood of the story. Its goal is to create anticipation for the unfolding story, providing the viewer with context and a sense of the story's tone.

219 007 THUNDERBALL TITLE SEQUENCE DESIGN
School: Loyola University New Orleans | Instructor/Professor: Matt Normand
Student: Ella Balhoff
Assignment: Students research a movie made before 1990 and make an opening title sequence that matches that time period. They are limited to typefaces available up to the date of the movie.
Approach: I rotoscoped select footage from the movie. I'm on the swim team so I used a GoPro to record footage above and below the school pool to get the rippling effects for the typographic reveals. The footage was then converted to black and white. My inspiration came from James Bond movie aesthetics, i.e. stark colors, silhouettes, quick cuts, etc.
Results: I had the top 3 best projects in class (out of 15).

219 FABRIC MUSEUM: F GENERATOR | School: ArtCenter College of Design
Instructors/Professors: Roy Tatum, Brad Bartlett | Student: Jocelyn Ziying Zhao
Assignment: The "F Generator" is an interactive tool for the Fabric Museum, enabling users to craft, customize, and output their version of the museum's logo. The logo's design references the Jacquard loom, which connects traditional weaving with computer code.
Approach: The software's core functionality encompasses two modes: Layering and Animation. The Layering mode offers a way to combine up to three layers of Fs, each with eleven sets of grid units and seven color palettes. Animation mode provides four sets of shapes mapped onto ASCII characters, enabling users to timestamp and export individual frames.
Results: By offering visitors the ability to craft custom logos, the museum fosters a personal connection through interactive engagement. Creative coding serves as a beacon of innovation, drawing the eyes of the tech and art sectors and enhancing the museum's recognition. Meanwhile, the use of timestamps creates a living digital archive, charting the museum's progression and visitor engagement across a growing timeline.

219 FABRIC MUSEUM: TEXTLOOM | School: ArtCenter College of Design
Instructors/Professors: Brad Bartlett, Ivan Cruz, Miles Mazzie
Student: Jocelyn Ziying Zhao
Assignment: TextLoom is an interactive installation held at Fabric Museum, an immersive experience that draws inspiration from the revolutionary Jacquard Loom. Connecting traditional weaving techniques with computer programming, the installation allows users to generate text through the process of weaving.
Approach: The tabletop tray is designed to resemble a traditional weaving shuttle. Linked with Arduino code, users must emulate the shuttle's action to transmit messages. A sound-reactive typewriter creates unique patterns. TEXT comes from textile, the installation fosters a hands-on experience with the weaving process and deepens audience engagement.
Results: By embodying the evolution of programming from the Jacquard Loom to contemporary computing, the experience makes the connection between craft and cutting-edge technology.

220 URBAN DICTIONARY BRANDING FILM | School: ArtCenter College of Design
Instructor/Professor: Ming Tai | Student: Yuqin Ni

220 ARCHITECTURAL DIGEST REBRAND | School: ArtCenter College of Design
Instructor/Professor: Ming Tai | Student: Mishen Liu
Assignment: The assignment is to rebrand a company using a contemporary perspective.
Approach: My rebrand strategy for Architectural Digest aims for the brand to be at the forefront of interior design, architecture, and travel inspiration and resources. This is achieved through vibrant colors, a sans serif typeface, and playful image treatment. The logo is reduced down to the most foundational elements and shapes to reference tools used in architecture.
Results: My project successfully captures the essence of architecture and interior design through a contemporary lens, as seen in my poster designs, animation, and image treatment.

220 THEORY 6 | School: West Chester University
Instructor/Professor: Jeremy Holmes | Student: Tully Ryan

220 ARORA PUBLISHING | School: West Chester University
Instructor/Professor: Karen Watkins | Student: Tully Ryan
Assignment: Senior thesis response to word prompt, 'Legacy.'
Approach: Arora Publishing House showcases a series of cover designs for four celebrated science-fiction novels. The project conceptualizes technology that utilizes an ultra-thin OLED screen embedded within the binding of each book, projecting an animated cover design beneath an opaque hardcover overlay.

221 ACCESSIBLENYC | School: Fashion Institute of Technology
Instructor/Professor: Christie Shin | Students: Sara Park, Mariko Dreifuss, Yoojin Song
Assignment: Navigating NYC can be confusing and frustrating, especially if you have disabilities. Most of NYC's public transit system is not disability-friendly, and only about a quarter of subway and train stations are fully accessible. How can we make NYC more accessible?
Approach: The Accessible NYC app creates a personalized experience based on user's accessibility type, interests, and needs that can assist people to enjoy and explore New York City.
Results: Through this project, we learned the importance of empathy interviews. They played a critical role in helping us understand the challenges faced by individuals with disabilities. We were able to seek out exclusions and use them to create new and better experiences.

221 INTERACTION INSTALLATION | School: Brigham Young University
Instructor/Professor: Eric Gillett | Student: Brett Hilton
Assignment: We live in an increasingly connected digital world, yet social isolation is reaching an all-time high. My goal was to create an experience using experimental typography that would subtly raise awareness for this issue.
Approach: I came up with an interactive display that required people to put their arms through a board to spell the word "INTERACT." This has a double meaning, implying both the need for the participant to interact with the installation, but also the need to interact with multiple people in order to spell the word. A sign to the side read, "will you interact with me?" There were no other instructions besides directions for how to position your arms. I left the installation in a public place to see if people would choose to interact with strangers.
Results: Several people interacted with the installation. While the concept was lost on some, it left others thinking about the meaning of it all, many coming to their own unique conclusion. The resulting footage and imagery from the experiment has a uniquely human quality to it that forces the viewer to ponder on themes of connectedness and interactions.

221 CYLINDER TYPE | School: Dankook University
Instructor/Professor: Hoon-Dong Chung | Student: Sumin Kwon
Assignment: 'CYLINDER TYPE' is an experimental 3D Typography. The three images are based on characteristics of the Korean Alphabet. The spinning top symbolizes tradition, the tree represents uniqueness, and the hourglass signifies finitude. Distinctive images are connected through animation, expressing the fluidity of language like water.
Approach: Integrating symbolic aspects and experimental aspects in a 3D environment.
Results: This received positive reviews at the Poster Stellars competition.

221 DOPE, DOPAMINE | School: Dankook University
Instructor/Professor: Hoon-Dong Chung | Student: Minkyeong Cho
Assignment: Recently, short-form videos have gained tremendous popularity. These formats create a swamp of infinite scrolling. Moreover, application addiction is meticulously

designed utilizing features such as 'likes' or 'push notifications' as triggers. This project was conceived to raise awareness about dopamine addiction caused by such applications.
Approach: While there is a general caution against dopamine addiction from alcohol, drugs, and gambling, there is less awareness about the risks of dopamine addiction from applications. Drawing parallels with drug and gambling addiction, the aim was to highlight the dangers of application addiction. Vivid colors were chosen to represent dopamine addiction. I visually expressed the dangers of dopamine addiction that using motion graphics.
Results: The work was exhibited at the graduation exhibition and garnered significant attention. Viewers were intrigued by motion poster composed of vibrant emoji colors, providing everyone who saw it with time to contemplate the issue of application addiction.

222 SELF PORTRAIT | School: School of Visual Arts
Instructor/Professor: Greg Lee | Student: Jennifer Han
Assignment: The goal is to create a 30-60 seconds motion graphic video on a "self-portrait" from now until the end of the semester while learning other techniques in class. Before we dive into designs, illustrations, and animation, we will come up with three strong concepts.
Approach: I began with a concept about a characteristic of me or something significant in my life. I believe I have pretty good luck, but I suffer unlucky events to achieve this luck. I illustrated the examples of unfortunate events to visualize the final "prize". I wanted to keep the achievement's identity ambiguous to convey that the reward makes all the pain worth it.

222 POST SEPARATION - VETERAN MINIDOC
School: Texas A&M University-Commerce | Instructor/Professor: Brent McMahan
Student: Tyler Holloway
Assignment: The project was to make a mini-documentary of a cause or issue we are passionate about. I, being a Veteran, decided to make a video on the struggles of being a Veteran.
Approach: The intro is a dramatization of a Veteran turning to substance abuse before attempting suicide and then fall into darkness. This section was desaturated and dramatic lighting was used to fit the eerie music. Sound effects were added to add to the overall theme of despair. A statistic of Veteran suicide is presented after the last scene fades. The second portion of the video is an interview with 3 Veterans. I purposely left my questions out of the Q&A to give space for the Veteran to share each of their experiences.
Results: I received A+ on the assignment and received excellent feedback from my peers.

222 THE MILLINERS | School: School of Visual Arts
Instructors/Professors: Gael Towey, Stephen Doyle | Student: Mingxin Cheng
Assignment: Dive into the captivating world of millinery with "The Milliners", a documentary highlighting the craftsmanship of two artisans at East Village Hat. Explore the rich culture of East Village as the film weaves together the artistry of hat-making.
Approach: While exploring the East Village, I discovered a fascinating hat shop. I contacted the owner, planned the shooting, and researched hat-making. I designed the story to showcase the East Village culture and the modern changes happening with hats industry. In the visuals, I used lots of close-up shots to focus on the detailed process of making hats.
Results: The hatshop owner is excited to watch the documentary, and it's making a difference by introducing many people to the term "milliners" and showcasing the beauty of hat making.

222 PARVENU
School: University of Cincinnati DAAP, Myron E. Ullman Jr. School of Design
Instructor/Professor: Yoshiko Burke | Student: Brady Rudisill
Assignment: Develop a title sequence of a hypothetical film, TV, or online narrative series. Convey a central idea and establish the meaningful psychological/emotional mood for the story. Explore aesthetic possibilities to execute communication objectives with moving imagery and graphics. Investigate an effective design solution to bridge between narrative and information, utilizing montage methods for visual narrative communication.
Approach: The design approach for "Parvenu" is centered around a dramatic limited series. The narrative follows Alexandra's journey from a tranquil life in a wealthy American family to the revelation of her royal Russian lineage and involvement in international crime. The design strategy for the title sequence employs visual metaphors and transitions to convey the narrative's progression. High-contrast graphic illustrations, symbolic iconography, and a refined color palette make up the visual language.
Results: Crafted with dynamic transitions and strategic effects, our title sequence masterfully builds tension, using symbolic allegories to mirror the series' themes. Beginning with the symbolic shattering of a Russian doll family cracks seamlessly traverse frames, symbolizing the protagonist's shattered understanding of identity. As the narrative unfolds into the protagonist's journey on the run, feeling lost in different settings that reflect her family lineage and the looming threat, the crack line becomes a compelling visual thread. Culminating in a climactic flight test, a symbolic bird in a stained-glass window becomes the focal point, encapsulating the protagonist's ultimate challenge – to rise above adversity by picking up the shattered pieces.

SILVER DESIGN FILM/VIDEO WINNERS:

223 SELF CONTINUITY | School: ArtCenter College of Design
Instructor/Professor: Miguel Lee | Student: Jamie Kim

223 FREEDOM OF EXPRESSION | School: Georgia Southern University
Instructor/Professor: Jeff Garland | Student: Mona Gandomkar

223 INFINITY: FROM BEFORE
School: University of Ljubljana, Academy of Fine Arts & Design
Instructor/Professor: Andrej Kamnik | Student: Strahinja Jovanović

223 THE GOOSE AND THE GOLDEN EGG | School: West Chester University
Instructor/Professor: Jeremy Holmes | Student: Ryan McMullen

223 MINDSET | School: M.AD School of Ideas Atlanta
Instructor/Professor: Hank Richardson | Student: Emily Jeffrey
Designers: Taylor Firtle, Maya Givens

223 THE MARTIAN TITLE SEQUENCE | School: School of Visual Arts
Instructor/Professor: David Conklin | Student: Jiyoon Kim

223 THE MENU | School: University of North Texas
Instructor/Professor: David Wolske | Student: Keaton Dillard

223 FOOD BABY
School: University of Cincinnati DAAP, Myron E. Ullman Jr. School of Design
Instructor/Professor: Yoshiko Burke | Student: Em Humphress

224 HER | School: University of North Texas
Instructor/Professor: David Wolske | Student: Andrea Torrijos

224 THE HUNGER TITLE SEQUENCE DESIGN | School: Loyola University New Orleans
Instructor/Professor: Matt Normand | Student: Joseph Donovan

224 AUDIBLE SILENCE | School: Pratt Institute
Instructor/Professor: Unattributed | Student: Michelle Kim

224 INSIDE DESIGN OF THE 20TH CENTURY | School: West Chester University
Instructor/Professor: Jeremy Holmes | Student: Emily Simon

224 LYNX APP PROMOTIONAL VIDEO | School: Texas Christian University
Instructor/Professor: Yvonne Cao | Student: Brooke Budde

224 BANK OF AMERICA KIDS | School: Fashion Institute of Technology
Instructors/Professors: Randy Elles, Joseph Staluppi | Student: Yoojin Song

224 FROG LEVEL GUITAR LOGO ANIMATION | School: Texas State University
Instructor/Professor: Alice Lee | Student: Nick Voss | Music & Sound: Ambient Backyard Nature Sounds, Pixabay, Under the Pixabay Content License, Wind Sound, SoundReality, Under the Pixabay Content License

224 AMSTERDAM URBAN MOBILITY CONCEPT | School: College for Creative Studies
Instructor/Professor: Raphael Zammit | Student: Xuze Jin

225 VANGUARD SIZZLER MOVIE | School: Iowa State University
Instructor/Professor: Andrea Quam | Student: Delaney Golden
Designers: Cristiano Drescher, Fabrizio Ducato, Anna Vacura, Rahf Almutairi, Gavin McQuillan, Megan Qualley

225 WHAT HANDWRITING TELLS ABOUT YOU | School: School of Visual Arts
Instructor/Professor: David Conklin | Student: Roy Kim

225 MEMENTO | School: West Chester University
Instructor/Professor: Karen Watkins | Student: Jimmy Hall

225 9 SQUARES | School: Brigham Young University
Instructor/Professor: Linda Reynolds | Student: Luke Miller

225 DAYDREAM OF OASIS | School: School of Visual Arts
Instructor/Professor: Greg Lee | Student: Keumbie Hwang

225 CYLINDER TYPE | School: Dankook University
Instructor/Professor: Hoon-Dong Chung | Student: Sumin Kwon

225 REUTERS | School: Brigham Young University
Instructor/Professor: Doug Thomas | Student: Juan Pablo Gutierrez Hurtado

225 POLAROID | School: School of Visual Arts
Instructor/Professor: Greg Lee | Student: Keumbie Hwang

226 CONSUMER JOURNEY | School: M.AD School of Ideas Atlanta
Instructor/Professor: Hank Richardson | Student: Arthur Flaksman

226 RETROVISION | JELL-O OLD COMMERCIAL REDESIGN
School: School of Visual Arts | Instructor/Professor: Andrei Dan | Student: Diexin Yu

226 MYTHS AND LEGENDS PODCAST | School: Brigham Young University
Instructor/Professor: Linda Reynolds | Student: Brett Hilton

226 BLING BLING | School: Parsons School of Design
Instructor/Professor: Faiyaz Jafri | Student: Shristi Singh

226 PHANTOM LIMBS: DESIGN INTERVENTIONS & SITE-SPECIFIC STORYTELLING
School: ArtCenter College of Design | Instructors/Professors: Brad Bartlett, Miles Mazzie
Student: Veronica Tsai

226 RED | School: M.AD School of Ideas Atlanta
Instructor/Professor: Hank Richardson | Student: Anna LeBer

226 TRANSPOSED
School: University of Cincinnati DAAP, Myron E. Ullman Jr. School of Design
Instructor/Professor: Yoshiko Burke | Student: Frankie Matthews

226 COUNT COSMIC
School: University of Cincinnati DAAP, Myron E. Ullman Jr. School of Design
Instructor/Professor: Yoshiko Burke | Student: Nova Ostermann

GOLD PHOTOGRAPHY WINNERS:

228 NOCTURNAL EMBERS | School: Dawson College
Instructor/Professor: Denis Gendron | Student: Charchit Kant
Assignment: Create a set of images as part of the Graduating Portfolio for the AEC in Commercial Photography Program.
Approach: I embarked on a project to integrate photography with 3D elements, envisioning an amalgamation that would produce captivating visuals. This fusion allowed me to capture scenes that would have posed considerable challenges using photography alone. The perfume was photographed in the college studio and was later edited in Photoshop. The water was created in 3D using Blender and the final composite was created in Photoshop.
Results: I received high praise from the judges and also had the highest rated portfolio.

SILVER PHOTOGRAPHY WINNERS:

230 LIVING PAGES, PHOTOMONTAGE | School: Campbell University
Instructor/Professor: Dejan Mraović | Student: Arianna Aguila

230 WHEN THE PARTY'S OVER: DESPAIR AND DOPAMINE
School: Portland Community College | Instructor/Professor: Kathleen Rick
Student: Alexa Tusing

230 THEY COME AND GO | School: M.AD School of Ideas Atlanta
Instructor/Professor: Hank Richardson | Student: Molly Jacobs

231 BRYNN | School: M.AD School of Ideas Atlanta
Instructor/Professor: Kelly Lewis | Student: Liv Donaldson

231 GRIFFIN | School: M.AD School of Ideas Atlanta
Instructor/Professor: Kelly Lewis | Student: Liv Donaldson

231 RAINS | School: M.AD School of Ideas Atlanta
Instructor/Professor: Kelly Lewis | Student: Liv Donaldson

231 ELEGANCE IN MOTION | School: M.AD School of Ideas Atlanta
Instructor/Professor: Ari Skin | Student: Liv Donaldson

231 MONOTONY IS A MUSE | School: M.AD School of Ideas Atlanta
Instructor/Professor: Hank Richardson | Student: Molly Jacobs

231 RAINS | School: M.AD School of Ideas Atlanta
Instructor/Professor: Kelly Lewis | Student: Liv Donaldson

231 MOREAU | School: Texas Christian University
Instructor/Professor: Hillary Keckeisen | Student: Rebecca Richard

231 RESTRAINED | School: Texas Christian University
Instructor/Professor: Dusty Crocker | Student: Kien Nguyen

232 MELODIC HARMONY | School: Dawson College
Instructor/Professor: Denis Gendron | Student: Charchit Kant

232 PEACEFUL MORNING STILL LIFE | School: Texas Christian University
Instructor/Professor: Hillary Keckeisen | Student: Rebecca Richard

232 LIQUID BRILLIANCE | School: Dawson College
Instructor/Professor: Denis Gendron | Student: Charchit Kant

249 INDEX

AWARD-WINNING SCHOOLS

ArtCenter College of Design .. 52-55, 58, 75, 78, 81, 85, 86, 92-94, 111, 114, 123, 125, 147-150, 152, 153-164, 166, 175, 177-180, 182, 189-191, 193, 194, 196, 197, 202, 203, 212-214, 217-220, 223, 226
Asia University ... 196
Auburn University ... 184, 186
Baylor University ... 26, 28, 35, 37, 154, 159, 183-187
Belmont University, Watkins College of Art ... 32, 129
Brigham Young University ... 110, 152, 156, 166, 170, 173, 174, 183, 184, 190, 195, 221, 225, 226
Budapest Metropolitan University ... 118
California Institute of the Arts .. 148, 171
California State University, Fullerton 115, 119, 126, 130, 148, 151, 170, 171, 190, 192-195, 200
Campbell University 99, 183, 210, 230
Capilano University ... 28, 152, 168
College for Creative Studies ... 218, 224
Columbia University ... 179
Dankook University ... 120, 137, 200, 203, 221, 225
Dawson College ... 228, 232
Dongduk Women's University ... 61, 121, 198, 202
Drexel University ... 171
Duy Tan University ... 103, 164, 166, 168-170, 136
Ewha Womans University ... 31
Fashion Institute of Technology ... 158, 218, 221, 226
Florida Atlantic University ... 201
George Brown College ... 162
Georgia Southern University ... 223
Hansung University, Design & Arts Institute ... 31, 132, 189, 197-199, 202, 203
InFocus Film School ... 100, 187
Iowa State University ... 225
Jacksonville State University ... 31, 98, 196
Kean University ... 131, 173, 196, 198-200
KREA Design School ... 158, 164
Kutztown University ... 199
Kyonggi University ... 31
Kyung Hee University ... 31
LABASAD Barcelona School of Arts & Design ... 182
Lehigh University ... 72, 124, 133, 148, 150, 166, 169, 215
Loyola University New Orleans ... 219, 224
M.AD School of Ideas ... 24, 43-45, 156, 204
M.AD School of Ideas Atlanta ... 73, 105, 106, 109, 134, 135, 149-151, 155, 158, 159, 167, 173, 174, 186, 193, 204-206, 208, 223, 226, 230, 231
M.AD School of Ideas Madrid ... 46
M.AD School of Ideas New York ... 36, 45, 46, 214
M.AD School of Ideas Toronto ... 43
Methodist Theological University ... 31
Metropolitan State University of Denver ... 63
Otis College of Art & Design ... 169
Parsons School of Design ... 143, 207, 226
Pennsylvania State University ... 160, 174, 200, 202
Portland Community College 56, 57, 173, 174, 184, 188, 230
Pratt Institute 30, 116, 156, 175, 190, 207, 224
Purdue University ... 165, 194, 198, 199, 210
Rhode Island School of Design 122, 149, 163, 197, 201
Ringling College of Art & Design 98, 187, 188
Rochester Institute of Technology .. 167, 169, 171, 174, 186, 198, 202, 214
Royal College of Art 62
Savannah College of Art & Design ... 199
School of the Art Institute of Chicago 44, 104, 156
School of Visual Arts 29, 36, 46, 50, 51, 60, 64-67, 69, 74, 76, 77, 79, 80, 82-84, 87, 95-97, 100, 108, 112, 117, 128, 136, 138, 140-142, 144, 147, 150-152, 154, 156, 157, 159, 160, 162, 163, 166, 167, 171, 172, 174-181, 189, 190, 192, 194, 195, 198, 200-202, 206, 207, 210, 211, 213-215, 222, 223, 225, 226
Southern Methodist University ... 22, 26, 27, 31, 34, 35, 38, 39, 41-45, 100, 182, 184, 186, 187
Swinburne University of Technology ... 171
Syracuse University, The Newhouse School ... 19-21, 29-31, 33, 35-37, 39, 41-46, 171, 209, 211
Temple University 166
Temple University, Tyler School of Art and Architecture 191, 193, 208
Texas A&M University-Commerce .. 28, 99, 139, 147, 166, 169, 184, 187, 192, 196, 222
Texas Christian University ... 26, 33, 41, 107, 113, 147, 154, 164, 168, 182, 183, 191-193, 195, 200, 206, 208, 212, 224, 231, 232
Texas State University 23, 29-32, 35, 59, 88, 98, 101, 102, 127, 158, 168, 169, 184-188, 198, 224
University of Architecture Ho Chi Minh City 184
University of Arts Poznan 200
University of Central Oklahoma 195
University of Cincinnati DAAP, Myron E. Ullman Jr. School of Design 212, 213, 219, 222, 223, 226
University of Ljubljana, Academy of Fine Arts & Design 90, 223
University of Louisville 164, 169
University of Minnesota, Twin Cities ... 211
University of North Texas 26, 27, 33, 35-37, 70, 71, 89, 91, 99, 101-103, 145, 148, 151, 155, 159, 165, 166, 168, 170, 175, 178, 182, 184, 186, 187, 192, 193, 195, 196, 198, 202, 223, 224
University of Notre Dame 183
University of Texas at Arlington ... 155, 182
University of the Arts London 156
University of the Incarnate Word 163, 185, 196
Virginia Commonwealth University, VCU Brandcenter 148
West Chester University .. 159, 160, 165, 175, 199, 204, 208, 220, 223-225
Woodbury University 201
York University 183

AWARD-WINNING INSTRUCTORS/PROFESSORS

Adams, Sean 214
Ahlberg, Peter 112, 128, 136, 154, 167, 172, 200, 201, 206, 214, 215
Ahlman, Carson 130
Albrecht, Rebekah 201
Alderette, Elaine 156, 160, 181
Allen, Mark 26, 27, 31, 34, 35, 38, 41, 42, 44, 45
Anderson, Chad 98, 196
Baghbani, Mehrdad Sedaghat 201
Baker, Eric 79, 83, 154, 156, 160, 192, 195
Ballard, Jan 147, 168, 208
Baronet, Willie 22, 26, 34, 39, 42, 43, 100, 182, 184, 186, 187
Bartlett, Brad 81, 85, 123, 155, 160-162, 203, 219, 226
Beck, David 192
Bergman, Peter 63
Bishop, Debra 172
Bleitz, Jeff 98, 187, 188
Boback, Sara 46
Bódog, Darázs 164
Boyd, Brian 193
Bravo, Luis 156
Brinkman, Mark 98, 102, 184-188
Brodner, Steve 176, 178, 181
Buck, Austin 187
Buck, Mikaela 169
Burke, Yoshiko 219, 222, 223, 226
Burns, Emily 160, 174, 202
Campbell, Nancy 131, 173, 196, 198-200
Cao, Yvonne 41, 107, 113, 191-193, 195, 224
Carlson, Emily 169
Carrasquilla, Santiago 198
Carson, Dillon 177
Čehovin, Eduard 90
Chen, Junhong 196
Chopin, Constantin 147
Chung, Hoon-Dong 120, 137, 200, 203, 221, 225
Clair, Kate 199
Clayton, Robert 58, 82
Cochran, Josh 95, 179, 180
Coffey, Susanna 179
Colt, Justin 66, 67, 108, 117, 140, 152, 159, 189, 190, 194, 214
Comrie, Tyler 50
Conklin, David 223, 225
Corlett, Bracken Hanuse 28
Crocker, Dusty 26, 33, 206, 231
Cruz, Ivan 219
Culbertson, Mia 208
Da Silva, Nour 24
Daher, James 46
Dan, Andrei 226
Davis, Jeff 158, 169, 185, 186, 188
Deegan, Ken 211, 213
Deseo, Jessica 189
Devejian, Ara 179
Devlioti, Villy 36
Dolezal, Ben 155, 182
Doyle, Stephen 222
Dunn, Tim 46
Duran-Garibi, Rosana 198
Eckwell, Jensine 178, 180
Ege, Joshua 28, 99, 147, 166, 169, 184, 187, 196
El Akad, Hatem 46
Elizalde, David 164, 182, 212
Elles, Randy 224
Escalante, Juan 171
Fargo, Marinette 46
Feng, Lisk 176, 178, 179
Fleming, Samantha 147
Frazer, Colin 171
Galyean, Bill 26, 154, 183, 200
Garland, Jeff 223
Gendron, Denis 228, 232
Gibbs, Andrew 189
Gibson, Yasmin 171
Gillett, Eric 173, 174, 221
Glaser, Lewis 212
Gooch, Courtney 80, 147, 163
Granger, Gus 89, 99
Gray, Cheri 148
Green, Virginia 183
Guido, Abby 191, 193
Han, Joseph 77, 87, 152
Han, Seung-Min 31, 132, 189, 197-199, 202, 203
Harvey, Brankica 211, 213
Herrera, Gerardo 75, 111, 154, 162, 164, 166, 190, 191, 194
Hieu, Le Phuong 164, 170
Hoang, Viet Quoc 168, 170
Holden, Whitney 70, 71, 145, 175
Holmes, Jeremy 220, 223, 224
Holohan, Kelly 166
Hoy, Dan 114
Ip, Willie 144
Jafri, Faiyaz 226
Jen, Natasha 50, 51, 60, 74, 76, 82, 84, 201, 211, 213
Jenko, Radovan 90
Johnston, Simon 54, 55, 152-155, 157, 163, 197, 213
Jordan, Anne 167, 169, 171, 174, 186, 198, 202, 214
Juarez, Briana Nicole 188
Kammerzell, Dirk 36
Kamnik, Andrej 223
Kapur, Priyoshi 44
Karnes, Eric 171
Keckeisen, Hillary 231, 232
Kfir, Hadar 116, 207
Kim, Hyung Joo 165, 198, 199, 210
Kim, Na-Min 31
Koen, Viktor 176
Konetzka, Michael 156
Koren, Cindy Buckley 156
Kowalski, Jenny 166, 169
Kudos, John 174
Kwon, Sohee 199
Lahat-Blum, Einat 30
Lavalais, Shirleen 159
Lawton, Deb 211
Lee, Alice 224
Lee, Greg 222, 225
Lee, Heidi Hayoung 175
Lee, Miguel 218, 223
Lehrer, Warren 172
Lenning, Matthew 151
Lewis, Kelly 231
Lin, Charles 153, 155
Lindy, Greg 212
Lowen, Lauren 129
Luck, Annie Huang 152
Macbain, Anthony 96, 176, 179
Magbua, Billy 62
Masi, Maurizio 72, 124, 133, 148, 150, 215
May, Douglas 26, 27, 33, 35-37, 101-103, 155, 165, 168, 170, 184, 186, 187, 192, 195
Mazzie, Miles 159, 219, 226
McMahan, Brent 222
Meek, William 23, 29-31, 35, 59, 88, 101, 102, 127, 158, 168, 169, 185, 188
Mehl, Richard 64, 65
Mendes, Pedro 69, 156, 160, 162, 163, 172
Merto, Alex 150
Moore, Theron 115, 119, 126, 130, 148, 151, 190, 192-195, 200
Moran, Bill 211
Mraović, Dejan 99, 183, 210, 230
Neal, Michael 147
Newman, Jon 138, 141, 166
Newton, Joseph 100, 142, 162, 194
Nguyen, Tri Phuong Dong 103, 164, 166, 168-170, 186
Normand, Matt 219, 224
O'Neill, Kevin 20, 21, 31, 37, 39
Padula, Lily 97, 176
Palmeros-McManus, Doris 185, 196
Park, Dong-Joo 31, 132, 189, 197-199, 202, 203
Parmar, Vinay 43
Parris, Able 29
Paulson, Ryan 36
Pereira, Joana 156
Pobjoy, Valerie 175
Quam, Andrea 225
Radford, Annabelle 171
Rahman, Muhammad 212, 213
Rea, Brian 180
Regen, Doug 32
Reifsnyder, Scotty 159, 165, 199
Reynolds, Linda 110, 156, 170, 184, 190, 195, 225, 226
Riccardi, Douglas 202
Richardson, Hank 43-46, 73, 105, 106, 109, 134, 135, 149-151, 155, 158, 159, 167, 173, 174, 186, 193, 204-206, 208, 223, 226, 230, 231
Rick, Kathleen 230
Rivero, Genaro Solis 26, 28, 32, 35, 37, 154, 159, 184-188
Rogers, Paul 178, 180
Rose, Richard 163
Ross, Adam 94, 182
Rota, Matt 177, 180, 181
Runnells, Jamie 31
Salati, Doug 176, 180
Salvati, Jim 92, 93, 177, 178, 180, 182, 197, 202
Sandhaus, Louise 148
Savage, Nathan 56, 57, 173, 174, 184, 188
Savala, Cheryl 170
Say, Cory 196
Scharpf, Thomas 148
Schlaug, Monica 191, 193
Serrato, Stephen 52, 53, 78, 125, 161
Shiffman, Tracey 148-150
Shim, Hyojun 61, 121, 198, 202
Shimizu, Yuko 178, 180, 181
Shin, Christie 221
Shipton, Taylor 174, 200
Simms, Rory 80, 147, 163
Singh, Angad 158, 164
Singleton, Leila 100, 187
Skin, Ari 231
Skolos, Nancy 122, 197, 201
Skorwider, Eugeniusz 200
Staluppi, Joseph 224
Stevens, Renée 211
Strong, Claudia 171, 209
Tai, Ming 81, 155, 157, 217, 220
Tatum, Roy 219
Thomas, Doug 152, 166, 170, 183, 225

250 INDEX

Tillinghast, David 58, 196
Tóth, Judit 118
Towey, Gael 222
Trabucco-Campos, Andrea 157, 162
Trevino, Teresa 163
Tri, Le Thanh 186
Trigo, Carolina 86
Tu, Rich 167
Vaccariello, Sarah 175
Valdivieso, Jimena Gamio 150
Vaughn, Veronica 139
Verma, Neeta 183
Von Hardenburgh, Charlotte 143
Wahlig, Trysh 164, 169
Walker, Dominique 152, 168
Walker, Elliott 194
Ward, Devon 184, 186
Warne, Jesse 195
Watkins, Karen 160, 175, 204, 208, 220, 225
Weber, Sam 178, 180, 181
White, Mel 19, 29-31, 33, 35-37, 41-46
Willard, Lisa 98, 187, 188
Willie, Mark 171
Wilson, Darren 183
Wolske, David 223, 224
Wood, Sarah 214
Xie, Shengmin 196
Zamir, Alisa 175
Zammit, Raphael 218, 224
Zhang, Li 194
Zhang, Stephen 91, 148, 151, 159, 166, 178, 182, 196, 198, 202
Zhu, Zipeng 144, 210, 211, 213
Zizila, Nicole 158, 218
Zsolt, Kathi 158

AWARD-WINNING STUDENTS

Abdullahi, Jama 75, 164
Acevedo, Courtney 98
Acierno, Philip 45, 46
Adams, Megan 46
Aguila, Arianna 230
al-Kowatli, Laila 46
Albertson, Colette 160
Alvarez, Chelsea 200
Ambrus, Lair 164
Angjaya, Kissa 157
Aquino, Lauren 191
Aragi, Tori 44, 46
Ardhata, Handaru 164, 166
Armstrong, Brylee 184
Avila, Andrea 44
Babcock, Ella 166
Baddley, Sophie 174
Baek, Becky 144
Baier, Marie Sophie 44
Baker, Isabella 113, 154, 191
Balhoff, Ella 219
Ballantyne, Caitlin 173
Balog, Eden 202
Barge, Addis Ababa 148
Barrera, Sabrina Franco 166
Bayle, Anais 28, 168
Beaudet, Nicole 209
Beck, Kayla 44, 46
Belton, Macy 26, 101, 165, 168
Benguhe, Larisa 193
Betai, Krishna 43
Bianchi, Mariana 33, 36
Bierma, Emily 198
Blan, Kaitlyn 26
Blow, Rachel 103, 151
Bolton, Anya 212
Bowman, Brianna 135
Brouillette, Kelsie 158, 169
Brown, Emily 155, 182
Brown, Emma 186
Brown, Kyla 148
Bubna, Vasari 117, 211
Budde, Brooke 224
Burke, Hannah 193
Burns, Noah 175
Burrows, Ellie 152
Byers, Jenna 19, 45
Caban, Samantha 131
Canseco, Lucia 168
Carletta, Quinn 211
Carling, MeiLi 166, 191
Chacon, Claudia 190
Chae, Sang Eun 123
Chae, Timmy 34, 42
Chang, Ray 80
Chapman, Tyler 38, 45
Charalambous, Anastasia 153
Chavez, Elmo 169
Chen, Caihui 143
Chen, Goyer 195
Chen, Jade 143
Chen, Jiaxi 180
Chen, Meiyun 155
Chen, Yi 176
Chen, Yuan 167
Chen, Yunyao 176
Cheng, Alicia 177
Cheng, Mingpin 222
Cheng, Yiwei 190
Cho, Minkyeong 137, 221
Choi, Jiyun 178, 197, 202
Choi, Kyeong Loc 132
Choi, Li June 149
Choi, Suin 69, 172, 200
Chou, Ting En 176
Chu, Emily Anne 101, 102, 127
Chu, Kerrie 191
Clark, Lauren 165, 187, 192
Clarke, Emma 27, 34
Cohen, Emma 160
Compton, Brandy 59, 102
Conner, Ryan Garret 30, 45
Cooper, Charlotte 215
Cordoviz, Darren 211
Cornwell, Cuinn 36, 170
Cossins, Megan 148
Courman, DeMia 211
Crawford, Travis 23, 31, 184, 185, 188
Crognale, Alyssa 175
Cruz, Christopher 199
Cuevas, Jennifer 194
Curbelo, Claudia 156
Czyz, Mandy 185
Daproza, Derek 194
Davis, Caroline 26, 39
De Jesus, Alyssa 169
De Lara, Jackelyn 166, 196
de Torres, Elena Fernández 46
Deegear, Jeanette 188
Delapa, Lang 29
DeLeon, Carlos 173, 200
Dell'Aquila, Chris 198
DeMare, Jack 148
Descamp, Daniel 196
Dillard, Keaton 223
Ding, Scarlet 180
Ding, Shuwen 148
Ding, Zifei 161
DiPietro, Meredith 175
Doe, Olivia 31
Donaldson, Liv 231
Dong, Yijiang 176
Donio, Sophia 19, 45
Donovan, Joseph 224
Dorsey, Logan 29, 185
Dreifuss, Mariko 221
Dreon, Olivia 175
Dubrosky, Seth 193
Dugan, Rebecca 70, 182
Dung, Le Van 168
Durr, Nya 201
Dzulfayan, Maria 93, 180, 182
Elassar, Yasseen Cherif 185
Ellington, Abigail 210
Ellis, David 196
Enriquez, Gabriella 20, 21
Erazo, Destiny 29
Espiritu, Olivia 187
Fand, Lela 151
Felner, Rachel 71
Flaksman, Arthur 226
Forero, Javier 24, 45
Fu, Silei 171
Furyk, Caleigh 32
Ga, Su-Min 189, 197
Gandomkar, Mona 223
Gao, Leni 153
Gao, Rain 92, 177, 182
Garcia, Jazmine 187
Garcia, Marilyn 91
Garcia, Paige 194
Gayda, Conner 31, 98, 196
Gazzoni, Julieta 195
Gendron, Delaney 26, 182
Gerber, Abby 165
Germann, Elena 195
Gershowitz, Julia 46
Giancola, Lauren 180
Givens, Maya 206
Gleaton, Jonny 206
Goerke, Morgan 41
Golden, Delaney 225
Gomez, Kiara 169
Gonyea, Ellie 193
Gonzalez, Alexandra Ryberg 171
Grant, Colleen 175
Green, Corinne 107, 154, 192, 200
Grimm, Charlotte 150
Gross, Kathryn 174
Guardado, Leonel 162
Gui, Huilin 176
Gulley, Meghan 44
Guo, Xiangyi 206
Guo, Xiaohan 180
Guo, Yaoxinyu 35
Gupta, Ariana 147
Gupta, Rabiya 66, 67, 198, 214
Gupta, Roshan 26, 31, 41, 44
Ha, Estelle 179
Habony, Ágota 118
Haidar, Judie 164
Hall, Jimmy 225
Han, Jennifer 213, 222
Hanrahan, Kayla 41
Hargraves, Helena 35
Harris, Briana 30
Harris, Gabrielle 174
Hart, Ciara 178, 180
Hartwyk, Greta 44
Haseman, Julie 165
Haught, Shyann 196
Havard, Mason 184
He, Jingyao 178
He, Xuehui 199
Heath, Jordan 36, 155
Helquist, Kiera 170
Herman, Harper 45, 46, 214
Herschend, Virginia 184, 187
Hew, Reilly 192
Higaki, Dianna 41, 46
Hilton, Brett 183, 221, 226
Hinaga, Saki 30
Hinson, Lauren 145
Hirsch, Brooke 43, 46
Ho, Thi Thu Thao 170
Hodes, Savanna 22, 42, 184, 186, 187
Hogan, Spencer 34
Holloway, Tyler 222
Holmes, Kate 110, 190
Hong, Jiani 157
Hong, Xinni 166
Houghton, Sophie 184
Howard, Grace 56, 57
Howes, Sean 202
Hoz, Nic De La 186
Hsueh, Wen-Chi 116 175, 190, 207
Hu, Yawen 176
Huan, Doan Van 103
Huang, Xin 178
Hughes, Katelyn 29
Humphress, Em 223
Hurtado, Juan Pablo Gutierrez 225
Hwang, Keumbie 172, 215, 225
Ibarra, Aliya 98
Ibrahim, Alyah 188
Ibrahim, Marina 129
Ichikawa, Mika 180
Iijima, Jo 85, 214
Ilukhor, Darlington 100
Isabell, Jalon 102, 186
Jacobbe, Hannah 38
Jacobs, Molly 230, 231
Jang, Yeonjoo 198
Jason, Jamie 150, 167, 174, 193
Jatia, Adya 214
Javadi, Hannah 156, 170
Jeffrey, Emily 223
Jenkins, Ivy 187
Jeon, Soomin 162
Jeong, Sae-Hee 31
Jin, Xuze 224
Jo, Hyeon-Ha 203
Jones, Aleah 45, 46
Jones, Ethan 34, 44, 184
Jones, Veronica 32
Jovanović, Strahinja 90, 223
Jung, Alice 211
Jung, Min-Jae 31
Kalbach, Madison 159
Kant, Charchit 228, 232
Keller, Juliette 37, 42
Killough, Abigail 187
Kim, Dong Hyun 46, 64, 65, 167, 201
Kim, Doyeon 157, 172
Kim, Eungyeol 199
Kim, Gang-Min 203
Kim, Grace 147
Kim, Hannah 29
Kim, Hyeonji 207
Kim, Jamie 218, 223
Kim, Jiyeon 154
Kim, Jiyoon 190, 223
Kim, Jiyoung 172
Kim, Jung Youn 194
Kim, Michelle 224
Kim, Minjoo 183
Kim, Roy 225
Kim, Ruby Minhyoung 157
Kim, Younghyun 152, 194
Koi, Caroline 35
Kokinda, Avery 195
Kortas, Aleksandra 200
Kouhpayeh, Pantea 162
Krishan, Ipshita 213
Kurnia, Georgina 190
Kurtz, Courtney 165
Kusnadi, Jonathan 193
Kwok, Tracy 200
Kwon, Doah 156
Kwon, Hyowon 50, 51, 74, 76, 201
Kwon, Sumin 221, 225
Laguatan, Roseld 199
Langstaff, Liza 204
Larsen, Ylliana 145
Laufer, Madison 160
Lawless, Hailey 209
LeBer, Anna 105, 155, 204, 226
Lee, David J. 58
Lee, Elaine 160, 179
Lee, Esther Yeseul 54, 55, 156
Lee, Eun-Hye 31
Lee, Hannah YinTian 87
Lee, Hyeon Seung 198
Lee, Hyunju 202
Lee, Jacob Hwan 163
Lee, Jaiwon 123, 125, 152, 197, 203
Lee, Jerilyn 178
Lee, Natasha 152
Lee, Se-Young 31
Lee, Sydney 150, 159, 163
LeiLi, Zoe 72, 215
Li, Orlando 154
Li, Yaheng 86
Li, Yanhua 200
Liang, Zhanhao 179
Liao, Yun Shen (Angel) 210
Lin, Chuanyuan 207
Lin, Hung-Wei 218
Lin, Jonathan 156
Lin, Mia 192
Lin, Yinghao 179
Liu, Alicia 136, 154
Liu, Mishen 154, 220
Liu, Yongfeng 120
Lourie, Noah 35
Lu, Daniel 194
Lund, Abigail 26, 206
Lund, Alex 31, 41
Lyster, Blake 26, 39, 42
Ma, Aoran 147
Ma, Hanson 155
Mac, Bella 34
Madrid, Michael 174
Maginnis, Lavens 184
Mainou, Danie 187
Mallon, Maggie 39, 42
Mandato, Samantha 187
Mardorf, Michele 156
Markarian, Shahen 62
Martinez, Jess 94, 175
Martinez, Morgan 26, 45
Mathews, Liz 44
Matthews, Frankie 226
Maynard, Aviela 150
McClain, Lee 198
McClish, Macy 35, 103
McConnell, Samuel 208
McKintosh, Kara 168
McMullen, Ryan 223
Mehta, Sara 144, 162, 167
Mejia, Daniel 145
Meng, Jiayi 112
Meyer, Courtney 63
Mihal, Natalie 211
Miller, Luke 195, 225

251 INDEX

Miner, Ariel	175
Minyard, Emma	195
Molinari, Lara	33, 36
Morton, Maggie	189
Murphy, Mackenzie	30, 45
Murschell, Abigail	183
Nachimson, Elyza	36
Nam, Minsik	152
Newcombe, Katherine	219
Nguyen, Andy (Nhan)	212
Nguyen, Ha Uyen	170
Nguyen, John Paul	27, 89, 99
Nguyen, Khoa	151
Nguyen, Kien	164, 231
Nguyen, Nho Hieu Kien	182
Nguyen, Phan Le Binh	186
Nguyen, Sang	193
Nguyen, Sophia	171
Nguyen, Thanh Thao	170
Nguyen, Thi Hoang Yen	169
Nguyen, Thi My Linh	166
Ni, Yuqin	81, 220
Niu, Qianying	104
Novakova, Jessica	171
O'Connor, Cassidy	149
Ochoa, Sophia	183
Oden, Callie	27, 38
Olinger, Evan	165, 199, 210
Olivas, Rozlynn Macbeth	163, 185, 196
Oliver, Lexi	139
Ortiz, Emma	178
Ortiz, Sarah	188, 198
Orum-Harris, Kaliah	29
Ostermann, Nova	226
Otero, Maddie	22, 31, 43, 44
Pagan, Mariangelis	159
Palau, Emily	188
Pan, Rachel	60, 84
Panahandeh, Narges	201
Papadopoulou, Valia	182
Park, Don	162
Park, Gyeongmin	199
Park, Heejai	52, 53, 153
Park, Hwi-Seo	199
Park, Hyo-Bin	31
Park, Jenna	95
Park, Joonhee	161
Park, Mi-Sun	202
Park, Sara	221
Park, Seongyun	29, 160, 210
Park, So Yeon	83
Park, Yoon-Gi	141
Paroz, Sophia	213
Pasino, Isabella	26
Patti, Abriella	185, 186
Pauls-Caruso, Dia	187
Peng, Zedan	77
Perez, Isabella	147
Pham, Huu Minh	152, 162, 163
Pham, Lilian	155
Pirtle, Taylor	73
Pius, Maxwell	37, 151, 195
Poorman, Wyatt	174
Popejoy, Cole	173
Powers, Gabriel	37
Qin, Tian	171
Quiros, Natalie	115
Race, Bella	98
Ramsingh, Jonathan	28
Ramsower, Riley	188
Randolph, Mallory	185
Ray, Maeci	155, 175
Redzinski, Matthew	198
Richard, Rebecca	26, 193, 231, 232
Roberts, Sam	102
Robinson, Bryan	134
Rodriguez, Christine	130
Ronca, Angelique	169
Rosario, Sara	173
Roth, Brett	147
Rudisill, Brady	222
Ruiz, Hunter	208
Russell, Fallon	168, 188
Ryan, Glenn	162, 212, 213
Ryan, Tully	199, 220
Saad, Emily	37
Sam, Sydney	38
Sanchez, Ramon	206
Sanders, Abigail	26, 28, 183
Sanders, Paige	165
Sandevski, Nikolas	43
Santana, Mariana	184
Sarvepalli, Nagasai Vardhan Rao	198
Sawai, Pranjal	169, 171
Sawhny, Kailyn	35
Schafer, Aurora	145
Schefren, Ava	31, 41
Schildhaus, Avery	41, 42
Schultz, Carson	200
Seabron, Asha	182
Seaton, Rachel	186
Seo, Hyeyoung	121
Seo, Minsu	192
Shang, Xiaoqi	156
Shao, Wenjun	180
Shawger, Grey	184
Shea, Charlotte	43
Shellenberger, Tessa	185, 188
Shiels, James	218
Shilpakar, Ilu	46
Shin, Paige	45, 46
Shin, Sungeun	108, 140
Shin, Yena	202
Shin, Yong Han	158, 218
Shreve, Amina	46
Sibley, Cole	186
Silva, Juan	100, 182
Simon, Emily	175, 204, 224
Singh, Aditi	174
Singh, Shristi	226
Skonberg, Miles	186
Sledge, Joshua	183
Smith, Craig	33
Snow, Annika	165, 170, 186
So, Leann	190
Sockwell, Brooke	159, 187
Sojatia, Eshaan	167, 214
Son, Mina	82, 189
Song, Un-Hyeong	203
Song, Yoojin	221, 224
Sostre, Aïna Zaragoza	44
Stegall, Rachel	26
Stencel, Jessica	200
Sterlacci, Catarina	106, 151, 158, 205, 206
Stowe, Danielle	98
Strusallen, Morgan	160
Sudderth, Kate	154, 185, 187
Sun, Anita (Ningjing)	197
Sun, Letao	178
Sun, Wenbin	156
Super, Taylor	208
Svetlova, Anastasia	29
Swiss, Samantha	209
Takahashi, Kyoko	150
Tan, Cynthia Huiwen	143
Thomas, Savannah	124
Thompson, Alyssa	42
Thompson, Bella	188
Thorpe, Will	45
Tice, Alexandra	183, 208
Tole, Robert	196
Tolson-Tucker, Breonna	99
Torrijos, Andrea	224
Torroni, Andrea	27
Tran, Emily	36
Tran, Fiona	171
Tran, Uyen Nhi	164
Tran, Vu Quynh Thi	168
Trapizonian, Viktoriia	148, 195
Tsai, Veronica	226
Tshimanga, Felicia	101
Tsunoda, Remi	42
Tucker, Michael	99
Tusing, Alexa	230
Tweedie, Matthew	126
Twining, Hannah	102, 188
Uribe, Isabella	45
Utter, Charlie	169
Valle, Emma	133
Vaughn, Elisabeth	192
Vazquez, Ana	194
Verti, Bryce	170
Vijil, Atenas	44
Vilcan, Iuliana	45
Villafuerte, Jillian	193
Vo, Hieu	184
Vo, Ky Bao Ngoc	164
Vo, Nhi	33
Voss, Nick	88, 185, 188, 224
Vu, Linh	38
Vy, Ngo Chau	164
Walton, Kennedy	35
Wang, Bella	150
Wang, Samantha	97
Wang, Shuixin	122, 201
Wang, Sizhe	196
Wang, Yixuan	160
Wang, Yuchien	36
Weinstein, Allie	34
Welsh, Will	160
White, Brian	114, 158
Whitelaw, Anna	190
Wilkie, Emma	26
Williams, Dasia	119
Williams, Reagan	109, 159, 173, 204, 205, 208
Wilson, Jayden	35
Won, Sojung	61
Won, Yubin	100, 142, 166, 174, 194, 213, 214
Wu, Genie	78, 191
Wu, Shengjie	154
Wu, Tzu-Chieh (Kate)	159
Wu, Zhehao	181
Xiao, Yawen	202
Xiong, Meiling	29, 39
Xu, Alan	155, 217
Xu, Chalzea	177
Xu, Jialu	79
Yan, Timothy	177
Yang, Esther	162
Yang, Songer	179
Ye, Rongzhang	176
Ye, Yvonne	149
Yearicks, Braydon	175
Yenerich, Ross	31
Yi, Jae Ho	138
Yi, Suhyeon	183
Yingshi, Taylor	179
Yoon, Na Kyeong	202
You, Yiwen	96
Younas, Muhammad Tayyab	202
Yu, Dixin	226
Zhang, Kailin	43
Zhang, Lillian	161
Zhang, Michelle	148
Zhang, Mingxing	200
Zhao, Jocelyn Ziying	111, 160, 219
Zhong, Celina	168
Zhou, Mifei	178
Zhou, Sijin	195
Zhou, Yuzhuan	178
Zhu, Yilin	181
Zimmer, Nicole	27
Zou, Sirui	181
Zou, Yaxin	163
Zurga, Tina	31, 35

Within the realm of visual storytelling, the Graphis New Talent Awards 2024 stands as a testament to creativity's boundless potential.

Jim Ma, *Senior Designer, Bailey Lauerman*

New creative talent is the lifeblood of our industry. I'm encouraged and excited by the many good ideas the entrants shared.

Scott Bucher, *President, Traction Factory*

252 SCHOOL DIRECTORY

ArtCenter College of Design
www.artcenter.edu
1700 Lida St.
Pasadena, CA 91103
United States
Tel +1 626 396 2200

Asia University
www.web.asia.edu.tw/EN/index.php
Shangde St., Rm. 3, 3F., No. 136
North Dist.,
Taichung City 404020,
Taiwan
Tel +886 4 2332 3456

Auburn University
www.auburn.edu
152 S. College St.
Auburn, AL 36849
United States
Tel +1 334 844 4000

Baylor University
www.baylor.edu
1311 S. 5th St.
Waco, TX 76706
United States
Tel +1 800 229 5678

Belmont University, Watkins College of Art
www.watkins.edu
Leu Center for the Visual Arts,
Belmont Blvd.
Nashville, TN 37212
United States
Tel +1 615 460 6770

Brigham Young University
www.byu.edu
150 E. 1230 N.
Provo, UT 84602
United States
Tel +1 801 422 4636

Budapest Metropolitan University
www.metropolitan.hu
Nagy Lajos Király Utja 1-9, 1148
Budapest
Hungary
Tel +36 1 273 2419

California Institute of the Arts
www.calarts.edu
24700 McBean Parkway
Santa Clarita, CA 91355
United States
Tel +1 661 255 1050

California State University, Fullerton
www.fullerton.edu
800 N. State College Blvd.
Fullerton, CA 92831
United States
Tel +1 657 278 2011

Campbell University
www.campbell.edu
143 Main St.
Buies Creek, NC 27506
United States
Tel +1 800 334 4111

Capilano University
www.capilanou.ca
2055 Purcell Way
North Vancouver, BC V7J 3H5
Canada
Tel +1 604 986 1911

College for Creative Studies
www.ccsdetroit.edu
201 E. Kirby St.
Detroit, MI 48202
United States
Tel +1 313 664 7400

Columbia University
www.columbia.edu
116th St. and Broadway
New York, NY 10027
United States
Tel +1 212 854 1754

Dankook University
www.dankook.ac.kr
152 Jukjeon-ro, Suji-gu
Yongin-si, Gyeonggi-do
South Korea
Tel +82 1899 3700

Dawson College
www.dawsoncollege.qc.ca
3040 Sherbrooke St. W
Montreal, QB H3Z 1A4
Canada
Tel +1 514 931 8731

Dongduk Women's University
www.dongduk.ac.kr
60 Hwarang-ro 13-gil
Seongbuk-gu, Seoul
South Korea
Tel +82 2940 4000

Drexel University
www.drexel.edu
3141 Chestnut St.
Philadelphia, PA 19104
United States
Tel +1 215 895 2000

Duy Tan University
www.duytan.edu.vn
254 Nguyễn Văn Linh, Thạc Gián
Thanh Khê, Đà Nẵng 550000
Vietnam
Tel +84 236 3653 561

Ewha Womans University
www.ewha.ac.kr
52 Ewhayeodae-gil
Seodaemun-gu, Seoul
South Korea
Tel +82 2 3277 2114

Fashion Institute of Technology
www.fitnyc.edu
227 W. 27th St.
New York, NY 10001
United States
Tel +1 212 217 7999

Florida Atlantic University
www.fau.edu
777 Glades Road
Boca Raton, FL 33431
United States
Tel +1 561 297 3000

George Brown College
www.georgebrown.ca
160 Kendal Ave.
Toronto, ON M5R 1M3
Canada
Tel +1 416 415 2000

Georgia Southern University
www.georgiasouthern.edu
1332 Southern Drive
Statesboro, GA 30458
United States
Tel +1 912 478 4636

Hansung University, Design & Arts Institute
www.edubank.hansung.ac.kr
116 Samseongyo-ro 16-Gil
Seongbuk-gu, Seoul 136-792
South Korea
Tel +82 02 760 5533 5534

InFocus Film School
www.infocusfilmschool.com
554 Seymour St.
Vancouver, BC V6B 1J5
Canada
Tel +1 604 915 6900

Iowa State University
www.astate.edu
2433 Union Drive
Ames, IA 50011
United States
Tel +1 515 294 4111

Jacksonville State University
www.jsu.edu
700 Pelham Road N
Jacksonville, AL 36265
United States
Tel +1 256 782 5781

Kean University
www.kean.edu
1000 Morris Ave.
Union, NJ 07083
United States
Tel +1 908 737 5326

KREA Design School
www.kreaiskola.hu
Október 6. utca 18. Félemelet
1051 Budapest
Hungary
Tel +36 70 318 2970

Kutztown University
www.kutztown.edu
15200 Kutztown Road
Kutztown, PA 19530
United States
Tel +1 610 683 4000

Kyonggi University
www.kyonggi.ac.kr
154-42 Gwanggyosan-ro,
Yeongtong-gu
Suwon-si, Gyeonggi-do
South Korea
Tel +82 31 249 9114

Kyung Hee University
www.khu.ac.kr
26 Kyungheedae-ro
Dongdaemun-gu, Seoul
South Korea
Tel +82 2961 0114

LABASAD Barcelona School of Arts & Design
www.labasad.com
C/ d'Aragó, 326, 1-2, Eixample
08009 Barcelona
Spain
Tel +34 900 827 226

Lehigh University
www.lehigh.edu
27 Memorial Drive W
Bethlehem, PA 18015
United States
Tel +1 610 758 3000

Loyola University New Orleans
www.loyno.edu
6363 St. Charles Ave.
New Orleans, LA 70118
United States
Tel +1 504 865 3240

M.AD School of Ideas
www.miamiadschool.com/miami
571 NW. 28th St.
Miami, FL 33127
United States
Tel +1 305 538 3193

M.AD School of Ideas Atlanta
www.miamiadschool.com/locations/atlanta
3340 Peachtree Road NE,
Suite 1010, Office 2055
Atlanta, GA 30326
United States
Tel +1 404 351 5055

M.AD School of Ideas Madrid
www.madridadschool.com
C. de Sta. Cruz de
Marcenado, 4
Local 4, Centro, 28015 Madrid
Spain
Tel +34 917 54 03 75

M.AD School of Ideas New York
www.miamiadschool.com/locations/new-york
35-37 36th St., 3rd Floor
Queens, NY 11106
United States
Tel +1 917 773 8820

M.AD School of Ideas Toronto
www.miamiadschool.ca
147 Liberty St.
Toronto, ON M6K 3G3
Canada
Tel +1 250 295 9034

Methodist Theological University
www.mtu.ac.kr
31 Naengcheon-dong
Seodaemun-gu, Seoul
South Korea
Tel +82 2361 9239

Metropolitan State University of Denver
www.msudenver.edu
890 Auraria Parkway
Denver, CO 80204
United States
Tel +1 303 556 5740

Otis College of Art & Design
www.otis.edu
9045 Lincoln Blvd.
Los Angeles, CA 90045
United States
Tel +1 310 665 6800

Parsons School of Design
www.newschool.edu/parsons
66 5th Ave.
New York, NY 10011
United States
Tel +1 212 229 8900

Pennsylvania State University
www.psu.edu
201 Old Main, University Park
State College, PA 16801
United States
Tel +1 8114 865 4700

Portland Community College
www.pcc.edu
12000 SW. 49th Ave.
Portland, OR 97219
United States
Tel +1 971 722 6111

Pratt Institute
www.pratt.edu
200 Willoughby Ave.
Brooklyn, NY 11205
United States
Tel +1 718 636 3600

Purdue University
www.purdue.edu
610 Purdue Mall
West Lafayette, IN 47907
United States
Tel +1 765 494 4600

Rhode Island School of Design
www.risd.edu
2 College St.
Providence, RI 02903
United States
Tel +1 401 454 6100

Ringling College of Art and Design
www.ringling.edu
2700 N. Tamiami Trail
Sarasota, FL 34234
United States
Tel +1 941 351 5100

Rochester Institute of Technology
www.rit.edu
1 Lomb Memorial Dr.
Rochester, NY 14623
United States
Tel +1 585 475 2411

Royal College of Art
www.rca.ac.uk
Kensington Gore,
South Kensington
London, SW7 2EU
United Kingdom
Tel +44 20 7590 4444

Savannah College of Art & Design
www.scad.edu
1600 Peachtree St. NW.
Atlanta, GA 30309
United States
Tel +1 877 722 3285

School of the Art Institute of Chicago
www.saic.edu
6 S. Wabash Ave.
Chicago, IL 60603
United States
Tel +1 800 232 7242

School of Visual Arts
www.sva.edu
209 E. 23rd St.
New York, NY, 10010
United States
Tel +1 212 592 2000

Southern Methodist University
www.smu.edu
6425 Boaz Lane
Dallas, TX 75205
United States
Tel +1 214 768 2000

Swinburne University of Technology
www.swinburne.edu.au
John St.
Hawthorn, VIC 3122
Australia
Tel +61 1300 794 628

Syracuse University, The Newhouse School
www.newhouse.syr.edu
215 University Place
Syracuse, NY 13210
United States
Tel +1 315 443 2302

Temple University
www.temple.edu
1801 N. Broad St.
Philadelphia, PA 19122
United States
Tel +1 215 204 7000

Temple University, Tyler School of Art & Architecture
www.tyler.temple.edu
2001 N. 13th St.
Philadelphia, PA 19122
United States
Tel +1 215 777 9000

Texas A&M University-Commerce
www.tamuc.edu
2200 Campbell St.
Commerce, TX 75428
United States
Tel +1 903 886 5102

Texas Christian University
www.tcu.edu
2800 S. University Drive
Fort Worth, TX 76129
United States
Tel +1 817 257 7000

Texas State University
www.txstate.edu
601 University Drive
San Marcos, TX 78666
United States
Tel +1 512 245 211

University of Architecture Ho Chi Minh City
www.uah.edu.vn
196 Pasteur, Phường 6
Quận 3, Thành phố Hồ Chí Minh
Vietnam
Tel +84 28 3822 2748

University of Arts Poznan
www.uap.edu.pl
al. Marcinkowskiego 29
60-967 Poznań
Poland
Tel +48 61 855 25 21

University of Central Oklahoma
www.uco.edu
100 N. University Drive
Edmond, OK 73034
United States
Tel +1 405 974 2727

University of Cincinnati DAAP Myron E. Ullman Jr. School of Design
www.daap.uc.edu
2624 Clifton Ave.
Cincinnati, OH 45221
United States
Tel +1 513 556 4933

University of Ljubljana, Academy of Fine Arts & Design
www.uni-lj.si/eng
Kongresni trg 12
Ljubljana 1000
Slovenia
Tel +386 1 241 85 00

University of Louisville
www.louisville.edu
2301 S. 3rd St.
Louisville, KY 40292
United States
Tel +1 502 852 5555

University of Minnesota, Twin Cities
www.twin-cities.umn.edu
231 Pillsbury Drive SE
Minneapolis, MN 55455
United States
Tel +1 612 625 5000

University of North Texas
www.unt.edu
1155 Union Circle
Denton, TX 76203
United States
Tel +1 940 565 2000

University of Notre Dame
www.nd.edu
Notre Dame, IN 46556
United States
Tel +1 574 631 5000

University of Texas at Arlington
www.uta.edu
701 S. Nedderman Dr.
Arlington, TX 76019
United States
Tel +1 817 272 2011

University of the Arts London
www.arts.ac.uk
272 High Holborn
London, WC1V 7EY
United Kingdom
Tel +44 20 7514 6000

University of the Incarnate Word
www.uiw.edu
4301 Broadway
San Antonio, TX 78209
United States
Tel +1 210 829 6000

Virginia Commonwealth University, VCU Brandcenter
www.brandcenter.vcu.edu
103 S. Jefferson St.
Richmond, VA 23284
United States
Tel +1 804 828 8384

West Chester University
www.wcupa.edu
700 S. High St.
West Chester, PA 19383
United States
Tel +1 610 436 1000

Woodbury University
www.woodbury.edu
7500 N. Glenoaks Blvd.
Burbank, CA 91504
United States
Tel +1 818 767 0888

York University
www.yorku.ca
4700 Keele St.
Toronto, ON M3J 1P3
Canada
Tel +1 416 736 2100

253 HONORABLE MENTIONS

Honorable Mentions appear on Graphis.com and in the digital copy. Only Platinum, Gold, & Silver winners appear in the physical book.

Schools:
Art and Design Lab
ArtCenter College of Design
Auburn University
Baylor University
Boston University
Brigham Young University
California Institute of the Arts
California State University, Fullerton
Campbell University
Capilano University
Colorado State University
Dankook University
Dongduk Women's University
Drexel University
Duy Tan University
Elon University
Fashion Institute of Technology
FH Joanneum
Hansung University, Design & Arts Institute
High Point University
Hong Kong Polytechnic University
Hongik University
InFocus Film School
Iowa State University
Jacksonville State University
Kean University
Kutztown University
Lafayette High School
Lehigh University
Loyola University, New Orleans
Maryland Institute College of Art
M.AD School of Ideas
M.AD School of Ideas Atlanta
M.AD School of Ideas New York
M.AD School of Ideas San Francisco
National Taiwan Normal University
OCAD University
Pacific Northwest College of Art
Parsons School of Design
Pennsylvania State University
Portland Community College
Pratt Institute
Purdue University
Rhode Island School of Design
Ringling College of Art & Design
Rochester Institute of Technology
Salisbury University
Savannah College of Art & Design
School of the Art Institute of Chicago
School of Visual Arts
Sejong University
Southern Methodist University
Syracuse University, The Newhouse School
Temple University
Temple University, Tyler School of Art & Architecture
Texas A&M University -Commerce
Texas Christian University
Texas State University
Thomas Jefferson University
University of Cincinnati DAAP
University of Ljubljana, Academy of Fine Arts & Design
University of Louisville
University of North Texas
University of Notre Dame
University of South Florida
University of Texas at Arlington
University of the Incarnate Word
Virginia Commonwealth University
Virginia Commonwealth University, VCU Brandcenter
Watkins College of Art
West Chester University
Western Washington University
Wilson School of Design
Woodbury University

Professors:
Aaron Smith
Abby Guido
Adam Brodowski
Adam Ross
Adam Smith
Adrienne Leban
Alex Merto
Alice Lee
Allen Hori
Andrea Quam
Andrea Trabucco-Campos
Andrew Gibbs
Andrew Walters
Angela Mortorana
Anne Jordan
Anneke Coppoolse
Annie Huang Luck
Anthony Kerr
Anthony Macbain
Ara Devejian
Aubrey Holliman
Aurora De Armendi
Austin Buck
Ben Hannam
Ben Dolezal
Beth Shirrell
Bill Brammer
Bill Galyean
Bob Warkulwiz
Brad Bartlett
Brankica Harvey
Brian Boyd
Burton Runyan
Byunghak Ahn
Casey McGarr
Celia Ruiz Lopez
Chad Anderson
Charles Lin
Charles Varner
Chen Wang
Christian Dunn
Christian Perez Morin
Christie Shin
Christina Lee Kim Koon
Chung-Liang Lin
CJ Yeh
Clara Bunker
Claudia Butts
Claudia Strong
Corey Gurley
Cory Say
Courtney Gooch
Daeki Shim
Dan Brawner
Dan Hoy
Daniel Soucy
David Chathas
David Elizalde
David Jones
David Smith
David Tillinghast
David Villouta
David Wolske
Deborah Beardslee
Dejan Mraović
Denise Bosler
Dirk Kammerzell
Don Haring
Dong-Joo Park
Doris Palmeros-McManus
Doug Regen
Doug Salati
Doug Thomas
Douglas May
Douglas Sirois
Dusty Crocker
Edward Boches
Eduard Čehovin
Eileen Feeney Bushnell
Elaine Alderette
Ellen Lupton
Elliott Walker
Elyssa Schmidt
Emily Burns
Eric Baker
Eric Gillett
Eric Karnes
Erica Holeman
Erik Carter
Erik Freer
Esther Pearl Watson
Federico Giraldo
Felipe Yamaoka
Frank Baseman
Franz Werner
Gabriel Gonzalez
Gail Anderson
Gary Harman
Gayle Donahue
Genaro Solis Rivero
Geoff Brewerton
Georgia Bockos
Gerardo Herrera
Greg Lindy
Gus Granger
Hafeez Saheed
Haik Avanian
Hank Richardson
Henry Nuhn
Holly Sterling
Hon Kit Lam
Hoon-Dong Chung
Huiwon Lim
Hyojun Shim
Hyung Joo Kim
Jackson Sipes
James Daher
Jamie Runnells
Jan Ballard
Jason Heuer
Jason Holly
Jeff Bleitz
Jeff Davis
Jeff Glendenning
Jeff Hughes
Jennifer Cadieux
Jennifer Pepper
Jenny Kowalski
Jensine Eckwell
Jessica Deseo
Jim Salvati
John Bohls
John Drew
John Gravdahl
John Kim
Jon Newman
Jose Hadathy
Joseph Han
Joseph Newton
Joseph Staluppi
Josh Cochran
Joshua Ege
Joshua Oceguera
Joshua Williams
Justin Colt
Justin Reynolds
Karen Dorff
Karen Kresge
Karen Watkins
Kate Clair
Kathy Mueller
Kelly Bryant
Kelly Holohan
Ken Deegan
Kevin O'Neill
Kim Gun
Kyle Blue
Lauren Cantor
Lauren Lowen
Lavinia Lascaris
Lee Hackett
Leila Singleton
Lewis Glaser
Li Zhang
Lily Padula
Linda Reynolds
Lisa Willard
Livia Ito
Lorraine Wild
Malina Omut
Marcelo Duhalde
Mario F. Bocanegra Martinez
Mark Allen
Mark Brinkman
Mark Stammers
Mark Todd
Martin Lau
Mary Yang
Matt Normand
Matt Rota
Matteo Bologna
Matthew Lenning
Maura Lisson
Maurizio Masi
Mel White
Melinda Beck
Mia Culbertson
Michael Cober
Michael Konetzka
Michael Worthington
Mihyun Kim
Mike Ford
Ming Tai
Minsun Eo
Mirko Ilić
Molly R. Jukes-Hudson
Monica Kellenberger
Monica Schlaug
Morgan Ford Willingham
Muhammad Rahman
Nancy Campbell
Natasha Jen
Nathan Savage
Neeta Verma
Neil Raphan
Nicole Zizila
Olga Mezhibovskaya
Pamela Olecki
Panayiotis Terzis
Patrick Finley
Paula Airth
Pedro Mendes
Pete Evans
Peter Ahlberg
Phillip DiBello
Ramsey Ruleas
Randy Elles
Raymond Adrian
Rebekah Albrecht
Renée Seward
Renée Stevens
Rhonda Wolverton
Rich Tu
Richard Rose
River Jukes-Hudson
Robert Clayton
Robert Finkel
Roberto Vilchis Echeverri
Roland Murillo
Rory Simms
Ryan Harvey
Ryan Mansfield
Samantha Herbert
Sandy Stewart
Scott Zukowski
Scotty Reifsnyder
Seung-Min Han
Shawn Denny
Shawn Hasto
Sheri Squires
Shirleen Lavalais
Simon Johnston
Sohee Kwon
Stephen Serrato
Stephen Zhang
Steve Brodner
Steve James
Talia Cotton
Tamislav Bobinec
Taylor Shipton
Teresa Trevino
Theron Moore
Thi Nguyen
Thomas Scharpf
Tim Bruce
Timothy Cohan
Tom Varisco
Tony Kerr
Tracey Shiffman
Tri Phuong Dong Nguyen
Trysh Wahlig
Tyler Comrie
Tyrone Drake
Valentina Aproda Maurer
Veronica Vaughn
Vesper Stamper
Viktor Koen
Virginia Green
Whitney Holden
William Meek
Willie Baronet
Yeliz Secerli
Yeon Joo Ru
Yoshiko Burke
Yuko Shimizu
Yvonne Cao
Zipeng Zhu

Students:
Aaron Payne
Abby Lichtfus
Abby White
Abdulla Al-Najjar
Abigail Killough
Abigail Murschell
Abigail Sanders
Abriella Patti
Adam Hansen
Aditi Singh
Adrian Guardado
Aidan Roe
AJ Ruffra
AJ Zapanta
Alan Xu
Aleah Jones
Aleigha Thompson
Alexa Pinarski
Alexa Tusing
Alexander Lieberman
Alexander Martinez
Alexandra Jacobson
Alexandra Tice
Alicia Chau
Alina Stopello
Aliya Ibarra
Allie Chilek
Ally Manziano
Alyssa Van Zandt
Alyssa Virnau
Amanda Stotz
Amber Taylor
Amelia Flinchbaugh
Ana Aguilar
Anastasia Svetlova
Andrea Acal
Andrea Avila
Andrea Trejo
Andrianna Georgekopoulos
Andy (Nhan) Nguyen
Angelica Lodes
Angelique Ronca
Anggie Arivia
Anh Nguyen
Anita (Chengran) Li
Anna LeBer
Anna Maack
Anna Ramsey
Annabelle Neher
Annie Frey
Annie Oatman
Annika Snow
Anya Dai
Aoran Ma
Areli Bautista Martinez
Arian Chandra
Ariana Reyes
Arianna Aguila
Arlene Tomista Antonio
Arlo Martin
Arthur Flaksman
Arthur Starling
Ashley Bierma
Ashley Warren
Atenas Vijil
Aurora Schafer
Austin Templeton
Autumn Kitabjian
Ava Caruso
Avery Kokinda
Avery Orta
Avery Schildhaus
Aviela Maynard
Bella Sanchez
Biheng Sun
Biyao Xie
Blake Lyster
Brandy Compton
Brennah Wagner
Brett Hilton
Brett Roth
Brian Diep
Briana Harris
Brianna Bowman
Brianna Velazquez
Brinlee Kelly
Brooke Budde
Brooke Hirsch
Brooke Matey
Brooks Baley
Bryn Dettman
Brynn Olsen
Brynn Squires
Caitlin Sukohardjo
Caleb Ramos
Cali Martin
Calvin Keller
Camila Balderrama
Carissa Kalisek
Carli Aldape
Carlos Duran-Pichardo
Carolina Uscategui
Caroline Davis
Caroline Kelly
Carson Karlin
Cassidy O'Connor
Cassie Valenzuela Poon
Catarina Sterlacci
Catherine Gloeckner
Cayla Israel
Cecilia Duarte Mol
Cecily Li
Celeste Van Ausdall
Celestine Pileri
Celine Loc
Celine Sanderson
Chang Qu
Charlea Helmberger
Charlotte Grimm
Charlotte Little
Charlotte Offin
Charmy Patel
Chiara Odgers
Chong Ho Yan
Christine Choe
Chuhan Ji
Claudia Curbelo
Colette Chidalek
Conner Gayda
Corinne Green
Courtney Acevedo
Courtney Kurtz
Craig Smith
Cuinn Cornwell
Da-eun Kim
Damaris Haro
Daniel Geiszler
Daniel Mainou
Daniela Mantica
Dean Lourenco
DeMia Courman
Denise Alayon
Derek Daproza
Devon Ellison
Diana Castro
Dianna Higaki
Diexin Yu
Difeng Zhang
Dishti Ajmani
Don Park
Donald Ross Jr.
Dong Hyun Kim
Doyeon Kim
Edward J. Kelly
Elaine Gong

254 HONORABLE MENTION

Honorable Mentions appear on Graphis.com and in the digital copy. Only Platinum, Gold, & Silver winners appear in the physical book.

Elaine Lee
Elise Hernandez
Elise Johnson
Elizabeth Lee
Elizabeth Taylor
Elizabeth Vogt
Ell Nittler
Ella Fiegener
Ella Janssen
Elliot Rosenberg-Rappin
Elly O'Bannon
Elmo Chavez
Elton Tinoco
Elyza Nachimson
Emaan Noorzaie
Emilee Waltz
Emily Bierma
Emily Brown
Emily Heemer
Emily Jeffrey
Emily Juliano
Emily Neufeldt
Emily Saad
Emily Simon
Emily Soccio
Emily Tran
Emily Tsao
Emma Brown
Emma Georghakis
Emma Wilkie
Emmeline Walker
Eric Hernandez
Erica Steele
Erika Donley
Erin Kim
Eshaan Sojatia
Ethan Jones
Ethan Leifer
Ethan Rujak
Eunseo Ko
Eva Jarman
Fang Nan
Felicia Tshimanga
Felicity Acevedo
Felipe Reblora
Fiona Huang
Forough Yazdanpanah
Ga-Eun Kim
Gab K. de Jesus
Gabriella Zonari de Lorenzo
Gabrielle Trinidad
Gaeun Kate Chung
Genny Odine
Georgia Kincaid
Georgina Kurnia
Giang Le
Glenn Ryan
Gordana Jokanovic
Grace Alderman
Grace White
Gracie Wade
Greta Hartwyk
Greta Long
Gyeongmin Park
Gyuwon Jo
Ha Tran
Hadil Jamali
Hae-Dam-Eun Han
Hailey Bogner
Handeul Kim
Hannah Burke
Hannah Duff
Hannah Javadi
Hannah Kim
Hannah Lee
Hannah Twining
Hanson Ma
Hanyu Yang
Haoteng Zhu
Harper Herman
Heejai Park
Helen Liu
Hillary Geary
Hollie Hernandez
Honey Ashvinkumar Gardharia
Hope Xi
Huiting Lian
Huynh Thi Cam Tu
Hyeon-Ha Jo
Hyeri Choi
Hyewon Choi
Hyewon Kwon
Hyowon Kwon
Indi Ho
Ipek Koprululu
Ipshita Krishan
Isaac Jung
Isabella Alva
Isabella Baker
Isabella Bivona
Isabella del Rey
Isabella Pasino
Isabelle Brawley
Isabelle Kwong
Isra Younas
Ita Kim
Jacinta Philip
Jack Hoas
Jacqueline Velez
Jacquelyn Lin
Jada Gunner
Jada Merritt
Jade Chen
Jae Ho Yi
Jaiwon Lee
Jamari Cannady Pratt
Jamie Jason
Jamie Kim
Jamileh Shiber
Jana Klammer
Jasmin Nguyen
Jayla Momon
Jazmine Garcia
Jeeyoon Lim
Jeffrey Torres
Jenna Byers
Jeremiah Holsclaw
Jess Martinez
Jess Riporti
Jessica Gian
Jessica Ngoc-Tran Le
Jhan Le
Ji-Hyeon Kwag
Jia Li
Jialu Xu
Jiawen Zhang
Jihwan Jeon
Jihye Kim
Jihyun Lee
Jimin Hur
Jimmy Hall
Jingxin Yu
Jingyun Xiao
Jinyuan Liu
Jiwon Wang
Jiyul Kim
JJ Eng
Jo Iijima
JoAnn Do-On
Jocelyn Ziying Zhao
Joel Pratt
John Mark Lasater
Jonathan Kusnadi
Jonathan Lin
Jonathan Ramsingh
Jonathan Wideman
Jonny Gleaton
Jordan Heath
Jose Munguia
Joseph Neus
Joshua Cotsworth
Joshua Sledge
Ju-Yeon Kim
Juan Pablo Gutierrez Hurtado
Juan Silva
Julia Orr
Juliette Keller
Jun An
Jun Wang
Jung Youn Kim
Jungmin Lee
Junhyuk Lee
Junyi Zhu
Kacey Le
Kaitlyn Blan
Karla Amaya
Karla Ruiz
Karolyne Diep
Kate Holmes
Kate Sudderth
Katelyn Cerami
Katelyn Hughes
Katelyn On
Kathryn Hendry
Kathy Chung
Katie Bedewi
Katrina Cabrera
Kayci Fox
Kayden Hadley
Kayla Hanrahan
Kayla Keen
Keaton Dillard
Kelsey Dicker
Kerrigan Hoffine
Kerstin Negado
Kianna Dallman
Kien Nguyen
Kiera Helquist
Kimberly Ramirez Inestroza
Kimi Mate
Kristen Duong
Lam Pan
Landon Blake
Laney Punarate
Lang De apa
Larisa Benguhe
Lauren Chin
Lauren Clark
Lauren Lutson
Lauren Ortega
Lauren Sears
Lauren Snyder
Lauryn Green
Le Wang
Lee McClain
Lela Fand
Lexi Oliver
Li June Choi
Li Lin
Lihao Zhu
Linh Vu
Lior Edrich
Litzy Patterson
Logan Dorsey
Lottie Brown
Lucia Canseco
Luciana Lopez
Lucy Hawblitzel
Luis Herrera
Lujia Zhuang
Luke Famme
Luke Miller
Luke Sheridan
Luyao Zhang
Mackenzie Murphy
Macy McClish
Maddie Christian
Maddie Otero
Madison Shetter
Madissen Kwon
Maeci Ray
Maggie Gray
Maggie Menz
Maggie Morton
Mahta Jafari
Maija Brandish
Makayla McCarty
Makayla Sanchez
Mallory Cha
Man Chun (Jason) Shing
Man Ying Wu
Manh Dat Pham
Mandy Czyz
Mansi Vinay
Mari Hosho
Maria Bautista Signorini
Maria Gronowska
Maria Mansfield
Maria Santana
Marilyn Garcia
Marin Cormier
Marina Ibrahim
Marina Sepe
Marisa Saggio
Maritza Quintuna
Markus Allen
Marta Huerta-Sanchez
Mary K. Mitchell
Mary Neuman
Marybeth Zipagang
Matt Foster
Matt Latvis
Matt Newberry
Matthew Bruner
Maya Berenblum
Maya Givens
Megan Adams
Megan Dale
Megan Marflak
Meghan Gulley
MeiLi Carling
Meiling Xiong
Meiyun Chen
Mekielle Vaughn
Meredith DiPietro
Micaela Cedillo
Micah Hoang
Micah Shannon
Michael Jahn
Michael Knipe
Michael Lovett
Michele Mardorf
Michella Zhang
Mike Ray
Miles Skonberg
Mina Kim
Mina Son
Miranda Arias
Mishen Liu
Miso Song
Molly Heller
Molly Jacobs
Mona Monahan
Morgan Goerke
Morgan Martinez
Mui Cheuk (Victor) Nam
Myesha Bennett
Nancy Compean
Natalie Nash
Nathalie Kirsheh
Nathalie Lopez
Nghi To
Ngoc Duy Nguyen
Ngoc Quynh Thy Tran
Nhi Vo
Nia Gombač
Nic De La Hoz
Nick Bazzoni
Nick Malandrino
Nick Rheem
Nick Voss
Nicole Mech
Nicolle Smith
Nikolas Sandevski
Nina Im
Noah Cousineau
Noah Lourie
Olaya Ordieres Ortega
Olivia Doe
Olivia Guerra
Olivia Heller
Olivia Vitale
Oriana T. Zhao
Paige Sanders
Paige Shin
Pamela Pardo
Paris Cipollone
Patterson Guyton
Peace Park
Peter Grissom
Philip Acierno
Phoebe Huey
Phuong Thanh Ha
Pranjal Sawai
Prarthana Rathore
Rabiya Gupta
Rachel Blow
Rachel Burt
Rachel Felner
Rachel Lieb
Rachel Pan
Rachel Seaton
Rachel Stegall
Rain Gao
Rainbow Pun
Ramzee Camarena
Reagan Oates
Reagan Williams
Rebecca Dugan
Riley Ramsower
River Chang
Robert Tole
Roblyn Powley
Rose Edwards
Roshan Gupta
Rozlynn Macbeth Olivas
Ruby Minhyoung Kim
Ruihan Wang
Ruoshu Sun
Ruoshui Liu
Ruoyu Wu
Ryan Wood
Ryder Vassilos
Rylee Armstrong
Saeyeon Jung
Sam Shelast
Samantha Freeman
Samantha Reaves
Samantha Terrio
Samuel McConnell
San Myeong Kim
Sara Cacoilo
Sara Freyre
Sara Park
Sarah Bridge
Sarah Margit Walters
Satoko Okuno
Savanna Hodes
Sayler Rivas
Seamus Foran
Sean Nagao
Sehyeok Lee
Seo Jin Lee
Seokun Kwon
Seokwon Hong
Seonghyun Jeon
Seoyeon Lim
Seslie Sliva
Seung Ri Lee
Seunghye Jin
Shelby Olson
Shenjie Chen
Shivangi Chopra
Shuning Ren
Shuwen Ding
Shyann Haught
Sian Marshall
Sieun Lee
Simon Osbourne
Simran Khungar
Sion Kim
Siyi Zhao
So Jeong Kim
So Yeon Park
Sofia Cortes
Sofia Rodriguez
Soo-Hyun Kang
Sophia Martinez
Sophia Ochoa
Sophia Sardello
Sophie Appel
Sophie Baddley
Sophie Houghton
Soyeon Moon
Spencer Hogan
Stephanie Dryer
Stephanie Mylonas
Steven Perales
Subin Choi
Suin Choi
Sukyeong Kim
Sumin Lee
Sunnie Ro
Sunny Li
Suramya Pathak
Sydney Crook
Sydney Herritt
Sydney Lee
Taylor Pirtle
Thai To
Thi Chi Hieu Phan
Thi Ngoc Huyen Dao
Thi Nhan Hau Nguyen
Thi Nhu Y Dinh
Thuy Nhat Nguyen
Tianyi Zhang
Timothy Chae
Tina Dernovšek
Travis Crawford
Tully Ryan
Tzu-Chieh (Kate) Wu
Vasavi Bubna
Verity Badov
Veronica Eseguerra
Veronica Joyce
Veronica Tsai
Victoria Puga
Viktoriia Leonenko
Virginia Herschend
Vivian Jade Li
Vu Le Gia Bao
Wang Yinan
Wen-Chi Hsueh
Wenbo Wu
Wenxin Jiang
Will McKinnie
Will Thorpe
William Carlos Johnstone
Wu Lok (Louis) Nam
Xiangyi Guo
Xiao Wang
Xiaoqi Shang
XingMei Wu
Xinni Hong
Xinyi Liao
Xinyi Yao
Xiyu Wang
Xuehui He
Yaheng Li
Yaif Hossain
Yang Doo Woon
Yaoxinyu Guo
Yasseen Cherif Elassar
Yawen Xiao
Yaxin Zou
Yeeon Kang
Yeil Kang
Yeji Jun
Yeji Shim
Yerin Jo
Yerin Lee
Yi Fan Sunny Ruan
Yin Yi Lin
Yip Chun (Henry) Hin
Yiwei Cheng
Yiwen You
Yixuan Wang
Yong Han Shin
Yoo-Jin Lee
Yoojin Song
Yoon Bee Baek
Yoon Seo Kim
Yoonbee Baek
Yu Bin Lee
Yu Tung Cheng
Yuan Chen
Yubin Won
Yue Wang
Yukun Chloe Ba
Yuna Kim
Yunah Lee
Yutong Hu
Yuxin Ding
Zach Hall
Zalika Yavlinsky
Ze Feng
Zedan Peng
Zhengrong Chai
Zhirou (Lexie) Li
Zihao Dong

Photography Annual 2024

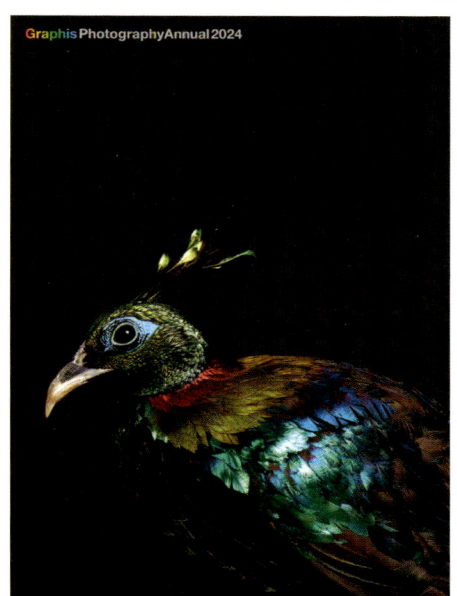

2024
Hardcover: 256 pages
200-plus color illustrations
Trim: 8.5 x 11.75"
ISBN: 978-1-954632-28-8
US $75

Awards: Graphis presents 12 Platinum, 102 Gold, and 216 Silver awards, along with 54 Honorable Mentions.
Platinum Winners: Craig Cutler, Lindsey Drennan, Jonathan Knowles, James Minchin, Artem Nazarov, Peter Samuels, Howard Schatz, John Surace, and Paco Macias Velasco.
Content: This book is full of exceptional work by our masterful judges, our Platinum, Gold, and Silver award winners, and our Honorable Mentions. It also includes a retrospective on our Platinum 2014 Photography winners, a list of international photography museums and galleries, and an In Memoriam list of photographers who have passed away this past year. The digital copy has an extra 52 pages of additional content for you to peruse.

Advertising Annual 2024

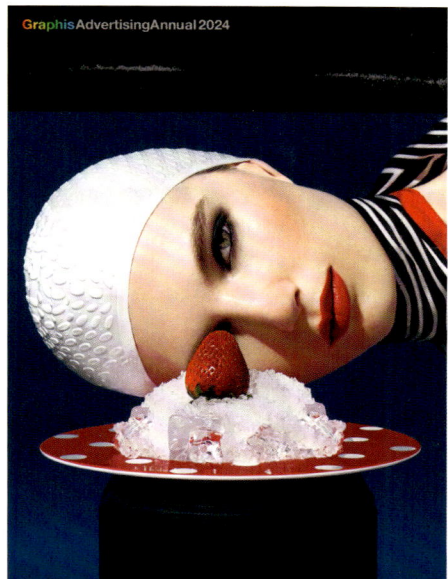

2024
Hardcover: 224 pages
200-plus color illustrations
Trim: 8.5 x 11.75"
ISBN: 978-1-954632-25-7
US $75

Awards: Graphis presents 15 Platinum, 61 Gold, and 99 Silver awards, along with 14 Honorable Mentions.
Platinum Winners: ARSONAL, Brunner, Célie Cadieux, Extra Credit Projects, Freaner Creative & Design, PangHao Art Studio, Partners + Napier, PETROL Advertising, ReThink, Rhubarb, SJI Associates, Sukle Advertising, and SUPERFY.
Content: This Annual includes amazing Platinum, Gold, and Silver Award-winning print and video advertisements from well-established firms and agencies. Honorable Mentions are also presented. Also featured in the annual is a selection of award-winning work from the competition judges and our yearly In Memoriam list of the advertising talent we've lost over the last year.

Design Annual 2024

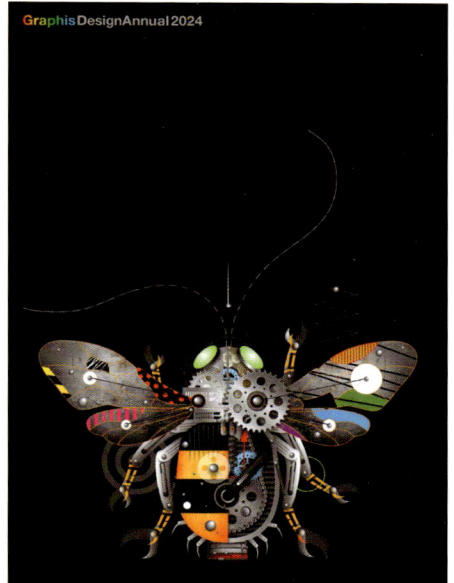

2023
Hardcover: 272 pages
200-plus color illustrations
Trim: 8.5 x 11.75"
ISBN: 978-1-954632-22-4
US $75

Awards: Graphis presents 12 Platinum, 108 Gold, and 436 Silver awards, along with 182 Honorable Mentions.
Platinum Winners: Presenting AV Print, The Balbusso Twins, Carmit Design Studio, Journey Group, Michael Pantuso Design, Namseoul University, Omdesign, PepsiCo Design & Innovation, Studio Eduardo Aires, Sun Design Production, Underline Studio, and Wonderlust Industries, Inc.
Content: This book includes award-winning work from the judges, as well as Platinum, Gold, and Silver-winning work from internationally renowned designers and design firms. Honorable Mentions are presented, and a list of designers that we have lost this past year and a directory of design museums are also included.

Poster Annual 2024

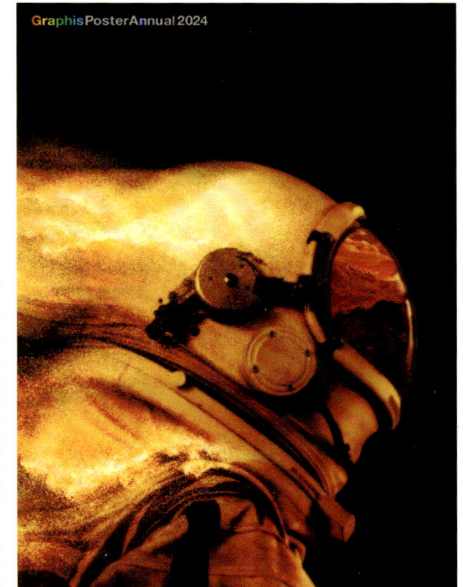

2023
Hardcover: 256 pages
200-plus color illustrations
Trim: 8.5 x 11.75"
ISBN: 978-1-954632-23-3
US $75

Awards: Graphis presents 14 Platinum, 100 Gold, and 266 Silver awards, along with 211 Honorable Mentions.
Platinum Winners: This year's group of international designers include Antonio Castro Design, Atelier Radovan Jenko, Chemi Montes, Holger Matthies, Kashlak, Kiyoung An Graphic Art Course Laboratory, Mirko Ilic Corp., MOCEAN, Peter Diamond Illustration, Šesnić&Turković, Supremat, The Refinery, and Underline Studio.
Content: This book features international Platinum, Gold, and Silver-winning work. Honorable Mentions are also presented. Award-winning work from the judges and a section of Platinum-winning works from 2014 are also included. Platinum and Gold-winning designers discuss their posters and explain the approach they took that resulted in their winning work.

Packaging 10

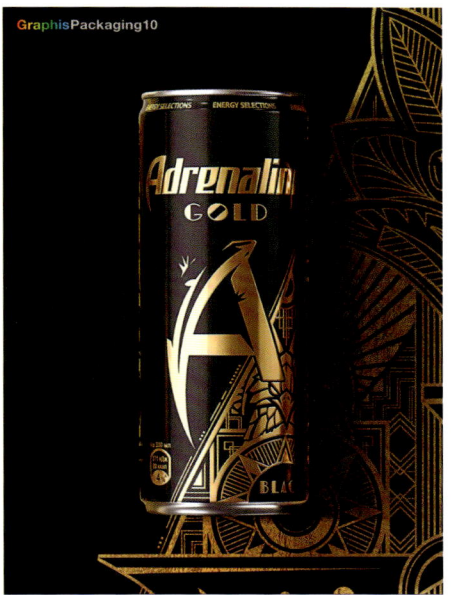

2022
Hardcover: 240 pages
200-plus color illustrations
Trim: 8.5 x 11.75"
ISBN: 978-1-954632-12-7
US $75

Awards: Graphis presents 12 Platinum, 100 Gold, 204 Silver, and 249 Honorable Mentions for innovative work in product packaging.
Platinum Winners: Michele Gomes Bush (Next), Chad Roberts (Chad Roberts Design Ltd.), XiongBo Deng (Shenzhen Lingyun Creative Packaging Design Co., Ltd.) and Lu Chen (Xiaomi), Vishal Vora (Sol Benito), Mattia Conconi (Gottschalk+Ash Int'l), and Frank Anselmo (New York Mets), Ivan Bell (Stranger & Stranger), Brian Steele (SLATE), and the team at PepsiCo Design & Innovation.
Content: This book contains award-winning packaging from the judges, as well as international Platinum, Gold, and Silver-winning packaging designs from designers and design firms from around the world. Honorable Mentions are presented, and a feature of award-winning work from our Packaging 9 Annual is also included.

Narrative Design: Kit Hinrichs

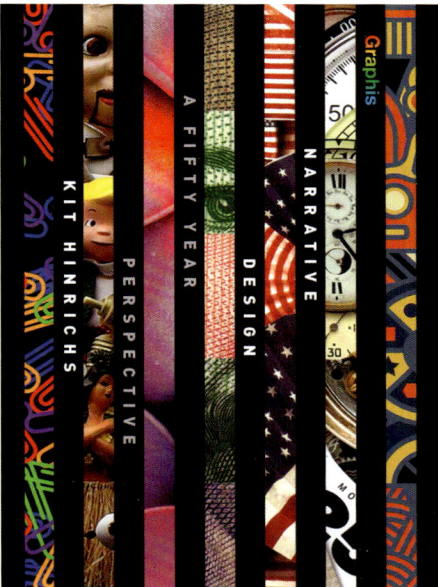

2023
Hardcover: 248 pages
200-plus color illustrations
Trim: 9 x 12"
ISBN: 978-1-954632-03-5
US $65

Narrative Design: A Fifty-Year Perspective is a collection of over 50 years of work from the obsessive graphic designer Kit Hinrichs. To the legendary AIGA medalist, author, teacher, and collector, design is the business of telling a story. It's not just about communicating a product or a corporate ethos—it's about contributing to the collective culture of storytelling. Presented in the book are not individual case studies but rather categories of work and graphic approaches to assignments that have wowed clients and dazzled viewers. The work is arranged to communicate Hinrichs' creative thinking, which always leads to a unique and effective solution to any design conundrum.

Books are available at graphis.com/publications

www.Graphis.com